KT-387-480

KA 0236736 X
WINCHE

THE WORKS OF A LOLLARD PREACHER
The Sermon *Omnis plantacio*
The Tract *Fundamentum aliud nemo potest ponere*
and
The Tract *De oblacione iugis sacrificii*

EARLY ENGLISH TEXT SOCIETY
No. 317
2001

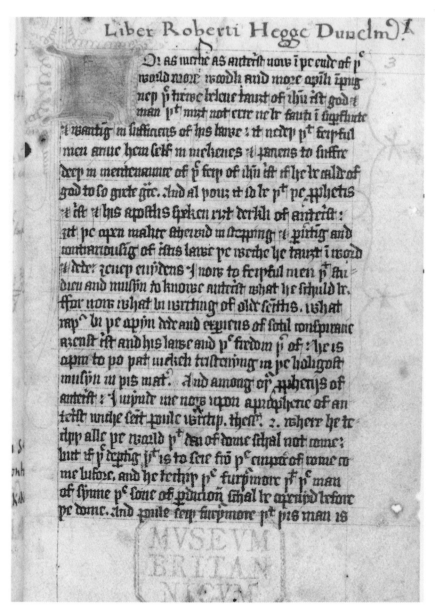

British Library, MS Cotton Titus D.v, f. 3ʳ

Reproduced by permission of The British Library

THE WORKS OF A
LOLLARD PREACHER

The Sermon *Omnis plantacio*
The Tract *Fundamentum aliud nemo potest ponere*
and
The Tract *De oblacione iugis sacrificii*

EDITED BY

ANNE HUDSON

Published for
THE EARLY ENGLISH TEXT SOCIETY
by the
OXFORD UNIVERSITY PRESS
2001

OXFORD

UNIVERSITY PRESS

Great Clarendon Street, Oxford OX2 6DP

Oxford University Press is a department of the University of Oxford.
It furthers the University's objective of excellence in research, scholarship,
and education by publishing worldwide in

Oxford New York

Athens Auckland Bangkok Bogotá Buenos Aires Cape Town
Chennai Dar es Salaam Delhi Florence Hong Kong Istanbul Karachi
Kolkata Kuala Lumpur Madrid Melbourne Mexico City Mumbai Nairobi
Paris São Paulo Shanghai Singapore Taipei Tokyo Toronto Warsaw

with associated companies in Berlin Ibadan

Oxford is a registered trade mark of Oxford University Press
in the UK and in certain other countries

Published in the United States
by Oxford University Press Inc., New York

© Early English Text Society, 2001

The moral rights of the author have been asserted
Database right Oxford University Press (maker)

First published 2001

All rights reserved. No part of this publication may be reproduced,
stored in a retrieval system, or transmitted, in any form or by any means,
without the prior permission in writing of Oxford University Press,
or as expressly permitted by law, or under terms agreed with the appropriate
reprographics rights organisation. Enquiries concerning reproduction
outside the scope of the above should be sent to the Rights Department,
Oxford University Press, at the address above

You must not circulate this book in any other binding or cover
and you must impose this same condition on any acquirer

British Library Cataloguing in Publication Data

Data available

Library of Congress Cataloging in Publication Data

Data applied for

ISBN 0-19-722320-6

1 3 5 7 9 10 8 6 4 2

Typeset by Joshua Associates Ltd., Oxford
Printed in Great Britain
on acid-free paper by
Print Wright Ltd., Ipswich

KING ALFRED'S COLLEGE
LIBRARY

284.
3
HUD

0236730 X

ACKNOWLEDGEMENTS

The present edition represents the second half of work that has been very long in progress; the first half, an edition of the sermon of William Taylor and the *Testimony* of William Thorpe, was published by the Early English Text Society as OS 301 in 1993. The texts here proved too long and complex to be included in the same volume, but, like those, have been on my desk for over twenty years now—during which time my views about them, and especially about their origins, have shifted.

I am glad to acknowledge permission to print the texts here from manuscripts in the British Library and Lambeth Palace Library, and to include plates. I am also grateful to the authorities of the Cambridge University Library and the Huntingdon Library, San Marino, for access to manuscripts collated here, and for permission to include plates. As with the previous EETS edition, I remain indebted to Mr. John Fuggles, then of the National Trust, for arranging the temporary deposit of the Blickling Hall copy of *A proper dyaloge*, bound together with the early print of Thorpe, in the Bodleian Library. My main debt, however, is to the assistants in the Bodleian Library, and especially in Duke Humfrey's Library, for their continued patience and assistance.

Work on these texts has been many times interrupted by other commitments, scholarly and administrative, and indebtedness is hard now to enumerate. Dr. Ian Doyle has remained an invaluable source of advice, Dr. Pamela Gradon a constant source of encouragement and interest. Long ago the Revd. Dr. David Thomson advised me on two difficulties in the Titus text. More recently conversations with Helen Barr, Kantik Ghosh, Ralph Hanna, Richard Sharpe and Fiona Somerset have alerted me to relevant materials. I am glad to acknowledge the grant given by the Oxford faculty board of English Language and Literature which covered the invaluable work done by Dr. Edward Jones in checking the texts and variants at the final stage. And it is a great pleasure to thank Dr. Helen Spencer, the Society's Editorial Secretary, for her stoical tolerance of an editor's importunities and Mrs Anne Joshua for her expertise with a more than usually taxing typographical situation.

CONTENTS

PLATES

British Library, MS Cotton Titus D.v, f. 3^r   *frontispiece*
(reproduced by permission of The British Library)

British Library, MS Egerton 2820, ff. 38^v–39^r   *facing p. xvii*
(reproduced by permission of The British Library)

Cambridge University Library, MS Dd.14.30(2),
ff. 26^v–27^r   *facing p. xviii*
(reproduced by permission of the Syndics of Cambridge University
Library)

Huntington Library, MS HM 503, ff. 51^v–52^r   *facing p. xx*
(reproduced by permission of *The Huntington Library, San Marino,
California*)

Lambeth Palace Library, MS 551, ff. 46^v–47^r   *facing p. xxii*
(reproduced by permission of Lambeth Palace Library)

ABBREVIATIONS

References to unprinted sources, and to printed primary sources, are explained in sections 1–2 of the bibliography. The normal form of reference to printed secondary materials is by author's name, followed in brackets by date of publication, and by page or column numbers; these references are expanded in section 3 of the bibliography.

The main manuscripts edited here are referred to under the following sigla:

D: Cambridge, University Library, MS Dd.14.30(2)
E: British Library MS Egerton 2820
F: Cambridge, University Library, MS Ff.6.2
H: Huntington Library, San Marino, HM 503
L: Lambeth Palace Library, MS 551
T: British Library MS Cotton Titus D.v

The two sixteenth-century editions of part of the material in L are:

P: covers both printed editions, P1 and P2
P1: *A proper dyaloge* . . . ([Antwerp, ?1529], STC 1462.3)
P2: *A compendious treatyse* . . . (Antwerp, 1530, STC 1462.5)
Q: the modern edition of P2 by Parker (1996), for which see section 2 of the bibliography

Throughout the edition line numbers are prefixed with one of the sigla above, unless a sequence from the same text is given in which case the sigil against the first should be carried forward until another is explicitly given.

The following abbreviations, and abbreviated titles of frequently cited works (details of which, where not given here, appear in the bibliography) have been used:

Add.	Additional (in manuscript references)
ALD	See *Apology for Lollard Doctrines*
AV	Authorized Version of the Bible
BIHR	*Bulletin of the Institute of Historical Research* (London, 1923–)
BJRL	*Bulletin of the John Rylands Library* (Manchester, 1903–)

BL   British Library London
CA   Gower, *Confessio amantis*
CCCM   *Corpus Christianorum, continuatio medievalis* (Turnhout, 1952–)
CCR   *Calendar of Close Rolls*
CCSL   *Corpus Christianorum, series latina* (Turnhout, 1953–)
CPR   *Calendar of Patent Rolls*
CHMLP   *The Cambridge History of Later Medieval Philosophy*, ed. N. Kretzmann, A. Kenny and J. Pinborg (Cambridge, 1982)
CS   Camden Series (London, 1838–)
CSEL   *Corpus scriptorum ecclesiasticarum latinorum* (Vienna, 1866–)
CT   Chaucer, *Canterbury Tales*
CUL   Cambridge University Library
CYS   Canterbury and York Society (London, 1907–)
DML   *Dictionary of Medieval Latin from British Sources*, 1 A–L, ed. R. E. Latham and D. R. Howlett (Oxford, 1975–97)
Doct.   *Doctrinale* . . . by Netter of Walden, Thomas
EETS   Early English Text Society (London, 1864–); OS Original Series; ES Extra Series; SS Supplementary Series; where no indication of series is given, the Original Series is implied.
EHR   *English Historical Review* (London, 1886–)
Emden *Oxford*   See Emden (1957–9)
EV   Early Version of the Wycliffite bible
EWS   *English Wycliffite Sermons*
FDR   *Friar Daw's Reply* see *Jack Upland*
FM   See Forshall and Madden
FZ   *Fasculi Zizaniorum*
GO   *Glossa Ordinaria* (Antwerp, 1617)
GP   General Prologue to the Wycliffite bible
HBC   *Handbook of British Chronology*, ed. E. B. Fryde *et al.* (London, 3rd ed., 1986)
HUO   *The History of the University of Oxford ii Late Medieval Oxford*, ed. J. I. Catto and T. A. R. Evans (Oxford, 1992).
IPMEP   *Index of Printed Middle English Prose*, ed. R. E.

	Lewis, N. F. Blake, A. S. G. Edwards (New York and London, 1985)
JEH	*Journal of Ecclesiastical History* (London, 1950–)
JTS	*Journal of Theological Studies* (Oxford, 1899–)
LALME	*A Linguistic Atlas of Late Medieval English*, ed. A. McIntosh, M. Samuels, M. Benskin (Aberdeen, 1986)
LB	see Hudson (1985)
LL	*Lanterne of Liȝt*
LP	*Letters and Papers, Foreign and Domestic, Henry VIII*, ed. J. S. Brewer *et al.* (21 vols. and Addenda, London, 1862–1932)
LV	Later Version of the Wycliffite bible
MC	*Of Mynystris in þe Chirche*, ed. *EWS* ii. 328–65.
MED	*Middle English Dictionary*, ed. H. Kurath, S. M. Kuhn *et al.* (Ann Arbor, 1952– ; latest volume used W.2)
More *CW*	*The Complete Works of St Thomas More*
ns	new series
NT	New Testament
ODCC	*The Oxford Dictionary of the Christian Church*, ed. F. L. Cross and E. A. Livingstone (Oxford, 3rd edn., 1997)
OED	*Oxford English Dictionary* (13 vols., Oxford, reissued 1933)
Op. ard.	*Opus arduum*, see Brno University Library MS Mk 28
OT	Old Testament
PBA	*Proceedings of the British Academy* (London, 1903–)
PG	*Patrologia Graeca*, ed. J. P. Migne (Paris, 1857–66)
PL	*Patrologia Latina*, ed. J. P. Migne (Paris, 1841–)
Pol. Poems	see *Political Poems and Songs*
PPl	*Piers Plowman*
PPl. Crede	*Piers Plowman's Crede*
PR	See Hudson (1988)
Ps. Bodley 288, Ps. Bodley 877	Wycliffite revisions of Rolle's English Psalter commentary, found respectively in MSS Bodley 288, Bodley 877
Rot. Parl.	*Rotuli Parliamentorum* (7 vols., London, 1832)
RS	Rolls Series (London, 1858–1911)
SC	*A Summary Catalogue of Western Manuscripts in the Bodleian Library at Oxford* (Oxford, 1895–1953)

SCH	*Studies in Church History* (London, 1964–)
SEWW	*Selections from English Wycliffite Writings*
Sharpe *HLW*	*A Handlist of the Latin Writers of Great Britain and Ireland before 1540*, ed. R. Sharpe (Turnhout, 1997)
STC	*A Short-Title Catalogue of Books printed in England, Scotland and Ireland and of English Books printed abroad 1475–1640*, ed. A. W. Pollard and G. R. Redgrave, revised W. A. Jackson, F. S. Ferguson and K. F. Pantzer (2 vols., I–Z London, 1976, A–H London, 1986)
Taylor	Sermon by William Taylor, edited in *TWT*
TCC	Trinity College Cambridge
TCD	Trinity College Dublin
Thomson (with page)	See Thomson, J. A. F. Thomson (1965)
Thomson (with no.)	See Thomson, W. R. (1983)
Thorpe	*Testimony* by William Thorpe, edited in *TWT*
TWT	*Two Wycliffite Texts*, ed. A. Hudson (EETS 301, 1993)
Upland	see *Jack Upland*, bibliography section 2
VO	*Vae Octuplex*, ed. *EWS* ii. 366–78
Vulg.	Vulgate version of the Bible
Walsingham, *Chron. Angl.*	Walsingham, *Chronicon Anglie*
Walsingham, *Hist. Angl.*	Walsingham, *Historia Anglicana*
Walther	*Initia carminum ac versuum medii aevi posterioris latinorum* ed. H. Walther (Göttingen, 2nd ed. 1969)
WB	Wycliffite Bible
Whiting	*Proverbs, Sentences and Proverbial Phrases . . . before 1500*, ed. B. J. and H. W. Whiting (Cambridge, Mass., 1968)
Wilkins	*Concilia Magnae Britanniae et Hiberniae A.D. 446–1717*, ed. D. Wilkins (4 vols., London, 1737)
WW	*Nouum Testamentum . . . Latine secundum editionem Sancti Hieronymi*, ed. J. Wordsworth, H. J. White et al. (3 vols., Oxford, 1889–1954)
Wyclif works:	*De apos.* *De apostasia*
	De blas. *De blasphemia*

De civ. dom.	*De civili dominio* (3 vols.)
De dom. div.	*De dominio divino*
De eccl.	*De ecclesia*
De euch.	*De eucharistia*
De mand.	*De mandatis*
De off. reg.	*De officio regis*
De pot. pap.	*De potestate pape*
De stat. inn.	*De statu innocencie*
De ver.	*De veritate sancte scripture* (3 vols.)
Opus evan.	*Opus evangelicum* (2 vols.)
Op. min.	*Opera minora*
Pol. Wks.	*Polemical Works* (2 vols.)
Serm.	*Sermones* (4 vols.)
Supp. Trial	*Supplementum Trialogi*
Trial.	*Trialogus*

INTRODUCTION

1. PLAN OF THE EDITION

The present volume was intended to contain an edition of two works, a long sermon *Omnis plantacio* and a tract *Tractatus de oblacione iugis sacrificii*, which are claimed in the second to have been written by a single author. The sermon survives in four manuscripts, the tract in only one; the tract presents only the normal textual problems found in a text uniquely preserved in a rather poor copy. The position in regard to the sermon is more complicated. A shorter variant version of some of the material in it was printed from the single medieval copy in which it survives by F. D. Matthew in 1880 under the title 'The Clergy may not own Property'.[1] Matthew was not aware that part of this variant version had been incorporated into a Reformist tract now known as *A proper dyaloge betwene a Gentillman and an Husbandman*, issued first probably in 1529 and reprinted with additions in 1530,[2] nor aware of the overlapping sermon text. It became clear that this variant version should also be included in the present volume, since the status of the sermon could not fully be understood in isolation.

In regard to the edition of the sermon and its congener, the following points explain the contents of the present volume.

1. Texts. Where the texts run parallel: (a) Egerton is printed on left hand pages, with its apparatus at the foot of the page, continued where necessary on the right hand page with a line above, and running titles **Egerton sermon**; (b) Lambeth is printed parallel (so far as that is possible, given isolated verbal differences and variant orthography) on right hand pages, with its apparatus at the foot of the page, and running titles **Lambeth tract**. Where Lambeth is missing for a substantial period, Egerton is printed on both pages with its apparatus and running titles, and the converse for the few places where Lambeth has a substantial insertion not in Egerton. The conclusion to Lambeth is printed at the end of the Egerton

---

[1] See *The English Works of Wyclif hitherto unprinted* (EETS 74, 1880, revd. edn. 1902), pp. 362–404.

[2] STC 1462.3 and 1462.5; a modern edition, based on the second of these by D. H. Parker (Toronto, 1996), used Matthew's edition but does not use the sermon version edited here.

sermon (pp. 144–53), using both left and right hand pages, with its apparatus and running heads. The two texts are line-numbered independently. At the end of the shorter version's material a directive in italics indicates where that version continues. The text of the sermon version is based on E, that of the tract version on L.

2. Apparatus. That below the text of L is intended to record marginal material in L, emendations made to L, and variants from the two printed versions of this version, P1 and P2 (simply P where the two agree). Apparatus for the text of E includes emendations to the base text E, variant readings from the other three manuscripts of the sermon version DHF, marginal material in EDHF. It also records those variants from L which either agree with one or more of the sermon manuscripts, or which might explain their readings; this is intended to facilitate the textual comparison of the two versions.[3] In this bank is also included a record of L's omitted material. It is important to stress that this should *not* be taken to imply that L is textually derived from E—it is simply that, since L is generally shorter than E, it is typographically easier to subordinate it to the longer text; the question of priority is discussed below (pp. xlii–xliv).

3. Introduction. Both versions are discussed in full. Where a sequence of line numbers is given, the source, E or L, is indicated only before the first and should be understood to continue until the other is entered.

4. Notes. These primarily relate to the sermon version in E, again with no implication of priority. Where the two texts are parallel, L's line numbers are given in brackets after those of E; where L omits material no second line number is recorded; where L adds material (save at the end), these are inserted after the last shared note; notes relating to L's substitution of L966–1310 for E2491–3099 are to be found after the last note to E.

5. Glossary. This relates primarily to the version in E (together with the Titus tract); variant spellings and line references from L are not included. The only forms of L included in the glossary are those in passages not paralleled in E, or where L's spelling might be regarded as offering a discrepant reading from E's.

---

[3] Isolative variants from L are thus very rarely recorded in this way, though combinative variants regularly appear.

1. ff. 2^r–100^v inc. incomplete at 24 *heuene and lede hem perinne* . . . ends incomplete 2949 *ȝou here þat if ony*. Material is missing in the course of the text because of the loss of leaves. A further quire, as well as the last two leaves of quire 14, would have been needed to complete the text.

The manuscript is written in the same hand as E,[7] and is of precisely the same format and layout. Quotations in Latin and references are underlined in red in the text and in the marginalia, and a few other words are similarly underlined, apparently for emphasis; there are alternate blue and red paraph marks. The text has been corrected by the original hand, and *cor* is entered at the end of quire 5.[8] There are no ornamented capitals, but with the loss of the first leaf there is no obvious opportunity for one. The manuscript towards the end was damaged at the inner gutter, perhaps from having been bound too tightly; some leaves have been remounted.

There is no sign of medieval ownership, nor is it clear from what source it came into the Cambridge University Library.

In addition to E and D, there is a third manuscript in this hand, now St. John's College Cambridge G.28, a small volume but larger than those involved here.[9] The original contents were a copy of *The Pore Caitif*, in its standard non-interpolated form;[10] on its front flyleaves appear two uniquely recorded poems, one against the friars and the other in their defence.[11] The layout of the manuscript is closely comparable to that of E and D; the opening capital is, however, less elaborately ornamented than that of E. The manuscript belonged in the fifteenth century to John Graunge, who also owned St. John's G.11 (a fifteenth-century copy of Latin theological and

manuscripts (and the sense) confirms. The manuscript is now kept in a box with the penultimate binding retained separately.

[7] The same hand appears once more in St. John's College Cambridge G.28, a copy of *The Pore Caitif*.

[8] Because of the cropping of its margins, it is not clear whether E had been similarly checked.

[9] See *A Catalogue of the Manuscripts preserved in the Library of the University of Cambridge* (Cambridge, 1856–67), i.537, and further handwritten notes kept in the Library (made before the last rebinding).

[10] See M. T. Brady, '*The Pore Caitif*: An Introductory Study', *Traditio* 10 (1954), 529–48 at p. 532 n. 39, and the same author's 'Lollard Interpolations and Omissions in Manuscripts of *The Pore Caitif*', in *De Cella in Seculum*, ed. M. G. Sargent (Cambridge, 1989), pp. 183–203 at p. 184.

[11] *IMEV* 3697 and 161, edited R. H. Robbins, *Historical Poems of the XIVth and XVth Centuries* (New York, 1959), nos. 68–9.

canonistic materials); both manuscripts came to the college library from the collection of Thomas, Earl of Southampton in 1635.

H: San Marino California, Huntington Library MS HM 503

131 parchment leaves, size 127 mm by 97 mm, written frame 92 mm by 60 mm; ruled in a single column of 21 lines.[12] Collation: ii paper and i parchment flyleaves, $1-8^8$ (ff. 1–64), 9^8 lacks 8 (ff. 65–71), 10^8 (ff. 72–9), 11^8 lacks 1 (ff. 80–6), 12^8 lacks 4–5 and 8 (ff. 87–91), $13-15^8$ (ff. 92–115), 16^8 lacks 2 (ff. 116–22), 17^8 lacks 8 (ff. 123–9), i parchment and ii paper flyleaves; quire signatures +, a–q and catchwords are visible throughout. Margins have been only slightly cropped, and the pricking is still visible in the early leaves on the outer edges.

1. ff. 1^r-129^r *In nomine patris et filii et spiritus sancti amen* inc. *omnis plantacio quam non plantauit pater meus celestis eradicabitur. Mathei xv.* Almiti god þe trinite fadir . . . expl. . . . *leste þou be disceyued bi her fals signes. Amen amen so mot it be. Deo gracias.*

2. f. 129^v single 6–line stanza, *IMEV* 3098.5, written out as prose, inc. *Sche þat Y loue alleþermoost and loþist to begile*, ending *Wiþ an Y and an O, Crist Y hir biteche, / And Y lay louesik in my bed Y bed non oþer leche*; probably part of a longer poem, but no other copy known.[13]

Item 2 is an addition, made later in a hand of the middle or end of the fifteenth century on a blank flyleaf. The layout of the manuscript as originally written is very similar to that of E and D, but the hand is more informal. It is a fere-textura type of the early fifteenth century. The initial at the opening of the text is in blue with gold, white, red, green and ink ornamentation in a style similar to E. Blue paraph marks appear through the text, and the letter following these is regularly touched in red. Biblical references, quotations in Latin and some quotations in English are in red. The text has been corrected by the original scribe and by more than one other hand. One of the correctors also added to the outer margin of f. 51^v against 1203 the note 'For þis sayde frere Claxton a

---

[12] A brief description of the contents appears in R. Hanna, *The Index of Middle English Prose Handlist 1: A Handlist of Manuscripts containing Middle English Prose in the Henry E. Huntington Library* (Woodbridge, 1984), pp. 32–3, and a fuller account in C. W. Dutschke et al., *Guide to Medieval and Renaissance Manuscripts in the Huntington Library* (2 vols., San Marino, 1989), pp. 239–40.

[13] See R. L. Greene, 'A Middle English Love Poem and the *O-and-I* Refrain Phrase', *Medium Aevum* 30 (1961), 170–6.

Huntington Library, MS HM 503, ff. 51ᵛ–52ʳ

Reproduced by permission of The Huntington Library, San Marino, California

prechour and doctor of dyuynyte in þe chayere at oxenforde þat holy wrytte is fals heresye and impossible';[14] the hand is little later than that of the text. The manuscript is in a sixteenth-century blindtooled calf binding, more recently rebacked.

The manuscript belonged in the early sixteenth century to an unnamed vicar of Billingshurst, according to an inscription on f. 129 below the end of the text.[15] There is a bookplate of Sir John Cope Bart inside the front cover;[16] it was sold as lot 24 in the Cope sale on 4 March 1913. It appeared in the Quaritch catalogue 328 (1914) as lot 585, and in their catalogue 344 (1916) as lot 39 with a facsimile. It was acquired by the Huntington Library in 1925.

F: Cambridge University Library MS Ff. 6.2

84 paper leaves, measuring approximately 203 mm by 145 mm; unruled, but written in a single column of variable size, around 165 mm × 125 mm. Collation: i stub, ii flyleaves plus stubs, $1-17^4$ (ff. 1–68), 18^2 (ff. 69–70), $19-20^4$ (ff. 71–80), 21^2 (ff. 79–80), 22^4 (ff. 81–4), ii flyleaves, i stub. Quire signatures a–s are visible on quires 1–18, a–c on quires 19–21. The watermarks in the three items all seem to be the same, though, since they are in the inner gutter it is impossible to identify their precise form.

1. ff. 1^r-70^v (quires 1–18), inc. $M^{th}.xv^\circ$ Omnis plantacio qua (sic) non plantauit . . . Allmyghti god the trinite the father; ends lest ye be dyssayvyd by þer false sygnez. Finis. Laus detur deo.

2. ff. 71^r-80^r (quires 19–21), inc. Too the lorde god and to all the congregacion of cristys churche I Jack vpon londe; ends sett ye in þe ryght way to hevyn Jack upon lond lookith for an answer schortly wiþ all spedynes; Jack Upland lines 1–411, headed in a different hand 'Chaucer'.[17]

---

[14] See Emden Oxford i.426, Sharpe HLW no. 1725, and references given in both. Claxton was a Dominican, one of the members of the Oxford university committee who sent a letter to Convocation in 1411 condemning 267 errors of Wyclif; for the possibility that Claxton was also involved in scrutiny of another case of putative heresy in Oxford in 1416 see F. D. Logan, 'Another Cry of Heresy at Oxford: the Case of Dr. John Holand, 1416', SCH 5 (1969), 99–113 at pp. 101–2.

[15] Billingshurst, south west of Horsham, is in the Chichester diocese, an area for which evidence of early heresy is poor (though this may be due in part to the very limited survival of episcopal registers for the diocese).

[16] See Historical Manuscripts Commission, Appendix to the 3'd Report (London, 1872), p. 243 no. 20; at that point the Cope collection was housed at Bramhill House, Hampshire.

[17] See the edition by P. L. Heyworth, Jack Upland, Friar Daw's Reply and Upland's Rejoinder (London, 1968); description of this manuscript pp. 1–2.

3. ff. 81ʳ–84ᵛ (quire 22), headed *The prynce Sathanas commyssion vnt* (sic) *his welbelovyde sectis of perdicion*; ends *Suche rest as we haue be wiþ yow euermore. Amen*; a Lollard version of the *Epistola Sathane ad Cleros*.[18]

Despite some variations in the appearance of the script, the whole seems to be written in a single secretary hand of the first half of the sixteenth century. In item 1 Latin quotations and the biblical references are underlined in red, together with some of the translations of biblical passages; chapters (see below p. xlv) are ruled off in red. This rubrication was probably done by the scribe as he worked, since there are a few marginal references in red certainly entered by the scribe (e.g. f. 53ᵛ). The scribe wrote the foliation in the centre top of each recto up to the end of item 1, but not thereafter and modern numbering completes the foliation; his quire signatures appear on the first leaf of each quire save the last.

According to notes kept in the Cambridge University Library, the manuscript belonged to Richard Holdsworth DD, Master of Emmanuel (died 1649), in whose collection it was 103 (a number which appears at the head of f. 1); it was adjudged to the University in 1664.[19]

(ii) A further manuscript contains some of the material of the sermon in a tract of ten chapters followed by three series of authorities, the first in English, the second and third in Latin.

L: Lambeth Palace Library MS 551

62 parchment leaves, measuring approximately 142 mm by 95 mm; written space 87 mm by 55 mm; 21 ruled lines (22 from f. 57 onwards). Collation: one loose sheet sewn through, 1–7⁸ (ff. 2–57), 8⁶ (ff. 58–62) lacks 6 cut away.[20] The volume is vellum bound originally with leather ties, and the pastedowns are pieces of parchment manuscripts of s.xi–xii, at the front (with stub after f. 8) a part of Augustine *De magistro* (PL 32.1201–2), and at the back (with stub after f. 57) part of

---

[18] Edited *SEWW* no. 17.

[19] The notes are supplementary to the description in *A Catalogue of the Manuscripts preserved in the Library of the University of Cambridge* (Cambridge, 1856–67), ii.510. The identification is noted with no. 103 in S. F. Parris's catalogue, CUL MS Dd.8.45, where it is described, f. 151ᵛ, as 'Liber Theologicus Anonymi Anglicè'.

[20] A brief description appears in M. R. James, *A Descriptive Catalogue of the Manuscripts in the Library of Lambeth Palace: The Medieval Manuscripts* (Cambridge, 1932), pp. 756–7, and a more recent account of the contents in O. S. Pickering and V. O'Mara, *The Index of Middle English Prose Handlist XIII: Manuscripts in Lambeth Palace Library* (Cambridge, 1999), p. 52.

Lambeth Palace Library, MS 551, ff. 46ᵛ–47ʳ

Reproduced by permission of Lambeth Palace Library

Augustine's *De mendacio* (PL 40.493–4). There are two sets of modern pencil foliations in the manuscript; that at the foot of the recto leaves, which includes the first sheet, has been used here.

1. ff. 2ʳ–59ᵛ inc. *Fvndamentum aliud nemo potest . . . Almyȝty god þe trinyte*; ends *qui cum patre et spiritu sancto viuit et regnat deus. Amen.*[21]

The text ends at the foot of leaf 2 of quire 8; ff. 60–62 are blank, apart from later scribbles f. 62ᵛ. Gaps were left for capitals, but they have not been filled in. There is a gap of one line on f. 47ʳ at the end of the material that overlaps with the sermon after L965 and a second after the ensuing heading (after L968); another two gaps of one line each on f. 51ʳ before and after the heading between the first sequence of authorities in English and the second in Latin after L1051 and L1054 respectively; the same pattern is followed f. 57ᵛ before the third, Latin sequence after L1242 and L1244, and a final blank line is left before 1305. The hand varies in appearance somewhat, but is probably the same throughout.

On f. 62ᵛ an inscription is entered in a sixteenth-century hand: 'Be hyt had yn mynd wat Robert Ansell hathe Resevod (*sic*) of sentomas quarter' followed by a series of names with amounts; the names are unhelpful: 'charllys/ Dayygche/ Danyell/ Thomas danyell/ John Foster/ Wyllyam Foster/ Mondy/ Bokynden/ Horwod/ Chyrbyrry senyor/ Haddon'; above the whole appears what is probably another name 'Borke' followed by another sum. In the outer margin is a fifteenth-century note 'Cleros grece / sors latine dicitur', picking up the information within the text at L1227–8.

Part of the text in the shape in which it appears in L was incorporated into two books produced around 1529–30. A modern edition of the second of these, with collation of the first, was produced by D. H. Parker (Toronto, 1996), and his line numbers (preceded by *Q*) are added in these descriptions. Neither book names an author, and the question of the origin of them will be discussed below (pp. lxi–lxiii).

P¹ STC 1462.3 [1529]?[22]

Title: A proper dyalo/ge betwene a Gentillman and an Husband man /eche complaynenge to other theyr myse/rable calamyte

---

[21] Text previously printed Matthew, pp. 362–404.

[22] For further discussion of the date see below p. lxi–lxii. This edition was not included in the first edition of STC; the second STC's attribution of this and the following to William Barlow cannot be accepted; see below p. lxii.

through the am/bicion of the clergye. ¶An A. B. C. to the spiritualte.

The volume consists of 24 unnumbered leaves, size 132 mm by 90 mm; collation A-C⁸ (with C³ missigned C⁴). The contents, printed continuously though with internal indications of shifts, are:

1. sig. A.1, a 21 line alphabetical poem against the clergy (Q7–27).
2. sigs. A.1ᵛ–A.2ᵛ, ten seven-line stanzas addressing the reader (Q28–97).
3. sigs. A.2ᵛ–B.4, the opening of the dialogue (Q99–684).
4. sigs. B.4ᵛ–C.4, *an olde treatyse made aboute the tyme of kinge Rycharde the secounde* (Q685–1042); text corresponding, after an opening sentence, to L630–965.
5. sig. C.4ᵛ, twelve lines of dialogue (Q1043–56).
6. sigs. C.4ᵛ–C.6ᵛ, (Q1057–1144), text as L969–1051.
7. sigs. C.6ᵛ–C.8ᵛ, the conclusion of the dialogue (Q1145–1682).

The book has no imprint or date, but has been associated because of its type with a series of reforming tracts put out under the name of Hans Luft of Marburg; the imprint was a cover for the printer J. Hoochstraten of Antwerp, who is named as the printer of the other edition.[23] It is likely that this edition was slightly the earlier of the two, since the other combines the material of this with material from another pamphlet put out from the same press in 1530.[24] There are two copies of this book surviving, now Oxford Bodleian Library Wood 774 and Blickling Hall I.e.17; both are collections of reforming materials, in the second of which the present text is bound together with *The examinacion of Master William Thorpe*.[25]

---

[23] See Hume (1973), nos. 6–7, 10–11, 13, 15–19; cf STC vol. 3 p. 110 for Luft and p. 85 for Hoochstraten. For the Antwerp press see R. Steele, 'Notes on English Books printed abroad, 1525–48', *The Library* 11 (1912), 197–213; M. E. Kronenberg, 'De geheimzinnige drukkers Adam Anonymus te Bazel en Hans Luft te Marburg ontmaskerd (1526–1535)', *Het Boek* 8 (1919), 241–80, and 'Notes on English printing in the Low Countries', *The Library* 4th series 9 (1929), 155–9, 'Forged Addresses in Low Country Books in the Period of the Reformation', *The Library* 5th series 2 (1948), 85–7, and most recently A. G. Johnston and J.-F. Gilmont, 'Printing and the Reformation in Antwerp', in *The Reformation and the Book*, ed. J.-F. Gilmont, trans. K. Maag (Aldershot, 1998), pp. 188–213.

[24] See further below p. xxv. Attention to this separate edition was drawn by M. E. Kronenberg, *Nederlandsche Bibliographie van 1500 tot 1540* (The Hague, 1923–61), no. 4215.

[25] For the second see *TWT*, pp. xxx–xxxi. In the first the present text is no. 5, preceded by copies of STC 1462.7, 22043, 5103, 23318, and followed by 22022, 16984 and 3965; the latest of these is the fourth, dated by STC as 1604 though this copy lacks a titlepage.

P² STC 1462.5 (formerly 6813)²⁶ 1530

Title: A proper dyalo/ge betwene a Gentillman and a husbandman / eche complaynynge to other their mise/rable calamite through the am/bicion of the clergye. / ¶An A. B. C. to the spiritualte.

The volume consists of 32 unnumbered leaves, size 147 mm by 94 mm; collation A–D⁸. The first five items are identical with those of P¹, though reset and from sig. A.5ᵛ somewhat compressed (item 4 is B.4–C.3ᵛ; item 5 C.3ᵛ, item 6 C.3ᵛ–C.5ᵛ; item 7 C.5ᵛ–C.7ᵛ).

8. sigs. C.8–D.8, *A compendious / olde treatyse shewynge howe that we / ought to haue the scripture in / Englysshe* (1292–1682) preceded by two seven-line stanzas and interrupted by a third.

Colophon sig. D.8 *Emprented at Marborow in the lan/de of Hessen by me Hans Luft / in the yere of owre lorde. M./CCCCC. and XXX.* Item 8, without the three stanzas had been printed as a separate pamphlet, under the Hans Luft of Marburg imprint, in 1530; it is STC 3021.²⁷ Again the work was a Lollard tract, a reworking of part of a long determination on translation written in Latin by Richard Ullerston.²⁸ There seems no reason to doubt the date given by the colophon to P², and this is accepted by STC. There is only a single surviving copy, London British Library C.37.a.28(5).²⁹

B. THE TRACT *TRACTATUS DE OBLACIONE IUGIE SACRIFICII*

Only a single copy of this is known:

T: London, British Library MS Cotton Titus D.v

100 parchment leaves, size 157 mm by 106 mm; ruled in a single column of 115 mm by 65–70 mm usually of 25 written lines. In the recent

²⁶ The first edition of STC listed the book under the heading of *Dialogue*. A facsimile of the single copy of this edition appeared with an introduction by Francis Fry (London, 1863), and it was from this edition that the text was reprinted in Arber Reprints 8 (London, 1871), pp. 125–84, and by D. H. Parker (1996).

²⁷ Hume no. 16; two copies survive, London British Library C.25.d.16(1) and San Marino Huntington Library 95901. A later edition of [1538?] was produced by R. Banckes of London, STC 3022; the only surviving copy is London British Library C.37.b.42.

²⁸ The English Lollard tract was edited by C. F. Bühler, 'A Lollard Tract: on Translating the Bible into English', *Medium Aevum* 7 (1938), 167–83, and earlier by M. Deanesly, *The Lollard Bible* (Cambridge, 1920), pp. 437–45. Though Deanesly was aware of a related Latin tract, she had not seen it. For Ullerston's authorship of that Latin work, see *LB*, pp. 67–84, and for the tract *LB*, pp. 229, 231–2, 242–4.

²⁹ Again the volume is a collection with the present tract as no. 5, the preceding items being 4240, 3036a, 24238, 20036 and the following items 24167, 14667, 2788 and 845.

rebinding in 1982 the medieval quires have been remounted on stubs. Collation: iii paper flyleaves, i binding strip from a medieval Latin manuscript, probably liturgical, with decorated capitals, probably discarded because on one side the writing is upside-down, ii older paper flyleaves, $1-12^8$, 13^4, iv paper flyleaves. Catchwords but no quire signatures survive. Post-medieval ink numbering of the folios begins at f. 1 with the text; this has been modified by a subsequent pencil numeration which starts with the two older paper flyleaves (but omits the binding strip); this latter numeration has been followed here. The last two leaves, ff. 101–2, were originally blank.

1. ff. $3^r–100^v$ *inc. For as meche as antecrist now in þe ende of þe world . . .; ends three lines from the bottom of f. 100^v . . . honour into þe world of wordlis. Amen*, and on the last two lines *Explicit tractatus de oblacione iugis sacrificij.*

The manuscript has been badly affected by damp and worms; in a number of places letters or short words are illegible or missing because of these causes.[30] The single hand is a practised bookhand of the first half of the fifteenth century; the ascenders of letters on the first line are extended into the upper margin. On f. 3^r the opening initial is in blue with red flourishing, but now faded. Authorities mentioned are sometimes underlined in red. The original scribe corrected his work after its completion. At the foot of many of the folios there is a running abridgement of the material above in a later medieval hand, and this is sometimes also found in outer margins; this is faint and in many parts illegible.[31] The summary appears to be an accurate one, and the viewpoint of its author is not evident. There are also later marginal notes on the subject matter.

On ff. 101^v and 102^r are a number of notes, many of them heavily rubbed and largely illegible. On f. 102^r appears a note prefixed by 'Thomas bonde awithe this booke of Eve^m' in a fifteenth-century hand; the identity of this man is unclear, and the expansion of the final name as 'Evesham' must be regarded as uncertain. Below this appears in a different hand a second note which, so far as it can be read, suggests an outlook more orthodox than the contents of the main text. In the early seventeenth century it belonged to Robert Hegge of Durham, whose signature appears at the head of f. 3^r. On

---

[30] Reconstruction (enclosed here within angle brackets) is usually simple, but readers will differ in their assessment of which letters require such marking.

[31] Because of its frequent illegibility, it has not been transcribed here.

f. 2ᵛ appear various notes about the date of the manuscript and its subject in sixteenth- and seventeenth-century hands, including one signed 'Steph. Hegg'. Stephen Hegge was a Durham notary, and the father of Robert, c. 1597–1629. Robert also owned other manuscripts, the best known of which is that of the N-Town cycle of plays, now BL Cotton Vespasian D.8. This latter, and the present manuscript, seem to have come into the Cotton collection in the 1620s.[32]

THE LANGUAGE OF THE MANUSCRIPTS

Given that all the material edited here is in prose, and that the base manuscripts are relatively consistent in their spelling systems, it seems difficult to make any conjectures about the language of the author. It seems inherently improbable that the author's dialect should have been widely discrepant from the language of all surviving manuscripts, with the rider that the similarity between the orthography of all five surviving medieval manuscripts could be the result of scribal translation, either coincidentally producing that similarity or owing it to a stage when the author's three works were transmitted together into a different language. But, even if this suggests the likelihood that both author and scribes owed their orthography to a similar background area, it remains impossible to prove, especially if author and scribes derived from areas contiguous or nearly so. The only trace of an earlier stage of language comes from a single textual problem at E864. Here ED read *if alþouȝ*, HF *alþouȝ*; the former makes no sense, but it is possible that the archetype of all four manuscripts read *if al*, a rarely attested conjunctional form which the two scribes ED and H modified. *LALME* shows *if al* as occurring in north Midland counties, alongside the more widely attested and distributed *al if*; this latter is common in the texts here.[33] But this single conjecture, and even

---

[32] See S. Spector, 'The Provenance of the N-Town Codex', *The Library* 6th ser. 1 (1979), 25–33, and the same author's introduction to his edition of *The N-Town Play* (EETS SS 11, 1991), pp. xvi–xviii. The present manuscript does not appear in the catalogue of the Cotton collection dated 1621 in BL Harley 6018, but it is found in the catalogue of the early 1630s in BL Additional 36789, f. 75, and that made prior to 1639 in BL Additional 36682B, f. 207ᵛ. In *Catalogue of the Manuscripts in the Cottonian Library, 1696*, ed. C. G. C. Tite (Cambridge, 1984), p. 128 it appears under its current shelfmark.

[33] See *LALME* iv.56 for *if al*, recorded in texts from Cheshire, Lincolnshire, Nottinghamshire, Warwickshire and West Riding of Yorkshire; iv.55 *al if*, in texts from all of these counties apart from the first, together with others from a similar region plus more central Midlands counties such as Leicestershire, Northamptonshire, Huntingdonshire and the Soke of Ely. For *al if* in these texts see Glossary.

the attested conjunctional form, offers little assistance. Any detailed comments must relate to the surviving copies. Leaving aside for the moment the latest of the manuscripts involved, F of the sermon, the remaining five manuscripts involve four scribes: that of E and D, plus those of H, L and T.

All these four orthographic systems can in general terms be localized as south-east Midland in dialect, with present tense verbal inflexions of -*eþ*/-*iþ* 3sg. (*LALME* dot map 646), -*en* pl. (map 652), 3pl. pronouns *þei, her, hem* (maps 30, 42, 52), OE long *a* as ⟨o⟩, long and short *y* as ⟨i⟩, and *eo* as ⟨e⟩. All four scribes use only *ȝ*-forms of the verb 'to give', a feature which places all of them south of the Wash, given the easterly nature of the language shown (map 425).

Beyond the general similarity, some discrepancies are found. To use the three base texts here, the most obvious can be tabulated as follows:

	E	L	T
'they'	þei	þai	þei[34]
'such'	such(e	siche	seche[35]
'which'	which(e	whiche	wiche[36]
'any'	ony	eny	any[37]
'much'	moche	myche	meche[38]
'through'	þoruȝ	þorow	þour[39]
'given'	ȝoue(n	ȝeue(n	ȝoue(n/ȝeue[40]
'work' vb.	worche	–	wirche[41]

Despite these variations, a similar localization seems most likely for all three scribes. The scribe of E and D, together with that of H, was placed by *LALME* in Huntingdonshire, though without further refinement or linguistic profile.[42] Looking at the sources more

---

[34] See *LALME* maps 30–1.
[35] *LALME* maps 67–8, 73.
[36] *LALME* maps 76, 79.
[37] *LALME* maps 97–9.
[38] *LALME* maps 101–3.
[39] See *LALME* ii.225–30.
[40] *LALME* maps 425, 427, 430, 432.
[41] *LALME* maps 313, 315; the forms are not frequent in either E or T, and so may not be so significant as the divergencies in the rest of the list. L has only the nominal form *worchinge*.
[42] See for E i.109, 201, for D i.66, 201, and for H i.92 and 201.

precisely mapped for that county, it is striking how many of the manuscripts contain Wycliffite material.[43] None of them shares all the features charted above from any of the three manuscripts (E, D and H) here; the norm of Huntingdonshire practice in the eight features listed above is *þei, siche, which(e, ony, mych(e, þoruȝ/þorou, ȝouen, worche*. The orthography of the scribe of E and D is close to that of *LALME*'s linguistic profile 518, the scribe of BL Royal 17 B.i, a copy of the concordance to the Wycliffite New Testament, placed in south-west Huntingdonshire.[44] The only major discrepancy between ED and this lies in ED's regular *moche* against the Royal manuscript *mich(e*; but *moche* is frequent in Cambridge and Bedfordshire, and hence not impossible in conjunction with the other evidence.

L's departures from this Huntingdonshire language norm are in *þai, eny* and *ȝeuen*, though all of them are to be found as minority spellings in the county or as common in neighbouring counties. Not dissimilar to the orthography of L is that of LP 4267, BL Additional 37677 of Alkerton's sermon, located in Cambridgeshire, though there are discrepancies.[45] T, however, seems the most difficult to localize, though it may derive from a similar region.[46] The most idiosyncratic of T's spellings is *þour* 'through'. T's form is nowhere common, though it is found in two manuscripts localized in Cambridgeshire; but in neither of these are several of T's other regular forms found.[47] T's *seche* is found in scattered areas, mostly more western, but is recorded for Cambridgeshire.[48] Again in general, however, the

---

[43] See iii.181–94 for linguistic profiles of twelve scribes, including BL Additional 40672 hand 3, BL Harley 2396, Bodleian Douce 321, New College 95 hand 1, all of the English Wycliffite sermon cycle, four Wycliffite Bibles or biblical material (Lambeth Palace 369, Oxford Lincoln Coll. lat.119, TCD 75, all of WB, plus BL Royal 17 B.i of the concordance to WB), Bodley 288 of the Wycliffite revision of Rolle's Psalter commentary, and Manchester Rylands Eng.86 of Wycliffite tracts. Though not mentioned by *LALME*, the manuscripts of Taylor's sermon and Thorpe's *Testimony* (Bodley Douce 53 and Rawlinson C.208) are localizable on the borders of Hunts. and Cambs.

[44] Grid reference 518 250; see the editions of the preface listed in *IPMEP* no. 449.

[45] Notably 4267 *þoruȝ* and *þei/þey*.

[46] Using the full documentation in the offices of *LALME* before the publication of its volumes, a location of T between eastern Huntingdonshire and mid Cambridgesire was suggested to me by Professor Michael Benskin.

[47] See *LALME* iv.100. It is also witnessed occasionally in other counties, but these are further away from the area that seems to be in question. Cambridgeshire LP 4230 differs notably in the pres.pl.ind. inflexions, whilst LP 4711 shares very few significant features with T.

[48] See *LALME* iv.17.

spelling seems to derive, as do the systems of ED and L from the east central Midlands.

Perhaps surprisingly, it is the late copy F which has relics that suggest that its antecedents were less central than the manuscripts EDHL and T. Most strikingly F, beside normal *shal* and *shuld* has a number of examples of *xal* and *xuld*, forms almost limited to Norfolk.[49] Less distinctive, but nonetheless departing from the forms found in any of the other manuscripts involved here, are forms of the pres.ind.pl. in *-eth*, again alongside more normal *-e(n*.[50] This form is remarkable in that it was strongly recessive in the fifteenth century. These forms are almost certainly not the F scribe's normal usage (overall all are small minorities), but were copied by him from his exemplar. Taken together they suggest that F's exemplar was both early (i.e. of the first half of the fifteenth century) and also derived from north Norfolk.

The geographical indications of the manuscripts, with the exception of F, may be worth bearing in mind in the later discussion of the author's identity. But the frequency with which Wycliffite manuscripts can be orthographically located within a relatively small area must suggest possible explanations other than that of authorial origin: the most immediate is perhaps that of a scribal centre for dissemination of Lollard texts of differing origins, more prosaically the possibility that Lollards apprehended the advantages for dissemination of adopting the orthography of a relatively central and unflamboyant area. This last hypothesis would have the advantage of accounting both for the general similarities, but minor discrepancies, noted above for E, L and T and replicable in many other Wycliffite copies. But it leaves much more uncertain the question of the location both of the scribes' activity and of the author's home territory.

---

[49] See *LALME* map 149. Here *xal(l* E131, 195, 196, 292 etc., *xuld* E819 (variant), 1411, 1511 etc.

[50] See, for instance, *mayntenith* E212, *agreith* E219 (variant), *takyth* E339 etc.; the examples are sufficiently numerous, and their context sufficiently plain, for it to be incredible to explain them as intended as singulars.

3. TEXT AND MANUSCRIPT RELATIONS

A. THE SERMON *OMNIS PLANTACIO*

The four manuscripts of the sermon stand in a clear and fairly close relation to each other; since two of the four are in the same hand, and a third is of very similar format, this is not entirely surprising. A stemma can be constructed on the following basis:

1. The position of F

It is clear that F, though about a century later in its writing, is very closely related to H. HF share a large number of errors against E and D, or against one of them when the other is defective. Cases may be seen from the variants to lines 67, 101, 110, 176, 201, 211 etc., in all of which F shares the mistake of H. There are only two convincing cases where H is incorrect but F apparently correct: in both F is restoring a biblical quotation or reference (155 F *inducantur* as Vulgate, EDH *ducantur*, 778 margin EDF rightly *1 Cor.9*, H *1 Cor.1*), and its correct reading may not reflect the exemplar immediately before the scribe.[51] A third, and more puzzling, case is 272 where EDH read *supposen*, F *supposyd*; the context, with the parallel verb *tooken* 273, make a past tense preferable; the text has been emended. But it may be that the correction is an independent one on the part of F, and that the erroneous present tense was in the hyparchetype.[52] There are some other cases where H and F preserve different readings, the latter agreeing with ED, but where F's reading is credibly either a simple correction (eg 449, 1583, 2604, 3063, 3078), or a coincidental agreement (eg 569, 587, 2984). Most significantly for the relation of F and H, F incorporated into his text after 1203 the note concerning Claxton found in the margin of H—this note, not found in E or D, is extremely unlikely to have been part of the original text. Because of the date of F, H cannot descend from it; in any case F has a large number of minor rewordings, largely the

---

[51] WW confirm *inducantur* as the normal reading, though show *ducantur* as an unusual variant (see note to 155). The extension by F of the Latin quotation in 360, whilst correct against the Vulgate, is unlikely to be the reading of the original since none of the manuscripts include the clause in the translation that follows.

[52] At 1042 EDF all read *so þat*, whilst H has simply *so*; this latter reading seems certainly correct, and the text here has been emended. Coincidental substitution by F of the common collocation seems the likely reason for the agreement with ED.

result of its later date, which isolate it. There seems little, however, to controvert the conclusion that F was copied from H.

In regard to the original text, therefore, F has nothing significant to offer, and the curtailment of its multitude of divergent readings might seem sensible. It does, however, have some interest in relation to the later history of the text. As a result, with the exception of one substitution listed below p. lxv, its changes are recorded in the variants.

2. The group ED in contrast to H(F)

There is a large number of cases where H, usually accompanied by F, can be shown to be in error against ED (eg 43, 67, 104, 110, 160 etc.). This makes it clear that the pair ED cannot be descended from H. There is a slightly smaller number of instances where ED can be shown to be in error against H (notably 26 where H's correct reading is on an erasure, 915, 1437, 1587, 1868, and probably 637 and 2572 though D is lost at these points). H then cannot be descended from either E or D individually or from their exemplar. The stemma from the hyparchetype must be a bifurcating one, with ED descending from one branch, H, and in turn F, from the other.

3. The relationship of E and D

These two manuscripts are in the same hand, and, as would be expected and as the last section shows, are closely related. But D cannot descend from E, since the latter has errors not found in the former (eg 154, 789, 857, 1584, 1736 margin etc.). It is rather less clear that E could not descend from D. The number of instances where E is correct against D is small, and some of these could be independent correction by the scribe of E copying from D: see variants to 855, 937, 1608, 1748, 2140, in all of which the modification could credibly have been done independently, and 1980 where correction is unlikely to have been possible; compare 2351 where E first wrote the erroneous reading of D and then added the necessary *and* by interlinear insertion, or 2354 where E reads *fellen* canc. *in*, D *fellen in*, HF rightly *in*. Similarly in 1381, where D and HF agree in an apparently incorrect reading, E's preferable alternative could be independent emendation. But there remain seven cases where it seems unlikely that E, had he been copying from D, could have arrived at the correct reading; these are at 1693, 1790, 1876, 1995, 2319, 2483, 2567. In all of these D's reading is possible, but in comparison with the alternative seems unlikely to be the original; in all save the fourth another manuscript supports E's version.[53] It thus seems likely that the scribe made two copies of the same exemplar, rather than that he copied that exemplar once and then made his second version from his own first copy. Equally, however, one of his copies, D, was a much more accurate version than the other.

The stemma suggested from the evidence above may be represented diagrammatically thus:

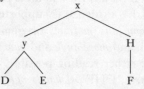

That x was itself a scribal copy rather than the original is suggested by 2999 H *is aliened*, E *is* canc. *aliened*, F *beyng strange* (D is lost), but *aliened* is required—in this case the error seems likely to have been in x. At 864 ED read *if alþou3*, HF *alþou3*; it seems possible that the original had *if al*,[54] expanded at x to *if alþou3*, and thereafter retained in ED but simplified in HF. The evidence that x was not the original is enlarged by scrutiny of the relation of the sermon to the Lambeth tract version, discussed below.

There are some cases where conflation in one or more of the four manuscripts may be suspected:

297 D *it*, E ⌜*as*⌝ *it*, H *as it*; necessary reading *as it*.

679 E *Cristis chirche . . . puttide*, DHF *þe chirche . . . putten*; E's first reading is clearer and in the second a past tense is neccssary.

789 D *3yue þou not to me*, E *3yue þou not 3oue to me*, H *haue þou not 3oue to me*, Vulgate *ne dederis* (pret.sj.), WB *3yue þou not*; D's reading is the easiest, but H's might be explained as an attempt to retain the past tense, E's is certainly impossible—x possibly with corrected reading?

866 E *men suppose þat such worldli lordlynesse of þe clergie*, DHF *suppose of þe clergie . . . lordlynesse* (D adds *of þe clergie*); either HF or E are possible, but D's repetition must be erroneous.

---

[53] The other manuscript is usually H, but at 1876 H has lost a folio but F supports E's reading. At 1995 either the reading of E or that of DHF is possible, but the verb *to seche* found in E is perhaps preferable.

[54] See note to 864 for the limited geographical distribution of *if al*, and above p. xxvii.

986 E *1*, DHF *as it is writun 1*; DHF anticipates the following *where it is writun þus* that follows the reference.

1066 E ⌐*summe ellis*⌐, om. DHF; an alternative to the *summe by foly ȝifte* of the preceding phrase seems needed, though it is possible that the original had a stronger one.

1291 E *conspiratours worchen*, DHF *conspiracie worchiþ*; the parallel with *Iewis* 1290 suggests an animate subject is needed, and *MED* suggests that E's reading is the more difficult.

1381 EL *lordship*, DHF *lordis*; EL's noun is parallel to 1379 and so is preferable, and E's evidence is supported by L.

1599 D *more quyk now and more*, E originally as D but *and more* crossed through and *more quyk* and *now* marked for reversal, H *now more quyk*; either reading possible.

1770 E *koude þei neuere*, DHF *þei koude not*; E's reading is stronger and seems preferable.

1908 E *forsoþe*, DHF *siþ*; again E's reading is the harder.

1911 E *þese anticristis meyne and retenu meuen*, D *þese anticristis and retenu meueþ* with *and* cancelled, H *þis anticristis retenu meueþ*; either E or H seem possible readings, but D's reading even in its corrected form (suggesting an obscure exemplar) seems unlikely since *þese* would naturally be understood as plural but the verb as singular.

1995 E *to seche*, DHF *such*; E's reading seems preferable.

2006, 2011 E *couent*, DHF *comounte*; either reading is possible,[55] but E's use of *comounte* at 2012–13 makes it unlikely that the scribe would have mistranscribed here.

2084 E *distraccioun*, DHF *distruccioun*; see note to the line for evidence that E's reading is preferable.

2393 E *þis fro þe staat*, DHF *þis fro þis staat*, L *þis fro þat state*; E's absence of repetition seems slightly preferable.

2797 D *deu. 15*, E *Num.15* but margin *Deut.15* different hand, HF *num.15*; correct reading *Deut.15*.

2871 D *can*, E *can not* with *not* cancelled, H *can not*; correct reading *can*.[56]

---

[55] See *MED couent* sense 1a 'number of person having something in common', and *communte* sense 4a 'religious community or brotherhood', though the former seems the more difficult.

[56] Recognition of cases is more difficult where D is lacking because of loss of leaves, and accounts for the relatively few instances from the last third of the text.

In some cases where a decision of correctness can be given it is possible that x had either an erroneous reading or one that was unclearly corrected, and that this obscurity was taken over into y; the scribes of the extant manuscripts in varying degrees attempted to put this right. The same explanation may be relevant to the cases where either reading is possible. If conflation by the scribes of any of the manuscripts is in question, E would seem to be the most likely case; in 297, 1066, 1599, 2871 this is visually clear in E's corrections. But E and D are written by the same scribe and can be shown to have copied the same exemplar (since in most respects their readings are very close). From this, in regard to the other cases, it must follow that the making of D preceded that of E, and that their common exemplar was itself corrected between the writing of D and that of E; the responsibility for most of the conflation was thus y's.

4. Choice of a base text for the sermon

As has been indicated, the DE branch of the stemma is textually somewhat better than that represented by HF. Logically, leaving aside the evidence of conflation, it would be preferable to choose D as the base text since that is in most respects the superior witness to the DE group. But D is now seriously defective because of damage to the manuscript; it lacks some 630 lines of the whole. Since E is so close to D, it therefore seems more sensible to use E as the base text; E lacks only ten lines at the end. For these last ten lines H must be used. It should be said that to use H as the base text would not remove the need for reconstruction, since H has lost seven leaves. Only by using F could the need for reconstruction be entirely avoided, but F is not a possible choice on either textual or linguistic grounds. From the stemma shown above it follows that E, save where conflation may be involved, must be emended not only where it can be shown to be erroneous but also wherever D and H agree against the reading of E—agreement between D and H must indicate the version found in both y and x.[57] The number of cases where E's corruption can be recognized would doubtless be increased had D survived without mutilation. In most instances E's variation is minor, though it is frequent; in some cases (see 52, 731, 982, 1144, 1584,

---

[57] Recent scepticism about the usefulness of constructing a stemma (see, for instance, G. Kane and E. T. Donaldson, eds., *Piers Plowman: The B Version* (London, 1975), pp. 17–20 and especially n. 10; their case is discussed by Hanna (1996), pp. 77–9 and stemmatics more generally, pp. 83–93) disregards this consideration.

1787, 1850) E's uncorrected reading needs to be restored. In the interests of consistency E has in those places where it stands in isolation from DHF (about one hundred in all) been emended.

B. THE LAMBETH TRACT AND THE PRINTED TEXTS

The material in EDHF runs parallel for substantial sections to a tract in ten chapters plus appended strings of authorities found uniquely in L. In turn part of the version witnessed by L was incorporated into the text known as *A proper dyaloge betwene a Gentillman and an Husband man*, STC 1462.3 and 1462.5.[58] A bibliographical description of these (as P1 and P2 respectively, P being used where no difference needs to be made) has been given above (pp. xxiii–xxv). This part consists in L630–965 corresponding to the sermon version E1877–2490 with all of L's variations, together with L's first appendix of supporting vernacular material (here L969–1051). P's text, though late, has interest both in suggesting that L's tract version attained circulation beyond the single manuscript in which it now survives, and in indicating L's defects as witness to that version.

In the *Dyaloge* the material overlapping with the present text is introduced both as an insertion and also as incomplete (P1 sig. B.4, P2 sig. B.4–4^v, Q656–84). The Husbandman, refuting an objection reported by the Gentleman that hostility to clerical temporalities is a new-fangled view, cites a work

> That . . . is aboue an houndred yere olde
> As the englysshe selfe dothe testefye. (Q661–2)

He laments that 'halfe the boke we want/ Hauynge no more left than a remenant/ From the begynnynge of the .vi.chapter verely' (Q671–3). He is, notwithstanding, encouraged by the Gentleman to cite it 'Begynne hardely at the syxte chapter/ Redynge forthe to the ende seryously' (Q676–7), and acknowledging that such old books 'include/ The pithe of a matter most fructuously' (Q679–80); this the Husbandman agrees to do, though apologizes for the lack of 'ornate speache' (Q684). The text is then headed

[58] Though the edition of this text by D. H. Parker (1996) is unsatisfactory in regard to its discussion of the relation to earlier material, the text line numbering, prefaced by Q, has been used in this chapter to facilitate comparison with that edition. Parker's text is declaredly that of P2, but it is clear from collation that it often uses the spellings of P1, less frequently readings of P1 without notice. The variants in the edition here derive from independent collation of the texts, and unless otherwise stated derive in spelling from P1.

¶Here foloweth an olde treatyse made aboute the tyme
of kinge Rycharde the secounde. (Q685–7)

At the end of the main text (L965, Q1042), P resumes the dialogue
with a single speech of each person (Q1043–56). The Husbandman
mentions the ensuing citations 'Prouynge it by their ovne doctovres
and lawes' (Q1052), and is encouraged by the Gentleman to read this.
There follows the English appendix (L969–1051, Q1057–1144).

The description offered, and the material that is included, does not
precisely fit with the arrangement offered in L: P's text begins not in
chapter 6, as would be expected, but in L's chapter 7; and P does not
incorporate the Latin sections which in L conclude the text (here
L1052–1310). P's material is not itself divided into chapters. But, quite
apart from the Husbandman's explicit mention of chapter division, the
layout of P in both prints reflects such a disposition. In P2 the material,
though extending over nearly eight leaves, has only three clear
paragraph divisions; these correspond precisely to the beginning of
L's chapters 8–10 (L670, 759, 873, Q733, 829, 949).[59] P1 has these and
two further paragraph divisions within L's chapter 8 at the sentence
divisions in L675 and L692 (Q740 and Q759) and one in L's chapter
nine (at L791, Q864). The suppression of these in P2 may suggest that
the text was rechecked against the medieval version between the issuing
of the two prints, though other evidence of this is not overwhelming,
and there are other suggestions that the compositor of P2 was anxious to
save space. The *Dyaloge* also acknowledges the separation of the main
text in chapters from the English appendix (L966–8, Q1044–56).

The relation of P to L, and of P1 to P2, has next to be considered,
and, as will appear, these questions are best taken together. The
manuscript used for the print was certainly not L. This, suggested by
the comments in the *Dyaloge* itself, is confirmed where agreements
between P and the sermon version of EDHF against L indicate that L's
text is probably corrupt. The most significant cases are at E2083–6 (L
after 753, Q823–6) and E2100–1 (L in 772, Q844–5), where L lacks
material found both in the sermon version and in P; since P's source was
plainly in the general form of L, L in these cases seems likely to represent
a defective copy of the tract version. The first of these is particularly
interesting in that it occurs where L apparently substitutes its usual
ending for each chapter; P retains the latter preceded by the material not

[59] Parker's new paragraphs at L895 (Q971) and L907 (Q983) reflect small breaks,
probably only insignificant failures of justification where a sentence ends close to the right
hand margin. There is a third such case at L1004 (Q1095) which Parker ignores.

present in L, thus suggesting that the hyparchetype of the tract version had both. These two passages have been incorporated as emendations into L. In addition there are some seven places where P agrees with EDHF (or with those available at the line in question) against L, and where again the preferable explanation must be the corruption of L.[60] Conversely, though it is impossible to prove whether P's exemplar was faulty or that the mistake was made by the compositor of P, there are places where L's text is closer to that of EDHF than P's.[61] There are a few cases where P's readings reflect those of a single manuscript of the sermon version against the remainder including L, but these are probably coincidental rather than significant either of descent or conflation; many of these involve agreement with F, the late copy of the sermon version.[62] Date is also the reason for the orthographic and morphological resemblances between F and P, though it is striking that P retains many medieval linguistic forms modernized by F.[63]

In general the two versions of P are extremely close, even in orthography. Certain obvious errors in P1 are corrected in P2;[64] P2 in turn was responsible for a few new mistakes.[65] In a few places P2 agrees with L, or with L plus the sermon manuscripts, against P1; but, since all are very minor instances, it is hard to see this as anything other than coincidence.[66] There is only one case where P1's isolative and apparently unoriginal reading would seem not to be restorable: this is E2272/L862 (Q938) where EDHLP2 all have *leue* against P1 *lawe*.

[60] See variants to E2041/L714 (Q781) *pair dedis*, E2044/L717 (Q784) *propir*, E2051/L724 (Q792) L reversal, E2065/L735 (Q804) *eny*, E2440/L932 (Q1008) L reversal, E2486/L956 (Q1033) L omission.

[61] Note the omissions of P at E2070/L740–1 (Q810), E2138–9/L808–9 (Q882–3), E2183–4/L834–5 (Q910), E2267/L858 (Q933), E2381/L875 (Q951), E2396–8/L890–2 (Q966); the second and last of these are obvious haplographies.

[62] See E1882/L635 (Q696) *nakid* omitted FP, E2072/L742 (Q811) *perfore* FP, E2078/L748 (Q817) FP1 *longith*, P2 *longe*, E2131/L801 (Q875) *hap* DP, E2390/L884 (Q960) HF *greeter*, P *a greater* (L *a grete*).

[63] For instance occasionally *tho*, against regular substitution of *thos(e* by F, as at L742 (Q811), L748 (Q817), L930 (Q1006, only in P1), though at L727, 730, 733 (Q795, 799 and 802) and many other cases substitution has occurred.

[64] See L705 (P1 twice *an*), L745 (*paye* P1), L761 (P1 om. *he*), L910 (P1 om. *it*), all corrected P2 and hence not appearing in Parker's edition (Q771, 814, 831, 986 though erroneously here the reading of P1 is printed).

[65] See L880 (Q955) P2 *him*; L941 (Q1018 silently emended to the P1 reading) P2 om. *be Crist*; L727 margin (Q footnote to line 861, again not acknowledged as not found in P2) P2 has lost the marginal biblical reference.

[66] See E2094/L766 (Q837) P2 et al. *hadde*, P1 *hath*; E2111/L783 (Q855) P2 and EDH *ensaumple*, P1 and F *exampyll*; E2246/L842 (Q917) P2 and L *hap*, P1 *hadde*.

For the most part P is a very faithful reproduction of the material as it appears in L. There is one extended passage, E2419–31/L915–23 (Q991–9), that shows more divergence but interestingly demonstrates the relation of L to P1 and P2, and also indicates the situation in regard to this version as compared with the sermon text; since it is hard to reconstruct what has happened from the variants, it is set out in full here:[67]

E2419 and lay peple robben hooli chirche if þei wiþdrawe þe tiþis
L915 and þe lay peple robben holy chirche if þai wiþdrew þe tiþis
P1   and the laye people robbe[
P2 (Q991) and the laye people robbe[

E from hem or turne hem to þe possessioun or vss and mynystracioun of
L fro hem[
P1
P2

E ony oþer staat . . . *to* E2422 L, P1 and P2 *omit all*

E robbid hem for as moche as þei han take her temperaltees from hem
L   ]for als miche as þai han take her temperaltes fro hem
P1   theym for as moche as they take theyr temperalteis fro theym
P2   ]them for as moch as they take their tempcralties[

E And þis takyng of þese temperaltees into þe hondis of þe
L And þis takynge of þes temperaltes into þe handis of þe
P1 And thys takynge of thes temperalteis into the handes of the
P2   ]into þe handes of þe

E clergie haþ neuere þe lesse malice of robberie alþou3 it be not
L clergi haþ neuer þe lesse malice of robrye[
P1 clergye hath neuer the lesse malyce[
P2 clergy hath neuer the lesse malice[

E don bi violence but raþer it haþ þe more cause for to be callid
L
P1
P2

E robberi and cause of malice in itsilf for as moche . . . wickidnesse
L   ]and cause of malice in itsiilfe
P1   ]in hit selfe
P2   ]in itselfe
    (2428); L, P1 and P2 *as* E

[67] Parker's text of P2 here is notably discrepant, and must reflect silent conflation with P1; the readings given here are taken direct from P1 and P2.

E For þus Lucifer robbide Adam of goodis of fortune of kynde
L For þus Lucifer robbid Adam boþe of goodis of fortune of kynde
P1 For thus Lucifer robbed Adam bothe of goodes of fortune, of kynde
P2 For thus Lucifer robbed Adam both of goodes of fortune of kinde

E and of grace as it is writun Gen.3 as þe clergie robbiþ[
L and of grace[(*margin* gen.iij)   as þe clergi haþ robbid and
P1 and of grace   as þe clergye hath robbed and
P2 and[(*margin* Gene.3)

E   ]now þe chirche of þese þre manere of goodis as it is tau3t
L   3it doþe þe chirche of þes þre maner goodis[
P1 yet do the chyrche of thes thre maner goodes[
P2]yet dothe the chirche of thes thre maner goodes[

E bifore. And as Lucifer dide þis
L   ]For ri3t as Lucifere did
P1   ]For ryght as Lucifer ded
P2   ]For right as lucifer dyd

For the most part this reveals a clear sequence: L reflects a substantially shorter version of the material found in the sermon version here, though which is the antecedent is not here evident. P1 represents a shortening of a text that credibly was identical to that found in L, whilst P2 has even further curtailed the text of P1. The inclusion of *the(y)m* by P in E2423/L917 (Q993) could reflect independent supply of an object for *robben*, producing coincidental agreement with E. It seems reasonable to conjecture that L here reproduces the common archetype of itself and P better than does either text of P, though it may be legitimate to wonder whether that archetype was in some way obscure in these lines, possibly by attempted interlinear correction of a copy realised to be defective.

Despite these complications, however, it seems fairly plain that the relations between L and P can be expressed as follows:

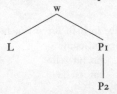

P2 may, on the evidence presented above, represent a text checked at least perfunctorily against *w* (or at least a text between *w* and P1).

C. THE RELATION OF LP TO EDHF

Differences of text make it clear that L cannot be the sole source of the sermon version, nor conversely the sermon version the sole source of L. Thus

(a) L lacks EDH E53–802, 848–50, 860–7, 876–82, 886–93, 941–1070, 1078–99, 1121–43, 1152–271, 1283–339, 1382–483, 1500–17, 1547–613, 1656–8, 1662–7, 1681–6, 1766–86, 1885–8, 1891–6, 1905–18, 1959–2037, 2058–60, 2107–83, 2189–244, 2249–53, 2283–379, 2398–402, 2449–72, 2491–3099.

(b) EDH lack L48–59, 65–9, 173–8, 185–9, 197–200, 221–30, 237–42, 310–14, 360–422, 449–50, 539–40, 551–2, 607–8, 650–69, 756–8, 870–2, 892–7, 961–1310.

Many, but not all, of the passages found only in L consist of biblical and patristic authorities, with a minimum of comment.

Looking for the moment only at the material shared between L and EDHF:

(a) L cannot be the source of EDHF because of errors found in L: see L's readings in comparison with E's text at E848–51/L113–14, E873–5/L129–30, E876–84/L130–2, E886–93/L133, E1359–61/L274, E1898/L641, E2420–3/L916–17, E2426–7/L919, E2487/L956, and perhaps at E2069–70/L740–1.

(b) EDHF cannot be the source of L because in shared material L seems at some points to preserve a preferable reading: thus at E44–6 there is no translation of the Latin quotations, but this is supplied in L45–6 and 48–9; E1110 *soudiours* is expanded as L208–9 *soudyoures and lyue by her wagis*, an expansion that the previous question about knights' status and means of livelihood seems to justify if not require; E1117 where L's explanatory (L215–16) 'for þai ben sotilly spolid of her lordeschipis in distroyng of her staate and power þat God sett hem in' again provides information that needs to be deduced from E's text, though it is resumed in E's *in alle þese poyntis* (1117); E1497 lacks the repetition of the words of Christ present in L308, where the point is clearer; E1524 *chirche* seems less suitable than L's *clergye* (321); at E1641 no Latin biblical quotation appears, though it is provided in L434–5; E1799 where the additional patristic reference in L551–2 provides a neater transition than is offered by the sermon; perhaps E2396–9 as against L890–5 where the shorter sermon version could derive from haplography in a passage with repetitive vocabulary; the reading at E2413 *þat* is unclear compared with L909 *to þe secular party þat*. The force of these is hard to assess: in many cases it could equally well be argued that L's version represents a later clarification, amplification or sophistication of E's more difficult antecedent reading, as that L reflects the original state of the text.

(c) Looking at cases where L agrees with one or a pair of sermon manuscripts: L26 shares the reading of ED at E26 (but see note), and of E at E2257 in L847; it has the same error as E at E914 (L155) but it does not share the two errors of ED at E915 (L156). There seems to be no case of agreement between L and H(F) in error, nor involvement of L in agreements between HD. The few cases of FL agreement are probably coincidental (E803/L70, E883–4/L132, E1151/L236, E1537/L334, E1746/L520–1, E2076/L746, E2091/L763, possibly E1687/L469 but H is lost).

All of the above would be compatible with the following diagram:

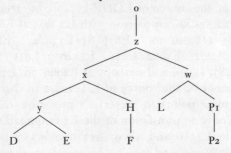

D. THE ORIGINAL FORM OF THE TEXT

If the preceding diagram is credited, it follows that x must have been a text of the sermon version, and w must have been in tract form. But what was the form of z, and indeed of o?

Decision between the two forms, sermon and chaptered tract, is not easy. Moving beyond the narrowly textual, arguments can be brought on either side. First there are grounds for thinking that the sermon form was the original. The text in EDHF runs smoothly through without hitch, whilst L divides the text into chapters, all of which end with a quotation of 1 Cor.3:11, so that the material need not follow on from chapter to chapter. The material in L not found in EDHF consists largely of authorities, and such an addition seems simpler than the development of the sermon's extensive comment. Most persuasively the author of the Titus tract refers back to his earlier work as having the incipit *Omnis plantacio*; this is only appropriate to the sermon version, L's tract version instead being prefixed with a different biblical text *Fundamentum aliud nemo potest ponere preter id quod positum est quod est Christus Ihesus* (1 Cor.3:11), a text which is dominant because of its repetition.

On the other hand, considered in isolation L looks very like a half worked-up stage in the development of a typical Lollard text, a text expounding a collection of authorities on the topic of clerical property. The three sets of authorities which are placed at the end, one English and two Latin, could be the undigested part that would ultimately have been developed into further chapters. However, these further authorities are *not* used in the longer sermon, even though they would certainly have been relevant to the subjects expounded in that sermon albeit not reached in the tract. If a tract of the kind represented by L really lies behind the sermon, then it must be conjectured that all that was known was the ten chapters and not the further authorities. L's extra authorities would on this account be a secondary enterprise, irrelevant to the question of the original form of the text. But these authorities can hardly be dismissed as irrelevant to L as it stands, since four of them appear both within the chapters and in Latin in the second group: thus L360–77 translated Latin L1127–44, L382–98 Latin L1189–202, L551–202 Latin L1220–1 and L650–67 Latin L1110–26.

Relevant evidence derives from the allusions within the longer sermon version to the mode of delivery, with the strong personal involvement of the preacher with his congregation. These passages will be discussed in more detail below (pp. lii–liv). But it is significant that with few exceptions all of them are lacking from the version in L.[68] Of itself, this is not enlightening: the tract writer could have eliminated just as well as the preacher could have added them, even though in the former case some care must have been needed to remove all trace of origin. Many of these allusions to the circumstances of preaching admittedly occur within longer passages not found in the tract version, notably within E53–802 and E2491–3099[69], but there are a few that

---

[68] The two exceptions are E1888/L637–8 'But here haue I no leiser to telle, al if I coude', and E1919/L670 'But here I woot wel . . .'.

[69] See also E1032, 1105, 1205, 1329, 1503, 1670, 2216.

occur in the sermon within material found in L.[70] In only a single case is there any rewriting: E803 *but first I wole shewe here* appears in L70 *here it schal be schewid*. As will be described below (p. liv), verbs compatible with a written rather than a spoken form of delivery are found in the sermon—but, since the preacher announces his intention to leave the text with his congregation for their discussion, this need not reveal anything about the original shape of the material. Beyond these indications of delivery the differences in shared material between sermon and tract versions are in content (as opposed to textual detail) few, and impossible to interpret in terms of direction of change. At E1101–12 the preacher retails a conversation he claims himself to have had with *a greet maistir of þis mengid lawe*; this in L203–9 appears as questioning by a *gentilman* of *a greete bischop of þis londe*. It is hard to make much of this: the bishop and the great master could obviously be one and the same person, and his side of the conversation is, for the purposes of the story, the more revealing. The equivalence of narrator and *gentilman* is more problematic in the context of the preached sermon—everything else in the sermon, as in L's tract, points towards a clerical preacher (see below pp. lii–lvii).[71] But direction of change is still unclear: the story has similarities to others that circulated in and beyond Lollard texts (see note to E1100), and could have been modified to the particular context in either direction.

Finally, it seems to me, we are left with a balance of probabilities rather than any incontrovertible evidence. My own tentative conclusion is that the text began life in the form represented by L, though whether that form included what I have described as the two appendixes, English and Latin authorities, remains unclear; it was then reworked into the sermon. The concentration of references to preaching and the congregation within lengthy sections not found in L seems to me to point towards their addition to an already existing text; were they original and eliminated from an L-type derivative they might be expected to appear more evenly through the sermon. This implies that *o* and *z* had the shape now represented by L, and that *x* represents the modification and enlargement. But it seems clear that both versions, tract and sermon, had equal status as independent works; hence they demand parallel editions, and are both included in the present volume. Whether they share the same author will be discussed later (pp. liv–lv).

[70] See E1275–6 (*om.* after L246), E1361–3 (*om.* L274), E1539 (*om.* L336).
[71] The examples in *MED gentil-man* n. suggest that the word regularly implies secular status.

E. FURTHER TEXTUAL QUESTIONS

1. Numbering systems

L divides the material shared with the sermon version into ten chapters: compared with the sermon version's line numbering, and ignoring here L's omissions or additions (hence the discrepancy between the apparent lengths of chapter in E as against L), these are: 1: L1–69 (E1–54), 2: L70–189 (E803–942), 3: L190–314 (E1067– 500), 4: L315–450 (E1518–656), 5: L451–540 (E1665–765), 6: L541– 608 (E1787–855), 7: L609–69 (E1856–918), 8: L670–758 (E1919– 2086), 9: L759–872 (E2090–282), 10: L873–965 (E2379–490). Though F presents the sermon version of the text, division into chapters is also found in it. This division is into 36 chapters, though there are irregularities near the start: new chapters (see record in the variants) begin at 2: E67, 3: 121, 4: 196, 5: 270, [6 and 7 not indicated], 8: 445, 9: 503, 9 again: 653, 10: 768, 11: 882, 12: 933, 13: 1021, 14: 1086, 15: 1150, 16: 1214, 17: 1309, 18: 1419, 19: 1524, 20: 1612, 21: 1712, 22: 1790, 23: 1879, 24: 1971, 25: 2062, 26: 2163, 27: 2229, 28: 2407, 29: 2435, 30: 2581, 31: 2643, 32: 2734, 33: 2815, 34: 2886, 35: 2963, 36: 3040. Though the length of these 'chapters' varies between less than thirty and around a hundred and fifty lines in the modern edition, the breaks sometimes correspond to a new stage in the argument (though not all coincide with a paragraph break in the present edition). It seems possible that the missing breaks occurred at E317 and E393, though the double ninth chapter (which could hardly be amalgamated into a single unit, since this at c.260 lines would be far longer than any other) may suggest that only one break is missing and that the numbering of chapters 8 and the first 9 should be reduced by one. It will be noted that F's chapter divisions do not correspond at any point with those of L, and that the obscurity about F's numbering between chapters 5 and 10 cannot be resolved from L since L contains none of the material in those chapters. F's divisions must be seen as a later accretion, independent of L.

None of the earlier copies of the sermon version have any trace of the chapter system found in either F or L. But all show some marginal numbering of points in the argument, though this is often a sequence only witnessed by one manuscript.[72] Only one section is

---

[72] That in E is noted in the variants; F also has six sequences between 629–53, 1033–9, 2094–107, 2176–80, 2227–31 and 2609–11.

noted by all copies, that between E200 and E463: thus 200 1 E, (*number cut off*) part H, 1 pars F; 281 ij part H, 2 pars F; 291 3 ED, iij part H, 3 pars F; 302 4 pars F; 317 4 ED, iiij part H, 5 pa. F; 393 5 D, v part H; 442 6 E(D *lost*), vj part H; 463 7 E(D *lost*), vij part H, vij pars F. Most of the divisions mark stages of the exegesis of 2 Pet. 2:1–3, quoted at E186–90; this is clear in the first five and last, but less obvious at 442. Though H is the only manuscript to have the divisions throughout this section, the presence of occasional divisions at the same points in D and E shows that they must have been present in x and also in y. F's confusion may well be associated with the competing chapter division in F and the problems of that at around the same stage of the text.

2. Marginalia

All four manuscripts of the sermon version, and the Lambeth manuscript of the tract version, have marginal annotations mostly by the original scribe. A few of these are simply *nota* comments, and these are only recorded (in the variants) for the base manuscript. A few in the sermon version between E200 and 463 apparently record section divisions, and are listed above.

Most of the marginal material notes the sources, mainly biblical, of quotations or references within the text, and often seems to duplicate information incorporated into the text itself. So, for instance, at line E2496 EDHF within the text give the reference to Matthew 8[:19], whilst EF repeat that information in the margin. There is no regularity about the placing of this information,—within text or in margin—either at an individual reference or in the practice of a single scribe. It seems clear that in the majority of cases the author intended to note the detailed reference, an intention in line with his scholarly habits, but where this was to be recorded seems impossible to recover. The following examples may establish this:

1. reference in text and margin: E25 Mal.2[:7] EDHFL (though F omits text reference, and marginally H lacks the chapter number); 185 2 Pet.2[:1] in ED, in text only in H, in margin only F

2. reference in margin only: E86 Matt.23[:5] in EF, *euangelium* H, *om.* D; 180 1 Cor.1[:10] in ED, *om.* HF

3. reference in text or margin: E391 *declina a malo et fac bonum* in text only HF (with side reference to *dauid* H), in margin only ED;

E1372 1 Tim.2[:1–2], 5[:17], Eph. 5[:1–9] and Tit. 3 [:1] in text only HF, in margin only ED and partially L

4. reference in text only: 1813 Luke 8[:3] in EDHF, though in margin L; 2069 2 Cor.8[:10–14] in EDHF, though L (with *prima* for *secunda*) places in margin only.

Each manuscript apart from E has isolated individual references: D see variants to E2925, H see variants to 1220 (but this is a later corrector not the original scribe), F see variants to 15; L in the material which overlaps with E has several examples, see for instance L75 (E809), L520 (E1746). H tends to place references within the text and not in the margins, whilst F often does the reverse. This divergence between H and F, though in other textual respects they are closely related, emphasises that it would be hazardous to use the placing of references as indication of textual affinity. Equally the evidence above suggests that each scribe might add his own reference, even when this is nowhere given in other manuscripts, independently. It would thus be hazardous to use even the incidence of a reference as serious grounds for or against textual relationship.

As a result of this evidence, it has been decided to follow the base text E in printing the text: all references contained within E's main text are preserved in that position, all marginal references in E are given in the variants (marked *margin*). E may not in any individual case reflect the original in this regard, but any other practice seems to give rise to inconsistencies and anomalies. In the variants are recorded the presence of marginal references in the other manuscripts (whether in agreement with E or not), the insertion of those marginal references within the text (indicated by *in text*), and the absence of references from within the text. This may appear cumbersome: for instance

185 *margin* 2 pet. 2 EDF ii Pet.ii] *om.* F

indicates that two manuscripts, ED, have the information from within the text repeated in the margin, whilst F has the information only in the margin and H implicitly only within the text. It is hoped, however, that this provides a complete record of the manuscripts' information, information which cannot be generalized because of their diversity of practice.

F. THE TEXT OF *DE OBLACIONE IUGIS SACRIFICII*

Since there is only a single surviving manuscript of the text, the textual history can hardly be traced and there is obviously no question of choice for the base text. It is clear that the surviving manuscript is not the author's autograph: quite apart from the professional layout of the copy, the scribe has made a number of mistakes that certainly derive from copying.[73] There are also a number of places where the text as it stands in the manuscript does not make sense, where simple emendations have been made to correct this, but where it is possible to conjecture that there is an underlying error of more substantial proportions; this is particularly credible in the case of passages that are translations from Latin sources, since the English usually follows these very closely.[74] The obscurity of parts of the author's arguments, and the difficulty of rendering some of his patristic quotations in English, make it sometimes difficult to be sure whether the surviving manuscript is corrupt.[75] Beyond the probabilities that Titus is not the author's holograph, and is not a particularly accurate copy, no further hypotheses about textual transmission can be made. The text has been treated as conservatively as is compatible with comprehensibility, and the explanatory notes (which include generous quotation from the sources cited) are intended to elucidate obscurities.

4. THE ORIGINS AND CIRCULATION OF THE TEXTS

No heading or colophon to either text in any form provides any information about either date of composition or authorship. Within the texts incomplete evidence concerning the sermon and the *Tractatus* on the eucharist derives from Titus: first the author states that concerning clerical property (T220) 'I declarid onys in a sermon þat begynneþ þus *Omnis plantacio quod non plantauit Pater meus celestis eradicabitur*'.[76] Whilst neither text nor subject are

---

[73] See, for instance, the emendations made at T113, 652, 663, 825, 1234; note also the various cases where the scribe has made mechanical errors, as at T543, 641, 1057 etc.

[74] For examples see notes to T1321 or 2084-9.

[75] See, for instance, notes to T1526, 2175-8, 3284-90 and 3730-5.

[76] See also T1232 note.

peculiar to the Egerton sermon, the similarity of viewpoint, technique and authorities between the two texts confirm this claim of common authorship. Even if the first two are subjective judgments, hard objectively to measure, the third is more indicative. This may also help towards the case that the Lambeth tract likewise should be attributed to the same author. Though many of the authorities shared between these three are commonplace, at least in Lollard texts, some are not: Gorham is cited in all three, whilst Odo of Paris is quoted in both Lambeth and Titus.[77] The evidence for common authorship of Egerton and Titus may be accepted immediately, that for Lambeth will be discussed further below.

(A) DATE

The most explicit evidence concerning the date of any of these texts derives from the Titus tract. At T174 the author questions whether 'king Herri þe fourþe þat nouȝ late diȝid' attempted to defend God's law, and comments, slightly sceptically, 'It was seide þat he dede, and if he dede I suppose he dede neuer a better dede'. This reference to Henry's recent death necessitates a date after 20 March 1413. Later he tells a story concerning 'þe grettist enmy þat Crist haþ in Ynglond, þat is þe archebischop of Cauntirberi, Arundel' (T405). Assuming the tenses of the verbs here to be significant, the Titus tract must have been completed before Arundel's death on 19 February 1414.[78] This second story may allow for further restriction within this period of eleven months: Arundel is said to have affirmed that, even if Christ returned in person, he would rather believe the pope and his clergy than the saying of Christ—this affirmation is said to have been made 'nouȝ wiþin a fewe daiis in presens of þe worþiist audiens in þis reme' (T406). The context of this remarkable utterance is the issue of the eucharist, and the author's claims that the contemporary ecclesiastical hierarchy departs from biblical teaching on it. An enquiry for heresy thus seems a likely occasion for Arundel's observation. The eleven months provide ample opportunities, notably during the protracted case against Sir John Oldcastle during the summer months of 1413; this would fit well since Titus in no detail alludes to the rebellion of January 1414. The

[77] See for Gorham E1798, 2996, 3082, T1228, for Odo L382, 1163, 1189, T477. Reference is given L382 note to other Lollard texts using Odo; no comparable attributed citation of Gorham is known to me.

[78] Dates from *HBC* pp. 40, 233.

name of Oldcastle was first brought to the Canterbury convocation in association with an accused clerk on 6 March 1413, before the death of Henry IV,[79] but the main accusations were made in the summer following the resumption of business by convocation in June. The enquiry involved protracted meetings of Arundel and various clerics, some of which occurred in the presence of the new king Henry V.[80] Since the accusations included Oldcastle's views on the eucharist and his willingness to accept the determinations of the pope and hierarchy on this and other issues,[81] ample opportunity for Arundel's statement would have arisen, though, hardly surprisingly, the official account preserves no record of it. The most likely occasion was perhaps that on 23 September when Oldcastle, asked further about his views on the eucharist and on oral confession, was required to comment on the claim that the determinations of the church on these should be believed. To this Oldcastle replied 'quod bene voluit eas credere et observare; sed quod dominus noster papa, cardinales, archiepiscopi, et episcopi, caeterique praelati ecclesiae haberent potestatem talia terminandi, noluit ad tunc aliqualiter affirmare.'[82] Formal sentence against Oldcastle was given, and order for its publication made subsequently on 10 October. Whatever the precise date of Arundel's reported, and probably exaggerated, observation, it seems safe to date the Titus text to the late summer or early autumn of 1413.

How much earlier in composition the sermon may have been is unclear: *onys* in the reference back might imply some gap in time, but it is entirely imprecise.[83] Statements within the sermon concerning the claims of 'worldli prelatis' that 'þei maken alle þese newe constituciouns and statutis aȝens þese newe prechours and her fautours to exclude heresies and errours and al manere fals doctrine'

---

[79] Wilkins iii.338, where Oldcastle is named as lord of Cobham.

[80] The fullest accounts remain those of W. T. Waugh, 'Sir John Oldcastle', *EHR* 20 (1905), 434–56, 637–58 (see here especially pp. 449–55), and J. H. Wylie and W. T. Waugh, *The Reign of Henry the Fifth* (3 vols., Cambridge, 1914–290) i.242–57 (the responsibility for this part is Wylie's).

[81] Wilkins iii.355.

[82] Wilkins iii.355. The issues were then clarified in an English version for Oldcastle, on which his answers (iii.356) were much more outspoken: he denied the authority of ecclesiastical determinations when these countered scripture, and ascribed such invalid determinations to the period before the endowment of the church. The fuller account of the examination in Bale's *Brefe Chronycle* sigs. D.2–E.5 (itself expanded from *The Examinacion . . . of Syr Jhon Oldcastell*, STC 24045 sigs I.1–4) offers numerous opportunities for Arundel's alleged observation here, but the sources of this part are obscure.

[83] See MED *ones* adv.3(a).

(E1159) are most naturally interpreted as referring to Arundel's *Constitutions*, issued in 1407 and formally published in 1409.[84] Earlier legislation against the Lollards could have been presented in similar terms, but the use of *constituciouns and statutis*, and the recurrence of the words in the sermon as in Titus, points towards the coordination of ecclesiastical and civil legislation found in the reign of Henry IV.[85] This is confirmed by another passage shortly before this (E1130): 'þei cursen þe prest þat prechiþ, and him þat resceyueþ him, and alle þat fauoren him, and alle þo þat heeren him, and ouer þis enterditen þe place þere Cristis gospel is prechid freli', which echoes closely the ruling of the first two *Constitutions* concerning the preacher, his receivers and his place of operation.[86]

The date of the Lambeth tract is more unclear. The claim in the printed version that it was 'made aboute the tyme of kinge Rycharde the seconde' (Q685) cannot be regarded as authoritative, and is almost certainly too early.[87] Lambeth lacks the allusions argued above to be to Arundel's *Constitutions*, having instead of E1130–3 the less precise 'As if bischoppis and abbotis spaken today togedre "Hyde we Goddis lawe, lest þes seculer lordis comme and take oure lordeschippis and fordo oure statis"' (L226–8). This passage is, in fact, a quotation from sermon 175 of the standard Lollard sermon cycle.[88] The dating in turn of these sermons is not firmly established, but the late 1380s or 1390s seem most likely.[89] Equally unhelpful is the variation between the two versions at E1100 ff and L203 ff. The discussion is on the legitimacy of ecclesiastical appropriation of temporal property: in E there is presented an envisaged conversation

[84] Wilkins iii.314–19; the date of origin is examined in C. R. Cheney, 'William Lyndwood's *Provinciale*', in *Medieval Texts and Studies* (Oxford, 1973), pp. 158–84 at p. 172 n. 7.

[85] See E1180, 1182, 2989; T323, 335, 347, 1269, 2928 (see note), 3041 and most notably T945, 952. For the progressive legislation in the first decade of the fifteenth century see especially McNiven (1987).

[86] Wilkins iii.316, note particularly the second 'ecclesia, coemeterium, seu locus quiscunque in quo sic praedicatum fuerit, ipso facto ecclesiastico subjaceat interdicto, sicque maneat interdictus'. This passage is not found in L, but the same point is made T322 ff.

[87] Matthew (p. 359) doubted Wyclif's authorship, but suggested that, if by him, it must be from early in his career, 1365–75, since it lacks features of texts such as the *Supplementum Trialogi*. Parker repeats this (pp. 9–10, 32–3) but prefers 'perhaps late 1381 or early 1382 as a document supporting one of the major concerns in the 1381 Peasants' Revolt.'

[88] See note for the full extent of the quotation.

[89] See *EWS* iv.10–20.

between the preacher and *a greet maistir of þis mengid lawe* who spoke
to him *now late*, whilst in L essentially the same conversation is
between *a gentilman* and *a greete bischop*; the status of the respondent
is repeated in each at the the end, as *þis autentik man* in E1111, but as
þis bischop L210. A chronological sequence of *bischop* to *maistir of þis
mengid lawe* is perhaps the reverse of that which might be expected if
a particular individual were in mind; but this instance does not seem
sufficient to overturn other indications that Lambeth antedates the
sermon version. Assuming that the two opponents are one and the
same person, and postulating that *maistir of þis mengid lawe* might
refer disparagingly to one who was master of both civil and canon
law, little help is given for chronology.[90] Several bishops within the
period 1390 to 1410 held degrees in both laws.[91] The most that it
seems possible to say about L's date is that it probably predates
Arundel's *Constitutions*, but not by many years.

(B) AUTHORSHIP AND AUDIENCE

References within each text, and particularly within the Egerton
sermon, to the projected audience help to indicate the status, though
not the precise identity, of the author. The Egerton text is presented as
a sermon, not only by virtue of the opening biblical text (to which
reference is made subsequently at E65, 130, 2578, 3004 *my teeme*, 2963
I purposide . . . in þe bigynnyng of my sermoun . . . my teeme, and also in
the allusion in Titus 220), but also by numerous admonitions and
questions directed to a congregation (see below). Most striking are the
indications of oral delivery: the preacher is very aware of the passing of
time (E275, 2661) and the possible impatience of his listeners with the
sermon's length (see lines E2495, 2939, 3086–8). More informative
about the preacher is his statement near the sermon's close that, since
time is short and he cannot delay to answer questions, he will leave a
written version with his congregation for them to study; when he
returns he will deal with problems at more leisure (E2939–48). He
continues to admonish his hearers to pay attention if any opponent

---

[90] *MED mengen* gives no confirmation of this sense: whilst recording various uses of the
past participle as adjective, no instance of *mengid lawe* is offered. The only other possible
meaning seems to be by taking 'mixed law' to allude to the temporal concerns of canon,
supposedly spiritual, law. See note to E1098.

[91] Included are bishop Henry Bowet of Bath and Wells (1401–7), Walter Skirlaw of
Durham (1388–1406), Edmund Stafford of Exeter (1395–1419), Robert Braybrooke of
London (1382–1404), Robert Hallum of Salisbury (1407–17), and Richard le Scrope of
York (1398–1405).

comes and tries to answer his case: they should particularly note any biblical passages such an opponent cites, and report these and the arguments to the preacher on his return—he will then refute his opponent to them (E2948–55). From this it is clear that the preacher is peripatetic (rather than the holder of a local benefice), and certainly implies that he moves around in fear of opposition; his congregation is apparently friendly, accustomed to argument about theological and ecclesiastical matters, but not itself at the time of the sermon under open suspicion of heresy. Perhaps surprisingly, there is no overt exhortation to conceal the copy of the sermon left by the preacher.[92] That the preacher's leaving of a copy of his sermon should be credited as having occurred is strongly supported by the physical appearance of the three fifteenth-century copies surviving: two, E and D, are in the same hand; these two and H are all small in size, easily carried, and concealed, in a pocket or bag. The same is true of L, where the sermon is found as a shorter tract from which all allusions to a congregation, listening or later reading, are absent. None of them originally had any other content. All are credibly books that could have been carried around by a preacher for presentation to suitably favourable congregations or persons. Further indication of the preacher's peripatetic existence is given by the allusion to his current lack of books: E2652 'whanne I haue more leiser to studie and more help of bookis, þou shalt haue a more large answer', or earlier 'I haue no tyme ne wheron to write' (E275). It is tempting to see the marginal note in H referring to 'frere Claxton, a prechour and doctor of dyuynyte in þe chayere at oxenforde' (f. 51ᵛ against E1203), a note that is incorporated into the text of the later F, as an authorial addition made on a subsequent visit of the kind promised.[93] Though there are no direct references to the preacher's fear of persecution, he speaks in haste: whilst 'and I hadde leiser' (E750, 1205, 1888) may be insignificant expressions of *occupatio*, other expressions seem more pointed 'I was purposid for to haue markid mo notable þingis þan I do at þis tyme; for now I knowe þat I haue not so moche leiser as I wende þat I hadde. Neþeles for al þe haast

---

[92] Compare the situation outlined in the sermon of MS Longleat 4, written by the author of *Dives and Pauper*: here the preacher portrays himself as inhibited in his activities, but his audience, for whom he provided the written sermons, as out of the reach of prosecution. See A. Hudson and H. L. Spencer, 'Old Author, New Work: the Sermons of MS Longleat 4', *Medium Aevum* 53 (1984), 220–38, especially the passage quoted pp. 231–2.

[93] Even if the note cannot be proven as authorial, it is clear that its initiator must have been one familiar with contemporary debate in Oxford.

. . .' (E2847), and especially 'I wolde marke here, and tyme wolde serue; but I mai not tarie' (E2780).

These last passages, however, highlight the problem of this evidence: though *Omnis plantacio* is presented as a delivered sermon, it survives in the written form and this form is also inscribed within the text in the preacher's promise to leave it with them for comment (E2939 ff). That double form, spoken and written, is reflected in the words of the text. Whilst verbs such as *declare*, *describe*, *show*, even *tell* may be used indifferently in either situation, parts of *speak* or *say* as against *write* seem more pointed, but both are found: *I wole . . . speke* (E289), *I spak of bifore* (E355, 1275, 1670, 2603, 3041 and similar), *of þat þat I seide a litil bifore* (E2206, 2501, and cf 2351), but *I haue writun þe more large* (E121 and cf 753), *as it is writun bifore* (E2123 and cf 2242); the preacher's views are *in þis writynge* (E1826). But the fiction—if that is what it is—of the spoken occasion is the more persistently maintained: first person pronouns in reference to the preacher abound, just as do second person pronouns for the congregation, sometimes the formal plural *ȝe* but more often the intimate *þou*. The preacher is constantly 'buttonholing' his listeners: 'as I seide to þee bifore, and I kepe not þat þou forȝete it' (E2351); 'and we were togidir at partie' (E2858); 'I mene moche more þan I expresli seie here' (E3084). Twice there is an envisaged interchange between preacher and listener: at E2567–80 where the listener reproaches the preacher for attacking the 'sects', and again at E2833–66 where the preacher defends himself against opposition to his condemnation of the friars. At the very end the exasperated hearer is written in to the discourse (E3085–90): 'But up hap þou seist to me here "þou presumest proudli to expowne þe derk visiouns of þe Apocalips; it hadde be for þi profit þat þou haddist left þis mater and maad an eende whanne þou bihiȝtist us þat þou so woldist! For wite þou wel, as for þis processe, þou getist þee no þank of ony clerk or religiouse or ony of her retenu þat loueþ þis endowynge!"', a charge that the apparently exhausted preacher only briefly rebuffs (E3090–6).

The question of L's authorship has been mentioned before, and it is less unambiguously answerable than that of the identical responsibility for the Egerton sermon and Titus tract. None of the allusions to audience, or the preacher's relation to it, discussed above, are present in L. It has been argued above that L probably represents the earlier form of the text, of which the sermon as found in EDHF is an expansion. But it is possible that L might have been an independent tract by another Lollard author. In favour of such a view is the way in which the two sets of appended authorities have not been quarried for the sermon's longer argument, despite the relevance of many of them to the urging of that argument. The idea that those appendices are of different origin from the text seems unconvincing in view of the converse: that some biblical and patristic sources *are* used in those parts of L *not* paralleled in E.[94] If for no reason other than economy, it seems simplest to envisage a single author, responsible for all parts of L, E and T, but reviewing his strategy between the texts.[95]

In contrast to the sermon, the Titus tract provides very little indication of reception: only 'þe dome of þo þat reden þis' (T3852), from whom the author seeks correction (T3850) suggests a reading rather than a listening audience and one not closely and personally known to the author. In contrast to Egerton, there is little tailoring of the argument to attract or retain attention. Again the author repeatedly alleges shortness of time (T83, 139, 713, 3847), intention to write more on a later occasion (T859, 2919), and lack of immediate resources of books (T2601).

That the author was a Lollard hardly admits of dispute. Given the date of the two longer texts, views such as are argued here, and assumptions that are made, emphatically and even flamboyantly proclaim the writer's sympathies. But none of the texts, and particularly the two longer ones, is entirely typical of Lollard writing, especially in their lengthy concentration each on one polemical issue, the sermon on temporalities and the Titus tract on the eucharist, to which any other discussion is subordinated. Both imply the unacceptability of the current ecclesiastical hierarchy, with the pope in both named as *anticrist* (eg E1917, T1412), and both assume that scripture is the sole legitimating authority for the christian, but neither argue these cases. The attitude towards the friars is plainly Wycliffite (even if some of the language is inherited from earlier antifraternal writing), but the criticism is subordinated to the main issues of each text. There are very occasionally sentences or turns of phrase which make clear the author's disapproval of the cult of saints

---

[94] See indexes for Gen. 4:2–4, 4:9, Num. 18:20, Jer. 31:16, Hos. 6:6, Luke 14:14, 22:25, 1 Pet. 5:3; Bernard at L650, 1110, Cyprian at L969, 1256, Jerome at L173, 1225, Odo at L382, 1181, Origen at L360, 1127, in all of which cases the second is the Latin source quotation, the first the English translation.

[95] His avoidance of canon law authorities in E and, save for generalities, T, might reflect growing Lollard hostility to this source.

or of long prayers, but these are very plainly side-hits and not issues in their own right. The speaker ostentatiously acknowledges that the concluding section of the sermon veers off target (E3085 ff). Conversely, however, the major topic of each text is discussed from a number of angles, and with a wealth of detail.

Any search for an author must take account of the evidence in all three works of his erudition.[96] Both sermon and eucharistic tract show knowledge of academic terms (E1880, T258 ff), Titus of grammar (T2884) and etymology (T1166), and Titus disparages Oxford's current activities (T2727 ff, cf T474). Biblical and patristic allusions and quotations abound, most accompanied by precise references of work, book, chapter or letter number either within the text or marginally.[97] Accuracy of citation is a matter of concern, most explicit in T2599 'And houȝ seint Denyse writiþ of þis sacrament aftur þe logic of Goddis law I told in partie before, but for I haue not nouȝ þe copie of his boke, I write not his wordis here.'[98] Canon law is rarely cited, save in the Latin appendix to Lambeth; two common Lollard authors, FitzRalph and pseudo-Chrysostom on Matthew are under-represented. Augustine is by a long way the favourite authority, and the length of quotations as well as their frequency in Titus (over a hundred) must be accommodated in any conjectures about authorship. Odo of Cheriton, an infrequent authority in Wycliffite writings, is cited in both Lambeth and Titus, 'Gorham on the Apocalypse' in all three.[99] Most interesting is the long quotation in Titus (2615) from 'Fulgencius þat is cald *Auctor De diuinis officiis*': the interest here lies not in the misattribution of a work by Rupert of Deutz, but in the fact that Wyclif himself used the same text under a variety of names including that of Fulgentius, and that as a result there was apparently debate in Oxford early in the fifteenth century about the true author and antiquity of a text that appeared to support Wyclif's eucharistic views.[100] Recent work on later medieval eucharistic language reveals also some of the background to the author's criticism of contemporary debate, and

---

[96] A preliminary survey of this appeared in my paper published in 1985; only the most important points of this are summarized here.

[97] For the frequency of these see the indexes of biblical and non-biblical quotations and allusions.   [98] Cf E2951.

[99] See the index of non-biblical quotations for references to all of these.

[100] For this debate see Hudson (1985), pp. 309–12, and see further note to T2615. It is worth noting that the Titus author does not betray any awareness of debate about the attribution of his source.

makes clear his detailed awareness of the issues.[101] Likewise alluding
to academic discussion, though it has proved harder to discover the
precise details, is the section on the status of Christ's humanity and
divinity after the ascension; here, as on the eucharist, the author
seems particularly exercised by grammatical and logical analysis.[102]

If the evidence so far is convincing, then the search for an author
must be for a Lollard of academic background, at some point a
peripatetic preacher, possibly no longer in Oxford but with continuing
access to academic materials, still writing between 1409 and 1414, and
with awareness of political affairs, or at least of political gossip.
Candidates would seem to include Peter Payne, William Taylor,
John Purvey or Richard Wyche. Of these Payne seems unlikely: he
is not known to have been a peripatetic preacher of the kind implied
by the sermon, and was probably in Oxford for most of the relevant
period until his departure abroad, probably in the autumn of 1413.[103]
His subsequent writings abroad show little significant overlap in his
authorities with the texts here.[104] Taylor certainly has the background
to explain these texts, though his whereabouts between his London
sermon of 1406 and the erroneous preaching in 1417 with which he
was charged in 1420 is unclear.[105] He appears to have preached
wherever opportunity offered, and maintained his academic interests
right through to the 1420s. Apart from his 1406 sermon, the most
extensive record of his teaching comes in the text which he wrote to
Thomas Smyth of Bristol probably shortly before his arrest in 1423;[106]
the subject of this later text is the claim that all prayer should be
directed to God alone. The subject matter thus does not overlap with
the concerns of the texts here. Taylor's 1406 sermon is much closer to
the interests of Lambeth and Egerton, but Taylor there deliberately
avoids the eucharist (see line 340). The authorities used by Taylor in
the sermon overlap with those here, but arguably not significantly: the
extensive citation of Augustine, Jerome and Bernard is hardly unusual

---

[101] See notes to T1981 ff and bibliography under Bakker, de Libera, and Rosier.
[102] See notes to T3480–93 and 3497, and bibliography under Courtenay.
[103] Published English biographies of Payne are now somewhat out of date; they include
Emden *Oxford* iii.1441–2 and the same author's *An Oxford Hall in Medieval Times* (Oxford,
revd. ed. 1968), pp. 146–56.
[104] See W. R. Cook, *Peter Payne, Theologian and Diplomat of the Hussite Revolution*
(unpublished Ph.D.thesis, Cornell, 1971). I am indebted to Dr Cook for the generous loan
of microfilm and xeroxes of many of the works by Payne listed pp. 399–400.
[105] For the sermon see EETS 301 pp. 3–23, and for his life ib. pp. xvii–xxv.
[106] The text is printed in *Chichele reg.* iii.162–6; it was apparently in Latin, since
pp. 162, 166 it is claimed to have been transcribed *de verbo ad verbum* into the register.

in Lollard works; perhaps more interestingly Grosseteste and Hildegard are cited in Taylor's sermon as here,[107] though again both are
found in other Wycliffite sources; missing from the certain Taylor
texts are the more unusual Odo and *Fulgencius*. There is some
similarity of vocabulary, notably *quyletis* (Taylor 544 and see here
note to E2749 *quilagis*). But there seems to be one major objection to
Taylor's responsibility for the texts here: throughout the long
sequence of investigations into his heterodoxy, no accusation against
him appears regarding the eucharist. Yet the Titus tract shows the
author here to have been an outspoken adherent of Wyclif's opinion
concerning this sacrament; such a view is also enunciated, if sparingly,
in the Egerton sermon. It is, of course, possible that neither of these
works were available to those engaged in the pursuit of Taylor, and
that by 1417 he realised that silence on this subject would be prudent.
But the discrepancy seems sufficient to discard such an attribution of
authorship.

The case for Purvey's authorship seems even less clear. Thanks
to Maureen Jurkowski's findings, we now know that Purvey played
an important rôle in the Oldcastle rising of 1414, despite the
obscurity of his history after the 1401 trial and his relinquishment
of the West Hythe living by October 1403.[108] The list of books found
in Purvey's lodgings in 1414 contains texts by a number of the
authors used in the present texts, but the overlap of actual works is
small: the inventory includes Chrysostom on Paul but not the *Opus
imperfectum* on Matthew, *Parisiensis super epistolas* but not the *Summa
viciorum*. Some of the overlapping material in the inventory may, to
judge by their value, have been extracts: *Moralium Gregorii, 1
paunflot August' super Spalterinium* (sic).[109] Absent again are the
unusual texts cited here, Odo, *Fulgencius*, Hildegard, Gorham.
There seems no positive evidence to connect Purvey to these texts.
Even less is available to argue the case for William Thorpe, whose
career after the interview with Arundel in 1407 (assuming that to
have actually occurred) is entirely unknown.[110]

Richard Wyche is an intriguing possibility, but in the last resort

---

[107] Taylor 38, 261, 389, 397, and 221, 244.

[108] 'New Light on John Purvey', *EHR* 110 (1995), 1180–90; see earlier my paper
reprinted *LB* pp. 85–110.

[109] See Jurkowski p. 1184; the first was valued at 3s. 4d., the second at 12d.—the first is
said to be paper, but even so seems cheap for such a long work (compare the *Pastoralia
Gregorii* valued at 10s. od.).

[110] See *TWT* pp. lii–liii.

the case is not persuasive. Emden suggested he probably studied at Oxford, though no direct evidence of this is available.[111] He was examined by bishop Skirlaw of Durham in 1402–3, as a result of his active preaching in the north.[112] The account of this examination only, and exceptionally, survives in the defendant's own words.[113] This letter, sent to friends whilst he was still imprisoned, reveals a number of contacts with Wycliffites including probably Thorpe and Purvey.[114] The letter has certainly been cast to show Wyche in a favourable light, but, in its evasions, hesitations but equally its specificities, gives the impression of a basically reliable account.[115] The outcome of Skirlaw's investigation only emerges from later information about Wyche. The next directly recorded event is the letter which Wyche sent to Jan Hus from London dated 8 September 1410.[116] In November 1419 Wyche was once again in trouble, this time with archbishop Chichele; it is there stated that he had been detained in prison for a long time in the north after his condemnation (presumably by Skirlaw), though Wyche went on to claim that because of a royal letter called 'corpus cum causa', he had been brought to Westminster and there released.[117] Wyche's subsequent history is irrelevant to the present texts, given their date. Wyche would thus seem to have been in a position to write all three texts. Comparing the two letters and a lengthier undated reply to articles of which he was accused with the texts here, no clear conclusions

[111] Emden, *Oxford* iii.2101.

[112] An account of Skirlaw's investigations of Lollard heresy, in which Wyche was involved, is given by M. G. Snape, 'Some evidence of Lollard activity in the Diocese of Durham in the early fifteenth century', *Archaeologia Aeliana* 4th ser.39 (1961), 355–61, though the details can be amplified.

[113] Printed by Matthew (1890) from the only surviving manuscript, Prague University Library III. G.11.

[114] Wyche was urged to consider, and presumably to emulate, Purvey's recantation (Matthew p. 537); an acquaintance and friend of Wyche's was married to a sister *domini Wilhelmi Corpp* (p. 543), where the surname initial is probably a misreading of *Torpp*, a Bohemian form of Thorpe's name found elsewhere.

[115] Wyche's self-presentation in this account is discussed by C.von Nolcken, 'Richard Wyche, a Certain Knight, and the Beginning of the End', in Aston and Richmond (1997), pp. 127–54, and is currently being compared by Joanna Summers with other texts whose authors claim to have been imprisoned.

[116] Text most reliably printed by V. Novotny, *M. Jana Husi Korespondence a dokumenty* (Prague, 1920), no. 22 which lists the known manuscripts; an English translation appears in M. Spinka, *The Letters of John Hus* (Manchester, 1972), pp. 213–15.

[117] *Chichele Register* iii.56–7; cf *CCR 1419–22* p. 82. A recantation that Wyche must have made between October 1404 and March 1406 is printed from BL Royal 8 F.ii ff. 16–17 in *FZ* pp. 501–5 (in the third line p. 501 *Willelmus* is a mistranscription of *Walterus*).

emerge.[118] Wyche's letter to Hus is couched for the most part in general exhortatory and biblical terms, and offers little specific detail; the undated reply uses biblical and canonistic sources to support the views. The longer letter written during his 1402/3 imprisonment produces some more intriguing parallels. Wyche in his letter shows the use of the same academic terminology of *minor—maior* (p.532) as found in E1880 (L633), and similarly urges that, such is the distance of contemporary ecclesiastics from the teaching of Christ and his apostles, should Christ appear before them, they would condemn him (p.541, compare E1135, T408). Three quotations from Augustine in Wyche's letter are also cited in the texts here; the third of these concerns the eucharist, a major interest of Skirlaw's investigation, a minor subject of E and the prime topic of T.[119] More general similarities are the skill in conveying conversation, whether reported as in the case of the account, or imagined as in the texts here. But, despite these, Wyche's attested theological and ecclesiastical interests do not entirely overlap with the present texts: whilst the eucharist is a major component of both these and the various investigations (and Wyche's view and that expressed in T are in general agreement), the dominant concern of E and of L, namely ecclesiastical temporalities and their illegitimacy, is scarcely acknowledged in the documentary sources.[120] Given the extremity, and the explicit implications, of the author's views on this subject, it seems improbable that, were that author Wyche, his investigators would not have insisted on their recantation.

Beyond these possibilities there are others for which comparative evidence is either insufficient or non-existent.[121] The conclusion, hostile though it is to human curiosity, must be agnostic. Much though it is possible to deduce about the background and habits of

[118] For the undated reply see *FZ* pp. 370–82, where it appears between the 1395 Lollard *12 Conclusions* and Purvey's articles extracted by Lavenham.

[119] See p. 535 cited at T3455, p. 538 at T3574, p. 539 at T625.

[120] These questions do not figure in Wyche's own account, though the recantation that seems to have followed between 1404 and 1406 (*FZ* 501–5) contains as the ninth item 'Nullus sacerdos debet aliquid mendicare', confirmed at more length later (pp. 504–5 as items 4 and 6). The undated and undateable response of Wyche to accusations (*FZ* 370–82) likewise contains material on mendicancy (pp. 372–3 as item 2), on the recompense suitable for clerical offices (pp. 375–6 as item 7), on tithes and mortuaries (pp. 378–80 as item 11), and on the illegitimacy of fraternal orders (pp. 380–1 as item 12); but the central issue for the texts here, that of the incompatibility between clerical involvement in temporalities and Christ's precepts, is not broached.

[121] Jurkowski's survey (1997) has shown a number of Merton sympathisers, amongst whom Thomas Lucas or William James would certainly have had the erudition and inclination for these texts; but in neither case do attested texts survive.

the writer of these three texts, he withheld his personal name from all three, probably for reasons of his own security and that of his audience. To the listeners of the Egerton sermon, accepting the scenario written into its extant version, the author's identity must have been clear. But from the text, as from his other writings, the information was withheld. That anonymity remains.

(C) THE PRINTED VERSION OF L

Despite the lack of textual authority attached to the printed versions of the second part of the Lambeth text, they remain an interesting testimony to the continued circulation of, and interest in, Lollard texts in the early sixteenth-century Reformation period. D. H. Parker has recently reviewed much of the evidence from that period,[122] but it may be worth setting out the main points here, albeit briefly.

Only the second printed version carries an imprint date. Internal reference in both editions suggests that neither can have appeared before late 1529.[123] Lines 485–90 of the main text seem to refer to Simon Fish's *A supplicacyon for the Beggers* and to Thomas More's response, *The supplycacyon of soulys*:

> So shuld we be sure of soche answeres
> As were made vnto the poore beggers
>   For their pituous supplicacyon.
> Against whom þe clergyes resons nought worthe
> The soules of purgatory they brought forthe
> The beggers complaynte to discomfyte.

Fish's work (STC 10883) likewise has no imprint date, but More's reply (STC 18092) was written, according to its heading, whilst he was still chancellor of the duchy of Lancaster, a post he relinquished on 24 October 1529. Foxe later stated that Fish's *Supplicacyon* reached court circles around Candlemas (2 February) 1529,[124] and the haste this implies for the composition of More's reply seems confirmed by the text. The earliest possible date for the printing of the *Proper dyaloge* seems to be the very end of 1529.[125] That it was

---

[122] See Parker's edition, pp. 22–50, and his (1996) article.

[123] See Parker, p. 8. For a recent summary of the context see D. Loades, 'Books and the English Reformation prior to 1558', in Gilmont (1998), pp. 264–91.

[124] See the edition of More's work by G. Marc'hadour (More *CW* 7, 1990), p. lxv and Foxe iv.659.

[125] Parker, pp. 189–91 in note to his text 475 ff, and less fully in his paper (1996) at p. 63 n. 2 suggests that lines 479 ff refer to the first session of the so-called Reformation Parliament from 3 November 1529.

not much later is implied by the incorporation into the second edition only (P2) of the second Lollard text at its end, that on biblical translation (Q1292–1678, of which 1345–678 is the medieval text). This text appeared independently (STC 3021) with the date 1530, from the same printer in Antwerp as P1 (see above p. xxiv). It seems unlikely that the first edition in P1 of the partial text here would have been put out independently had this second English tract been available at the time to the printer. The amalgamated edition (P2, STC 1462.5) is dated 1530 at the end. This suggests that P1 was printed in the last months of 1529 or early months of 1530.

Such a date is consonant with the fact that the *Proper dyaloge* (though in which edition is unclear) was known to various dissenters investigated both by More and by bishop Stokesley of London in 1531.[126] A list of fifteen books whose circulation was forbidden dating probably from the previous year includes the *A. B. C. against the Clergy*, the alternative title for the *Proper dyaloge* (again not specifying the edition).[127] Thereafter the text appears again in other lists.[128]

The responsibility for the issuing of these two texts, *Proper dyaloge* and the *Compendious olde treatyse*, both separately and together, has been a contested question from the start and the argument has been continued amongst modern bibliographers and critics. In the first edition of STC (1926), the second edition of *Proper dyaloge* was listed anonymously under the heading of *Dialogue*.[129] This entry, together with a new entry covering the first edition, was moved in the revision of STC to appear under the name of William Barlowe, with the note that the work has also been attributed to William Roye; a supplementary note at the end of the volume makes the alternative suggestion of Jerome Barlowe as Roye's collaborator.[130] Jerome Barlowe is certainly a more likely candidate; his name, together with that of William Roye, was connected by Thomas More with *Rede me and be nott wrothe* (STC 1462.7), better

---

[126] Note especially Richard Bayfield, once monk of Bury St Edmunds, see *Confutation* CW 8.17–18 and notes pp. 1247–9, and Foxe iv.680–8. The list of books confiscated from Bayfield, Foxe iv.684–5, includes 'a Dialogue betwixt the Gentleman and the Ploughman'.

[127] Wilkins iii.739, though the date is less clear than that indicates; P. L. Hughes and J. F. Larkin, *Tudor Royal Proclamations 1 The Early Tudors* (New Haven and London, 1964) give the text, pp. 181–6, dating it p. 186 'before 6 March 1529', almost certainly too early. See Clebsch (1964), p. 264 for discussion.

[128] See *PR*, pp. 490–1 and Parker pp. 22–3.

[129] The first edition was dated 1926; the item was 6813.

[130] The entries are 1462.3 for P1, 1462.5 for P2; the supplementary note is i.613.

known to contemporaries as *The Burying of the Mass*.[131] This was put out as an anonymous production in 1528 from the Strassburg printer Johann Schott.[132] In 1533 Jerome Barlowe admitted to 'have made certayne bookes, and have suffred theym to be emprynted', including the *a Dyaloge between the Gentyllman and Husbandman* and *the Buryall of the Masse*;[133] the association of Roye with these two works is persistent in the critics, but his precise rôle is uncertain. It is also unclear whether either More or Barlowe is claiming *authorship* rather than responsibility for dissemination.[134] The more celebrated name of William Tyndale has been claimed as the instigator for the printing of the *Compendious olde treatyse*, but the evidence seems slight.[135] D. H. Parker, the recent editor of the *Proper dyaloge*, has argued for the indebtedness of the non-medieval parts of that text to *Rede me* and to Simon Fish's *Supplicacyon for the beggers*, and for common authorship by Jerome Barlowe and William Roye of *Proper dyaloge* and *Rede me*.[136] Since these questions obviously concern the material surrounding the Lollard texts and not those texts themselves, they need not be pursued further here. The interesting point for the student of the medieval texts is that they were still circulating amongst reformist circles in the 1520s to 1530s, and thought sufficiently relevant to contemporary debate to be put into print.

5. EDITORIAL PROCEDURES

I. TEXTS

These are printed from BL Egerton 2820 in the case of the sermon *Omnis plantacio*, Lambeth Palace 551 for the tract version which overlaps with it, and Cotton Titus D.v in the case of the *Tractatus de*

---

[131] See *Supplication of Souls*, CW 7, p. 161/33 and note, p. 352; also the edition under the former title by D. H. Parker (Toronto, 1992).

[132] See Hume in CW 6.ii p. 1070 no. 5; for Schott see M. U. Chrisman, 'Reformation printing in Strasbourg, 1519–60', in Gilmont (1998), pp. 218–19, 222.

[133] For the claim see T. Wright ed., *Three Chapters of Letters relating to the Suppression of the monasteries* (CS 26, 1843), p. 6; also Clebsch (1964), p. 236. For the confusion of the two Barlowes see E. G. Rupp, *Studies in the Making of the English Protestant Tradition* (Cambridge, 1947), pp. 62–72.

[134] See Clebsch (1964), pp. 235–40, Parker, pp. 27–32, for surveys.

[135] See Deanesly (1920), p. 438 and Parker's review, pp. 37–8. D. Daniell, *William Tyndale: A Biography* (New Haven and London, 1994), p. 179, takes Barlowe as responsible for the *Proper dyaloge* but seems not to discuss the *Compendious olde treatyse* (though cf p. 156 n. 2). [136] Parker, pp. 22–32 and 51–66.

oblacione iugis sacrificii. Modern punctuation and capitalization has been substituted for that of the manuscripts, modern paragraph division has been introduced and modern word division used. Modifications of the base manuscript that consist of the addition to, or alteration of, what is written in the base text are enclosed in square brackets; those emendations that consist in the suppression of words or letters in the manuscript are recorded in the variants. In *Omnis* the variants normally record the justification for the emendation from the other manuscripts. Marginal or interlinear additions to the text are enclosed by half brackets. Where such additions are not by the original scribe, this is recorded in the variants with the signal *dh* (different hand); if the addition is by the original scribe, this is not noted in the variants unless (as with *Omnis*) it sheds light on the textual history. Occasionally additions have been curtailed by cropping; this is indicated by [. . . or . . .]. Marginal references, which often duplicate those in the text, are recorded in the variants (see further pp. xlvi–xlvii above for the divergent treatment of these in the various manuscripts of *Omnis plantacio*). Damaged words or letters are enclosed in angle brackets ⟨ . . . ⟩. These are most common in *Tractatus*, since the manuscript has been damaged by damp, but the reading is not usually in question.[137] Words in Latin, or which are probably to be interpreted as Latin, are italicized within the texts where the surrounding material is English (but not in the two sets of Latin authorities appended to Lambeth).[138] Change of folio is marked within the text by | and the folio number given in the margin.

Abbreviations in English words are standard and their expansion is not indicated. In references printed within the text, which are usually in Latin, titles are expanded except for those of biblical books; the standard *li.* (*libro*) and *ca.* (*capitulo*) have not been expanded, and indications of ordinals are not shown. Expansion of *p̄* as *per* or as *par* is governed by their modern form; *ihu(s)* is expanded *Iesu(s)* (save in Lambeth where the unabbreviated form *Ihesu(s)* is found, and where the abbreviated form consequently retains *-h-*), *añcrist* as *anticrist* (where *antecrist* is written, it is so spelled out in the manuscript), *g'g'* as *Gregor.*

---

[137] Since the damage may affect part only of a letter, differences of opinion will exist about the extent of such indications of damage. In order to limit the reader's distraction by these signs, my own recording has been kept to a minimum.

[138] Since references are normally in Latin, the ampersand linking two has been interpreted as *et* rather than *and* (eg E831).

As far as is practicable, the parallel texts of the sermon *Omnis plantacio* and the tract version in Lambeth are presented facing each other, though, since even when the two contain the same material the orthography of the two does not match, this cannot be absolutely precise. Each text has been lineated throughout independently of the other. Where the two run parallel (a) the sermon version is printed on left hand pages under the running title **Egerton sermon**, with its variants at the foot of the page, continued where necessary at the foot of the right hand page with a line above; (b) the Lambeth tract version is printed on right hand pages under the running title **Lambeth tract**, with its apparatus at the foot of the page. Where one of the two (usually Lambeth) lacks material for a substantial period, the other is printed on both pages with its appropriate running title and with its variants. The conclusion to Lambeth, which has no counterpart in the sermon version, is printed at the end of the Egerton in the same fashion.

II. *APPARATUS*

(A) General

Abbreviations are expanded without notice in English material, but have been retained in Latin references. Material variants only are included, though the convention of regarding substitution of lexical synonyms as material variation has been followed. Because of their late date, F and the two editions of P include a large number of minor changes of vocabulary. A case could be made for omitting these, especially when they are isolative; but in view of the irregularity with which these changes have been made, it was decided to include them (with the one exception that all substitute *exampyl(l* for *ensaumple* and this has not been recorded).

(B) Individual texts

(a) In the case of the *Tractatus* the apparatus consists solely of a record of scribal corrections and of editorial emendations.

(b) Variants, and the marginal material, for the sermon *Omnis plantacio* are given in the order (E)DHF(L), though this is altered to show proximity or otherwise to the accepted reading. E's reading is usually the lemma unless its text has been emended; in such cases the manuscript support for the emendation (if any) is shown immediately after the lemma. L's isolative variants (or variants it shares only with P) are not recorded below the *Omnis* text, but those which may shed light on the textual history of the two versions are included there.

(c) The apparatus for the Lambeth text consists of the scribal corrections and marginal material in the manuscript, and the editorial emendations to its text. In addition readings that depart materially from L are recorded from the two printed versions; where these two agree their reading is signalled as P, but where only one of the two diverges they are differentiated as P1 and P2.

The following conventions have been used throughout the variants:

]	a single square bracket separates lemma from variant.
,	comma separates variants to the same lemma
om.	omitted.
rev.	word order reversed.
marked for rev.	words written in order stated but marked for reversal.
canc.	cancelled, either by subpunction or by crossing through.
dh	different hand.
sh	same hand.
eras.	erased.
corr.	corrected.
on eras.corr.	written over an erasure by a corrector.
/	change of line.
//	change of leaf.
⌐. . .⌐	insertion above the line or in the margin.
⟨. . .⟩	letters now illegible, or substantially damaged, and restored in editing.
[. . .]	editorial addition to, or alteration of, the base text.
] or [	preceding or following a word, or part of a word, often in the margin, to indicate that something has been lost in cropping.

Where a lemma consists of words that run without a break into the ensuing line, no indication of the second line number is given; where only the first and last words of a lemma are given, any change of line number for the final word is indicated in round brackets after it.

BIBLIOGRAPHY

Abbreviations are explained in the list on pp. ix–xiii. The spelling of manuscript or edition of primary sources is retained, but modern punctuation and capitalization has been supplied (and sometimes modified in the case of older editions). References to patristic texts, for the sake of simplicity, are given to the PL and PG volumes unless the text here requires scrutiny of more recent editions. Secondary material that is only used in a single note is not listed here.

1. PRIMARY UNPRINTED SOURCES

a. Manuscripts

Foliation or pagination, as used in the manuscript, is followed, and supplied where absent, but not corrected when wrong; numbers without indication are recto; where the text is in two columns, these are indicated by *a* and *b*. The following list indicates only the content of the manuscript that has been used here.

Brno University Library Mk 28: *Opus Arduum* (Wycliffite Latin commentary on the Apocalypse)

Cambridge, Trinity College O.1.29: English anthology, some texts Wycliffite

Cambridge, University Library Kk.1.11: Odo of Cheriton sermons

Dublin, Trinity College 245: English Wycliffite tracts

London, British Library Additional 24202: English Wycliffite tracts
  Cotton Titus D.i: *Thirty-Seven Conclusions*
  Harley 401: *Floretum* (Wycliffite handbook)
  Harley 1203: two English Wycliffite texts
  Harley 2398: English anthology, some texts Wycliffite
  Royal 6 E.v: Grosseteste sermons
  Royal 7 E.ii: Grosseteste sermons

London, Lambeth Palace 34: Wycliffite revision of Rolle's English Psalter commentary

Oxford, Bodleian Library, Bodley 288: Wycliffite revision of Rolle's English Psalter commentary
  Bodley 293: William of Pagula *Summa summarum*
  Bodley 420: Odo of Cheriton sermons
  Bodley 647: English Wycliffite material
  Bodley 703: Woodford texts against Wyclif
  Bodley 716: Wyclif *Postilla* and commentary on Apocalypse attributed to Hugh of St Cher

Bodley 806: English sermons, of Wycliffite colouring
Bodley 830: Grosseteste *Dicta*
Bodley 877: Wycliffite revision of Rolle's English Psalter commentary
Douce 53: Taylor's sermon and *Sermoun of þe Horsedoun*
Laud misc.200: Latin Wycliffite sermons
Rawlinson C.208: Thorpe's testimony
Oxford, Lincoln College lat.101: Grosseteste commentary on pseudo-Dionysius

b. Episcopal Registers

With the exception noted below, material is cited from manuscripts in the form diocese (or for Canterbury, Lambeth), bishop's name, folio, page or opening). A full guide to the registers is to be found in:

D. M. Smith, *Guide to Bishops' Register of England and Wales* (London, 1981). The register most frequently cited has been printed:
The Register of Henry Chichele, ed. E. F. Jacob (4 vols., CYS and Oxford, 1938–47).

2. PRIMARY PRINTED SOURCES

References are by line in the case of verse, by page, column or item number, followed (where given) by line number after an oblique stroke (ignoring all headings). Only opening line numbers are usually given.

Albertus Magnus, *Opera omnia*, ed. A. Borgnet (38 vols., Paris, 1890–9).
Alexander of Hales, *Summa theologica*, ed. Collegium Sanctae Bonaventurae (4 vols., Quaracchi, 1924–48).
Anselm, *Opera omnia*, ed. F. S. Schmitt (6 vols., Edinburgh, 1946–61).
An Apology for Lollard Doctrines, ed. J. H. Todd (CS, 1842).
Aquinas, *Opera omnia* 23 (Padua, 1869).
Aquinas, *Opuscula theologica*, ed. R. A. Verardo and R. M. Spiazzi (2 vols., Turin and Rome, 1954).
Aquinas, *Scriptum super Sententiis magistri Petri Lombardi*, ed. R. P. Mandonnet et al. (4 vols., Paris, 1929–47).
pseudo-Aquinas *see* Albertus magnus.
Arnold, T. (ed.), *Select English Works of John Wyclif* (3 vols., Oxford, 1869–71).
Augustine, *City of God*, trans. G. E. McCracken et al. (Loeb Classical Library, 7 vols., London and Cambridge, Mass., 1957–1972).
Bale, John, *Illustrium maioris Britanniae Scriptorum . . . Summarium* (Ipswich, 1548).
Bale, John, *Scriptorum Illustrium maioris Brytannie . . . Catalogus* (2 vols., Basel, 1557–9).
Bartholomaeus Anglicus, translated John Trevisa, *On the Properties of Things*, ed. M. C. Seymour et al. (3 vols., Oxford, 1975–88).

Bernard, *Opera*, ed. J. Leclercq, C. H. Talbot and H. M. Rochais (8 vols., Rome, 1957–77).

The Holy Bible . . . made from the Latin Vulgate by John Wycliffe and his Followers, ed. J. Forshall and F. Madden (4 vols., Oxford, 1850; repr. New York, 1982).

Biblia Sacra iuxta Vulgatam Clementinam, ed. A. Colunga and L. Turrado (Madrid, 4th edn., 1965). [*Vulg.*]

Bonaventura, *Opera omnia*, ed. Collegium Sanctae Bonaventurae (10 vols., Quaracchi, 1882–1902).

Brown, E., *Fasciculus Rerum Expetendarum* (2 vols., London, 1690).

Calendar of Close Rolls (London, 1902–).

Calendar of Patent Rolls (London, 1901–).

The Riverside Chaucer, ed. L. D. Benson *et al.* (Boston, 1987).

Dionysiaca, recueil donnant l'ensemble des traductions latines des ouvrages attribués au Denys de l'Aréopage, ed. P. Chevallier et al. (2 vols., Bruges, 1937–51).

Dives and Pauper, ed. P. H. Barnum (2 vols., EETS 275, 280, 1976–80)—cited by commandment and chapter number.

Dymmok, Roger, *Liber contra duodecim errores et hereses Lollardorum*, ed. H. S. Cronin (Wyclif Society, London, 1922).

English Wycliffite Sermons, ed. A. Hudson and P. Gradon (5 vols., Oxford, 1983–96)—sermons cited by number in continuous sequence, with *E* for the epistle sequence; introductory material and material in vols. 4–5 are cited by volume number and page.

Fasciculi Zizaniorum, ed. W. W. Shirley (RS 1858).

Fontes Franciscani, ed. E. Menestò and S. Brufani (Assisi, 1995).

The Acts and Monuments of John Foxe, ed. S. R. Cattley and J. Pratt (8 vols. in 16, London, 1853–70)—cited save where details require the use of the 1563 and 1570 editions.

Francis, St. *see Fontes Franciscani*

John of Friburg, *Summa Confessorum* (Nuremburg, 1517).

Friedberg, E. (ed.), *Corpus Iuris Canonici* (2 vols., Leipzig, 1879–81; repr. Graz, 1959)—the different parts are cited in the modern forms listed by J. A. Brundage, *Medieval Canon Law* (London, 1995), pp. 190–200.

Gascoigne, *Loci e libro veritatum*, ed. J. E. Thorold Rogers (Oxford, 1881).

The Complete Works of John Gower, ed. G. C. Macaulay (4 vols., Oxford, 1899–1902; vols. 2–3 were also issued as EETS ES 81–2, 1900–1).

'Nicholas Hereford's Ascension Day Sermon, 1382', ed. S. Forde, *Medieval Studies* 51 (1989), 205–41.

Jack Upland, Friar Daw's Reply and Upland's Rejoinder, ed. P. L. Heyworth (London, 1968).

Knighton's Chronicle 1337–1396, ed. G. H. Martin (Oxford Medieval Texts, 1995).

Langland, William, *Piers the Plowman: A Parallel-Text Edition of the A, B, C and*

Z Versions, ed. A. V. C. Schmidt (London, 1995). [*PPl*]—the line numbers of all texts are those of this edition.

The Lanterne of Li̇ct, ed. L. M. Swinburn (EETS 151, 1917).

Legenda aurea, ed. T. Graesse (Leipzig, 2nd ed. 1850).

Legg *see Sarum Missal*

[*Lollard Chronicle*], *The Chronicles of Rome: The Chronicle of Popes and Emperors and The Lollard Chronicle*, ed. D. Embree (Woodbridge, 1999)—the latter only is cited here from Emmanuel College Cambridge MS 85, the line numbers being prefixed by *Em*.

Lollard Sermons, ed. G. Cigman (EETS 294, 1989)—from BL MS Additional 41321, Bodleian Library MS Rawlinson C 751 and John Rylands Library MS Eng 412.

Matthew, F. D. (ed.). *The English Works of Wyclif hitherto unprinted* (EETS 74, 1880, revd. edn., 1902).

The Complete Works of St Thomas More, ed. L. L. Martz, R. S. Sylvester, C. H. Miller *et al.* (New Haven and London, 1963–).

Mum and the Sothsegger, ed. M. Day and R. Steele (EETS 199, 1936).

Netter of Walden, Thomas, *Doctrinale Antiquitatum Fidei Catholicae Ecclesiae*, ed. B. Blanciotti (3 vols., Venice, 1757–9; repr. Farnborough, 1967)—quoted by book and chapter number, followed in brackets by volume and column number).

Heresy Trials in the Diocese of Norwich, 1428–31, ed. N. P. Tanner (CS 4th series 20, 1977).

Pecock, Reginald, *The Repressor of over much blaming of the Clergy*, ed. C. Babington (2 vols., RS 1860).

Peraldus, William, *Summae Virtutum ac Vitiorum* (2 vols., Paris, 1668–9).

Pierce the Ploughman's Crede, ed. W. W. Skeat (EETS 30, 1867).

Piers Plowman see Langland.

The Plowman's Tale, ed. M. R. McCarl (New York, 1997).

Political Poems and Songs . . . from the Accession of Edward III to that of Richard III, ed. T. Wright (2 vols., RS, 1859–61). [*Pol. Poems and Songs*]

Polychronicon Ranulphi Higden Monachi Cestrensis, ed. C. Babington and J. R. Lumby (9 vols., RS, 1865–86).

A proper dyaloge betwene a Gentillman and an Husbandman, ed. D. H. Parker (Toronto, 1996).

Rede me and be not wrothe, ed. D. H. Parker (Toronto, 1992).

Robbins, R. H. (ed.), *Historical Poems of the XIVth and XVth Centuries* (New York, 1959).

Rosarium Theologie see von Nolcken.

Ross, W. O. (ed.), *Middle English Sermons* (EETS 209, 1940).

Rotuli Parliamentorum (7 vols., London, 1832).

Rupert of Deutz, *Liber de divinis officiis*, ed. H. Haacke (*CCCM* 7, 1967).

St Albans Chronicle see Walsingham.

The Sarum Missal, ed. J. W. Legg (Oxford, 1916).

Selections from English Wycliffite Writings, ed. A. Hudson (Cambridge, 1978).

Snappe's Formulary and other Records, ed. H. E. Salter (Oxford Historical Society 80, 1924).

Tanner, see *Norwich*.

[*Thirty-Seven Conclusions of the Lollards* =] *Remonstrance against Romish Corruptions*, ed. J. Forshall (London, 1851)—text quoted from BL Cotton Titus D.i but with page references to Forshall's edition.

Tractatus de regibus, ed. J.-P. Genet, *Four English Political Tracts of the Later Middle Ages* (CS 4th ser. 18, 1977), pp. 5–19.

Trevisa, *Dialogus inter Militem et Clericum, Sermon by FitzRalph and þe Bygynnyng of þe World*, ed. A. J. Perry (EETS 167, 1925).

[Usk, Adam] *The Chronicle of Adam Usk 1377–1421*, ed. C. Given-Wilson (Oxford Medieval Texts, 1997).

von Nolcken, C. (ed.), *The Middle English Translation of the 'Rosarium Theologie'* (Heidelberg Middle English Texts 10, 1979).

Walsingham, Thomas, *Chronicon Anglie*, ed. E. M. Thompson (RS, 1874).

Walsingham, Thomas, *Historia Anglicana*, ed. H. T. Riley (2 vols., RS, 1863–4).

Walsingham, Thomas, *St Alban's Chronicle 1406–1420*, ed. V. H. Galbraith (Oxford, 1937).

Wilkins, D. (ed.), *Concilia Magnae Britanniae et Hiberniae* (4 vols., London, 1737).

'The Trial of Richard Wyche', ed. F. D. Matthew, *EHR* 5 (1890), 530–44.

Wyclif, John, *Latin Works*: all those used here were edited for the Wyclif Society between 1883 and 1921, apart from *Trial.* and *Suppl. Trial.* which were edited together by G. V. Lechler (Oxford, 1869).

3. SECONDARY SOURCES

The normal form of reference to printed secondary materials is by author's surname, followed in brackets by date of publication, and usually by page numbers. Where an author issued more than one publication in the same year, superior numbers follow the date in brackets. In a number of cases several articles by the same author have been reprinted in a single volume; references are to that reprint volume.

Alford, J. A., *'Piers Plowman': A Glossary of Legal Diction* (Cambridge, 1988).

Aston, M., *Thomas Arundel: A Study of Church Life in the Reign of Richard II* (Oxford, 1967).

Aston, M., *Lollards and Reformers: Images and Literacy in Late Medieval Religion* (London, 1984).

Aston, M., *England's Iconoclasts: I. Laws against Images* (Oxford, 1988).

Aston, M., *Faith and Fire: Popular and Unpopular Religion, 1350–1600* (London, 1993).

Aston, M. and Richmond, C., eds., *Lollardy and the Gentry in the Later Middle Ages* (Stroud, 1997).

Bakker, P. J. J. M., '*Hoc est corpus meum*: L'Analyse de la formule de consécration chez des théologiens du xive et du xve siècles', in Marmo (1997), pp. 427–51.

Brundage, J. A., *Medieval Canon Law* (London and New York, 1995).

Catto, J. I., 'John Wyclif and the Cult of the Eucharist', *SCH, Subsidia* 4 (1985), pp. 269–86.

Chadwick, H., '*Ego Berengarius*', *JTS* ns 40 (1989), 414–45.

Clebsch, W. A., *England's Earliest Protestants, 1520–1535* (New Haven, 1964).

Courtenay, W. J., 'Theology and Theologians from Ockham to Wyclif', in *HUO* ii.1–34.

Crompton, J., '*Fasciculi Zizaniorum*', *JEH* 12 (1961), 35–45, 155–66.

Davies, R. G., 'Thomas Arundel as Archbishop of Canterbury, 1396–1414', *JEH* 24 (1973), 9–21.

Deanesly, M., *The Lollard Bible* (Cambridge, 1920).

de Libera, A., and I. Rosier-Catch, 'L'Analyse scotiste de la formule de la consécration eucharistique', in Marmo (1997^1), 171–201.

de Libera, A., and I. Rosier-Catch, 'Les enjeux logico-linguistiques de l'analyse de la formule de la consécration eucharistique', *Cahiers de l'Institut du moyen âge grec et latin* 67 (1997^2), 33–77.

Dyer, C., *Lords and Peasants in a Changing Society: the Estates of the Bishopric of Worcester 680–1540* (Cambridge, 1980).

Emden, A. B., *An Oxford Hall in Medieval Times* (Oxford, 1927, revd. edn. 1968).

Emden, A. B., *A Biographical Register of the University of Oxford to A.D. 1500* (3 vols., Oxford, 1957–9).

Emden, A. B., *A Biographical Register of the University of Cambridge to 1500* (Cambridge, 1963).

Fairfield, L. P., 'John Bale and the Development of Protestant Hagiography', *JEH* 24 (1973), 145–60.

Fairfield, L. P., *John Bale, Mythmaker for the English Reformation* (West Lafayette, 1976).

Gilmont, J.-F. ed., trans. K. Maag, *The Reformation and the Book* (Aldershot, 1998).

Gradon, P., 'Langland and the Ideology of Dissent', *PBA* 66 (1980), 179–205.

Gwynn, A., *The English Austin Friars in the Time of Wyclif* (Oxford, 1940).

Gy, P.-M., 'L'office du Corpus Christi et S. Thomas d'Aquin: État d'une recherche', *Revue scientifique de philosophie et théologie* 64 (1980), 491–507.

Gy, P.-M., 'L'office du Corpus Christi et la théologie des accidents eucharistiques', *Revue scientifique de philosophie et théologie* 66 (1982), 81–6.

Hanna, R., *Pursuing History: Middle English Manuscripts and their Texts* (Stanford, 1996).

Heath, P., *The English Parish Clergy on the Eve of the Reformation* (London, 1969).

Hudson, A., *Lollards and their Books* (London, 1985).

Hudson, A., 'A Wycliffite Scholar of the early Fifteenth Century', *SCH Subsidia* 4 (1985), pp. 301–15.

Hudson, A., 'Wycliffism in Oxford 1381–1411', in *Wyclif in his Times*, ed. A. Kenny (Oxford, 1986), pp. 67–84.

Hudson, A., *The Premature Reformation: Wycliffite Texts and Lollard History* (Oxford, 1988).

Hudson, A., '*Hermofodrita or Ambidexter*; Wycliffite Views on Clerks in Secular Office', in Aston and Richmond (1997), pp. 41–51.

Hudson, A., '*Peculiaris regis clericus*: Wyclif and the Issue of Authority', in *The Growth of Authority in the Medieval West*, ed. M. Gosman, A. Vanderjagt and J. Veenstra (Groningen, 1999), pp. 63–81.

Hume (1973) *see* More *CW* 8.

Jones, W. R., 'Relations of the two Jurisdictions: Conflict and Cooperation in England during the thirteenth and fourteenth centuries', *Studies in Medieval and Renaissance History* 7 (1970), 79–210.

Jurkowski, M., 'Heresy and Factionalism at Merton College in the early Fifteenth Century', *JEH* 48 (1997), 658–81.

Kennedy, L. A., 'A Carmelite Fourteenth-century Theological Notebook', *Carmelus* 33/1 (1986), 70–102.

Kenny, A., *Wyclif* (Oxford, 1985).

Kenny, A., ed., *Wyclif in his Times* (Oxford, 1986).

Kightly, C., 'The Early Lollards: A Survey of Popular Lollard Activity in England, 1382–1428' (unpubd. D. Phil. thesis, York, 1975).

Leff, G., *Heresy in the Later Middle Ages* (2 vols., Manchester, 1967).

McFarlane, K. B., *John Wycliffe and the Beginnings of English Nonconformity* (London, 1952).

McFarlane, K. B., *Lancastrian Kings and Lollard Knights* (Oxford, 1972).

McNiven, P., *Heresy and Politics in the Reign of Henry IV* (Woodbridge, 1987).

Macy, G., *Theologies of the eucharist in the early scholastic period* (Oxford, 1984).

Macy, G., *The Banquet's Wisdom: A Short History of the Theologies of the Lord's Supper* (New York, 1992).

Macy, G., 'The Dogma of Transubstantiatioon in the Middle Ages', *JEH* 45 (1994), 11–41.

Marmo, C., ed., *Vestigia, imagines, verba: Semiotics and Logic in Medieval Theological Texts (xiith–xivth Century)* (Turnhout, 1997).

Moorman, J., *A History of the Franciscan Order from its Origins to the year 1517* (Oxford, 1968).

Owst, G. R., *Preaching in Medieval England* (Cambridge, 1926).

Parker, D. H., *'A proper dyaloge between a Gentillman and a Husbandman*: the Question of Authorship', *BJRL* 78/1 (1996), 63–75.

Raban, S., *Mortmain Legislation and the English Church 1279–1500* (Cambridge, 1972).

Richardson, H. G., 'Heresy and the Lay Power under Richard II', *EHR* 51 (1936), 1–28.

Robson, J. A., *Wyclif and the Oxford Schools* (Cambridge, 1961).

Rosier, I., 'Signes et sacrements: Thomas d'Aquin et la grammaire spéculative', *Revue des sciences philosophiques et théologiques* 74 (1990), 392–436.

Scase, W., *'Piers Plowman' and the New Anticlericalism* (Cambridge, 1989).

Snape, M. G., 'Some Evidence of Lollard Activity in the Diocese of Durham in the early fifteenth century', *Archaeologia Aeliana* 4th series 39 (1961), 355–61.

Somerset, F., *Clerical Discourse and Lay Audience in Late Medieval England* (Cambridge, 1998).

Spencer, H. L., *English Preaching in the Late Middle Ages* (Oxford, 1993).

Swanson, R. N., *Church and Society in Late Medieval England* (Oxford, 1989).

Szittya, P., *The Antifraternal Tradition in Medieval Literature* (Princeton, 1986).

Thompson, A. H., *The English Clergy and their Organization in the Later Middle Ages* (Oxford, 1947).

Thomson, J. A. F., *The Later Lollards 1414–1520* (London, 1965).

Thomson, W. R., *The Latin Writings of John Wyclyf* (Toronto, 1983).

Walsh, K., *A Fourteenth-Century Scholar and Primate: Richard FitzRalph in Oxford, Avignon, and Armagh* (Oxford, 1981).

Whiting, B. J. and H. W., *Proverbs, Sentences and Proverbial Phrases . . . before 1500* (Cambridge Mass. and London, 1968).

Wood-Legh, K. L., *Studies in Church Life in England under Edward III* (Cambridge, 1934).

Workman, H. B., *John Wyclif: a Study of the English Medieval Church* (2 vols., Oxford, 1926).

THE SERMON *OMNIS PLANTACIO* AND THE TRACT *FUNDAMENTUM ALIUD NEMO POTEST PONERE*

f. 4ʳ *Omnis plantacio quam non plantauit pater meus celestis eradicabitur*
Mathei xv c°.

Almyȝti God þe Trinyte, Fadir ⌜and⌝ Sone and Hooli Goost, boþe in
þe oold lawe and in þe newe haþ foundid his chirche upon þre statis
answeringe or acordinge to þese þre persoones and her propirtees. So
þat to þe Fadir in Trynyte to whom is aproprid power answeriþ þe
5   staat of seculer lordis, fro þe hiȝest knyȝt þat is or shulde be
emperour to þe lowest squier þat bi weie of office or of his staat
beriþ þe swerd. For þis staat in hooli chirche seynt Poul (*ad Ro.* 13)
calliþ powers, and seiþ þat þis power beriþ þe swerd not wiþoute
cause but to avenge þe wraþ of God into him þat mysdoiþ, and to
10   supporte and maintene him þat wel doiþ; þis is þe sentence of Poul
þere. And also þis staat or power is þe vicar of þe godhed, as it mai
f. 4ᵛ be groundid here, | and as seynt Austyn seiþ in þe *Book of þe*
questiouns of þe oold lawe and þe newe and oþer dyuers placis. And so,
as it bilongiþ to þe godhed of Crist to avenge him on hise enmyes
15   and to rewar[d]e hise trewe seruauntis, as God himsilf seiþ, as þe
Apostle rehersiþ ' "To me," seiþ God, "it bilongiþ to do veniaunce
and I shal rewarde." ' And also þe prophete seiþ þat God shal
rewarde euery man aftir hise werkis. So it bilongiþ here upon erþe to
þe staat of seculer lordis as vicaries of þe godhed to do in poneshinge
20   and rewardinge to þe enmyes and to þe seruauntis of God. To þe
secunde persoone in Trinyte, to whom is aproprid wisdom or
kunnyng, answeriþ þe staat of clergie or of presthod, þe which bi
bisy studie and contemplacioun shulde gete hem heuenli kunnyng,
wherbi þei shulde teche þe peple þe weie to heuene and lede hem
f. 5ʳ þerinne. And herfore seiþ God bi his | prophete (*Malachie* 2°) *Labia*
26   *sacerdotis custodiunt scienciam, et legem* [re]quir[e]*nt ex ore eius quia*
angelus domini exercituum est, 'The lippis of þe prest kepiþ kunnyng,
and þe peple schal seche þe lawe of his mouþ, for he is þe aungel of
God.' And herfore Crist, supposinge þat þis heuenli kunnyng shulde

---

D *missing to 24* heuene   *omnis*] in nomine patris et filii et spiritus sancti amen
omnis H   1 fadir] the father F   and sone] the sonne F   hooli] the holy F
2 statis] estatis F   5 staat] estate F   6 squier] esquier F   weie] the way F
6 staat] estate F   7 staat] estate F   ad Ro.13] *margin* F   8 calliþ] callyd F
beriþ] *om.* (*caret mark but no correction*) H   9 cause] a cause F   10 wel doiþ]
rev. F   11 þere] þere Questionibus veteris et noue legis c.35 et c.91 dicit quod rex est
vicarius diuinitatis et sacerdos est vicarius Christi humanitatis, *margin* Austin H   and] *om.* F
staat] estate F   12 and . . . in] ⌜Augustinus⌝ questionibus . . . humanitatis, Thus
saith saynt Austen in (*see* H *line 11*) F   13 lawe] *om.* H   newe] newe lawe HF
margin c.35 and c.91 D   oþer] in oþer HFL   and so as] so that F   15 rewarde]

Fvndamentum aliud nemo potest ponere preter id quod positum est quod f.2ʳ
est Christus Ihesus.

Almy3ty God þe Trinyte, Fadir, Sonne and Holy Gooste, boþe in þe
olde lawe and þe newe haþ fowndid his chirche vpon þre statis
awnswerynge or acordynge to þes þre persones and her propirtes. So
þat to þe Fadir in Trinyte to whom is apropred power awnsweriþ þe
state of seculer lordis, fro þe hi3est kny3te þat is or schuld be þe 5
emperoure to þe lowest sqwyer þat by wai of office of his state beriþ
þe swerde. For þis state in holy chirche saynt Poule calliþ powers,
and saiþ þat þis power beriþ þe swerde not wiþowte cause but to
avenge þe wraþ of God into hym þat misdoiþ, | and to supporte and f.2ᵛ
mayntene hym þat wel doþe; þis is þe sentence of Poule þere. And 10
þis state or power is þe vicar of þe godheede, as it may be growndid
here, and, as saynt Austyn saiþ in þe *Booke of qwestyons of þe olde
lawe and þe newe*, and in oþer dyuers placis. And so, as it bylongiþ to
þe godheed of Criste to avenge hym on his ennemys and to rewarde
his trewe saruandis as God hymsiilfe saiþ, as þe Apostle rehersiþ 15
'"To me," saiþ God, "it longiþ to do vengance, and I schal
rewarde."' And also þe prophete saiþ þat God schal rewarde
euery man aftir his werkis. So it bylongiþ here vpon erþe to þe
state of seculere lordis as vicars of þe godhede to do in ponyschynge
and rewardynge to | þe ennemyes and seruandis of God. To þe f.3ʳ
secunde persone in Trinyte, to whom is apropred wisdam or 21
kunnynge, awnsweriþ þe state of þe clergy or of presthode, þe
whiche by bissy study and contemplacyon schulde gete hem heuenly
kunnynge, wherby þai schulde teche þe peple þe way to heuen and
lede hem þerinne. And herfor saiþ God by his prophete Malachie 25
Labia sacerdotis custodiunt scienciam et legem [re]quir[e]nt ex ore eius,
quia angelus Domini excercituum est, 'þe lippis of þe prest kepyn
kunnynge, and þe pepill schul seke þe lawe of his mouþe, for he is þe
awngell of God.' And herfor Criste, supposynge þat þis heuenly

---

Text *margin* prima ad cor. iiiᵒ cᵒ L   7 *margin* Ro. xijᵒ L   25 *margin*
Malachie ijᵒ cᵒ L   requirent] exquirunt L

---

rewarge (*lower bow of* g *eras.*) E   as²] and as F   *margin* deu.xxxij, Ro.xij F   16 god]
allmighti god F   bilongiþ] ʳbiˈlongiþ H, longiþ L   19 staat] estate F   vicaries]
vikers HFL   20 and¹ . . . seruauntis] the enmys of God and in rewardyng the
seruantis F   23 bisy] *om.* F   25 herfore] therfor F   god] god allmighty F
Malachie 2] *om.*F   *margin* Mal.2 EDFL, Malechie H   26 custodiunt] custodi/
diunt E   requirent] *on eras.*H, requirunt F, exquirunt EDL   27 þe] a F
kepiþ] kepen DH   28 seche] require F   29 herfore] therfor F

30 be in þe staat of presthod, comaundide hem alle in his assencioun in
þo wordis þat he seide to hise apostlis, and in hem to alle oþir
prestis, as seynt Austyn seiþ in a sermon þat bigynneþ þus *Si
diligenter attenditis* etc. þat þei shulde teche and preche þe gospel to
his peple, þe which gospel is heuenli kunnyng. For þis staat in þe
35 chirche is þe vicar of þe manhed of Crist, as seynt Austyn seiþ in þe
book þat is aleggid bifore; and, so as Crist cam in his manhed to
teche and preche þe gospel and to suffre mekeli persecucioun
þerfore, so shulde þe staat of prestis, þat is þe vicar of his |
f. 5ᵛ manhed, do as he comaundide hem in his ascencioun and ofte
40 tymes biforhond. To þe þridde persoone, to whom is aproprid
trewe loue or good will to þe Fadir and Sone, answeriþ þe staat of
þe comunte þe which owiþ trewe loue and obedient will to þe statis
of lordis and prestis, as seynt Poul techiþ (*ad Eph*.6 *et ad Hebr.
vltimo*) *Serui obedite dominis vestris carnalibus cum omni timore et
45 tremore etc.* (*ad Heb. vltimo*) *Obedite prepositis vestris; ipsi enim
peruigilant tanquam reddituri racionem pro animabus vestris.*

And so þese þre statis ben or shulden be sufficient in Goddis
chirche, or ellis men moste seie þat God is and was fauti in
ordynaunce of boþe hise lawis. And, in ful euydence and opun
50 tokenyng þat God takiþ þis ordynaunce in his chirche as ⌐ful⌐,
sufficient and in no wise fauti in scarste or excesse þerof, Crist þe
f. 6ʳ wisdom of þe Trinyte, bi þe which wis|dom þ[is] chirche is þus
ordeyned and foundid upon þese þre statis wiþout mo, tauȝte þe
newe statis and sectis of þe oold lawe, þe whiche weren not expresli
55 groundid in þe lawe of God, to be drawun out of þe chirche bi þe
roote. For he seiþ þus of þe pharisees, as þe teme aboue witnessiþ,
þe whiche pharisees were þe moost worshipful sect of religioun of þe

30 staat] estate F   31 þo] thos F   32 *margin* Austin HF   34 staat]
estate F   36 þat is] *om.* F   38 staat] estate F   40 biforhond] before FL
margin 3 D persoone] person in trinite FL   41 staat] estate F   42 comunte]
comynaltye F   statis] estatis F   43 ad Eph. . . . tremore etc. (45)] ad eph. vj cᵒ
serui obedite . . . tremore etc. *after* biforhond (40), *with* ad eph.6 et ad Hebr.vltimo H, eph.
vj F, *repeated after translation   margin* ad eph.6 EDFL   45 *margin later hand*
hebr. 13 E, hebre vltimo F   46 reddituri racionem] *rev.* DF, ⌐racionem⌐ *dh*
reddituri H   pro] *om.* H   47 statis] estatys F   48 moste] myght F
49 ordynaunce] his *canc.* ordynaunce E   51 in² . . . excesse] without excesse or
skarsnes F   52 þis] DHF, þis *corr.to* þe E, þe L   53 statis] estatis F
53–802 wiþout . . . clergie] *om.* L   53 mo] ony more F   þe] þese HF
54 statis] estatis F

44 *margin* Ephe. vj caᵒ L   46 *margin* hebr' vltimo caᵒ L   54 *margin* Galat.
iᵒ L

kunnynge schuld be in þe state of presthode, commaundid hem alle 30
in his ascencyon in þo wordis þat he saide to | his apostles, and in f. 3ᵛ
hem to alle oþer prestis, as saynt Awstyn saiþ in a sermon þat
bigynneþ þus *Si diligenter attenditis* etc. þat þai schulden teche and
preche þe gospell to his peple, þe whiche gospel is heuenly
kunnynge. For þis state in þe chirche is þe vicar of þe manhede of 35
Criste, as saynt Austyn saiþ in a booke þat is alegyd tofore; and, so as
Criste cam in his manhede to teche and preche þe gospell and to
suffre meekly persecucion þerfore, so schulde þe state of prestis, þat
ben vicaris of his manhede, do as he commaundit hem in his
ascencyon and oft tymes byfore. To þe þridde persone in Trinyte, 40
to whom is apropryd true loue or goode will to þe Fadir and Sonne, |
awnsweriþ þe state of þe comonte þe whiche owiþ true loue and f. 4ʳ
obedyente will to þe statis of lordis and prestis, as saynt Poule techiþ
saynge *Serui obedite dominis vestris carnalibus cum omni timore et
tremore*, þat is 'Seruandis obeyiþ to ȝour temperall lordis wiþ alle 45
drede and tremblynge.' Also saynt Poule saiþ þus *Obedite prepositis
vestris, ipsi enim vigilant tanquam reddituri racionem pro animabus
vestris*, þat is 'Obeiþ to ȝoure souereyns; forsoþe þai waken as for to
ȝeue acowntis for ȝoure soulis.' By þes souereyns is vndirstonde þe
state of presthode, þe whiche schulde bisyly wake in studiynge and 50
prechynge of Goddis lawe to alle cristen peple and to ȝeue goode
ensaumple in her lyuynge. And in þis euery man | is bonden to obey f. 4ᵛ
to her doctrine. And þerfore Poule saiþ 'Be ȝe fylowers of me, as I
am of Criste.' And efte he saiþ 'þouȝ we or an awngell of heuen
preche to ȝou bysidis þat þat we han prechid, be he acursid.' And so 55
bi þis sentence prestis schulden not haue worldly lordeschippis, siþ
Criste and his apostles han vttirly forfendid hem boþe in her lyuynge
and techynge, as it suiþ playnly heraftir. For it was neuer Cristis lore
to make prestis riche and knyȝtis pore.

   And so þes þre statis ben or schulde be sufficient in Goddis 60
chirche, or ellis men mosten say þat God is and was fawty in
ordenance of boþe his lawis. And, in full euydence and open
tooknynge þat God takiþ þis ordenance in his chirche | as full, f. 5ʳ
sufficient and in no wise fawtye in scarste or excesse þerof, Criste þe
wisdam of þe Trinyte, by whiche wisdome þe chirche is ordend and 65
fowndid vpon þes þre statis, techiþ vs in all his lawe to kepe and to
mayntene þis ordenance, wiþowten addynge þerto or abregynge
þerfro. Wherfor Poule saiþ 'No man may putt anoþer grounde
bysidis þat þat is putt, þe whiche is Criste Ihesu.'

[*Lambeth Tract* resumes on p. *33*]

oold lawe, þat 'Eueri plauntyng, þe which myn heuenli Fadir haþ not
plauntid, shal be drawun up bi þe roote.' And þe same word most bi
60 þe same skill be vndirstondun of oþir sectis, as of þe essees and
saducees. And so Crist hatide þese sectis, and dampneþ þe
fundacioun of suche sectis wiþ þe abite and rule. And so he
dampneþ alle þat longiþ to such a sect, and makiþ it to dyuerse
fro þe comoun sect of God, and also to be dyuerse among hemsilf.
f. 6ᵛ þe fundacioun of suche sectis Crist dampneþ in my | teeme, in as
66 moche as he meueþ opunli þat þei ben not plauntid into þe chirche
bi þe Fadir of heuene. And siþ þer ben here in þis world but two
chirchis, þat is to seie Cristis and anticristis, and two heedis of hem,
þat is to seie God and þe deuel, it is liȝt to vndirstonde who
70 plauntide þese sectis.

As touchinge þe abite of þe pharisees þe which Crist repreuede, as
þe Maistir of Stories telliþ, þei hadden large and grete hemmes in
her abite, and þerupon þei sowide brood scrowis wiþ þe comaundementis writun þerupon wiþ greet lettre, as who wolde seie 'We kepen
75 þese comaundementis'; and vndir þis abite in her hammes hyng a
buysh of þornes þat prickide hem ofte, as if þei wolden mene þus
'þouȝ we wolde forȝete þese maundementis, þese þornes shulen
f. 7ʳ warne us þat we doen not.' And ȝit | vndir alle þese hooli signes þei
weren þe falsest and þe moost wickid peple and þe moost contrarious
80 to God among alle þe peple alyue. But þe symple peple koude not
perseyue þat, into þe tyme þat Crist hadde declarid þe falsnesse and
þe malice of hem, þat was hid vndir suche hooli signes, but wenden
for þe greet honeste and deuocioun þat þei shewide in dyuyne
seruyce and for her long praiers þat God hadde be fair serued in
85 hem—as þei ben disceyued now bi oþir þat folowen her trace. Crist
þanne in repref of ⌐þis⌐ ypocritli abite seiþ þus: 'þei maken grete
hemmes and brood scrowis.'

And in repref of her rulis and tradiciouns or ordynauncis, þe

58 *margin* Mt.xv.c H   þat] *om.* F   þe] *om.* F   59 roote] rotis F   word]
wordys F   60 skill] reason F   þe²] *om.* F   63 makiþ] that makith F
dyuerse] swarue F   67 and] 2m ca. and F   siþ] in so muche þat F   but two]
tᶠuᶠo H, ij F   71 þe³] *om.* F   72 stories] ⌐the⌐ storys F   74 þerupon] vpon
them F   lettre] letters F   wolde] *om.* F   we kepen] kepen we *marked for rev.* E
75 þese] the F   77 maundementis] commandmentis F   shulen] schuld F
78 not] them not F   79 falsest] most false F   þe moost¹] *om.* F   and² . . .
alyue (80)] alyve ⌐and the most contrarie to god among al þe peple⌐ F   80 alyue] of
lyue H   81 into] vnto F   82 wenden] the people thought F   84 long]
longe said F   85 þat . . . trace] *om.* F   86 þis ypocritli] thes ipocritis and ther F
margin Mt.23] EF, euang. H, *om.* D   88 or ordynauncis] *om.* F   þe] *om.* F

whiche þei kepte streytli and made oþir folk to kepe, nameli such
ordynaunce þat sownede to her wynnyng, Crist spekiþ þus (*Marci* 7): 90
'Ypocritis, Ysaie þe | prophete propheciede wel of 3ou, as it is writun f. 7ᵛ
Populus hic labiis me honorat cor autem eorum long[e] est a me, "þis
peple honouriþ me wiþ lippis but her herte is fer fro me." *In uanum
autem me colunt, docentes doctrinas, et precepta hominum; relinquentes
enim mandata Dei tene[tis] tradiciones hominum; bene irritum fecistis* 95
mandatum Dei, ut tradicionem vestram seruetis; 'In vayn þei worshipen
me, techinge þe looris and maundementis of men; for 3e leuen þe
maundementes of God and holden þe tradiciouns or rulis of men.'
And þere Crist specifieþ summe of her lewid obseruauncis, þe
whiche were chargiouse to þe ypocritis of þat religioun. And so 100
Crist seiþ ferþermor þere 'Veyn haue 3e maad þe heeste of God, þat
3e kepe 3oure owne tradiciouns.' And wiþ suche vngroundid ritis and
tradiciouns þei chargide not oon|li þer owne sect but also oþer peple. f. 8ʳ
For Crist playneþ upon hem [and seiþ] (*Mt.*23) *Alligant enim onera
grauia et importabilia, et imponunt ista in humeros hominum*, 'þei 105
bynden togidir greuouse or heuy chargis þat moun not be bore,
and putten hem upon þe shuldris of men.' And for couetise þei
tau3te þe peple to breke þe maundement þat God hadde 3oue of
worshiping of fadir and of modir; for þei tau3te men to avowe and to
offre her goodis to þe temple, þat it my3te turne to her vss, and bade 110
hem þat þei shulde enfourme her fadir and modir þat it was so more
profitable þan þou3 it hadde be spendid in her vss or nede. And I
suppose þat oure pharisees han not for3ete þis loore. For oon seide
now late in presence of moche peple þat it was beter to offre to an
ymage of stoon or tre þan to 3yue þat good to a | pore man, hadde he f. 8ᵛ
neuere so moche nede. And þus as Crist playneþ upon suche 116

89 streytli] ful *canc.* streytli E   nameli] specially F   90 þat] as F   marci 7]
margin F   91 *margin* ysaie DH   92 longe] DHF, long E   þis . . . me²
(93)] *after* seruetis (96) HF   93 lippis] ther lippys F   95 tenetis] H, tenentes F,
tenent ED   96 in . . . me (97)] thei worchip me in wayn F   97 looris]
lernyngis F   maundementis] commandmentis F   3e] thei F
98 maundementes] commandmentis F   99 þe] *om.* F   101 *margin* ysaie H
veyn] *om.* F   heeste] promyses F   þat] veyn that F   102 kepe] may kepe F   ritis]
customys F   104 for] and therfor F   playneþ] pey *canc.* compleynith F   and
seiþ] DH (*after* Mt.23)F, *om.* E   *margin* Mt.23 EDF   Mt.23] *om.* F   enim] *om.* HF
105 ista] ea   F   106 or] and   F   107 couetise] covetusnes   F
108 maundement] commandmentis F   109 of²] *om.* F   110 bade] haue HF
111 þat¹] and þat F   it] *om.* F   so] *om.* F   112 þan] so than F
113 loore] teachyng F   114 late] a late F   115 tre] of tre F   hadde] thowe
he had F   116 nede] nede þerof (of *canc.*) to F   as] *om.* F   playneþ]
complaynith F

pharisees (*Mr.* 7) *Non permittitis eum quicquam facere patri suo, aut matri, rescindentes verbum Dei per tradicionem vestram, quam tradidistis,* 'þei suffren not men to do þat hem ouȝte to fadir and to modir, but
120 kitten awei þe word of God for her tradicioun þat þei han ȝouun.'

This processe I haue writun þe more large þat men mai se þe malice of þe oolde pharisees, and þe beter combyne þe oolde pharisees and þe newe togidir. And so of þis processe writun bifore we mai se þat Crist haþ repreued and dampned not oonli
125 þe fundacioun of suche priuat religiouse, but also þe abite and þe rule, bi þe whiche þe priuat sectis weren dyuersid and departid fro þe pure sect of men of þe oold lawe, as oure sectis now bi such fundacioun, abite and rule ben dyuydid ech from oþir, and also fro
f. 9ʳ þe | purid sect of Iesu Crist. And, in tokenyng þat Crist wolde no
130 suche sectis be in his lawe, he seiþ in my teeme þat 'Euery such plauntyng shal be drawun up bi þe roote.' For, whanne a plaunt is pullid up so, it is a tokene þat he þat so doiþ wole þat it shal growe no more. And in more witnesse of þis Crist wiþ teching of his gospel turnede summe of þe[se] pharisees to his clene and purid sect, as
135 Nichodeme, Gamaliel and Poul; and þo þat wolden not turne fro suche sectis he distriede bi Tite and Vaspasian, and made an eende of alle suche sectis, as he hadde prophecied bifore.

And, as he hadde be an enmye to God þe Fadir and to Crist and his lawe þat wolde plaunte, founde or susteyne suche sectis þat God
140 þe Fadir foundide not, and þerfore wolde haue hem rootid up þat þei shulde growe no more in his chirche, so is he an enmye to þe same
f. 9ᵛ Fadir, | to Crist and his lawe þat foundiþ or susteyneþ [ony] suche priuat sectis þat ben not now expresli foundun in þe gospel—but if it so be þat suche sectis can shewe in þe newe lawe ony beter or more
145 autorite of her fundacioun þan myȝte þe pharisees in þe oold lawe, and þat as I suppose shal þei not, ȝhe al-bisi a liȝt colour of founding

---

117 pharisees] phareseys saing F   Mr. . . . tradidistis (118)] *margin* D   *margin* Mci. vij F   118 per] propter *alt.to* per H, propter F   119 þei] ye F   hem ouȝte] þei owith F   fadir] ther father F   to³] *om.* HF   120 kitten] kit//kitten D, kyttyng F   her] yower F   þei] ye F   121 *margin* 3 ca. F   122 pharisees] *om.* F   126 dyuersid] devided F   127 as] *om.* F   128 ech] yche on F 129 purid] pure HF   130 be] to be F   he seiþ] sayd F   *margin* Mt.xv c. H 134 þese] DHF, þe E   and purid] ˹and˺ pure H, and pure F   138 hadde be] is F 140 wolde] he wold F   142 and] also and F   lawe] lawis F   ony suche] DHF, suche E   143 expresli foundun] fowndyd expresly F   it] *om.* HF 144 shewe] finde HF   145 in] of D   146 shal þei] *rev.* F   not] DHF, not do E   ȝhe . . . a] then lett them busy themselfe about suche a F

of suche sectis. And such a colour of Goddis lawe wiþoute expresse autorite is not ynow to founde so many chargeouse sectis, but if þei wolde bi contrarie witt grounde hem upon such wordis of Crist, where he seiþ (*Mt.* 23) *Patrem nolite vocare vos super terram: vnus est* 150 *enim pater vester, qui in celis est.* *Nec vocemini magistri: quia magister vester vnus est, Cristus.* 'Nile 3e calle 3ou a fadir upon erþe', or upon þese wordis, 'Be 3e not callid maistris, forsoþ, oon is 3oure maistir, [Crist]', or ellis (*Mt.* 24) whe|re Crist seiþ *Surgent pseudoprophete, et* f. 10ʳ *þ[s]eudoChristi, et dabunt signa et prodigia, ita ut in errorem ducantur et,* 155 *si fieri potest, electi,* 'False prophetis or false Cristis or false cristen men shal arise, and þei shal 3yue signes and wondris so þat, if it mai be, þe chosun of God be brou3t into errour.'

Suche textis þat sownen a3en þe founding of suche newe sectis mai men fynde many. And I calle alle þo newe sectis, be þei neuere 160 so oold in tyme, þat ben brou3t into þe chirche and not expresli foundid of Crist. Crist seiþ also þat 'þer shal come a tyme whanne men shal seie "Lo here, lo þere!"', as þou3 he wolde mene þat men shal seie 'Lo, here is perfeccioun at Rome!', and oþir shal seie 'Lo, here is perfeccioun or ground of cristen lyuyng at Auinon!', or ellis 165 in more special 'Lo, here among mounkis is perfeccioun, or Crist is here fair serued!' Summe seien 'Lo, here it is at | þe chanouns!'; f. 10ᵛ summe seien 'Lo, here at freris is Crist fairest serued!' þus men seien now in oure daies bisili, 'Lo here, lo þere!' But what seide Crist þat trewe men shulden do in þis tyme? Crist seiþ [þus] (*Luc.* 17) *Dicent* 170 *'Ecce hic, ecce illic!' Nolite ire, neque sectemini,* 'Nile 3e go awei, ne folowe 3e, or be 3e no sectis.' A man goiþ neuere awei into þe tyme þat he wiþdrawe him from Crist. Alle cristen men in eueri staat in þe

147 of¹] *om.* F   a] *om.* F   149 wolde] wole HF   witt] wise F   hem] themself F   150 where] as F   *margin* Mt.23 DF   Mt.23] in mathew F   vos] *om.* F   152 nile . . . a] call no man your F   153 be 3e] loke ye be F   154 Crist] DHF, *om.* E   Mt.24] *om.*, *margin* eodem cap.supra F   155 pseudochristi] pheudochristi E   in] *om.* H   ducantur] inducantur F   158 be²] shal be F   159 þat sownen] as sownd F   of suche] *twice, 2nd canc.* E   newe] *om.* HF   160 mai men] *rev.* HF   162 *margin* nota de hoc Mt.24 et Mr (Mt. EF) 13 (23 F) per processum ED, *in text after* Crist¹(162) HF   come] a *canc.* come E   163 þere] here F   shal] shuld F   165 cristen lyuyng] perfection F   auinon] avynion or grownd of cristen levyng F   or²] luc. vij c. (*margin* luc xvii F) dicent ecce hic ecce illic nolite ire neque sectemini or HF   166 special] especiall F   168 freris] þe fryers F   fairest] fayer F   169 now] *om.* F   þere] here F   what] w *canc.*/ what E   170 þus] DHF, *om.* E   170 luc. 17 . . . sectemini (171)] *om., see above 165* HF   *margin* luc.17 ED   171 nile . . . awei] go not away F   ne] nor F   172 3e¹] them F   or . . . 3e²] and looke ye be F   into] tyll F   173 þat] be þat F   staat] estate F

bigynnyng of Cristis chirche weren foundid upon him wiþoute ony
175 mene. þei þanne þat putten a founder of her staat or ordre bitwene
hem and Crist aftir þis vndirstonding goiþ fro Crist; and þese it ben
þat folowen oþir þan Crist and bicomen sutes or sectis aȝens Cristis
heeste.
    þerfore whanne þis meschif was growinge into þe chirche in seynt
180 Poulis tyme he, as he hadde lerned of Crist in heuene, knowinge
f. 11ʳ what sor|we it shulde do in þe chirche of God, wiþstood þis meschif,
and redresside aȝen þe peple fro suche sectis to be of þe pured sect of
Iesu Crist wiþoute ony mene, as it is writun hereaftir more opunli.
Loo, suche contrarie groundis men mai fynde for þese sectis. Or ellis
185 liȝtli þese newe sectis ben groundid upon seynt Petris wordis (ii *Pe.*
ii), where he seiþ þus: *Fuerunt vero et pseudoprophete in populo, sicut et*
in vobis erunt magistri mendaces, qui introducent sectas perdicionis, et
eum qui emit eos Dominum negant, superducentes sibi celerem perdicio-
nem. Et multi sequentur eorum luxurias, per quos via veritatis blasfema-
190 *bitur; et in auaricia fictis verbis de vobis negociabuntur,* 'Forsoþe, false
prophetis han be in þe peple, as also in ȝou shal be maister liers þat
shulen brynge yn sectis of perdicioun or dampnacioun, and him þat
bouȝte hem þei shal denye, brynginge into hemsilf haasti perdicioun |
f. 11ᵛ or dampnacioun. And many shal sue her lecheries, bi whom þe weie
195 of truþe shal be blasphemed; and in couetise wiþ feyned wordis þei
shal marchaundise of ȝou.' And, certis, and we applie þe lyuyng and
þe maners of oure newe sectis to þis prophecie of seynt Petir, þe
which is þe trewest manere of expownyng of derk prophecies for þe
dede or þe þing in itsilf expowneþ prophecies, we mai se many of þe
200 newe sectis groundid in þese wordis. First seynt Petir seiþ þat þer
shal be maistir liers among cristen peple. Soþe it is þat maistrie
sowneþ into difficulte or hardnesse or peril; and, so as a þing is more

175 mene] removyng F   staat] estate F   176 aftir] and aftr HF   and² . . .
ben] thes be they F   177 sutes or] men of F   178 heeste] hoost F
179 growinge into] in F   180 *margin* 1 cor.1 ED   tyme] days F   lerned]
lernerd E   in heuene] *om.* F   181 do] bryng F   in] into F   182 aȝens þe
peple] the peple agayn F   pured] pure HF   183 mene] removyng F   opunli]
opun H   184 for] more opun for HF   185 *margin* 2 pet.2 EDF   185 ii
Pet.ii] *om.* F   186 where] where as F   he] hem, -m *canc.* E   þus] *om.* F
187 erunt] ereunt H   189 veritatis] verita // *lost to 215* maken D
191 maister liers] lyeng masters F   193 hemsilf] þem F   194 sue] folow F
196 marchaundise] make merchandyse F   and¹] 4m ca. and F   certis] of a very
truthe F   and²] if F   lyuyng] lernyng F   197 þe¹] *om.* F   198 of²] a F
prophecies] prophecy F   199 þe²] þese HF   200 *margin* 1 pars F,] part H
201 maistir liers] lying masters F   *margin* 1 E   maistrie] maister HF   202 so]
om. F

hard or perilous to be don, so it is more maistrie. For, as it is more
maistrie to me to bere at oonys two buysshels of corn þan oon bi
himsilf, for it traueliþ, faintiþ or peyneþ me more, and so it were 205
more maistrie to me to wiþstonde or ouerlede þe baily or þe mair of
þis toun þan anoþir | symple man of myn astaat. And so it were more f. 12ʳ
maistrie to make a lesyng upon oon of hem and maintene it þan upon
my pore felowe, for þer were more worldli peril þerinne. And so it
wole sue þat it were þe moost maistrie þat a man myȝte do in liynge 210
to bilie God and maintene it obstynatli. Siþ þanne þese newe sectis
maken a greet lesyng upon God, and obstynatli maintenen þat lesyng
wiþout colourable ground, and not oo lesyng but manye, no wondir
þouȝ seynt Petir calle such maister liers.

And if þou wolt wite what lesyng þese newe sectis maken upon 215
Crist and techen þe symple peple to do þe same, among many oþir
lesyngis þei writen and reden in scool, and seien in sermouns and
priuy comynyngis obstynatli, þat Crist was a begger aftir þe comoun
vndirstonding of þis word begger. And to þis lesyng assenten now þe
religious | possessioners; and whi þei doen so þe cause is toold aftir f. 12ᵛ
þis. And þis most nedis be a lesyng. For Crist hadde ful lordship 221
upon al þe world bi titil of creacioun for he made al; also he hadde bi
titil of innocence þe same lordship or more þat Adam hadde in
paradiis; and also he was a riȝtful man and ful of grace. And so bi
riȝtwisnesse o[r] grace he hadde titil to alle þe þingis of þis world, for 225
scripture seiþ þat alle þingis ben of þe riȝtwise men. And ouere þis
he was a trewe prest and bishop, and truli wiþoute faute dide þat
office to þe peple. And ꞃsoꞁ bi titil of þe gospel he myȝte take as he
dide þo þingis þat weren needful to his lyuyng; and so he myȝte not
begge aftir þe comoun vndirstonding of begging. And herfore 230
whanne he askide ony þing ((Johannis 4) Mulier da mihi bibere, as

203 maistrie] mastrye to me (me canc.) prove it by example F   for] om. H   204 to²]
forto H   205 himsilf] itself alone F   faintiþ] it faynteth F   more and] even F
206 or ouerlede . . . or] om. F   208 oon of hem] suche a man F   209 more]
om. F   margin nota E   and . . . were (210)] in like wise it is F   210 moost]
most/moste F   211 bilie] bigile HF   siþ] seing F   212 maintenen] þei
canc. maintenen E   213 colourable] substanciall F   wondir] mervell it is F
214 maister liers] lieng masters F   215 wolt wite] wold know F   lesyng]
lesyngis HF   217 scool] scolys F   218 comynyngis] comme/ingis H
219 lesyng] lying F   assenten] agreith F   now] om. F   220 religious] religious (-
us added)// use E   223 þat] than F   226 þat] for D, om. F   of . . . men] ryghtus mens F
þe] om. H   ouere þis] euer F   228 peple] pepull that he tooke vpon hym F
so] ꞃsoꞁ ED   229 þo] thos F   230 herfore] therefore F   231 margin
Jo.4 EDF   Johannis 4] om.F   Johannis . . . bibere] after samarie (232) HF   michi]
michi canc. F

f. 13ʳ watir of þe womman of Samarie, | (*Luc.* 19) *Zachee festinanter descende, quia* ⌜*hodie*⌝ *in domo tua oportet me manere*, or an hous of Zachee; (*Mt.* 21) *Inuenietis asinam alligatam et pullum cum ea; soluite*
235 *et adducite mihi*, or þe asse and hir colt upon þe which he rode to Ierusalem), he askide þese þingis bi weie of comaunding as a lord, or ellis bi weie of dute and not in maner of begging.

Anoþir opun lesyng þese maistir liers wiþ her sectis affermen obstynatli on Crist, seiynge þat his lawe is moost fals and heresie,
240 blasphemye and contrarious to itsilf, notwiþstondinge þat þe prophete seiþ *Lex domini immaculata* þat þe lawe of God is vndefoulid or wiþoute wem. Siþ þanne þer is no þing foul saue lesyng, for al synne is lesyng, it sueþ þat þe lawe of God is not defoulid wiþ lesyngis. It nediþ not to stonde long to dispreue þis lesyng for it is opun ynow.

f. 13ᵛ þese maistir liers and her sectis li|en also to þe peple and confermen
246 her lesyng wiþ her lettre and her general seel, in tokenyng þat þei ben alle liers in doyng or in consenting; and seien þat whosoeuer haþ her lettre and her seel, and so is a broþer of her ordre, is partener of alle her meedful dedis, and þei specifien many of þese dedis
250 boostinge of hem in her lettris. But al þat is fals: for, whilis þei stonden obstynat in þese synnes and many mo, þei doen no meedful dede toward euerlasting liif. For suche synnes as I haue rehersid here, and manye mo þat ben ⌜comoun⌝ among hem, stonden not wiþ charite, wiþoute which charite no dede þat man doiþ is meedful to
255 him, as seynt Poul techiþ (1 *Cor.*13) *Si linguis hominum loquar et angelorum* etc. And þus for faute of charite neþer þei ne her briþeren ben parteners of her meedful werkis, alþou3 þei seie þe contrarie and
f. 14ʳ bleren her briþeren i3en wiþ her gai peyn|tid lettre to bigile hem of her worldli good and also of her soulis helþe.

260   Anoþir greet lesyng þese maistir liers and her sectis maken vpon

232 watir] the water F   *margin* luc.19 DF   luc.19] *om* F   232 Luc . . .
manere (233)] *after* Zachee (234) HF   232 festinanter] festinans HF
234 Mt. . . . mihi (235)] *after* Ierusalem (236) HF   *margin* mt.21 DF   Mt.21] *om*.F
236 weie] the way F   237 weie] the way F   in maner] by þe way F
238 *margin* ij lesinge H   maistir liers] lieng masters F   wiþ her sectis] *om.* F
241 lex] Ps. lex H, *margin* dauid D   or] and F   242 wem] ony vemme F   siþ]
seyng F   þer] þat there F   saue] except F   243 sueþ] semyth F
244 dispreue] reprove F   245 maistir liers] lyeng masters F   246 lesyng]
lying F   lettre . . . her³] *om.* F   247 þat] *om.* F   haþ] haue F   249 alle]
om. F   specifien] specified F   þese] þe H, þer F   250 but] and F
251 mo] mor F   253 mo] more F   254 which] þe whiche HF
255 *margin* 1 cor.13 ED   si . . . etc. (256)] *om.* HF   256 faute] defaute F   ne]
nor F   257 parteners] partakers F   seie . . . bleren (258)] blynd F   258 lettre]
letters F   259 good] goodis F   260 maistir liers] lying masters F

þe sacrament of þe auter, seiynge þat þe sacrid oost is not Cristis
bodi, notwiþstondinge þat Crist techiþ opunli, and alle feiþful men
bifore þese sectis han take as trewe bileeue, it to be Cristis bodi. And
fro þis bileeue þei varien on wundir dyuerse wise, notwiþstonding
þat alle þe men þat ben now or euere were han no more of pure   265
substaunce of þe bileeue in þis poynt þan Crist himsilf techiþ
expresli in þe gospel. In witnesse wherof seynt Poul, þat was þe
grettest doctour and hiest lerned saue Crist, spekinge of þis bileeue
durste not adde, wiþdrawe or chaunge ony word of þe bileeue þat
Crist hadde tauȝt him in heuene. And so seynt Poul passiþ not in þis 270
mater þe gospel, but calliþ it 'breed' and 'Cristis bodi'. And | so   f. 14ᵛ
diden oþer seyntis þat suppose[de]n scripture to be trewe, and
tooken as ground of her feiþ, and durste not seie, as þese maistir
liers and blasfemouse sectis doen now, þat hooli scripture is fals.

And, certis, I haue no tyme ne wheron to write þe grete lesyngis 275
and fautis þat þese sectis opunli or derkli putten upon Cristis lawe
and his lyuyng. For, and þei supposide effectueli þat his lyuyng was
moost perfit, þei wolde not bi so many dyuerse sectis on dyuerse wise
straie awei fro his lyuyng. And þe same I seie of his lawe, if þei
supposide it to be ful trewe and ful autentik. No wundir þanne   280
alþouȝ seynt Petir calle such folk maistir liers. And so of þes wordis
of seynt Petir þus declarid is þe next word of seynt Petir opun þat
sueþ aftir, for he seiþ þat þese maistir liers shal brynge yn sectis of
perdicioun. He seiþ not 'oo | sect', but 'sectis of perdicioun', or   f. 15ʳ
dampnacioun, þe whiche I am ful feerd ben ful many—for I can not 285
noumbre þe sectis þe whiche, alþouȝ þei ben dyuerse among hemsilf
and fro Cristis pure sect bi fundacioun, abite and rule, ȝit alle þei
assenten, and so in oo manere or in anoþer maintenen þese greuouse
lesyngis, and oþir heresies and errours of þe whiche I wole sumwhat
speke soone if God wole.   290

264 on . . . wise] mervelus dyuersly F   265 þe] om. F   266 himsilf] om. F
269 adde] om. F   ony] on F   270 in heuene] om. F   and] 5 ca. and F
272 supposeden] F, supposen EDH   273 as¹] it as HF   maistir liers] lesyng
masters F   274 hooli] þe HF   275 certis] of a truthe F   ne wheron]
om. F   276 fautis] DHF, fautis(gap of 1 letter)es E   277 and] iff F
278 bi] be F   279 straie] and strange F   280 þanne] it is than nor mervell F
281 alþouȝ] thow F   folk] floke F   maistir liers] lying mast' F   margin ij part H; 2
pars F   282 word] wordis F   of² . . . Petir²] om. F   283 sueþ] folowith F
margin 2 D   þat . . . seiþ (284)] om. F   284 not] no F   margin 2ᵃ pars F
285 þe] om. F   I¹] as I HF   ful] very F   288 assenten] agre F   in anoþer]
oþer F   290 soone] hereafter F

Ferþermor, seynt Petir seiþ in his prophecie þat þese maister liers and her sectis shal denye him þat bouȝte hem. And so doen þese sectis, in as moche as þei leuen þe pure sect of Iesu Crist and his gospel and bynden hem to newe fantasies of mannes ordinaunce, in
295 abite, in rule and oþir vngroundid ritis wiþoute noumbre. And in þis þei speciali forsaken him þat bouȝte hem, for as moche as þei speken so moche velony of his lawe, as it is seid in partie bifore. For, ⌐as⌐ it is
f. 15ᵛ al oon | to loue Crist and his lawe, for þat lawe is substanciali Crist, as it mai be preued bi þe gospel, so it is al oon to denye Crist and to
300 denye his lawe. And siþ þat þese sectis in word and dede denyen so opunli Cristis gospel, it wole sue as seynt Petir seiþ þat þei denyen him þat bouȝte hem. And so for þese synnes, as seynt Peter seiþ, and for many mo þat we myȝte reherce here, þese maistir liers wiþ her sectis shal brynge vpon hemsilf haasti dampnacioun. For lenger þan
305 her deeþ dai shal þei not ascape; for suche hidouse synnes asken ful depe dampnacioun, but if þei amende ⌐hem⌐, and þat doen ful fewe of hem fructuousli as I am afeerd. For, siþ þese synnes ben opun ⌐and⌐ occasioun of manye and greuouse synnyngis to þe peple, if þei shulde do fructuous penaunce acordinge to her synnes, þei shulde do
310 it opunli in presence of þe peple, þat her opun penaunce and
f. 16ʳ forþenking we|re occasioun to þe peple to be sori, and for to do penaunce for her synnes, and to leue hem, as þe synnes of þese sectis bi opun ensaumple and occasioun ȝouun han brouȝt þe peple into her synnes and maad hem obstynat in hem. But þis opun penaunce
315 wole þei not do, but raþer maintene alle her foule heresies and errours and lesyngis as experience techiþ.

Ferþermor seynt Petir ⌐seiþ⌐ in his prophecie aleggid bifore þat

291 *margin* 3 ED, iiij part H, 3 pars F   seynt . . . sectis (292)] þes lying masters as saynt petur saith in his prophecy F   293 sectis] new sectis F   295 oþir] in other F   ritis] customys F   þis] þese HF   297 so moche] *om.* F   in partie] partly F   *margin* Io.14 sermonem quem audistis. Et non potest solui/ scriptura quam pater etc. D, io.14 s[ermo]/nem quem audistis E, jo.xiiij F, Ioon H   for] Ioon xiiij (cᵒ *only margin* F) sermonem quem audistis etc. For HF   as] *added sh* E, *om.* D 298 crist¹] *om* F   crist²] cristis F   299 as] et non potest solui scriptura quem (quam F) pater etc. as HF   so] and *canc.* so E   300 siþ] seing F   301 sue] folow F   Petir] *om.*F   302 *margin* 4ª pars F   for] as for HF   303 for] *om.* F mo] more F   maistir liers] lying masters F   304 dampnacioun] perdicion or damnation F   305 deeþ dai] day of dethe F   hidouse] myschevus F 306 ful . . . fructuousli (307)] þei full fayntly F   307 fructuousli] fruytfulli H afeerd] afrayd F   siþ] seyng F   308 and²] *om.* HF   synnyngis] synnes F 310 presence] þe presence D   311 forþenking were] repentaunce myght be F 313 ȝouun] gyvyng F   315 and errours] *om.* F   317 *margin* 4 ED, iiij part H, 5 pa. F

manye [men] shal sue þe lecheries of þese maistir liers and her sectis
þat þei shal brynge yn. Housoeuer it stonde among þese maistir liers
and her sectis of bodili lecherie, þe which is ful ryue among hem, and 320
þat in manye orrible and dyuerse maners as I drede ⌈me⌉ soore, I
wole not discryue now. But þer is anoþir maner goostli lecherie þat is
wondir harmful in Cristis chirche, þe which lecherie seynt Poul
calliþ auoutrie aȝens | þe word of God. For, riȝt as a womman þat   f. 16ᵛ
doiþ auoutrie aȝens hir husbonde leueþ þe seed of hir husbonde, bi 325
þe which she shulde bringe forþ [lawful] fleschly children, and takiþ
to hir alien seed, wherof she bryngiþ forþ bastardis vnlawful and
mysborun children, so þese maistir liers and her newe sectis leuen þe
seed of þe spouse of þe chirche Iesu Crist, þe which ⌈seed⌉ is his
word as he seiþ, bi þe which þei shulden gete in Cristis chirche 330
lawful goostli children, gotun of þis seed to heuenward, and taken
alien seed as triflis, flateryng and vngroundid talis and lesyngis,
wherwiþ þei bryngen forþ manye ⌈children⌉ of þe fadir of lesyngis.
And so, as seint Petir seiþ, many men suen þe lecheries of þese
maistir liers and her sectis. For, as bodili spousebrekers, boþe men 335
and wommen, leuen comounli þe honest, gentil and chaast wiif or
husbonde for a foul loþeli hoore or harlot, | so þese goostli f. 17ʳ
spousbrekers leuen þe honest, fair, chaast and gentil lawe of God,
þe which is his seed, and taken to hem Lucifers seed specified bifore,
þe which is sowun among þe peple bi suche maistir liers and sectis of 340
his founding and retenu. þus dide Lucifer bi suche sectis in þe oold
lawe as it is toold bifore, and so he doiþ now, whoso takiþ heede bi
sectis of þe newe lawe. And of þis malice þat þe deuel shulde worche
in his chirche bi sowing of such wickid ⌈seed⌉ spekiþ Crist (*Mt.*13),
where he telliþ a parable of a man þat seew good seed in his feeld, 345
and of þe wickid man þat seew cockil þerupon; and Crist expowneþ

---

318 men] DFH, *canc.* E   sue] folowe F   maistir liers] lieng masters F
319 maistir liers] lying masters F   320 þe] *om.* DF   321 as] *om.* D   drede
me] *rev.* F   322 discryue now] now make relacion of it F   goostli] of gostli HF
þat] and þat HF   323 wondir] wonderus F   þe] *om.* F   *margin* 2 ad cor.2 non
enim sumus sicut plurimi adulterantes verbum dei ED, *in text* H, *reference margin, rest in
text* F   324 riȝt] lyk F   326 lawful] DHF, *om.* E   327 to] vnto F
alien] an alieen H, a strange F   328 maistir liers] lying masters F   newe sectis]
sectis newe, *marked for rev.* E   239 þe³] *om.* F   332 alien] an alieen H, a
strange F   lesyngis] lesyng DH, lyeng. *scilicet* þe devyll F   334 suen] schulen
sue H, shall folowe F   335 maistir liers] lyeng masters F   336 gentil and]
fayer F   337 loþeli] *om.* F   339 þe] *om.* F   340 maistir liers] lying
masters F   sectis] her *canc.* sectis E   of] as be of F   343 þe¹] *om.* F
344 of] ⌈of⌉ H, *om.* F   Mt.] in matheu, *margin* mt.xiij F   345 seew] ded sow F

þis parable himsilf and seiþ þat he þat seew [þe] good seed is þe maidens sone, and þe wickid man þat seew yuel seed herupon is þe deuel.

350   And certis, and we take heede, we mai se hou þe peple nowadaies
f. 17ᵛ so ferforþli suen þe lecheries of þese maister liers and her |sectis, in doyng of goostli auoutrie aȝens Iesu þe spouse of þe chirche and his seed, þat þe prophecies of Ysaie and of seynt Poul ben now verified of such goostli lecherous folk, and of suche bastard children þat ben
355 gotun of þese maistir liers and her sectis bi þe wickid seed þat I spak of bifore. For Ysaie in þe persoone of God playneþ þus upon suche bastard braunchis and seiþ (*Ysaie* 30) *Populus enim ad iracundiam prouocans est, et filii mendaces, filii nolentes audire legem Dei, qui dicunt videntibus (id est prophetis vel predicatoribus) 'Nolite videre (id est*
360 *predicare) ea que recta sunt; loquimini nobis placencia; videte nobis errores. Auferte a me viam, declinate a me semitam, cesset a facie nostra sanctus Israel'*, 'Forsoþe þe peple stiriþ me to wraþ, and þe sones or children ben false or liers, and wole not heere þe lawe of God, þe whiche seien to prechours "Nyle ȝe preche to vs þo þingis þat ben
f. 18ʳ riȝtwise; speke ȝe to | us þingis þat ben plesing, prechiþ to us
366 errours. Doiþ þe weie fro me, bowe ȝe þe paþ awei fro me (þat is to seie þe weie of comaundementis and þe paþ of þe councel), and letiþ þe hooli of Israel ceesse fro oure face (or fro oure presence)"', þe which hooli of Israel is God Iesu Crist, þat is figurid bi alle þe hooli
370 cerymonyes þat weren ȝoue to þe children of Israel. For, as seynt Poul seiþ, 'Crist is þe eende of þe lawe', so þat þe hooli of Israel, Iesu Crist, shal not come among suche bastard braunchis bi openy[n]g of his lawe her þankis. And so as experience techiþ us þis prophecie of Ysaie is verified of þese maistir liers, and of her bastard braunchis
375 þat þei geten wiþ her cursid seed in goostli hordam.

347 seew] sowith þe F   þe good] DHF, de *canc.* good E   348 seew] sowith þe F   herupon] þervpon F   350 certis] of a trueth F   and²] if F   351 so . . . þe] dothe mervelusly sowe the sede and F   maister liers] lyeng masters F   352 aȝens] and folowing þe same agaynst F   iesu] iesu crist HF   353 of²] *om.* F   355 gotun] now gote D   maistir] masters F   wickid] *om.* F   356 playneþ] complaynith F   suche] them suche F   357 *margin* ysa.30 EDF   ysaie 30] *om.*F   360 ea] et aspicientibus nolite aspicere ea F   362 stiriþ] movith F   sones or] *om.* F   363 or] and F   þe whiche] wich also F   364 to¹] vnto F   nyle . . . preche] preache not F   þo] thos F   366 doiþ] take F   bowe ȝe] and remove F paþ awei] pathe way F   367 comaundementis] þe comaundementis HF   paþ] pathe way F   councel] counseils HF   368 þe²] *om.* F   369 God] godis son F   372 openyng] openyg E   373 her þankis] *om.* F   374 maistir] masters F   375 hordam] awowtrye F

And seynt Poulis prophecie, þe which is verified of þe same peple is þis (2 *ad Thi*.4) *Erit tempus cum sanam doctrinam non sustinebunt, sed ad sua desideria coaseruabunt sibi | magistros, prurientes auribus, et a* f. 18ᵛ *veritate quidam auditum auertent, ad fabulas autem conuertentur,* 'A tyme', seiþ seynt Poul, 'shal be whanne þe peple shal not susteyne 380 hoolsum doctrine, but at her desiris þei shal hepe to hemsilf maistris tickelinge hem in her eeris (or makinge hem to icche in her eeris), and forsoþe þei ⌜shal⌝ turne her heering fro truþe, and þei shal be turned to fablis.' And it nediþ not to studie here wheþer þese wordis of seynt Poul ben now verified. For experience techiþ us hou þe 385 peple, and nameli þe grete boþe among lordis and clerkis, ben falle awei fro Goddis lawe boþe in loue, and in lernyng and lyuynge, and deliten hemsilf in flaterynge and fablis and poisies, þe whiche ben harmful, veyn and vnfruytful, and stiren þe peple raþer to game or to wondring þan to leue her synne and to do good, and so to perfourme 390 þe too partie[s] of riȝtwisnesse—and þis shulde be þe eende of | al f. 19ʳ preching.

Seynt Petir seiþ ferþermor in his text þat þe weie of truþe is blasphemed bi þese maistir liers and her sectis. And þat is soþe. For in as moche as þei founden newe sectis upon newe patrouns, wiþ 395 newe rulis not expressid in þe gospel ne acordinge þerwiþ, in keping of þe whiche rulis and religioun þei seien þat þer stondiþ þe plente of perfit lyuyng, þei menen in her doing and seiyng þat Crist was fauti [i]n his ordynaunce, and þat he and hise apostlis and oþir perfit men þat sueden Crist wiþoute ony addiciouns of newe ritis or rulis of 400 religioun kepte not perfitli Goddis lawe, siþ þei weren not of suche ordris ne kepten þe priuat newe foundun rulis of such religioun. For, if Crist tauȝte fulli þe rule of perfeccioun and lyuede þeraftir, it hadde be ynow for a man þat wolde haue be perfit, as þis maistir was,

376 þe¹] *om.* F   377 *margin* 2.thi.4 EDF, Poul H   2 ad Thi.4] *om.* F
tempus] enim tempus F   380 seiþ . . . be] shal be saith saynct paule F
381 at her] ⌜her⌝ H   hepe] kepe F   382 to] *om.* F   383 truþe] the truthe F
385 verified] verified or no F   us] *om.* F   386 nameli] specialy F
387 and¹] *om.* F   and²] and in F   388 and¹] *om.* F   þe] *om.* F
389 raþer] raþer þe, þe *canc.* E   game] sport F   to²] *om.* F   391 þe¹ . . . of¹]
om. F   parties] H, partie ED   *margin* declina a malo et fac bonum ED, dauid H
and] *om.* F   392 preching] prechinge For dauiþ seiþ declina a malo et fac bonum
etc. HF   393 *margin* 5 D, v part H   394 þese] þe same H   maistir]
masters F   soþe] trueth F   395 in] *om.* F   396 ne] nor F   397 þat
þer] *om.* HF   399 in] DHF, and E   400 sueden] folowid F   or] and D
401 kepte not] ded not kepe F   perfitli] perfet F   siþ] seyng F   402 ne] nor F
þe] not F   404 þis] his F

405 for to haue sued his rule and his lyuyng. But þese sectis, menynge
f. 19ᵛ þat Crist shulde haue | be vnperfit in his loore and his lyuyng, han
cloutid up a rule þe which conteyneþ al þe perfeccioun of Cristis
rule—and sumwhat of perfeccioun ouer as þei seien. And so, as her
rule passiþ in perfeccioun Cristis rule þe which he kepte, so þei þat
410 kepen þis rule passen Crist in perfit lyuyng. In þis also þei blasphe-
men opunli Crist, þat is weie of truþe, þat þei presumen to brynge
yn and founde suche newe sectis as he and hise apostlis at þe
plesaunce of his Fadir drowen out of þe chirche bi þe roote. And so,
as þouȝ þei wolde shewe in dede þat Crist dide amys þat he drowe
415 out of þe chirche þese þre sectis, pharisees, saduceis and esseis, þei
han graffid yn oþir þre in stide of hem (and wolde God of no more
malice!), as mounkis, chanouns and freris, wiþ many spicis of
dyuerse and harmful sectis conteyned vndir þese þre general
f. 20ʳ names. And þis is an opun | blasphemye. For wel we mai vndirstonde
420 here þat, if suche sectis hadden be plesynge to þe Trinyte, þe which
haþ foundid his chirche upon þre statis answeringe to þe same
Trinyte, as I seide bifore, Crist þat knewe þe hool councel and will of
þis Trinyte, and was ysent as an aungel of þe greet councel to make
þe councel of þe Trinyte knowun to his chirche, wolde not haue hid
425 so hiȝ a profit and perfeccioun fro his chirche as þese presumen to be
in her sectis, ne he wolde haue dampned and vndo or distried þe
sectis of þe oold lawe in word and dede as he dide, but haue amendid
suche sectis and haue lete hem stonde forþ in his chirche. For,
alþouȝ þer were moche synne in þese sectis, ȝit þei kepte many
430 vertuouse poyntis as oure doen now, for suche synnes mai not haue
her forþ but vndir colour of vertu. For þis is þe craft of þe deuel
f. 20ᵛ wherbi | he practisiþ synne: ᵣ⟨þ⟩at he mengiþ synne⁷ wiþ vertu, or
ellis colouriþ synne vndir vertu, þat it be not knowe such as it is. For
synne haþ so moche malice in himsilf þat þer mai no man assente
435 þerto but if it be knytt to good, delitable, honeste or vertuous. þus
þanne, as I haue seid in partie, if it hadde be plesaunt to þe Trinyte

405 sued] folowid F   406 loore] law F   407 þe] *om.* F   of . . . ouer
(408)] *om.* F   408 seien] say themself F   409 þe] *om.* F   410 kepen]
kept F   411 opunli crist] *rev.* F   weie] þe way F   þat²] in so moche as F
413 plesaunce] plesure F   414 þat²] bycause F   417 as] *om.* F   chanouns]
chanantis F   420 þe²] *om.* F   423 þis] the F   an] *om.* H
425 profit] parfyt F   426 ne] *om.* F   haue] not ᵣalso⁷ haue F   430 haue
her] goo F   432 þat he mengiþ] to myxt F   434 assente] agre F
435 but if] except F   436 in partie] partly F   it] it (*on eras. of* su) che sectis, che
sectis *canc.* E   hadde] had//, *lost to 657* were gilti D

þat suche sectis shulde be in þe chirche of God, þe aungel of þe greet
councel, Iesu Crist, wolde haue correctid þese þre sectis, pharisees,
s[a]duceis and esseis, and late hem stonde forþ, as he correctide þo
þre statis þat I spak of first, lordis, prestis and comuners, and 440
confermede hem in his chirche.

In þis also Crist, þe weie of truþe, is defamed and blasphemed þat
þese maistir liers and her sectis writen, reden and defenden opunli
and priueli þat þe lawe of þe gospel is þe falsest lawe, heresie,
blasphemye and | contrarious to itsilf, as I reherside bifore. And in f. 21ʳ
þis, as wel as in oþir blasphemyes þat þei blasten out wiþ her 446
stynkinge breeþ, þe which stynkiþ fouler in Goddis siȝt þan dide þe
spotil þat Iewis spitten upon Cristis face, shewiþ opunli of whos
fundacioun and retenu þei ben. þat is to seie of þe fadir of lesyngis,
þe which first enpungnede þe truþe of Goddis lawe, seiynge to Eue 450
þat Adam and she shulde not die þouȝ þei braken þe bidding of God,
where God hadde seid þe contrarie. But ⌜ȝit⌝ þis deuel Lucifer spak
not so vilenousli of God and of his lawe as hise disciplis doen now.
And as her fadir Lucifer, bi enpungnyng of truþe of Goddis word,
brouȝte yn al þe errour groundli þat is in mankynde, so doen now 455
hise disciplis bryngen yn al þe vnstabilnesse of bileeue, heresie,
errour or mys|bileeue regnynge in þe tyme of þe newe lawe. For, f. 21ᵛ
whanne þe autorite of Goddis lawe is waueringe, al oure bileeue most
nedis be vnstable. þanne in þese maner wisis and ful many mo is
Crist, þe weie of truþe, blasphemed among þese maistir liers and her 460
sectis þat seynt Petir spekiþ of, as I haue opened to ȝou sumwhat
now and more shal soone if God wole.

Ferþermor seynt Peter in his text, for as moche as men shulde not
stonde in doute or in weer whiche ben þese maistir liers and her
sectis, specifieþ hem and shewiþ hem at iȝe, liik in a maner as seynt 465

439 saduceis] suduceis E   late] haue lett F   stonde] ⌜to haue⌝ goon F
440 comuners] commons F   442 *margin* 6 E, vi part H   443 maistir]
masters F   writen] do wryte F   445 blasphemye] and blasfemye HF   and²]
8 ca. and F   446 þat] *om.* F   447 þe¹] *om.* F   448 iewis] the cursed
Iewys F   spitten] ded spytt F   shewiþ] and schewith F   449 lesyngis]
lesinge H   450 þe¹] *om.* F   to] vnto F   451 bidding] commandment F
452 God] allmighti god F   ȝit] *om.* F   453 vilenousli] myschevusly F
454 as her] þerfor, for *canc.* F   of¹] the F   word] lawe F   455 brouȝte] hathe
browght F   þe] *om.* F   groundli] *om.* F   456 bryngen] for þei *canc.* bryngen E,
bryngyng F   þe] *om.* F   458 most] mutt H   459 þanne] þus þanne HF
þese] this F   wisis] wise F   ful] in ful H, *om.* F   461 opened to] schewid F
462 soone] hereafter F   463 *margin* 7 E, vij part HF   464 in weer] fere F
maistir] masters F   465 liik . . . maner] in maner lyke F

Iohun Baptist shewide Crist. For seynt Petir seiþ þat þese maistir liers and her sectis in couetise shal marchaundise, þat is to seie, sille or bie of 30u wiþ feyned wordis. Siþ þanne þat þe dede expowneþ

f. 22ʳ best derk profecies as it is seid, loke 3e who ben þo þat | 3yuen 30u

470 moost custumabli feyned wordis and veyn biheestis, þat 3e shal be parteners of her suffragiis or meedful werkis for 30ure worldli good, as of her fastyng, wakinge, praiers, preching and many mo þingis þat þei boosten of. And þei it ben þat in couetise sillen and bien of 30u in fayned wordis, for þei sillen her suffragiis or meritis, and bien þerwiþ

475 30ure worldli good; and þus doen marchaundise wiþ 30u or of 30u in feyned wordis. And wel seiþ seynt Petir þat þe wordis of þese ypocritis ben feyned, for þei ben false and wiþout ground. For þe proud presumpcioun of þese sectis þus boostinge of her meritis makiþ þat her dedis ben refusid of God, as Crist techiþ in þe gospel

480 of Luyk bi ensaumple of such a religious ypocrite, a pharisee, and a publican (*Luce* 18) *Duo homines ascenderunt in templum ut orarent,*

f. 22ᵛ *vnus phariseus* etc. Boþe, as Crist | seiþ, 3iden up into þe temple to preie. þe pharise preesside up into þe hooli place of þe temple, and preiede and boostide of hise meritis, as hise successours and briþeren

485 doen now, and seide þat he was not synful as oþer men weren, and nameli as þat publican. But þe publican feelide so mekeli of himsilf þat he demede himsilf vnworþi to loke to heuene, but knockide on his brest and seide 'Lord, be merciful to me synner!' And, as Crist seiþ, þis publican 3ide hoom iustified bifore þe pharisee. Lo! so þe

490 praier of þis booster was refusid of God as hise felowis praiers ben, þe whiche seien wiþ þis pharisee her broþer þat þei ben not synful liik as oþer men ben. For if þei feelide mekeli of hemsilf, þei wolde be as redy, and her lettris of fraternyte weren ou3t worþ, to purchace

f. 23ʳ suche lettris of oþir men, supposinge mekeli | oþer mennes praiers to

495 be better þan hers, as þei ben now redi to profre for worldli good suche lettris to oþir men, to be parteners of her praiers and meritis or

466 crist] crist wiþ his fynger F   maistir] masters F   467 to] for to F
468 siþ] seing F   469 þo] thos F   470 custumabli] custumable H
biheestis] promisys F   471 parteners] partakers F   werkis] dedis F
472 wakinge praiers] prayng watchyng F   473 it ben] ar thos F   of²] wiþ F
475 doen] thei do F   476 þe] þese H   of] of/of F   480 bi . . . publican
(481)] *after* etc (482) HF   ensaumple] þe ensaumple HF   481 *margin* luc.18 EF
18] *om.* F   482 3iden] went F   484 and boostide] boostyng F
486 nameli] specially F   feelide] vsyd hym F   of himsilf] *om.* F   487 demede]
thowght F   on] *om.* HF   488 as] so F   489 3ide] went F   lo so] se
how F   490 of²] at H, before F   491 þe] *om.* F   492 liik] *om.* F
493 and] yf F   ou3t] ony thyng F   496 meritis] her meritis HF   or] and F

meedful dedis. And, but if þei hadde ouȝt to ȝyue for suche lettris, þei wolde labore for to haue sum þing to ȝyue for suche lettris, as hem semeþ þat þe comoun peple shulde do now for to haue wherwiþ to purchace her lettris. But her pharisees pride wole not assente 500 herto; and þerfore her dedis ben, as I suppose, ful litil good worþ to hem┌silf or┐ to ony oþer peple.

For þe blessid virgyn Marie seiþ in hir song (*Ps.*) *Despexit superbos mente cordis sui* þat God haþ dispisid proude men in þe mynde of her herte. And Crist seiþ *Omnis qui se exaltat humiliabitur* etc. þat euery 505 man þat enhaunciþ himsilf shal be mekid or ymaad lowe, and euery man þat me|kiþ himsilf shal be maad hiȝe or enhaunsid. And þis f. 23ᵛ word of Crist, as seynt Austyn seiþ upon þe same word, is opunli shewid bi al þe processe of scripture. And þe prophete seiþ in þe Sauter (*Ps.*) *Respexit in oracionem humilium et non spreuit precem eorum* 510 þat God haþ ┌had┐ reward into þe praier of meke men, and haþ not dispisid þe praier of hem; and siþ God haþ himsilf in þe contrarie wise to meke men and to proude men, it sueþ of þese wordis of þe prophete þat God haþ no reward to þe praier of proude men but dispisiþ it. Acordinge to þis seiþ þe apostle (*Jacobi* 4) *Deus superbis* 515 *resistit, humilibus autem dat graciam* þat God wiþstondiþ proude men, and ȝyueþ grace to meke men. And þe Wise Man seiþ *Oracio humiliantis se nubes penitrabit*, þat þe praier of þe man þat mekiþ himsilf shal peerse þe cloudis. And of þis comendacioun of mekenesse we | mai se þat þe praiers or suffragiis of þese pre- f. 24ʳ sumptuouse ypocritis, be þei neuere so long or solempli don, ben not 521 worþi or acceptable at God. For, in as moche as þei ensuren þe peple bi word, lettre and seel þat þei ben parteners wiþ hem for þe good þat þei ȝyuen of alle þe suffragiis þat þei specifien in her lettris, þei presumen and proudli demen wiþouten ony condicioun þat þei and 525

497 but] *om.* F   499 hem semeþ] thei thynke F   500 wole] wolde H assente] agre F   501 herto] therto F   worþ] *om.* F   503 for] 9 ca. For F *margin* Ps. E   Ps.] *om.* F   504 her] his F   505 *margin* euangel' E, luc. 18 F þat] *om.* F   506 enhaunciþ] dothe enhawnce F   mekid . . . ymaad] browght F 509 processe] processis H   *margin* Ps. E   510 Ps.] *om.*F   humilium] humilum H   511 þat] *om.* F   reward] respect F   into] to F   praier] prayers F   512 siþ] seing F   þe] *om.* HF   513 sueþ] folowith F   of²] and of F   514 reward] respect F   515 *margin* Ja.4 EF   Jacobi] seint Iame. Ia. H, Iamys F   4] *om.* F   516 þat] *om.* F   517 *margin* ecc.35 EF, *in text after* penetrabit (518) H   518 þat¹] *om.* F   þe²] a F   519 of¹] *om.* F   522 or] *om.* H, to be F   at] to HF   in] *om.* F   ensuren] promyse F   523 parteners] partakers F   524 þe] *om.* F   specifien] specified F   þei³] þat þei H, and þus þei F   525 demen] judge F

her praiers wiþ oþir suffragiis ben worþi ⌐or⌐ acceptable in þe siȝt of God. But God, þat loueþ mekenesse in praiers and in alle oþir þingis, as it is seid in partie bifore, dispisiþ suche proude praiers and oþir suffragiis also. But we shulen not forȝete here þat seynt Petir

530 seiþ in his text þat þese maistir liers and her sectis shulen marchaundise, or sille and bie of men, wiþ feyned wordis, for þei bien mennes goodis wiþ her suffragiis, and also sillen her suffragiis

f. 24ᵛ for mennes worldli goodis. | And þus þei bien and sillen, and so doen her marchaundise wiþ feyned wordis, as it is seid bifore, and þat in

535 couetise, as seynt Peter seiþ—ȝhe certein, in ful greet couetise for, haue þei neuere so moche of corn, bacoun, chese, money or ony oþir beggid good, ȝit euer þe beggers crauen aftir more, and ben redi to take al þat þei mai gete, and þei delen neuere—and þis is þe sotelist mene a man to be worldli riche.

540 And þe possessioners, as mounkis, chanouns and oþir suche sectis ben euere redi to resceyue and to amorteise alle þe seculer lordships þat þei mai, and to apropre into her deed hondis alle þe fat beneficis þat þei mai bi ony sleiȝtþe gete. And also for þis skill þe couetise of þese ypocritis is greet, þat þei wole haue so moche good of men for

f. 25ʳ riȝt nouȝt. It is a greet couetise for to haue moche go|od for litil, and

546 so it is þe moost couetise for to haue so moche good for riȝt nouȝt, as þese sectis han—for þei han þis good for her meritis, þe whiche ben noon, for þei ben excludid bi her pride and oþer synnes as it is declarid bifore. Off þis text þanne of seynt Petir þus declarid we mai

550 se what he feelide of þese maistir liers and her sectis, and what ioie he hadde of hem; for he saie wel in his spirit what harm suche maistir liers and her sectis shulden do in Cristis chirche. And we shal not doute here but þat, if seynt Petir hadde seyn in his spirit ony goode sectis to come into Cristis chirche, ouer þo sectis or statis þe

555 whiche Crist hadde sett and confermed in his chirche, he wolde sumwhat haue spoke of hem and maad men haue discrecioun bitwene þe goode sectis and þe yuele.

526 worþi or] om. F   or] and H   528 in partie] partly F   530 maistir] masters F   531 or] wiþ yow F   sille and bie] bye or sell F   535 couetise¹] covetuusnes F   certein] of a truthe F   ful] om. F   couetise²] covetusnes F   537 beggid] beggyng F   þe] thes F   ben] may be F   539 a] for a F   worldli] om. F   540 chanouns] and chanouns H   542 to] do F   deed] om. F   543 mai] may gett F   sleiȝtþe] meane F   gete] om. F   skill] cause is F   544 þat] for as moche as F   moche] so canc. moche ED   546 good for riȝt] goode // ryght F   547 þis good] þes goodis F   þe] om. F   548 bi] for F   550 feelide] perceyvyd F   maistir liers] lying masters F   554 ouer] besyd F   þe] om. F   556 men] þem F   haue] to haue HF   discrecioun] dystance F

And wundre þou not | here, alþou3 seynt Petir calle þese sectis f. 25ᵛ
maistir liers, for a printis of craft of liyng, þat is not ful lerned and
ybooldid in his craft, whanne he shal make a lesyng, he wole telle his 560
lesyng priueli among fewe folk wiþ a lowe voice, and he is wel war
who stondiþ or sittiþ aboute him—and 3it wiþ al þis he lieþ wiþ
a dreed. But þese maistir liers, þat ben ful lerned and ful harned in
her craft, whanne þei wole make such hidous and harmful lesyngis as
ben specified bifore, þei kepen not do þat in priuyte, but warnen ful 565
moche peple bi a bedel or a greet belle; and þanne in presence of al
þe peple, wiþoute ony drede of God or of man, hauyng no reward
who stondiþ aboute hem, þei blasten out wiþ hi3 voice her
blasphemouse lesyngis into greet offence of Goddis maieste and
harme to þe peple; and þis as me semeþ is maistirfulli don. No 570
wondir þan|ne alþou3 seynt Petir 3yue hem þe maistrie in þis craft of f. 26ʳ
liyng.

Ferþermor, in opun euydence and knouleche þat God hatiþ suche
sectis in his chirche, þou shalt vndirstonde here þat seynt Poul, þat
in heuen hadde lerned of Crist hou he wolde haue his chirche 575
groundid and gouerned in erþe, stifli wiþstood suche sectis in þe
bigynnyng and wolde not suffre hem to growe into Cristis chirche
duringe his tyme. For, as we mai rede (1 *Cor.*1) *Signatum est mihi*
fratres ⸢de vobis⸣ quod contenciones sunt inter vos. Hoc autem dico, quod
vnusquisque vestrum dicit · 'Ego quidem sum Pauli', 'Ego autem Apollo', 580
'Ego vero Cephe', 'Ego autem Christi'. Diuisus est Christus? Numquid
Paulus pro vobis crucifixus est? aut in nomine Pauli baptizati estis?
Gracias ago Deo meo, quod neminem vestrum baptizaui nisi Crispum et
Gayum etc. Aftir þe tyme þat þe peple in þe bigynnyng of Cristis
chirche were cristened, summe of Petir, sum of Poul, summe of 585
Apollo, | þei cleymede hem patrouns of her perfeccioun biside Crist, f. 26ᵛ
and seiden, as oure sectis seien now, 'I am of Poul', 'I am of Apollo',

558 alþou3] thowe it be so þat F   559 maistir] masters F   craft] þe craft F
ful] fully F   560 lesyng] lye F   561 lesyng] lye F   562 wiþ¹] for F
563 a dreed] feare F   ful¹&²] fully F   harned] hardied H, booldyd F
564 hidous] great F   harmful] perillus F   565 kepen] care F   do] to do HF
þat] it F   in priuyte] secretly F   ful moche] many F   567 reward]
advisement F   568 hi3] a hey F   569 lesyngis] lesing H   into] to þe F
570 harme] great harme F   semeþ] thynke F   maistirfulli] boldely F
571 wondir] mervell F   alþou3] it is thow F   574 here] *om.* F   þat in heuen]
which F   576 in] on HF   stifli] boldly F   577 into] in F   578 for]
om. F   mai] *om.* F   1 cor.1] *margin* F   581 diuisus] numquid diuisus F
583 baptizaui] baptisarim F   584 þe²] *om.* HF   585 summe²] and
summe HF   587 as] lijk as H

'I am of Petir'. And Poul, seynge þis errour among þe peple, knowinge þat a litil errour in þe bigynnyng if it be suffrid is cause
590 of þe grettest in processe of tyme, as þe Ph[i]losofre seiþ, wiisli wiþstood þis foly and redresside hem aȝen to Crist, and tauȝte hem to be oonli of Cristis sect and to cleyme hem noon oþir patroun of her perfeccioun. And sharpli he vndirnymmeþ hem and writiþ þus to hem: 'It is certified to me þat þer ben stryues among ȝou, and I
595 seie, as ech of ȝou seiþ, "Forsoþe, I am of Poul", "and I am of Appollo", "and I am of Cephe, þat is to seie of Petir", "and I am of Crist". Wher Crist be departid? Wher Poul be crucified for ȝou? or ȝe ben cristened in þe name of Poul? I do þankingis to my God þat I
f. 27ʳ haue cristened noon of ȝou, | saue Crispus and Gayus, lest ony man
600 seie þat ȝe ben cristned in my name.' So þat þe apostle in þese wordis redressiþ þe peple to þe pure sect of Crist, and reioisiþ in hymsilf þat þer was so litil occasioun on his side wherbi þe peple myȝte chalenge him as patroun or founder of her perfeccioun. And, as þis peple bi seynt Poulis loore shulde haue cleymed no founder, or
605 avowid hem upon ony patroun of her perfeccioun, saue oonli upon Crist, alþouȝ her perfeccioun were mynystrid and declarid to hem bi mene persoones þat were Cristis seruauntis, so ⌈myȝte⌉ oure newe sectis, if þei hadden vouchi[d] saaf, if þei hadde þe perfeccioun þat þei blabren of, haue cleymed oonli Crist for her founder, patroun
610 and avourie, alþouȝ þe perfeccioun of þe gospel hadde be declarid or mynystrid to hem bi oþir men, and not þus dynyed Crist and his
f. 27ᵛ chirche aȝens | þis blessid loore of seynt Poul, and ful will of Crist lerned in heuene, seiynge þus, liik as dide þe Corinthies whom Poul blamede, 'I am of Benet', 'I am of Bernard', 'I of Fraunceis', 'I of
615 Domynyk', 'and I of Austyn', or ellis, as þe frere Carme seiþ þat woot neuere redili of whom he is, 'I am of Helye, or of Helize, or ellis of seynt Marie' (but a man mai suppose resonabli here þat þese freris ben of Nabal of Carmeli, þat was so drunk þat he knewe not

---

588 I] and I F   590 philosofre] pholosofre E   592 sect] sectis F
593 sharpli . . . hem] he vndirnymeþ hem scharpli H, thus he writethe scharply vnto
þem F   and² . . . hem (594)] saying F   595 ech] yche on F   and] om. F
596 þat . . . crist¹ (597)] om. F   597 wher¹] is F   be departid] devyded F
wher²] was F   be²] om. F   598 ȝe ben cristened] were ye baptised F   do þankingis
to my] thanke F   598 þat . . . noon (599)] I neuer cristenyd ony F   599 saue]
except F   600 seie] schuld say F   603 or] and H   604 loore]
techyng F   608 vouchid saaf] plesyd F   vouchid] vouchif E   612 loore] law F
613 lerned . . . heuene] om. F   lerned] and lerned H   615 and] om. F   Carme]
carmelite F   616 neuere] not F   whom] whennes HF   617 ellis] om. F
seynt Marie] our lady F

redili himsilf or his owne astaat). And so, as seynt Poul meneþ here, whoso markiþ hise wordis, suche sectis dyuyden foul Crist and his chirche. 620

And so suche sectis bryngen yn manye errours and heresies. For euere it haþ stonde þus þat dyuerse and contrarie opynyouns han be multiplied, after þe dyuersite or noumbre of sectis. As among þe heþen men weren dyuerse sectis of philosofris, as summe were of 625 Pla|to, summe were of Aristotle, summe were of Anaxagaras, summe f. 28ʳ of Democritus. And alle þese sectis, and many mo þat weren þanne, weren of dyuerse opynyouns and in many þingis contrarie. And summe of her opynyouns for ensaumple I shal shewe here. As Plato and his sect, whom Austyn preisiþ aboue alle oþir, seiþ þat þe world 630 hadde a bigynnyng; but Aristotle and his sect seien þe contrarie, ȝhe among cristen ȝit into þis dai. Also Plato and his sect seien þat two poyntis or indiuisible þingis stonden togidir in a riȝt lyne wiþoute ony mene, and also þat two instantis or indiuisible þingis in tyme comen so nyȝ togidir, oon aftir anoþer in cours of tyme þat þer goiþ 635 no tyme bitwene hem. But Aristotle and his sect in boþe þese opynyouns reuersen Plato and his sect. For Aristotle and his sect seien þat alwei bitwene two poyntis in a riȝt lyne, stonde þei neuere so nyȝ togider, is a long | lyne bitwene, ȝhe and as many poyntis as f. 28ᵛ ben in al þe world. And on þe same wise þei seien of tyme þat, hou so 640 euere nyȝ two instantis comen, oon aftir anoþir in cours of tyme, þer comeþ a long tyme bitwene hem, and as many instantis as were fro þe biginnyng of þe world and shal be into þe eende. And þis semeþ a lesyng alowd and an opun ynow, þouȝ it were for þe wheston! And þe toþir two sectis of philosofris þat I spak of ⌐in sum þing⌐ varien 645 fro þese two—ȝhe it is hard, as I supposc, to fynde two suche sectis þat acorden in al.

Ouer þese þer weren oþir sectis in tyme of þe oold lawe þat shulde haue lyued aftir þe pure lawe of God ȝouun bi Moyses, as pharisees, s[a]duceis and esseis. And, as þese were dyuerse in sectis, so þei were 650

---

619 himsilf or] of HF   620 whoso markiþ] who se F   dyuyden] devydyd F foul] vngraciusly F   626 were²] om. F   627 and¹] om. F   alle] of alle H 629 margin 1 E, Plato F   630 Austyn] saynt austen F   631 but] om. F margin Aristotell F   632 into] vnto F   634 in tyme] om. F 636 margin 2 E   637 opynyouns] om. F   reuersen] seiþ (say F) þe contrarie and reuersen (repugne F) HF   638 bitwene] betwen them F   640 of tyme] oftyn tyme F   hou so] who so F   641 nyȝ] markyth F   comen] commyng F 643 into] vnto F   and² . . . wheston (644)] om. F   645 þe toþir] þe oþer HF þing] thyngis F   646 suche] om. HF   650 saduceis] suduceis E   þese were] thes was F

of dyuerse and contrarie opynyouns, and helden dyuerse errours and
f. 29ʳ heresies. For þe es|seis weren opun heretikis, for þei refuside al
Goddis lawe and helden to her owne tradiciouns and rulis. But þe
saduceis, alþouȝ þei resceyuede Moyses lawe as autentik, þei wolde
655 not so admitte þe prophecies; and þis sect seide and helde stifli þat
þer was no resureccioun, aungel ne spirit. But in alle þese heresies þe
pharisees reuerside þo two oþir sectis. But þei were gilti of many
oþir, as þe pharisees helden þis heresie, mainteneden and tauȝten þat
it was beter to þe children and to her eldris boþe to avowe and offre
660 her good to þe temple, where þe þing offrid turnede to her profit,
þan to releue þerwiþ her fadir and her modir in her greet nede. Also
in þat þei erride foul þat þei contynuede and mainteneden her sect,
þat was brouȝt ⸀yn⸀ aȝens þe plesaunce of þe Fadir of heuene and
f. 29ᵛ wiþoute autorite of his blessid lawe. þese er|rours þei defendide and
665 tauȝte and many oþer, as Crist rehersiþ (Mt. 23) bi long processe; for
þe whiche heresies and errours and ypocrisie þat þei vside Crist
wisshiþ hem wo þere ofte tymes, þe which wo as þe Maistir of
Stories telliþ is euerlasting dampnacioun.

And ouer þese sectis now in þe newe lawe ben brouȝt yn, on þat
670 wise as I haue toold bifore, ful manye and dyuerse sectis, þe whiche,
as þei ben of dyuers fundacioun, abite and rule, so þei ben ful
dyuerse in opynyouns. For þe possessioners, as mounkis, chanouns
and oþir endowid sectis, seien þat it is more hooli and perfit to lyue
bi lordships amorteisid, and bi chirchis aproprid þan to lyue
675 custumabli bi clam[ar]ous begging. But alle þe foure ordris of
beggers reuersen þis and seien þat, for as moche as Crist and hise
apostlis, in whom as men mote nedis suppose was þe souereynte of
f. 30ʳ per|feccioun, forsook suche lordships and possessiouns, as dide also
þe perfit peple in þe bigynnyng of Cristis chirche and so puttide
680 hemsilf wilfulli to streyt pouert, it mut nedis sue þat þe lyuyng of

651 helden] ded hold F   652 margin 3 E   653 helden] kept F   to] hem
to HF   margin 4 E   but] ⸀9 ca.⸀ But F   654 þei²] yet thei F   wolde] wol H
655 and¹] om. F   helde] ded hold F   657 reuerside] ded repugne F   þo] þe H
two oþir] toþer two H, oþer two F   659 offre] to offre D   660 good] goodis,
-is canc. DF   661 her²] om. F   663 plesaunce] pleasure F   665 margin
mt.23 EDF, added corr. H   Mt.23] Mt.xxij H, in mathew F   23] om. F
666 and¹] canc. F   667 þere . . . þe¹] om. F   wo²] om. F   668 stories] þe
storys F   dampnacioun] dethe or dampnation F   669 ouer] besyde F
670 ful] om. F   þe] om. F   672 chanouns] and chanouns H   673 oþir
endowid] suche oþer F   675 clamarous] DHF, clamous E   676 reuersen]
repugne F   þat] om. F   677 mote] must F   þe souereynte of] þe chefe F
679 Cristis] þe DHF   puttide] putten DHF   680 to] in to F   mut] must F
sue] folowe F   lyuyng] beggyng F

suche [pore] beggers is more perfit, and more acordinge to Cristis liif
þan is þe lyuyng of suche religiouse possessioners. And boþe þese
parties eche on her side han euydencis (suche as þei ben) to coloure
wiþ her ypocrisie and her apostasie fro Crist and his purid lawe.
Neþeles, hou so euere it stonde of suche colours, wel I woot þat ech 685
of þese sectis haþ ⌐or ma[i] haue¬ many opun euydencis of hooli
scripture, and resoun of oolde seyntis writun and of her lyuyng, and
also (þat is moost of autorite to suche ypocritis) ⌐of her¬ owne rulis to
proue, ech upon oþir, þat þei ben apostatas fro Crist and þe
perfeccioun of his gospel, and fro þe vertuous mene þat he chees 690
to him and hise apos|tlis, and to alle þo þat wolde sue him in þe f. 30ᵛ
plente of þis perfeccioun. And in declaring of þese euydencis, þat
þese apostatas han ech aȝens oþir, þei laboride ful bisili and ofte
tyme in scool, in preching and in priue comunyng, as it is knowun to
þe clerkis of oure rewme and in alien rewmes boþe. 695
But now siþ, þoruȝ þe grace of God and declaring of trewe clerkis,
þe fundacioun of boþe þese maner of sectis is knowun cursid and
rotun in þe roote, and worþi to be drawun up and neuere to growe
aftir, liik as Crist and hise apostlis, trewest doctours þat euere weren,
diden to þe pharisees, þese contrariouse sectis, liik as Heroudis and 700
Pilat þat weren enmyes togidir, þerc Crist shulde be dampned in
maintenaunce of þer boþe astaat, assentide togidir. As also þe
pharisees and saducees þat weren enmyes togidir and pursuede ech
of hem oþir, in | strengþing of her boþe sectis, acordiden to pursue f. 31ʳ
Crist and brynge him to þe deeþ, as a man mai se bi processe of þe 705
gospel, so þese newe sectis, notwiþstonding þat þei ben contrariousli
foundid, þat oon upon possessiouns and þat oþer upon beggerie, as
hemsilf seien, and notwiþstonding þat þei han wrouȝt ech aȝens oþir
in scool and in preching, and þat long and ofte tymes to dispreue ech
oþeris fundacioun and lyuyng, ȝit, bicause þat vnyte is so needful þat 710

681 pore] DHF, *om.* E   682 religiouse] *om.* F   683 parties] sectis F
her] oþer F   euydencis] evidens F   as] *om.* F   684 her²] *om.* F   purid]
pure HF   685 wel I woot] I am sure F   ech] euery on F   686 mai] ma E
euydencis] evidenc' F   687 scripture] scripturis F   of¹] and of F   writun]
writyng F   688 is] which is ⌐of¬ F   of] *om.* F   691 hise] to his HF   þo]
om. HF   sue] folowe F   692 þis] *om.* F   euydencis] evydenc' F
693 laboride . . . and] busy þemself F   695 alien] oþer F   696 siþ] seyng F
698 drawun] daraweH   growe] *om.* F   699 trewest] þe truest F   700 liik] *om.* F
701 þere] when F   702 þer boþe] *rev.* F   astaat] astates HF   assentide] ded
agre F   703 and²] *om.* HF   ech . . . oþir (704)] on anoþer F   704 of hem]
om. H   strengþing] stryvyng F   her boþe] *rev.* F   705 þe¹] *om.* F   processe]
þe processe DH   707 þat oþer] þe oþer HF   708 ech] iche on F
709 and¹] *om.* F   long] longe tyme HF   dispreue] dysprayse F   710 oþeris] þer F

þe deuelis rewme mai not stonde if his retenu be dyuydid, þese sectis
ben acordid, as Herodis and Pilat and þe pharisees and saduceis, and
boþe bi oon assent maintenen oþeris fundacioun and lyuyng, and
acorden in dampnyng of truþe of Goddis lawe and resoun, wherbi
715 trewe men laboren to brynge þese sectis fro [þe] viciouse extremytees
þat þei stonden yn—þat is to seie lordship and beggerie—and to |
f. 31ᵛ brynge hem to a vertuous mene þat Crist helde and hise disciplis and
apostlis, þe which mene as seynt Poul seiþ is liiflood and hilyng (1 ad
Thi. 6) Habentes autem alimenta et quibus tegamur hiis contenti s[i]mus.
720 But þis vertuous mene þei haten as deeþ and rennen to þe[se]
viciouse extremytees or eendis, þat is to seie greet superfluite, þe
which is in lordship of possessioners, or ouer greet faute, þe which is
in custumable beggers, alþouȝ þis nede be not so greet as þei
pretenden.

725 Neþeles, for opun vndirstonding of þis processe þat is writun
here, ȝe shal vndirstonde, as þe Philosofre and kyndli resoun techen,
vertu stondiþ in a resonable mene bitwene two vicis. As sum man is a
waastour of Goddis goodis, and spendiþ [hem] þere is no nede and
upon hem þat haþ no nede, and to an yuel eende as for pompe and
730 pride of þis world and for his owne veyn glorie, as dide þe riche,
f. 32ʳ boostful, worldli and glo|rious glotoun þat is biried in helle, of whom
þe gospel spekiþ (Luc. 16). And sum man is so greet a chynche þat
he leiþ al up to himsilf, and for þe greet auarice þat he is encumbrid
wiþ he mai not fynde in his herte to spende his goodis to Goddis
735 worship, in releuyng of þo þat ben nedi to encresyng of his owne
mede. And of such an auarous chynche we mai rede (Luc. 12) þat
leide up al his good for himsilf and was dampned also. And sum men
ben so resonabli fre-hertid þat þei gladli spenden þe goodis of God

714 acorden] agreith F   truþe] the trewith F   715 þe] DHF, om. E
717 helde] om. F   disciplis] apostles F   718 apostlis] disciples F   þe] om. F
hilyng] clothyngis F   margin 1 thi.6 EDF   718 1 . . . 6 (719)] om.F
719 autem] om. F   simus] D, sumus EHF   720 haten] refuse and hatt F   and
rennen] om. F   þese] DHF, þe E   721 þe] om. F   722 or] and F   faute]
nead F   723 custumable] thes customabyll F   725 opun] playn F
727 vertu] þat vertu F   728 hem] DHF, om. E   þere . . . nede] as no nede is F
729 haþ no nede] no neede ⌈han⌉ H   haþ] han D   730 owne] om. F
731 boostful] bostyng F   worldli] DHF, ⌈and⌉ worldli E   and] om. HF   glotoun]
gloteny F   732 margin luc.16 ED   luc. 16] om. F   16] xviij H, margin 18 F
chynche] nygard F   733 al up] vp all F   734 wiþ] with all F   to¹] for to F
734 Goddis worship] þe honor of god F   735 þo] thos F   to] and to the F
encresyng] incras F   736 mede] meritis F   and] twice F   chynche] nygard F
margin luc.12 EDF   luc 12] in the gospell F   737 good] goodis F   738 so]
om. F   gladli spenden] rev.F

where and whanne and among suche as it nediþ, as dide Zachee
(*Luc.* 19) and Corneli (*Act.*10), whos almesse and spending of her 740
goodis ben comendid of God, for þei, as alle suche men doen,
souȝten cheefli Goddis worship in ge[t]ing and spending of her good.
And such a man þat doiþ þus doiþ vertuousli and is callid a liberal
man, and þe toþer two doen | viciousli and ben callid viciouse men; f. 32ᵛ
þe firste is callid a wastour, þe secunde is callid a nygard, a chynche 745
or an auarous man. So þat þe liberal man, þe which is vertuous,
stondiþ in a mene bitwene þe wastour and þe avarous man, and
forsakiþ her viciouse condiciouns, þat is to seie waast and auarice;
and so he holdiþ him in a vertu bitwene þese two vicis, þe whiche
vertu is callid liberalte. Anoþer saumple liik to þis I myȝte putt, and 750
I hadde leiser, of a fool-hardi man and of a coward, and of a vertuous
strong or boold man: two þe firste ben viciouse and þe þridde is
vertuous. þis ensaumple I write here þat men haue þe more opun
knouleche hou vertu is a mene bitwene two vicis, þat men leue þe
viciouse extremytees or eendis and holde hem in þe vertuous mene, 755
for þus dide Crist and hise apostlis and disciplis here in erþe, and
also oþir perfit and vertuouse men þat weren | in Cristis chirche, þe f. 33ʳ
whilis it stood vndir þe pure lawe of Crist, and was not infect wiþ
þese maistir liers and her sectis and her dritti tradiciouns. For þei
lefte þe possessiouns and þe lordships, and so al maner of seculer 760
lordlynesse or lordshiping, þe which mounkis and chanouns and oþir
religiouse ypocritis þat ben possessioners ful lecherousli clippen to
hem, and han leuer to be deed and go to helle wiþ hem þan leue
hem. And þat þei shewen wel, in as moche as þei doen neuere
fructuous repentaunce of þis greet synne; for if þei diden, þei moste 765
nedis and wolde leue al such lordship, þe which, as þing moost
contrarious to þe perfeccioun of þe gospel, Crist forfendiþ alle perfit
men in þe gospel, as I shal shewe hereaftir if God wole. And also

739 *margin* luc.19 EDF, act.10 ED, act.18 F   740 luc.19] *om.*F   and¹] and
also F   act.10] *om.*F   10] xviij H   almesse] almessis H   742 cheefli]
specially F   worship] honor F   geting] DHF, gedering E   744 þe toþer] þe
oþer DHF   745 þe²] and þe H   a chynche] *om.* F   746 þe²] *om.* HF
747 stondiþ] studyethe F   þe²] *om.* D   749 vicis] *om.* F   þe] *om.* F
750 *margin* exemplum ED   saumple] ensaumple DHF   and] yf F
751 fool-hardi] hardy F   man] *om.* F   and¹] *om.* H   752 two þe] *rev.* F
753 haue] myght haue F   þe] *om.* F   754 vicis . . . þe] *om.* F   756 in] on
DH, vpon F   757 þe whilis] whilis HF   759 maistir] masters F
761 or lordshiping] *om.* F   þe] *om.* F   762 clippen] take F   763 han]
had F   765 repentaunce] penanc' F   766 nedis] *om.* HF   þe] *om.* F   þing] a
thyng F   767 forfendiþ] forbiddith F   768 and] ⌐10 ca.⌐ And F

Crist and such perfit folk leften þat oþir vicious extremyte þat is to
f. 33ᵛ seie beggerie, as it is in partie shewid | aboue, and shal wiþ Goddis
771 help more heraftir. And so þei leften þe two viciouse extremytees as
grete and hidouse synnes, and chosen to hem þe vertuous mene, þat
is to seie liiflood and hilyng, and helden hem apaied þerwiþ. And þis
þei took of þe peple, not bi titil of lordship or of beggerie, as oure
775 maistir liers and her sectis doen, but bi titil of þe gospel or of prestis
office duli perfourmed to þe peple—þe which titil is þis, as Crist
himsilf seiþ, 'þe werkman is worþi his meede or his mete.' And seynt
Poul askiþ þis questioun (1 Cor.9) Si nos vobis spiritualia seminauimus,
magnum est si carnalia vestra metamus?, 'If we haue sowe to 3ou
780 spiritual þingis, is it greet and we repe 3oure fleshli þingis?', as who
seiþ nay. And þis vertuous mene was ordeyned to Crist and perfit
suers of him of þe blessid Trinyte wiþoute bigynnyng.

f. 34ʳ   And Salomon in þe | persoone of Cristis manhed preieþ to God
þat þis vertuous mene be 3oue to him and to hise perfit folowers, and
785 þat þei avoide þe viciouse extremytees in þe staat of presthod or of
clergie, þat is to seie lordship and beggerie þat oure newe sectis han
take hem to. For Salomon preieþ þus to God (Prouerb. 30)
Mendicitatem et diuicias ne dederis mihi, sed tribue tantum victui meo
necessaria, 'Lord! 3yue þou not to me beggerie [ne] richessis, but
790 3yue to me oonli needful þingis to my liiflood.' And þis mene
acordiþ moost wiþ þe staat of innocence, þe which was moost perfit
lyuyng of mankynde. And þerfore Crist, innocent man, chees þis
lyuyng and tau3te þis mene bi word and bi ensaumple, and chargide
hise disciplis and also oþir þat wolden be perfit wiþ þis maner of
795 lyuyng, so þat þei, holdinge hem apaied wiþ þis mene, drawe hem to
f. 34ᵛ innocent lyuyng, | as moche as freelte of mankynde corrupt bi synne

770 as] at F   in partie] partly F   aboue] afore F   772 hidouse] perlus F
773 hilyng] clothyng F   apaied] content F   775 prestis] þe preastis F
776 þe²] om. F   777 þe] dignus est operarius mercede sua (sua corr.H) þe HF
his¹] of his F   meede] reward F   or his mete] om. HF   778 margin 1 cor.9
EDF, 1 cor.1 H   1 cor.9] om.DHF   spiritualia] spirituali F   seminauimus]
seminamus H   780 greet] a great mater F   and] thowe F   fleshli]
temporall F   781 to . . . him (782)] om. F   782 bigynnyng] beginning to
crist and perfyt folowers of hym and F   783 to] vnto F   784 and²] om. HF
785 avoide] may avoyd F   þe¹] þes F   787 for . . . god] after necessaria (789) HF
for] om.F   margin prou.30 EDF   Prouerb.30] om.F   788 sed] om. HF
tantum] tamen HF   789 3yue] haue H   þou not] om. F   not] D, not 3oue EH
beggerie] neþer beggery F   ne] DH, nor F, and E   richessis] riches F   791 þe]
om. F   792 innocent] þe most innocent F   795 apaied] content F   drawe]
drawyd F   hem] hym F   to] to in H, and folowid his F   796 freelte] fre wyll F
bi] wyth by F

wole suffre. Also we seen wel at iȝe þat þo two viciouse lyuyngis,
as for hem þat shulde perfourme þe perfeccioun of þe gospel, han
worldli bisynesse anexid to hem, þe which distractiþ suche ypocritis
fro heuenli lyuyng. And þis is a cause whi boþe in þe oold lawe and 800
eke in þe newe God made an ordynaunce þat þer shulde no such
lyuyng be among his clergie.

But first I wole shewe here hou God hatiþ worldli lordship or
lordshiping in þe staat of his c[lergie], and in alle þo þat shulde
805 perfourme þe perfeccioun of þe gospel. For in þe oold lawe, where
God made an ordynaunce for al his peple hou and wherwiþ þei
shulde lyue in euery staat, he assignede þe worldli possessiouns to þe
seculer peple, and bade þat þe prestis shulden bi no weie haue ony
f. 35ʳ possessiouns wiþ þat oþer | partie of þe peple, saue þe peple was
810 chargid of God to ordeyne þe prestis and dekenes housis, not to be
lordis þerof, but to dwelle þerinne, and on þe same wise þei hadden
subarbis, to feede þere þe beestis þat shulde be offrid sacrifice to God
in þe temple. And God seide he wolde be þe part of þe prestis and
dekenes, þat is to meene þat 'þo þingis þat I shal asigne to hem, þe
815 whiche þingis ben offrid to me, shal be her part and her lyuyng.' And
so God asignede to þe prestis and dekenes þe firste fruytis, and tiþis,
and oþir certein deuociouns of þe peple, þe whiche was liiflood ynow
for hem, her wyues, children and meyne. And he chargide soore and
hard þe peple for to þenke on þis clergie, and þat þei defraude not
820 hem of þe part þat God hadde asigned to hem, for þei hadde noon
oþir possessioun among þe oþir peple, ne ony shulde haue. So þat
f. 35ᵛ Goddis | part was þus asigned to þe tribe or kynred of Leuy, of þe
which kynred weren Goddis prestis in þe oold lawe and of noon oþer.
And þis ordinaunce of God, as touching þe liiflood of þe prestis,
825 was kept ful streitli, so ferforþ þat þo þingis þat weren offrid to God
in þe temple bi deuocioun of þe peple, þe whiche were not bi þe lawe
of God expresli asigned to þe kynred of Leui, weren kept fro þe vss
of þat kynred to þe comoun profit of al þe peple, as to repaire þe
temple, and to raunsome þe kyng and þe rewme at nede, as scripture
830 beriþ witnesse in þe tyme of þe good kyngis Ioas and Iosias (4 *Regum*
12 *et eiusdem* 22); and þis was wiisli don. For, siþ God hadde asigned
liiflood to þe kynred of Leuy aftir his owne witt, and he mai not be
fauti in his worching or ordynaunce, it hadde be a proud dampnable
f. 36ʳ presumpcioun for to haue or|deyned more liiflood to hem. And

803 or lordshiping] *om.* FL   804 clergie] DHFL, chirche E   in²] *om.* DF
þo] þos F   807 staat] astaat HF   þe²] *om.* HF   808 bade] commavndyd F
þe] *om.* HFL   shulden . . . weie] in no wyse schuld F   809 þat oþer] the oþer F
þe²] only the F   810 housis] hous H   811 wise] maner F
812 sacrifice] in sacrifyce F   813 and¹ . . . and²] and F   of] of þe part *canc.* of E
814 meene þat þo] say thos F   þe] *om.* F   815 to] vp to F   817 þe²] *om.* F
ynow] *om.* F   818 her] for ther F, *om.* H   wyues children] and for ther
chyldern F   and meyne] *om.* F   soore . . . peple (819)] þe peple straytly F
819 for to] to FL   defraude . . . hem¹ (820)] xuld not defrawde them F   821 þe

Capitulum ii

Here it schal be schewid how God hatiþ worldly lordeschip in þe 70
state of his clergye þat schulde performe þe perfeccyon of þe gospell.
For in þe olde lawe, wher God made an ordynance how and wherwiþ
þai schulde lyue in euery state, he assigned þere worldly possescyons
to þe | seculer party, and bad þat prestis schulde by no way haue eny f. 5ᵛ
possescions wiþ þat oþer partye of þe peple, saue þe peple was 75
chargid of God to ordeyn þe prestis and deeknys housis, not to be
lordis of hem, but to dwelle in hem, and on þe same wise þai hadden
subarbis, to fede þer þe beestis þat schuld be offred sacrifice to God
in þe temple. And God saide he wolde be þe parte of þe prestis and
deknys, þat is to mene þat 'þo þingis þat I schal assigne to hem, þe 80
whiche þingis ben offred to me, schal be her parte and her lyuynge.'
And so God assignyd to þe prestis and deknys þe first fruytis, and
tiþis, and oþer certeyn deuocyons of þe peple, þe whiche was liiflode
inowȝe | for hem, wiþ alle her seruandis and oþer meynȝe. And he f. 6ʳ
chargid sore and harde þe peple to þenke on his clergi, and þat þai 85
defraude not hem of þe parte þat God haþ assignyd to hem, for þai
hadden noone oþer possesyon amonge þe oþer peple, ne eny schuld
haue. So þat Goddis parte was þus assignyd to þe trybe or kynrede
of Leuy, of þe whiche kynrede wern Goddis prestis in þe old lawe
and of noone oþere.   90
    And þis ordynance of God, as tochynge þe liflode of prestis, was
kept ful streytly, so ferforþe þat þo þingis þat wer offrid to God in
þe temple by deuocyon of þe peple, þe whiche wer not by þe lawe of
God expresly assigned to þe kynrede of Leuy, weren kept | fro þe vse f. 6ᵛ
of þat kynrede to þe comon profete of alle þe peple, as to þc rcpaire 95
of þe temple, and to rawnson þe kynge and þe rewme at nede, as
scripture beriþ witnesse in þe tyme of goode kyngis Ioas and Iosias.
For, siþ God had assigned liiflode to þe kynrede of Leuy aftir his
owne witte, and he may not be fawty in his worchinge or ordenance,
it had ben a dampnable presumpcion for to haue ordend more liiflode 100

---

75 *margin* Nu'i xviij° L   97 *margin* iiijᵗᵒ Reg.xij° caᵒ et xxij° cᵒ L

---

oþir] oþer H, the F   ne] nor F   ony] *om.* F   822 goddis] god F
824 ordinaunce . . . prestis] *om.* F   825 þo] þos F   826 þe³] *om.* F
828 repaire] DH, þ *canc.* repare F, þe repaire f, -e *on eras,* f *canc.* E, þe repaire of L
829 and þe rewme] *om.* F   830 in . . . Iosias] *after* 22 (831) H   *margin* 4 r.12 et
22 EFL, 4.12.22 D   4 . . . 22 (831)] *om.* FL   831 siþ] seing F   832 witt]
wyll F   833 worching] ordinanc' F   ordynaunce] workyng F

835 notwiþstondinge þat kyng Dauid, purposinge to encreese þe worship
of God in his peple, ordeynede syngers and pleiers in dyuerse
musical instrumentis to serue bisili bifore God in þe temple, ȝit
presumede he not to take ony þing þat God hadde asigned to þe
temperal partie of his peple, and endowe wiþ suche goodis þes
840 mynystris of þe temple; but he chees þese men of þe tribe or kynred
of Leuy, and leet hem lyue on her owne part, and so kepte his regalie
and þe staat of þe temperalte hool wiþoute ony apeiring or
amenusyng þerof. And Salomon his sone, þe wisest kyng þat euer
was, dide þe same.

845 And siþ kyng Dauid, þe chosun of God, aftir his owne herte and
ful of þe spirit of prophecie, and Salomon his wise sone also durste
not in a litil chaunge þe ordynaunce of þe goodis, mouable ˹and
f. 36ᵛ vnmouable˺, þe whi|che God hadde bitake to her gouernaunce, ne
durste take ony of þe temperaltees, þe whiche God hadde lymytid to
850 temperal men, and make þe prestis riche wiþ hem and to amende her
part, as þouȝ God hadde not sufficientli ordeyned for hem in his
lawe; and wiþ þis, notwiþstonding þat kyng Dauid was so ful of
vertuous kyngli condiciouns þat he is sett in scripture as a patroun
and ensaumple of alle goode kyngis, hou dar oure kyngis, þat han not
855 þese ȝiftis of God, so expresli aȝens Goddis lawe, þe oold and þe
newe, presume to ouerturne al þe glorious ordynaunce of God
aboute suche temperaltees and make þe staat of prest[hod] lordis
and riche, expresli aȝens þe liif and þe loore of Crist and þe apostlis,
and aȝens þe processe of þe oold lawe in þis poynt confermed by þe
860 newe? For siþ God goiþ forward and not bacward in his worching,
f. 37ʳ and wolde drawe his peple, and nameli his clergie, in|to more and
more perfeccioun, þer mai no man resonabli suppose þat it plesiþ to
God now in tyme of þe newe lawe þat hise clerkis be worldli riche
wiþ worldli lordships and possessiouns, if al it hadde be so þat Crist
865 hadde, neþer in word ne dede, tauȝt þis in þe newe lawe. Hou moche
raþer þanne shulden men suppose þat such worldli lordlynesse of þe
clergie hogeli offendiþ God, siþ he haþ so opunli, in word and in
ensaumple, tauȝt hem and comaundid þat þei shulde not be lordis so?

And vndirstonde þou here þat whanne þer is ony þing dampned of
870 God in þe oold lawe, if þe same be dampned in þe newe lawe, alle þe
euydencis þat ben aȝens such a faute in þe oold lawe ben euene aȝens
þe same in þe newe. And so alle þe lawis þat God ȝaf bi Moyses

---

835 purposinge] purposyd F   839 endowe] endowid HF   wiþ . . . temple
(840)] thes mynisters of þe tempyll wiþ suche goodis F   840 or] and F   kynred]

to hem. And notwiþstondinge þat kynge Dauyd, purposynge to encrese þe worschip of God in his peple, ordend syngers and players in dyuers musical instrumentis to serue byfore God in þe temple, ȝit presumyd he not to take eny þinge þat God had assigned to þe temperall parte of his peple, and endowe wiþ siche goodis þes | 105 mynystres of þe temple; but he chese þes men of þe tribe or kynrede f. 7ʳ of Leuy, and lett hem lyue on her owne parte, and so kept þe temperalte hoole wiþowte eny peyrynge þerof. And Salamon his sonne, þe wisest kynge þat euer was, dide þe same.

And siþ kynge Dauid, þe chosen of God, aftir his owne herte and 110 full of þe spirite of prophecye, and Salomon his wise sonne also durste not chawnge þe ordenance of þe goodis, mouable and vnmouable, þe whiche God had bytake to her gouernance, and make prestis ryche, as þouȝ God had not sufficiently ordend for hem in his lawe; and wiþ þis, notwiþstondynge þat kynge Dauyd was 115 so full of vertuous and kyngly condycions þat he is sett in scripture as a patrone and ensaumple | of alle goode kyngis, how dar oure f. 7ᵛ kyngis, þat han not þes ȝiftis of God, so expresly aȝens Goddis lawe, þe olde and þe newe, presume to ouerturne all þe gloriouse ordinance of God abowte siche temperaltes and make þe state of 120 presthode lordis, aȝens þe lyfe and þe lore of Criste and his apostlis, and aȝens þe proces of þe olde lawe in þis poynte confermyd bi þe newe, in whiche he haþ so openly in worde, dede and in ensaumple tawȝte and commaundit hem þat þai schuld not be lordis so?

And vndirstonde þu here þat whan þer is eny þinge dampned of 125 God in þe olde lawe, if þe same be dampnyd in þe newe, alle þe euydence þat ben aȝen syche a defawte in þe olde lawe ben euen aȝens þe same | in þe newe. And so all þe lawis þat God ȝaue by f. 8ʳ

þe kynred H   841 kepte] he kepte HF   regalie] regall estate F
842 apeiring] hurtyng F   843 amenusyng] myschevyng F   845 siþ] seyng F
846 of þe] om. F   848 þe] om. F   bitake] referryd F   ne] nor F
849 take] not take D   þe] om. F   850 þe] ᵀþeᵀ H, om. L   852 wiþ þis]
om. F   853 is] om. HF   854 alle] oolde HF   kyngis²] kyng F 855 þese]
þefte D   856 ouerturne] turne ouer F   857 presthod] DHFL, prestis E
858 expresli] om. FL   þe loore] a canc.lawe F   860 siþ] seyng F
861 nameli] specifiely F   862 no . . . resonabli] no resonabyll man F to] om. F
863 tyme] the tyme F   be worldli] schuld be F   864 if al] if alþouȝ ED,
alþouȝ HF   865 ne] nor F   866 suppose] suppose of þe clergie DHF
866 of þe clergie] om. HF   867 hogeli offendiþ] dothe greatly offend F   siþ]
seyng F   in²] om. F   868 þat] hem canc. þat E, hem þat L   so] om. H
869 vndirstonde] marke F   here] this well F   871 euydencis] evidenc' F,
euydence L   ben¹] may be F   a faute] astaate HF   euene] om. F
872 in] dyrectly in F   newe] new lawe F   ȝaf] om. F

a3ens þe worldli lordshiping of prestis in þe oold lawe, and also alle
f. 37ᵛ þat þe prophetis han declarid | in þat poynt acordinge wiþ þo lawis
875 ben euene a3ens þis þat prestis shulde haue worldli possessiouns, or
be lordis so in þe newe lawe. And so oure prestis mai not truli
suppose þat þo lawis þat God 3yueþ bi Moyses, a3ens þe possessiouns or lordship of þe prestis of þe oold lawe, ben impertynent to
þe lordship of prestis in þe newe, no more þan ⌐þe lawis⌐ þat God 3af
880 in þe oold lawe a3ens mawmetrie ben impertynent to mawmetrie in
þe newe lawe. And þus standiþ it of oþir synnes þat ben dampned in
boþe lawis. And siþ þat Moyses lawe is moral in þis poynt þat longiþ
to þe perfeccioun of presthod, and wiþ þat þis lawe most nedis be
kyndli resoun, Crist my3te not distrie þese lawis or reuerse hem,
885 neþer dispence wiþ hem, þat þe prestis shulde not be boundun to
þese lawis. And for as moche as he hadde take of his Fadir a
f. 38ʳ comaundement for to teche and lyue as he dide, and | so for to teche
expresli in word and in ensaumple þat þe staat of presthod of þe
newe lawe shulde not ocupie seculerli lordships, as þe comaunde-
890 ment of his Fadir boond him and his colege to þis perfeccioun, so
diden also alle þo lawis þat þe same Fadir comaundide bi Moyses,
and bade þat þe staat of presthod shulde haue no worldli possessiouns. And siþ Crist and his colege my3te not be dispensid wiþ or
exempt fro þe boondis of þe oold lawe in þis mater, I merueile where
895 þe prauylegies comen a lond, wherbi oure coligiens, monkis or
chanouns, or ony oþir temperali endowid prestis þat dwellen in
suche conuenticlis, claymen to be exempt fro þis boond of þe oold
lawe þat in so many placis so opunli forfendiþ hem such lordship.

For in *Num.* 18 it is writun þus: *Dixit Dominus ad Aaron 'In terra*
900 *eorum nichil possidebitis, nec habebitis partem inter eos. Ego pars et*
f. 38ᵛ *hereditas tua in medio filiorum Israel.* | *Filiis autem Leui dedi omnes*
decimas Israel in possessionem pro ministerio, quo seruiunt mihi ⌐*in*⌐
tabernaculo. Nichil a[liud] possidebunt, decimarum oblacione contenti,
quas in vsus eorum et necessaria seperaui', 'þe Lord seide to Aaron,
905 (and in him to al þe tribe or þe kynred of Leui, of þe which kynred
were þe prestis and dekenes), "3e shal haue no possessioun in þe
lond of þe children of Israel; I am þi part and þin eritage in þe
myddis of þe sones of Israel. And I haue 3oue to þe sones of Leuy
alle þe tiþis of Israel into possessioun for þe seruyce þe which þei
910 doen to me in þe tabernacle. þei shal haue noon oþir possessioun; þei
shal be ⌐apaied⌐ wiþ þe offring of þe tiþis, þe whiche I haue departid
into her vsis and nedis."' Also in þe book of *Deutronomii* 18 God

Moyses aȝens þe worldly lordeschip of prestis of þe olde lawe be
euen aȝens þis þat prestis schulde be lordis so in þe newe lawe. Siþ 130
þat Moyses lawe is morall in þis poynte þat longeþ to þe perfeccyon
of presthode, Criste myȝte not distroy þes lawis, neiþer dispens wiþ
hem, þat prestis schulden not now be bunden to þes lawis. And siþ
Criste and his colage myȝt not be dispensid wiþ ne be exempte fro þe
bondis of þe olde lawe in þis mater, I merueyle wher þe pryuelegis 135
commen a londe, wherby owre colagis of monkis, chanons, or eny
oþer endowid prestis þat dwellen in siche conventycles, claymen to
be exempt fro þis bonde of þe olde lawe | in þis poynte þat in so f. 8ᵛ
many placis so opynly forfendiþ hem siche lordeschip.

For þus it is writen *Dixit Dominus ad Aaron 'In terra eorum nichil* 140
possidebitis, nec habebitis partem inter eos. Ego pars et hereditas tua in
medio filiorum Israel. Filiis autem Leui dedi omnes decimas Israel in
possescionem pro ministerio, quo seruiunt mihi in tabernaculo. Nichil
aliud possidebunt, decimarum oblacione contenti, quas in vsus eorum et
necessaria seperaui, 'þe Lorde sayde to Aaron, (and in hym to alle þe 145
tribe or kynred of Leuy, of þe whiche kynred wer þe prestis and
deeknys,) "Ȝe schal haue no possescyon in þe londe of þe childern of
Israell; I am þine part and þine erytage in þe myddis of þe sonnys of
Israell. And I haue ȝoue to þe sonnys of Leuy alle þe tiþis of | Israel f. 9ʳ
into possescion for þe seruyce þe whiche þai done to me in þe 150
tabernacle. þai schal haue noone oþer possessyon; þai schal be payde
wiþ offrynge and tiþis, þe whiche I haue departid into her vsis and
nedis."' Also in þe booke of Deutronomy God saide þus: *Non*

---

140 *margin* Nu'i xviijᵒ L   153 *margin* Deut. xviij L

873 lordshiping] lordlines F   prestis] DHFL, þe prestis E   874 prophetis]
prophecies HF   þo] thos F   877 þat] *om.* F   þo] thos F   3yueþ] gave F
878 impertynent to] agaynst F   879 no more] *om.* F   880 impertynent to]
not agaynst F   882 lawis] the lawys F   and] ⌐11 ca.⌐ And F   siþ] seyng F
883 þe] *om.* D   and . . . resoun (884)] *om.* FL   most nedis] ⌐is⌐ most nedid, -d *on*
eras. of -s H   884 reuerse] turne F   887 teche] lyue HF   lyue] teche HF
889 seculerli] seculer F   890 and] in HF   891 þo] thos F   893 siþ]
seing F   894 where] and so may all ye from whence F   895 a lond] and be
alowid F   896 chanouns] channantis F   temperali] temporall F
897 conuenticlis] coventis or conventicles F   898 forfendiþ] is forfendyd F
lordship] lordschyppys F   899 *margin* num.18 EDFL   18] *om.* F
902 israel] israelis F   903 nichil] federis nihil F   aliud] HFL, autem ED
904 þe] that is to say our F   to] vnto F   905 or] of F   of þe] *om.* F
906 possessioun] possessions F   907 þi] the F   þin] the F   909 þe²]
om. HF   911 apaied] apayd and content F   þe³] *om.* F   912 into] to F
margin deu.18 EDFL   18] *om.* FL   god] allmighti god F

seide þus: *Non habebunt sacerdotes et Leuite, et omnes qui de eadem*
tribu sunt, partem et hereditatem cum reliquo populo Israel, [quia]
f. 39ʳ *sacrificia ⌐domini⌐ | et oblaciones comedent; [et] nichil a[liud] accipient*
916 *de possessione fratrum suorum,* 'þe prestis and þe dekenes and alle þo
þat ben of þe same tribe shal not haue part and heretage wiþ þat oþir
peple of Israel, for þei shal ete þe sacrifice[s] and þe offryngis of him;
[and] þei shal take no þing ellis of þe possessioun of her briþeren.'
920 Also in *Iosue* 13 it is writun þus: *Tribui autem Leui non dedit*
possessionem, quoniam Dominus Deus Israel, ipse est possessio eius ut
locutus est illi, þat, whanne Moyses departide þe possessioun of þe
lond of Israel among þe peple, he ȝaf no possessioun to þe tribe of
Leuy, for þe lord God of Israel is þe possessioun of þat tribe, as he
925 haþ spoke to him. And þese lawis, ȝouun of God bi Moyses, þe
prophetis tauȝten, as among oþir we mai rede (*Ezechiel* 44) where,
aftir þe prophete haþ tauȝt hou þe prestis and þe dekenes shulde
f. 39ᵛ haue hemsilf to Godward | in lyuyng and sacrifice doyng, seiþ þus:
Non erit autem eis hereditas, ego autem hereditas eorum et possessionem non
930 *eis dabitis in Israel, ego enim possessio eorum,* 'Forsoþe, þer shal be noon
eritage to hem; forsoþe, I am þe eritage of hem, and ȝe shal ȝyue no
possessioun to hem in Israel, for I am þe possessioun of hem.'

Off þese textis þanne of þe oold lawe we mai se hou opunli and
streitli God forfendide hise prestis possessiouns and lordships in þe
935 oold lawe, and hou þese textis and lawis bynden oure prestis to þe
same; and whi it is sumwhat toold bifore. And þe prestis of þe oold
lawe koude not shake awei þis boond bi a contrarie gloos liik as oure
prestis can now. Siþ þanne þat oure prestis, as it is seid, ben
boundun to kepe þese lawis, as touchinge [þe] avoiding of worldli
940 possessiouns or lordships, and ouer þat þei ben boundun to þe same
f. 40ʳ bi a more perfit lawe þan were | þe prestis of þe oold testament, þe

913 seide] saith F   914 quia] DHF, et EL   915 oblaciones] oblationes
eius F   et nichil] FL, ⌐et⌐ nichil H, nichil ED   aliud] FL, *on eras.* H, autem ED
916 fratrum] fratum D   þe²] *om.* HFL   þo] thos F   917 þat²] the F, *om.* H
918 sacrifices] DH, sacrifice EFL   919 and þei] FL, ⌐and⌐ þei H, þei ED
possessioun] possessions F   920 *margin* iosue 13 EDFL   13 . . . þus] *om.* F
þus] *om.* H   922 þat] *om.* F   925 þese] ⌐of⌐ thes F   þe . . . tauȝten (926)]
om. F   926 *margin* eze. 44 EDL, 44 F   44] *om.* F   927 aftir] as F   þe³]
om. HFL   928 haue] be haue F   to godward] toward god F   929 erit autem]
rev. F   930 eis dabitis] *rev.* FL   931 þe] ther F   of] *om.* F   hem²] hem in
israel H, in israel F   933 off] ⌐12 ca.⌐ Off F   934 forfendide] forbad F
936 þe¹] þere H   937 boond] boon D   bi] per H   937 oure prestis¹]
owrs F   938 siþ] seyng F   seid] manyfest F   939 þe] DHFL, *om.* E
940 or] and HF   ouer þat] more ouer F   þei] *om.* H   941 a] the F   were]
om. F   of] were of F   þe³] *om.* F

habebunt sacerdotes, et omnes qui de eadem tribu sunt, partem et
hereditatem cum reliquo populo Israell, [quia] sacrificia Domini et 155
oblaciones commedent; et nichil aliud accipient de possescione fratrum
suorum, 'þe prestis and deeknys and alle þo þat ben of þe same tribe
schal not haue parte and heritage wiþ þat oþer peple of Israel, for þai
schal ete þe sacrifyce[s] and þe offryngis of þe Lorde; and þai schal
taake no þinge ellis of þe possessyon of | her breþern.' Also it is f. 9ᵛ
writen þus: *Tribui autem Leui non dedit possescionem, quoniam Dominus* 161
Deus Israel, ipse est possescio eorum ut locutus est illi, þat is, whan
Moyses assignyd þe possescyon of þe londe of Israel amonge þe
peple, he ȝaue no possescion to þe tribe of Leuy, forwhi þe lorde
God of Israel is þe possescion of þat tribe, as he haþ spoken to hym. 165
Also þes lawis, ȝouen of God by Moyses, þe holy prophetis tauȝten,
as amonge oþer we may rede of Eȝechiel, þat tawȝte how þe prestis
and deeknys schuld haue hemsiilfe to Godwarde in lyuynge and
sacrifice doynge; for he saiþ þus: *Non est autem eis hereditas, ego*
autem hereditas eorum et possescionem non dabitis eis in Israel, ego enim | 170
possessio eorum, 'Forsoþe, þer schal be noone heritage to hem; forsoþe f. 10ʳ
I am þe heritage of hem, and ȝe schal ȝeue no possescion to hem in
Israel, for I am þe possessyon of hem.' And saynt Jerom saiþ
acordynge herto *Clericus nichil preter Dominum possidere debet, scilicet*
non aurum non argentum, nec possessiones, quia cum huiusmodi non vult 175
Dominus esse pars, 'A clerke schal haue no possession but God, þat is
to say, neþer gold ne siluer or possessions, for wiþ siche God will not
be parte þat han more þan is necessary to performe her office wiþ.'
 Of þis processe before we may se how expresly God forfendiþ
lordeschip to his prestis in þe olde lawe, and þai cowde not schake 180
away þis bonde by a contrari glose liike | as oure prestis kan nowe. f. 10ᵛ
And bi þe same bonde oure prestis ben bonden to kepe þes lawis, as
tochynge þe auoydynge of worldly lordeschipis, and ouer þat þai ben
bonden to þe same by a more perfyte lawe þan wer þe prestis of þe
olde testament. þerfore þai schulde be þe more wiþdrawe fro seculer 185
lordeschip þan prestis of þe olde lawe, namely siþ þe olde lawe
byhotiþ for þe kepynge þerof prosperyte of þis liife, and þe gospell
bihotiþ þe kyngdome of heuen. And so no man may putte anoþer
grounde bisyde þat þat is putte, þe whiche is Criste Ihesu.

155 quia] et L   159 sacrifyces] sacrifyce L   161 *margin* Josue xiij° L
169 *margin* Ezechiel xliiij c° L   173 *margin* Epᵃ xxxiiijᵃ L

[*Lambeth Tract resumes on p. 45*]

which was figure and derknesse, and þe lawe of þe gospel is truþe
and liȝt, as seynt Poul seiþ, þei shulde be more wiþdrawe fro seculer
lordship þan prestis of þe oold lawe, nameli siþ þe oold lawe bihotiþ
945 for þe keping þerof prosperite of þis liif, and þe gospel bihotiþ þe
kyngdom of heuene. And so þei shulde drawe more to þe staat of
innocence and to heuenli lyuyng, in þe which staat of innocence or of
blis is, ne was no such worldli lordship but oonli kyndli lordship,
wherbi God, þat is in kynde aboue alle creaturis, hadde and haþ
950 lordship upon alle creaturis, and man in þe staat of innocence hadde
such manere lordship upon alle creaturis þat were sugetis to him in
kynde; and so þer was in paradiis, ne is, ne shal be in heuen no such
f. 40ᵛ lordship as ⌈is⌉ þis vnperfit worldli lordship, þat inclu|diþ constrey-
nyng or violence or lordship of oo man upon anoþir, þe which
955 lordship is aȝens kynde, for alle men ben euen in kynde. And so þis
worldli lordship is so vnperfit and so euene and so moche aȝens þe
perfeccioun of mankynde þat it hadde be plesaunt to God þat such
lordship hadde neuere be among men. In witnesse wherof in þe staat
of innocence was no such lordship, as it is seid bifore, ne shulde haue
960 be at ony time duringe þat perfeccioun of man. And so þis lordship,
for þe vnperfeccioun þerof as it myȝte not, so it was not euenli
brouȝt into þe peple bi God neþer perfit man. But it was first brouȝt
yn among men bi þe heþen folk, and aftirward at þe ensaumple of
heþen peple þe children of Israel, þat weren callid Goddis peple, for
f. 41ʳ as moche as þei hadde refusid þe lawe of Moyses wiþ | þe
966 sacramentis aȝens þe plesaunce of God and aȝens þe councel of
her prophete Samuel, brouȝte yn þis lordship among hem.

And in more witnesse þat þis lordship was not brouȝt yn bi þe
euene or riȝt ordinaunce of God, or ellis bi his plesaunce, whanne
970 God ȝaf þe oold lawe to his peple bi Moyses, he ordeynede no such

942 was] wer F   figure and] fygured in F   þe¹] if þe F   is] be F   truþe]
true F   943 liȝt] puer lyght F   seiþ] testifieth F   be] þe F   fro] themself
from F   944 lordship] lordschyppis F   nameli] specially F   siþ] seing F
bihotiþ] promyseth alonly F   945 bihotiþ] promiseth suerly F   947 and] or
of and F   in] in sprete in F   948 ne] nor F   949 in] om. HF   kynde]
kyng F   aboue] of F   950 man] also man F   951 lordship] of lordschypp F
sugetis] sugget HF   952 in¹] ⌈not⌉ in H, not in F   ne¹] nor F, om. D   ne²]
nor F   no] any (on eras.) H   953 is] om. F   954 þe] om. F
955 men] om. F   euen] equall F   956 euene . . . so³] om. F   959 was] þer
was F   it] om. H, I F   is] om. F   ne] nor F   960 þis] þat F   961 it
was] rev. H   euenli] expressly F   962 into] to F   neþer] nor by F   man]
men F   margin 1 r.8 EDF, in text after man H   965 refusid] resceyued HF
þe¹ . . . moyses] ⌈moyses⌉ lawe H, moyses lawe F   966 plesaunce] pleasure F
967 her] þe F   969 euene or] om. F   plesaunce] pleasure F

lord upon hem, but wolde þat þe peple shulde be gouerned bi iugis
þat shulde teche and do execucioun to þe peple of þe pure lawe of
God upon hem; so þat duringe þis ordynaunce of God, þe which was
after his owne plesaunce, þei hadden neþer lord ne lawe upon hem
saue oonli God and his lawe. For þis peple of Israel was first 975
gouerned [bi] pure Goddis lawe and iugis, as fro þe tyme of Moysees
into þe tyme of Samuel. And þanne þei wolde nedis haue a kyng | as f. 41ᵛ
þe heþen men hadden, and so, as þei hadden a newe lord, so þei
hadden a newe lawe, þat is to seie þe kyngis lawe, wherbi þe king
hadde moche worldli power upon her bodies ⌐and her goodis⌐, 980
moeblis and vnmoeblis, þe which lawe includiþ moche artyng and
violence and bondage, as it is writun (1 *Regum* 8). And so þere[as] þei
and her goodis weren fre, þei weren aftir boond, and þereas bifore þei
weren not boundun to obeie but to God and his lawe, aftir þat þei
weren boundun to obeie to her kyng, in exilyng, in prisonyng, into loss 985
of her good and also into deeþ: 1 *Esdre* 7, where it is writun þus:
'Euery man þat haþ not do þe lawe of God and þe lawe of þe kyng, of
him shal be ȝoue doom wiþ avisement, or into deeþ, or into exilyng, or
into condempnyng of his liiflood, or certenli into prisoun.'

And so aftir tyme þat þe peple hadde chosun to | hem a kyng, þei f. 42ʳ
weren gouerned bi Goddis lawe and þe kyngis into þe tyme þat þe 991
kyngis losten þat maieste upon þe peple worþili, and þat bicause þat
þei wolde not kepe þe maieste of God hool upon his peple, in
distriyng and in avoiding of mawmetrie. For whosoeuer doiþ
mawmetrie he doiþ tresoun aȝens þe maieste of God, for bi his 995
power he amenusiþ þat maieste, in as moche as he doiþ to a creature
a worship, þe which God haþ oonli reserued to himsilf, as is avowing
praier, offryng or sacrifice, þe whiche worships God haþ reserued

971 lord] lordschip HF   973 upon . . . God²] *om.* F   þe] *om.* F
974 plesaunce] pleasur F   ne] nor F   976 bi] DHF, wiþ E   977 into]
vnto F   þe] *om.* H   978 þe] *om.* F   980 her²] on her H, vpon þer F
981 moeblis] movabyll F   vnmoeblis] not movabyll F   þe] *om.* F   artyng and]
om. F   982 *margin* 1 r.8 EDF   1 . . . 8] in þe fyrst book of þe kyngis F
þereas] DH, þere as, as *canc.* E, wher as F   984 þat] *om.* F   985 in¹] vnder
payn of F   in²] and H, *om.* F   into] and F   loss] þe losse H   986 good]
goodis F   into] ⌐of⌐ F   *margin* 1 esdr. 7 EF   1] as it is writun 1 DH, as it is writen
in F   7] *om.* F   987 of him] *om.* F   988 shal] he schall F   be . . . into¹]
wiþ advysement be put to F   or¹] *om.* F   into²] in F   989 certenli] ellis
truly F   into] to F   990 tyme] þe tyme F   991 into] tyll F
992 losten] worthely lost F   worþili] *om.* F   þat³] *om.* F   994 distriyng]
distrieninge H   in] *om.* F   995 bi] to F   996 amenusiþ] demynischet F
þat] þe F   maieste] honour of god F   as²] *om.* F   997 a worship þe] þat F
998 þe] *om.* F   worships] worschype F

oonli to himsilf, as seynt Austyn seiþ in his *Book of sixe questiouns* in
1000 þe chapitre of þe distinccioun of sacrificis. And al þis worship is
bitokened bi þis oon Gru word *latria*, as seynt Austyn seiþ þere.
Aftir tyme þanne þat kyngis weren obstynat in her malice, and
f. 42ᵛ hadden no reward | to kepe þis maieste of God hool in hem and in
her peple, God made an eende of hem.

1005 And þanne cam þe gouernaunce of þe peple into prestis hondis,
and þei iugide þanne þe peple, and ledde þe peple into batel, and
took such worldli gouernaunce upon hem. And as þe prestis weren
þanne out of þe pure staat of presthod aftir Moyses lawe, and out of
þe gouernaunce þat God hadde sett hem yn bi Moyses, so þei moste
1010 and dide make ordynauncis and lawis acordinge to þe gouernaunce
þat þei were and wolden be of. And as þei took more and more
sauour in maistership and gouernaunce of þe peple, and drowen into
more and more couetise, so þei multipliede her tradiciouns, þe
whiche sownede into couetise. And so þis peple hadden among
1015 hem princis of prestis or bishops, þat weren cheef of þis gouernaunce; and þei hadden scribis, þe whiche weren kunnynge in suche
f. 43ʳ gaynful tradici|ouns; and also þei hadden among hem religious folk
þat weren callid pharisees, þe whiche hadden þe opynyoun of þe
peple þat þei weren kunnynge in Goddis lawe and þerwiþ hooli. And
1020 bi þese þre maner of peple, as bi iugis and councelers, þe Iewis weren
gouerned. And þese gouernours, þat is to seie bishops, scribis and
pharisees, woxen so couetouse upon þis maistership and upon her
richesse þat þei myȝte not suffre Crist, þat vndirnam her couetise, to
preche in her synagogis. But first þei curside him, and also alle þo
1025 þat effectueli louede or leeuede his loore. And whanne þei saien þat
Crist wolde not for þis cursyng ceesse of his preching, and nameli

999 *margin* Aug. libro de 6 (*partly cut off* E) questionibus capitulo (*om.* D) de
sacrificiorum distincione ED, aug. F   inᵗ . . . sacrificiis (1000)] Augustinus libro vj
questionum capite de sacrificio 2ᵃ distinctione F   in²] Augustinus libro de vj
questionibus c° de sacrificio ij distinccione in H   1002 tyme] þe tyme F
kyngis] DHF, þe kyngis E   1003 reward] respect F   1006 into] to HF
1007 gouernaunce] busynes F   1009 Moyses] moyses lawe F   moste] most
nedis HF   1011 were] were of F   1013 þe] *om.* F   1014 sownede]
sowndyth F   couetise] covetusnes F   þis] þe F   1016 þe] *om.* F   kunnynge]
very cunnyng F   1017 gaynful] covetusnes and lucratyve F   and] þat thei made
and F   1018 þe¹] *om.* F   1019 þat þei weren] to be very F   in . . . lawe] *om.* F
þerwiþ] also F   1020 and] *om.* F   weren] *om.* F   1021 and¹] ⌐13 ca.⌐ And F
1022 her] þe F   1023 vndirnam] spak agaynst F   couetise] covetusnes F
1024 and also] and not alonly hym but F   þo] thos F   1025 effectueli]
affectusly F   leeuede] lernyd F   loore] lawe F   1026 nameli] specially F

aȝens her couetise, þei conspiride aȝens Crist, and dcmcdc þat it was beter for to kille him þan þat þei shulde leese her lond and þe subieccioun of þe peple. And þus þoruȝ þis couetise þei killiden innocent | Crist and hise apostlis aftir, into confusioun to hemsilf and f. 43ᵛ her peple to bodi and to soule. 1031

Now haue I toold ȝou in greet þe coors of þe gouernaunce of þe peple vndir þe oold lawe, hou it was first gouerned bi iugis aftir þe pure lawe of God wiþoute deedli lord or mannes lawe; and þanne it was beste gouerned and moost after þe plesaunce of God. Aftir þat it 1035 was gouerned bi kyngis, and Goddis lawe and þe kyngis. And þanne in tyme of goode kingis, as Dauid, Ezechie and Iosie, it was wel gouerned, but not [so] fulli aftir Goddis plesaunce as it was in þe tyme of goode iugis. And at þe laste þis gouernaunce fel into þe prestis power, þe whiche, as þei lyuede not as pure prestis of Goddis 1040 lawe, ne as dide þe firste iugis, ne as kyngis, but of ech of þes hadden sumwhat, so þei maden hem a mengid lawe of Goddis lawe, [of] þe kyngis and | of her owne tradiciouns. And vndir þis gouernaunce þei f. 44ʳ brouȝten hemsilf and her peple to a shamful eende. And as in þe ooold lawe so in þe newe þe cristen peple haþ had þis ᵣcoors᷄ [of] 1045 gouernaunce. For firste in Cristis tyme and þe apostlis, and in tyme of oþir perfit peple þat suede her paþis, þe cristen peple was gouerned aftir þe pure lawe of þe gospel and bi þo þat tauȝte it, as it were bi iugis. Afterward, whanne heþen kyngis and lordis turneden to þe bileeue of Crist and maden her peple to do þe same, 1050 þe peple weren wel gouerned vndir goode kyngis but raþer beter, for more perfitli, for after a more pure and perfit lawe, and more acordinge wiþ þe staat of innocence. For þe kyngis gouernede in greet partie þer peple bi her owne lawis, þe whiche lawis as wel as regalie camen yn bi þe heþen folk. But after tyme | þat þe kyngis and f. 44ᵛ lordis weren bidotid and ablindid bi þe ypocrisie of þe clergie, many, 1056

1027 couetise] covetusnes F   demede þat] sayd F   was] wer F   1028 for to] to F   1029 þis couetise] þer covetusnes F   1030 to] of F   1031 to¹] bothe F   to²] om. F   1032 in greet] om. F   1034 deedli] any mortall F 1035 plesaunce] pleasure F   1036 kyngis¹ . . . kyngis²] godis lawe and kyngis F 1038 so] DHF, om. E   goddis plesaunce] þe pleasure of god F   1040 þe] om. F as þei] om. F   1041 ne¹] nor F   ne²] nor F   ech] euery on F   þes] thes þei F 1042 so] so þat EDF   mengid] myxt F   of þe] of canc. þe E, þe HF   1043 of her] her HF   1044 her] þe F   and²] for D   in] it was in F   1045 þe²] om. D   of] DHF, om. E   1047 suede] folowid F   paþis] ways F   þe] om. D 1048 þo] þos F   1049 heþen] the hethyn F   1051 weren] was HF   but . . . perfitli for (1052)] om. F   1054 þe] om. F   1055 tyme] þe tyme F 1056 lordis] þe lordis HF   bidotid] ouercome F   ablindid] blyndyd F

as Constantin and oþir, ӡauen her lordships to prestis. And many kyngis and lordis, as I suppose, han lost þe maistrie of regalie upon þe peple bi cause þat þei han not kept Goddis maieste hool among 1060 hem and her peple, but suffride hem to do mawmetrie, and more iustli as it semeþ myӡte not such a kyng be poneshid þan to leese his maieste aboue his peple, þat kepiþ not bi his power his peple fro þis moost offence aӡens þe maieste of God. And ful many of londis and grete lordships and citees, þat were sumtyme in gouernaunce of 1065 kyngis and oþer grete temperal lordis, ben summe bi foly ӡifte, ⌐summe ellis¬, fallen into prestis possessiouns.

And as kyngis and lordis gouernede bifore suche lordships bi f. 45ʳ worldli lawis groundly | brouӡt yn bi þe heþen folk, so þe clerkis now gouernen suche lordships bi þe same lawis and ben lordis þerupon, 1070 liik as þe lordis and kyngis weren—and so euene aӡens Cristis wordis [þei ben lordis], where he seiþ þus (*Luc.* 22): *Reges gencium dominantur* ⌐*eorum*¬; *vos autem non sic,* 'þe kyngis of þe heþen han lordship vpon hem; but ӡe not so.' And also aӡens his ensaumple þat, whanne he was souӡt to haue be a kyng, and so to haue take upon 1075 him þe lordship of þe peple, þe which was brouӡt yn bi þe heþen, þat þe clerkis han now in hond, he fledde into þe hill and preiede, in tokenyng þat such lordship was contrarie to þe staat of clergie, þat shulde lyue in contemplacioun. And so now at Rome, at Bolayn, and ful many oþir placis where prestis ben cheef lordis, þei leden þe f. 45ᵛ peple to batel and gouernen hem in al wise worldli | as þe kyngis and 1081 temperal lordis diden bifore. And bicause þat þei ben not of þe pure soort of presthod of þe gospel, as were Crist and hise apostlis and her folowers, ne of þe pure soort of kyngis, as weren kyng Dauid and þe kyngis þat folowiden hise maners, but mengen boþe þese staatis 1085 togidir for þe worldli profit, prosperite and welþe þat þei han þerbi, þerfore þei han maad hem a lawe liik to þe staat þat þei stonden yn, þe which is gedering of þe emperours lawe and of her owne tradiciouns. And, for to poisowne þe peple þe more sliӡli þerwiþ, þei colouren þis mengid ware here and þere wiþ hooli scripture. 1090 And, as þei falsli callen hemsilf hooli chirche, notwiþstonding þat þei ben of noon of þe þre statis of Goddis chirche, þe whiche ben specified bifore, so as falsli þei callen þis mengid lawe 'þe lawe of f. 46ʳ hooli chirche', siþ þe pured lawe of Iesu Crist | is þe lawe of hooli chirche, as he [and noon oþer] is heed þerof. For as his chirche haþ 1095 but oo bodi, so it haþ but oon heed, þe which is Crist, as seynt Poul seiþ: *Apostolus* (*ad Eph.* 1) *docet quomodo Deus Pater omnia subiecit sub*

Capitulum iii

Moreouer we may se how euen aȝens Cristis wordis in þe gospell 190
prestis ben þus lordis, wher Criste saiþ þus: *Reges gencium dom-*
inantur eorum, vos autem | non sic, 'þe kyngys of heþen han lordeschip f. 11ʳ
on hem, but ȝe not so.' And also aȝens his ensaumple þai ben lordis,
for whan he was sowȝte to be made a kynge, and so to take on hym
worldly lordeschip, he fledde into þe hill and prayde, in toknynge þat 195
siche lordeschip was contrarie to þe state of þe clergi, þat schuld lyue
in contemplacyon. But clerkis nowe lyuen not oonly contrariously to
þis techynge and ensaumple of Criste, but also þai maken stronge
lawis reuersynge boþe his wordis and dedis, and letten in all þat þai
may hem þat wolde teche þe trouþe of Criste. 200

191 *margin* luc' xxij° L

1058 þe] þer F   maistrie of regalie] regall magesty F   maistric] maicste DH
1059 þat] *om.* DF   goddis] the goodis of þer F   1061 it semeþ] semyth me F
it] me H   1062 aboue] vpon F   þis moost] þat F   1063 aȝens] þat is most
agaynst F   ful] in ful HF   of] *om.* HF   1065 lordis] lordisis H   ben] by F
bi] *om.* F   1066 summe ellis] *om.* DHF   1068 þe] *om.* F   1070 þe] þo
H, those F   euene] dyrectly F   1071 þei ben lordis where] DHF, prestis ben þus
lordis wher L, where E   *margin* luc. 22 DHFL   luc. 22] *om.* HFL   1072 þe²]
om. DL   1073 ensaumple] example F   þat] *om.* HF   1074 haue be] be
made FL   1075 þe³] *om.* F   1076 now] *twice, 2nd canc.* E   1078 at
rome] *twice, 2nd canc.* E   1079 ful] *om.* F   1080 wise worldli] wordly maner F
1082 were] was F   1083 ne] nor F   weren] was F   1084 mengen] myxt F
1086 þerfore] ⌐14 ca.⌐ Therfor F   1087 þe¹] *om.* F   gedering] gedrid þing H, a
gaderyd   thyng   F   of²]   *om.* F   1088 sliȝli] sliȝlier D, easly F
1089 mengid] myxt F   ware] lawe F   1091 statis] estatis F   þe²] *om.* F
1092 mengid] myngled F   1093 siþ] seyng F   pured] pure F   1094 and
noon oþer] DHF, *canc.* E   1095 þe] *om.* F   1096 *margin* ad eph. 1 EDF
apostolus ad eph. 1] *om.* F

pedibus Christi: et ipsum dedit caput super omnem ecclesiam, que est corpus ipsius. And þis mengid lawe þei studien and practisen and magnyfien aboue alle oþir lawis.

1100 And as þei han þese lordships, so þei hopen to haue alle. In tokenyng wherof, as a greet maistir of þis mengid lawe toolde me now late, þe clergie haþ maad such a lawe þat þei shal gete out of þe laymen hondis alle þe temperal possessiouns and lordships þat þei mai, and in no caas þei shal delyuere ony suche lordships to laymen
1105 aȝen, what nede so euere þei haue. And þanne I askide of him, in caas þat þe clergie hadde alle þe temperal possessiouns, as þei han

f. 46ᵛ now þe more part, hou shal þe se|culer lordis and knyȝtis lyue, and wherwiþ, siþ God haþ in boþe hise lawis alowid her staat and her liiflood. And þanne he wiþ studie answerde me and seide þat þei
1110 shulde be þe clerkis soudiours. And certis þis lawe of getyng yn of þese temperaltees into þe clerkis hondis, and þese oþir wordis þat þis autentik man þus teelde to me, ouȝte to be take heede to. For, siþ þei han now þe more part of þe temperal lordships, and wiþ al þat þe spiritualtees and þe grete mouable tresours of þe rewme, þei mai
1115 liȝtli make a conquest upon þe toþir partie, nameli siþ þe temperal lordis ben not in noumbre, good, witt, ne manhod liik as þei han be bifore, and þe partie of þe clergie in alle þese poyntis encresen, and so couetousli þei ben sett upon þese goodis þat þei welden now, and

f. 47ʳ mo þat þei hopen to haue, þat þei wolen not suffre | her couetise to
1120 be enpungned opunli ne priueli, as fer as þei mai lette it.

And herfore þei pursuen wiþoute merci pore prestis, þat in lyuyng and word techen þe pouert of pore Crist and hise apostlis to be kept in al þe staat of þe clergie. And so as þe maliciouse bishops, pharisees and scribis weren knytt togidir aȝens Crist þat prechide aȝens her
1125 couetise, and curside him and putte him out of her synagogis, and on al wise lettide him and hise apostlis to teche þe gospel, þe which techiþ prestis wilful pouert, so bishops and religiouse, and kunninge men of þis mengid lawe pursuen vnmesurabli pore prestis þat suen Crist and hise apostlis in lyuyng and teching, and þat more
1130 maliciousli þan diden her felowis in þe oold lawe. For þei cursen þe prest þat prechiþ, and him þat resceyueþ him, and alle þat

f. 47ᵛ fauoren him, and alle þo þat heeren him, and ouer þis enterdi|ten þe

1097 super] supra F   1098 mengid] menglyd F   and magnyfien] *om.* F
1101 mengid] menglyd F   1102 late] a late F   þe¹] þat þe F   þe²] *om.* F
1104 caas] vyse *canc.* case what so euer chance F   delyuere] neuer delyuer F
lordships] lorschype F   1105 what . . . haue] haue thei neuer so great nead F
1106 caas] chawnc' F   1107 more] most F   1108 siþ] seing F   haþ] *om.* F

And by þis lawe þat þai han made sum of hem han saide þat þai
schuld gete owte of þe seculer hondis alle | the temperal lordeschip f. 11ᵛ
þat þai may, and in no caase delyuer noone aʒen. And þerfore a
gentilman axid a greete bischop of þis londe, in caase þat þe clergy
hadde alle þe temperal possescyons, as þai han now þe more parte, 205
how schal þe seculer lordis and knyghtis lyue, and wherwiþ, siþ God
haþ in bothe his lawis alowid her staate and her liiflode. And þen he
awnswerid and sayde þat þai schuld be clerkis soudyoures, and lyue
by her wagis. And certis þis lawe of getynge in of þes temperaltes,
and þes oþer wordis of þis bischop, ouʒte to be taken hede to. For, 210
siþ þai han now þe more part of þe temperal lordeschips, and wiþ
þat þe spiritualtees and þe greete | mouable tresouris of þe rewme, f. 12ʳ
þai may lightly make a conquest vpon þat othir party, namely siþ þe
temperal lordis ben not in noumbre and in ryches lyke as þai wer
sum tyme. For þai ben sotilly spolid of her lordeschipis, in distroyng 215
of her staate and power þat God sett hem in; and þe party of þe
clergy in alle þes poyntis ben encresyd. And so couetously þai ben
sette vpon þes goodis þat þai welden now, and mo þat þai hopen to
haue, þat þai will not suffre her couetise to be enpugnyd openly ne
priuely, als ferr as þai may lett it. 220

For þe gospel of Ion saiþ þat bischopis and pharises sayden of
Criste 'If we leuen hym þus, alle men schul byleue in hym, | and f. 12ᵛ

---

221 *margin* Jo. xj° L

staat] estate F 1110 certis] of a truthe F of²] *om.* F 1111 þe] þcsc HF
oþir] *om.* F 1112 þus] *om.* F to¹] *om.* F to²] ful gretly to F siþ] seyng F
1113 þe²] *om.* HF 1115 þe toþir] al þat (the F) oþer HF nameli] ye and
chefly F siþ] seyng F 1116 good] DHF, ⸢of⸣ good E ne] nor F
1117 bifore] in tymys past F þe partie of] *om.* F and²] mervelusly greatly and F
1118 goodis] wordly goodis F welden] haue F 1119 mo] more F couetise]
inordinat covetusnes F 1120 enpugned] spokyn agaynst F ne] nor F fer]
farforthe F 1121 herfore] therefore F wiþoute] and wiþowt F pore]
persecut pore F 1123 staat] estate F þe²] *om.* H 1124 þat] wich F
1125 couetise] covetusnes F on al wise] wiþ all þe ways and inventions þat thei cowd
fynd F 1126 þe²] *om.* F 1127 techiþ] teachyd F wilful] ⸢of⸣ wilful H, of
wylful F 1128 mengid] menglyd F pursuen] persecut F vnmesurabli]
vnresonnabli HF pore] wiþout pety or compassion poor F suen] folow F
1130 diden] *om.* F 1131 prest] preastis F him¹&²] þem F 1132 him¹]
them F and¹] yee and F þo] þei F him²] them F and . . . þis] but yet se þe
wickyd malyc' of þes synfull wretches and of þer malicius workis ouer all þes synguler
malycis thei cruelly and vengably F enterditen] þei entirditen H

place þere Cristis gospel is prechid freli. And wel shewen þei herinne
þat þei ben þe children of þe cursed bishops, religiouse and scribis of
1135 þe oold lawe; and wel shewen þei in þis malice what þei wolde do to
Cristis owne persoone, and he apperide here bodili, and lyuede and
tauȝte as he dide—ȝhe, alþouȝ he tauȝte but þis oo word 'þe kyngis
of þe heþen han lordship upon hem, but ȝe not so.' For bi þe hate
┌þat┐ þei shewen to his lawe, and to þo þat techen it, þei shewen what
1140 hate þei han to Crist þat is autour þerof. And so as Caiphas and hise
compeers killiden Crist for drede of leesyng of her worldli good, so
oure prelatis, her felowis and folowers, but wiþoute mesure of more
malice, killen Crist in hise pore membris þat techen þis conclusioun.
And in þat þei suffren not Crist to be alyue in þe soulis of his peple
f. 48ʳ bi quyk feiþ, þe which co|meþ bi knouleche of his lawe þat þei so
1146 crueli hiden fro þe peple. And þis is more cruel killing of Crist þan
to kille him bodili in his owne persoone; for þerto Crist assentide,
and þat pleside þe Fadir of heuen and þerof cam þe moost good and
worship to mankynde þat myȝte be, þat is to seie þe sauacioun of þo
1150 þat ben chosun to blis, but of þe secunde manere of killyng of Crist
bi hiding of his lawe mai no good come euenli. For it is aȝens þe
plesaunce of þe Fadir and þe last will of Crist here on erþe, þat
comaundide alle hise prestis for to preche, and make his gospel
knowun to al þe world, and not to hide it from ony man. Off
1155 whomeuere han þese meyne lerned for to make þis gospel hid ┌and
vnknow⟨e⟩┐ I can not seie, but if it be of her fadir Lucifer. For wel I
wot bi bileeue þat þe will of Crist stondiþ ȝit stabli vpon þe same
poynt þat it stood in his assencioun, and euere shal into þe doom.
f. 48ᵛ   But I | woot wel here þat oure worldli prelatis seien here þat þei
1160 maken alle þese newe constituciouns and statutis aȝens þese newe
prechours and her fautours to exclude heresies and errours and al

1133 þere] þat F   prechid freli] *rev.* F   wel . . . herinne] and in þis act thei do
manifest and schew F   1135 oold] *om.* F   1136 and¹] if F   1137 but]
twice, 1st canc. E, but only F   1138 *margin* luc F   ȝe] yow F
1139 shewen] schewid H   þo] thos F   1141 compeers] compenys F
1142 felowis and folowers] folowurs and felowys F   but] yee þe mor pety it is but
thei F   wiþoute] þei wiþouten H   1143 in] and HF   1144 þat] þat ┌þat┐ E
his] þe F   1145 þe] *om.* FL   1146 hiden] do hyde F   1147 assentide]
agreith F   1149 þo] thos F   1150 *margin* 2 D   but] ┌15 ca.┐ But F
manere of] *om.* F   1151 euenli] *om.* FL   1152 plesaunce] pleasure F
1153 for to] to D   1154 and] *om.* HF   1155 whomeuere] who so euer F
han . . . meyne] þis meyne han H, thes men haue F   and vnknowe] *om.* F
1156 wel I wot] I know well F   1157 stabli] stable HF   1158 in] in at F
into] ┌vn┐to F   1159 here] *om.* F   1160 alle þese] *om.* F   1161 heresies
and errours] errors and heresyes F

Romayns schulen comme, and take oure place and oure folke.' For þai dredden hem of Criste ȝif his wordis wenten forþe þat Romayns schulden comme and fordo prestis and phariseis. As if bischoppis 225 and abbotis spaken today togedre 'Hyde we Goddis lawe, lest þes seculer lordis comme and take oure lordeschippis and fordo oure statis.' And fro þat day, þe gospel saiþ, þai þouȝten to sle Criste. So now by more malyce þai killen hem þat techen þe trouþe of Cristis gospell. And in þat þai suffre not Criste to be alyue in þe sowlis of 230 his peple bi qwike faythe, whiche commiþ by knouleche of his lawe þat þai so cruely hyden fro þe peple. And þis is more cruel killynge of Criste þan to kille hym bodely in his owne persone; | for þerof f. 13ʳ came þe mooste goode to mankynde, þat is saluacion of þo þat ben chosen to blisse, but of þat oþer maner of killynge of Criste by 235 hidynge of his lawe may no goode comme. For it is aȝens þe plesance of Criste, and mooste lykynge to þe fende and lesynge of soulis. And þerfore saynt Poule saiþ *Si opertum est euangelium nostrum, hiis qui pereunt est opertum, in quibus Deus huius seculi excecauit mentes infidelium* (2 Cor.4), 'Ȝif þe gospel is hid, it is hid to hem þat 240 perschen, in þe whiche God of þis worlde haþ blyndid þe mynde of vnfeiþful men.'

[*Lambeth Tract* resumes on p. 55]

manere fals doctrine. But God woot þis is not soþe, for ⌐ȝit⌐ knewe I
neuere prest þat goiþ aboute and freli prechiþ þe gospel, as doen
many of þese þat ben callid Lollardis, but þat he desiriþ wiþ al his
1165 herte for to come into opun and indifferent audience, þere to declare
al þat he holdiþ or techiþ opun or priue; and if he erre he is glad to
be amendid, and if he seie wel desiriþ to be alowid. And also if þei
hatide heresies as þei pretenden, þei wolden distrie many and grete
heresies þat regnen in oure rewme—but not among þe Lollers. And
1170 þei wolde bigynne at þis heresie of þis lordship in þe staat of þe
f. 49ʳ clergie, þe which I now enpungne, þat ma|kiþ þe clergie bi
dampnable apostasie ouere foul straie awei from Cristis blessid
ordre. þei wolde also distrie þe foul heresie of mawmetrie, þe
which is þe greet crime of harmyng of Goddis maieste, wherbi
1175 men doen þe worship þat God haþ oonli reserued to his owne
persoone to aungels, seyntis, relikis or ymagis as it is sumwhat
touchid of bifore; and þis moost hidous synne, for it is moost euene
aȝens God, is ful ryue among þe peple, and in no wise þei refreyne
þe peple of þis, but bi word and ensaumple and bi her constitu-
1180 ciouns, þe whiche þei autorisen as þei weren Goddis lawe, þei arten
þe peple to do þis synne, and forfenden ony man to enpungne it, as a
man mai conseyue of þe newe constituciouns.

And þei distrien not but maintenen þe foul heresie wherbi aȝens
f. 49ᵛ seynt Poul þei encumbren and en|triken hemsilf in worldli bisynesse
1185 and office, as in þe chaunserie, in tresorie and in oþir ful manye
worldli office, aȝens þe pure staat of presthod and into greet wrong
aȝens God and þe peple, to þe which þei shulde do duli a prestis

1162 fals] of false F   soþe] so F   ȝit] *om.* F   knewe I neuere] I neuer knewe F
1163 doen many] *rev.* F   1164 lollardis] lollers DHF   1165 opun] open
audienc' F   þere] þerfor F   1167 desiriþ] he desyeryth F   1170 in þe
staat] *om.* F   þe¹] *om.* F   1171 þe¹] *om.* F   now] do now F   þat] which F
þe clergie] men F   1172 ouere foul] too perlusly to F   1173 þei] and þei F
þe²] *om.* F   1174 þe] a F   of¹] in F   1176 sumwhat touchid] touchid
sumwhat, *marked for rev.* E   1177 of] *om.* F   moost hidous] perlus F   for it]
om. F   moost euene] dyrectly F   1178 is] and it is F   þei] þe D
1180 þe] *om.* F   þei weren] it were F   1181 and] and yet besyd all þis cruell
malyce thei F   forfenden] forbyd F   1182 conseyue] persayve F   þe] DHF,
þese E   1183 þei] thus þei F   not] not ye fowle heresys F   þe foul heresie]
þem yee some tyme wiþ dethe of innocent pepyll F   1184 *margin* 2 ad thi. 2 labora
sicut bonus miles Cristi Iesu. Nemo militans Deo implicat se negociis secularibus ED, *in
text after* office H, *reference margin, quotation text* (secularibus negociis) *after* office (1186) F
encumbren] cowmbyr F   entriken] lape F   hemsilf] hem H   1185 ful] syn
canc. ful E, *om.* F   1186 office] officis D   staat] estate F   and] *om.* D
1187 þe which] whome F

office. (*Act.* 6) *Non est equum nos derelinquere verbum Dei, et ministrare mensis.* For, if it was vnequite, as þe apostlis seiden in her comoun decre, hem for to leue þe preching of Goddis word and mynystre to 1190 [þe] bordis of widues, wherfore þei ordeynede oþir men in þat bisynesse, and seiden þat þei wolden take heede bisili to preching of Goddis word and praier, hou moche more, 3he wiþoute mesure more, vnequite and wrong to God and to man is it to oure prestis to leue contemplacioun, studie, praier ⌐and⌐ preching of Goddis word 1195 and mynystringe to bordis of widues, and go to þe court of a seculer lord and ocupie hem in a seculers office? Ne þei bisien hem to distrie | þe foul heresie of þe sacrament of þe auter, where þei and her f. 50ʳ confederacie seien, euene a3ens þe gospel and seynt Poul, þat þe sacrid oost is neþer breed ne Cristis bodi. Ne þei doen ony remedie 1200 a3ens þe foul heresie þat þe freris maintene vpon Crist, of þe begging þat þei putten upon him, ne of þat ⌐þat⌐ þei blasfemen so hidousli a3ens þe truþe of God, seiynge þat his lawe is falsest and heresie. Suche ful many heresies þat ben orrible to heere, and errours þat ben ful harmeful in Cristis chirche, I my3te reherce here and I hadde 1205 leiser. And þei setten not to her litil fyngir to amende ony of hem; wherof we mai take an opun euydence, but if þe deuel ablynde us, þat þei maken not alle þese newe ordynauncis to distrie heresies and errours, but Herodis and Caiphas drede of lesyng of her temperaltees is cropun into her hertis, and makiþ oure hooli fadris and worshipful 1210 pre|latis to pursue and kille Crist in þe manere as I haue toold aboue. f. 50ᵛ For, dreedles, experience techiþ us þis þat, and þei be sure of a prest þat he shal not enpungne her worldli profit[is], nameli in worldli possessiouns, beggerie and mawmetrie, he shal li3tli haue leue to go

1188 *margin* act. 6 EDF   Act. 6] *om.* F   1189 if] *om.* HF   vnequite] not convenient F   1190 hem for to] þat þei schuld F   1191 þe] *om.* E 1192 þat] *om.* HF   preching . . . praier (1193)] prayer and preachyng of godis word F 1194 more] *om.* HF   vnequite] vnequall F   to²] *om.* F   is it] *rev.* F   to³] for F 1195 praier] and preier HF   1196 mynystringe] mynister F   1197 seculers] seculere HF   ne] nor F   hem²] þemself F   1199 euene] *om.* F 1200 ne¹ᐟ²] nor F   doen] go not abowt sekyng F   1202 ne] nor F   of] agaynst F   þat] which F, *om.* D   hidousli] vngraciusly F   1203 *margin dh* for þis sayde frere Claxton a prechour and (a F) doctor of dyuynyte in þe chayere at oxenforde þat holy wrytte (scripture F) is fals heresye and impossible H, F *in text after* heresie 1204 ful] *om.* F   1205 ful . . . chirche] in cristis churche full harmfull F   here and] if F   1207 but if] except F   ablynde] blynd F   1209 drede] for dred F 1210 into] to F   hertis] herte DH   1211 pursue] preache and to persue F kille] to kyll F   aboue] befor F   1212 dreedles] dowtles F   and] if F 1213 profitis] DHF, profit E   nameli] specially F   1214 li3tli] *om.* F   to] quicly to F

1215 and preche as large as he wole; and if he wole go begge aftir his preching, he shal be þe lesse enpungned and ylett—for anticristis retenu, þat is wundir strong and large sprad, haþ þanne a ful grete euydence þat such a prest is oon of hers. For Crist, spekynge not synguler for his owne persoone, but in persoone of alle hise trewe
1220 folowers, seiþ þus: *Ego venio in nomine Patris mei, et me non recipitis; si alius veniat in nomine suo, ipsum recipietis*, 'I come in þe name of my Fadir (þat is to seie for profit of þe peple), and me', seiþ Crist, 'ȝe
f. 51ʳ resceyuen not; anoþir (or an alien) shal come in his | owne name (þat is to seie for his owne profit), and him ȝe shal resceyue.' And þis
1225 alien, as seynt Austyn seiþ in *De verbis Domini* vpon þe same word, is anticrist, þe which is fynali aliened fro God out of heuene wiþ his heed Lucifer. Al þis sorwe and wiþoute noumbre more is brouȝt into þe chirche bi þe dreed þat þe clergie haþ of lesyng of her temperaltees, and þoruȝ þe vile couetise þat þei han to gete yn
1230 more.

And so of þis processe we mai se hou þat þe peple is worst gouerned vndir þese bastard prestis and her manglid lawe, as were þe peple of Israel vndir her prestis in þe same caas of þe oold lawe. And hardli studie þe gospel, and marke þe malice þat þo þre manere of
1235 peple, bishops, religiouse and scribis diden aȝens Crist and his gospel; and þe same malice in kynde but moche more maliciousli
f. 51ᵛ is wrouȝt now aȝens þe | same Crist and his lawe bi oure bishops, religiouse and kunnynge men in þe bishops lawis. þei leften Goddis lawe in greet partie, and studiede and magnyfiede her owne
1240 tradiciouns for worldli wynnyng, and oure doen þe same (*Mt.* 23): *Ve vobis scribe et pharisei ypocrite, qui decimatis mentam, et anetum, et cuminum, et reliqui[s]tis que grauiora sunt legis, iudicium, misericordiam*

1215 and²] ⌈16 ca.⌉ and F   1216 for] by cause of F   1217 wundir] wonderus F   haþ þanne] þan þei haue F   ful grete] om. F   1219 persoone²] the person F   1220 þus] om. HF   margin Ioh.v *later corr.* H   1221 veniat] venit F   1222 profit] þe prophet F   of] to H   and me] om. F   ȝe] and ye F   1223 not] not me F   alien] stranger F   1225 *margin aug.* F   alien] stranger F   in] om. F   1226 þe] om. F   aliened] a stranger F   1227 wiþoute . . . more] moche F   1228 bi] thrugh F   dreed] fere F   1229 and] om. F   1230 more] more and more F   1232 prestis] brawnches of preastis F   manglid] mengid H, menglyd F   1233 her] þe F   1234 hardli] hardili H, therfor F   þe¹] ye truly and boldely þe F   þe²] ye the F   þo] thos F   1238 men] om. D   goddis] goodis H, god F   1240 *margin* mt. 23 EDF   mt. 23] om. F   1242 cuminum] ciminum DHF   reliquistis] HF, relinquitis ED   misericordiam] et *canc.* misericordiam E

et fidem, 'þei chargide moche litil þingis, as tiþing of myntis, anctt and comyn, and leften', as Crist seiþ, 'þo þingis of þe lawe þat were more to charge, as merci, iugement and feiþ.' Doen not oure þe 1245 same? Haue not oure more charge in a rite of Salisberi vss or of anoþir, þat þei bynden hem⸀silf⸃ to, ybrokun or ykept, þan þei han in þe ten comaundementis?– or in symony, or vsurie, or in alle þo heresies þat ben aȝens þe feiþ, of þe which I spak bifore? And hou vnmerciful þei ben þei | shewen in dede. For al þat euere þei mai of f. 52ʳ worldli goodis þei scrapan into her corbanan, and þerwiþ lyuen as 1251 worldli, lordli, as ony kyngis or duykis; and to þe pore blynde, feble and lame þei ȝyuen wel nyȝ riȝt nouȝt, notwiþstondinge þat þei seien þat her goodis ben suche pore mennes goodis; and vndir colour of releuyng of suche pore men, þese goodis ben ȝoue into 1255 her conuen[ti]clis. And hou cruel þei ben to þe peple in goostli almesse þei shewen opunli ynow, in þat þat þei hiden þe breed of Goddis word so streitli fro þe hungri peple. Ȝhe, it doiþ hem ful moche harm, and moche þei grucchen, if ony nedi man haue so moche of þis breed, þat he vndirstonde his Pater noster in his 1260 modir tunge. And so, as þe [cursid] confederacie of þe oold lawe closide þe kyngdom of heuene bifore þe peple (þat is to seie, as Crisostum seiþ, þe knowing of God|dis lawe), so doiþ þis cursid f. 52ᵛ conspiracie aȝen Crist in þe newe lawe. And wite þei wel þat þe same Crist, þat wisshide wo to þat confederacie (þe which wo, as þe 1265 Maistir of Stories seiþ, is euerlasting dampnacioun), wisshiþ effectuali þe same wo to oure conspiratours, þat þus conspiren aȝens him and his gospel in oure daies. þei putten Crist out of her synagogis, and curside him and hise fautours; and oure enmyes of Crist specified aboue han now don þe same maner of malice, but 1270 moche more crueli as it is in partie toold bifore. And þus biþenke

---

1243 chargide moche] set moche by F   anett] and anes F   1244 þo] thos F
1245 more to] of F   doen . . . bifore (1249)] *om.* F   1248 þo] þe H
1250 of] gett of F   1251 into] it into F   1252 lordli] as lordly F   kyngis]
oþir kyngis HF   or] and F   1255 into] to F   1256 conuenticlis]
conuenclis E   1258 ful] *om.* F   1260 vndirstonde] vndurstondith F
1261 cursid] DHF, first E   1262 of heuene] *om.* F   1263 seiþ]
reportythe F   1264 aȝen crist] *om.* HF   wite þei wel] knowe ye sure F   þe
same] *om.* F   1265 þat¹] ⸀which⸃ F   þat²] þe F   1266 stories] þe stories F
1267 effectuali] also F   1268 putten] ded put F   1269 curside] cursen H
1271 partie] part F   bifore] afore F   biþenke þee] remembyr yow F

þee wiþ bisy studie what maner malice was practisid aȝens Crist bi bishops, scribis and religiouse in tyme of his bodili presence here; and þe same malice in kynde þou shalt fynde, ȝhe, uphepid in oure 1275 bishops, religiouse and kunnynge men of þat manglid lawe þat I | f. 53ʳ spak of bifore.

And as þe peple of Israel was worst gouerned vndir her prestis, whan þe gouernaunce was come hool[li] into her hondis, and vndir þat gouernaunce camen into her moost confusioun, and losten þe 1280 hooli lond for euere, so ben now cristen rewmes foul confoundid bi þe worldli gouernaunce and lordship þat þe prestis han take upon hem; and alwei as þei geten more and more of þis, so to more confusioun drawen cristen rewmes. And þis is soþe of worldli shenship, whoso takiþ bisy heede, and as wiþ Goddis help it shal 1285 be more opunli shewid herafter. But þis is moost sorwe and ruþe, and wiþoute ceessyng to be biwope and birewid, þei ben licli to putte þe peple of cristendom out of þe pure feiþ and lawe of Crist, as þei han now in greet partie and it were wel asaied, and so to make þe f. 53ᵛ peple to leese þe lond of heuene for euere, þe which is | figurid bi þe 1290 hooli lond þat þe Iewis loste for lesse malice wrouȝt aȝens Crist þan oure conspiratours worchen now. For þat þat þe Iewis diden aȝens Crist was bi vnkunnyngnesse, as seint Petir seiþ; and þat þat oure prestis doen is of pure studied malice. And seculer lordis han no grace to se þis malice of þe prestis, neþer for to se hou a litil and a 1295 litil þei han vndirmyned hem, and ben in poynt to ouerþrowe hem and to vndo her astaat. For þei han almoost sliȝli ypikid out þe material swerd, wiþ þo þingis þat perteynen þerto, out of þe hondis of [þe] seculer lordis, and so ferforþ þat þei han wrouȝt to her vndoing.

1300   For þou shalt vndirstonde here, for to haue þe more cleerli my menyng, þat, whanne Crist ȝide aȝens hise enmyes þat tooken him, he hadde in his cumpany two swerdis and þat as he himsilf seide was f. 54ʳ ynow, for to do þe Iewis to vndirstonde bi þe | puruyaunce of þo swerdis þat her malice was not vnknowun to him. For þis was a skill, 1305 as seynt Austin seiþ, whi he hadde þese swerdis in his cumpany. And þese two swerdis weren also ynow to figure þe two swerdis of Cristis chirche, þat is to seie þe material swerd, of þe which seynt Poul spekiþ (ad Ro. 13), and þe spiritual swerd, of þe which he spekiþ. For þese skilis þanne Crist hadde þo two swerdis in his cumpany, 1310 and not þat he or ony of his meyne wolde or shulde fiȝte wiþ þo. In tokenyng herof, whanne Petir drowe his ⌜swerd⌝ and wolde fiȝte,

And þus whoso biþenkiþ hym what maner malyce was practisid a3ens Criste by bischopis and scribis and religious in tyme of his bodily presence here, þe same malice in kynde | he schal fynde, 3he, vphepid in oure byschopis and religious.   f. 13ᵛ
246

And as þe peple of Israel wern werste gouernyd vndir her prestis, whan þe gouernance was commen holy into her hondis, and vndir þat gouernance come in her mooste confusion, and losten þe holy londe for euer, so ben now cristen rewmys foule confoundid by   250
worldly gouernaunce and lordeschip þat prestis han take vpon hem; and alwey as þai getyn more and more of þis, so to more confusion drawen cristen rewmys.

1272 wiþ . . . studie] *om.* F   malice] of malyc' F   1274 kynde] maner F uphepid] and more F   1275 manglid] menglyd F   1278 hoolli] DHF, holy L, hool E   1279 camen] þei came F   1282 þis] þis wordly covityse F 1283 is soþe] trueth F   1284 shenship] possessions F   and] *om.* F 1286 wiþoute ceessyng] alway F   biwope and birewid] mornyd and lamentyd F   þei] for they F   licli] like F   1288 and¹] if F   asaied] lokyd vpon F 1278 þe²] *om.* F   1290 wrou3t] wrowght þei F   1291 conspiratours] conspiracie DHF   worchen] worchiþ DHF   þat²] wich F   1292 vnkunnyngnesse] ignoranc' F   þat²] wich F   1293 studied] studye of F   1296 to] *om.* F sli3li ypikid] goten F   1297 þo] thos F   þerto] þervnto F   1298 þe] DHF, *om.* E   þat] ⌐þat⌐ D, *om.* HF   1299 vndoing] vndoyng but yf god of his gracius and endlis goodnes put to his hond and support þes lordis þei schuld neuer recouer it F 1301 3ide] went F   1303 ynow] sufficient F   for to do] to certyfye F   to vndirstonde] *om.* F   þo] thos F   1304 to] vnto F   skill] reson F 1305 *margin* in de questionibus veteris et noue legis ED, *in text after* seiþ HF   *margin* aug. HF   þese] þos F   and] and also F   1306 also] ⌐also⌐ H, *om.* F 1308 *margin* (ad D) ro. 13 EDF   and] in the epystle ad romanos and F   of þe] *om.* F spekiþ] spekiþ, *margin* dh eph. vj H, *margin* F   spekyth of in þe epistle ad ephesios F 1309 for] ⌐17 ca.⌐ For F   skilis] causys F   þanne] *om.* F   þo] than þes F 1310 meyne] compeny F   þo] thos F   1311 tokenyng] tokene D   herof] w *canc.* herof E

Crist blamede him, and seide 'Turne þi swerd into his place!' And if
Crist wolde not fiȝte in sauacioun of his owne liif, ne wolde suffre
hise apostlis to fiȝte for sauacioun of her maistris liif þat was an
1315 innocent man, hou dar he þat cleymeþ to be Cristis viker in erþe and
f. 54ᵛ þe successour of seynt Pe|tir, drawe þe material swerd þat was
forfendid him in Petir, and kille þerwiþ giltles cristen peple for to
conquere to him so worldli lordship, þe which Crist haþ so expresli
in word and in dede forfendid him? Truli, I can not deuyse me hou
1320 þat he and alle suche myȝten be more contrariouse to Crist þan þei
ben. But þou shalt vndirstonde here þat Petir in manye þingis þat he
dide and seide, ⌐and⌐ in many þingis þat weren seid to him of Crist,
figuride Cristis chirche, as seint Austyn seiþ ⌐De verbis Domini 13⌐
and in many oþir placis. And into euydence of þis, as Cristis chirche
1325 haþ a name fourmed of Crist in þat þat þei ben callid cristen, so
Crist formede a name to Petir of his owne name and callide him bi
þis name Petrus, þe which name is fourmed of þis name petra, þe
which is a name of Crist. þanne Cristis chirche, þus figurid bi Petir,
f. 55ʳ haþ þo two swerdis þat I spak of | riȝt now; and in good gouernaunce
1330 of þese swerdis stondiþ þe prosperite of Cristis chirche. And so Crist
wolde þat þese two swerdis weren in her kyndli placis, and nameli þe
material or temperal swerd, þe which bi Goddis lawe, boþe oold and
newe, as we mai se bi þe processe of þe book of Numeri and of þe
Kyngis, and bi seynt Poulis wordis (Ro. 13), þe whiche I reherside
1335 bifore, is asigned to þe lay peple and speciali to þe seculer lordis as to
his owne kyndli place. And also in þat þat Crist forfendide þe prest
Petir, and in him alle oþir prestis, to fiȝte wiþ þis swerd, he dide us
to vndirstonde þat it was his will þat þis swerd wiþ hise purtynauncis
shulde abide as in his place, in þe lay partie of his chirche.

1314 an] om. F   1317 forfendid] forbydden F   1318 lordship] a
lordschype F   þe] om. F   expresli] straytly F   1319 in²] om. HF
forfendid] forbyden F   me] om. F   1320 be more] rev. HF   1323 de . . .
13] DHF, in margin marked for insertion E   13] sermo xiij DH, sermone 13 F
1325 a] þe F   þat þat] þat H, so moche as F   cristen] cristen men F
1327 þis¹] his HF   þe¹&²] om. F   1328 cristis chirche] crist is F   bi] om. F
1329 haþ] and hathe F   þo] DH, canc. E, þes F   riȝt now] before F
1331 nameli] specially F   1332 þe] om. F   bi] he by F   1333 margin
numeri/ regum/ r. 13 F   1334 Ro. 13] om. F   Ro.] ad romanos DH   þe] om. F
1335 is] as I H, haith F   to¹] it to F   1336 þat þat] þat canc. þat H, so moche
þat F   forfendide] forbade F   1337 swerd] temporall sword F   dide] schewyd
vnto F   1338 to vndirstonde] playnly F   purtynauncis] purtynance F
1339 as] om. HF   of] in F

1340   And in as moche as Crist seide þese wordis to alle men: *Reddite que*
f. 55ᵛ *sunt Cesaris Cesari, et que sunt Dei Deo* (*Luc.* 20), 'Ʒildiþ to Cesar | þo
þingis þat ben of Cesar, and to God þo þingis þat ben of God', he
confermede to þe lay partie þis swerd wiþ hise purtynauncis, in þe
persoone of Cesar, in whom þat tyme was cheefli þis swerd wiþ alle
1345   þe temperaltees þat longen þerto. And certis, I drede me not þat þe
lay partie of þe chirche, and nameli þe lordis, han as moche or more
colour of þe first partie of þis text to chalenge oonli to hem þe
temperal swerd wiþ hise purtynauncis þat longen þerto, as seculer
possessiouns and lordships, seculer iugement and seculer office, as
1350   oure prestis han euydence of þe secunde part of þis text to chalenge
þe tiþis of þe peple, as þingis oonli longinge to hem. And if þei were
indifferent in her iugementis, as þei demen þat it is wrong and
dampnable a seculer man to take upon him a prestis office, in
preching or mynystringe of sacramentis, and in disposinge of tiþis
f. 56ʳ þat were | lymytid to þe staat of clergie, so þei shulde deme it ful
1356   dampnable a prest to ocupie þis temporal swerd wiþ þe purtynauncis
þat longen þerto specified bifore. And in ful witnesse þat þis is ful
dampnable in þe staat of presthod, Crist, in whom is ful ensaumple
and loore of perfeccioun of presthod, fledde alle þese þingis and
1360   tauʒte hise apostlis and alle prestis to do þe same. Hou he fledde þe
vss of þis swerd and tauʒte hise apostlis to do so I tolde riʒt now; and
hou he avoidide seculer lordships þat is anexid to þis swerd I haue
toold bifore. And seculer offices he forsook, and tauʒte hise prestis to
do þe same, whanne he fledde fro þe peple þat wolde haue sett him
1365   in þe office of a kyng. And whanne he was requirid to haue ʒoue
iugement bitwene two briþeren stryuynge for eritage, he wolde not
f. 56ᵛ ʒyue þat seculer ⌐iugement⌐, but seide to him *Homo quis me* | *constituit*
iudicem aut diuisorem super vos?, 'Man, who made me a iuge or a
departer upon ʒou?' And so he avoidide þis swerd, and lefte it to þe
1370   temporal part of þe chirche wiþ alle hise purtynauncis.
   And þis same lessoun tauʒte hise apostlis, for seynt Poul asigneþ
þis swerd to þe seculer lordis, as it is ofte seid bifore (*ad Ro.* 13), and

1340 *margin* luc. 20 EDFL   1341 luc.20] *after* men (1340) H, *om.* FL   ʒildiþ]
gyfe F   þo] thos F   1342 þo] thos F   1343 hise] þe HF   purtynauncis]
purtynance FL   1345 certis] suerly F   drede me] fer F   1346 and . . .
lordis] *om.* F   1347 colour] autoryte F   1348 purtynauncis] pertynanc' F
1349 and²] or D   1350 oure] oþer F   part] party FL   1351 to] vnto F
1352 demen] iuge F   1353 a¹] þat a F   man] *om.* F   1354 of¹] þe D
1355 deme] iuge F   1356 purtynauncis] pertynanc' FL   1357 specified] as it
is *canc.* specified E   1359 loore] law F   1360 hou] as F   1361 so] so

And for Crist wolde not þat prestis schulde haue sychc worldly
gouernance, he saiþ to alle men: *Reddite que sunt Cesaris Cesari, et que* 255
sunt Dei Deo, 'Зeldiþ to Cesar þo þingis þat ben of Cesar, and to God
þo | þingis þat ben of God', confermynge to þe seculer party of þe f. 14ʳ
chirche þe material swerde wiþ his purtenance, in þe persone of
Cesar, in whom þat tyme was chefly þis swerde wiþ alle þe
temperaltes þat longen þerto. And certis, I drede not but þat þe 260
seculer party of þe chirche, and namely þe lordis, han als myche or
more coloure of þe firste party of þis texte to chalenge oonly to hem
þe temporal swerde wiþ his purtenances þat longeþ þerto, as seculer
lordeschipis wiþ seculer iugement and seculer offyce, as oure prestis
han euydence of þe secunde party of þis tixte to chalenge þe tiþis of 265
þe peple, as þingis oonly longynge to hem. And if þai wer
indifferent, as þai demen þat it is wronge and | dampnable a seculer f. 14ᵛ
man to take vpon hym a prestis office, in prechynge or minystrynge
of sacramentis, and in disposynge of tiþis þat weren lymyted to þe
state of þe clergy, so þai schulden deme it full dampnable a prest to 270
ocupie þe temporal swerde wiþ þe purtenance þat longiþ þerto
specified tofore. And in full witnes þat þis lordeschip is dampnable
in þe state of presthode, Crist, in whom is full ensaumple and lore of
perfeccyon of presthode, fled all þes þingis, for he auoidid þis swerde
in seculer office, and tauзte his apostles, and in hem alle oþer prestis, 275
to do þe same whan he fled fro þe peple þat wolde han sett hym in þe
office of a kynge. And whan he was requirid to зeue iugement
bitwene two breþern | stryuynge for heritage, he wolde not зeue þat f. 15ʳ
seculer iugement, but saide *Homo quis me constituit iudicem aut
diuisorem super vos?*, 'Man, who made me a iuge or a departer vpon 280
зou?' And so he auoidid þis swerde, and left it to þe temporal party
of his chirche wiþ all þe purtenances.

And þis same lesson tauзte þe apostle, for saynt Poule assigneþ þis
swerde to þe seculer lordis, as it is saide bifore, and techiþ men to

---

255 *margin* luc' xxº L   279 *margin* luc' xij L   284 *margin* Thimo. ij et vj L

ʳasˈ H, þe same as F   riзt now] yow afore F   1362 lordships] lordship HF
haue told] told yow F   1363 offices] office HF   1365 in] in // in F
1366 iugement] iugementis HF   1367 *margin* luc. 12 EDFL, *in text* H
1369 departer] devyder F   1370 part] partye FL   1371 þis . . . apostlis]
tauзt his apostles þis same F   lessoun] *om.* H   asigneþ] asigned H
1372 þis] þe F   as it . . . seid] in many placis as I haue schewid yow F   *margin* 1 (ad
DHF) thi. 2 et eiusdem 6 (5 D) ad eph. 6 et ad Titum 3 ED, *in text* HF *after* 13, *adding*
1 pet. 2 F, et prima petri ij c, *margin* Thimo. ij et vj Ephe. vj Titum iij L

techiþ men to preie first fo⌐r suche⌐ men, þat þe peple mai lede a
pesible liif vndir hem, and techiþ cristen men to obeie to hem,
1375 wheþer þei ben cristen or heþen, ȝhe alþouȝ þei ben triuauntis. And
seynt Petir techiþ þe same lessoun and biddiþ þe peple to obeie to þe
kyng, as to him þat is passynge oþir, and to duykis, as to þo þat ben
sent of þe kyng into þe veniaunce of schrewis and preisyng of goode
men. And, as touchinge þis seculer lordship, seynt Petir techiþ hou
f. 57ʳ þer shulde be no lordis in þe clergie; and | þis word most ⌐nedis⌐ be
1381 vndirstondun of seculer lordship, þe which was brouȝt yn bi þe
heþen, þe which Crist his mastir bifore forfendide al his clergie. For
man loste þe kyndeli lordship bi þe first synne, and lordship bi grace
upon creaturis is forfendid to no man. And worldli office or bisynesse
1385 seynt Poul forfendiþ al þe staat of presthod, þe which speciali wiþ þe
swerd of ⌐þe word of⌐ God shulde conquere þe peple out of þe power
of þe deuel. For of þis seynt Poul writiþ þus to Thymothe þe prest,
and in him to alle prestis (2 ad Thi. 2): Labora sicut bonus miles Christi
Iesu. Nemo militans Deo implicat se negociis secularibus, 'Trauele þou as
1390 a good knyȝt of Iesu Crist. No man fiȝting to Godward encumbriþ
himsilf in seculer bisynesses.' And so no man, þat is verili of þis staat
and fiȝtiþ truli to Godward, entrikiþ himsilf in seculer lordship, for |
f. 57ᵛ þat is moost seculer office or bisynesse þat is in þis world. And so he
þat ocupieþ moost seculer lordship seculerli is moost encumbrid, or
1395 wrappid and entrikid in worldli office, as emperours and kyngis
moost, and oþir lordis aftir þe proporcioun of her worldli lordship,
ben more or lesse þus ywoundun in worldli office or bisynessis. Ȝhe,
alþouȝ þei liggen lame in her bed and doen her office bi her
mynystris, ȝit ben þei not exempt fro such worldlynesse as long as
1400 þei ocupien þat staat. And as touching seculer iugement seynt Poul
blamede cristen peple bicause þei fel so fro perfeccioun þat þei wolde
ony suche iugementis haue among hem, and askide hem whi þei
suffride not raþer wrongis; and upon þis he comaundiþ þe peple þat,
if þei haue ony seculer iugementis among hem, þat þei shulde
1405 ordeyne upon suche domes þe more vnworþi of þe peple for to
f. 58ʳ deme suche worldli | causis. And of þis þou maist wel se þat it was
not seynt Poulis will, no more þan it was Cristis, þat prestis shulde
be seculer iugis.
    Off þis processe þanne þou maist se here hou þat Crist and hise
1410 apostlis in lyuyng and in teching, þe which teching is hooli writt,
tauȝten þat prestis shulden leue and vttirli forsake þis temperal
swerd wiþ hise purtynauncis, and remitte þis temperal swerd to lay

pray firste for suche men þat þe peple mai lede a pesablc liifc vndir 285
hem. And he techiþ cristen men to obey to hem, whedir þai ben
cristen or heþen, ȝe allþouȝ þai ben tirawntes. And saynt Petir techiþ
þe same lesson and biddi[þ] þe peple to obey to þe kynge, as to hym
þat is passynge | oþer, and to duykys, as to þo þat ben sent of þe f.15ᵛ
kynge into þe vengance of schrewis and preysynge of goode men. 290
And, as touchynge þis seculer lordeschip, saynt Petir techiþ how þer
schulde be no lordis in þe clergy; and þis worde most nedis be
vndirstonden of seculer lordeschip, þe whiche Criste his maister
bifore forfendid to alle his clergi.

285 *margin* Ephe' vj   Titum iij L   287 *margin* 1 pet^i ij L   288 biddiþ]
biddid L   291 *margin* 1 pet^i v L

[*Lambeth Tract resumes on p. 65*]

1373 men]   DHFL,   seculer   men   E   1374 cristen]   cristenyd   F
1375 triuauntis] tyrauntis HFL   1376 *margin* 1 pe. 2 ED,   petri ij L, petrus F
1377 passynge] above F   þo] thos F   1378 schrewis] cursyd pepyll F
1381 lordship] lordis DHF   þe^1] *om.* F   1382 þe] *om.* F   bifore forfendide]
forbyd   befor   F   1384 forfendid]   forbydden   F   and]   but   F
1385 forfendiþ] forbyde to F   þe²] *om.* F   speciali] specially and alonly F
1386 shulde] schal F   1388 prestis] oþer preastis and sayd F   *margin* 2 (ad D)
thi. 2 EDF   2 ad Thi. 2] *om.* F   2²] ij c and seiþ H   1390 Iesu crist] *rev.* DF
crist] *om.* H   encumbriþ] may encombyr F   1391 in] wiþ F   bisynesses]
busynes F   1392 entrikiþ] foldyth F   1393 þat^1] truly it F   moost] þe
most F   þis] the F   1394 or . . . entrikid (1395)] *om.* F   1396 moost] most
specially F   lordis] worldli lordis HF   lordship] lordschypys F   1397 ben] be
it F   ywoundun] yboundun H, thei be bownd F   bisynessis] busynes F
1400 *margin* i cor. 6 per magnum processum ED, *see* 1406 HF   1402 ony] haue
ony F   haue] *om.* F   1403 not] no F   wrongis] wrong DH   comaundiþ]
commandyd F   1404 haue] had F   þat þei] thei F   1405 domes]
judgementis F   1406 deme] judge F   causis] Paulus 1 cor. vj c° per magnum
processum H, *margin* 1 cor.6 F   þou maist] yow may F   wel se] *rev.* D
1407 cristis] cristis wyll F   1409 þou maist] yow may F   1410 in²] *om.* HF
þe] *om.* F   is] *twice* D   writt] scriptur F   1411 tauȝten] wyche teachith F
1412 purtynauncis] purtynanc' F   remitte] commytt F   lay] þe lay HF

partie, as þei diden wiþ alle hise purtynauncis, as seculer lordship, office and iugement. For siþ þe prestis of þe oold lawe kepten hem
1415 fro þis lordship, as her lawe tauȝte hem, and also þe iugis dide þe same, hou moche raþer shulde oure prestis do so, þat ben boundun to þat perfeccioun bi ⌐þe⌐ same lawe, and also bi expresse doctryn of Crist in word and dede as it is shewid bifore?

And as touchinge þe iugis in þe oold lawe, it is no doute þei knewe
1420 þis lordship so vnperfit and so expresse aȝens þe plesaunce of God |
f. 58ᵛ þat þei hadde a manere of abhominacioun or a loþing þerof; and þerfore opunli þei [quytte] hemsilf, and shewide þat þei were not gilti of ony such inperfeccioun or such lordship upon þe peple, as we mai rede of þe firste and þe laste iuge upon Israel, Moises and
1425 Samuel, and ⌐of⌐ þe good iuge Gedeon þat was bitwene hem two. For Moyses excusiþ hymsilf of such lordship in witnesse and presence of þe peple: for, whanne weiward folk putten upon Moyses þat he wolde be a lord upon hem, he seide þus: *Tu scis, Domine, quod nec asellum quidem vmquam acceperim ab eis, nec afflixerim quempiam*
1430 *eorum,* 'Lord, þou woost truli þat I haue not take of hem a litil asse, ne turmentid or wrongfulli trauelid ony of hem',—as kyngis and oþir seculer lordis doen ofte her sugetis, for þei han power upon her bodies and her goodis, as it is writun I *Regum* 8. And in þe same book 12 cᵒ Samuel declariþ himsilf to be giltes of þis vnperfit worldli
1435 lordship upon þe peple, bi witnesse of God and of þe kyng, and of þe peple þat he hadde be iuge upon, where he spekiþ þus to þe peple:
Loquimini de me coram Domino, et coram Christo eius, vtrum bouem
f. 59ʳ *cuiusquam tule|r[i]m, aut asinum: si quempiam calumpniatus sum, si oppressi aliquem, si de manu cuiusquam munus accepi; et contempnam*
1440 *illud hodie, restituamque vobis.* [*Et*] *dixerunt: 'Non es calumpniatus nos, neque oppressisti, neque tulisti de manu alicuius quippiam'*, 'Speke ȝe to me bifore þe Lord, and bifore þe Crist of him (or þe anointid of

1413 þei] crist and his apostles F   hise] þe F   purtynauncis] partynanc' F
1414 and] of F   siþ] seyng F   1417 also] morouer F   expresse] open F
1419 and] ⌐18 ca.⌐ And F   it] þer F   1420 expresse] manifest F   plesaunce]
pleasur F   1421 a] in F   of] *om.* F   or a loþing] and abhorryng F
1422 þeiⁱ] *om.* H   quytte] DHF, comittide E   1425 þe] *om.* D
1426 excusiþ] excusyd F   1427 weiward] frowerd F   1428 þus] *om.* F
margin num. 16 EDF, *in text* H   1430 woost] knowist F   1431 ne . . .
trauelid] nor beatyn wrongfully F   1432 her] to þer F   1433 and . . . goodis]
om. F   1434 book 12 cᵒ] xij F   12] þe xij D   declariþ] declaryd F
1437 *margin* 1 r. 12 E, 1 r. 8 D   loquimini . . . quippiam (1441)] *after* 1 Regum 8 (1433)
ED   domino] deo H   1438 tulerim] DF, tuleram EH   quempiam]
quemquam H   1440 et] DHF, *canc.* E   1441 speke] spekiþ H, this is to
say spek F   1442 of himⁱ] *om.* F   anointid] oyntyd F

him), wher I took an oxe of ony man, or an asse, if I falsli chalengide ony man, if I oppresside ony man; if I took ʒift of þe hond of ony man, I shal dispise or forsake it todai, and I shal restore it to ʒou. 1445 And þe peple bar witnesse wiþ him and seiden: "þou hast not falsly chalengid us, neþer oppressid, neþer þou hast take ony þing of þe hond of | ony man." And Samuel seide to hem: "þe Lord is witnesse f. 59ᵛ aʒens ʒou, and his Crist is witnesse in þis dai, for ʒe han not foundun ony þing in myn hond."' þus þanne, bi witnesse of God and of þe 1450 kyng Saul and al þe peple, ful opunli þis ⌐prophete⌐ excuside him þat he was no þing gilti of such lordship upon þe peple, as þei brouʒten yn upon hemsilf, in þat þat þei chosen ⌐hem⌐ a kyng, þe which manere of lordship haþ þe staat of clergie takun upon hem now.

And of Gedeon, þat was also a iuge upon Israel, we mai rede in 1455 Iudicum 8 hou þat, aftir tyme þat God hadde wrouʒt a greet victorie upon þe enemyes of Israel bi þis man Gedeon, alle þe men of Israel seiden to þis Gedeon: 'Dominare tu nostri, et filius tuus, et filius filii tui: quia liberasti nos de manu Madian.' Quibus ille ait: 'Non dominabor vestri, nec dominabitur in vobis filius meus, set dominabitur vobis 1460 Dominus', ' "Haue þou lordship upon us, and þi sone, and þi sones sone, bi cau|se þou hast delyuered us fro þe hond of Madian." And f. 60ʳ he answerde hem þus: "I shal not haue lordship of ʒou, neþer my sone, but þe Lord shal haue lordship of ʒou."' Lo, of þis processe þou maist se hou loþe þe trewe iugis, þat God hadde sett upon his 1465 peple, hadde be to haue take þis worldli lordship upon her briþeren, and hou loþe þei were for to haue be foundun in ony wise gilti þerof. And no man shulde doute here but þat þese men myʒte haue take þis lordship vpon hem wiþ moche lesse offence of God þan mai oure clergie now; for þei [ben] of more perfit staat, and þis lordship is now 1470 forfendid oure clerkis bi a lawe and a mynystre of þe lawe, þat is to seie Crist and his gospel, þe whiche ben wiþout mesure more perfit þan Moyses and þe oold lawe.

1443 an] ony HF   if . . . man¹ (1444)] om. F   1445 I²] om. F   1448 is witnesse] witnesith F   1452 upon] of HF   1453 þe] om. F   1455 in] om. HF   1456 tyme] þe tyme F   margin iudicum 8 EDF   1458 gedeon] man gedeon F   filius filii] filij HF   1460 vestri] om. F   1461 haue] þat is to say haue F   sones sone] sonnys F   1462 hond] hondys F   1464 lord] lord god F   lo] om. F   1465 þou maist] yow may F   loþe] om. F   hadde] ded F   1466 hadde . . . haue] wold not F   1467 haue] om. F   in . . . gilti] gylty by ony means F   1468 shulde] schall F   1469 of] to HF   1470 ben] DHF, weren E   more] a more HF   staat] astate F   1471 forfendid] forbydden F   a²] by a F   1472 þe] om. F   mesure] comparison F   1473 lawe] lawe was F

And here I merueile in my wittis, and þe more I muse here þe
f. 60ᵛ more I merueile hou | þe staat of þe clergie, þat is boundun to
1476 perfeccioun of þe gospel, and nameli þe religiouse folk, þat boosten
hou þei perfourmen þat perfeccioun, moun for shame take upon hem
to be þus lordis, þe which manere of lyuyng, alþou3 God suffre it, is
so vnperfit and so fer fro perfeccioun of kynde þat God my3te not
1480 ordeyne it in his chirche, oold ne newe, or ellis þat þei take upon
hem þat oþir vicious extremyte þat I spak of, þat is to seie beggerie,
a3ens þe which God made ful ordynaunce in boþe hise lawis þat it
shulde not be in his chirche. Siþ þanne þat þis lordship of þe clerkis
is so opunli a3ens þe will of God shewid in boþe hise lawis, and so
1485 offendiþ God deedli, and euer shal whilis it duriþ, it were tyme þat
Cristis chirche took heede to Cristis wordis, þe which he spak to
f. 61ʳ Petir figuringe þis chirche, and | seide 'Turne þi swerd into his
place'; as þou3 Crist wolde seie þus: 'þou my chirche, figurid bi
Petre, se hou þe material swerd [wiþ hise purtynauncis] is out of his
1490 place; [þerfore] do as I comaunde þee and turne þi swerd into his
place—3he! turne þou þis swerd wiþ hise purtynauncis, as seculer
lordships, seculer office and seculer iugement, into þe staat of seculer
lordis or of lay men, as I haue ordeyned.' And certis, but if þe
chirche of Crist heere effectuali þis word of Crist shal it neuere
1495 stonde in redi rule, ne aftir þe plesaunce of God. And dredeles þe lay
peple, and nameli þe lordis, shulde take heede ful tendirli to þis vois
of Crist, for þis apostasie of þe clergie wole not oonli be cause of
dampnacioun of þese ypocritis, but also of alle þo þat mai amende
þis vnrulynesse among þese apostatas and doen not; as seynt Poul
f. 61ᵛ techiþ | (ad Ro. 1). And þe lordis shulde wiþ bisi studie considere
1501 þese here þat, al so long as þe clergie stondiþ in þis dampnable
apostasie fro Crist and his lawe, and is encumbrid in þo two viciouse
extremytees þat I haue spokun of, þei doen no dede þat is aceptable
or worþi meede in blis. For dedis þat ben good in kynde, as praier,

---

1474 in . . . wittis] *om.* F   1475 þe²] *om.* D   þat] wich F
1476 perfeccioun] þe perfeccioun HF   nameli] specialli F   boosten] boost and crak F
1477 perfourmen . . . perfeccioun] per/ʳformen perˑfeccioun H   þat] *om.* F
1478 þus lordis] lordis on this maner F   þe] *om.* F   1479 my3te] wold F
1480 ne] nor F   1481 þat¹] þe F   vicious] abhominabyll and vicius F
1482 hise] thes F   1483 siþ] seyng F   1485 shal] it shalt, -t *canc.* D
whilis] as long as F   duriþ] contynuith F   were] is hey F   1486 took] tak F
to¹] of F   þe] *om.* F   1487 þis] his F   1488 þou] þou3 H   figurid] DL,
be *canc.* figurid E, be figurid HF   1489 þe] þis D   wiþ hise purtynauncis]
DHFL, *om.* E   1490 þerfore] DHFL, and E   þi] þis DL   1491 3he] *om.* F
wiþ] wich be of þe spiritualty wiþ F   purtynauncis] purtynancˑ F   as] þat is to say F

Siþ þan þat þis lordeschip of þe clerkis is so openli aȝens þe will of 295
God schewid in boþe his lawis, and so þai offenden God deedly and
euer schulen while it duriþ in hem, it wer tyme þat Cristis chirche
toke hede to Cristis wordis, þe whiche he spak to Petir figurynge þis
chirche, and saide 'Turne þe swerde into his place'; as þouȝ Criste |
wolde say þus: 'þou my chirche, figurid bi Petir, se how þe material f. 16ʳ
swerde wiþ his purtenances is owte of his place; þerfor do as I 301
commaundid þe and turne þis swerde into his place wiþ his
purtenancis, as seculer lordeschipis, seculer office, and seculer
iugement, into þe seculer arme of my chirche as I haue ordeyned.'
And certis, but if þe chirche here effectualy þis worde of Criste, schal 305
it neuer stonde in redy rule, ne aftir þe plesance of God. And þerfore
lordis schulden take hede full tendirly to þis voyce of Criste þat saiþ
'Turne þis swerde aȝeyne into his place', forwhi þis apostasie of þe
clergie will not oonly be cause of dampnacion of hemsiilfe, but also of
alle | þo þat mai amende þis and done not. For saynt Poule saiþ 'He f. 16ᵛ
is not oonly worþi deþ þat doþe yuel þingis, but also he þat 311
consentiþ to þe doer.' Forsoþe, alle þo consenten þat done not her
power to amende syche defawtis. And þerfore no man may putt
anoþer grounde bisidis þat þat is putt, þe whiche is Criste Ihesu.

---

310 *margin* Ro. pᵒ L

seculer lordships] ʳseculere lordschipʳ H   1492 lordships] lordeschype F
1493 I haue] our sayuor crist haith F   certis] for a suerty F   but if] except F
1494 effectuali] affectuusly F   shal it] *rev.* F   1495 redi rule ne] a pure and
parfyte way F   plesaunce] pleasur' F   God] allmyghty god F   dredeles] suerly F
1496 nameli] specially F   to] of F   1497 cause] the cause F
1498 dampnacioun] þe dampnation F   þo] them F   mai] may or schuld F
1500 ad Ro. 1] *margin* FL   1501 þese] þis DH, well F   1502 crist] our
sauiour crist F   encumbrid] infectyd F   in þo] wiþ þes F   1503 haue spokun]
spak HF   doen] can do F   1504 meede] of reward F   blis] þe blys etarnall F
dedis] þe dedis F   good] doen HF   praier] meke prayer F

1505 sacrifice, fasting or almesse, or ony suche oþir, ben not meedful
wiþout charite, þe which charite stondiþ not wiþ ⌐þis⌐ dampnable
apostasie; and stondinge þis apostasie, þis peple synneþ deedli what
þat euere þei doen, for as moche as þoruȝ a dampnable sleuþe þei
contynuen in þis hidouse apostasie. And if men loþen a religiouse
1510 ypocrite and callen him apostata þat chaungiþ þe abite or þe rule þat
his synful foundour haþ bitake him, hou moche raþer shulden men
f. 62ʳ loþe suche, and calle hem | apostatas þat þus dampnabli straien awei
fro þe perfeccioun of þe gospel, to þe which, as þei seien, þei han
maad here professioun? And of þis processe men mai se þat þe clergie,
1515 and nameli þe religiouse ypocritis, blabren manye waast wordis, and
doen many oþir vein werkis as toward heuene blis. And þis I woot wel
is a trewe processe and a ruþeful, whoso wole biþenke him.

Neþeles of oo þing I preie ȝou here þat ȝe greue ȝou not, alþouȝ I
forȝete not liȝtli þis material swerd wiþ hise purtynauncis, and þat I
1520 desire bisili þat it were turned aȝen into his kyndli place where God
himsilf hadde putt it. For whanne Crist was in þe hondis of hise
enmyes, where comounli men forȝeten hemsilf and al þat þei han to
do, ȝit he biþouȝte him on þis swerd, and seide to Petir, and in him
to al his chirche, 'Turne þi swerd into his place.' And it were nede |
f. 62ᵛ þat Cristis chirche took tent to þis word bi tymes. For þis swerd wiþ
1526 hise purtynauncis mai be drawe so fer out of his place þat it wole be
impossible to brynge it into his place aȝen. For þus stondiþ it of þis
swerd in ful many londis, where clerkis han fulli þe seculer lordshipis
in her power, and is ful liik for to stonde in þe same wise wiþyn a
1530 fewe daies in Engelond, but if þe lay partie of þe English chirche
sette þe sunner hond upon þis swerd to brynge it into his kyndli
place. For wel we myȝte se, ner þe slepe of litarge þat is fallun upon
us, þat þe clergie haþ fro dai to dai more and more hond upon þis
swerd wiþ hise purtynauncis. And so þei ben licli, duringe þis sleep
1535 in þe lay partie, to pulle þis swerd out of þe lay hond sodenli, and so
to haue þe ful power þerof, as clerkis in oþir dyuerse londis han. And

1505 oþir] other work of þe faith F   1506 charite] charyte or love F   þe] om. F
dampnable] om. F   1507 þis²] þe HF   what þat euere] what so euer F
1509 in] om. H   hidouse] horrible F   loþen] hait and dyspyse F   1511 bitake
him] gevyn vnto hym F   raþer] more F   1512 loþe] hate and vtturly dyspyse F
1513 gospel] holy gospell F   1514 of] om. F   1515 nameli] specially F
religiouse] wretched F   blabren] blabyr and invent F   1516 as toward] as þei
wold optayn F   1517 trewe] very true F   and] but sore to be lamentyd and F
wole] wole wel D, wel H, wyll F   biþenke him] dylygently take hede of it F
1518 here] om. F   ȝe . . . liȝtli (1519)] yow be not movyd wiþ any prolyxite that I treate

Capitulum iiii.

Neþelesse of o þinge I pray ȝou here þat ȝe greue ȝou not, allþouȝ I 315
forȝete not liȝtly þe materiall swerde wiþ his purtenances, and þat I
desire hertly þat it wer turnyd aȝen into his kyndely place wher God
hymsiilf had putt it. For whan Crist was in þe hondis of his enmyes,
wher co|munly men forȝeten hemsiilfe and all þat þai han to do, ȝit f. 17ʳ
he byþouȝte hym on þis swerde, and saide to Petir, and in hym to all 320
his clergye, 'Turne þe swerde into his place.' And it wer nede þat
Cristis chirche toke tente to þis word by tymys. For þis swerde wiþ
his purtenance may be drawe so fer owte of his place þat it will be
vnpossible to brynge it aȝen. For þus it stondiþ of þis swerde in full
many londis, wher clerkis han fully þe seculer lordeschipis in her 325
power; and it is ful like for to stonde in þe same wise wiþin a few
ȝeris in Ynglonde, but if þe knyȝthode of þis rewme sett þe sonner
honde vpon þis swerde to brynge it into his kyndely place. For well
myȝte we se, | ner þat slepe of litergi þat is fallen vpon vs, þat þe f. 17ᵛ
clergi haþ fro day to day more and more honde vpon þis swerde wiþ 330
his purtenance. And so þai ben likly, durynge þis slepe in þe seculere
partye, to pull þis swerde owte of þe seculer honde sodenly, and so to
haue full power þerof, as clerkis in oþer dyuers londis han. And wete
lordis well þat, if þe clergi gete þis swerde oonys fully in her power,
þe seculer party may go pipe wiþ an yuy lefe for eny lordeschipis þat 335
þe clerkis will ȝeue hem aȝen! For it wer aȝens þe lawe þat þai han
made as touchynge siche lordeschipis, bi þe whiche lawe þai ben
bonden to gete into þe clergie als myche of þe possescions as þai
may, and in no caas to ȝeue eny siche | lordeschipis aȝen into þe f. 18ʳ
seculer honde; and þis lawe, as experience techiþ vs, is streytly ynouȝ 340
kepte amonge hem. For all day it is seen þat seculer men ȝeuen her
temperall possessions to þe clergi, but cowde I neuer seen ne here
þat eny siche lordeschipis wern ȝeuen aȝen to þe seculer party.

[*Lambeth Tract* resumes on p. 71]

of F   1519 wiþ] and F   1520 bisili] dylygently F   1521 hadde] ded F
crist] crist hymself F   1522 enmyes] cruell enmys F   al] all thyngis F
1523 biþouȝte] dylygently bethowght F   1524 and] ⌜19 ca.⌝ and F
1525 tent] hed F   word] *om.* F   1527 it of] *om.* F   1528 ful] *om.* F
1529 for to] to F   1530 þe english chirche] cristis churche wiþin þe englysch pale F
1531 sunner] stronger F   to] for to D   1532 myȝte] *om.* F   ner . . . litarge] by
reason of þe sloggyschnes and our sufferanc' and slowthfulnes F   1533 more and
more] layd F   1534 purtynauncis] purtenance FL   and] more and more and F
duringe . . . sleep] yf þis slepe do contynewe F   1535 þis] þe F   out] sodenly
owt F   þe²] þer F   lay] *om.* F   sodenli] *om.* F   1536 clerkis] þe clerkis HF

f. 63ʳ wite þou | wel þat, if þei gete þis oonys fulli into her power, þe lay
partie mai go pipe wiþ an iuy leef for ony lordships þat þe clerkis
wolen ȝyue hem aȝen! For, as I toold þee bifore, it were aȝens þe
1540 lawe þat þe clergie haþ maad as touchinge suche lordships, bi þe
which lawe þei ben boundun to gete into þe clergie as moche of þe
worldli possessiouns as þei mai, and in no caas to ȝyue ony of suche
lordships into þe lay hond; and þis lawe, as experience techiþ us, is
streitly ynow kept among hem. For al dai it is seyn þat lay men
1545 ȝyuen [her] temperal possessiouns to þe clergie, but coude I neuer se
ne heere þat ony suche lordships were ȝoue aȝen to þe lay partie.

And, for to loþe þe more þis swerd wiþ hise purtynauncis in þe
staat of þe clergie or of þe religiouse folk, þou shalt vndirstonde here
f. 63ᵛ þat þis se|culer lordship includiþ so moche of imperfeccioun þat
1550 euery man, er ⌐he⌐ come to blis, ȝhe, er he die, mut reney to þat
lordship. For þus grete clerkis vndirstonden þis word of Crist, where
he seiþ 'But if a man forsake or reney to alle þo þingis þat he worldli
haþ in possessioun, he mai not be my disciple.' In þe staat of
innocence it was no nede to do þis, for þat manere of lordship or
1555 possessioun þat mankynde hadde upon Goddis goodis includide
noon imperfeccioun, for þat lordship was kyndli to man aftir his
first makyng. And þus stondiþ it of þe lordship þat riȝtwise men
⌐han⌐ upon þe goodis of þis world, bi titil of grace or riȝtwisnesse,
for, as such grace or riȝtwisnesse, þe which is ground of þis lordship,
1560 ceessiþ not or dieþ not whanne þe riȝtwise man dieþ but raþer
encresiþ, so stondiþ it of þe lordship þat he haþ bi þat titil. For þis
f. 64ʳ lord|ship includiþ noon imperfeccioun ne peruertyng of mankynde.
But þe contrarie wise it stondiþ of seculer lordship, þat was brouȝt in
to mankynde aȝens þe plesaunce of God bi mannes witt, corrupt bi
1565 synne, and sumwhat fauti in alle hise werkis. And so þis lordship
includiþ imperfeccioun, contrarie to þe ful perfeccioun of mankynde

1537 wite þou] consyder F   þis] þis sword FL   power] owne power F
1538 iuy leef] myschefe F   1539 toold þee] haue sayd F   þe²] om. HF
1542 no caas] novyse F   1543 into] aȝen into L, agayn to F   hond] mennys
hondis F   us] om. F   1544 al] euery F   1545 her] DHFL, hem canc. E
to] DHFL, into E   but] but yet F   1546 ne] nor F   1547 forto loþe þe] to
abhorre F   1548 þou shalt] yow schall F   1549 includiþ] haith and
includyth F   1550 mut] must F   reney] renounce D, rene F   1552 but]
þus but F   or reney to] om. F   reney] renounce D   þo] thos F   he worldli] þe
world F   1553 my] om. D   1554 no nede] nedfull F   1555 includide]
includiþ HF   1557 stondiþ it] DHF, rev. E   þe] om. F   1558 þe] om. F
1560 not¹] om. H   or] nor F   1561 þis] his F   1562 ne] nor F
peruertyng] perueuertinge H   1564 plesaunce] pleasure F

ᵣin þe staat of innocenceᵀ or of blis, in þe which no ᵣsuchᵀ violent lordship was, shulde haue be, or shal or mai be. þerfore resonabli þis lordship shal be forsake where man fynali forsakiþ synne, and al þe occasioun þerof, and al þing þat smacchiþ of synne, and so at þe leest 1570 weie euery man mut at his deeþ dai, but if he do raþer renounce to þis vnperfit lordship þat is so fer fro innocence, þat is þe bigynnyng and eending of man.

Siþ þanne þat oure clergie, and nameli þei þat ben callid religiouse, dien as to þe world whanne þei entren into religioun, in 1575 tokenyng wherof þei renouncen alle her worldli þingis, | into fadir f.64ᵛ and modir, sistir and broþer, and wynden hem in her shroud as deed careyns euere redi to be cast into þe pitt, and þis renounsyng is, or shulde be, al so hool and as verri wiþoute ony doublenesse or symylacioun as a lay man renounciþ whanne he dieþ bodili, it 1580 were a foul abhominacioun þat such peple resume, loue and ocupie þat þing þat he haþ so vttirli renouncid and forsakun as þing moost worldli, þe which is seculer possessioun or lordship, þe which [as] I haue ofte seid bifore was brouȝt yn aȝens þe plesaunce of God, and most nedis be forsake here for þe vnperfitnesse þerof. For 1585 such oon is liik þe dogge þat seynt Petir spekiþ of *Canis reuersus ad vomitum* [*suum*], 'þe dogge turneþ aȝen to his vomyt.' And wite þou wel þat such a foul dede of a dogge mai not be so loþeli, ne so abhominable in þe siȝt of a deedli man, as is þe doyng of | suche f.65ʳ houndish ypocrite þat turneþ aȝen to worldli lordship aftir tyme þat 1590 he dieþ þus and renounciþ to þe world.

And as her abite þat is her shroud bitokeneþ þat þei ben deede, so

---

1567 þe] *om.* H   1570 smacchiþ] tastyth F   1571 mut] must F 1572 þis] his F   þat¹] which F   1573 eending] þe endyng F   1574 siþ] seyng F   nameli] specially F   1575 as to] as tuchyng F   1576 into] yee F 1577 shroud] schrowdis F   1579 al so] *om.* F   as verri] trew F 1580 symylacioun] symylacioun ᵣfayneyngᵀ H, symulation faynyng F   whanne] þe world whanne F   1581 resume] resume ᵣtake aȝenᵀ H, schuld tak agayn F   loue] love to þe world F   1582 he haþ] they haue F   vttirli] vtterly and openly F 1583 þing] þe þing HF   þe¹] *om.* F   possessioun] manere possessioun H   þe²] *om.* F   1584 as I] DHF, as *canc.* I E   seid] *twice, 2nd canc.* E   plesaunce] pleasure F   1585 for . . . liik (1586)] truly suche men as turne þis to þe world covetyng þe possessions þerof may be well lykned F   1586 þe] to þe HF   spekiþ] spek F   *margin* 2 pe. 2 EDF, *in text* H   ad] ad/ad D   1587 vomitum suum] HF, vomitum ED   wite . . . þat (1588)] truly F   1588 a¹] *om.* F   mai] is F be] to be F   loþeli] abhorryd F   ne] nor F   1590 houndish] an hundissh D, currysche F   ypocrite] ypocritis HF   turneþ] haue turnyd F   to] vnto F   tyme] þe tyme F   1591 he dieþ] thei haue dyed F   renounciþ] renowncyd F   to] *om.* F

her large tonsure or shauyng bitokeneþ her pouert and rasyng awei of alle temperal possessiouns or lordship; so þat, as newe shorun sheep
1595 þat leuen ⌐alle⌐ her flees, þei shulde leue al worldlynesse and þe occasioun þerof, þe which is cheefli worldli lordship, and wiþoute lett of worldli charge vndir þe pure perfeccioun of Crist wiþoute ony symylacioun renne liȝtli in þe weie to heueneward. But I preie þee who ben now more quik aboute þe world, and nameli aboute þis
1600 vnperfit lordship to gete it, and to kepe it, and to encreesse dai bi dai þe worldli manere of lordshiping or lordlynesse, nameli in oppressyng of her briþeren bi bondage, þe which lordship is moost aȝens
f. 65ᵛ kynde, þan | ben þese deed folk þat startlen aboute in þis world ywounde in her shroud? Or who, I preie þee, haþ more habundaunce
1605 of such lordship in affeccioun, or in affect, or in boþe þan þei þat han moost tonsure, as popis, bishops, abbotis and priours wiþ þe sectis þat þei leden? For þei ben more redi to chide, plete and striue, ȝhe, and to fiȝte also for to gete and holde such lordship þan ben oþir men, þat weren sumtyme in comparisoun of suche callid worldli
1610 men. Her cloistre is also closid strongli aboute euery weies, and opun aboue to heuenward, in tokenyng þat her lyuyng is not in þis world but in heuenli contemplacioun. But alle þese signes ben liik an hoop of iuy þat hangiþ þere where no drynk is to sille. Neþeles I woot wel þat þei wole seie here þat al her bisynesse, þat þei han here in þis
f. 66ʳ world aboute such worldli lordlynesse, as in stri|uyng, pleting,
1616 chiding and fiȝting, is for þe riȝt of hooli chirche. But certis I merueile here hou and bi whos autorite þis riȝt cam a place. For wel I woot þat God is ful lord of al þe world aboue and also of þe erþe here bineþe, as þe prophete Dauid seiþ 'þe erþe and þe plente þerof is þe
1620 Lordis.' And wel I woot þer is no lord here of þe erþe, but if he holde of him as cheef lord, and haue his lordship and holde it bi leue or autorite of þis lord God. And wel I woot, ferþermor, þat þis cheef Lord haþ ȝoue a decre upon his clergie, boþe in þe oold lawe and in þe newe, þe which he mai not reuoke, þat noon of his clergie, þe

1593 her²] om. F   1594 lordship] lordschipys F   1595 alle] om. D
flees] flesys so þat F   1596 þe] om. F   1597 crist] crist and his gospell so F
1598 renne . . . þe] dyssayt or leyng þei myght kepe þe true pathe and hey way F   þee]
yow F   1599 now more quik] more quik now marked for rev. and more canc. E,
more quyk now and more D, more quick or dyligent F   nameli] specially F
1600 daiⁱ] daly day F   1601 lordshiping] lordschipe F   or] and F   nameli]
specially F   1602 þe] om. F   1603 þese] the F   1604 ywounde]
wowndyd and wrappyd F   shroud] cowllis of ypocrisy F   þee] yow F
1606 sectis] sectis of perdicion F   1607 þei ben] who is F   to] yee or who is so
redy to F   1608 þan ben oþir] as ⌐be⌐ þes men truly moche more thei be sett vpon

Neþeles I wote well þat þe clergi will sai here þat all her bissynes, þat þai han in þis worlde abowte siche lordeschipe, as in stryuynge, 345 pletynge, chydynge and fiȝtynge, is for þe ryȝte of holy chirche. But certis it is merueyl how and by whos autorite þis riȝte cam a place. For well I wote þat God is full lorde of all þis worlde aboue and also of þe erþe bineþe, as þe prophete Dauyd saiþ *Domini est terra et plenitudo | eius,* 'þe erþe and þe plente þerof is þe Lordis.' And well I f. 18ᵛ wote þat þer is no lorde here of þe erþe, but if hc hold of hym as 351 chefe lorde, and haue his lordeschip and hold it by autorite of þis lorde God. And wel I wote, forþermore, þat þis chefe Lorde haþ ȝeue a decre vpon his clergi, boþe in þe olde lawe and in þe newe, þe whiche may not be reuokid riȝtfully, þat none of þe clergye, þe 355

þes lordschypys than were oþer men F   þan] þat D   1609 þat weren] whiche F   callid] wer called F   1610 closid] wallyd F   weies] way F 1611 tokenyng] tokynge H   1612 but²] ⌐20 ca.⌐ But F   signes] sygnes (whiche is gretly to be lamentyd) F   ben] is F   hoop] busche F   1613 where] where as F 1616 certis] truly F   1617 here] *om.* F   a place] *om.* F   1618 þe²] al þe D *margin* daiud EDH   1620 wel I woot] I am in certaynte F   þer] þat *canc.* þer E, þat þer D   1621 bi leue] bileue H, by autoryte F   1622 or] and HF autorite] leve F   þis¹] his F   wel . . . ferþermor] farthermore I am suer F 1623 decre] degre F   upon] to F   1624 þe²] *om.* F   þe³] *om.* F

1625 which is boundun bi his staat and office to sue Crist in þe perfeccioun of þe gospel, shulde ony such lord be, as it is shewid opunli bifore bi autorite of boþe þe lawis and bi ⌐þe⌐ liif of Crist and hise apostlis.

1625 sue] folow F   1626 ony] be ony F   be] *om.* F   1628 hise] of his F

379 *margin* Mt. 19 L   382 *margin* Odo in sermone Ecce nos reliquimus omnia L
386 gouernour] gouer/ L   392 *margin dh* Odo in sermone Ecce nos relinquimus
omnia L   omnia L

whiche is ybonden by his astate and office to sue Criste in þe
perfeccion of þe gospell, schulde eny siche lorde be, as it is schewid
openli before by autorite of boþe þe lawis and bi þe liife of Criste and
his apostles.

And þerfore þe holy doctoure Origene writiþ þus of goode prestis 360
and yuell: 'Wolt þu wite what difference is bitwix þe prestis | of God f. 19ʳ
and þe prestis of pharao? Pharao grawntiþ londis to his prestis;
forsoþe, God grauntiþ none partye in þe erþe to his prestis, but saiþ
"I am ȝoure parte". þerfore alle ȝe prestis of þe Lorde þat reden þes
þingis take hede, and se what is þe difference of prestis, lest þai, þat 365
han parte in þe erþe and taken tente to bissinessis and tilþis of þe
erþe, be not seyn to be prestis of þe Lorde but of pharao: for he will
þat his prestis haue possessions and hawnte þe tylynge of þe felde
and not of þe soule, he wol þat þai ȝeue bissynes to þe londe, and not
to þe lawe. But what Criste commaundiþ here ȝe: "He þat forsakiþ 370
not alle þingis þat he haþ in possession may not be my disciple."
Crist denyeþ him to be his disciple þat haþ | any þinge in f. 19ᵛ
possess[i]on, and him þat forsakiþ not alle þingis þat he haþ. And
what do we? how rede we þes þingis ouresiilfe? oþer how expowne
we þes þingis to þe peple?—þe whiche renounce not þes þingis þat 375
we han, but we willen gete to vs þo þinges þat we hadden neuer
bifore we cam to Criste'—that is, to forsake pouert and bodely
trauell forto haue riches and ese. But, certis, þis is contrarie to þe
apostles liife, as saynt Petir witnessiþ, saynge to Criste 'What schal
be to vs þat han forsaken alle þingis and swen þe?' Lo, Petir axed not 380
lordeschip and ese of þis liife to rewarde for his seruyce.

And þerfor þe holy doctoure Odo in a sermon saiþ þat bigynneþ
þus | Ecce nos reliquimus omnia: 'Abel is dede; þe bissynes of schipard f. 20ʳ
and spiritual mornynge or weylynge is slayne; but Cayme, þat is
possession, is kept, ȝee, and Caym þe erþetyller is made þe hirde or 385
gouer[nour] of sowlis. For it is not axyd in þe chirche if he kan well
teche, or if he kan wepe and weyle for synys, but ȝef he be Caym, þat
is, an erþetilyer þat kan well till þe londe. And it is no wondir þouȝ
possession sle ful many, siþ it is venym. For þe same day þat þe
chirche was endowid bi Constantyne, þer was herde a voyce in þe 390
eyre "Today is venym sched into þe chirche." For þe chirche was
made more in dignite but lesse in religion. And if it be axid of siche
oone | "Where is þe schepe þat was bytaken to þe?", he awnsweriþ f. 20ᵛ
"Wheþer I am kepar of my broþer?", as þouȝ he sayde "What charge
is to me of þe sowlis, so þat I haue well ordenyd for þe temperall 395

f. 66ᵛ   But here þe | endowid clerkis and religiouse seien þat Crist
1630 forfendiþ hem not such worldli lordship saue þat þei shulde not
be lordis aftir þe pompe and þe pride of þis world. But þis fleshli
gloos, and many suche oþir þat þei han, is no þing to purpos, for
God haþ forfendid pompe and pride to alle maner men and myssvss
of hise goodis, for he ȝaf neuere man leue to do synne. But up hap
1635 þou art a clerk, or a religious endowid wiþ many worldli lordships,
and art wo þat euere Crist was so yuel avisid ⌜to seie⌝, or þe
euangelist to write, þese wordis 'þe kyngis of þe heþen han lordship

1629 here] herto H,   therto F   þe] thes F   endowid] lordly F
1630 forfendiþ] forbyde F   such . . . not²] om. F   1631 þe²] om. FL   fleshli]
carnall and fleschly F   1632 han] haue inventyd F   1633 forfendid]
forbydden F   pride] pride and mysvse of his goodis F   men] of men FL   and²
. . . goodis (1634)] om. F   1634 man . . . do] leue neuer to man to F   up hap þou]

goodis?" Syche ben acursid as Cayme was, þat led owtc þe schepe
Abel, and brynge hym not aȝen, but disseyuen hym—of whiche God
saiþ by þe prophete Ezechiel "Her schipardis han disseyuyd hem."'
Alle þis saiþ þe goode doctour Odo.

To siche holy sentence of scripture and doctouris schulden lordis 400
take hede. For saynt Ysydre saiþ, and it is putt in þe lawe, 'Seculer
lordis, pryncis of þe worlde, schulden well wite and knowe þat þai
schal ȝelde herd rekenynge and acowntis to God for | holy chirche f. 21ʳ
þat þai han take of Criste to kepe and to defende. For, as saiþ þe law
þer, wheþersoeuer þat seculer lordis rule holy chirche wel or yuell, 405
Criste schal ax reknynge of hem. For vndir seculer lordis power Crist
haþ sett þe rulynge and gouernynge of his chirche.' And þerfore
saynt Austyn in þe *Boke of questyons of þe olde lawe and þe newe*, and
in oþer dyuers placis, saiþ þat kyngis and lordis ben vicaris of þe
godhede. And saynte Poule saiþ 'Not wiþoute cause knyȝtis beren 410
swerde, but to avenge þe wraþe of God into hym þat mysdoþe, and
to supporte and mayntene hem þat done [w]el.' And for worþines of
þis astate saynt Poule techiþ to pray, first of alle for kyngis and
knyȝtis, þat God ȝeue hem grace to gouern | hemselfe and her peple f. 21ᵛ
þat þai han in gouernance to þe plesance of God and to helþe of her 415
owne sowlis. And herfor saynt Petir biddiþ þe peple to obey to
kyngis as to hem þat ben passynge oþer, and to dukys as to þo þat
ben sent of kyngis into þe vengance of mysdoers, and to þe
praysynge of goode men.

And notwiþstondynge alle þes autorites þat ben rehersid afore 420
aȝen þe lordeschipis þat þe clerkis occupien expresly aȝens Goddis
lawe, as it schal be pleynly proued heraftir wiþ Goddis help, ȝit þai
sayen þat Criste forfendiþ hem not siche worldly lordeschip saaf þat
þai schuld not be lordis aftir þe pompe and pride of þis worlde. But
þis fleschly glose, and many siche oþer þat þai han, is no þinge to 425
pur|pose, for God haþ forfendit pompe and pride to all maner of men f. 22ʳ
and mysuse of his goodis, for he ȝaue neuer man leue to do synne.
But vp hap þu art a clerke, or a religious man endowid wiþ many
worldly lordeschipis, and art wo þat euer Crist was so yuel avised to
say, or þe euangelist to write, þes wordis 'þe kyngis of heþen han 430

---

401 *margin* Ys. ethicarum ca.° liij° xxiijᵃ.q.vᵃ ca.° principes L   404 of] of/of L
410 *margin* Ro' xiijᵃ L   412 wel] yuel L   *margin* Thimo. ij° et vj° L
416 *margin* I Petri ij° L   418 ben] bent L

þou þat F   1635 religious] religius man FL   worldli] *om.* F   1636 and]
om. F   1637 *margin* luce 22 F   þe²] *om.* FL

upon hem, but ȝe not so!', and woldist liȝtli, and it were in þi power,
do þis word and suche oþir out of þe gospel for euere—as weiward
1640 clerkis wolden in seynt Austyns tyme haue don out, and þei hadden
f. 67ʳ wist hou, þis word of þe gospel 'Vpon Moyses | chair han ysete
scribis and pharisees; al þat þei shal seie to ȝou, kepe and do ȝe; but
do ȝe not after her werkis.' þ[u]s seiþ seynt Austyn *De verbis domini
super isto textu*. And for as moche as þou maist not vndo for euere
1645 suche textis ȝit, ne þou wolt do aftir þe lettre of suche textis, þerfore
þou seist þ[ou] most haue a gloos. Wel þanne for Goddis loue, if þou
wolt glose þe textis of þe gospel, þat ben so euene aȝens þi
lordshiping or lordlynesse, glose hem as Crist dide and comaundide
þee to ȝyue ful credence to his gloos, whanne he seide 'If ȝe leeue not
1650 me, þat is to seie, for my wordis, leeue ȝe þe dedis!' And if þou
bileeue effectuali þis gloos, þou shalt not oonli forsake þe lordship
þat þou ocupiest, but also, raþer þan þou shuldist be ocupied
þerwiþ, þou shalt renne awei þerfro, and hide þee, as Cristis gloos
f. 67ᵛ seiþ | þat he dide (*Io.* 6). And if þou wolt not bileeue effectueli
1655 Cristis wordis neþer his gloos, þanne þou wilfulli and obstynatli
forsakist Crist vttirli, and so þou bicomest a lyme of anticrist. Also it
mai be þat summe heþen ocupie such lordship vertuousli, as dide Iob
and Cornelius, of whom we mai rede (*Act.* 10), but a clerk mai not be
a lord or vertuousli ocupie so seculer lordship. And if þou wolt wite
1660 whi, me semeþ þat þis is cause sufficient ynow: þat Crist haþ
forbodun hem þis lordship in pleyn wordis, as it is writun ofte
bifore, and gloside þo wordis wiþ his dedis, as it is seid. And so þe
fleshli gloos þat þe clerkis ȝyuen here upon Cristis wordis, þe which
gloos is rehersid a litil aboue, is no good worþ.
1665   And siþ Crist dide no þing indifferentli or wiþoute greet cause,
not wiþout ⌐a⌐ greet cause Crist fledde and hidde him þus whanne þe
f. 68ʳ peple wolde haue take him and maad him | kyng. For whanne he was
souȝt to his passioun, he profride himsilf, but whanne he was souȝt
to be a kyng, and so to take upon him þe material swerd wiþ hise

1638 and¹] thow F   liȝtli and] also soone yf F   1639 do] put owt F   out]
om. F   weiward] frawwerd F   1640 and] yf F   hadden wist] cowd tell F
1641 of] out of HF   *margin* mt.23 EDHFL   moyses chair] þe chayer of moyses F
1642 scribis] þe scribys F   kepe] kepe yt F   do ȝe] do it F   1643 do ȝe] look
þat ye do F   þus] DHFL, þis E   de] vpon þis text in de F   1644 super . . . textu]
om. F   and] therfore F   vndo for euere] for euer vndoo F   1645 ȝit ne] nor F
þou] *om.* F   wolt] wolt noʳt⌐, noʳt⌐ *canc.* E   1646 þou] DHFL, þei E   most]
maist DH   1647 so euene] directly F   1648 lordshiping] lordschipe F
comaundide] command F   1649 *margin* Io. 10 et 14 EDHFL   leeue] beleve F
1650 for] *om.* HF   leeue] beleve F   1651 þe] þi F   1653 renne awei . . .

lordeschip vpon hem, but ȝe not so!', and woldist liȝtly, and it wer in
þine power, do þis worde and siche oþer owte of þe gospell for
euer—as waiwerd clerkis wolden in seynt Austyns tyme haue done
owte, and þai wisten how, þis worde of þe gospell *Super cathedram
Moyses sederunt* etc., 'Vpon Moyses chayer han siten scribis and   435
pharyseis; alle þat þai schal say to | ȝou, kepe and do ȝe; but do ȝe not   f. 22ᵛ
aftir her werkis.' þus saiþ Austyn *De verbis Domini super isto textu.*
And for als myche as þu maist not vndo for euer suche textis, ne ȝit
þu wilt do aftir þe letter of siche textis, þerfore þu saist þu most haue
a glose. Wel þan for Goddis loue, if þu wilt glose þe textis of þe   440
gospell, þat ben so euen aȝens þi lordeschip, glose hem as Criste did
and commaundid þe to ȝeue full credence to his glose, whan he saide
'ȝif ȝe leue not me for my wordis, leue ȝe þe dedis!' And if þu bileue
effectualy þis glose, þu schalt not oonly forsake þe lordeschip þat þu
occupiest, but also, raþer þan þu schuldist be ocupied þerwiþ, þu   445
schalt renne awai þerfro, and hyde þe, as Cristis glose saiþ þat he
did. And if þu wilt not bileue ef|fectualy Cristis wordis neþer his   f. 23ʳ
glose, þan þu wilfully and obstynatly forsakist Crist vttirly, and so þu
bycummyst a lymme of anticriste. For no man may putt anoþer
grounde bysidis þat þat is put þe whiche is Criste Ihesu.   450

Capitulum v

Here we may se þat a clerk may not be a lorde or vertuosly occupi so
seculer lordeschip. And ȝif þu wilt wete whi, me semiþ þat þis is a
cause sufficient ynowe: þat Criste haþ forbodun hem þis lordeschip
in playne wordis, as it is writen ofte tofore, and glosid þo wordis wiþ
his dedis. For whan he was souȝte to his passion, he profred   455
hymsilfe, but whan he was souȝte to be a kynge, and to haue taake
vpon hym þe material swerde wiþ his purtenances, he fled and |
hidde hymself, and left þis swerde hooly in his place, techynge his   f. 23ᵛ
prestis by þis ensample to do þe same. And it is no doute but þat þis

---

434 *margin* Mt. xxiij L   443 *margin* Joh. xᵒ et xiiijᵒ L   447 *margin* Jo.
vjᵗᵒ L

þee] renewe and forsake it hydeng the þerfro F   *margin* io.6 EDF   1655 þou]
om. F   1656 þou] *om.* HF   1658 and] *om.* F   *margin* Act. 10 EDF
Act.10] in þe actis F   1660 cause] a cause FL   1662 þo] þos F   it is seid] I
sayd F   1663 þe²] *om.* F   1664 no good] nothyng F   1665 and siþ]
seyng F   indifferentli . . . but (1687)] *lost* H   greet] a greet D, a F
1666 not . . . cause] Crist wiþowt a great cause F   fledde] flede not F   him] hymself F
1667 him¹] *om.* F   kyng] a *canc.* kyng E

1670 pur[t]ynauncis þat I spak of bifore, he fledde and hidde himsilf, and
lefte þis swerd hooli in his place, techinge hise prestis bi þis
ensaumple to do þe same. And it is no doute þat ne þis ensaumple
was a comaundement to Cristis prestis to fle vttirli þis lordship. For
as seynt Gregor seiþ *Dominus Iesus Cristus, aliquando nos sermonibus,*
1675 *aliquando vero operibus ammonet. Ipsa enim facta eius precepta sunt,*
quia dum aliud tacitus facit, quid agere debeamus innotescit, 'Cristis
dedis or ensaumplis ben comaundingis what we shulde do.' And þat
Crist fledde þis temptacioun of þe peple and hidde himsilf shulde
teche þe prestis to fle not oonli þis synful and dampnable lordship in
1680 þe staat of presthod, but also þat þei flee þe occasioun or þe
f. 68ᵛ temptacioun þerof. For siþ Adam and | Eue helden hem not
apaied wiþ þe kyndli lordship þat God hadde ȝoue hem in paradise,
mankinde, infect bi þe first synne, haþ had an vnruly lecherous
appetite to worldli maistirdom and lordship. And þerfore, as to
1685 avoide bodili lecherie þe beste mene is to fle þe occasioun and þe
temptacioun þerto, so it is in þis synne. And þat ensaumpliʳdeˀ Crist
in his fleyng and hidyng—and not oonli þis, but also Crist in þis
doyng dampnede symonye, þe which is takyng, or an vnruli will to
take or to ȝyue, worldli good for grace, or bi occasioun of grace of
1690 God mynystrid to ony creature. For Crist hadde graciousli and bi
myracle fed þis peple, þoruȝ occasioun of þe which grace þis peple
was moued þus to take Crist, and make him a lord or to ȝyue him
worldli lordship. But Crist, a cleer ensaumple of clennesse of prestis,
bi whom as Goddis instrumentis grace is ȝoue to þe peple, as þis
f. 69ʳ grace | was bi þe prest Crist, fledde þis ȝifte.
1696   And in þis fleyng of Crist fro þis lordship, aftir þe myracle and
grace þat God þe fadir hadde mynystrid bi him, he dampnede þe
resceyuyng of þe lordship, þe which Siluestir took of Constantyn,
and commendide and confermede þe dede of þe blessid prophete
1700 Elize, þat refuside þe ȝiftis or þe endowyng of temperal goodis
profrid to him of Naaman aftir þe myracle and grace þat God hadde
do bi him to Naaman. Neþeles, for more opun knouleche of þat þat I
moue here, þou shalt vndirstonde þat þe casis þat bitidde bitwene

    1670 purtynauncis] DFL, puruyauncis E   he] than he F   1672 þat ne] but
þat FL   þis] *om.* F   1673 a comaundement] commandyd F   to¹] vnto F
to²] for *canc.* to E, for to DF   1674 *margin* omelia 17 E, gregor omelia 17 D,
gregorius F, Gregorius (*added*) omelia xvij L   seiþ] sayth þe xvij homelye F
1675 vero] *om.* F   enim] etenim F   1676 aliud] aliquid F   1677 or] and F
comaundingis] commandyd F   what] how F   þat] seyng F   1678 shulde] it
schuld F   1680 þat þei flee] to fle F   or . . . temptacioun (1681)] *om.* F

ensaumple was a commaundement to Cristis prestis to fle vttirli þis 460
lordeschip. For as seynt Gregory saiþ *Dominus Ihesus Christus,
aliquando nos sermonibus, aliquando vero operibus ammonet. Ipsa enim
facta eius precepta sunt, quia dum aliud tacitus facit, quid agere debeamus
innotescit*, 'Cristis dedis or ensaumples ben commaundementis what
we schulden do.' And þat Criste fled þis temptacion of þe peple and 465
hidde hymself schuld teche prestis to fle not oonly þis synfull and
dampnable lordeschip in þe state of presthode, but also þat þai fle þe
occasion or þe temptaci|[on] þerof. And þis ensaumpled Criste in his f. 24ʳ
fleynge and hydynge—and not oonly þis, but also Crist in his doynge
dampnyd symony, þe whiche is takynge, or an vnruely will to take or 470
to 3eue, worldly goode for grace, or bi occasion of grace of God
mynystred to eny creature. For whan Criste had graciously and by
myracle fed þe peple, þorow occasion of þat grace þis peple was moued
to take hym, and make hym a lorde. But Criste, a clere ensaumple of
clennesse of prestis, by whom as Goddis instrumentis grace is 3ouen to 475
þe peple, as þis grace was by þe preste Criste, fled þis 3ifte.

And in þis fleynge of Criste ⌐fro¬ þis lordeschip, aftir þe myracle
and grace þat God þe fadir had ministrid by hym, he dampned | þe f. 24ᵛ
ressauyng of þe lordeschip, þe whiche Siluestre toke of Constantyne.
And Criste commendid and confermyd þe dede of þe blessid 480
prophete Helyze, þat refusid þe 3iftis proferid to hym of Naaman
after þe miracle and grace þat God had done by hym to Naaman.
Neþelesse, for þe more open knowleche of þat þat I moue here, þu
schalt vndirstonde þat þe casis þat bitydden bytwene Constantyne
and Siluestre and Naaman and Helize ben wondir like. For boþe þes 485
seculer men wer grete lordis and mesels, and boþe weren helid bi
myracle of God and bi grace mynystred to hem by þes two prestis.

---

461 *margin* Gregorius omelia xvijᵃ L   467 þat] but *canc.* þat L
468 temptacion] temptaci// L   481 *margin* iiij° R. v° ca.° L

1681 siþ] sense F   hem not] *rev.* D, þem not well F   1683 had] *om.* F
1684 and þerfore] lyke F   1686 þerto] þerof F   ensaumplide crist] crist schewyd
by exampyll F   1687 his] *om.* F   and²] hymself and F   þis²] his FL
1688 þe] *om.* F   1689 for] to ony creature for F   grace¹ . . . grace²] þe gyft F
1690 mynystrid . . . creature] *twice* F   and] fled þis pepyll F   1691 fed . . . peple]
om. F   1693 cleer] clene D   ensaumple] ensaumpleʳreʼ H   clennesse] þe
clennes F   1694 as . . . instrumentis] *om.* F   1695 bi . . . crist] *om.* F
3ifte] þerfor F   1698 þe which] þat F   1700 or þe endowyng] *om.* F
1701 to] vnto F   *margin* nota 4 r.5 historiam de Naaman et helizeo ED, *in text* (*margin*
v.c H) HF, *margin* iiij R.v.ca. L   1702 þat þat I moue] my meanyng F
1703 þou shalt] yow schall F   bitidde] hapenyd F

Constantyn and Siluestir and Naaman and Helize ben wondir liik.
1705 For boþe þese seculer men weren grete lordis and mesels, and boþe
weren helid bi myracle of God and bi grace mynystrid to hem bi
prestis. For Naaman was helid of God bi grace mynystrid to him bi
ˈHelize, and Cons[tan]tyn was helid of God bi grace mynystrid to
f. 69ᵛ hym biˈ Siluestir, as his storie telliþ. And boþe þei we|ren helid on oo
1710 wise: for in watir shewid of God to þese prestis, and bi þese two
prestis shewid to þese two siik men, as we mai rede in þe ferþe book
of Kyngis þe fifþe chapiter, and in þe storie of Siluestir. And aftir
þese gracis þus mynystrid bi þese two prestis Naaman profride
Helize wondir grete ȝiftis of mouable goodis, and Constantyn
1715 profride to Siluestir boþe mouable and vnmouable goodis in
wondir greet plente and excesse. But, notwiþstondinge þat
Naaman preiede ful hertili Helize and enforcide him þat he shulde
haue take þese ȝiftis, vttirli he forsook hem and wolde not resceyue
hem. But Siluestir in þe same caas took þat þe emperour profride
1720 him, boþe ˈþeˈ greet worldli arai and þe wundir grete lordships. And
oo greet cause whi Helize wolde not assente to Naaman, for to take
ony ȝiftis of him in þis caas, was for þanne Helize hadde be a
f. 70ʳ symonyan. For siþ | his man Giezi, þat ran aftir Naaman and took
ȝiftis of him, þoruȝ occasioun of þat grace so mynystrid, was a
1725 symonyan, notwiþstondinge þat þat grace was not ȝoue bi him [i]n
ony wise to Naaman, but þat he took þo ȝiftis bi þat occasioun, hou
moche raþer his maistir Helize, þat hadde more kunnyng and was
boundun to more perfeccioun, shulde haue be a dampnable symonyan, if he hadde resceyued þat good, siþ þat þat grace was ȝoue to
1730 Naaman bi him. And hou moche more was Siluestir a greet
symonyan, resceyuynge suche ȝiftis as he dide of Constantyn, siþ
þat þis grace of myraculous helþe was mynystrid bi himsilf, þoruȝ þe
which occasioun Constantyn ȝaf and he resceyuede þese ȝiftis. And
no doute, þouȝ he hadde in þis caas resceyued but mouable goodis,
1735 he shulde haue synned moche more greuousli þan Giezi dide, or
f. 70ᵛ Helize shulde if he hadde re|seyued þat Naaman profride him, for
Siluestir trespasside aȝens a more perfit lawe. And what bi Giezi and
bi Balaam, what bi Iudas and Symon Magus, þat weren symonyans
acursid of God and ysmytun wiþ Goddis veniaunce, what bi many
1740 fair euydencis of scripture and resoun þat such a man ouȝte to haue
had, he hadde many grete warnyngis of hidousnesse and peril of þis

For Naaman was helid of God bi gracc ministred to hym bi Helize,
and Constantyne was he|[lid] of God by grace ministred to hym bi f.25ʳ
Siluestre, as his storie telliþ. And boþe þai wer helid in oon wise: for 490
in water schewid of God to þes prestis, and bi þes two prestis
schewid to þes two sike men. And aftir þes gracis þus minystred by
þes two prestis Naaman proferid to Helize wondir grete ȝiftis of
mouable goodis, and Constantyne proferid to Siluestre boþe mouable
and vnmouable goodis in wondir grete plente and excesse. But, 495
notwiþstondynge þat Naaman prayed full hertly Helize and enforsid
hym þat he schuld haue take þo ȝiftis, vttirly he forsoke hem. But
Siluestre in þe same case toke þat þe emperoure proferid hym, boþe
þe grete worldly | aray and þe wondir grete lordeschipis. And oo f.25ᵛ
grete cause whi Helize wold not asent to Naaman, to take eny ȝiftis of 500
hym in þis case, was for þan Helize had ben a symonient. Siþ his
man Giezi, þat ran aftir Naaman and toke ȝiftis of hym, þorow
occasion of þat grace so minystred, was a symonyent, notwiþstondynge þat þat grace was not ȝeue by hym in eny wise to Naaman, but
þat he toke þo ȝiftis bi occasion of þat grace, how myche raþer his 505
maister Helize, þat had more kunnynge and was bounden to more
perfeccion, schuld haue be a symonyent, ȝif he had ressauyd þat
goode, siþ þat grace was ministred to Naaman by hym. And no
dowte, þouȝ Siluestre had in þis case ressauyd but mouable goodis,
he | schulde haue synned more greuously þan Giezi did, or Helize f.26ʳ
schulde ȝif he had ressauyd þat Naaman proferid to hym, for 511
Siluestir trespassid aȝens a more perfite lawe. And what bi Giezi
and Balam, what by Iudas and Symon Magus, þat wer symonyentis
acursid of God and ysmyten wiþ Goddis vengance, and what bi
many faire euydencis of scripture and reson þat siche a man owȝt to 515
haue had, he had many grete warnyngis of hydousnes and perell of

---

488 *margin* iiiᵒ R. vᵒ L   489 helid] he// L   492 to þes] to þes to þe L

1711 in] *om.* HF   1712 kyngis] þe kyngis F   þe¹] *om.* H   in] *om.* HF   and²]
ᵣ21 ca.ᵊ and F   1713 þus mynystrid] *rev.* F   1714 Helize] to helize HFL
1716 wondir] mervelus F   1717 ful . . . Helize] helysei hartly F   1721 oo] as
on F   greet cause] cause greet *marked for rev.* E   assente] agre F   1723 siþ]
seyng F   1725 in] DHFL, on E   1726 þo] þes F   1727 raþer] ᵣraþerᵊ
H, more *canc.* F   1729 siþ] seing F   þat þat] þat HFL   þat³] þis D
1731 siþ] seyng F   1735 greuousli] *om.* F   Giezi dide] *rev.* F   1736 þat]
þat wich F   *margin* nota historias 4 r.5 (et F) numeri 22 (22 *om.* E) Mt. 26 et (*om.* F) act.
8 (8 *om.* E) ED, *in text after* lawe (1737) HF   1739 goddis] god F
1740 euydencis] evydenc' F   1741 hidousnesse] þe jeopardy F   þis] his F

synne ouer þat hise predicessours hadden; and al þis aggreggide his
synne. And þou maist se here þat þis man dide not after þe
ensaumple of Crist ⌐here⌐. For he fledde whanne he shulde haue
1745 be maad a kyng and hidde himsilf, and so wiþstood it, but he
profride himsilf to passioun; but þis man dide on contrarie wise. For
whanne he was souȝt to passioun he hidde him, as þe storie of him
telliþ; and whanne he was callid to þe staat of empire or of seculer
f. 71ʳ lordship and worldli dignyte, he in | a manere profride himsilf, in as
1750 moche as he manly wiþstood not þis hidous and synful purpos of þe
emperour but cowardli consentide to his foly. And certein I drede me
not þat he hadde neuere beter cause of martirdom, þan to haue
wiþstonde þis foly of þe emperour, in caas þat he wolde bi violence
haue enforsid him to þis lordship. For as a man mai conseyue in
1755 partie of þat þat is seid bifore, and of euydencis þat wiþ Goddis help
shal sue heraftir, þis wickid dede was peruertyng of Cristis
ordynaunce in his chirche, and harmful and distruccioun to euery
astaat þerof, and wole be fynal confusioun þerof but if it be
remedied. And so þis man hadde neuere so greet cause to fle and
1760 to hide himsilf as whanne he was callid to þis rialte; and þat he myȝte
haue lerned of him þat shulde haue be his maistir, Iesu Crist, þat
f. 71ᵛ sumtyme in þe same caas | fledde and hidde himsilf. And, þouȝ
vnkunnyngnesse myȝte sumdel excuse þe emperour, ȝit þat myȝte
not excuse þis prest, þat ouȝte for to knowe, as a þing cheefli
1765 bilonging to his perfeccioun, þat he shulde not be a lord on þat wise.
  But here clerkis þat ben encumbrid in þis maner of symony and in
many oþir wolen seche wel many and dyuerse glosis to excuse þis
symonye—and no wondir to me. For I haue knowe þat þo þat han
had þe name of riȝt grete clerkis han bisied hem to excuse Symon
1770 Magus as giltles of þis synne, for koude ⌐þei⌐ neuere se hou þei
myȝte haue ony rest wiþ her conscience if Symon Magus shulde be
dampned, for he wende wickidli þe ȝifte of God to be had bi monei,
and þei knewe wel þat þe more part of þe clergie doiþ more þan þis.
For þei doen not oonli þis synne in opynyoun but in will, word and
f. 72ʳ dede ofte | tyme rehersid, and contynuen in þis synne al her liif dai.
1776 And wondre þou not, alþouȝ couetouse clerkis encumbrid in þis
synne, þat ben redi to dampne hooli scripture as for fals and heresie,
dampne þe sentence of seynt Petir demynge Symon Magus worþi to
be dampned for þis dede. For it were a ful greet ese for her
1780 encumbrid conscience and Symon Magus myȝte be excusid here.
But whateuere glosis symonyans studien in þis mater, I drede me not

þis synne oucr þat his predecessouris hadden; and all þis agregeden his syn. Here it may be knowen þat Siluestre did not aftir þe ensaumple of Criste, þat fled whan he schuld haue be made a kynge and hidde hymself, and so wiþstode it, but he proferid hymself to his 520 passion; but | Siluestir did on þe contrari wise. For whan he was f. 26ᵛ sowȝte to passion he hidde hymsiilfe, as þe storie of hym telliþ; and whan he was callid to þe state of þe emperoure or worldly dignite, he in a maner proferid hymself, in als myche as he manly wiþstode not þe hidous and synfull purpose of þe emperoure but cowerdly 525 consentid to his foly. And certis I drede not þat he had neuer better cause of martirdome, þan to haue wiþstonde þis foli of þe emperour, in case þat he wolde by violence haue enforsid hym to þis lordeschip. For as a man may conceyue in partye of þat þat is saide before, and of euydence þat wiþ Goddis help schal sue heraftir, þis 530 wickid dede was peruertynge of Cristis ordenances in | his chirche, f. 27ʳ and harmfull and destruccion to euery state þerof, and will be fynal confusion þerof but ȝif it be remedied. And so þis man had neuer so grete cause to fle and to hide hymself as whan he was callid to þis rialte; and þat he myȝte haue lernyd of Criste, þat schulde haue be 535 his maister, þat in þe same case fled and hidde hymself. And, þouȝ vnkunnyngnes myȝte sumdele excuse þe emperour, ȝit þat myȝt not excuse þis preste, þat owȝte to knowe, as a þinge chefly bilongyng to his perfeccion, þat he schuld not be a lorde on þat wise. For no man may putt anoþir grounde byside þat is putt whiche is Criste Ihesu. 540

---

520 *margin* Joh. xviij° L

1742 aggreggide] augmentyd F   1743 þou maist] may F   þat] þat/þat F
1744 here] *om.* DFL   1746 passioun] his passion FL   man] *om.* D   on] *om.* F
contrarie] þe contrary FL   wise] *om.* F   1747 passioun] suffer dethe F   of
him] *om.* F   1748 þe] þat HF   empire] emperour D, þe emperoure L
1750 hidous] great F   1751 his] this F   certein] of a truyth F   drede] fere F
1752 þat] *om.* HF   1754 him] *om.* F   conseyue] persayue F   in partie] partly F
1755 is] was F   1756 sue] folow F   1757 ordynaunce] ordynauncis DFL
and²] *om.* HF   1758 astaat] staat FL   1763 vnkunnyngnesse] ignoranc' F
sumdel] somewhat F   1764 for to knowe] to haue knowen F   cheefli] most chef F
1765 bilonging] longyng F   1767 wel] *om.* F   þis . . . excuse (1769)] *om.* F
1768 han had] hadde D   1770 koude þei neuere] þei koude not DHF
1771 myȝte] coud F   wiþ] in F   shulde] schal F   1772 wende] thouȝt F
ȝifte] gyftis F   bi] wiþ F   1773 knewe] know F   part] partye F
1775 contynuen] contynuyng F   dai] days F   1776 wondre] mervell F
alþouȝ] thow F   1777 for] *om.* HF   1778 demynge] iugyng F
1779 ful] *om.* F   1780 encumbrid] combred F   and] yf F   1781 glosis]
om. F   symonyans] symonyacis F   drede] fere F

þei shal neuere cleerli excuse Siluestir of symonye in þis caas into þe tyme þei han excusid Giezi of his symony, and also Helize in caas þat he hadde resceyued þe ȝiftis þat Naaman profride to him, as 1785 Siluestre took upon ⌈him⌉ þe lordship and þe worldlynesse þat Constantyn profride to him.

And so who so lokiþ wel þ[is] dede of Siluestir was not oonli f. 72ᵛ symonye, as it is de|clarid now, but also it was heresie, for it was expresse aȝens þe lyuyng and þe teching of Iesu Crist as it is opunli 1790 tauȝt bifore. And siþ þe dowyng of þe clergie wiþ seculer lordships is groundid upon þis dede, we mai se bi þis processe hou þe clergie is wondir foul infect wiþ symonye and heresie. For þis synne in þe clergie mai not be vndo til þat þis lordshiping, lordlynesse or lordship in þe clergie be distried, þe which haþ enuenymed al þe 1795 chirche. And if we take heede to þis processe, we shulen not moche wondre alþouȝ þe aungel of God, apperinge in þe eir ⌈in tyme⌉ of þe doyng of þis wickid dede, seide þes wordis 'þis dai is venym shed or helt in þe chirche of God', as Gorham seiþ upon þe twelþe chapitre of þe Apocalips.

f. 73ʳ And herfore Crist, þat was in liik caas wiþ | þese two prestis Helize 1801 and Siluestir, in dampnyng of þis wickid dede þat haþ so moche harmed and enuenymed his chirche, lefte þe wey of Siluestir, þat took þis worldli lordship upon him, and chees þe weie of Helize þe prophete, forsakynge þo ȝiftis þat Naaman profride to him, and so 1805 fledde boþe [þis] symony and heresie. And so, as Helize lefte þe greet richesse þat Naaman profride [to] him, and took worþili þe pore ordynaunce and fynding þat a good man and his wiif profride to him, þat is to seie a litil soler and a litil bed, a bord and a chair and a candelstik, þe whiche ben acordinge to a studier or a contemplatif 1810 man, as it is writun (4 *Regum* 4), so Crist forsook seculer lordship and helde him apaied wiþ pore liiflood þat deuout peple mynystride to him to his sustynaunce in his labour, and þus dide also þe apostlis, f. 73ᵛ as a man mai conseyue of | þe gospel (*Luc.* 8) and in many oþer

1782 cleerli] *om.* F into] tyll F 1783 his] this F 1785 lordship] lordschipys F 1787 þis] DHF, þe, -e *on eras. and final* -s *eras.* E, þe L 1789 expresse] manifest F 1790 and] ⌈22 ca.⌉ And F siþ] seyng F þe¹] this F, *om.* H dowyng] vndoyng F clergie] chirche D wiþ . . . lordships] *om.* FL 1791 upon] on F 1792 wondir foul] fowll F 1793 þat þis] þis F lordshiping] *om.* F or] and F 1794 þe²] *om.* FL enuenymed] venomyd F 1795 chirche] clergie DL 1796 wondre] mervell F tyme] þe tyme DFL þe²] *om.* FL 1797 of] *om.* F seide] dyd say F or helt] *om.* F 1798 in] into F 1800 herfore] þerfor HF þat . . . siluestir (1801)] *om.* F

Capitulum vi.

And so whoso lokiþ wel þe dede of Siluestir, it was | expresly aȝens f. 27ᵛ
þe lyuynge and þe techynge of Ihesu Criste, as it is openli tawȝt
bifore. And siþ þe endowynge of þe clergi is groundid vpon þis dede,
we may se by þis processe how þe clergi is wondirfull enfect wiþ
symonye and heresie. For þis sinne in hem may not be vndo till þe 545
temperall lordeschip in hem be distried, whiche haþ envenemyd alle
þe clergi. And ȝif we taake hede to þis processe, we schal not myche
wondir allþouȝ þe awngell of God, aperynge in þe eyre in þe tyme of
doynge of þis wickid dede, saide þes wordis 'þis day is venym sched
or helt in þe chirche of God', as Gorram saiþ vpon þe xii chapitre of 550
þe Apocalips. And þerfor saiþ | saynt Ierom in *Vitis Patrum* 'Siþ þe f. 28ʳ
chirche encresid in possessyouns it haþ decresid in vertues.'

And herfore Criste, þat was in liike case wiþ þes two prestis Helize
and Siluestre, in dampnynge of þis wickid dede þat haþ so myche
harmyd and envenemyd his chirche, left þe way of Siluestre, þat toke 555
þis worldly lordeschip, and chese þe way of Helize þe prophete, þat
forsoke þo ȝiftis þat Naaman proferid hym, and fled boþe symony
and heresy. And so, as Helize left þe grete richesse þat Naaman wold
haue ȝyue hym, and tooke worþili þe pore ordenance and fyndynge
þat a goode man and his wyfe proferid to hym, þat is to say a lytill 560
soler, a bedde, a borde, a chaire and a kandilstek, þe whiche | ben f. 28ᵛ
acordynge to a studier or a contemplatyfe man, so Criste forsoke
seculer lordeschipis and held hym payde wiþ þe pore liflodc þat
deuoute peple ministred to hym to his nedeful sustenance in his
laboure, and þus didden also alle þe apostles, as a man may conceyue 565
of þe gospell and in many oþer placis of her liifis. For aftir tyme þat
God þe fadir had wrouȝte þis grete miracle bi Criste his preste in

---

550 *margin* Gorra L   559 *margin* iiij° Reg' cap. iiij° L   566 *margin* luc'
viij° L

1802 enuenymed] venemyd F   1804 þo] thos F   1805 boþe] *om.* F   þis]
DHF, *om.* EL   1806 to] DHF, *om.* E   worþili . . . ordynaunce (1807)] the poor
ordynaunce worþly F   1808 and²] *om.* FL   1809 þe] *om.* F   1810 *margin*
nota historiam 4 regum 4 ED, nota historiam H, iiij Reg.cap.iiij L   4²] 5 F
1811 helde him apaied] was content F   pore] þe power FL   deuout] DHFL, þe
deuout E   1812 to²] for F   1813 conseyue] persayve F   in] *om.* F

placis. For aftir tyme þat God þe fadir hadde wrou3t þis greet
1815 myracle bi Crist his prest in releuyng of fyue þousynd and mo þat
weren in mysese of hungir, he avoiᴿdiᵈde such worldli reward þat
shulde haue be 3oue to him bi occasioun of mynystring of þis grace.
Siþ þanne þat Crist and Helize acorden togidir in þis caas, and
Siluestir reuersiþ hem boþe here, and suche contrariouse dedis in
1820 caasis þat ben so liik mai not be glosid togidir, we mote nedis, if we
wolen go a sure weie, magnyfie in word and dede þe doyng of Helize
and of Crist in þis caas, siþ þat Helizeis dede is comendid in
scripture and Crist is truþe and autour of scripture. And we mote
dampne þe doyng of Giezi and Siluestir, þus fer straiyng awei fro
1825 Helize and Crist and his gospel.

And in þis writynge I blaspheme no more Siluestir, alþou3 I
f. 74ʳ reherce and blame his synne, | þan I do Petir and hise felowis whanne
I seie þat þei synfulli forsook Crist, or Poul whanne I seie þat he
wickidli pursuede Cristis chirche. For I blame him ᴦofᴧ no þing
1830 wherfore he shulde be a seynt, as I do not þese apostlis, alþou3 I
blame her synnes, þe whiche þei hemsilf dampnede and were sori þat
euere þei synnede so. For Petir wepte sore for his synne as þe gospel
seiþ. And seynt Poul, mekeli knoulechinge his synne, seiþ þat he was
not worþi to be callid apostle of Crist, and þat bicause þat he
1835 pursuede Cristis chirche. And on þe same wise Siluestir dide, or ellis
shulde haue do, for his synne. For whanne we wolen preise seyntis,
we shal loke wheryn þei sueden Crist and his lawe in word, dede or
maners, and so ferforþ þei ben worþi preisyng and no ferþer. For
Crist is þe mesure of vertuous lyuyng and worching; and herfore he
f. 74ᵛ calliþ alle men to sue | him, and alle men to lerne of him, and euery
1841 man and nameli prestis to teche þat þat he tau3te, and þanne we mai
not erre. And herfore seynt Poul tau3te þat þe cristen peple shulde
cleyme hem no priuat patroun, as Petir, Poul or Apollo, as it is seid
bifore, and techiþ þat þe peple shulde sue him but no ferþer þan he
1845 sueþ Iesu Crist. And Petir remittiþ þe peple ᴦto Cristᴧ for to take of

1816 in mysese] almost lost F   of] by F   1817 to] vnto F   1818 siþ]
seyng F   þat] om. F   1819 reuersiþ] refusith F   and . . . liik (1820)] it folowith
þat þei F   1820 be] om. F   mote] must FL   1822 siþ] seyng F
1823 mote] must F   1824 siluestir] of syluester FL   1830 be] not be F   not]
not blame F   1831 þe] om. F   1832 so] om. F   synne] synnes HF
1833 synne] synnes HF   margin mt. 26 EDFL, in text H   margin 1 cor. 15 EDF, in
text H, margin cor. xv L   1834 apostle] an apostyll F   and þat] om. F   þat²]
om. F   1836 synne] synnys F   wolen] schall F   1837 shal] must F
sueden] folowid F   1839 is] om. F   þe] om. H   and²] om. DHF   herfore]
here. for H, om. F   he] om. F   1840 alle] om. D   sue] folow F

releuynge of fyve þousande and mo þat wern in mysese of hunger, he
avoydid siche worldly rewarde þat schulde haue be ʒoue to hym bi
occasion of minystrynge of þis grace. Siþ þan þat Criste and Helize   570
acorden togydre in þis case, and Siluestre reuersiþ hem boþe here, |
and siche contrarius dedis in casis þat ben so liike mow not be glosid   f. 29ʳ
togedre, þan we most nedis, ʒif we will go a sure way, magnifie in
worde and dede þe doynge of Helize and of Criste in þis case, siþ þat
Helizes dede is commendid in scripture and Crist is truþe and autor   575
of scripture. þan we moten dampne þe doynge of Gyezi and of
Siluestre, þus ferr strayynge away fro Helize and Criste and his
gospell.

And in þis writynge I blasfeme no more Siluestre, and þes holy
men and sayntis þat han ben siþ þis endowynge of þe chirche cam in,   580
allþouʒ [I] rehers and blame her synne, þan I do Petir and his felowis
whan I say þat þai synfully forsoken Criste, or Poule whan | I say þat   f. 29ᵛ
he wickidly pursuyd Cristis chirche. For I blame of no þinge wherof
þai schuld be sayntis, no more þan I do þes apostles, allþouʒ I blame
her synnys, þe whiche þai hemself dampnyd and wer sori þat euer   585
þai synned so. For Petir wept sore for his synne as þe gospell saiþ.
And saynt Poule, mekely knowlechynge his synne, saide þat he was
not worþi to be callid apostle of Criste, and þat bicause þat he
pursuyd Cristis chirche. And on þe same wise Siluester and þes
sayntis diden, or ellis schuld haue do, for her synne. For whan we   590
will preyse sayntis, we schul loke wherin þai suyd Criste and his lawe
in worde, dede or maners, and so ferr þai ben worþi preysynge | and   f. 30ʳ
no ferþer. For Crist is þe mesure of vertuous lyuynge and
worchynge; and herfore he calliþ alle men to sue hym, and to
lerne of hym, and namely prestis to teche þat þat he tawʒte, and   595
þan we may not erre. And herfore saynt Poule tauʒte cristen peple to
sue hym, but no ferrer þan he sueþ Ihesu Criste. And saynt Petir
remittiþ þe pepill to Criste for to take of hym ensaumple, saiynge
þus: 'Crist haþ suffred for vs; leuynge ʒou ensaumple þat ʒe filow þe

---

581 I] *om.* L   586 *margin* Mt. xxvjᵒ L   588 *margin* 1 Cor. xvᵒ L
591 *margin* Mt. xi L   593 *margin* Mt. vltimo L   596 *margin* Eph. vᵒ L
598 *margin* iª. petⁱ. ijᵒ L

1841 nameli] specially F   þat²] wich F   *margin* Mt. 11 Mr. vltimo ED, mt. xi mt.
vltimo L   1842 herfore] þerfor F   *margin* 1 cor. 11 (et ad DH) eph. 5 (50 E)
EDH, eph. v L   þe] *om.* HFL   1843 patroun] patronys F   asⁱ] a F
1844 and . . . þat] teachyng F   peple] cristen *canc.* peple E   shulde sue] to folow F
1845 sueþ] folowid F   iesu] *om.* F   for to] to F

him ensaumple, seiynge þus: ‘Crist haþ suffrid for us, leuynge ȝou ensaumple þat ȝe folowe þe stappis of him þat dide no synne, neþer was ony gile foundun in his mouþ.’ And so a man mai euere saafli sue his lyuyng and his teching wiþoute ony erring. But, and we sue in alle þingis [Petir, Poul or] Siluestir or ony oþir synful man, we mosten nedis erre in many þingis as þei diden. Loke þanne if f. 75r Siluestir suede pore Iesu Crist, þat forsook al worldli lord|ship, whanne he forsook þe pouert of þe gospel and bicam a lord upon þe west empire of þe world; and if he so dide, þanne preise him in þat doyng and ellis not.

And bi þis processe we ⌜mai⌝ answere to þe comoun argumentis þat couetouse clerkis maken in þis mater to maintene wiþ her synne, in þe whiche argumentis þei aleggen þe synnes of her predicessours for to maintene wiþ her synne, and seien þus: ‘Seint Thomas, seynt Huwe or seynt Swithyn weren lordis þus, and þei weren hooli men here and ben seyntis in heuene now; þanne mai we bi þe same skill meedfulli and hoolli take upon us þis worldli lordship and sue hem in þis.’ But þou shalt vndirstonde þat þis maner of a⌜r⌝gument halt wel whanne we arguen of God, for it sueþ wel Crist dide þus, seide or wolde þus, þerfore þis was wel don, seid or willid; and so in þis f. 75v dede, word or will it is | hoolsum, spedi and plesaunt to God þat we sue him. But whanne we arguen of a creature, þis argument is to short. For it sueþ not ‘Petir seide þus or dide þus, þerfore he dide or seide wel, and in þes wordis or dedis it is hoolsum to sue him.’ For þis maner of arguyng is ⌜vn⌝preued, in þat þat Petir forsook Crist, and in þat þat he smoot of Malcus eere, þouȝ þat þis maner of arguyng of a creature is to short. And þerfore þou most argue þus: ‘Petir seide or dide þus, and in þis he suede þe liif or þe loore of Iesu Crist; þerfore Petir in þis dide or seide wel, and in þis it is hoolsum to sue Petir.’ And so most oure clerkis argue whanne þei aleggen for her lordship þe lyuyng of her patrouns and seyntis, and seie þus: ‘Seynt Thomas, seynt Huwe and seynt Swithyn weren þus lordis,

1846 *margin* I Pe.2] EDL, *in text after* þus H 1847 folowe] may folowe F 1848 saafli sue] folow F 1849 and] yf F sue] folow F 1850 Petir . . . or] *eras.* E, petir and poul or D, petir and poul and HF or[2]] eþer DH 1852 suede] folowid F 1854 and] *om.* F 1855 and] or F 1857 wiþ þer synne] ⌜þer⌝ synn wiþ F 1859 wiþ her synne] þer synn wiþ F 1861 skill] reason F 1862 hoolli] hoolili H sue] folow F hem] hym F 1864 sueþ] folowiþ F 1865 þis] it F 1867 sue] folow F 1868 sueþ] folowith F þus[1]] *om.* HF þerfore] þerfore for ED dide] sayd F 1869 seide] ded F sue] folow F 1870 vnpreued] non *canc.* ⌜vn⌝preued E 1871 þouȝ] seyng F þat[3]] *om.* F 1872 and] *om.* HF 1873 suede] folowid F or . . . loore] *om.* F Iesu] our

steppis of hym þat did no synne, neþir was eny gyle founden in his 600
mouþe.' And so a man may euer saafly sue his lyuynge and techynge
wiþowte eny errynge. But, and we sue in alle þingis eiþer Petir,
Poule or Siluester or eny | oþer synfull man, we must nedis err in f. 30ᵛ
many þingis as þai diden. Loke þan if Siluestre suyd Criste, whan he
forsoke þe pouert of þe gospell and bycam a lorde vpon þe west 605
empire of þe worlde; and if he so did, þan preyse hym in þat doynge
and ellis not. Forwhi, no man may putt anoþer grounde bisidis þat
þat is putt þe whiche is Criste Ihesu.

Capitulum vii

Bi þis processe bifore saide men mow lerne to awnswere to þe comon
argumentis þat couetous clerkis maken in þis mater to may[n]tene 610
wiþ her synne, in þe whiche argumentis þai aleggen for hem þe
sinnes of her predecessoris sayinge þus: 'Seynt Hue, seynt Thomas
and saynt Swythune | wer þus lordis, and þai wer holy men here, and f. 31ʳ
now ben seyntis in heuen; þan may we be þe same skile medefulli
taake vpon vs þis temperal lordeschip and sue hem in þis.' But ȝe 615
schal vndirstonde þat þis maner of arguynge holdiþ well whan we
argue of God, for it suyþ well Criste did þus, saide þus or wolde þus,
þerfor þis was wel done, saide or willid; and so in þis dede, worde or
will it is holsum, spedy and plesaunt to God þat we sue hym. But
whan we argue of a creature, þis argument is to schorte. For it sueþ 620
not 'Petir saide þus or did þus, þerfore he did or saide well, and in
þes wordis and dedis it is holsum to sue hym.' For þis maner | of f. 31ᵛ
arguynge is vnpreuyd, in þat þat Petir forsoke Criste, and in þat þat
he smote of Malcus ere, so þat þis maner of arguynge of a creature is
to schorte. And þerfor ȝe most argue þus: 'Petir saide or did þus, and 625
in þis saiynge or doynge he suyd þe life and þe lore of Ihesu Criste;
þerfor Petir in þis did or sayde well, and in þis it is holsum to sue
Petir.' And so musten oure clerkis argue whan þai aleggen for her
lordeschip þe lyuynge of her patrons and sayntis, and sayen þus:
'Seynt Thomas, and seynt Hwe and seynt Swithune wer þus lordis, 630

---

610 mayntene] maytene L   620 a] an L   628 and . . . þus (629)] Where as
the clergy perceiveth that lordlynes and worldly dominyon can not be borne out by
scripture then fle (flie P2) they to argumentes of mennes perswasyon saienge after thys
maner P   630 seynt¹ . . . and¹] om. P

---

saviour iesu F   1875 to] for to F   sue] folow F   petir] hym F   most . . .
holde (1899)] lost H   1876 and seyntis] om. D

and in þis þei suede Cristis loore or his lyuyng; þerfore we mai
f. 76ʳ leefulli be þus lordis.' And I wo|ot wel þat Gabriel shal blowe his
1880 horn er þei han preued þe minor, þat is þat þese seyntis or patrouns
in þis sueden þe loore or þe liif of Iesu Crist.

And of þis þou maist se þat suche nakid argumentis, þat ben not
cloþid wiþ Cristis lyuyng or his teching, ben riȝt nouȝt worþ, alþouȝ
ypocritis ablynden wiþ hem moche folk—ȝhe, suche men þat ben
1885 callid wise men in þis world. And of þis we mai se also hou nakid þis
euydence is: 'Seynt Siluestir reseyuede suche seculer lordships and
helde hem as hise into his lyues eende, þerfore it is leeful to vs to do
þe same.' But here haue I no leiser to telle, al if I coude, what
cheuysshaunce and costis þe clergie makiþ, and what werris þei
1890 holden to contynue þis symonye and heresie ⌈so vnauysy[li] brouȝt
into þe chirche⌉. Loke þanne I preie þee wiþ studie here, and
f. 76ᵛ biþenke þee bisili hou oure clergie myȝte ferþer straie awei | fro
Crist, and be more contrariouse to him and to his lawe in word,
maners and dedis þan þei doen now, siþ þat he fledde and hidde
1895 himsilf for he wolde not be temptid to þis [l]ordship, as it is seid
bifore. And notwiþstonding þat þis lordship in þe clergie is groundid
as it is seid upon heresie and symonye, þei sechen alle þe weies þerto
þat þei can, ȝhe, and goen opunli into þe feeld armed, and killen
cristen men for to gete and holde such lordship.

1900 And notwiþstonding þat seynt Petir was so pore þat he hadde
neþer gold ne siluer, as he seiþ (*Act.*3), and his oþir worldli good he
lefte whanne he bigan first to sue Crist, as touchinge þe titil of
worldli lawe þat he hadde to þat good, and neuere resceyuede after
worldli lordship or possessiouns, ȝit þe blasphemes callen al her hool
f. 77ʳ lordship 'seynt Petris ground' or 'lordship'. And as | þei blasphemen
1906 þis seynt in word, so þei doen in dede, in as moche as þei peinten
and grauen him wiþ a diademe upon his heed and an ymage of þe

1878 suede] folowyd F   loore] law F   þerfore] þer F   mai] *om.* F
1879 and] ⌈23 ca.⌉ and F   þat] *om.* D   1881 sueden] folowid F   loore]
lawe F   1882 nakid] *om.* F   1883 cloþid] cloosyd F   worþ] *om.* F
1884 ablynden] blynd F   wiþ . . . folk] moche folk wiþ them F   1886 lordships]
lordschipe F   1887 hise] his owne F   to¹] for F   1888 haue I] *rev.* F
1889 cheuysshaunce and] *om.* F   1890 vnauysyli] DL, vnauysy E, wiþowt
advysment F   1891 þee] yow F   wiþ studie here] here wiþ a dyligent studye
and fervent wyll F   1893 word] wordis F   1894 siþ] seyng F
1895 lordship] DF, wordship E   as . . . seid] *om.* F   1897 þei] yet thei F
sechen] serche F   þerto] *om.* F   1901 ne] nor F   Act. 3] *om.* F   *margin* Act.
3 FL   1902 sue] folow F   as] and as EL   1904 lordship] lordschipis F
ȝit] and yet FL   1906 peinten] paynt hym F   1907 þe] *om.* F

and in þis þai suyd Cristis lyuynge and his lore; þerfor we may lefulli
be þus lordis.' And I wote wel þat Gabriel schal blow his horne or
þai han preuyd þe mynor, | þat is þat þes seyntis or patrons in þis f. 32ʳ
suyden þe lore or þe life of Ihesu Criste.

And of þis ȝe may se þat siche nakid argumentis, þat ben not 635
cloþid wiþ Cristis lyuynge or his techynge, ben riȝt nouȝt worþe,
allþouȝ þe clerkis ablynden wiþ hem myche folke in þis worlde. But
here haue I no leyser to tell, allȝif I kouȝde, what chefesaunce and
costis þe clergi makiþ, and what werris þai holden to contynu þis
symony and heresi so vnauysely brouȝte into þe chirche. And ȝit þai 640
sechen all þe ways þerto þat þai kan, ȝhe, in so myche þat [þai] gone
openli armyd into þe felde to kill cristen men for to gete and holde
siche lordeschipe.

And, notwiþstondynge þat seynt Petir was so pore þat he had
neþer golde | ne siluer, as he saiþ in þe *Dedis of þe Apostles*, and his f. 32ᵛ
oþer worldly goode he lefte whan he began to sue Criste, and as 646
tochinge þe tytle of worldly lawe þat he had to þat goode, he made
neuer clayme ne neuer resseyuyd aftir worldly lordeschip, and ȝit þai
callen alle her hoole lordeschip 'seynt Petirs grounde' or 'lordeschip'.
And þerfore saynt Bernerd writiþ to Ewgeny þe pope saiynge þus: 650
'Ȝif þu wilt be a lorde, sike it by anoþer title, but not bi þe apostles
ryȝte, for he myȝt not ȝeue þe þat he hadde not; þat he hadde, he
ȝaue, þe whiche was bissynes vpon chirchis. Wheþir he ȝaue
lordeschip, here what he saiþ: "Be ȝe not lordis in þe clergi, but
be ȝe made fourme or ensaumple of Cristis | flokke." And, lest þu f. 33ʳ
trow þis to be sayde not of trowþe, take kepe what Criste saiþ in þe 656
gospell: "þe kyngis of heþen han lordeschip vpon hem, forsoþe ȝe
not so." Se how pleynly lordeschip is forbodyn to alle apostles. For
ȝif þu be a lorde, how darst þu take vpon þe apostilhede? or if þu be
a bischop, how darst þu take vpon þe lordeschip? Playnly þu arte 660
forbodyn boþe. And ȝif þu wilt haue boþe togydir, þu schalt lese

631 suyd] ensued P   lore] doctryne P   may] may be P   632 be] *om.* P
and] but P   634 lore] doctryne P   635 ȝe may] thou mayst P   nakid] *om.* P
637 ablynden] blynde P   þis] þe P   638 allȝif] though P   639 clergi]
chyrche P   641 þai] *om.* L   644 þat¹] *om.* P   645 ne] nor P2
dedis] actes P   *margin* Act.iij° LP   647 þat goode] soche wordly godes P
648 worldly] any wordly P   649 lordeschip] kyngdome P   650 *margin* libro
ij° LP2, Libro[P1   þus] *om.* P   651 it] *om.* P2   title] waye to attayne P1, waye to
attayne it P2   þe] thys P   652 myȝt] may P   654 lordeschip] lordshyppe or
no P   *margin* iᵃ petᵗ v L, i.Petri P2, i.petr¹ P1   655 or] and P   ensaumple]
example P   þu] ye P   656 to be] be not P   not] *om.* P   659 apostilhede]
apostleshyp P2

emperour vndir hise feet; and þat is wundir falsli don. Forsoþe he
tauȝte þe peple to be suget to kyngis and duykis, and tauȝte also þat
1910 þer shulde be no lord in þe clergie. For, and Petir hadde do and tauȝt
as þese anticristis meyne and retenu meuen in word and dede, seynt
Petir hadde be fals and contrarious to his maistir Iesu. Lord! hou
seemeþ þee þanne of þis processe? Were it ony greet synne to calle
þese folk anticristis, siþ þei reuersen Crist and hise apostlis in þis
1915 mater and in oþir poyntis rehersid bifore? What supposist þou?
Myȝte þis peple be more contrariouse to Crist þan þei ben? Or myȝte
þer come a more harmful or opun anticrist þan is þis confederacie of
f. 77ᵛ clerkis, | þat in word and dede ben so opunli contrariouse to Crist?
But here I woot wel þat clerkis þat ben lordis, and oþir religiouse
1920 ypocritis þat louen vnkyndli ⌐þis⌐ lordlynesse, wolen glose here, and
seie þat þei ocupien not suche lordships in propre liik as seculer
lordis doen but in comoun, liik as þe apostlis (Act.4) a[nd] þe perfit
peple diden in þe bigynnyng of Cristis chirche, þe which hadde alle
þingis in comoun, liik as suche clerkis and religiouse han now. In
1925 tokenyng wherof, as no man seide of ony þing þat tyme 'þis is myn',
so oure clerkis, and nameli oure religiouse peple, whanne þei wolen
speke in termes of her religioun, a priuat persoone wole not seie 'þis
or þis is myn', but in persoone of alle hise briþeren he wole seie 'þis
is oure'. And ouer ⌐þis⌐ þei seien more sutili þat þei ocupien not
f. 78ʳ þis lordship bi titil of seculer lord|ship, but bi titil of perpetuel
1931 almesse. But whateuere þis peple seie here, we mote take heede to þe
rule of pref þat failiþ not, þe which rule Crist techiþ us in þe gospel
in dyuerse placis where he seiþ: 'Leeue ȝe þe werkis.' And þis rule is
wundir needful to a man, þere þat he haþ ado wiþ þe pharisees, or
1935 wiþ ⌐ony⌐ men of her condiciouns. For as Crist seiþ 'þei seien but
þei doen not.' And so as Cristis werkis, as he seide, bar witnesse of
him and shewide what he was, and hou he lyuede, so þe dedis and þe

1908 wundir] wonderus F   *margin* 1 pe. 2 E, 1 pe.2 et 5 DF, *in text after* peple
(1909) H   forsoþe] siþ DH, seyng F   1910 and¹] if F   1911 þese] þis HF
meyne] *om.* DHF   and¹] and *canc.* D, *om.* HF   1912 iesu] iesu crist F
1913 þee] it F   1914 þese] þis HF   reuersen] turne from F   1918 to]
vnto F   1920 lordlynesse] worldli lordinesse H, worldli lordship D
1921 ocupien] occupyed F   1922 *margin* act. 4 EL   and] DHFL, as E
1923 diden] *om.* D   þe²] *om.* F   1926 nameli] specialli F   1929 ouer]
besyd F   1930 lordship²] lordschipis F   1931 whateuere] what þat euere D,
what ⌐so⌐ euer F   mote] moste DF   1932 þe¹] *om.* F   *margin* io. 5.10 and 14 c
ED, io. 5 and 14 *margin at 2253* F, Joh. x & xiiij *margin* L, *see* 1935 H   1933 leeue]
beleue F   1934 wundir] very F   þat] as F   ado] to do F   1935 wiþ²]
om. F   þei] vt patet Ion v c et xiiij c þei H

boþe, and be of þat noumbre of whiche God pleniþ be þe prophete
Ose saiynge "þai regneden but not be me", saiþ God. And ȝif we
holden þat þat is forboden, here we þat is bodyn of Criste: "He þat is
gratter of ȝow, loke þat he be made as ȝongar | in sympilnes, and ⌐he⌐ f. 33ᵛ
þat is forgoer, loke he be a seruant." þis is þe forme of þe apostles 666
liife: lordeschip is forbodon and seruyse is boden.' þis saiþ saynt
Bernarde þere. And þerfore no man may putt anoþere grownde
bisidis þat þat is putt þe whiche is Criste Ihesu.

Capitulum viii

But ȝit I wote well þat, and clerkis and religious folke þat louen 670
vnkyndely þes lordlynes willen glose here, and say þat þai occupien
⌐not⌐ siche lordeschipis in propir as seculer lordis done but in
comoun, like as þe apostles and þe perfite peple diden in þe
begynnynge of Cristis chirche, þe whiche hadden alle þinge in
comoun, like as suche clerkis and religious saien þai han nowe. In 675
tokenyng wherof, as no man sayd of eny | þinge þat tyme 'þis f. 34ʳ
is myne', so oure clerkis, and religious namely, whan þai will speke
in termis of her religion, a priuate persone will not say 'þis or þis is
myne', but in persone of alle his breþern he will say 'þis is oure.'
And ouer all þis þai saien more sutilly þat þai occupie not þis bi title 680
of seculer lordeschip, but be title of perpetual almes. But whateuer
þis peple saien here, we mot take hede to þe rewle of prefe þat fayliþ
not, þe whiche rule Criste techiþ vs in þe gospel in dyuers placis
wher he saiþ: 'Leue ȝe þe werkis, forwhi by her werkis ȝe schul
knowe hem.' And þis rule is wondir nedefull to a man þat haþ ado 685
wiþ eny men of þe pha|riseis condicions. For as Criste saiþ 'þai f. 34ᵛ
saien but þai done not.' And so as Cristis werkis beren witnes of
hym, as he hymsiilfe saiþ, and schewdyn what he was, and how he
lyued, so þe dedis and þe maner of lyuynge or þe þinge in itsiilfe

---

662 þat] the P *margin* Osee viij L, Ozee[P1   665 gratter] greatest P   loke]
se P   666 forgoer] a foregoere P   a] as a P   þe²] *om.* P   667 lordeschip is]
lordshyppes P   669 þe] *om.* P   Capitulum viii] *om.* P   670 and¹] *om.* P
673 *margin* Act. iiij° L þe²] *om.* P   perfite] profite *altered to* perfite L
674 chirche] chyrche as wryteth Saynct Luke in the fourthe chaptre of the Actes of the
apostles P   þinge] thynges P   676 as] *om.* P   that] at that P   677 religious
namely] namely relygyous people P   680 all] *om.* P   683 rule] faileþ not *canc.*
rule L   *margin* Joh. x° et xiiij° L   684 leue] beleue P   686 men] man P
margin Mt. xxiij° L þai] in the thre and twenty chaptre of Mathewe. They P1, Math. xxiij.
They P2   688 schewdyn] sheweth P   689 þe²] *om.* P

maner of lyuyng or þe þing in itsilf beriþ witnesse wiþoute faile hou it stondiþ among hem in þis poynt.

1940 And if we take heede þus bi þis rule, we shal se at iȝe hou þe clergie seiþ here oþer wise þan it is. For in sum place in priuat persoone, and in sum place in comounte or persoone aggregat, þe

f. 78ᵛ which is al oon bi seynt Austyn vpon | þe Sauter, þe clergie ocupieþ þe seculer lordship seculerli and so in propre. For in þe same wise as

1945 þe baroun or þe knyȝt ocupieþ and gouerneþ his barony or knyȝt fee, so aftir þe amorteisyng ocupieþ þe clerk, or mounk, or chanoun, or colege, or couent þe same lordship, and gouerneþ it bi þe same lawis, in iugement and poneshing, as prisonyng, hanging and oþir such worldli turmenting, þe which ⌐sum¬ tyme bilongide oonli to þe

1950 seculer arm of þe chirche. Ȝhe, ofte tymes we mai se hou þei bisien hem to be kyngis in her owne, and reioisen hemsilf ful moche in þat ciuilite or seculerte, if þei mai gete it; and þat is an euydence þat þei wolde gladli be kyngis of al þe rewme or þe world. Ȝhe, þereas her londis and lay mennes londis fraunchisen togidir, þei stryuen who

f. 79ʳ shal haue þe galowes, or oþir ma|ner turmentis for felouns; and so

1956 striuen ofte who shal haue seculer power to prisone or to honge such a feloun. þei kepen also vndir bondage her tenauntis and her issu wiþ her londis. And þis is [þe] moost ciuilite or seculer lordship[i]ng þat was among þe heþen or mai be in þis world, as Crist meneþ in þo

1960 wordis þat I haue ofte aleggid bifore, whanne he seiþ 'þe kyngis of þe heþen han lordship of hem, but ȝe not so.' So þis heþen lordship is not oonli upon þe londis or þe mouable goodis of þe sugetis, but also upon her bodies and her issu. And so for þe vnperfeccioun þerof, alþouȝ Crist haue ȝoue leue to lay men to be lordis þus, he

1965 myȝte not do ⌐so¬ to þe clerkis þat shulde ⌐sue¬ him in þe perfeccioun of þe gospel. And certis, þouȝ ony man wolde assente aȝens þe gospel

f. 79ᵛ þat clerkis shulde haue such seculer lordship | upon worldli possessiouns, ȝit me semeþ he shulde not assente þat clerkis shulde ⌐haue¬ þis moost vnkyndli lordship, wherbi [a] man haþ

1970 lordship upon his broþir þat is euene in kynde wiþ him.

1938 or þe þing] *om.* F   1940 at iȝe] playnly F   1942 þe] *om.* FL
1943 bi] as FL   vpon] saith vpon F, saiþ vp L   1944 þe¹] *om.* HF
1946 or¹] *om.* F   or³] eþer F   1948 iugement] judgementis F   prisonyng]
prisonment F   hanging] and hangyng FL   1949 þe¹] *om.* F   1952 mai]
myght F   1953 þereas] as HF   1954 mennes londis] men H, mentis F,
mennes L   fraunchisen] be franchysed F   1955 þe] *om.* F   galowes] galhous H
1956 who] w *canc./* who E   to²] *om.* F   1958 and] as F   þe] DHFL, *om.* E
lordshiping] lordshipg E   1959 or . . . meneþ] *om.* F   þo] þes F   1960 he]

beriþ witnesse wiþoute fayle how it stondiþ amonge hem in þis 690
poynte.

And if we take hede þus bi þis rule, we schal se at yȝe how þe
clergie saiþ here oþer wyse þan it is. For in sum place in priuate
persone, and in sum place in comunte or persone aggregate, whiche
is alle oone as saynt Austyn saiþ vp þe Sawter, þe clergi occupieþ þe 695
seculer lordeschip seculerli and so in propre. For in þe same wise as
þe baron or þe knyȝte occupieþ and gouerneþ his baronrye or his
knyȝt [f]e, so after þe amor|tesynge occupieþ þe clerke, þe monke or f. 35ʳ
chanon, þe colage or þe couente þe same lordeschip, and gouerniþ it
by þe same lawis, in iugement and ponyschinge, as prisonynge and 700
hangynge wiþ siche oþer worldly turmentynge, þe whiche sum tyme
bylongyd oonly to þe seculer arme of þe chirche. Ȝhe, oft tymys we
may se how þai bissyen hem to be kyngis in her owne, and reioycen
hem full myche in þat cyuylite or seculerte, ȝif þai may gete it; and
þis is an euydence þat þai wold gladly be kyngis of alle þe rewme or 705
þe worlde. For wher her londis and seculer mennys franchisen
togydir, þai stryuen who schal haue þe galows, or oþer maner
turmentis for felouns. þai kepen also vndir bondage her tenauntis
and her | issue wiþ her londis. And þis is þe mooste cyuylite or f. 35ᵛ
seculer lordeschipinge þat eny kynge or lorde haþ on his tenauntis. 710

692 yȝe] oure eye P   693 here] *om.* P   is] is in dede P   694 comunte]
comone P   695 vp] vppon P   696 wise] maner wyse P   698 knyȝt fe]
knyȝtte L, knyghtes fe P   699 þe²] *om.* P   702 oonly] *om.* P
703 hem] theymselfes P   705] an] an an P1   706 franchisen] fraunchyse
ar P2

[*Lambeth Tract resumes on p. 99*]

crist F   1961 but] and HF   þis] the F   1962 þe³] þer F   1963 so]
om. F   1965 so] ʳsoˡ EH   sue] folow F   1966 certis] verely F   assente]
agre F   1967 clerkis] DHF, þe clerkis E   such] *om.* HF   1968 semeþ]
thynk F   assente] agre F   1969 a man] DHF, a *canc.* man E

And it is no doute þat, as þis vnperfit and vnkyndli lordship stondiþ not in oo persoone bi himsilf wiþ þe perfeccioun of þe gospel, so it stondiþ not wiþ þis perfeccioun in two or þre, or in a couent; for it is þe same manere of vnperfit lordshiping and seculer
1975 manere of lordship, in whom it euere be. And as symony, manslau3-tir or heresie dampnabli infectiþ a couent, where þei in comoun assenten þerto, þe which synne is neuere þe lesse in ony of þo priuat persoones, alþou3 þe persoone aggregat or þat couent assenten and perfourmen in comoun þat synne, so stondiþ it of þis synful lordship
1980 in oo singuler persoone and in a comounte of clerkis or of religious
f. 80ʳ folk. And in ful euydence þat | þei han propre possessioun in suche lordships, þei vsen al manere of ciuile or seculer lawis or menes in getyng and keping of suche goodis, be it in stryuyng, pleting or fi3ting, liik as anoþer seculer lord doiþ. And certis, but if þei
1985 cleymede a propre possessioun or lordship in suche goodis ouer þe titil of innocence or bi grace, þei wolde no more plete, stryue or fi3te for suche goodis þan doen oþir men þat holden hem apaied wiþ þe titil of grace to suche goodis, or þanne þei pleten, or stryuen, or fi3ten for þe li3t of þe sunne or of þe mone, or ellis for þe eir, þe
1990 whiche ben comoun to alle men. Wheþer now þo þat cleymen þe perfeccioun of þe gospel, and seien þat þei perfourmen þe plente or souereynte of þat perfeccioun, stryuen bi alle maner lawis of ciuilite or propirte for geting and keping of worldli goodis?—and not oonli
f. 80ᵛ a3ens lay men, | but also þei, þat seien hemsilf for to be þus perfit,
1995 stryuen þus for to seche lordship among hemsilf, as a bishop or a colege a3ens an abbot or a priour or ellis a couent, where, and þei hadden left al maner ciuilite and proprete, liik as diden þe apostlis wiþ þe perfit men in þe bigynnyng of Cristis chirche, þei shulden haue alle her goodis in comoun wiþoute ony striif as þei hadden.
2000 And as suche wordis in þe bigynnyng of þis perfeccioun, 'þis is myn', 'þis is þyn', my3te haue maad striif for worldli goodis þat tyme, so þese wordis 'oure' and '3oure' maken now grete striif ofte among colegis and couentis þat cleymen þis perfeccioun. And herfore, alþou3 we reden (*Act.* 4) þat no persoone of þe perfit folk

1971 and]⸢24 ca.⸣ and F   1973 not] it not D   þis] þe F   1974 lordshiping]
lordschipe F   1975 whom it euere] whomeuer it F   1977 assenten] agre F
þe¹] *om.* F   þo] þes F   1978 persoone] persoones HF   assenten and] agree or F
1980 singuler] seculer D   1984 certis] verely F   1988 or¹] er H, raþer F
þei] to F   1989 of þe²] *om.* F   for] of F   1990 þo] thei F   1991 or
souereynte] *om.* F   1993 and¹] or F   1995 þus] *om.* F   to seche] such
DHF   1996 and] as yf F   2004 herfore] þerfor F

in þe tyme of þe apostlis seide of ony þing þat he hadde þat it was 2005
his, ȝit rede we not þere þat ony persoone or couent seide of ony
good 'þis is oure', or 'þis is ȝoure' but, as it is | red þere, alle þingis f. 81ʳ
weren comoun to hem, and þer was no nedi among hem for it was
departid to ech as nede was. For as þis word 'myn' includiþ propirte
of possessioun, and excludiþ comunyng of þing þat is so callid to 2010
anoþir persoone or couent, so þis word 'oure' wolde haue mened
propirte of suche goodis to a certein comounte wiþoute such
comunyng to a peple þat hadde not be of þe same comounte; and
þat hadde be vnperfitnesse among such peple, þat weren of oon herte
and will, and hadden alle þingis in comoun to alle of þat perfeccioun. 2015
    And of þis processe and experience þou maist se þat oure ypocritis
failen foul of þis perfeccioun. For if þei were of þis perfeccioun, þei
wolden be of oon herte and wil, and haue alle her goodis in comoun,
and suffre noon to be mescheuousli nedi among hem. And þanne siþ
mounkis, chanouns and freris | ben, as þei seien, of þis same f. 81ᵛ
perfeccioun, þe munkis and chanouns, þat han in her mynystracioun 2021
greet superfluite of suche as þei callen comoun goodis, wolde not
suffre her briþeren freris þat ben of þe same perfeccioun in so
mescheuous nede as þei pretenden, nameli siþ þe mounkis and
chanouns weren wount to preue in scool and to teche and preche 2025
opunli þat þe begging of þe freris is dampnable. For certeyn herof
doute I me not, and þei hadde þis perfeccioun wiþ charite þat longiþ
þerto þat sechiþ not hise owne (as seynt Poul seiþ 1 *Cor.* 13), and so
weren of oon herte and will, þei wolde not suffre her briþeren þus to
ligge alwei in þis cursid synne of beggerie, siþ it is in her power bi 2030
comunyng of suche goodis so to releeue her briþeren, þat hem nede
not ne haue ony occasioun for to synne þus. And bi þis mene þei
myȝte brynge her | briþeren out of þe synne of beggerie, þe which f. 82ʳ
þei dampnen in word and dede, into þe perfeccioun þat þei stonden
yn, þe which is greet as þei boosten. But sikir what þat euere þese 2035
ypocritis seien, I woot wel þei ben rotun in þe roote, and it is

2006 or] of HF   couent] comounte DHF   2009 ech] euery one F
2010 þing] the thyng F   2011 couent] comunte DHF   word . . . goodis (2012)]
om. F   2016 and experience] *om.* F   þou maist] ye may F   2017 foul]
moche F   2019 þanne siþ] moreouer seyng F   2020 chanouns] and
chanouns H   2024 meschevous] moche myscheuus F   nameli] specially F
siþ] seyng F   2026 þe²] *om.* HF   for . . . and (2027)] for I dowt not truly yf F
2027 doute I] *rev.* D   longiþ] bilongiþ HF   2028 *margin* 1 cor. 13 EDF   1
Cor. 13] *om.* F   2030 siþ] seyng F   2031 hem] they F   2032 ne] *om.* F
2033 þe²] *om.* F   2035 þe] *om.* F   sikir] truly F   2036 þei] þat þei D

falsnesse and doublenesse wel nyʒ al þat þei delen wiþ. For wel we
mai se hou suche sectis cleymen in her goodis a maner of propre
possessioun, contrarie to þe comunyng of þe comoun goodis in tyme
2040 of þe perfit men in þe bigynnyng of Cristis chirche. And so,
whateuere þe clergie seie, þe dede shewiþ wel þat þei han not her
goodis in comoun, liik as Crist wiþ hise apostlis and perfit men
hadden in þe bigynnyng of Cristis chirche. For in holding or hauyng
of her goodis is propirte of possessioun and seculer lordship, þe
2045 which stondiþ not wiþ þe plente of þis perfeccioun, as it sueþ of þis
f. 82ᵛ processe, and of þat | þat is declarid bifore.

And, as for þat oþir gloos þat clerkis han here, where þei seien þat
þei holden þese lordships and possessiouns bi titil of perpetuel
almesse, þou shalt vndirstonde þat merci or almesse is a will of
2050 releeuyng of a wrecche out of his mysese, as Lyncolniencis seiþ in þe
bigynnyng of hise *Dictis*. So þat if a man shulde effectueli do almesse,
he most loke þat he þat he shulde do almesse to were in mysese þat
shulde be releued. In tokenyng wherof Crist oonli asigneþ almesse to
þo in whom he markiþ mysese. And so of þis [it] wole sue þat, if a
2055 man releeue oo wrecche and makiþ anoþer or two ⌈or⌉ mo, he doiþ
noon almesse but raþer makiþ mysese; and moche raþer if he make
riche þo þat han no nede, for as moche as þei ben sufficient to
f. 83ʳ hemsilf, he doiþ noon almesse; and ferþermor, if he ma|ke such peple
riche wiþ waast ʒyuyng of hise goodis þat shulde not be riche bi þe
2060 gospel, and also ben sufficient in hemsilf, þis haþ no colour of
almesse, for þis mai beter be callid a woodnesse or wasting of Goddis
goodis. And ouere þis, if a man take þo goodis, þe whiche God in þe
beste wise euene and wiþout errours haþ asigned to þe staat of
seculer lordis, þe whiche he haþ appreued in his chirche, and ʒyue
2065 þo goodis to anoþer peple þat haþ no nede to hem,—ʒhe, to þe
which peple suche goodis ben forfendid,—þis shulde be callid noon

2038 suche] ⌈suche þese⌉ H, thes F   2043 or hauyng] or harmynge, r *and first
minim of* m *canc.* H, *om.* F   2044 þe] *om.* F   2045 stondiþ] stonden H
sueþ] foloweith F   2047 þat oþir] ⌈an⌉oþer H, anoþer F   2048 and
possessiouns] ⌈and possessiouns⌉ *dh* D, *om.* L   2049 þou shalt] yow schall F
merci] þe merci HF   or] of HF   2050 mysese] dysease F   Lyncolniencis]
lincoln HF   *margin* dicto 2 EDL, *in text after* dictis (2051) H, ij ca. F   2052 þat
he þat he] þat he ⌈to whom he⌉ H(*dh*)L, to whom he F   to] to men F   were in
mysese] dyseasyd F   2054 þo] those F   markiþ mysese] knowith disease F   it
wole] DHFL, wole E   sue] folowe F   2055 releeue . . . he (2056)] *om.* F
2056 makiþ] make H   2057 riche þo] thos rich F   2061 wasting] a waasting
DL   2062 and] ⌈25 ca.⌉ and F   þo] þos F   þe¹] *om.* F   in] on DHF
2063 euene and] and euen H, and F   errours] errour DHF   2064 þe] *om.* F
appreued] alowid F   ʒyue] gyveth F   2065 þo] thos F   anoþer] oþer F   to²]

And þerfore we may se how þai claymen in her goodis a maner of propre possession, contrary to þe comounynge of þe comon goodis in tyme of þe perfyte men in þe begynnynge of Cristis chirche. And whatsoeuer þe clergye sayen, þair dedis schewyn well þat þai han not her goodis in comoun, lyke as Criste wiþ his apostles and perfyte 715 men hadden in þe begynnynge of Cristis chirche. For in holdynge or havynge of her goodis is propir of possessyon and seculer lordeschipynge, þe whiche stondiþ not wiþ þe plente of Cristis perfeccion in prestis, as it sueþ of þis processe | and of þat þat is declarid before. f. 36ʳ

And, as for þat oþer glose þat clerkis han here, where þai saien þat 720 þai holden þes lordeschipis by title of perpetual almes, but here ȝe schul vndirstonde þat mercy or almes is a will of relevynge of a wreche oute of his mysese, as Lyncolnyence saiþ in þe bygynnynge of his *Dictis*. So þat ȝif a man schuld do effectualy almes, he most loke þat he to whom he schuld do almes to wer in mysese, and had 725 nede to be releuyd. In tokenynge wherof Criste oonly assigneþ almes to þo in whom he markiþ mysese. And so of þis it will sue þat, ȝif a man releue oo wreche and makiþ anoþere or mo, he doþe noon almes | but raþer makiþ mysese; and myche more he doþe noone f. 36ᵛ almes ȝif he make riche þo þat han noone nede, for als myche as þai 730 ben sufficiente to hemsiilf—þis haþ no colour of almesse, for þis may bettir be callid a woodnesse or a wastyng of Goddis goodis. And ouer þis, if a man take þo goodis, þe whiche God in þe best wise euen and wiþowte errourys haþ assigned to þe state of seculer lordis, and ȝeue þo goodis to eny peple þat haþ noone nede of hem,—ȝhe, to whiche 735 peple siche goodis ben forfendit,—þis schuld be callid noone almesse, but peruertynge of Goddis ordynance and þe destruccyon of þe state of seculer lordis, þe whiche God haþ aprouyd in his chirche. For, as | saynt Poule saiþ, almesdede schuld be so rewlid, f. 27ʳ þat it wer relevynge to þo þat ressavyn it, and no tribulacion to þo 740 þat ȝeuen it; and myche raþer it schuld not be vndoynge of þo þat

---

713 and] and so P   714 þair] the P   dedis] dede P   schewyn] sheweth P
717 propir] properte P   721 *margin* Almes P2   722 a²] some P
724 *margin* Dicto ijᵒ LP2,]icto ij P1   do effectualy] *rev.* P   725 þat he] *om.* P
to¹] knew *canc.* to L   727 þo] thos P   *margin* luc' xiiij. LP1   so] so here P
728 releue] will releve P   makiþ] make P2   730 þo] thes (thos P2) persones P
732 bettir be] *rev.* P   733 þo] thos P   735 þo] thos P   eny] another P
whiche] the which P   739 *margin* pᵃ cor. viij L, ij Cori.viij P   so rewlid] *rev.* P
740 þo¹] thos P   and . . . it¹ (741)] *om.* P   741 þo] thos P

---

of FL   ȝhe to . . . peple (2066)] specially vnto them to whom F   2066 forfendid]
forbydd F

almesse, but peruerting of Goddis ordynaunce or distruccioun of a
staat þe which God haþ appreued in his chirche. For, as seynt Poul
seiþ (2 *Cor.* 8), almesse dede shulde be so rulid, þat it were not
2070 releeuyng to þo þat resceyuen it and tribulacioun to þo þat ȝyuen it;
f. 83ᵛ and moche raþer it shulde | not be vndoing of þo þat doen it. And
herfor Crist techiþ in þe gospel men to do almesse of þo þingis þat
ben needles to him þat deliþ almesse; and in þis nede a man shal
haue reward to þe staat of him þat doiþ almesse and to þe charge of
2075 his owne hous. What almesse þanne, I preie þee, was it to vndo þe
staat of þe empire, and make þe clerkis riche wiþ hise lordships?—
nameli, siþ Crist hadde confermed to þe emp[er]our his astaat wiþ
þo þingis þat longide þerto, notwiþstondinge þat þe emperour þat
tyme was heþen, and haþ forfendid expressli his clergie in word and
2080 ensaumple such worldli lordship. And as þis was noon almesse, so we
mote seie of oþir kyngis, dukis and eerlis and barouns and knyȝtis,
þat ben vndo, and þe clerkis maad riche and worldli lordis wiþ her
goodis. And þouȝ it so hadde be þat þe clergie myȝte haue ocupied
f. 84ʳ þus world|li lordship and also, þouȝ it hadde be no distraccioun or
2085 apairing of ony oþir astaat of þe chirche, ȝit it hadde be noon almesse
for to ȝyue to hem suche goodis.

For þe clerkis weren sufficientli purueid for liiflood bi Cristis
ordynaunce in þe gospel, for he is so perfit in al his worching þat he
mai ordeyne noon astaat in his chirche, but if he ordeyne sufficient
2090 liiflood to þe same astaat. And þis is opun in Goddis lawe, who so
takiþ bisili heede, and þat vndir euery lawe of God, as vndir þe lawe
of innocence and of kynde, vndir þe lawe ȝouun bi Moyses, and also
vndir þe lawe ȝouun bi Crist. In þe tyme of þe staat of innocence we
knowen wel bi bileeue þat God hadde so ordeyned for mankynde þat
2095 it shulde haue had liiflood ynow, ȝhe, wiþoute ⌐ony⌐ teenful labour;
f. 84ᵛ and þis is þe lawe of kynde, | þat Crist spekiþ of (*Mt.*7) where he seiþ

2067 or] and FL   2068 þe] *om.* F   appreued] alowid F   2069 Cor.] ad
cor. D   dede] dedis F   2070 þo¹] thos F   þo²] þos F   2071 of] to HF
þo] thos F   doen] gyve F   2072 herfor] þerfore F   in] men *canc.* in E   þo]
þos F   2074 and] *om.* F   to²] vnto F   2075 þanne . . . it] was it then I pray
ye F   vndo] do *canc.* vndo E   2076 empire] emperour FL   2077 nameli]
specially F   siþ] seyng F   emperour] empour E   astaat] state FL
2078 þo] þos F   longide] longith F   þe] *om.* D   þat³] at þat F   2079 haþ]
⌐god⌐ haþ H, god hath F   expressli his clergie] his clergie expressli, *marked for rev.* E
2080 ensaumple] in exampyll F   we mote seie] may it be sayd F   2081 and¹]
om. HF   and²] *om.* HFL   2084 þus] þis F   distraccioun] distruccioun DHF
2086 to hem] them F   2087 purueid] provydyd F   2089 ordeyne] ordenyd F
2090 is] *om.* F   2091 bisili] bisi H, *om.* FL   vndir¹] and vndur F   2093 bi

done it. And herfore Criste techiþ in þe gospell to do almes of þo
þinges þat ben needeles or superflue; and in þis dede a man schulde
haue rewarde to þe nede of hym þat he doþe almes to, and to þe
charge of his owne house. What almes þan, I pray þe, was it to vndo 745
þe state of þe emperoure, and make þe clerkis riche wiþ his
lordechipis?—namely, siþ Criste confermyd to þe emperour his
state wiþ þo þingis þat longyd þerto, notwiþstondynge þat þe
emperoure þat tyme was heþen, and he haþ forfen|dit expresly his f. 37ᵛ
clergy in worde and in ensaumple siche lordeschip. And as þis was 750
noone almes, so we mote say of oþer kyngys, dukis and erlis, barons
and knyʒtis, þat ben vndo herby, and þe clerkis made riche and
worldely lordis wiþ her goodis. [And þouʒ it had be so þat þe clergi
myʒte haue occupyed þus worldely lordschip, and also þouʒ it had be
no destruccion ne apeyrynge of eny oþer state, ʒit it hadde be no 755
almes for to ʒeue to hem siche goodis.] Wherfore it may riʒtfully be
sayde 'No man may putt anoþer grounde bisidis þat þat is putt, þe
whiche is Criste Ihesu.'

Capitulum ix

Here we may se bi þe grounde of þe gospell and be þe ordenance of
Criste þat þe clergy was sufficyently purveyd for lyfelode. For God is 760
so perfyte in all his worchynge þat he may ordeyn no state in his
chirche, but if he ordeyn sufficient liflode to þe sa|me state. And þis f. 38ʳ
is open in Goddis lawe, who so takiþ heede, and þat vndir euery lawe
of God, as vndir þe law of innocens and of kynde, vndir þe lawe ʒeue
by Moyses, and also vndir þe lawe ʒouen by Criste. In þe tyme of þe 765
state of innocence we know wel by bileue þat God had so ordeynd
for mankynde þat it schulde haue had lyflode inow, ʒhe, wiþowte eny
tenefull laboure; and of þe lawe of kynde Criste spekiþ in þe gospell
seynge þus: 'Alle þinges þat we wollen þat oþer men done to ʒou, do

742 *margin* Quod superest date elemosinam. luc. xiiij° LP   herfore] therfore P
743 superflue] superfluite P   744 reward] regarde P   745 þan . . . þe] was it
then I praye (paye P1) you P   746 make] to make P   748 longyd] longeth P1,
longe P2   þat²] at that tyme P   749 þat tyme] *om.* P   750 ensaumple]
example P   753 and . . . goodis (756)] *om.* L   756 riʒtfully be] *rev.* P
757 þat þat] þat P   þe] *om.* P   Capitulum ix] *om.* P   761 he] *om.* P1
762 he] h *canc.* he L   766 had] hath P1   767 ʒhe] *om.* P
768 tenefull] tedious P   769 *margin* Mt. vij° LP   we] ye P

Crist] of Iesu Crist F   2094 wel] *om.* F   2095 it] he F   ony] ⌐ony⌐ E,
om. HF   teenful] tedius F   2096 *margin* mt. 7 EDL

þus: 'Alle þingis þat ȝe wolen þat oþir men do to ȝou, do ȝe to hem.'
And if þis lawe hadde be kept, þer shulde no man haue be
mesheuousli nedi. And in þe tyme of þe lawe ȝoue bi Moyses God
2100 made ful and sufficient ordynaunce for al his peple, hou and wherbi
þei shulde lyue, for he delide þe lond among þe lay peple, and
asignede þe firste fruytis and tiþis to þe prestis and dekenes. And
alþouȝ þat he wolde þat þer shulde be alwei pore men in þe lond of
Israel, ȝit he made an ordynaunce aȝens mescheuous nede, and
2105 comaundide al þe peple þat þer shulde be on no wise a nedi man and
a begger among hem, as it is writun (*Deut.* 15). And so in þis lawe he
ordeynede sufficientli ynow for his peple. And in þe tyme of þe newe
f. 85ʳ lawe Crist asignede þe temperaltees or secu|ler lordships to temperal
lordis, as it is tauȝt bifore, and alowide þe comounte her liiflood
2110 gotun bi trewe marchaundise and husbondrie, for he was partener
þerof. And in word and in ensaumple he tauȝte hise prestis to be
procuratours for nedi peple and pore at þe riche men, and specifiede
þese pore, and tauȝte hou þat þei þat were myȝti shulde make a
puruyaunce for such pore folk, þat þei were not constreined bi nede
2115 for to begge, as grete clerkis marken upon þis word of þe gospel
(*Luc.* 14), where Crist seiþ þus: 'Whanne þou makist þi feeste, þat is
to seie of almesse, calle pore feble, lame and blynde.' He seiþ not
'late suche pore men calle upon þee', but 'calle þou', menynge in þat
þat þou shuldist make a puruyaunce for such peple, þat þei ben not
2120 mescheuousli fauti. And for þe clergie he ordeynede sufficientli,
f. 85ᵛ teching ⌐hem⌐ | in word and [in] ensaumple hou þei shulde holde
hem apaied wiþ liiflood and hilyng, mynystrid to hem for her trewe
labour in þe gospel, as it [is] writun bifore.

Off þis þanne þou maist se hou God in alle hise lawis haþ
2125 sufficientli ordeyned for alle þe statis þat he foundide and approuede,
and hou it were aȝens þe goodnesse and wisdom of God to ordeyne
ony astaat, but if he ordeynede sufficient liiflood þerto. Siþ þanne þis
ordynaunce of God was sufficient, as wel for þe clergie as for oþir
men, it semeþ a blasphemous presumpcioun to brynge yn a newe and
2130 a contrarie ordynaunce of liiflood for þe clerkis upon þe ordynaunce

---

2097 ȝe²] yow F   2098 shulde . . . be] had bene no man F   haue be] be D
2102 tiþis] þe tiþis D   2103 þat¹] *om.* HF   alwei pore men] poor men allway F
2105 þat . . . on] in F   and a begger] to be F   2106 *margin* deu. 15 DFL
2107 sufficientli] frely and sufficiently F   2111 ensaumple] exampyll F
2112 *margin* luc. 14 D   procuratours] procters F   2115 *margin* luc. 14 EDFL
þis] þus D   2118 late] late not D   þee] yow F   þou] yow F
2119 þou] yow F   shuldist] schuld F   2120 sufficientli] hem sufficientli HF

ȝe to hem.' And if þis lawe had be kepte, þer schuld no man haue be 770
myscheuously nedy. And in þe tyme of þe lawe ȝeue by Moyses God |
made a full and a sufficient ordenance for alle his peple, [houȝ and f. 38ᵛ
wherby þai schuld lyue. For he delyd þe londe amonge þe laye
peple], and assigned þe fyrste fruytis and tiþis to þe prestis and
deeknes. And allþouȝ ⌐þat⌐ he wolde þat þer schulde be alle way pore 775
men in þe londe of Israell, ȝit he made an ordenance aȝens
myschevous nedis, and commaundet alle þe peple þat þer schulde
be on no wyse a nedy man and a beggere amonge hem, as it is
wryten. And so in þis lawe he ordeynyd sufficiently inow for his
peple. And in þe tyme of þe new lawe Criste assignyd þe seculer 780
lordeschipis to temperall lordes, as it is tauȝte byfore, and alowid þe
comonte her liflode goten bi true merchandise and hosbondrie and
oþer craftis. And in worde and ensaumple he tauȝte his prestis | to be f. 39ʳ
procuratouris for nedy peple and pore at þe ryche men, and
specifyed þes pore, and tauȝte how þai þat wer myȝty schuld make a 785
purviance for syche pore folke, þat þai wer not constrenyd by nede for
to begge, as grete clerkis merken vpon þis worde of þe gospell where
Criste saiþ þus: 'Whan þu makist þine feeste, þat is of almes, call pore
feble, lame and blynde.' He saiþ not 'latt siche pore men call vpon þe',
but 'call þu', menynge in þat þat þu schuldist make a purvyance for 790
siche peple, þat þai be not myschevously fauȝty. And for þe clergy he
ordenyd sufficiently, techinge hem in worde and in ensaumple how þai
schuld holde hem apayde wiþ lyflode and helynge, mynystred to hem
for her true labour | in þe gospell, as it is wryten tofore. f. 39ᵛ

Of þis þan þu mayst se houȝ God in alle his lawis haþ sufficiently 795
ordend for alle þe statis þat he foundit and aproued, and houȝ it wer
aȝens þe goodnes and þe wisdome of God to orden eny state, but if
he ordend sufficyent liflode þerto. Siþ þen þis ordenance of God was
sufficyent, als well for þe clergi as for oþer men, it semiþ a foule
presumpcyon to brynge in a new and a contrary ordenance of liflode 800
for clerkis vpon þat ordenance þat Crist had made for hem byfore, of

772 houȝ . . . peple (774)] om. L 774 assigned] he assygned P 777 nedis]
nede P 778 on] in P margin Deutº. xvº LP 784 procuratours]
proctoures P 787 þis worde] thes wordes P margin luc.xiiijº LP
788 pore] poore people P 790 þuʹ] thou vpon theym P 792 in²] om. P
794 tofore] before P 796 he] be P wer] is P 797 þe²] om. P
801 þatʹ] the P had] hath P

2121 in ensaumple] DHL, in exampyll F, ensaumple E 2123 is] DHFL, om. E
2124 þanne] om. F 2127 astaat] staat HFL sufficient liiflood] rev. F siþ]
seyng F 2128 as² . . . rebels (2127)] lost H

þat Crist hadde maad for hem bifore, of þe which ordynaunce þe
clergie ful manye ʒeer aftir þe bigynnyng of Cristis chirche, whanne
it was best, heelden hem apaied; for þis meeneþ þat Cristis
f. 86ʳ ordynaunce was | insufficient and worþi to be vndo. And if we
2135 take good heede, þei hadde no more nede to playne, or to holde hem
myspaid wiþ þis ordynaunce, þan hadde þe oþir two statis of his
chirche, þe whiche into þis dai holden hem apaied wiþ þis
ordynaunce of Crist, and desiren in greet partie þat þis fair and
sufficient ordynaunce of Crist were fulli kept. And more sikirnesse
2140 or ensuraunce mai no man make of ony þing þan Crist haþ of þis
liiflood to þe clergie. For Crist not oonli affermeþ to þe peple þat he
wole not faile hem in liiflood and hilyng, but also preueþ þis bi
argumentis þat mai not be assoilid, so þat þei be trewe seruauntis to
him. For Crist meneþ þus in his arguyng þere, 'Siþ God failiþ not
2145 briddis and lilies and gras þat growiþ in þe feeld, neþer heþen men,
hou moche raþer shal he not faile hise trewe seruauntis?' So þat
f. 86ᵛ puruyaunce | of such perpetuel almesse, þat oure clerkis speken of,
meeneþ faute of bileeue and dispair of þe gracious gouernaunce of
God.

2150   Siþ þanne, as it is seid bifore, it is noon almesse to releeue oon
wrecche and make anoþer or mo, or for to ʒyue almesse to hem þat
han no nede; and moche raþer it is noon almesse to make hem riche
þat shulde not be riche, and þat wiþ temperal possessiouns, þe
whiche ben forfendid to such peple, and nameli if such almesse-
2155 ʒyuyng be distriyng or apeiring of ony astaat appreued of God in his
chirche, it wole sue þat þe endowing of þe clergie wiþ worldli
lordship ouʒte not to be callid almesse but raþer al-amys, or waasting
of Godis goodis, or distriyng of Goddis ordynaunce, for as moche as
þe clergie was sufficientli ordeyned fore bi Cristis owne ordinaunce.
2160 And also oþir fautis in ʒyuyng of almesse, þe whiche ben asigned
f. 87ʳ bifore, weren | foundun in þe clergie. For þis almesse þat þe clerkis
speken of here made many wrecchis, and it was ʒouun to þo þat
hadden no nede, and it made hem riche worldli þat shulde not haue
be so riche, and it is distruccioun or enpeiring, not oonli of oon astaat

2131 hadde] haþ D   2133 þat] now þat F   2135 playne] complayne F
2136 oþir two] rev. F   his] þe F   2137 þe] om. F   into] vnto F   holden]
held F   2139 sikirnesse] surenesse F   2140 or ensuraunce] om. F   no]
not F   man] a man F, om. D   2141 þe¹] his F   2142 hilyng] lyuyng F
2144 siþ] seyng F   2145 heþen] þe heþen DF   2146 raþer] more and raþer F
2150 siþ] seyng F   2152 and] om. F   hem] hym F   2154 forfendid]
forbydden F   peple] pe/pepyll F   nameli] specially F   2155 -ʒyuyng] om. F

þe whiche ordenance þe clergy full many ȝere aftir þe bigynnynge of Cristis chirche, whan it was best gouernyd, helden hem apayde; for þis meneþ þat Cristis | ordenance was insufficyent and worþi to be f. 40ʳ vndo. And if we take goode heede, þai hadden no more nede to plene 805 hem of þis ordenaunce þan hadden þe oþer two statis of his chirche, þe whiche into þis day holden hem apayde wiþ þis ordenance of Criste, and desyren in grete party þat þis fayre and sufficient ordenaunce of Criste were fully kepte. And more sikirnes or ensurance may no man make of eny þinge þan Criste haþ of þis 810 liflode to þe clergy. For Crist not oonly affermiþ to þe peple þat he will not fayle hem in liflode and helynge, but also preueþ þis by argumentis þat may not be asoylyd, so þat þai be true seruandis to hym. For Crist meniþ þus in his arguynge þer, 'Siþ God fayleþ not briddis | and lilyes and grasse þat growen in þe felde, neiþer heþen f. 40ᵛ men, hou myche raþer schal he not fayle his true seruandis?' And so 816 þis purvyance of perpetual almes, þat oure clerkis speken of, meneþ fawte of bileue and dispeire of þe gracious gouernance of God.

Siþ þan, as it is sayde bifore, it is noone almes to releue oo wreche and make anoþer or mo, and to make hem riche wiþ temperall 820 lordeschip, þe whiche ben forfendit to siche peple, and namely if siche almes-ȝevynge be distroynge or apeyrynge of eny state aprevyd of God in his chirche, it will sue þat þe endowynge of þe clergy wiþ worldly lordeschipe owȝt not to be callid almes, but raþer all-amysse, or wastynge of Goddis goodes, or | distroynge of his ordenance, for f. 41ʳ as myche as þe clergi was sufficiently ordeynyd by Criste. Forwhi þis 826 almes þat clerkis speken of here made many wrechis, and it was ȝoue to hem þat hadde no nede, and þus it is enpeyringe, not oonly of oone estate of þe chirche, but of alle þre, of þe whiche I spoke of in þe bigynnynge. And so þis almes-ȝevynge haþ made all owre rewme, 830 ȝhe, and as I suppose, full nye all crestyndome full pore and nedy and myscheuous, ouer þat it schuld have be if þe clergy had holde hem payde wiþ Cristis ordenance.

---

802 ȝere] yeres P   803 apayde] well apayde P   807 þe] om. P   into] vnto P   808 and¹ . . . Criste (809)] om. P   809 were] were it P   or] and P 810 þis] hys P   814 margin Mt. vjᵒ L   820 make¹] to make P 822 state] astate Pı   823 of¹] by P   829 of] om. P   831 ȝhe] nedy ye P 833 payde] apayde P

or apeiring] om. F   2156 wole sue] may folow F   2158 as¹] a F 2159 fore] befor F   2160 þe] om. F   asigned] spokyn of F   2161 þe²] om. DL   clerkis speken] clergy spak F   2162 þo] thos F   2163 and] ⌐26 ca.⌐ And F   2164 or enpeiring] om. F   enpeiring] appering D

2165 of þe chirche, but also of alle þo þre astatis, of þe whiche I spak in þe bigynnyng. And so þis almesse-ȝuyng haþ maad al oure rewme, ȝhe, and as I suppose, ful nyȝ al cristendom ful pore and nedi and mescheuous, ouer þat it shulde haue be, if þe clergie hadde holde him apaied wiþ Cristis ordynaunce.

2170   And, for to knowe þis truþe þe more cleerli, þou shalt vndirstonde here þat Crist haþ not oonli foundid his vniuersel chirche upon þo þre statis answeringe to þe Trinyte, as I telde in þe bigynnyng, but also euery parishe chirche was foundid on þe same wise; and so as al
f. 87ᵛ Cristis chirche, so euery particuler chirche was | ensaumplid in þe
2175 Trinyte. For it hadde a lord answeringe to þe Fadir in Trinyte, þe which wiþ his worldli power shulde defende it fro bodili enmyes, and chastise rebels aȝens Goddis lawe and þe kyngis. And it hadde also a prest answeringe to þe Sone in ⌐þe⌐ Trinyte, þat wiþ heuenli wisdom shewid in word and dede shulde gouerne and lede þe peple in þe riȝt
2180 weie to heuene. And euery such chirche haþ a comunte answeringe to þe Hooli Goost, þat wilfulli bi her trewe labour and marchaundise shulde susteyne þ[e] two oþir astatis þat stonden in gouernail in þe chirche. But now þoruȝ þis perpetuel al-amys þat þe clerkis and religious folk callen almesse, þis gouernaunce is vndo in summe
2185 londis hoolli, and in Engelond for þe more part, and it is licli to be al vndo in processe of tyme. For bi amortaisyng of lordships þe lordis ben vndo in grete partie, and þo þat ben yleft, bicause þat hem |
f. 88ʳ lackiþ her owne part þoruȝ foly ȝift of her auncetris, ben ful nedi. And so þei ben ful greuous upon þe peple, and ouerleden hem soore
2190 bi manye dyuerse extorciouns and pilagis, wherbi þe peple is wundir nedi and pore, ȝhe, in ful many cuntrees fallen into mescheuous faute. And bi apropriaciouns of parishe chirchis þo prestis þat weren wount to be resident in suche parishis, to feede þe peple wiþ trewe loore and good ensaumple, and to feede þe pore nedi wiþ comoun
2195 almesse of þe chirche, and to susteyne and perfourme honestli dyuyne seruyce among þe peple, ben takun awei fro þe peple. And vnneþe in ful many placis is þer left a losel prest þat can lyue best at þe alehous, and mai nowher wel abide for his lecherie and oþir viciouse maners. And þus is þe fair policie of þe chirche distried bi
2200 þat þat þese ypocritis callen 'perpetuel almesse'.
f. 88ᵛ   And so þese ypocritis, and nameli þe religiouse en|dowid, as mounkis and chanouns and suche oþer sectis, han foul robbid and maad pore Cristis chirche, and þat wiþ a sotil and a dampnable manere of þefte þat is ypocrisie, for þei han robbid þe lordis of her

But now þorou þis perpetual al-amysse þat þe clerkis and religious
folke callen almes, Cristis ordenaunce is vndo in sum londis hooly, 835
and in Ynglonde for þe more party, | and it is likly to be all vndo in f. 41ᵛ
processe of tyme. For by amortesynge of lordeschipis þe lordis ben
vndo in grete party, and þo þat ben lefte, bycause þat hem lakkiþ her
owne party þorow foly ʒifte of her auncetreris ben full nedi.

834 and . . . folke (835)] om. P   838 þo . . . lefte] many noble men P   þat hem
lakkiþ] thei lacke P   839 party] parte P

2165 also] om. FL   þo] thes F   of þe²] om. F   in] of in FL   2166 haþ]
had F   2168 ouer þat] moche moore than F   2169 him] them F
2170 þe] om. F   þou shalt] yow schall F   2171 here] om. F   þo] þos F
2172 statis] astatis DF   in] yow in F   2173 and . . . chirche¹ (2174)] om. F
2175 þe²] om. F   2177 chastise] correct F   2178 þe²] om. F
2179 and dede] om. F   and lede] om. HF   2180 chirche] DHF, a chirche E
2182 þe] DHF, þo E   astatis] staatis HF   gouernail] gouernaunce F   in²] of F
2183 þis] þe HF   2185 part] partye FL   it] om. HF   al] om. F
2187 þo] thos F   hem lackiþ] þei lacke F   2189 ouerleden] ouerlayd F
2191 ful] om. F   2192 þo] þos F   2194 loore] lernyng F
2197 vnneþe] well nye F   ful many placis] euery place F   þer] om. D
2200 þat²] wich F   2201 nameli] specially F   2202 and¹] om. F

2205 temperaltees and þe curatis of her sustynaunce. And bi þese two
menes, as it is opun of þat þat I seide a litil bifore, þei han robbid þe
comunes and maad hem riȝt pore. And wondre þou not alþouȝ I calle
þis þefte, for þefte is takyng or wiþholding of good aȝens þe will of
him þat owiþ it, or aȝens þe will of þe lord, and nameli of þe cheef
2210 lord. Siþ þanne þese ypocritis taken and holden þese goodis aȝens þe
will and ordynaunce of God, þat is cheef lord, and haþ asigned þese
goodis to þe two statis in his chirche þat stonden in gouernaunce, it
sueþ pleynli þat þis is þefte. And þus þese þeeues ypocritis han
f. 89ʳ robbid Cristis chirche of goodis | of fortune, of goodis of kynde, and
2215 of goodis of grace as ben vertues. Hou þei han robbid þe chirche of
goodis of fortune, and maad it worldli pore and mescheuousli fauti, I
tolde it riȝt now. And hou þei han robbid þe chirche of goodis of
kynde it is opun at iȝe, for þei han vndo ful nyȝ þe staat of lordis, þe
whiche as lymes of a mannes bodi shulde susteyne, socoure and
2220 defende þe hooli bodi of Cristis chirche. And þei han robbid þe
chirche of goodis of grace in as moche as þei han putt awei þe honest
prestis bi apropriacioun of her chirchis, þat shulde and sumtyme
dide plaunte vertues in þe chirche bi her trewe teching and good
ensaumple, and bi honest perfourmyng of dyuyne seruyce.

2225 And so þei han almoost distried þe Trinyte of Cristis chirche here
on erþe, þat shulde answere to þe Trinyte of God in heuene in þese
f. 89ᵛ þre p[ropirtee]s, | power, wisdom and will. For þei han bireued þe
chirche of þe power, in as moche as þei han bireued it of þe staat of
lordis by amortaisyng of her liifloodis. And þei han robbid þe chirche
2230 of wisdom, as ferforþli as þei han wrouȝt to vndoyng of þe staat of
curatis, þat shulde be resident upon þe peple, and þat bi apropriacioun of her chirchis. And so in ful many placis is will left aloone
among þe comoun peple wiþoute power or wisdom; and in sum place
ben left power and will wiþoute wisdom; and in sum place wisdom
2235 and will wiþoute power. And so as power and will wiþoute wisdom is

---

2206 þat²] wich F   han] om. F   2207 wondre] marvell F   þou] yow F
2208 takyng] takyng awey HF   2209 it] om. H   nameli of] specially F
2210 siþ] seyng F   2213 sueþ] folowith F   2214 of²] om. F   of⁴] om. F
2215 hou] and how F   2217 it] om. HF   riȝt now] yow before F
2218 ful] well F   staat] staatis F   þe²] om. F   2219 a] om. HF   socoure]
and succour F   2220 hooli] hoole F   2222 apropriacioun] appropriacions F
2225 Cristis . . . for (2251)] lost H   2227 propirtees] DF, partis E   bireued]
spoyled F   2228 þe'] om. F   bireued] spoiled F   2229 and] ⌜27 ca.⌝
and F   2230 ferforþli] ferfurthe F   vndoyng] þe vndoyng F   2232 ful] om. F
2233 place] placis F   2234 place] placis F

tirauntrie, so will bi himsilf is ofte tyme rebellioun or woodnesse; and wisdom wiþoute power and will is but idil, and so is power wiþoute wisdom and will ydil also. And þus þou maist se þat ech of þese þre astatis haþ so moche nede, ech to oþir, þat noon of hem mai wel be
2240 wiþoute ech of þat oþir. |

f. 90ʳ   And of þis processe þou maist conseyue moche more þan is expresli writun here. And of þis þou maist se also hou harmful a peple in Cristis chirche ben þese ypocritis, þat callen þis robberie perpetuel almesse. And ferþermor þou maist vndirstonde of þis
2245 processe þat wiþdrawyng of þese goodis fro þese ypocritis, and restoring of hem to þ[e] statis þat God hadde asigned hem to, shulde be callid not robberie of hooli chirche, as þese ypocritis seien, but raþer riȝtwise restitucioun of goodis wrong[eful]li and þeefli wiþhol-dun. And þese harmful ypocritis han no cause to pleyne, alþouȝ þis
2250 were don in dede.

For men doen hem greet grace if þei suffren hem alyue bicause of þe robbyng and greet harm þat þei han don to al Cristis chirche. And, þouȝ þei feelen it not ⌜ȝit⌝ moost to hemsilf, ne þer mai ony ooþ or avow bynde ony man to maintene þis þefte and distriyng of
f. 90ᵛ   Goddis ordyn|naunce, and þis greet harmyng of Cristis chirche, as þe
2256 avow of Iepte shulde not haue boundun him to kille and sacrifice his owne douȝtir, ne þe ooþ of Heroude shulde not haue boundun him to kille innocent Iohun. But as Iepte shulde haue brokun his ooþ or avow and offrid anoþir þing þat hadde be plesynge to God and
2260 acordinge wiþ his lawe, as seynt Austyn seiþ *Libro suo de questionibus veteris et noue legis* upon þe same storie, so Herode shulde haue brokun his ooþ and saued innocent blood and sore repentid him for his vnauysi swering, and so shulde oure lordis now breke her ooþis if þei han vnauysili and wiþoute councel of hooli scripture sworun to
2265 maintene þis þefte—ȝhe, and heresie and symony, as it is proued bifore, þe which oure clerkis falsli callen perpetuel almesse,—and not þus, as þei doen, sue her predecessours or progenitours in her foly
f. 91ʳ   dedis and ooþis þat þei han maad to main|tene þis mescheuous peruertyng of Cristis ordynaunce. And as þe staat of þe clergie haþ

2236 tirauntrie] tyranny F   bi] in F   tyme] tymis F   2238 þou maist] yow may F   2239 astatis] staatis F   2240 ech of þat] *om.* F   2241 þou maist] yow may F   2242 þou maist] yow may F   2243 ben . . . ypocritis] þes ypocritis be F   2244 þou maist] yow may F   2246 þe] DFL, þo E   hadde] haþ FL   2248 wrongefulli] DFL, wrongli E   þeefli] theftly F   2249 harmful] perlos F   pleyne] complayne F   2251 greet] *om.* F   2252 greet] þe greet HF   2253 and . . . ne] *om.* F   ne þer] neþir H   ony] no

Ferþirmore it may be vndirstonde of þis processe þat wiþ- 840
drawynge of þes lordeschipis from þe clergi, and restorynge of
hem to þe statis þat God haþ assignyd hem to, schuld not be
callid robbery of holy chirche, as oure clerkis sayen, but raþer
riȝtwise restitucioun of goode wrongfully and þeuely wiþholde.

And þerfore þer may noon oþe or avow bynde eny man to 845
mayntene þis þefte and distryinge of Goddis ordenance, and þis
greete harmynge of Cristis chirche, as þe vow of Iepte schulde not
have bounde | hym to kill and to sacrifice his owne douȝter, ne þe f. 42ʳ
oþe of Herode schuld not haue bounde hym to kill innocent Ion. But
as Iepte schulde have broken his oþe or avow and han offred anoþer 850
þinge þat had be plesynge to God and acordynge wiþ his lawe, as
saynt Awstyn saiþ vpon þe same storie, so Herode schuld have broke
his oþe and a savyd innocent blode and ṣore a repentid hym for his
vnavysid swerynge, and so schulden lordis nowe breke her oþis þat
þai han vnavisely and wiþoute cowncel of holy scripture sworne to 855
may[n]tene þis þefte—ȝhe, heresye and symonye, as it is proued
bifore, þe whiche oure clerkis callen perpetual almes,—and not þus
sue her predecessouris or progenitouris in | her foly dedis and oþis f. 42ᵛ
þat þai han made to mayntene þis myscheuous peruertynge of Cristis
ordenance. For as þe state of þe clergi haþ no power ne leve to make 860

841 of²] agayne of P   842 þe] tho P   haþ] hadde P1   845 avow] vowe P
846 distryinge] destruccion P   847 *margin* Iudic. ijᵒ L   848 to²] *om.* P
849 *margin* Mt. vjᵒ L   850 avow] vowe P   852 *margin* De questionibus
veteris et noue legis L   854 nowe] nowe a dayes P   856 mayntene] may/
tene L   857 þus] *om.* P   858 predecessouris . . . her] *om.* P   860 ne]
or P

F, noon L   2254 or] no F   avow] vowe F   þis þefte] þus þis sect F
2255 *margin* iudicum 2 EDL, *in text after* lepte HF   þe avow] vowe F   2257 ne]
neyther F   heroude] heroude Mat.xiiij c HF   not haue] haue DHF   2258 his] þis F
2259 avow] vowe F   2260 *margin* mt. 6 EDL   suo] *om.* F   2263 vnauysi]
vnadvisement in F   2264 vnauysili] vnadvisyd F   2266 þe] *om.* F
2267 sue] folowe F   2268 þis] wiþ þis HF

2270 no power or leue to make þe peple or þe lordis to synne deedli, or to
distrie Goddis ordynaunce aboute his chirche, or ellis to maintene þe
breking and þe vndoing of þat ordynaunce, so þei han no leue or
power to councele or constreyne in ony caas þe lordis or þe peple to
swere to maintene þis endowing of þe clerkis and religious folk, þe
2275 which is ful greet þefte, heresie and symony, and wundir harmeful to
Cristis chirche, as it is shewid in þis processe and in oþir writun
bifore. But þe lordis speciali shulde se here what were plesynge, not
to þese ypocritis but to God, and þat shulde þei do. For what þat
euere þei swere bi sugestioun and disseit of þese ypocritis, herto þei
2280 ben boundun bi vertu of her office upon peyne of dampnacioun, and
f. 91ᵛ þer mai no man | dispence wiþ hem of þat boond stondinge her
astaat.

But here liȝtli men þat ben yȝouen to sensible þingis liik beestis,
and deliten to beestli hemsilf in suche sensible þingis þat mouen þe
2285 vtward wittis, as rynging of grete bellis, noys of organs and curious
synging, greet bilding and costlew and curious peintyng, and han not
her resoun arerid aboue sensualite to vndirstonde þese mescheues þat
ben in þe chirche wolen grucche aȝens me here, and wolen merueile
what haþ ablyndid me, þat I mai not se hou fair God is serued among
2290 þis peple þat I enpungne, and þat bi occasioun of þis perpetuel
almesse þat I blame here. Certis, I wolde fayn þat suche beestli men
wolden lifte up her vndirstonding wiþ me and se oo truþe þat I se in
þis mater, þe which truþe þat wolde make many blynde to se if it
f. 92ʳ were yknowe is þis: þat God is nowher fair serued, | saue þere þat his
2295 lawe is fair kept, and wiþ þis bisie hemsilf to haue knoulech of
Goddis lawe; and þanne, [as] I am sikir, þei shulde grucche aȝens þis
folk wiþ me, and knowe cleerli ynow þat no þing þat þese ypocritis
doen is worþi euerlastyng blis or plesaunt in þe siȝt of God, as it is
declarid bifore. And herfore seiþ God to suche ypocritis (*Isaie* 1) þat
2300 her solempnytees or halidaies, wiþ her offryngis, sacrificis and praiers
weren hatouse and abhominacioun to him, as it is tauȝt þere bi long
processe. And as touching her praiers God seiþ þus þere: 'Whanne
ȝe strecchen forþ ȝoure hondis, I shal turne awei myn iȝen fro ȝou;
and whanne ȝe shal multiplie praiers, I shal not heere ȝou.' And
2305 þanne God telliþ þe cause of al þis and seiþ þus: 'Forsoþe, ȝoure
hondis ben ful of blood.' For þou shalt vndirstonde here þat þo
ypocritis þat robben Cristis chirche as it is seid bifore, and maken his
f. 92ᵛ peple to be | in mysese and ouer greet nede ben mansleers. For
scripture seiþ (*Ecc.*34) þat þe breed of nedi men is þe liif of a pore

þe peple or þe lordis to synne deedly, or to distroye Goddis
ordenance in his chirche, so þai have no leve or power of God to
cowncell or to constreyne in eny case þe lordis or þe peple to swere
to mayntene þis endowynge of þe clerkis and religyous folke, þe
whiche is full grete þefte, heresy and symony, and wondir harmfull 865
to Cristis chirche, as it is schewyd in þis processe and in oþer writen
bifore. But þe lordis specialy schulde se here what wer plesynge, not
to þes clerkis but to God, and þat schulde þai do. For herto þai ben
bounden by vertu of her office vp payne of dampnacion, and þer may
no man dispence | wiþ hem of þat boonde stondynge her state. For f. 43ʳ
no man schuld putt anoþer grounde bisidis þat þat is putt, þe whiche 871
is Criste Ihesu.

861 þe²] om. P   862 margin Loke[/ apon[/ reaso[P1, Loke well apon this/
]eason P2   leve] lawe P1   863 to²] for to P   864 þe²] om. P   870 no]
no no P2   871 þe] om. P
                                    [Lambeth Tract resumes on p. 117]

2270 or leue] om. F   2272 þe] om. D   leue or] om. F   2274 endowing]
possessions F   þe²] om. F   2275 wundir] wonderus F   2277 speciali
shulde] rev. D   2279 herto] þerto F   2281 þer] here F   2283 liȝtli]
om. F   2284 beestli hemsilf] vse themself like beastis F   2285 grete] her
greet HF   2287 arerid] aresoun canc. arerid E, rerid H, reryd vp F
2288 wolen¹&²] wold F   2289 ablyndid] blynded F   2291 certis] verely F
2293 þe] om. F   þat] om. F   2294 is þis] this it is F   nowher] neuer F   saue
þere þat] but þeras F   2296 as] DHF, om. E   sikir] suer F   2299 herfore]
þerfor F   margin isa. 1 ED   2300 or] or//or D   2301 hatouse] horribill F
2303 strecchen] shal strecche D   2304 praiers] preier HF   2306 þou schalt]
yow xall F   þo] þes F   2307 is] om. H   2309 scripture] holy scriptur F
margin ecc. ED

2310 man, and who[so] defraudiþ him is a mansleer. And so, siþ þese ypocritis han defraudid Cristis chirche in ech astaat of þe liiflood þat God hadde asigned to his peple, and þat was needful to hem, þei ben mansleers. And so þe blood of his nedi chirche hangiþ on þis wickid peple, and upon her ouer worldli and waast arai in housyng, cloþing, 2315 in preciouse vessels and greet hors, and oþir þingis, þe whiche þei han in as greet plente and worldlynesse as ony seculer lordis. And so þei mai not, whilis þei stonden in þis pliyt, after þe councel of seynt Poul lifte up to Godward clene hondis in euery place. For as a man þat hadde sleyn a lordis sone, and baþide hise hondis in his blood, 2320 obstynat in þe same malice, is vnable to be herd of his boone at þe f. 93ʳ same lord, so in a maner is it of | þese mansleers þat, bi defrauding of Cristis chirche, sleeþ Cristis sones, and hise briþeren, and han her handis baþid þus in þe pore and nedi peplis blood, ben riȝt vnable to be herd at God þe Fadir, for þei stiren not ⌜God⌝ to merci but raþer 2325 to veniaunce.

For as seynt Gregor seiþ in hise *Pastorals* 'Whane he þat displesiþ is sent to make menes, wiþout doute þe will of him þat is wrooþ is stirid to do worse þingis.' For, as scripture seiþ and Gregor rehersiþ it þere, þe sacrificis of wickid men ben abhominable, and þe avowis 2330 of riȝtwise men ben plesible. þanne, alþouȝ it so were þat þese ypocritis diden many sacrificis and almesse of þese goodis, þe whiche þei callen so falsli perpetuel almesse, ȝit her dedis ben not acceptable in þe siȝt of God. For, as scripture telliþ, he þat doiþ sacrifice of þe substaunce or liiflood of a pore man is as a man þat sacrifieþ þe sone f. 93ᵛ in þe siȝt of his fadir. And herfore Crist biddiþ | þee þat 'If þou offre 2336 þi ȝift at þe auter, and þou haue mynde þat þi broþer haþ ony þing aȝens þee, þou shalt go first and be recouncilid to þi broþir, and þanne afterward þou shalt offre þi ȝift.' For a man shulde first offre himsilf bi iust lyuyng to God, and afterward his sacrifice or ȝift; and

2310 whoso] DHF, who þat E   siþ] seyng F   þese] þe F   2311 þe] þer F 2312 was] as F   2313 his] þis F   þis] ⌜þe hondis of⌝ *dh* þis H   2315 in] and D   and¹] in HF   oþir] in oþer F   þe] *om.* F   2317 þis pliyt] good helth F   2318 for] ensaumple for H   2319 hondis] sones D 2320 boone] peticion F   2321 is it] *rev.* HF   2324 at] of HF   stiren] move F   raþer] *om.* HF   2325 to] o F   2326 displesiþ] doith a displeasure F   2327 menes] amends F   2328 stirid] provokyd F   do] *om.* HF   *margin* gregory F   2329 sacrificis] sacrifice HF   avowis] vowis F 2330 plesible] peassabyll F   alþouȝ] yf F   2331 þe] *om.* F   2332 so] *om.* F 2333 *margin* ecc. 34 ED   2334 as] *om.* F   sone] *om.* F   2335 herfore] therfor F   *margin* mt. 5 ED   þat] *om.* F   2336 haue] haist F   haþ] haue D

þat seyntis marken of Abel and Caym, for it is seid of Abel þat God 2340
hadde reward first to him and aftir to hise ȝiftis, but not so of Caym.
þanne bi þis doctrine of Crist, if þe sacrificis and þe praiers of þis
peple shulde be worþi in þe siȝt of God, þei most first be recouncilid
to Crist, and to alle her briþeren þat han ⌐a⌐ cause aȝens hem for þis
robberie. And þei most do effectuel penaunce wiþ hool restoring of 2345
þese goodis, þe which þei han so wickidli take of her briþeren aȝens
þe glorious ordynaunce and lawe of God. And into þe tyme þat þei
doen þis, God shal neuere be fair serued among | hem, alþouȝ þei f. 94ʳ
han as gloriouse and solempne signes of deuocioun and honeste in
dyuyne seruyce as hadden her predicessours, þe pharisees of þe oold 2350
lawe. For as I seide to þee bifore, ⌐and⌐ I kepe not þat þou forȝete it,
God is nowher fair serued saue þere þat his lawe is fair kept, as it is
shewid in Lucifer and hise felowis, þat in þe glorious place of heuene
fellen awei fro þis seruyce, and in Adam and Eue þat in þe blessid
place of paradiis, fallinge fro þe keping of þe fair lawe of God, 2355
ceessiden fro þe fair seruyce of God into þe tyme þat þei diden
fructuous repentaunce of her synne. þus also God helde him not
apaied wiþ þe solempne ritis and sacrificis þat Hely and hise sones
diden in his fair tabernacle, and þat bicause þat his lawe was not fair
kept among hem (as it is writun 1 *Regum* 2). And so ful ofte tyme 2360
was God displesid wiþ þe prestis of þe glorious temple of Salomon, |
notwiþstonding þat þei maden þere many solempne sacrificis, and f. 94ᵛ
seiden many goode praiers; and þe cause whi was for his lawe was
not fair kept among hem, as we mai se in ful manye placis of
scripture. And so þis rule failiþ not, þat is to seie þat God is nowher 2365
fair serued saue þere as his lawe is fair kept; and þat mai not be
among þese ypocritis duringe apostasie þat þei stonden yn. And so it
were spedi to þe peple to make hem for to ceesse of her labour for, as
þei harmen þe peple of God bi þis robberie, so þei doen wiþ her
praiers and oþir þingis þat þei callen suffragiis, as it is opun of þe 2370
processe writun herbifore.

And of þis þou maist se hou falsli oure clerkis and religious folk

2340 marken] mak F   Caym] of cain F   2341 hadde] hath F   reward first]
fyrst respect F   of] to HF   2346 þe] *om.* F   2347 lawe] þe lawe HF
into] vnto F   2349 as] a F   2351 and] *om.* D   kepe] care F   þat] yf F
2352 nowher] neuer F   saue þere þat] but ther as F   2354 in²] fellen *canc.* in E,
fellen in D   2359 þat²] *om.* F   2360 *margin* 1 r. 2 EF   so] *om.* F   ful]
om. HF   tyme] tymys F   2364 ful] *om.* F   2365 nowher] neuer F
2366 saue] but F   2367 apostasie] þe apostasie HF   stonden] stoden H
2368 to²] for *canc.* to D, forto F   for to] *om.* F   2372 þou maist] yow may F

speken, whanne þei seien þat þei holden þese goodis bi titil of
perpetuel almesse. For siþ þis endowing is heresie and symony,
f. 95ʳ peruertyng of | Cristis ordynaunce, and robberie and in a manere
2376 manslauȝtir, and perpetuel apostasie fro Cristis pouert þat was verri
and not feyned, as it is declarid ⌐a˥boue, it mai not be callid truli
almesse; and if it is not almesse, it is not perpetuel almesse but
perpetuel al-amys. Also men deemen it greet synne to ȝyue lond
2380 entailid bi mannes lawe fro þe persoone or kynred þat it is entailid to,
ȝhe, alþouȝ it be not so ȝoue for euere but for a litil tyme, and þouȝ it
so be þat þe persoone or kynred þat such lond is ȝoue to be nedi, and
haue leue bi Godis lawe to ocupie such manere lond or lordship. And
þis is demed ful greet synne among þe peple, not oonli to þe ȝyuer,
2385 but also to þe taker, for boþe þei doen dampnable wrong to hem þat
it is entailid, as þe peple demeþ—ȝhe, alþouȝ it be ȝoue for good and
f. 95ᵛ trewe seruyce þat þe resceyuer | haþ don to þe ȝyuer bifore, or ellis
bi weie of almesse, or releuyng of þe persoone or kynred þat it is
ȝoue to. Hou moche raþer þanne, I preie þee, wiþoute comparisoun
2390 is it greet synne, as wel to þe resceyuers as to þe ȝyuers, to take
worldli lordship, þe which God, þat ha[þ] ful lordship upon al þe
world, haþ ȝoue bi perpetuel lawe or riȝt to þe staat of seculer peple
or lordis, and ȝyue þis fro þe staat, to þe which God haþ entailid þis
lordship, to anoþir straunge peple of anoþir liyn, þe which haþ neþer
2395 nede ne leue of God for to ocupie it?

And if oure prestis cleymen tiþis as goodis in a manere entailid to
hem, for as moche as God in þe oold lawe hadde ȝoue and entailid
suche tiþis to þe kynred of prestis bi euerlasting riȝt, notwiþstonding
þat þis entail was interrupt in Crist, and in hise apostlis and oþir
f. 96ʳ pore prestis þat sueden hem in | þe perfeccioun of þe gospel long
2401 after, and was not, as men supposen, expresli confermed bi Crist and
hise apostlis, and so ferforþ⌐ly˥ [þei] cleymen riȝt in þese tiþis þat no
man mai lawfulli wiþholde hem or mynystre hem, saue þei, ne þei

---

2374 siþ] seyng F   endowing] makyng of þem possessinours F   2375 cristis]
cristis/ cristis F   2376 verri] true F   2377 truli almesse] rev. F
2378 is not¹] be no F   not²] no F   but . . . al-amys (2379)] om. F   also] and so HF
deemen] judge F   2380 entailid] tailed F   2381 alþouȝ] thowe F
2382 so be] rev. FL   to] om. F   and] or F   2383 licens F   and] yet F
2384 demed] jugyd F   ful] om. F   2388 persoone] persons F   or²] om. HF
2389 þee] yow F   2390 greet] greeter HF   2391 þe¹] om. F   þat] om. F
haþ] DHFL, hadde E   ful . . . world (2392)] domynion vpon and F   2393 ȝyue]
ȝoue H   þis] it F   fro þe] fro þis DHF, fro þat L   2394 þe] om. F
2395 ne leue] nor faculte F   for to] to DF   2399 entail] tayle F   in²] om. F
2400 pore] om. HF   sueden] folowid F   hem] hym F   2401 supposen]

Capitulum x

And þerfore men demen it a grete synne to ȝeue lande entaylid by
mannys lawe fro þe persone or þe kynred þat it is entaylid to, ȝhe,
allþouȝ it be not so ȝouen for euer but for a litill tyme, and þouȝ it be 875
so þat þe persone or kynred þat siche londe is ȝeue to be nedy, and
haue leue by Goddis lawe to occupie siche maner londe or
lordeschip. And þis demyd full grete synne amonge þe peple, not
oonly to þe ȝeuer, but also to þe takere, for boþe þai done dampnable
wronge to hem þat it is entaylid to, as þe peple demiþ,—ȝhe, allþouȝ 880
it be ȝoue for goode and true seruyce þat þe resseyuour | haþ done to f. 43ᵛ
þe ȝeuer bifore, or ellis bi way of almes, of relevynge of þe persone or
kynred þat is ȝeue to. Houȝ myche raþer þan, I pray þe, wiþowte
comparyson is it a grete synne, as wel to þe ressaueris as to þe
ȝeueris, to take þe lordeschip, þe whiche God, þat haþ full 885
lordeschip vpon all þe worlde, haþ ȝoue bi perpetual lawe or riȝte
to þe sta[t]e of seculer lordis, and ȝeue þis fro þat state, to þe whiche
God entaylid þis lordeschip, to anoþer straunge peple of anoþir lyne,
þe whiche haþ neþer nede ne leue of God for to ocupie it?

And if oure prestis clayme tiþis as goodis in a maner entaylid to 890
hem, for als miche as God in þe olde lawe had ȝoue and entailed
siche tiþis to þe kynred of Levy and to noone oþer lyne. For Criste
cam of þe lynyage of | Iuda, to whiche lyne was no tiþis grauntid. f. 44ʳ
And so, as men supposen, þis entaile was not expresly confermyd bi
Criste and his apostles to his prestis in þe new lawe. For as it is 895
writen in *Policronicon* þe seuenþe boke, Gregor þe sexte ordenyd first
tiþis to be payde to curatis oonly. And ȝitt þai claymen so ferforþli

---

Capitulum x] *om.* P 874 mannys] mennes P2 þe²] *om.* P 875 not . . .
it²] *om.* P 878 þis] thys is P 880 hem] him P2 883 þat] that it P
þe] yow P 884 grete] greater P 885 lordeschip] lordeshyppes P
887 state] stade L þat] þe P 889 haþ neþer] hadde neuer P for to] to P
890 oure] *om.* P as . . . tiþis (892)] because god grauntyd them P 892 and . . .
lyne] yet ther argument is voyde P 894 expresly] *om.* P 895 his²] the P
as . . . boke (896)] *om., margin* Policro. Lib.vij P2,]licro./]b.vij P1 896 sexte]
tenthe P 897 ferforþli] fer forthe P

---

supposyd F 2402 ferforþly] ferfurth F þei] *om.* EDHF 2403 saue] saue
only F ne] neþer F

mai be turned or ȝoue to ony oþir staat or kynred, saue oonli to hem,
2405 alþouȝ men wolde do þat vndir colour or bi titil of perpetuel almesse,
for þis shulde be demed of þe clergie dampnable synne, and
distriyng of hooli chirche and sacrilege. Hou moche raþer þanne is
it an hidous and dampnable synne to ȝyue or to take awei þe seculer
lordships and possessiouns fro þe staat of seculer lordis, þe whiche
2410 God hadde ȝoue and entailid to hem bi þe same lawe and riȝt bi þe
which he hadde ȝoue þe tiþis to þe prestis in þe oold lawe? And þis
entail was neuere interrupt or ybrokun into Cristis tyme and hise
f. 96ᵛ apostlis, and þanne þei confermy|de þis entail bi lawe so stronge þat
no man saue anticrist and hise disciplis mai enpungne þis entail, as it
2415 is shewid bifore. And so, as no man shulde presume to wiþdrawe,
wiþholde or turne þe tiþis fro þe liyn or kynred or staat of presthod,
as þei seien, so moche raþer shulde þer no man presume bi ȝyuyng
or taking to aliene þe temperal lordships fro þe staat of seculer lordis.
And þus clerkis han not so moche colour to seie þat [þe] lordis and
2420 lay peple robben hooli chirche, if þei wiþdrawe þe tiþis from hem, or
turne hem to þe possessioun or vss and mynystracioun of ony oþer
staat of þe chirche, as þe lay peple haþ to seie þat þe clergie haþ
robbid hem, for as moche as þei han take her temperaltees from hem.

    And þis takyng of þese temperaltees into þe hondis of þe clergie
f. 97ʳ haþ neuere þe lesse malice of robberie, alþouȝ it be not | don bi
2426 violence; but raþer it haþ þe more cause ⌜for to be callid robberi and
cause⌝ of malice in itsilf, for as moche as it is don bi symylacioun of
hoolynesse, þe which is double wickidnesse. For þus Lucifer robbide
Adam of goodis of fortune, of kynde and of grace (as it is writun *Gen.*
2430 3), as þe clergie robbiþ now þe chirche of þese þre manere of goodis,
as it is tauȝt bifore. And as Lucifer dide þis harm to Adam and Eue
vndir colour of loue and frendship and helping of hem, so doen now
hise aungels, oure ypocritis þat I speke of, [þat] transfiguren hemsilf
into aungels of liȝt, and disseyuen þe peple bi fals biheest of heuenli
2435 help þat þei wolen procure to hem for her goodis. And if a bishop
and his colege or an abbot and his couent mai not aliene from hem
ony of þe temperaltees þat þei han, ne ȝyue to her founder ony of þe

2404 staat] astaat F   2405 þat] it F   2407 hou] ⌜28 ca.⌝ how F   þanne
is it] is it þanne HF   þanne] *om.* D   2408 an hidous] a perlous F
2409 þe²] *om.* F   2410 hadde] hath F   2412 into] vnto F   2414 saue]
except F   2418 aliene] ony strangur F   lordships] lordschipe F
2419 colour] cause F   þe lordis] DHFL, lordis E   2423 from] of F
2424 þese] þe F   2425 not] *om.* F   2426 for to] to F   2428 þe] *om.* F
2429 of²] goodis of F   of³] goodis of F   *margin* the robbynge of adam. ge. 3 F

þes tiþis þat no man lawfully may wiþholde hem or minystre hem, save þai, ne þai may be turnyd or ȝouen to eny oþer state or kynred, saue oonly to hem, allþouȝ men wolden do þat vndir coloure or bi 900 titill of perpetuall almes, for þis schulde be demyd of þe clergy a dampnable synne, and distroynge of holy chirche and sacrilege. Hou myche raþer þen is it an hidous and a | dampnable synne to ȝeue or f. 44ᵛ to take away þe seculer lordeschipis fro þe state of seculer lordis, þe whiche God had ȝeue and entaylid to hem bi þe same lawe and riȝte 905 by þe whiche he had ȝouen þe tiþis to þe prestis in þe olde lawe? And þis entaile was neuer interrupte or ybroken into Cristis tyme and his apostles, and þen þai confermyd þis entayle bi lawe so stronge to þe seculer party þat no man safe anticriste and his disciples may openly enpugne þis entaile, as it is schewid bifore. 910 And so, as no man schuld presume to wiþdrawe, wiþholde or turne þe tiþis fro þe state of presthode, as þai sayne, so myche raþer schuld no man presume bi ȝeuynge or takynge to aliene þe temperal lorde|schips fro þe state of seculer lordis. And þus clerkis han not f. 45ʳ so myche coloure to sai þat þe lordis and þe lay peple robben holy 915 chirche, if þai wiþdrew þe tiþis fro hem, for als miche as þai han take her temperaltes fro hem.

And þis takynge of þes temperaltes into þe handis of þe clergi haþ neuer þe lesse malice of robrye and cause of malice in itsiilfe, for als miche as it is done by symylacion of holynes, þe whiche is double 920 wickidnes. For þus Lucifer robbid Adam boþe of goodis of fortune, of kynde and of grace, as þe clergi haþ robbid and ȝit doþe þe chirche of þes þre maner goodis. For riȝt as Lucifere did þis harme to Adam and Eue vndir coloure of loue and frendischip and helpynge of hem, so done nowȝ | his awngelis, þes ypocritis þat transfigure f. 45ᵛ hemsiilf into awngellis of liȝte, and disseyuen þe pepill by fals 926 byheest of heuenly help þat þai willen procure to hem for her goodis as þai sayen. And if a bischop and his colage or an abbot and his couent may not alien fro hem eny of þe temperalteis þat þai han,

---

898 þes] *om.* P   lawfully may] *rev.* P   903 þen is it] is it then P   a] *om.* P2 907 or] nor P   into] vnto P2   908 apostles] holy apostles P   909 party] parte P2   910 it] *om.* P1   915 holy . . . fro (916)] *om.* P   916 han take] take P   917 fro . . . temperaltes (918)] *om.* P2   919 of¹ . . . malice²] *om.* P 921 *margin* gen. iij° LP2, Gen[P1   922 of² . . . robbid] *om.* P2   925 þes] thos P

2431 to . . . eue] *om.* F   2433 speke] spake F   þat] DHFL, *om.* E   *margin later hand* 2 cor.11 E   2434 biheest] promesse F   2435 and] ⌐29 ca.⌐ and F 2436 aliene] gyve F   2437 ne] nor F

f. 97ᵛ possessiouns þat he haþ ȝoue | into her deede hondis, what nede þat
euer he hauͬeˀ, yboundun oonli bi a positif lawe or a dritti tradicioun
2440 þat þei hemsilf han maad; and if ony suche lordships be wiþdrawe,
aliened or take from hem bi rechelisnesse of her predicessours, þei
ouȝte on al wise, ȝhe, into þe deeþ, labore to gete þo possessiouns
into her hondis ˹aȝenˀ, as þei seien; hou moche raþer shulde not a
seculer lord or a lay man aliene from him and his issu or fro þe staat
2445 of [temperal] lordis þe seculer lordships, þe whiche God haþ lymytid
to þat staat?—siþ he is boundun bi þe lawe of kynde to ordeine for
hise children, and ouer þis [he] is yboundun bi Goddis lawe to
susteyne þe staat of seculer lordis þat ben autorisid now in þe chirche
bi Crist and hise apostlis, where þese religiouse ypocritis ben not so
2450 expresli groundid. And if an abbot ˹orˀ his couent mai not ȝyue or
f. 98ʳ aliene ony of her possessiouns, haue þei neuere so greǀte superfluite,
to her pore briþeren þat cleymen to be oon in þe perfeccioun of þe
gospel wiþ hem, and þat for þe laweͬsˀ and ordynauncis þat þei
hemsilf han maad, hou moche more shulde not a seculer lord ȝyue
2455 awei fro þat astaat worldli lordships aȝens þe lawis and ordynauncis
þat God haþ maad aboute suche possessiouns, as it is tauȝt bifore?
And wundir it is þat þese ypocritis mai euere resceyue and take fro
þe lordis her goodis, notwiþstondinge þat Goddis lawe is aȝens hem
in þat,—and þei mai neuer ȝyue or delyuere aȝen þo goodis for þe
2460 statutis and tradiciouns þat þei maken among hemsilf bi her owne
couetous witt. And in þat þei magnyfien her owne tradiciouns aboue
Goddis lawe, and maken þe lordis þat assenten to hem to do þe
same. And so liik her predicessours, pharisees of þe oold lawe, þei
f. 98ᵛ breken þe fair lawe and ordynaunce of God for her foule | and
2465 vngroundid tradiciouns, and techen þe lay peple to do þe same. And
nar þese ypocritis shamles, þei myȝten be foul ashamed to seie þat
þei mai in no caas delyuere þe lordships þat þei ocupien into
temperal mennes hondis, boundun oonli bi her tradiciouns and
lawis, and wiþ þis seie þat þe lordis mai ȝyue into her deede
2470 handis alle her temperaltees, ȝhe, into ful vndoing of þat staat,
notwiþstondinge þat God haþ expresli autorisid þis staat in þe oold
lawe, and confermyd it and her liiflood to hem in þe newe lawe.

2439 haue yboundun] hathe F   2441 aliened] *om.* F   2442 on] in F   al]
ony F   into] in F   þe] *om.* F   þo] þes F   2443 into] agayne into F   aȝen]
om. F   2444 aliene] gyve F   2445 temperal] DHF, seculer EL   þe¹] *om.* D
þe²] *om.* F   2446 siþ] seyng F   2447 he] HFL, *canc.* E, *om.* D
2449 Crist] Iesu Crist F   2450 expresli] *om.* F   or aliene] *om.* F
2452 pore] *om.* F   2455 astaat] stat F   2457 wundir it is] it is a wondyr F

ne ȝeue to her founder eny of þo possessions þat he haþ ȝoue hem, 930
what nede þat euer he haue, ibounden oonly by a posityue lawe or a
tradycion þat þai han hemsiilfe made; and if eny siche lordeschips be
wiþdrawe, alienyd or take fro hem by rechelesnes of her predecessouris, þai owȝten on alle wise, ȝhe, into þe deþe, labore to [gete] þo
possescions into her hondis | aȝen, as þai saien; hou myche more þan f. 46ʳ
schuld not a seculere lorde or a lay man aliene fro hym and his issue 936
or fro þe state of seculere lordis þe seculer lordeschippis, þe whiche
God haþ lymytid to þat state?—siþ he is bounden by þe lawe of
kynde for to ordeyne for his children, and ouer þis he is bounden by
Goddis lawe to susteyne þe state of seculer lordis, þe whiche is 940
autorisid in þe chirche bi Criste and his apostelis.

930 ne] nor P2   þo] thos P2   932 han hemsiilfe] *rev.* P   933 *margin*
Nota P1   934 into] to P   gete] *om.* L   þo] þe P   936 man] *om.* P
939 for to] to P   941 bi Criste] *om.* P2

2459 þo] þos F   2461 witt] wittis HF   2462 assenten] agre F
2466 nar] if F   shamles] were not schameles F   2468 boundun] wich þei haue
bownd F   her] þer owne F   2469 seie] thei say F   2470 ful] þe full F
2472 confermyd] confermedid H   and²] in HF

Off þis processe þanne, if a man take bisy heede, he shal perseyue
þe falsnesse of þis gloos, whanne oure clerkis and religious folk seien
2475 þat þei holden þese lordships oonli bi titil of perpetuel almesse.
For, certis, siþ þes tiþis and offryngis (þe whiche as I suppose
counteruailen þe seculer lordis rentis of þe rewme, or ellis passen as
f. 99ʳ it is ful licli, for | if þei ben lesse in oo chirche, þei passen þe seculer
rent in anoþir), ben sufficient for alle þe prestis in cristendom, and
2480 þei ben euene delid, it were no nede to amorteise seculer lordships to
þe staat of clergie, þe which amorteising is vndoing of þe lordis and
apostasie of þe clergie; and if þis amorteisyng were not needful,
þanne were it not almesse, as it is declarid. And ouer þes tiþis and
offryngis þat ben of certein, þe clerkis han many grete and smale
2485 perquisitis, þe whiche smacchen of symonye and extorcioun, as þe
firste fruytis of vacaunt beneficis, preuyng of testamentis, and money
for halowing of chapels, chirchis and chaliss, and oþir ournementis of
þe chirche, and for sakering of ordris, and ful many mo þat for
multitude mai not wel be noumbrid. For wel ny3 alle her blessyngis
2490 ben sett to sale and to priis, into cristenyng and confirmacioun.
f. 99ᵛ   Ferþer|mor now I wole telle 3ou hou falsli and weiwardly þese
couetouse ypocritis glosen anoþer text of Cristis gospel, þe which
goiþ euene a3ens her worldli lordship; and soone heraftir, if God
vouchesaaf, I wole make 3ou an eende, for I se wel þe dai passiþ
2495 swiþe, and me were loþe to ouertraueile 3ou, or to be tedious to 3ou
in þis labour. þe gospel seiþ (Mt. 8) þat a scribe seide to Iesu þus:
'Maistir, I shal sue þee whidireuere þou shalt go!' And Iesu seide to
him 'Foxis han dennes, and briddis of þe eir han nestis, forsoþe þe
maidens sone haþ not where to leene his heed.' And Crist spekiþ
2500 here of hauyng bi titil of propre and ciuile or seculer lordship. For,
as it is opun of þat þat I haue seid bifore, Crist haþ ful lordship upon
al þe world bi his godhed, ˹and in his manhed˺ bi titil of innocence,
grace and ri3twisnesse he haþ lordship upon alle þingis þat ben lower
f. 100ʳ in kynde þan man. And, ˹for˺ | as moche as he dide truli a prestis

---

2473 bisy] good F   2476 certis] verely F   siþ] seyng F   þes] om. HF
þe] om. F   2477 counteruailen] sermownt above F   lordis] om. HF   passen] be
as moche F   2478 ful] om. F   2479 rent] rentis F   and] yf F
2480 euene] well F   2481 þe²] om. F   2483 were it] rev. F   not] no FL
and offryngis] om. D   2485 þe¹] om. F   smacchen] smell F
2487 chirches] and chirchis DHF   and¹] om. DHFL   chaliss] chalisis HF
2488 ful] om. F   þat] whiche F, om. F   2489 wel be] be wel, marked for rev. E, be
well F   2490 into] as F   2491 ferþermor now] rev. F   2492 þe] om. F
2493 heraftir] aftur F   2494 vouchesaaf] will F   wole] schall F   3ou] om. F
2495 swiþe] fast F   me] I F   ouertraueile . . . tedious] be ouertedius F

Of þis processe þen, if a man take hede, he schal perceyue þe
falsnes of þis glose, whan oure clerkis and religious folke saien þat
þai holden þes lordeschipis oonly by tytill of perpetual almes. For,
certis, siþ þes tiþis and þis offryngis (þe whiche as I suppose 945
cowntirvaylen þe seculer lordis rentis of þe rewme, or | ellis f.46ᵛ
passen as it is full likly, for þou3 þai be lesse in oo chirche, þai
passen in anoþer), ben sufficient for alle þe prestis in cristendome,
and þai wer euen delyd, þen it wer no nede to amortise seculer
lordeschipis to þe state of þe clergi, þe whiche amortesynge is 950
vndoynge of lordis and apostasie of þe clergy; and if þis amortasynge
wer not nedefull, þen wer it noone almes, as it is declarid. And ouer
þe tiþingis and offeringis þat ben now of certeyne, þe clerkis han
many grete and smale perquisitiuys, þe whiche smachen of symony
and extorcion, as þe first fruytis of vacant beneficis, prouynge of 955
testamentis, for halowynge of chapels, chirchis, chauncellis, and oþer
ournementis of þe chirche, and for sacrynge of ordres, and full many
mo þat for multitude may not | wel be nowmbred. For well ny3 all f.47ʳ
her blessyngis ben sett to sale and to prise, into crystenynge and
confirmacion. 960

Wherfor I may now sai, as I sayd at þe bigynnynge *Fundamentum
aliud* etc. No man may putt anoþer grounde bysidis þat þat is putt,
þe whiche is Criste Ihesu, þe whiche grounde of lyvynge Criste
graunte vs to kepe, þat we may ascape þe euerlastynge paynys of hell.
Amen. 965

945 þis] om. P   948] ben] and ben LP   949 and] yf P   951 and¹]
om. P2   margin Then[/ ture c[/ mort[/ syeng[P1   953 tiþingis] tythes P
certeyne] certeynte P   956 for] and money for P   961 fundamentum . . . etc.] om. P
[*Lambeth Tract resumes on p. 144*]

2496 seiþ] om. F   margin mt. 8 EF   þus] om. F   2497 shal sue] wull folow F
whidireuere] where euer F   shalt] wilt F   to] vnto F   2498 briddis] þe
birdis HF   2499 leene] lye F   2500 here] þer F   hauyng] hau/uyng E
of²] and F   and] om. F   or] of H, and F   2501 þat²] wich F   haue] om. F
upon] of F   2502 his²] om. D   2504 in kynde] om. F

2505 office to þe peple, and myȝte do noon excesse in taking, he hadde titil
bi þe gospel to alle þat he took to his nede. And so bi þese titlis
riȝtwisli he restide hiˢs heed⌐ and al his blessid bodi, now in oo place,
now in anoþir, boþe in lond and in watir, and euere in his owne
place. þerfore þis hauyng, where Crist seiþ ⌐þat⌐ 'þe maidens sone
2510 haþ not where to reste his heed', is vndirstondun as it nedis mut of
þe titil of worldli lordship or possessioun, bi þe which titil Crist
myȝte not ocupie here ony þing for þe vnperfitnesse of þat titil, as it
is declarid bifore. But wolt þou se what gloos oure maistir liers and
her couetouse sectis of ypocrisie ȝyuen to þis? I preie þee take heede
2515 hou waiward, ⌐contrarie⌐ and rotun is þe gloos þat þese ypocritis
ȝyuen here! For such as is her gloos, suche ben þei wiþynforþ in her
consciencis and affecciouns; and if þou knowe no more falsnesse in
f. 100ᵛ þese rotun | sectis, saue þis oon vngroundid gloos, þou ouȝtist be
euere þe beter war of hem, and haue þe lesse affeccioun to hem. þei
2520 seien þat þis text ouȝte not to be vndirstondun of þis maner of
worldli lordshiping, but it ouȝte to be vndirstondun of Crist as for þe
tyme þat he hyng upon þe cros, þe which was a cros tau T þat hadde
noon heed, and so Crist þere hadde not where to leene or reste his
heed. But euery man mai se wel þat þis vnþrifti gloos is no þing to
2525 purpos, for þis was comoun to Crist and also to þe þeeues þat weren
hangid bi him, and to Achitofel and Iudas, þat dampnabli hengen
hemsilf. And so þese maistir liers and heretikis shulden vndirstonde
here þat Crist, whos wordis ben ful of heuenli fruyt, meneþ more
perfeccioun in hise ⌐blessid⌐ wordis þan faute of reste of a þeeues
f. 101ʳ heed upon þe gibat or þe cros. For þou | shalt vndirstonde here, as
2531 we mai perseyue of þe text þat I reherside riȝt now, hou a scribe
boostide þat he wolde sue Crist whidir euere he shulde go, and, if þis
scribe shulde haue sued Crist þus to purpos, he shulde not oonli sue
hise stappis in þe material weie, but moche raþer he most sue Crist

---

2505 and . . . taking] om. F   2506 bi¹] of F   to²] for F   2509 þat] om. D
2509 mut] must F   2512 þe] om. D   2513 wolt þou] wyll yow F   gloos] a
glose HF   2514 þee] yow F   2515 contrarie] DHF, and ⌐contrarie⌐ E
2516 ben . . . affecciouns (2517)] is þer affections in þer consciens F   2517 þou] ye F
knowe] knew HF   2518 saue] but alonly F   þou ouȝtist] yow owyt to F
2519 war] ⌐and⌐ war E   2520 seien] sayd F   2521 lorshiping] lordscipe F
2522 þe²] om. F   2523 þere] om. F   2526 margin 2 r.17 ED, in text after
hemsilf (2527) HF   2527 hemsilf] hymself F   2528 heuenli] wisdome and
hevenly F   2529 blessid] b[, cut away D   faute of] to teache of þe F   of² . . .
þeeues] o[, cut away / -ues D   2530 gibat or þe cros] gibe[, cut away D, crosse F   þou
shalt] yow schall F   2532 sue] folowe F   whidir euere] where euer F
2533 sued] folowyd F   þus] om. HF   sue] folow F   2534 sue] folow F

in hise maners; and if he wolde so, þanne most he leue al maner of 2535
worldli possessioun or lordship as Crist dide. And þat lessoun tauȝte
Crist to þis scribe in þese blessid wordis, and so moste oure drasti
sectis do, er þei atteyne to þe perfeccioun þat þei so falsli boosten of.

And wundre þou not here, alþouȝ I speke sumwhat vnpacientli
aȝens þese cursid glosers þat, as opun enmyes of Crist, as moche as 2540
þei mai, peruerten Cristis liif and his loore. For, certis, and þe loue
þat Crist shewide to us upon þe cros were sunkun to þe roote of oure
her|te, and if we heelde wiþ Crist for þe clennesse of his Fadris f. 101ᵛ
chirche, it were no wundir alþouȝ we dide outrarously or more
steernli aȝens þese enmyes of Crist and his lawe þan dide Crist 2545
whanne he made him a scourge, and chaside out biers and sillers of
his Fadris temple, þe which figuride þese false bribours and viserd
deuels þat ben now, þoruȝ sleiȝt of þe feend, cropun into þe chirche,
and marchaundise of þe peple wiþ feyned wordis and ypocritis
signes, and so robben þe peple as it is seid bifore. And wel seide 2550
Crist to þo þat figuride þese þeeues þat þei hadden maad his temple,
þe which figuride Cristis chirche, a denne of þeeues. For in suche
dennes þeeues loten and hiden hemsilf, and so þese þeeues daren,
loten and hiden hemsilf so priueli vndir her ypocrisie in abite and
oþir hooli signes, þat vnneþe ony man mai cleerli perseyue þese 2555
þeeues. And I wol|de wundre here of þe blyndnesse of þe lordis and f. 102ʳ
oþir peple, þat þei perseyue not þe fals couetise of þese ypocritis,
saue þat Crist, þat mai not lye, prophecieþ of þis blyndnesse, seiynge
þus, as it is rehersid bifore, þat sotil fals peple, þe which he calliþ
pseudo, shal arise; and þei shal ȝyue suche signes þat þe peple shal be 2560
brouȝt into errour, ȝhe, and it mai be, þe chosun of God. And so, for
as moche þat, alþouȝ many be callid, ȝit fewe ben chosun, as Crist

2535 wolde] wyll F   2537 to] *om.* F   so] þat HF   drasti] *om.* F
2538 er] or euer F   þat] of þe gospell þat F   2539 þou] yow F   alþouȝ] thow F
2541 peruerten cristis] peruer[*cut away*]stis D   loore] lawe F   certis] truly F   and]
yf F   loue þat] *cut away* D   2542 were . . . to²] *cut away* D   sunkun] stucke F
2543 heelde] hold F   2544 alþouȝ] thow F   outrarously] contraiousli D
2545 steernli] ernestly F   þese] þe D   2546 *margin* luc. 19 mt.21 and io. 2 (iij
HF) ED, *in text after* temple (2547) HF, *margin* luc. mat. Jo. F   2547 þese] þe HF
2548 sleiȝt] means F   2551 þo] þes F   temple] hous and his temple HF
2552 þe] *om.* F   2553 loten] louten H, lurk F   daren] *om.* F   2554 loten]
louten H, lurk F   in] *altered from* and E   2555 vnneþe] scarsly F   þese þeeues]
them F   2556 I wolde] a man may F   2558 saue] but ⌜a⌝lonly F   þat mai]
wich can F   2559 rehersid] seid D   þe] *om.* F   calliþ] called F
2560 arise] rise HF   2561 and¹] yf F   2562 þat] *om.* F   many] þat many F

seiþ, and vnneþe þe chosun of God shal mow aspie þe falsnesse of
þese pseudo, I wundre sumwhat þe lesse, alþou3 ful many, and
2565 nameli fleshli and beestli men, in þe whiche sensualite haþ ouercome
resoun, ben blyndid wiþ þis ypocrisie.

But up hap þou þenkist here þat I speke to presumptuousli a3ens
þe clergie, and nameli a3ens þe monkis, of whom han be ful many
hooli men þat ben now seyntis, canonysid bi oure hooli fadris, popis |
f. 102ᵛ of Rome, and also þei ben of ful oold fundacioun. 'For seynt Ierom
2571 seiþ in hise epistlis þat seint Iohun Baptist was oon of hem, and þe
hooli prophete Helize, and þe sones of prophetis þat dwell[id]en wiþ
him, of whom we mai rede (4 *Regum* 6), and oþir seyntis of þe oold
lawe, þe whiche seint Ierom rehersiþ ⌐þere⌐. And ouer þese þer
2575 weren mounkis in þe newe lawe in tyme of þe apostlis, þe whiche as
seynt Denys seiþ in *De Ecclesiastica Ierarchia*, were moost perfit of þo
þat ben maad perfit. And of þis it wole sue, ferþermor, þat þou hast
foul mysgouerned þee in þi wordis ny3 þe bigynnyng of þi sermon,
where þou meuedist, as I haue vndirstondun, þat þe sectis whos
2580 signes þou blamest þus weren not plauntid yn bi þe Fadir of heuene.'
Sire! as for þese euydencis þat þee semeþ goen a3en me, þou shalt
vndirstonde here þat þese mounkis of þe oold lawe, of þe which
f. 103ʳ seynt | Ierom spekiþ, hadden neþer founder ne rule saue oonli God
and his rule, and among oþer þingis of perfeccioun þei hadden vttirli
2585 forsake worldli lordship. And in tokenyng þat seynt Iohun Baptist
wolde not brynge yn a sect of religioun foundid upon him and his
rule, he quenchide þe hi3 opynyoun þat hise disciplis hadden in him,
and tau3te hem to bicome oonli Cristis disciplis; and so seynt Iohun
Baptist wolde haue no founder saue God aloone and his pure lawe,
2590 and þe same he wolde of hise disciplis.

And þus it stood of þe mounkis þat seynt Denys spekiþ of, þe

2563 and vnneþe] þat scarsly ye F   mow] *om.* F   aspie] spye F
2564 alþou3] yee all thow F   ful] *om.* F   2565 nameli] specially F   þe] *om.* D
2567 up hap] perauentur F   þou þenkist] yow thynk F   to] here to F, *om.* D
2568 clergie . . . þe²] *om.* F   nameli . . . and richesse (2593)] *lost to* -chesse D   ful
many] *om.* F   2570 ful] *om.* F   2572 dwelliden] HF, dwellen E
2573 him] hem H   *margin* 4 r.6 E   and] of F   2574 þe] *om.* F   ouer]
besyde F   2575 tyme] þe tyme HF   þe³] *om.* F   2576 seynt] *om.* F   þo]
þos F   2577 sue] folow F   2579 meuedist] meanyst F   haue vndirst-
ondun] vnderstond F   þe] þese HF   2580 signes] synnes HF
2581 *margin* Responsio EF   sire] ⌐30 ca.⌐ syr F   þee semeþ] seme to F   þou shalt]
yow schall F   2582 þese] þe F   of þe²] *om.* F   2583 spekiþ] spekyth of F
ne] nor F   2586 him] *om.* F   2587 hi3] great F   2589 founder]
foundir ne rule HF   pure] purid H   2591 þe²] *om.* F

whiche hadde wilfulli left alle worldli possessiouns, lordship and
richesse, and maad hemsilf pore, not oonli in wordis or signes, as
oure doen now, but in effect, as Crist and hise apostlis hadden tauȝt
hem; and so þei leften not pouert and bicame riche, ne þei lefte her   2595
owne possessiouns and took oþir mennes, ne þei | lefte þe staat of   f. 103ᵛ
laborers and bicam lordis, as oure doen now, ne þese mounkis
hadden patroun or rule saue oonli Iesu Crist and his purid rule.
And in tokenyng þat seynt Denys was of þe same feiþ as was his
maistir Poul, þat wiþstood þe sectis þat wolde haue growe into þe   2600
chirche ouer þe purid sect of Iesu Crist, as it is seid bifore, and in ful
euydence þat seynt Denys knewe þat it was Goddis will þat þer
shulde be no mo astatis in his chirche, saue þo þre þat I haue spokun
of biforhond, he acountiþ þese mounkis in þe staat of þe comounte
or laborers, notwiþstondinge þat, as he seiþ, þese mounkis weren   2605
moost perfit of þo þat ben maad perfit. And as for þis word, þou
shalt vndirstonde here þat þer weren in seynt Denys tyme prestis
and dekenes, to whom it perteynede bi weie of her office to
perfourme þe dedis of ierarchies, þat is to seie to | liȝte, purge and   f. 104ʳ
make perfit. For þei liȝtide þe peple bi hooli ensaumple and trewe   2610
doctrine, þei purgide þe þeple bi helþful penaunce and made hem
perfit bi þe sacramentis, ȝhe, wiþ alle þese þre togidir. And so þese
ben clepid liȝters, purgers and makynge perfit, [and þe peple bi þese
ben liȝtid, purgid and maad perfit]. And so þese mounkis ben
acountid þere not among þe ierarchies þat liȝten, purgen and   2615
maken perfit, but among þe peple þat ben maad perfit bi hem þat
stonden in þe staat of ierarchies. And for as moche [as] þei hadden
effectueli left þe world and þe occasioun þerof, where oþir hadde not
do so, þei weren callid þe moost perfit of þo þat ben maad perfit, þat
is to seie of þe peple þat ben maad perfit bi þe ierarchies, as it is seid   2620
riȝt now. And þis maner lyuyng of monkis was contynued in dyuerse
placis into seynt Ieroms tyme, as it semeþ in dyuerse placis of his

2593 wordis] word F   2594 in] om. F   2595 her] not her DF
2596 ne þei] nor F   2597 ne] om. F   2598 hadden] also had no F   purid]
pure F   2599 in] om. F   2601 ouer] besyde F   purid] pure HF
2603 astatis] statis F   þo] þes F   haue spokun] spak F   2604 biforhond]
before F   acountiþ] cowntyth F   staat] staatis H   þe²] om. F   2605 as] om. F
2606 þo] thos F   þou shalt] ye schall F   2607 seynt] seynt / seynt, 2nd canc. E
2609 ierarchies] þe ierarchies F   2611 helþful] heelful HF   made] thei made F
2613 clepid] callyd F   and þe . . . perfit (2614)] DHF, om. E   2617 as²] DHF,
om. E   2618 effectueli] om. F   occasioun] occasions F   hadde . . . beggide
breed (2670)] lost D   2619 þo] twice, 2nd canc. E, þos F   2620 seid] om. F
2621 contynued] conteynyd F   2622 into] vnto F

f. 104ᵛ writing. For, notwiþstondinge þat he was a prest and doctour, | he
acomptiþ himsilf not among þe ierarchies but among þe oþer peple;
2625 and deemeþ hymsilf wondir gilti, but if he brynge sum þing to þe
auter in þe sustynaunce of þo þat perfourmen þe werkis of ierarchies
⌐to þe peple¬.

And þus monkis into þis dai leuen þe labour of þe ierarchies in
hooli chirche, and þat sumwhat for her owne eese as I suppose. For a
2630 curatis office wel perfourmed askiþ greet labour and teenful bisynesse. But þei forsaken not þe curatis liiflood, ne seculer lordship, þe
which is þe moost worldlynesse þat mai be as I seide bifore. And þei
ben redi ynow aȝens þe councel of Crist to stryue in iugement, not
oonli for þe coote, but also for þe mantil, þe which bitokeneþ þe
2635 largenesse of worldli possessioun, as Hildegar seiþ in hir prophecie.
And þei cleimen hem a patroun, rule and abite oþir þan dide Helize,
f. 105ʳ or seynt Iohun Baptist, or þe perfit | mounkis in þe tyme of þe
apostlis. And so þei han not ⌐a¬do wiþ þese mounkis, ne þese wiþ
hem, for þei ben of ful contrarie ordris. And so seynt Iohun Baptist
2640 mai wel vttirli forsake hem as for ony of his sect, and seie wiþ Poul
(1 Cor. 1) 'I do þankingis to my God, for I haue cristened noon of
ȝou', for þei suen him no dele, but raþer þe man þat seide þat he
wolde forsake al þe world and bicam an ostiler. And oo þing, as me
þenkiþ, I mai saafli seie here: þat þer is no more skill whi a seculer
2645 lord, willing to perfourme þe plente of þe perfeccioun of þe gospel,
most effectueli forsake his worldli lordship, but bi þe same skill and
moche raþer þe clergie and þe religious peple most vttirli and
effectueli forsake þe worldli lordships, þat þei bi dyuerse menes
han gete out of þe hondis of seculer lordis er þei han þe perfeccioun
f. 105ᵛ þat þei boosten of. | And I preie þee if þis answer be ony þing to
2651 purpos, take it a worþ at þis tyme; and wiþ Goddis help, if it nede
be, whanne I haue more leiser to studie and more help of bookis, þou
shalt haue a more large answer in þis mater.

2623 þat] here þat F   he²] yet F   2625 deemeþ] iugith F   wondir]
wonderus F   but if] except F   2626 þe¹] om. HF   þo] þos F
2628 into] vnto F   2630 teenful] sore F   2631 ne] nor F   þe²] om. F
2634 þe³] om. F   2635 hir] þer F   2638 ado] ⌐to¬ doo F   þese¹] þe HF
ne] nor F   2639 ful] om. F   2640 vttirli] and vttirli HF   2641 margin
1 cor. 1 E   þankingis] þankis HF   my god] god my father F   2642 suen]
folow F   no dele] nothyng F   þat] om. F   2643 bicam] bicome HF   and²]
⌐31 ca.¬ and F   2644 saafli seie] rev. H, say here savely F   here] om. F   skill]
cause F   2646 skill] reason F   and] as H   2649 er] or euer F
2650 þee] yow F   2651 it¹] om. F   a] at H, in good F   it²] om. HF
2652 þou shalt] yow schall F   2653 large] largier F

Now haue I toold ȝou hou þe endowid clerkis, and monkis and chanouns, wiþ oþir endowid sectis, ben falle awei [fro] þe vertuous 2655 mene þat Crist chees to himsilf and to hise apostlis and oþir perfit men into þe viciouse extremytee of to grete worldli habundaunce. And now heraftir, as I bihiȝte ȝou, I shal shewe hou þe foure apostasies of customable beggers ben gon afer fro þis vertuous mene into þat oþir viciouse extremytee of to moche faute, þe which þeʳiˀ 2660 pretenden in her customable begging. But, for as moche as þe dai drawiþ fast to an eende, and I [haue] not al forȝite hem bifore, I wole passe ouer þe more shortli in þis mater. For, whoso takiþ he|de to þat f. 106ʳ þat I haue seid in þis mater, mai se hou þese ben not groundid upon þe stoon but raþer upon þe erþe or ellis upon þe grauel; and he mai 2665 se also hou falsli þei lyen upon Crist in maintenyng of her vngroundid beggerie, seiynge þat he beggide watir, an hous and an asse.

And as falsli þei lyen upon þe hooli prophete Helye, whanne þei seien þat he beggide breed and watir of a womman, of whom it is 2670 writun þus (3 *Regum* 17): 'þe word of þe Lord is maad to Helye seiynge, "Arise, and go into Sarapta and þou shalt dwelle þere; I haue comaundid a womman, a widue, þat dwelliþ þere þat she feede þee." Helye haþ risun up and go into Sarapta and, whanne he hadde come to þe ȝate of þe citee, þe womman apperide to him, and he 2675 seide to hir, 'Ȝyue me a litil of water in a vessel þat I drynk." And whanne she ȝide for to brynge him watir, Helye criede aftir hir, | seiynge, "I preie þee brynge to me a mossel of breed in þin hond."' f. 106ᵛ Vpon þis storie þese maistir liers maken a lesyng upon God and Helye, þat Helye shulde haue beggid watir and breed here of þis 2680 widue. But þese renegatis shulde studie þis storie bisili and marke þe wordis þerof, and þanne, but if þe deuel þat, as Crist seiþ, is fadir of lesyng, haue blyndid hem, þei shal se wel þat Helye ȝide not to þis womman bi his owne autorite but bi þe autorite of God, comaunding him to do so, þat hadde also comaundid þe widue, as he seiþ, to 2685

2654 haue I] *rev.* HF   and¹] *om.* HF   2655 fro þe] HF, þe E 2657 extremytee] HF, extremytees E   2658 bihiȝte] promysed F   ȝou] *om.* F 2659 afer] fer F   2660 extremytee] -s *canc.* E   faute] nede F   þe] *om.* F 2662 haue] HF, mai E   2663 þe] *om.* F   to] of F   2664 þat] whiche F mai] he may HF   2665 ellis] *om.* F   þe] *om.* F   he] ye F   2666 also] *om.* F   2671 *margin* 3 R.17 E,]reg. 17 F   2672 into] in D   2674 haþ risun] rose F   go] went F   2676 drynk] may drynck F   2677 ȝide] went F for to] to F   2678 to me] me F   2679 storie] -s *canc.* E   maistir] masters F 2681 widue ... þis] *om.* F   marke] mak F   2682 but if] except F   2683 wel] *om.* F   ȝide] went F   2685 to²] for to F

feede Helye, not al for Helies nede or profit, but cheefli for þe nede and profit of þat widue, as þe storie telliþ aftir. And þei mai se also hou God seide not to Helie, 'Go begge of þat widue breed and watir.' And so Helye beggide no more of þis womman þan a child beggiþ

f. 107ʳ whanne, at þe comaun|dement of his fadir, he biddiþ or preieþ his
2691 fadris stiward, panter or botiler or ony oþer officer of his fadris to ȝyue him mete or drynk, and nameli þere as such a seruaunt haþ a special maundement of his lord or maistir to mynystre suche vitails to his child, as þis womman hadde of þe hiȝ lord God to feede Helye.
2695 And in tokenyng þat Helye beggide not here whanne he spak firste to þis womman, he spak to hir on þe comaunding maner and not on þe begging maner.

Neþeles I wondre þe lesse þouȝ þese maistir liers bilye here Helye, seiynge þat he beggide watir and a mossel of breed of þis womman,
2700 for þei booldli maken a lesyng upon Crist, seiynge þat he shulde haue beggid watir of þe womman of Samarie, whanne he comaun- dide þe womman to ȝyue him drynk. And, if a man take heede to |

f. 107ᵛ þis storie (Jo. 4) and to þe processe þat I haue seid bifore, he mai se þat þe freris lyen opunli here upon Crist. And as falsli ⌜and⌝ wiþoute
2705 ground of scripture or of resoun, þei seien þat Crist beggide lompis of breed fro dore to dore. But, and men wolde ȝyue to þis meyne oonli lumpis of breed, þei wolde wiþyn a while chaunge her opynyoun, and seie þat Crist beggide hool looues and money. For þei han not so moche colour of scripture to seie þat Crist beggide
2710 lompis of breed, as þei han for to seie þat Crist beggide money whanne he seide to þe ypocritis þat temptiden him þus: 'Shewe ȝe to me a prynt or a coyn of money.' And þei, as þe gospel seiþ, profride or offride to him a peny. And þus þese ypocritis bilien here þe manhed of Crist. And in þe storie of Helye and þe widue, þat I
2715 reherside riȝt now, þei maken a lesyng upon his godhed, menynge in

f. 108ʳ her wordis þat God sh|ulde haue tauȝt Helye to do synne in breking of his lawe, comaundinge expresli þat þer shulde on no wise be a

2686 cheefli] specially F   2689 beggiþ] beggeþ or preieþ H   2690 or preieþ] om. HF   2691 or¹] om. F   2692 nameli] specially F 2693 maundement] comaundement DHF   or] and F   2694 to² . . . kyndli (2720)] lost D   2696 on¹&²] by F   2587 neþeles . . . lesse] and no mervell it is F   þese . . . here] þei make a lowd lye of F   2700 lesyng] lye F   shulde haue beggid] beggyd F   2703 haue seid] seide H   2704 and²] om. HF 2706 and] if F   þis] þese H, thes F   meyne] men F   2709 colour] reason F þat] om. HF   2710 margin luc. 26 E, luc. 20 margin and text after þus F, text after þus (2711) H   2712 a²] om. HF   profride or] om. F   2713 bilien] lye F þe] of þe F   2714 crist] crist iesu F   2717 on] in F

nedi and a begger among þe peple. And þis lawe is so kyndli and
moral þat God myȝte not ordeyne or comaunde þe contrarie. For, as
a man desiriþ kyndli þat myȝti men shulden haue reward to his   2720
poerte, and make a puruyaunce aȝens his meschif þat he were not
nedid to begge, so shulde he bi weie of kynde do to anoþir; and so þis
is lawe of kynde þe which mai not be dissolued. For as Crist myȝte
not, so he dissoluede no such lawe, but perfourmede hem and
declaride þe ful perfeccioun of þe moraltees of þe oold lawe.   2725

And in witnesse þat it was Cristis will þat þis fair lawe of God as
touchinge beggers, þe which is writun [Deut.] 15, shulde not ceesse
in þe newe lawe, Crist ⌐as⌐ for his tyme here kepte it hool in him|silf   f. 108ᵛ
and hise apostlis and disciplis, ⌐and þe apostlis⌐ kepten þe same as for
her tyme. For as it is writun (Act. 4), þe comoun goodis weren so   2730
wiisli delid among þe peple þat þer was no nedi among hem. And
long aftir þis tyme seynt Clement, as we ⌐mai⌐ rede in his storie,
ordeynede for þe cristen peple so þat noon of hem shulde begge.
And, if we take heede what meschif comeþ of beggerie on dyuers
wise, we shulde not resonabli wondre, alþouȝ God forbede þus   2735
streitli begging, makinge a ful ordynaunce in boþe hise lawis to
exclude þis meschif fro his peple, as it is seid bifore. And whateuer
part ⌐þo⌐ þat ben fauorable to þis beggerie þat I enpungne now han
of þe praiers and suffragiis of þo beggers, of þis I am sure þat alle þo
þat, of proud will or malice or þoruȝ vnkun[nyng]nesse þat þei han   2740
þoruȝ her owne rechelisnesse, ben fauorable to þis abusioun, | ben ful   f. 109ʳ
parteners of þis greet synne of begging aȝens Goddis ordynaunce,
and of þe lesyngis þat þei maken upon Crist and oþir seyntis in
maintenaunce of þis apostasie. For seynt Poul seiþ (ad Ro. 1) [þat]
'Not oonli þo þat doen suche grete synnes, but also þei þat assenten   2745
to þe doers of hem, ben dampnabli gilti.'

And as falsli as þei lien upon Crist and Helye, þei lyen upon seynt
Poul, whanne þei beren him on hand þat he beggide liik as her

2718 and¹] or F   2721 meschif] nede F   2722 nedid] nedy F   weie] þe
way F   anoþir] anoþer man F   2723 lawe] þe lawe F   þe] om. F
2724 no] -t canc. E, not F   lawe] lawes F   2727 margin num. 15 corr. dh to deut.
15 E   Deut.] D, num. EHF   deu. D   2728 as] om. F   here] om. F
2729 hise] in his F   as] om. F   2730 margin actuum 4 F   2731 nedi] nedy
man F   2732 mai] ⌐mai⌐ corr. E, om. HF   2734 and] ⌐32 ca.⌐ and F   on]
om. F   2735 þus . . . begging (2736)] beggyng þus straytly F   2738 þo] those
F, om. D   now] om. F   2739 þo¹] thos F   of . . . sure] I am sure of þis F
2740 vnkunnyngnesse] DH, ignorance F, vnkunnesse E   2741 þoruȝ] by F
2744 ad] om. F   þat] DHF, om. E   2745 þo] thei F   2746 dampnabli]
dampnable HF   2748 beren . . . hand] say F

lymytours doen, whanne he made and ordeynede quilagis for [þe]
2750 hooli folk in Ierusalem. But þese shamles lyers shulde vndirstonde
here þat þe peple þat seynt Poul ordeynede fore was bicome pore for
Crist, and, for as moche as þei weren þere among her enmyes, and
hadden no leiser to gete hem liiflood wiþ her bodili labour, and many
of þis peple as it is ful licli weren pore feble, lame and blynde, for þe
f. 109ᵛ whiche prestis ben in|dett bi her office for to procure hem good, as it
2756 is tauȝt bifore. þese false liers shulde vndirstonde þat Poul, hatinge
begging boþe in himsilf and in al oþir cristen peple, made a
puruyaunce bi þese quilagis for to exclude begging fro Cristis
peple. And so in þis he perfourmede þe office of presthod, bi þe
2760 which he is yboundun to be a procuratour for pore nedi peple. And
þis was a þing þat alle þe apostlis chargide moche, as þei shewide in
þat þat þei chargide herwiþ Poul and Barnabas whanne þei ȝiden
from hem, as it is writun (ad Galathas 2). For, siþ seynt Poul in his
greet nede, notwiþstondinge þat he was a prest and apostle, wrouȝte
2765 and gate liiflood for himsilf and oþir wiþ hise owne hondis, and
tauȝte þat he þat trauelide not shulde not ete, and blamede þo þat
hadde leiser to trauele and wolde not, it is no doute he wolde not
haue maad such quilagis for þe peple ⌜in⌝ Ierusalem if þei hadde had |
f. 110ʳ leiser to gete hemsilf liiflood wiþ her owne hondis. And, in tokenyng
2770 þat he beggide not þese quilagis, he vside wordis of gouernaunce,
comaundinge and charginge, and not of begging. For he seiþ þat he
haþ ordeyned þat suche quylagis shulde be maad among þe myȝti
peple for þe pore, as it is writun (1 Cor.16). And þere he on þe
comaunding maner chargiþ þe peple to make such ordynaunce for þe
2775 pore nedi peple.

    And if þou wolt se hou moche seynt Poul hatide þis begging þat I
dispreue now, marke wel hise wordis (2 ad Thess. 3) where he spekiþ

2749 quilagis] collettis (-et/t- on eras.) H, colegis F   þe] DHF, om. E
2751 here] om. F   2754 lame] and canc. lame E   2755 prestis . . . indett] it is
preastis dewtye F   2758 quilagis] collettis (-let- on eras.) H, collagiis F
2759 presthod] a preast F   2760 pore] þe canc. pore E, ⌜pore⌝ D
2761 chargide moche] sett moche by F   2762 herwiþ] þerwiþ F   ȝiden] went F
2763 margin gal. 2 E   siþ] om. F   2764 þat] om. H   2766 trauelide]
laboryd F   þo] þos F   2767 trauele] labor F   it] this F   no] not D
2768 quilagis] collectis (-lect- on eras. of -leg-) H, collagis F   hadde . . . leiser to (2769)]
myght haue F   2769 liiflood] lyvyng F   2770 quilagis] collectis (-lect- on
eras. of -leg-) H, collagys F   vside] vsiþ D   2771 begging . . . extremyte þat
(2870)] lost D   2772 quylagis] collectis (-lec- on eras. of -leg-) H, collegis F
myȝti peple] peple myȝti marked for rev. E   2773 margin 1 cor. 6 E, 1 cor. 16 F
on þe] in F   2775 people] folk F   2777 dispreue] reprove F   margin 2 ad
th. 3 F

in special aȝens þese beggers, hauynge as I suppose, veri knouleche
of hem and of her falshed bi spirit of prophecie; þe which text wiþ þe
wordis þerof I wolde marke here, and tyme wolde serue; but I mai 2780
not tarie. Neþeles I councele þee here and, as I mai, charge þee on
Goddis bihalf, and as þou wolt not be gilti of þis dampnable
begging, | take heede and forȝite neuere oo word þat seynt Poul f. 110ᵛ
chargiþ þee wiþ in þis epistle. In þe which epistle he biddiþ þee þat
þou wiþdrawe þee fro þese vnruli freris þat, aȝens al Goddis rule and 2785
her owne rule also, as it is opun in seint Fraunces rule, beggen þus.
Where seynt Poul seiþ in þe eende of his epistle: 'If ony man shal not
obeie to oure word bi þis epistle, marke ȝe him, and be ȝe not medlid
wiþ him!'? And so ech vnruli walker aboute for to begge, into þe
tyme þat he amende him, shulde be as a cursid man among þe peple. 2790
And herfore seiþ seynt Iohun acordinge herto þat, whosoeuer come
to þe cristen peple and brynge not þe doctrine of þe gospel, þe which
he and hise felowis tauȝten, þei shulde not seie 'hayl' to him; for
whoso seiþ 'hail' to him shal haue part of hise wickid werkis. And siþ
þis begging is aȝens þe hool ordynaunce of God aboute his chir|che, f. 111ʳ
boþe in þe oold lawe and in þe newe, and sclaundre to Crist and his 2796
gospel, and seyntis þat sueden hym in perfeccioun, as it is seid
bifore, freris, whanne þei comen þus abeggid, bryngen not þe
doctryn þat seynt Iohun spekiþ of wiþ hem. And if he þat seiþ
'heyl' to such oon shal be partener of his wickid werkis, hou moche 2800
raþer he þat resceyueþ him and mainteneþ him wiþ hise worldli
good and strenkþe? And if he þat bryngiþ not þe doctryn of þe
gospel wiþ him, as seynt Iohun techiþ, shal not be freendli salued,
hou moche raþer shulde he haue no good cheer among Cristis
freendis þat seiþ þat þe gospel is þe falsest lawe and heresie; and 2805
aȝens al þe lawe of God, oold and newe, and ensaumple of Crist, and

2779 spirit] þe spirit HF   þe¹] om. F   2780 þerof] om. F   here] here wiþ þe
wordis F   and] yf þe F   serue] serue me F   2781 þee¹] yow F   charge] I
charge HF   þee²] yow F   2782 þou wolt] ye wyll F   2783 heede] om. F
2784 þis] his F   2785 vnruli] orible H, rebellis and horrible F   2787 in] þus
in HF   margin Nota bene poul H   2789 so] om. HF   ech] iche suche an H,
euery suche F   into] vnto F   2790 a cursid] acursid H   þe] om. F
2791 herfore] þerfore F   acordinge] in his secund epistle acordyng F margin Jo. þe
second epist' F   herto] þerto F   come] comith F   2792 to þe] vnto F   þe⁴]
om. F   2793 hayl to him] vnto hym all hale F   for] om. F   2794 whoso]
whosoeuer F   hail to him] vnto hym all haill F   haue part] be partaker F   siþ]
seyng F   2796 in²] om. F   newe] newe lawe F   2797 sueden] folowyd F
2798 abeggid] abeggyng F   2799 of] om. F   2800 heyl] all haill F
partener] partaker F   wickid] om. F   2803 shal] schulde HF   freendli salued]
salutyd F   2806 of God] bothe F

þe perfeccioun of his chirche mainteneþ þis synful custumable
begging? And, certis, nar þat Hildegar seiþ in hir prophecie þat
þese liers shulen þus walke aboute wiþoute shame, I wolde merueile
f. 111ᵛ þat þei prechen | her synne of beggerie so opunli.

2811   For in autorisyng and solempnysynge of þis dampnable beggerie,
and of alle þe lesyngis and blasphemyes þat þei putten upon Crist,
and his lawe and hise seyntis in þis poynt, in þe moost hooli dai,
alþouȝ experience techiþ þei haue no nede, he þat is moost autentik
2815 persoone among hem shal bere þe bag þat dai and begge. And al þat
is seid in scripture in comendacioun of wilful pouert for Crist, þei
falsly glosen to maintene wiþ þis vngroundid beggerie. þe which
custumable beggerie Crist myȝte not ordeyne in his chirche, for it is
a vicious faute, and Crist myȝte ordeyne no such faute, as it is
2820 declarid bifore, for he is wiþoute faute, and made an ordynaunce for
his chirche, þe which ordynaunce kept, as men ben boundun to kepe
it, his chirche in euery degre and staat shulde haue be wiþoute faute
of goodis of fortune, kynde and grace, of þe whiche goodis þe
f. 112ʳ apostasie of þe | clergie haþ robbid it now. And þe leest faute or
2825 incontynence is not possible at Crist. And, if þou þenke in þin herte
þat Crist is fair serued among þese custumable beggers, I haue toold
þee a rule bifore wherbi þou maist knowe wheþer it be so or noon.
But I councele þee here þat þou be wel war of þe signes of þese
pseudo þat Crist spekiþ of. And wherfore trowist þou þat Crist
2830 biddiþ þee so ofte and so diligentli in þe gospel þat þou shuldist take
heede to þe werkis, but for þou shuldist not be disceyued bi þe
signes of þese pseudo?

But up hap þou seist here, as folk þat ben disceyued bi ypocritis
doen, as Crisostum seiþ upon þis word of þe gospel (Mt. 7) *Attendite*
2835 *a falsis prophetis*, where Crisostum aresoneþ a man þat is disceyued
wiþ ypocritis þus: 'Vp hap þou seist "Hou mai I seie þat he is no
cristen man, þe which, as I se, knoulechiþ Crist, and haþ an auter,

2808 certis nar þat] if F   seiþ] dyd not say F   hir] hy F, *om.* H
2809 shulen] schulden HF   2811 solempnysynge] in solempnysinge H
2814 experience] as experience HF   2815 and²] ⌈33 ca.⌉ and F   2817 falsly
glosen] glosen falsly *marked for rev.* E   þe] *om.* F   2819 ordeyne] not *canc.*
ordeyne E, not ordene F   no] *om.* F   faute²] a fawte F   2821 þe] *om.* F
which . . . richelis- (2843)] *lost* H   2823 kynde] goodis of kynd F   grace] goodis
of grace   2824 and . . . Crist (2825)] *om.* F   2825 þenke] thynkest F
2827 a] *om.* F   2828 þat þou] *om.* F   þese] þos F   2829 trowist]
thynkest F   2831 þe¹] þer F   for] because F   2833 up hap]
peraventur F   2834 word of þe gospel] text F   2835 where . . . seist
(2836)] etc. peraventur þou sayst sayth crisostome F   2837 þe] *om.* F

and offriþ sacrifice of bre|ed and wiyn, and cristeneþ, þat rediþ þe f. 112ᵛ
hooli scripturis, and haþ alle þe ordris of hooli prestis?" þou art,' as
þis seynt seiþ, 'an vnwise man. For, if he knoulechide not Crist and 2840
his heþenesse were opun, and þou were disceyued in him, þis disceyt
were woodnesse. Forsoþe now, for as moche as he knoulechiþ Crist,
but not as Crist haþ comaundid, it is of þin owne richelisnesse if þou
be bigilid of him! For he þat falliþ into a priue diche is seid a
recheles man, bicause he lokide not warli; and he þat falliþ into an 2845
opun diche is not oonli seid a recheles man, but a wood man.' Upon
þis text of þe gospel, wiþ Crisostum þerupon, I was purposid for to
haue markid mo notable þingis þan I do at þis tyme; for now I knowe
þat I haue not so moche leiser as I wende þat I hadde. Neþeles for al
þe haast I councele þee þat þou marke þis of Cristis wordis and of 2850
þis blessid seynt: | to ȝyue no credence of hoolynesse to persoone or f. 113ʳ
sect, whateuer signes of hoolynesse þat he haue, but if þou haue a
riȝt redi euydence þat he lyue aftir þe hool lawe of God. And anoþir
þing þou maist marke of þese wordis: hou þat vnkun[nyng]nesse ᵣbi
rechelisnesseᴸ mai brynge a man into þe diche. And wel þou woost, 2855
and þou falle into þat diche, þou comest neuere out þerof.

But here up hast þou grucchist aȝens me in þin herte, and woldist
bittirli aske of me, and we were togidir at partie, wherbi þe beggers
þat han neþer londis ne rentis, and ben prestis and clerkis moche
beter þan I, and also semeli men and worþi mennes sones, shulde 2860
lyue? Hereᵣaȝensᴸ I aske of þee: who foundide hem? þou seist liȝtli
'Domynyk, Frauncis, and oþir, þou woost neuere who wel.' And I
seie to þee feiþfulli þat if Crist hadde foundid hem bi himsilf, and

2838 þe] om. F   2839 ordris] ordre F   prestis] churche of preasthode F
þou art] yf þou thynkyth þus F   2840 seynt] holy man F   an] þou art an F
for . . . woodnesse (2842)] om. F   2843 margin exemplum F   haþ] om. F   of]
om. F   richelisnesse] fawte F   2844 seid] callyd F   2845 recheles]
foolische F   lokide not warli] was not beware F   warli] warli aboute him, aboute
him canc. E   2846 opun] om. F   seid] callyd F   recheles] foolysche F
2847 þerupon] þer F   2849 hadde] ᵣschulde haueᴸ dh hadde H, schuld had F
for . . . þee (2850)] I counseile þee (yow F) for al þe hast HF   2850 þat þou marke]
to marke F   þis . . . wordis] þes wordis of crist F   2851 blessid] holy F
persoone] no person F   or] nor to F   2852 þou] yow F   a riȝt] riȝt a H, a
trew F   2853 redi] om. F   2854 maist] must F   vnkunnyngnesse] H,
vnkunnesse E, ignorance F   2855 rechelisnesse] folyschenes F   þou] yow F
woost] know F   2856 and þou] yf ye F   þat] þe F   þou comest] ye come F
2857 here up hast] peraventur F   hast] hap H   grucchist] saist and grudgis F   in]
sore in F   2858 bittirli] om. F   and] if F   we] we ij F   at partie] om. F
þe] þese HF   2859 ne] nor F   2860 men] om. HF   2861 hereaȝens]
here of ye F   of þee] agayn F   seist] answerist me F   liȝtli] om. F
2862 Frauncis] and Fraunces HF   woost] knowist F   neuere] not F

aftir his owne witt and plesaunce, he wolde haue ordeyned so for
f. 113ᵛ hem þat þei shulde not haue | be custumable beggers, as it is opun
2866 ynow of diuers processe þat I haue declarid bifore. And so, if þei ben
nedid to customable clamarous begging, þei mai wite it no þing saue
her owne apostasie, wherbi þei ben straied awei fro þe pure religioun
of Crist, and fro þe vertuous mene, þe which is fautles, þat Crist
2870 chees to him and to hise apostlis, into þe vicious extremyte þat I now
bi autorite of Goddis lawe and resoun dampne here. But freris can
seie here þat þese euydencis goen not aȝens perfit beggers as þei ben,
but aȝens oþir maner beggers. Certein, hauyng reward to þe craft
and sotilte þat þei han in begging, þei mai be callid perfit beggers;
2875 but, for al þat, her begging is not þe perfeccioun of þe gospel, neþer
stondinge þerwiþ, as it is declarid bifore. And if þou loue þese sectis,
or þe persoones þat ben of þese sectis, as þou pretendist, þou shalt
f. 114ʳ ȝyue hem ful sad and bi|sy councel, ȝhe, and helpe in dede what þou
maist, þat þei leue þis vicious extremyte, and turne aȝen to þe
2880 vertuous mene þat Crist tauȝte, and so bitake hemsilf to þe pure
religioun of Iesu Crist foundid on þe best wise.

For þou maist wel vndirstonde bi þat þat Crist seiþ in þe gospel of
þe pharisees, and þou take heede wiþ bisi studie, þat, haue þei
neuere so long praiers and solempne sacrificis wiþ gloriouse ritis, þat
2885 al þat auailiþ not, but if it be don in trewe lyuyng aftir þe pure lawe
of God. And certis I drede of boþe þese maner of peple, þat ben fled
fro þe vertuous mene of sufficience of liiflood and hilyng into þe
viciouse extremytees or eendis, þe whiche I haue blamed bifore, lest
her praiers be so long þat God mai not heere hem. For, as ȝe knowen
2890 wel, it is a comoun prouerbe and sumwhat it haþ of truþe, þat a short
f. 114ᵛ praier peersiþ heuene. þou woost wel þat a þing is | long whanne þe

2864 witt] will F   plesaunce] pleasure F   2866 of] in F   processe]
processes HF   so] om. F   2867 nedid to] so nedy þat þei must nedys vse þis F
wite it] well know it is F   saue] but F   2869 and . . . Crist²] om. F
2870 to hise] his H   þe] þis HF   2871 but] and so F   can] can not, not canc.
E, can not HF   2872 here] om. F   þese euydencis] þes evydenc' F   beggers] of
beggers F   2873 certein] but truly F   reward] respect F   2877 or . . .
sectis] om. HF   þou pretendist] yow pretend F   þou shalt] yow schuld F
2878 ful sad and bisy] good F   what] as moche as F   þou maist] ye may F
2879 leue] may leeve F   þis] þe H   2882 þou maist] yow may F
2883 and] yf F   wiþ . . . studie] om. F   2884 solempne] DHF, so solempne E
ritis þat] customys F   2885 but if] except F   2886 and] ⌜34 ca.⌝ and F
certis] truly F   drede] fere me F   2887 sufficience of] sufficient F   hilyng]
lyvyng F   2888 þe] om. F   2889 mai] wyll F   2890 wel] om. F
sumwhat it haþ] it is F   2891 þou woost] yow know F

eendis of it ben fer atwynne, as it is of a myle or of a ȝeer, in comparisoun of a foot or an hour. And so, as þe eendis ben ferþer atwynne, so þe þing is þe lenger. And þanne a þing is shortist whanne þe eendis ben euene togidir, as it is of a liyn of two poyntis, or of a tyme of two instantis. Vndirstonde þou here þanne þat a praier haþ two eendis: þat oon is þe spirit of man þat preieþ, and þat oþir eende is God, þat oonli to oure purpos now shulde be preied. And whanne it is so þat mannes spirit and God ben knytt togidir bi charite, wiþoute ony dampnable synne goynge bitwene, þanne ben boþe þe eendis of þis praier togidir. And such a praier ⌈is⌉ short aftir þis menyng, alþouȝ it ocupie moche tyme. But if dampnable synne go bitwene þese two eendis of praier, þat is to seie God and mannes spirit, þanne is þat praier long aftir þis menyng—ȝhe, loke hou fer such | a dampnable synne þat encumbriþ such a spirit is fro God, and so fer ben þe eendis of such a praier atwynne. And wite þou wel, þat a praier þat is long þus is so long and so fer fro heuene þat it mai neuere effectuali come þidir. Loke þanne here bisili I preie þee hou fer þese viciouse extremytees of vnkyndli worldli lordship in þe endowid clerkis and religiouse, and þese vngroundid and dampnable [synnes] of beggerie, ben fro Crist and þe vertuous mene þat he and hise apostlis chesen for her lyuyng here upon erþe—and so long and so fer fro God in effect ben her praiers! And so, I drede me not, ful fewe praiers or noon of þo persoones þat stonden obstynat in þes dampnable extremytees peersen effectuali heuene, for hemsilf or for ony þat þei preien fore. þus stood it of þe praiers of þe heþen men, þat blaberide many praiers whilis her herte was fer fro God. And bi such long | praiers þe scribis deuouride þe housis of widues, as Crist seiþ (*Mr.* 12), as oure ypocritis now wiþ her long praiers, and oþir myri noys þat þei maken in þe eeris of þe peple, deuouren not oonli

2895

2900

f. 115ʳ

2906

2910

2915

f. 115ᵛ

2920

2892 atwynne] betwixt F   2893 an] of an HF   so] *om.* HF
2894 atwynne] betwixt F   þe²] *om.* F   2896 of¹] *om.* F   þou] yow F
2897 þat¹] þe F   man] þe man F   þat oþir] þe oþer F   2898 is] is//is H
shulde] must F   2899 mannes] a mannes D   god] godis F   2900 synne]
sygne F   2903 go] DHF, goiþ E   2905 encumbriþ] trubleth F
2906 ben] is F   atwynne] betwixt F   wite þou] know yow F   2907 is²] and is F
2908 þidir] there F   þanne here] *rev.* F   þee] yow F   2909 þese] þe F
2910 þese] þis HF   2911 synnes of] D, synnes *canc.* of E, *om.* HF
2913 drede me] dowt F   ful] *om.* F   2914 þo] þos F   2915 effectuali
heuene] *rev.* F   2916 onmy] ony oþir, oþir *canc.* E   *margin* Mt 6 D, *in text after*
þus H   þe²] ⌈þe⌉//þe H   2918 þe¹] *om.* HF   scribis] scribys and pharaseys F
2919 *margin* mr. 12 E Mr.12] Mᵗ 12 D, Ma xiij c ⌈23 *dh*⌉ H, Mth 12 F   now] now doen
H, do now F   2920 myri] *om.* F   oonli] *om.* F

þe housis of widues but also of ful many worþi lordis and kny3tis, bi whom oure rewme, 3he, al cristendom was sum tyme moche gouerned and sokourid.

And so Crist, rehersynge þe wordis of Isaie, seiþ ful truli of þese
2925 renegatis þat han left Crist and hise apostlis and her vertuous mene, þat 'þis peple worshipiþ me wiþ lippis, but her herte is fer fro me.' And if, as Crist seiþ, þis prophecie was wel seid of þe pharisees, þe whiche, alþou3 þei weren couetouse, 3it bi ony þing þat I can perseyue of hem bi þe gospel, þei weren not falle into ony of þese
2930 two extremytees of lordship and of beggerie, hou moche raþer is þis prophecie opunli verified of oure clerkis and religiouse þat, a3ens al
f. 116ʳ þe ordynaunce of God in boþe hise la|wis, ben encumbrid obstynatli in boþe þese extremytees; and boþe þese manere of sectis, what in lyuyng, what in maintenaunce, ben falle fro þe vertuous mene into
2935 boþe þe[se] viciouse extremytees? For now, and þat is wundir, saue þat þe deuel anticrist strenkiþ himsilf what he mai, þe beggers maintenen þe possessioners, and þe possessioners maintenen þe beggers in her synnes.

Now siris þe dai is al ydo, and I mai tarie 3ou no lenger, and I
2940 haue no tyme to make now a recapitulacioun of my sermon. Neþeles I purpose to leue it writun among 3ou, and whoso likiþ mai ouerse it. And I biseche 3ou at þe reuerence of God þat 3e greue 3ou not wiþ ony truþe þat I haue seid at þis tyme, for if 3e doen so, I mai truli seie wiþ Moyses þat 3oure grucching is not a3ens me, but it is a3ens
2945 þe Lord þat is truþe. And certis, if I haue seid ony þing amys, and I
f. 116ᵛ mai now | haue redi knouleche þerof, I shal amende it er I go. And if I haue such knouleche herafter, I shal wiþ beter will come and amende my defautis þan I seie þis at þis tyme. And of anoþir þing I biseche 3ou here þat, if ony aduersarie of myn replie a3ens ony
2950 conclusioun þat I haue shewid to 3ou at þis tyme, reportiþ redili hise

---

2921 widues] þe wydowis F   2922 al] and all F   moche] *om.* F
2923 gouerned and] *om.* HF   2924 *margin* mt.15 E, *marked for insertion in text after*
mene (2925) H   2925 *margin* isa. 15 D   2926 worshipiþ] doth wirschipe F
lippis] þer lyppys F   2927 seid] ⸢y⸣seide H   þe²] *om.* F   2930 þis] *om.* D
2933 boþe] bi *canc.* boþe E   2934 þe] þis F   mene] *om.* F   2935 þese]
DHF, þe E   wundir] moche wonder F   saue] but F   2936 himsilf] hym F
what] as moche as F   þe²] *om.* D, þes F   2939 mai . . . I²] *om.* F
2940 now] *om.* F   neþeles] and also I am loothe to be tedius vnto yow neuertheles F
2942 and] and moreouer F   2943 so] *om.* F   2944 it is] *om.* F
2945 certis] truly F   and²] if F   2946 now haue] *rev.* F   2948 defautis]
fautis D   þis¹] *om.* HF   2949 here *om.* F   þat if] *rev.* F   aduersarie . . . end]
lost D   2950 shewid] seide HF

euydencis, and nameli if he take ony euydence or colour of hooli
scripture, and, if almy3ti God wole vouchesaaf to graunte me grace
or leiser to declare mysilf in þese poyntis þat I haue moued in þis
sermoun, I shal þoru3 þe help of him in whom is al help declare me,
so þat he shal holde him answerid. But I presume not þis upon my 2955
kunnyng, saue oonli upon þe truþe of God þat is my3ti to defende
itsilf. And me þenkiþ þer mai no man resonabli blame me moche for
ony þing þat I haue seid here at þis tyme, for I hope þat God haþ
rulid my tunge, so | þat I haue depraued no mannes persoone ne staat f. 117ʳ
approued and groundid of God and his lawe; and so haʳue I blamʸyd 2960
no þing saue synne, and as for þat mai ne wole ony man blame me,
saue he þat in effect loueþ þe deuel and synne.

For I purposide noon oþer wise in þe bigynnyng of my sermoun
but, aftir þe meenyng and vndirstonding of my teeme, to enpungne
synne and bastard sectis or braunchis þat, bi alien seed and not bi þe 2965
pure seed of Iesu Crist, þat is spouse of þe chirche, ben brou3t into
þe chirche; þe whiche bastard braunchis shal be blowun up, roote
and al, bi ful moche strong blowing of þe foure wyndis, þe which mai
bitokene þe foure gospels, or þe oold lawe, þe gospels, þe writyng of
þe apostlis and þe apocalips. And þese bastard braunchis, seynge þis 2970
meschif comynge to hem, holden þese foure wyndis þat þei blowe
not upon hem. And þus is þe prophecie of seynt Iohun fulfillid |
(*Apocalips*. 7) where he seiþ þat foure aungels stondinge upon þe f. 117ᵛ
foure corners of þe erþe helden þe foure wyndis þat þei shulde not
blowe upon þe erþe, neþer upon þe see, neþer upon ony tree; þe 2975
which foure aungels mai wel bitokene þe[se] foure bastard braunchis
þat growen not up in Cristis chirche of þe seed, þat is his word, þat
is to seie endowid clerkis, monkis and chanouns and freris. þese ben

2951 euydencis] evydenc' F   nameli] specially F   or colour] *om*. F   hooli] *om*. F
2953 or] and F   2954 me] myself F   2955 holde him] say he is F
2956 kunnyng] knowlege F   2957 þenkiþ] þinkiþ þat HF   2958 hope]
trust F   2959 rulid] so rulyd F   so] *om*. F   depraued] dampned HF   ne]
nor F   2960 and groundid] *om*. HF   his] groundid in his HF   haue I blamyd]
I blame HF   2961 saue] but F   mai . . . man] no man may F   2962 saue]
but F   2963 for] ⌐35 ca.⌐ For F   purposide noon] neuer purposyd F
2964 vndirstonding] þe vnderstondinge HF   2965 alien] strawnge F
2966 is spouse] I suppose F   2967 blowun] drawen HF   roote] by þe roote F
2968 ful] great F   strong] and strong HF   þe²] *om*. F   2969 writyng]
writyngis F   2971 blowe not] schuld not blow F   2972 *margin* apo. 7 E
2973 þe] *om*. HF   2975 neþer upon þe see] *twice, 2nd canc*. E   neþer²] nor F
ony tree] þe treys F   þe³] *om*. F   2976 þese] HF, þe E   2977 seed] whiche
seed F   2978 and¹] *om*. F   þese] þe F

þe foure aungels at þe hardist weie of Sathanas, bi ypocrisie
2980 transfigurid into aungels of liȝt; and þei han sett her feet, þat is to
seie her affecciouns, upon þe foure corners of þe erþe, ⌈and so upon
þe foure quarters of þe erþe⌉, and in þat upon al þe erþe þat is foure
quarters þerof. For what bi amorteising of lordships and apropriaciouns of chirchis, what bi dyuerse maner of begging, þei desiren to
2985 haue al þe fatt of þe erþe into her hondis, as it is tauȝt bifore, and
f. 118ʳ shewid in partie what me|nes þei maken to þis conclusioun. And, as I
suppose, þese foure wyndis vnneþe in Antiochis tyme weren
streitloker holdun þan þei ben now bi þese foure aungels þoruȝ
strenkþe of her newe statutis and constituciouns, as ȝe alle knowen
2990 wel, so þat þese wyndis mut not freli blowe upon þe erþe, see or tre.
þe whiche þre, as sum men seien, bitokenen men þat bigynnen to
lyue wel, and þo þat profiten in good lyuyng, and men þat ben perfit
in lyuyng. Or ellis, and beter as I suppose, þe erþe mai bitokene þe
comunte of þe peple þat tiliþ þe erþe, and þe see mai bitokene þe
2995 lordis, to whom bilongen þe grete worldli possessiouns, þe whiche
ben bitokened bi þe see, þat is a greet flood or habundaunce of watir,
þe which signyfieþ temperal possessiouns, as Gorham seiþ upon þe
Apocalips. Bi þese trees þat growen to heuenward mai wel be
f. 118ᵛ vndirstondun þe staat of þe | clergie þe which, aliened fro þis
3000 world bi contemplacioun, shulde in a manere lyue in heuen, as
seynt Poul seiþ.

But ȝit þis malice shal haue an eende, as seynt Iohun meneþ
aftirward in þe same prophecie. And so such bastard braunchis þat
my teeme spekiþ of shal be rootid up, alþouȝ þei florishen ȝit a while;
3005 for þe ax þat seynt Iohun spekiþ of is sett to þe roote. For Helye, þat
is Iohun, boolddli enpungneþ þe avoutrie of þe greet strumpet þat
sittiþ upon many watris, þe which vnclene womman bitokeneþ þe
endowid clergie þat restiþ upon worldli possessiouns and lordships
þat ben vndirstondun bi many watris. And also þese watris bitokenen

---

2979 þe¹] *om.* HF   hardist weie] best F   bi ypocrisie] *om.* F   2984 bi]
wiþ H   2985 fatt] staate F   2987 vnneþe] scarsly F   2988 streitloker]
more straytly F   2989 strenkþe] þe strengþe HF   2990 mut] may F   not]
no F   tre] tres F   2991 þe] *om.* F   2992 þo] þem F   profiten] goth
furth F   2994 tiliþ] tellith F   2995 þe²] *om.* F   2996 bitokened]
tokenide F   2997 þe¹] *om.* F   upon] on H   2998 bi] and bi HF
þese] þe HF   2999 þe²] *om.* F   aliened] is *canc.* aliened E, is aliened H, beyng
strange F   3004 rootid up] pluct vp by þe rootys F   3005 þat] þat // þat F
Iohun] Ioon baptist HF   3006 *margin* apo.17 EHF   booldli] bodely F
3007 þe¹] *om.* F   3008 clergie] clarkis or clergy F   3009 bitokenen]
bitoken HF

moche peple þat anticrist ⌐desiriþ⌐ to regne upon, þe which strumpet 3010
or hoore doiþ auoutrie aȝens him þat shulde be hir spouse, Iesu
Crist, leuynge his liif and his loore, and so þe seed of þis spouse | for f. 119ʳ
þe seed of þe alien þat Crist spekiþ of (*Io.* 5), þe which alien, as seynt
Austin seiþ upon þe same word, is anticrist. And wondre þou not,
alþouȝ I mene here þat þe lawe, bi þe which þe clergie is rulid in þis 3015
apostasie, be anticristis lawe, siþ þe clergie lyueþ so ful contrarie to
Crist vndir þis lawe. And no doute, as it is in partie declarid aboue,
þis apostasie and þis greet auoutrie is ground and roote of al þe
meschif in cristendom.

No wondir þanne, alþouȝ Helye, whom God sendiþ to hewe upon 3020
þis wickid roote, hewe upon þis ground of synne; for þus seint Iohun
Baptist hewe upon þe apostasie and þe goostli auoutrie of þe clergie
of þe oold lawe, in whom at þat tyme was cheefli þe malice of
anticrist and his chirche, þe which ⌐haþ⌐ growe forþ wiþ Goddis
chirche—ȝhe, growiþ and shal growe fro þe first wickid man Caym 3025
into þe last þat shal be dampned. And | so oure Helye now, bi whom f. 119ᵛ
I vndirstonde þe trewe prechours of þe gospel, hewiþ upon þis roote,
not oonli wiþ Ioones ax, but wiþ þe swerd of þe gospel, þe which is
sharp on boþe þe sidis, for it haþ þe egge of boþe þese lawis. And þis
swerd God bihiȝte to þis Helye (*Apo.* 11), where he seiþ þus: 'I shal 3030
ȝyue to my two witnessis, and þei shal preche a þousynd daies two
hundrid and sixti.' And manye men wenen þat þese two witnessis
shal be Enok and Helye, þat shal appeere bodili here upon erþe and
preche aȝens anticrist. But seint Ierom was of þe contrarie opynyoun,
for he writiþ in hise epistlis þat þei han fulli maad an eende as 3035
touchinge þe lyuyng here upon erþe. For, as seynt Ierom seiþ, whoso
wole seie þat þei shal appere here bodili and deedly, mut seie and
suppose þat þe temple wiþ þe sacrificis of þe oold lawe shal be
renewid. And þe | same sentence haþ Gorham upon þis text of þe f. 120ʳ
Apocalips; and þerfore Gorham vndirstondiþ bi þese two witnessis 3040
þe trewe prechours þat I spak of bifore, and þese prechours ben
asigned bi a noumbre of two bicause þat þei shal preche two þingis,

---

3010 peple] þe/peple E   þe] *om.* F   3011 or hoore] *om.* F   3012 loore]
lawe F   for] can haue no place for F   3013 þe alien] þis strangur F   þe³] *om.* F
alien] strangur F   3014 word is] wordis F   and . . . lawe (3017)] *om.* F
3016 ful] *om.* H   3017 in partie] partly F   3020 þanne] þan it is F   hewe]
dyd hewe F   3024 þe] *om.* F   3025 growiþ] growne F   3026 into]
vnto F   3027 þe³] *om.* F   3029 boþe þe] boþe HF   þese] þe HF
3030 bihiȝte] promysed F   11] ii ca. F   3036 þe] þis HF   lyuyng] lyffe F
3037 mut] must F   3040 and] ⌐36 ca.⌐ and F   3042 þat] *om.* F

þat is to seie Cristis godhed and his manhed, or ellis þe oold lawe and
þe newe, or ellis for þe charite þat þei shal haue in þis office to God
3045 and to her neiȝbore. And þese þousynd two hundrid and sixti daies
bitokeneþ, as þis clerk seiþ, þe gospel, þe which Crist prechide in so
many daies, þe whiche daies maken þre ȝeer and an half, or ellis nyȝ
so moche. And þese daies maken a tyme and tymes and half a tyme,
þat is to seie þre ȝeer and an half, þe whiche menen þe same gospel,
3050 bi þe which þe womman þat is hooli chirche was norishid in desert of
contemplacioun and heuenli lyuyng, into þe tyme þat vnauysid men |
f. 120ᵛ at þe mouyng of þe dragoun of helle casten upon þis womman watir
as a flood, þat is to seie greet habundaunce of worldli possessiouns,
wherbi þis womman is ydrawun fro heuenli lyuyng. And so upon þis
3055 meschif as a ground anticrist hadde power to make moneþis two and
fourti, þe whiche monþis maken as moche as þo daies and tymes and
half a tyme þat I spak of riȝt now. For þese moneþis maken þre ȝeer
and an half, þe whiche monþis and tyme bitokeneþ anticristis lawe,
þat is concurraunt wiþ Cristis lawe and contrarie þerto in alle þo
3060 pointis þat autorisen or fauoren þe encumbraunce of þis womman in
þe forseid flood. And euere, siþ ⌐þat⌐ þis flood was cast upon þis
woman, she haþ don more and more auoutrie aȝens hir spouse, þat
shulde be Iesu Crist and his seed, and delitiþ hir in þis synne—but
f. 121ʳ neuere so moche as now. And for þe greet lust þat | þis hoore haþ in
3065 þis auoutrie, as Iesabel pursuede Helye þat vndirnam hir of hir
auoutrie wiþ alien goddis, and as Herodias pursuede and killide seynt
Iohun Baptist þat dampnede hir bodili avoutrie, so þis strong hoore
pursueþ now þis Helye þat I speke of now to dyuerse maner of
deeþis, opun and priuy, bicause þat he blameþ hir of hir foul goostli
3070 auoutrie, hewinge upon þis roote þat is ground of alle þe abhominaciouns þat regnen in þe chirche. And herfore þis hoore procuriþ to
hir power and leue of kyngis to kille þus Helye, þat dampneþ þis
hordam, þe whiche assenten cowardli to hir foul peticioun for

---

3044 for] om. F   3045 þese] þis HF   þousynd] two canc. þousynd E
3046 bitokeneþ] bitoken HF   þe²] om. F   3047 þe] om. F   3049 þe] om. F
gospel] gospel ⌐apo.xij c⌐ H, gospell apoca. 12 F   3051 into] vnto F   margin apo.
13 E, marked for insertion in text after helle (3052) H, so inserted F   3056 þe] om. F
þo] þes F   3058 þe] om. F   3059 þo] þes F   3061 siþ þat] syns F
was] wast F   3063 delitiþ] delitide H   hir] om. F   3064 hoore] harllott F
3065 vndirnam hir of] dyd speke agaynst F   3066 alien] strange F   goddis]
goodis F   3067 hoore] harlott F   3068 pursueþ now] doth now persue F
speke] spak F   now] om. F   3069 blameþ] blame F   3070 þe] om. F
3071 herfore] þerfore F   hoore] harlott F   procuriþ to] gettith F   3072 þis]
hyr F   3073 hordam] advowtrye F   þe] om. F   assenten] agreith F

vnauysid ooþis þat þei han maad to maintene þis avoutrie and
apostasie, as her auncetris han don bifore hem. þus was Heroude 3075
ouercome, and for a foly ooþ assentide to þe wickid will of þe cursid
wom|man þat he susteynede. And þis encumbraunce of þis womman, f. 121ᵛ
wiþ þe apostasie and avoutrie þat suen þerof, shal not ceesse into þe
tyme þat þe erþe opene his mouþ and swolow up þis flood, and so
helpe þis womman, as þe Apocalips spekiþ—þat is to seie, into þe 3080
tyme þat seculer princis take þese temperaltees aȝen into her hondis
and redresse þe clergie to heuenli lyuyng, as Gorham seiþ upon þe
twelþe c[hapitre] of þe Apocalips.

And in þis processe I mene moche more þan I expresli seie here.
But up hap þou seist to me here 'þou presumest proudli to expowne 3085
þe derk visiouns of þe Apocalips; it hadde be for þi profit þat þou
haddist left þis mater and maad an eende whanne þou bihiȝtist us þat
þou so woldist! For wite þou wel, as for þis processe, þou getist þee
no þank of ony clerk or religiouse or ony of her retenu þat loueþ þis
endow|[ynge!' Sire, and it be þi wille, I presume not as þou seist. But f. 122ʳ
þe dede, or þe þing in itsilf, expowneþ þe visioun þat was derkli 3091
writun. And bi þis manere of mene þe apostlis vndirstoden þe
prophecies þat weren derkli seide of Crist, as it is writun in diuerse
placis of þe gospel. And also, if þou loke wel, I haue not seide al þis
on myn owne. And I preie þee, greue þee not wiþ me, for I wole tarie 3095
þee no lenger. But God for his greet mercy sende þee grace to haue
cleer knowleche of þese pseudo þat, wiþouten autorite of þe Fadir of
heuene, ben plauntid in þe chirche, leste þou be disceyued bi her fals
signes. Amen, amen, so mot it be. *Deo gracias.*]

3074 vnauysid ooþis] oothes wiþowt deliberation F   vnauysid] vnavisi H
3076 for a] *om.* F   assentide] agreid F   will . . . cursid] *om.* F   3077 womman]
woman and to hyr cursed will F   þat he susteynede] *om.* F   3078 suen] suede H,
folowith F   into] vnto F   3080 þe¹ . . . spekiþ] Iohun spekith in his apocalipse F
margin apo. 12 E, *in text after* flood (3079) H   into] vnto F   3082 to] of F
3083 chapitre] c' E   3084 mene] move F   moche] *om.* F   seie here] can well
mak an ende of for þe day is ouerpast F   3085 up hap] peraventur F   to me here]
here to me H, vnto me here F   þou] syr þou F   3086 visiouns] viciouns H
þat] if F   3087 bihiȝtist] promisist F   3088 so] *om.* F   wite . . . wel] þou
mast well know F   þis] þe F   3089 ony] of ony H   þis] þes F
3090 endowynge] endow// *rest lost* E, possessions F   sire] to þes I answere syr F
and] yf F   3093 seide] spokyn F   3095 on] of F   owne] owne hede F
and] þerfore F   greue þee not] be not grevyd F   tarie] be no/no more tedius vnto F
3096 no lenger] *om.* F   3098 þou be] ye be F   3099 amen¹ . . . gracias] *om.* F

Hereaftir it schal be schewid what peryl it is to prestis to be in seculer office, and to lordis to suffre hem þerinne or to excite hem þerto.

Seynt Cypriane saiþ þat 'þorow þe councell of bischopis þer is f. 47ᵛ made a statute þat alle þat ben charchid wiþ presthode | and 971 ordeynyd in þe service of clerkis schulde not serue but to þe auter, and to mynystre sacramentis and to take hede to prayers and orysons. Hit is forsoþe writen "No man berynge his knyȝthode to God entrike hym wiþ seculer nedis", þe whiche oure bischopis 975 and oure predecessouris, biholdynge religiously and purveynge hoolsumly, dempten þat whosoeuer take mynystres of þe chirche fro spirituall office to seculere, þat þer be noone offrynge done for hym ne eny sacrifice halowyd for his sepulture. For þai disserven not to be nempnyd byfore þe auter of God in þe prayer of prestis, þe 980 whiche willen clepe away prestis and mynystres of þe chirche fro þe auter.' þis saiþ saynte Cipriane.

Here men mow se how perylous it is to þe kynge and seculer f. 48ʳ lor|dis to wiþholde eny preste in seculer bissynes. þis is prevyd þus: for euery seculere lorde by þe law of þe gospell is Goddis bayly. But 985 if eny bayly hiryd a werkeman wiþ his lordis goode, and putt hym to his owne seruyce, he must nede be vntrue to his lorde. Riȝt so is euery seculere lorde to oure lorde Ihesu Criste, but if he amende hym, þat takiþ a preste and puttiþ hym in his seculer office, brekynge þe heest of his lorde God, þat commaundiþ 'þu schalt couett noon 990 oþer mannys seruande.' And he wiþdrawiþ hym fro þe seruyce of God, and fro þe kepynge of cristen mennys soulis, þe whiche he haþ take charge of, for whiche soulis oure lorde Ihesu Criste toke fleisch f. 48ᵛ and blode and suffred | harde deþe, and schedde his owne hert blode. þis perylous doynge of seculer lordis is boþe aȝens Goddis lawe and 995 mannys. It is aȝen Goddis lawe for, as saynt Poule saiþ, 'No man þat is a perfyte knyȝte of God, as euery prest schulde be bi his ordre, entirmete hym wiþ worldly nedis and bissynessis',—and for þis

966 hereaftir . . . þerto (968)] *om.* P   969 *margin* xxjª.q.iijª cap. Ciprianus L, Dist.xxi./]j.iii.ca./ Cipriane P2,]t.xxi./]iij.ca./]pria. P1   þorow] by P 972 sacramentis] the sacramentes to preache goddes worde P   973 *margin* ij.thi.ij. cº L,]him P1   974 entrike] entryketh P   976 dempten] deme P   take] taketh P   978 halowyd] holowed P   981 þis] thus P   983 preste] preste of christe P   984 *margin* luc. xvjº L, Lu.x[P1   986 nede] *om.* P lorde] owne lorde P   987 euery] any P   Ihesu Criste] *rev.* P2   995 *margin* ij. thi. ijº LP2, ij.Thi[P1   997 entirmete] entremedleth P   nedis] deades P2 bissynessis] busynes P

ende, þat he may so plese þat lorde to whose service he haþ putt
hymsilfe, and þat is God. For siche worldly bissynes in clerkis is
aȝens her ordre, and þerfore þe apostles sayden, as it is wryten in þe 1000
Deedis of þe Apostles, 'It is not euen vs to forsake þe worde of God
and mynystir to bordis of pore folke.' And if it was vnequite, as þe
apostles sayden in her common decre, hem for to leue þe prechynge
of Goddis worde and ministre to þe | bordis of pore men, hou myche f. 49ʳ
more vnequite and wronge to God and man is it prestis to leve 1005
contemplacion, studie, prayer and prechinge of Goddis worde and
mynistrynge to pore folke for þe service of a seculere lorde.

Hit it also aȝens þe popis lawe, for he spekiþ to a bischop and
biddiþ hym þat [he] warne openly prestis and clerkis þat þai be not
occupied in seculer office, ne procuratouris of seculer lordis nedis 1010
and her goodis. And if prestis and clerkis ben so bolde to occupie
hem in siche bissynes, and if þai fall aftir bi losse of lordis goodis,
þan saiþ þe lawe it is not worþi þat þai be holpen and socoured of
holy chirche, siþ þorou hem holy chirche is sclaundred. And saynte
Gregori wrote to þe defensoure of Rome in þis maner: 'It is tolde to 1015
vs þat oure moost reue|rent broþer Basile, þe bischop, is occupied in f. 49ᵛ
seculer causis, and kepiþ vnprofetably moote hallis, whiche þinge
makiþ hym foule, and distryeþ þe reuerence of presthode. þerfore
anoone as þu hast ressayvid þis maundement, co[m]pell hym wiþ
scharp execucion to turne aȝen, so þat it be not lefull to þe by noone 1020
excusacion to tarye it fyve days, lest if in eny maner þu suffir hym
eny langer to tary þerinne, þu to be coupable wiþ hym anentis vs.'

And so bischoppis and oþir prelatis ben holden to teche and
enforme lordis to wiþdraw hem fro þis synne, and scharply to
repreue prestis and curatis vndir hem, þat þai ocupie no seculer 1025
office. þis is prouyd þus: þe holy prophete Ezechiel saiþ 'If þe | f. 50ʳ
wayte (or þe waccheman) se ennemys cum, and if þe peple be not
warnyd and kepe not hemsiilfe, but ennemys cummen and sle þe
peple, þen saiþ God þat þe pepill is take in her wickidnes; and of þe
waite, þat schuld have blowe in his horne, will God axe acountis and 1030

999 god] good P   1001 *margin* Act. vjᵒ LP2, Acto.v[P1   forsake] leue P
1004 men] folke P   1008 *margin (eras.before)* iijᵒ decr. in fine L, Lin.iij. de/]re. in
fine P2,]iij.de/] n fine P1   1009 he] P, *om*. L   openly] *om*. P   1010 office]
offices P   nedis]   deades   P2   1017 vnprofetably]   vnproffytable   P
1019 compell] copell L   1021 it] *om*. P   if] *om*. P   1022 to²] *om*. P
anentis] agaynst P   1023 prelatis] prestes P   holden] bounde P   1026 þe¹]
by the P   saiþ] sayenge P   *margin* Ezechie xxxiij P   1030 in] *om*. P   will god]
rev. P2

reknynge of þe blode and of þe deþe of þe peple.' But now to goostly
vndirston[din]ge, euery bischop schuld be a waite or a waccheman to
tell and to warne byfore to alle þe peple, by his goode lyvynge and
techynge, þe perell of synne. And þis is þe reson whi bischoppis and
1035 oþir prelatis and prestis schulde not be occupied wiþ worldly nedis
and causis. For siche occupacions and chargis maken prestis slepynge
and slumbrynge in synne. And þerfore it is grete perell to lordis to
f. 50ᵛ make | ouer hem goostly waytis and wacchemen as bischoppis,
persones and vikers þat ben slepers and slombreris in lustis of þe
1040 fleysch and blyndid wiþ poudir of couetise of worldly riches, and so
occupied in worldly nedis þat þai neiþer kan ne may kepe hemsiilfe
ne noone oþer man. For of þis perell and siche oþir a prelate þat haþ
witt and kunnynge schuld scharply repreue and warne alle maner
men to þe schedynge of his owne blode, as Criste did. And if he leue
1045 and blame not, þen he assentiþ to her trespassis and synneþ deedly.
For, as saiþ þe prophete Malachie, 'Prestis lippis kepyn kunynge,
and þe pepill schal axe þe lawe of God of his mouþe, for he is þe
f. 51ʳ awngell of God if he kepe well þe ordre and þe degre of prest|hode.'
And þerfore it is not lefull to eny man to drawe to seculere office þe
1050 messangeris of Criste þat haþ so vttirly forfendit hem boþe in worde
and in dede seculere office in presthode.

If eny man stonde in doute of þis sentence before, here suen
autoritees of holy scripture and holy doctouris in Latyn aȝens
þe seculer lordeschip of prestis.

1055   Ciuilis aut secularis possessio fuit interdicta sacerdotibus et leuitis,
ut patet Numeri xviij 'Dixit Dominus ad Aaron "In terra eorum
nichil possidebitis, nec habebitis partem inter eos. Ego pars et
hereditas tua in medio filiorum Israell. Filiis autem Leui dedi
f. 51ᵛ omnes decimas Israelis in possessionem pro | ministerio quo seruiunt
1060 mihi in tabernaculo federis."' Sequitur 'Solis filiis Leui mihi in
tabernaculo seruientibus et portantibus peccata populi. Legittimum
sempiternum erit in generacionibus vestris. Nichil aliud possidebunt,
decimarum oblacione contenti, quas in vsus e[o]rum et necessaria

1032 vnderstondinge]   vnderstonge   L   1033 to   warne]   warne   P
1035 nedis] deades P2   1037 to lordis] om. P   1039 and¹] om. P   and
slombreris] om. P   1040 and¹] and in slomebernes and P   1228 riches . . . nedis
(1041)] deades P2   1044 leue] so leue P   1045 þen] than P1
1046 margin Malach. ij° LP   þe prophete] om. P   1048 þe²] om. P
1049 office] offices and busynes P   1051 in¹] om. P   office] offices P
1052 to end om. P   1063 eorum] earum L

seperaui.' Item Deuteronomi xviij 'Non habebunt sacerdotes et
leuite, et omnes qui de eadem tribu sunt, partem et hereditatem 1065
cum reliquo populo Israel, quia sacrificia Domini et oblaciones eius
comedent, et nichil aliud accipient de possessione fratrum suorum.
Deus enim ipse est hereditas eorum, sicut locutus est illis.' Super
quo glosa: 'Ministris altaris nec terrenis possessionibus adquirendis
concessum est inhiare.' Vnde Matthei x 'Nolite possidere aurum 1070
neque argentum neque pecuniam' etc., et post pauca 'Dignus est
operarius cibo suo.' Et alibi 'Qui altari deseruiunt cum altare | f. 52ʳ
participantur.' Non enim oportet quod qui semper altari debent
seruire officio diuino inhient terreno lucro, quibus Dominus hereditas est. Quid ergo illi deesse potest, qui omnia habentem habet. 1075
Hec ibi. Item Ezechielis xliiij 'Non autem erit eis hereditas, ego
hereditas eorum; et possessionem non dabitis eis in Israel, ego enim
possessio eorum. Victimam pro peccato et pro delicto ipsi comedent,
et omne votum in Israel ipsorum erit.' Super quo Jeronimus libro xiij
super Ezechielem 'Qui autem talis extiterit, ut ministret in sanc- 1080
tuario, et ingrediatur atrium interius, et offerat Deo sacrificium, ita
ut verus sacerdos sit, ymmo imitator eius, de quo scriptum est "Tu
es sacerdos in eternum secundum ordinem Melchisedech," iste
nullam habebit partem, nisi Deum qui est hereditas eius, nec accipiet
possessionem in Israel, hoc est, inter vulgus ignobile; sed sacerdo- 1085
talem, ut dicat de eo Dominus "Ego sum possessio et hereditas eius".
Quem cum venerit, loquatur ac dicat: | "Tenebo illum nec dimittam f. 52ᵛ
illum", et psallet cum propheta, "Pars mea Dominus".' Hec ille.

Item Deuteronomi x 'Non habuit Leui partem in possessionibus
cum fratribus suis, quia ipse Dominus possessio eius sicut promisit 1090
ei.' Item Josue xiiij 'Non acceperunt aliam in terra partem, nisi vrbes
ad habitandum, et suburbana earum ad alenda iumenta et pecora.'
Item Ecclesiastici xlv 'Nam sacrificia Domini edent, que dedit ipsi et
semini eius. Ceterum in terra gens non hereditabit, et pars non est illi
in gente; ipse enim pars eius est et hereditas.' Item Matthei xx 'Scitis 1095
quia principes gencium dominantur eorum, et qui maiores sunt
potestatem exercent in eos. Non ita erit inter vos. Sed quicunque
voluerit inter vos maior esse, sit vester minister. Et quicunque
voluerit inter vos primus esse, erit vester seruus. Sicut Filius hominis
non venit ministrari sed ministrare, et dare animam suam redemp- 1100
cionem pro multis.' Idem patet Matthei x et Luce xxij. Item prima

1089 margin Deutᵒ L   1091 margin Josue L   1093 margin Eccⁱ L
1095 margin Mᵗ L   1101 margin Marc' luc' L

f. 53ʳ Petri quinto | 'Pascite qui in vobis est gregem Domini, prouidentes
non coacti, sed spontanee secundum Dominum, neque turpis lucri
gracia sed voluntarie, neque dominantes in clero, sed forma facti
1105 gregis ex animo.' Item ad Thimotheum vj 'Habentes autem alimenta
et quibus tegamur, hijs contenti simus. Nam qui volunt diuites fieri,
incidunt in temptacionem et in laqueum diaboli.' Item Luce xiiij 'Sic
ergo omnis ex vobis qui non renunciat omnibus que possidet, non
potest meus esse discipulus.'
1110 Item Bernardus libro ij ad Eugenium papam 'Esto, ut alia
quacunque racione hec tibi vendices, sed non apostolico iure. Nec
enim ille tibi dare potuit quod non habuit; quod autem habuit, hoc
dedit, sollicitudinem super ecclesias. Numquid dominacionem? Audi
ipsum: "Non d[omi]nantes in clero sed forma facti gregis" ex animo.
1115 Et ne dictum sola humilitate putes, nonne eciam veritate, vox enim
Domini est in euangelio (Luce xxij): "Reges gencium dominantur
eorum," et infert "vos autem non sic." Planum est: apostolis
f. 53ᵛ interdicitur dominatus. | Ergo tu, et tibi vsurpare audes, aut
dominans apostolatum aut apostolatus dominatum? Plane ab alter-
1120 utro prohiberis. Si vtrumque simul habere velis, perdis vtrumque.
Alioquin non te exceptum putes de illo numero de quibus sic
conqueritur Deus (Osee octauo): "Ipsi regnauerunt sed non ex
me." At si interdictum tenemus, audiamus edictum (Luce xxij):
"Qui maior est vestrum," ait "fiat sicut iunior, et qui precessor est
1125 sicut qui ministrat." Forma apostolica hec est: dominacio interdici-
tur, indicitur ministracio.' Hec ibi.
Item Origenes super Genesis omelia xvj: 'Denique vis scire quid
intersit inter sacerdotes Domini et sacerdotes pharaonis? Pharao
terras concedit sacerdotibus suis, Dominus autem sacerdotibus suis
1130 partem non concedit in terra, sed dicit eis "Ego pars vestra".
Obseruate ergo qui hec legitis, omnes Domini sacerdotes, et videte
que sit differencia sacerdotum, ne forte qui partem habent in terra, et
f. 54ʳ terrenis cultibus | ac studijs vacant, non tam Domini quam pharaonis
sacerdotes esse videantur. Ille enim est qui vult sacerdotes suos
1135 habere possessiones, et exercere agri, non anime culturam, ruri et
non legi operam dare. Christus autem dominus noster sacerdotibus
suis quid precipit audiamus: "Qui non," inquit "renunciauerit
omnibus que possidet, non potest meus esse discipulus." Negat

---

1105 *margin* Thi' L   1107 *margin* luc' L   1114 dominantes] dnantes L
1116 *margin* luc' L   1122 *margin* Osee L   1123 *margin* luc' L
1127 *margin* Origen' L

Christus suum esse discipulum quem viderit aliquid possidentem, et eum qui non renunciat omnibus que possidet. Et quid agimus? 1140 quomodo hec aut ipsi legimus, aut populis exponimus, qui non solum non renunciamus hijs que possidemus, sed eciam adquirere volumus ea que nunquam habuimus antequam veniremus ad Christum?', etc. per processum.

Item Parysiensis libro de vicijs, titulo de auaricia mercenariorum. 1145 'Sciebat Dominus oculum ecclesie impediendum esse temporalibus istis ab officio suo. Modicum enim pulueris vel | palee, oculum f. 54ᵛ omnino cessare facit ab officio suo. Ideo voluit duces ecclesie pauperes esse, eo quod paupertas expedita est, sicut Seneca dicit. Et subdit: Si vis omnino vacare ut pauper sis, oportet ut pauperi sis 1150 similis. Et si cetera membra corporis ad plura officia conueniant, ut lingua ad gustum et loquelam, et manus ad multa similiter, oculus tantum vnum habet et contactum terre maxime timet. Sic oculus ecclesie contemplatiuus legi diuine debuit intendere, et a terrenis istis seperari, licet pes hominis a ceteris membris eius seperatus non 1155 sit, tamen habet seperatam artem que ei deseruit et artifices qui ei totaliter circa calciamenta eius intenti sunt. Quanto magis debent esse aliqui qui totaliter spiritualibus sint intenti. Sed hodie magis occupata est ecclesia in temperalibus quo ad magnam partem sui quam fuerat sinagoga. Vnde quando fuit datum a | Constantino f. 55ʳ imperium occidentali ecclesie facta est vox de celo dicens "Hodie 1161 infusum est venenum ecclesie Dei."' Hec ille.

Item Odo in sermone 'Estote misericodes', 'Stercora putredinis sunt diuicie quibus volucres celi, id est demones, excecant oculos cupidorum. Et bene dicuntur diuicie stercora demonum, quum 1165 omnes diuicias reputant tanquam stercora, nec querunt nisi animam, vnde diues quando moritur quasi in tres porciones diuiditur: mundus rapit diuicias, vermes cadauer, et demones animam. Et quilibet contentus sua porcione alterius partem non desiderat; vnde versus: 1170

Spiritus est Sathane, caro vermis, mammona mundi;
Vnica plus duplici pars sua cuilibet placet.

Item non tantum a demonibus sed a perfectis diuicie stercora reputantur. Vnde Apostolus "Omnia reputaui tamquam stercora ut Christum lucrifacerem." Pro hijs stercoribus causidici clamant in 1175

1145 *margin* Parisiens' L   1154 legi] -s *eras.* L   1163 *margin* Odo L
1171 *margin* versus L

f. 55ᵛ foro, clerici quoque cantant in choro, medici cum egrotis vigilant | in thalamo, pro hijs stercoribus frequenter illicita committuntur in mundo.' Sequitur 'Pocius cum Thobia gaudeamus qui curata cecitate quam per stercora contraxerat, visum recuperauit. Sic cum diuicie 1180 auferuntur oculum iusticie recuperamus. Cum gladius furioso aufertur, sanitate restituta, gracias refert illi qui abstulit. Similiter si dolemus pro ablacione temporalium quibus excecamur; quibus interficimur, furiosi sumus. Et reddita nobis discrecione saltem in alia vita, illi qui nobis stercora ab oculis nostris extersit, illi qui 1185 gladium abstulit, gracias referemus. Alibi appellantur venenum, vnde eodem die quo a Constantino dotata est ecclesia, in aere audita est vox angelica dicens "Hodie infusum est venenum in ecclesia." Maior quidam effecta est in dignitate, sed minor religione.'

Item Odo in sermone 'Ecce nos reliquimus omnia', 'Abel moritur, f. 56ʳ id est cura pastoralis luctus spiritualis interimitur, set | Caym, id est 1191 possessio, conseruatur. Ymmo pastor animarum Caym agricola efficitur. Non enim in ecclesia queritur, si sciat bene docere, pro peccatis lugere, sed si sit Caym, id est agricola, si sciat terras bene colere. Nec mirum si multos interficit possessio, cum sit venenum. 1195 Vnde eodem die quo dotata est ecclesia a Constantino, audita est vox in aere "Hodie infusum est venenum in ecclesia". Maior quidam dignitate, set minor religione. Si queritur "Vbi est ouis tibi commissa?", respondet "Numquid custos fratris mei sum?", quasi "Que cura est mihi de animabus, dummodo disponatur bene de 1200 temporalibus." Tales sicut Caim sunt maledicti, qui educunt ouem Abel, et non reducunt sed seducunt. Vnde Ezechiel "Pastores eorum seduxerunt eos."'

Item Gorham super illo Apocalypso xij 'Misit serpens ex ore suo post mulierem aquam tanquam flumen' etc. 'Per aquam fluminis f. 56ᵛ signatur | abundancia temporalis que fluit cotidie sicut aqua, vnde 1206 Psalmista "Diuicie si affluant, nolite cor apponere." Hanc aquam habundantissime misit draco in ecclesiam Dei, Domino permittente, quando a Constantino datum est imperium occidentali[s] ecclesie. Vnde tunc audita est vox angelorum in aere dicencium "Hodie 1210 infusum est venenum in ecclesia Dei", sicut legitur in apocrifo Siluestri. Et quia iam appropinquat venenum hoc ad cor ecclesie, ita ut iam sit suffocacio proxima, clamat ipsa ecclesia cum Psalmista "Saluum me fac Deus, quoniam intrauerunt aque usque ad animam meam. Et Dominus de sua bonitate, nunc primo incipit audire

1189 *margin* Odo L   1208 occidentalis] occidentali L

ecclesiam suam et misit adiutorem suum, scilicet, terram, que 1215
absorbere vult totum flumen, id est principem terrenum, qui vult
auferre ab ecclesia omnia temporalia sua, licet intencio non eadem sit
cum Domino, qui propter bonum ecclesie mittit illum ex misericordia.' Hec ille.

Item Jeronimus in Vitis Patrum: 'Ecclesia ex quo creuit in 1220
possessionibus decreuit in virtutibus.' Item Jeronimus ad Ne|pocia- f. 57ʳ
num, epistola xxxiiij. 'Aut aurum repudiemus nos, scilicet, clerici
cum ceteris supersticionibus Iudeorum, aut si aurum placeat,
placeant et Iudei, quos cum auro aut probare necesse est nobis, aut
dampnare.' Item Jeronimus ad Nepocianum, 'Clericus qui Christi 1225
seruit ecclesie, primo interpretetur vocabulum suum et nominis
diffinicione prolata, nitatur esse quod dicitur. Si enim cleros
Grece, Latine sors appellatur, propterea clerici dicuntur, quia de
sorte sunt Domini, vel quia Dominus ipse sors, id est pars
clericorum est. Et quia uel ipse pars Domini est, uel Dominum 1230
partem habet, talem se exhibere debet, ut ipse possideat Dominum et
possideatur a Domino. Qui enim Dominum possidet et cum
propheta dicit, "Pars mea Dominus", nichil extra Dominum possidere potest. Quod si quippiam aliud habuit preter Dominum, pars
eius non erit Dominus. Verbi gracia. Si aurum, si argentum, si 1235
possessionem, si variam suppellectilem habuerit, cum istis partibus,
Dominus pars eius fieri non dignatur.' Et paulo post: '"Habens
victum et vestitum, hijs contentus ero", | et nudus nudam crucem f. 57ᵛ
sequar. Obsecro te itaque repetens, iterum iterumque monebo, ne
officium clericatus genus antique milicie putes, id est, ne lucra seculi 1240
in Christi queras milicia, ne plus habeas quam quando clericus esse
cepisti.'

Here suen autorites in Latyn of holy scripture and doctouris
aȝens seculeris office of prestis.

Paulus apostolus dicit ij Thimotheum ij ad excludendum prelatos et 1245
sacerdotes ab omni seculari officio isto modo: 'Nemo militans Deo
implicat se negocijs secularibus, ut ei placeat cui se probauit.' Iste
autem textus breuis et compendiosus Apostoli, ex fide quam
importat, excluderet omnes sacerdotes et pure clericos ab omni
officio seculari. Quum seculare officium est destructiuum cure 1250
pastoralis, ideo ex canone apostolorum dicitur | 'Episcopus aut f. 58ʳ
sacerdos aut diaconus nequaquam seculares curas assumant. Sin

1220 *margin* Jero' L   1251 *margin* lxxxviij di. capᵒ Epc. L

autem assumpserint deiciantur', quia, ut dicit Gregorius ibidem 'Inutile et valde laboriosum est, hominem literatum raciocinacionum 1255 causas assumere, et in eis que non expedit se obligare.' Item ibidem, dicit beatus Ciprianus, capitulo *neque*, 'In dispensacione ecclesie hanc regulam obseruandam nouerit vnusquisque, ut nulli quantumlibet exercitate persone duo simul officia committat. Ideo nomine sacerdotis careat qui Dei ministros a suis euocet officiis.' Et idem 1260 Ciprianus dicit quod ministri ecclesie debent solum altari et sacrificijs deseruire et precibus, studijs et oracionibus vacare. Et si quis eos a spirituali officio ad seculare duxerit, non offeretur pro eo oblacio, nec sacrificium pro sepultura eius celebrabitur. Non enim ante altare Dei merentur nominari in sacerdotum prece qui sacer- 1265 dotes et ministros ecclesie ab altari volunt auocare.

Ideo dicit beatus Augustinus 'Fornicari hominibus nunquam licet, f. 58ᵛ negociari autem | aliquando licet, aliquando non licet. Antequam enim ecclesiasticus quis sit, licet ei negociari; facto ecclesiastico iam non licet.' Item ibidem scribitur sic 'Tuicionem testamentorum 1270 episcopus non suscipiat. Episcopus nullam rei familiaris curam ad se reuocet, sed leccioni et oracioni et verbo predicacionis tantummodo vacet.'

Item beatus Petrus in epistola ad Clementem dicit 'Sicut enim impietatis est crimen tibi, o Clemens, neglectis verbi Dei studijs, 1275 sollicitudines seculares suscipere, ita vnicuique laicorum peccatum est, nisi inuicem sibi eciam in hijs que ad communis vsum vite pertinent, operam fideliter dederint.' Ideo concludit lex canonica apostolorum statuta sunt que dicunt '"Nemo militans Deo implicat se" etc. 'Proinde aut clerici sint sine accionibus domorum, aut 1280 actores sine officio clericorum. Et vniuersi dixerunt hec obseruemus.'

Item ibidem sic scribitur 'Hij qui in ecclesia Domini ad ordinem f. 59ʳ promouentur clericorum, in nullo | ab administracione diuina auocentur, nec molestijs et negocijs secularibus alligentur, nec ab altaribus et sacrificijs recedant, set die ac nocte celestibus rebus et 1285 spiritualibus seruiant.' Item beatus Petrus in epistola ad Clementem sic scribit 'Te quidem oportet irreprehensibilem viuere, et summo studio niti, ut omnes vite huius occupac[i]ones abicias. Non fideiussor existas, nec aduocatus licium fias, ne in ulla occupacione prorsus inueniaris mundialis negocij occasione perplexus. Neque enim

---

1266 *margin* lxxxviij. di. cᵒ Fornicari L   1273 *margin* xjᵃ q'. iᵃ. cᵒ. Sicut L
1278 *margin* xjᵃ q'. iijᵃ cᵒ. Credo L   1286 *margin* xjᵃ. q'. jᵃ. cᵒ Te quidem L
1287 occupaciones] occupacones L

iudicem neque cognitorem secularium negociacionum te ordinare 1290
vult Christus, ne prefocatus presentibus hominum curis, non possis
verbo Dei vacare. Hec vero opera, que minus tibi congruere diximus,
exhibeant sibi inuicem vacantes laici, et te nemo occupet ab hijs
studijs per que salus datur hominibus' etc.

Item Gregorius Romano de[fen]sori 'Perlatum est', inquit, 'ad nos 1295
reuerendissimum fratrem nostrum Basilium episcopum velut vnum
de laicis in causis secularibus | occupari, et pretorijs inutiliter f. 59ᵛ
obseruire. Que res quoniam et ipsum vilem reddit, et reuerenciam
sacerdotalem adnichilat, statim ut experiencia tua hoc preceptum
susceperit, ad reuertendum eum districta execucione compellat, 1300
quatenus te illic consistente quinque diebus sub qualibet excusacione
immorari non liceat; ne, si quolibet modo eum ibidem amplius
moram habere permiseris, cum ipso apud nos grauiter incipias esse
culpabilis' etc.

Ista ad presens sufficiunt cum diligenti scripturarum excercita- 1305
cione ad excitandum sacerdotes ne curis secularibus se subiciant, sed
oracioni, studio et predicacioni intendant. Et sic, spiritualibus
inimicis deuictis, soli Deo placere studeant, ut cum ipso in celestibus
regnare valeant, prestante Domino nostro Ihesu Cristo, qui cum
Patre et Spiritu Sancto viuit et regnat Deus. Amen. 1310

1295 defensori] desori L   1301 excusacione] execucione *canc.* excusacione L

THE TRACT *DE OBLACIONE IUGIS SACRIFICII*

For as meche as antecrist now in þe ende of þe world more woodli   f. 3ʳ
and more opinli inpugneþ þe trewe beleue tauʒt of Iesu Crist, God
and man, þat miʒt not erre ne be fauti in superfluite and wanting in
sufficiens of his lawe, it nedeþ þat feiþful men arme hemself in
mekenes and paciens to suffre deeþ in mentenaunce of þe feiþ of Iesu 5
Crist, if he be calde of God to so grete grace. And alþouʒ it so be þat
þe prophetis and Crist and his apostlis speken riʒt derkli of antecrist,
ʒit þe open malice schewid in stopping and peruerting and contrariousing of Cristis lawe, þe weche he tauʒt in word and dede, ʒeueþ
euydens inow to feiþful men þat studien and musyn to knowe 10
antecrist, what he schuld be. For now, what bi writing of olde
seinttis, what raþur bi þe opyn dede and experiens of sotil
conspiracie aʒenst Crist and his lawe and þe fredom þerof, he is
opin to þo þat, mekeli tristenyng in þe Holi Gost musyn in þis
mater. And among oþur propheciis of antecrist I mynde me now 15
upon a prophecie of antecrist wiche seint Poule writiþ (*Thess.*2),
where he techiþ alle þe world þat dai of dome schal not come, but if
þe departing, þat is to seie from þe empire of Rome, come bifore; and
he techiþ þe furþurmore þat þe man of synne, þe sone of perdicioun
schal be openyd before þe dome. And Poule seiþ furþurmore þat þis 20
man is | contrarius, and enhaunsid aboue alle þyng þat is seide or f. 3ᵛ
ellis wirschipt as God. And for þe more declaring of þis þou schalt
beleue as þe Apocalips seiþ (*Apo.*1[2]) þat þe deuyl haþ a grete wraþ
aʒenst þe peple þat kepiþ Goddis commaundementis and han his
lawe, þat is to mene in trewe lyuyng and quyk werk; and aʒenst hem 25
þe deuil makiþ worre, for to wiþdraw hem from þis blessid lawe, and
so to lett þe fulfilling of þc chosyn numbre, and so to tari þe dai of
dome, in wiche dai he schal haue final euerlasting confusioun wiþ alle
his. For now, as seint Austen seiþ in *De questionibus vetere et nove*
legis, he is fed wiþ mannys errour, and so in þat he haþ a maner of 30
liking wiche he schal lak euer after.

    And, ⌈in⌉ as meche as he knowiþ wel bi experience þat holi lyuyng
and trewe preching lettiþ hym most of his purpos and hastiþ þis
dome upon him, þerfor it is no douʒte if he mai he wol inhabite
specialli þo þat ouʒten to do þat office. And, siþ þe fende haþ had þis 35
power upon þe clerge of Goddis chirche in þe old lawe, wherbi he
excludid and ʒut doþ welny al þe Iewis from þe trewe beleue of Iesu

Crist, he can do ȝit þe same malice. And siþ he kan do þis, and þer
he schal haue a ful grete power upon men whan, as þe Apocalips
40 seiþ, þat he schal be losid and disceyue many men, it is no douȝte he
f. 4ʳ schal do þis whan | he schal inhabite þe grete dampned man þat seint
Gregor spekiþ ofte tymes of toward þe ende of his *Morallis*, and seint
Poule also as I rehersid afore. For wete ȝe wel þat þe fende knowiþ
þis wel inow: þat it were vnpossible him to do ony riȝt notable ⌜or
45 gr[ete]⌝ schame to Cristis chirche in peruerting þerof, and þe clergi
stode truli and stifli in her owne office, riȝt in a maner as it were
vnpossible ony grete dedli sekenesse to growe in mannes bodi, ȝif þe
stomak þerof were hole. And þerfore, as he chiffli inhabitid þe
bischoppis and þe phariseis of þe olde lawe, so ferforþ þat as þei
50 supposidden and seiden þer was no bischop ne pharise þat beleued
on Iesu Crist saue þe kursid comynte of þe peple, so haþ he now
inhabitid our prelacie and phariseis, þat þei alle, as ferforþ as euer I
koude aspiȝe, boþ in worde and dede forsaken Crist specialli in þre
poyntis þat I schal asigne sone hereaftur. And in many oþur poynttis
55 of beleue þei forsaken Crist in worde ⌜or in⌝ dede or in boþe. For
þouȝ seche, as seint Poule seiþ, knowleche Crist in worde, ȝit in dede
þei denyon hym. And so as þe Iewis were lad aweie from Crist and
trewe beleue and clene lyuyng bi þer bischopis and þe clergie, so ben |
f. 4ᵛ nouȝ þo þat ben callid cristen bi her blynde duke antecrist, þe wiche
60 antecrist I schal specifiȝe sone if God wole.

And þis dampned man, [þat] so ful of þe fende schal sitt in þe
chirche after þe menyng of scripture and olde seinttis, schal not be a
singular person bi himself, but an aggregat persone of many riȝt
wikkid, acording in oo malice and conspiracie aȝenst Crist, þe wiche
65 ben in a maner onyd in her hede Sathanas. And þis maner of speche
and logic haþ seint Ion in a epistle, wher he callid many antecristis
oon antecrist and many disceyueres oo disceiuer. And Crist also haþ
þis maner of speche of his enmy antecrist þat 'Many schul come in
my name, and schul seie eche of hymself þat "I am Crist".' And þis
70 is verefiid as we seen at iȝe of eche chiff antecrist and his wickiddest
lymes as for her owne time. For eche ⌜seche seiþ⌝ in effect as for his
tyme he is Crist, as I schal schew ȝow hereaftur if God wol. And
eche of þise fals antecristis, as oure trewe Crist seiþ, schal disceyue
many men; and alle þes disceiuers and fals cristis, our trewe Iesu
75 seiþ, is an alion þat comeþ not in þe Fadris name of heuene but in

___

45 or grete] *margin cropped*   50 þer] þat þer   55 or in] and *canc.*, or
margin dh

his owne name. For he sechiþ not þe glorie of God and þe saluacioun of þe peple, but his owne glorie and wordli profite; but | naþeles he f. 5ʳ colouriþ himself as an ipocrite vndur þe name of Crist. And so þes two textis of Crist þat I rehersid riȝt nowe ben not contrarius. And þis maner of speche and logic of antecrist haþ seint Austen in *De* 80 *uerbis domini circa medium et* Gregor *circa finem Moralium,* and many oþur grete clerkis. And of þis processe, and many oþur euydencis þat miȝt be brouȝt a place here if a man had leiser, me mai suppose feiþfulli þat antecrist schal be a grete gadrid persone, of many grete and powerous priuat or singuler personys, þe wiche mowen most 85 passingli and most perlousli disceyue Cristis chirche, and lede it bi a blinde weie to helle, as comynli alle þe prelatis, þat schuld bi worde and bi ensample lede þe peple bi þe clere weie of þe gospel, þei leden hemself and þe peple bi þe contrarie weie, as we seen opinli at iȝe.

Herefore in þe text rehersid tofore, seint Poule rehersiþ þat þe 90 man of synne and þe sone of dampnacioun and ful of þe fende, bi whom alle men vnderstonden antecrist, schal sitt in þe temple, þat is to seie in þe chirche, schewing hymself as he were God. And for þe vndurstonding of þis ȝe schal mark here þat alle þe astate of þe prelacie, from þe pope vnto þe lest bischop, haþ a se in þe temple, 95 þat is in þe chirche. And siþ it is al oon to haue a see and | to sitt, as f. 5ᵛ it is al one to haue mouyng and to moue, euery seche prelat sittiþ in þe temple of God. And þis, I suppose, were noon inconuenient saf for þe malice þat þise sitters after þe cours of þe world nouȝ han annexid to here sete. For Crist seide to alle þe world þat 'Upon 100 Moises chaier schal sitt scribis and phariseis', and Crist commaundeþ alle þe peple þat, whilis þei sitten in þat chaier, to here and to kepe and to fulfil whateuer þei scide to hem. For þou schalt vndurstonde here þat þis Moises chaier, þat Crist spekiþ of, is þe lawe of God, as seint Austen seiþ in *De uerbis Domini circa sermonem* 38. And seint 105 Ierom vpon Mathev and upon þe same word of Crist haþ þe same sentens. þan, whosoeuer rede þe a lesson of þis chaier, þou schalt wiþ grete reuerens here it, kepe it and performe it in dede for reuerens and obediens þat þou owist to þe maister of þis chaier, þat is God hymsilf. For whoso þus prechiþ (as many prelatis han, þe 110 wiche iustli han seten upon Moises chaier, at þe hardest in þat þat þei han not þe malice annexid to þe se in þe temple, of þe wiche se seint Poule spekiþ), neiþur he is in þat contrarie to God, ne enhaunsid aboue al þyng þat is seide God, ne he schewiþ hymself

92 *margin* 20 de [/ dei 19   113 neiþur] for neiþur

f. 6ʳ as he were God, for he spekiþ not of his owne auctorite. But | þer is
116 anoþer mene þat I spake [of] before þat sitten in þe temple, þat is in
þe chirche of God, not upon Moises chaier but upon a bereschrewe
of her owne proude wille—and þes ben chiffli þe grete aggregat
persone of ypocrit prelatis, contrarius to Crist in lyuyng and teching,
120 þe wiche ben specialli and most passingli þe bodi of antecrist! For of
þis persone it is opinli soþ þat he sittiþ in þe temple, þat is to seie in
þe chirche, and contrarioþ God in worde and in dede, and is
enhaunsid aboue alle þing þat is seide God or wirschipt as God.
First we mai se at iȝe houȝ contrarius þis foreseide persone þat þus
125 sittiþ in þe temple is to Crist, for Crist was wilfulli pore in wille and
dede, and forsoke al maner of wordli lordschip, and þei don euyn þe
contrarie; Crist suffrid meche wrong wilfulli don to hymself, and þis
persone wol not her þankis suffre þat men don hir riȝt in lawful
discharging o[r] wiþdrawing of þes wordli lordschipis and possessio-
130 nus, þe wiche þei holdyn and occupien euyn aȝenst Cristis lyuyng
and his teching; Crist besiid himsilf nyȝt and dai to make þe wille
and þe lawe of his Fadur knowen to alle þe world, and þis persone
wiþ alle scleiȝtis, constitucions and statutis and ordenaunsis þat he
f. 6ᵛ kan deuyse | besieþ hym to stop and to furbarre the fredom of the
135 gospel, þat it be not know among Goddis peple, and he magnifiiþ his
owne tradicions and constitucions, charging þe peple vnder grete
peyne þat þei haue hem redili wrete, þat þei be ofte itauȝt and
streiȝtli kept, and þat bi grete peynes and censuris. But for as meche
as me lakkiþ leisar, alþouȝ I miȝt long lyue in þis world, for to
140 declare in special þe contrariuste bitwene Crist and þis persone þat is
antecrist, þerfor I cesse of þis, supposing þat bi þese fewe ensamplis
feiþful men schul mowe perceiue oþur poyntis wiþout numbre, in
ᴦþeᴧ wiche þis bodi and persone of antecrist is opinli at iȝe contrarious to Crist.

145   Seint Poule seiþ furþurmore þat þis antecrist, þat þus sittiþ in holi
chirche, is enhaunsid aboue al þing þat is callid God or truli
wirschipt as God. And upon þis worde seint Gregor vnderstondeþ
Moises in his *Morallis* bi þis word of Poule þat seiþ 'þat is callid
God'. For God callid Moises 'þe God of pharao', and bi þat wirschip
150 þat is undurstonde bi þis uerbe *colitur* in Latin he vndurstondeþ
almyȝtti God, for onli to him is þat wirschip don in þat significacioun þat þis uerbe haþ here. So þat þis antecrist þat þus sittiþ in þe
chirche enhaunsith hymsilf aboue Moises, þat brouȝt to þe peple þe

129 or] of

olde lawe, and also aboue Crist þat ȝaff þe newe law. For þis antecrist
settiþ litil or riȝt nouȝt bi eiþur | of þes lawis, but in as meche as þei f. 7ʳ
as hymsilf a⟨c⟩orden wiþ his proude wille. And herfore he wol 156
denyȝe boþ þes lawis, or ellis glose hem as himsilf likiþ. And, for
more hiȝe enhaunsing of himsilf and his lawis aboue Crist and his
lawis, he susteineþ in him and ⌜in⌝ his, and writiþ, redeþ and
defendeþ opinli and preueli in scolis and elliswhere þat Cristis 160
lawe is þe falsist lawe þat euer was or mai be, and þat it is eresie
and blasfemie and contrarie to itsilf. And siþ þis conclusion is
stablischid, and so proudeli and openli defended þat vnneþe any
man dar seie or meue þe contrarie, antecrist mai liȝtli bring in to þe
peple a feiþ whateuer conclusion he settiþ upon! For þouȝ a man 165
wold worre aȝenst antecrist bi þe textis of God[is] lawe, he and his
disciplis han so depraued þe auctorite þerof bi suspeccion of
falshede, and peruertid ⌜so⌝ scripture bi his fals glosis, þat welny al
men, lerned and lewde, taken þat lawe as of litil auctorite. For, and
þei dede, þei wold not suffre it so to be sclaundrid of falshede and of 170
heresie as þei don. And wel I wote þat þis antecrist þat sittiþ in þe
chirche, as I told before, sate neuer bi our daiis ne long beforehand
for to dampne þis sclaundre of Crist and his lawe, but raþur to
susteyne it. Wher þat king Herri þe fourþe, | þat nouȝ late diȝid, sett f. 7ᵛ
honde for to haue defendid Crist and his lawe from þis sclaundre I 175
wote neuer. It was seide þat he dede, and if he dede I suppose he
dede neuer a better dede. But I prai þe here, who dirst opyn his
mouþe aȝenst þis antecrist and his disciplis and his lawe, and speke
as unreuerentli þerof as þei don of Cristis? And þus þis open
enhaunsing of antecristis tradicions, and commending þerof, and 180
charging þerof aboue Cristis lawe, makiþ to us open euydens houȝ
þis man, so ful of þe fende, enhaunsiþ himsilf aboue alle þing þat is
God in kinde, or ellis seide a God bi office.

But furþermore here, fort to declare þe more opinli þe contra-
riouste bitwene þis antecrist and Iesu Crist and his enhaunsing aboue 185
God, I schal put two or þre ensamplis houȝ þis antecrist, ȝe, into
killing of cristen men, opinli defendeþ and techiþ þe contrarite of þat
þat Crist in word and dede tauȝt as beleue to alle þe world, and haþ
left iwrete into perpetual mynde to his chosyn. For Crist techiþ þis
conclusion in word and dede, þat whosoeuer wol kepe þe souerente 190
of perfeccioun of þe gospel, as dede nameli þe men in þe beginnyng
of Cristis chirche, ⌜þei⌝ schuld noo lordschip or wordli possession

161 is] þat *canc.* is   166 godis] god   179 þis] bi þis

f. 8ʳ haue, as we mai perceyue in dyuerse placis of þe gospel. | And as
litteralli as Crist tauȝt ⸢in⸣ his conclusion, so litteralli he and his
195 disciplis, and perfiȝt prestis long after and oþur perfiȝt peple also
kept þis conclusioun, wiþout any glosing or oþur vndurstonding þan
Crist tauȝt hem in worde and in dede. And þei kepten not þis
perfeccion onli in signys, as many men don nouȝ, in schauyng of
crownys and oþur tokenes of perfeccioun; but þei kept þis blessid
200 conclusioun in worke and truthe. But nouȝ, alþouȝ the couetous
prelatis, prestis and religious of þe old law coude neuer ȝeue a glose
to Moises lawe, undur colour of wiche glose þei myȝt haue be wordli
lordis, as our clerge is now, ȝit þis antecrist wiþ his comperis and his
disciplis ben so witti and sotil þat þei kan ȝeue a glose aȝenst Moises
205 and Crist also; vndur colour of þe wiche close þei ben temperal lordis
of þe more partiȝe of cristendom, and wol be of alle þe world ȝif þei
mai. Ȝe, sir, raþur þan þei schuld faile in þis poynt or in any oþur
poynt of Cristis lawe, þe wiche is aȝenst her lust, þei wil glose
Goddis lawe euyn bi his contradictorie, or ellis denyȝe it utturli and
210 seie þat it is eresie. And þei supposyn her glosis to be of so grete
auctorite þat whosoeuer be so hardie to meue þe contrarie is worþi to
f. 8ᵛ be brent. And, for as | meche as þei obstinatli auctorisen þus þer
owne proude wille, þei setten Cristis wille and his teching at riȝt litil
or nouȝt; and so in þis þei ben not onli contrarie, but enhaunsen
215 hemself aboue Moises and Crist þat techen þe contrarie.

þe secunde point in þe wiche þis antecrist is contrarie to Crist and
to Moises, and so enhaunsiþ himself aboue hem, is þis: þat þis
foreseide antecrist openli aȝenst the ensample of Crist and his
apostlis, and also aȝenst her teching entriþ h[i]mself in wordli
220 besinesse in letting of his owne office, as I declarid onys in a
sermon þat begynneþ þus *Omnis plantacio quod non plantauit Pater
meus celestis eradicabitur.* And for þat ⸢þat⸣ I seide and wrot in þat
sermon, I write þe lasse of þise two poyntis last rehersid, in þe wiche
poyntis þis ofte rehersid antecrist opinli contrarieþ Crist.

225 þe þrid poynt of beleue in wiche þis man of synne, ful of þe fende
and sone of perdicioun contrarieþ Crist, is in þe beleue of þe
sacrament of þe auter, þe wiche sacrament feiþful men most nedes
beleue to be Cristis bodi and brede, as it is pleynli tauȝt in þe gospel
229 of God, as I schal wiþ Goddis help schewe hereafter, bi writing of
f. 9ʳ olde seinttis and confermyng | of þe gospel, þe wiche auctoriziþ alle

199 þei kept] *twice*   211 so] þe *canc.* so   219 himself] hemself
225 of¹] is of

oþur ⌐trew⌐ writing and seiȝing of clerkis. But in þis poynt of beleue, as open and eche daiis experiens techiþ, þis grete persone of antecrist ofte before nempnyd, þe wiche sittiþ in þe chirche of God, as it is before seide, schewing himself as he were God, haþ no reward to Iesu Crist and hys lawe and to þe apostlis writing or wordis, ne to 235 olde seinttis writing, as Dyonyse, Ierom, Austen or seint Ciprian þe martir þat speken and writen acordingli to þe gospel of God. But þis antecrist haþ onli reward to his owne wille, writtingis and determy-nacions. And for þis contrariyng of Crist and olde feiþful men and exalting himsilf aboue alle þat is or mai be seide God, he seiþ in 240 dede, þat is þe most effectual speche, and in word preueli, 'Haue ȝe no reward to Crist or to his apostlis in þis poynt of beleue of þe sacrid oste of þe auter, ne beleue ȝe her wordis, for þei ben fals and disceyueable. But take ȝe hede to my wille, wordis, writinggis and determynacions! For whateuer Crist and his apostlis and alle þe 245 chirche þat is callid cristen han tauȝt, beleuyd or determenyd, ȝe schal take noon hede þerto, but to my wise and holi determinacioun.' For, certis, but if þe deuyl haue blyndded vs, we mai se þat þis antecrist spekiþ þus in dede, alþouȝ he | speke not þus opinli in dede. f. 9ᵛ For, þouȝ a feiþful man knoweleche alle þat euer Crist and his 250 apostlis tauȝt, and left as beleue wrete into perpetual mynde of his chirche, and ouer þis alþouȝ a man knowleche and beleue alle þat euer olde or newe feiþful men han tauȝt and wreten ⟨a⟩cordingli to Iesu Crist and his apostlis, ȝit þis antecrist haþ no reward hereto, ne holdeþ hym not apaide, but if he go from þes wordis and from þe 255 beleue of alle þes and graunt his drasti determinacioun, be it neuer so contrarious to the gospel. And þis antecrist haþ brouȝt ⟨our bileue⟩ into an insolible and into a grete perplexite. For, but if a man forsake Crist and his apostlis, ȝe, and alle þat þei han tauȝt and wrete, and nameli in þis poynt of beleue touȝching þe sacrid oste, he schal be 260 deuyded from Crist as fer as þis antecristis power mai til to bi censuris and ⟨dampn⟩acioun in eresiȝe. But ȝit whosoeuer stonde in þis perplexite is to blame and he chese þe wors parte!

And, certis, a feiþful man mai se ful meche perrel in seche presumptuous determinacions of þis antecrist. For as þis dampnable 265 bodi of antecrist before seide mai, as he presumeþ, peruerte and contrarie Cristis beleue in þis poynt, so he mai in many oþur or ellis in alle poynttis or articlis of beleue. | Houȝ, I prai the, haþ antecrist f. 10ʳ peruertid þe gospel bi his proude, presumptuous, fals and contrarie glosis to þe gospel in þe matir of þe wordli lordschip of þe clergie? 270

Sekir, so ferforþ þat vnnethe any man mai or kan opyn his iȝe to se þis foule abusion in þe clarge. And, sekir, as antecristis glosis per⟨uer⟩ten þe witt of þe gospel in þis ma⟨t⟩ir, so þei don in þe oþur two poynttis asigned before and in ful many oþur. But, for as
275 meche as þis proude antecrist, contrariing God ⟨and⟩ enhaunsing himsilf in auctorite aboue Iesu Crist, magnifiȝing his wilful determinacions aboue þe gospel, bi þat mene chifli he distroieþ þe feiþ and þe auctorite of ⌈Cristis⌉ lawe as þouȝ it were of none a⟨ucto⟩rite. Men most muse and studiȝe besili, ⟨to percey⟩ue þat uenym and so to do
280 her besinesse wiþ Goddis help to purge Cristis chirche þerof.

And first me semeþ here þat it were spedi ⟨a⟩nd nedeful to exam[i]ne besili þe argument þat antecrist demeþ an insolible in any mater þat he wol haue preued. þe wiche argument is þis in forme: þe ful holi chirche of Rome haþ determenyd þus þat alle
f. 10ᵛ cristendom ouȝten, vp peine of dampnacioun and as | þei wol not
286 worþeli [be] dampnyd for heretikis, beleue þus. Here I woot wel þat ȝif þat þei wold akount Crist as for her heede of þis holi chirche, þe wiche þei aleggen for hem, þis argument were goode inouȝ, holding bi þis necessarie mene þat Crist myȝt not erre. But, for as meche ⟨a⟩s
290 s⟨e⟩int Austen seiþ in De uerbis Domini þat antecrist wol þat Cristis chirche be heedles, I take þe chirche after þe commune vnderstonding þat nouȝ is ryue and nameli among antecristis disciplis, þat is to seie from þe state of þe prelacie, þe pope and his comperis bisi⟨de⟩ þi⟨s⟩, þe wiche nouȝ, houȝsoeuer þis witt c⟨a⟩me in, ben spe⟨cialy
295 c⟩allid holi chirche so ferforþ þat eche bischop l⟨i⟩kiþ to be callid holi chirche,—col⟨o⟩ur⟨in⟩g þ⟨is⟩ witt bi þe gospel wher Crist techiþ euery man þat, after tw⟨ey⟩n preueie vndurnemyngis of his fauȝti broþur, ⟨he⟩ schuld telle his fauȝte to þe chirche if he ⟨hede no⟩t. Supposing þan at þis tyme þ⟨is certeyn wit⟩t of þe chirche, we mai
300 sone se þat þis euydens is ful blynde: þis chirche determeneþ þus, þan alle feiþful men most nede beleue þus. For þis argument holdeþ not bi a necessarie mene as doþ þe oþur argument of þe chirche, ⟨i⟩n wic⟨he⟩ Crist is acountid as heede. For in þis chirche, as I speke
f. 11ʳ nouȝ, euery persone is fauȝti; and so alle þei | togedre ben fauȝti. And
305 so, siþ þei mai faile so ferforthe þat þei mai determene on her maner aȝenst Crist and alle his chosyn chirche, þis argument þat I last rehersid is no better þan þis in forme or in matir: þis holi chirche haþ determenyd þis poynt or article aȝenst Crist and his apostlis, þan euery man ouȝt to beleue þus. And so þis argument failiþ boþe in

277 bi] and bi   þe²] chifli *canc.* þe

forme and in matir, as dede þe argument of þe clerge of Iewis meued 310
in Cristis time, þe wiche was þus: we bischopis and prelacie haue
ʒeue a decre, and determened þat whosoeuer confesse þis Iesu as
Crist, he schal be do out of the syna⟨g⟩og⟨e an⟩d so be akursid,
þerfo⟨r⟩ eche seche on is akursid. Feiþful men most nedes suppose
here þat þis argument is not worthe! For þei moost suppose þat 315
whosoeuer effectuousli knowlechiþ þis Iesu f⟨or to⟩ be Crist, and so
endeþ, abideþ not onli in Cristis c⟨hirche⟩ here alþouʒ antecrist kurs
hym, but also regneþ for euer wiþ þe same Iesu in blisse.

And þus, as þis argument aboue rehersid is not worþ a piʒe hele,
so stondeþ it of many oþur þat þis antecrist makiþ, nameli among 320
mony oþur þat he makiþ and wolde þat alle men schuld ʒeue credens
to. It stondiþ so of an argument of þe deuyl, antecrist, þat is nouʒ
late putt in excecucioun, þe wiche is þis in sentence: we haue
determened and made a constitucioun | þat no prest schal preche f. 11ᵛ
þe gospel, but bi special leue of alle or of sum of þo þat sitten in þe 325
temple, as it is told before; eche þan þat doþe þe contrarie is an
eretike, worþi to be brent, and alle þo þat heren seche a prest to
preche þe gospel in þe same dede b⟨en⟩ akursid, and þe parson or þe
prest þat amittiþ hym is akursid and worþi to be depriued of his
benefice, and þe place, be it neuer so holi before, in þat preching of 330
Cristis gospel bi seche a prest is enturditid. Naþeles feiþful men
schal vndurstondin here þat, alþouʒ antecrist and his retinew semen
to be an insolible, ʒit seint Peter and his felowis couʒde asoile þis
grete argument riʒt liʒtli. For þei answerid þus to þe prelacie þat had
made seche constitucions aʒenst þe fre preching of þe gospel, as we 335
mai rede (*Act*.4 and 5) 'Wheþer it be riʒt in þe siʒt of God to here
ʒow raþur þan God, deme ʒe! For we mai not leu⟨e to⟩ speke þo
þinggis þat we haue hird and seien.' And whan þat þe prelacie
declarid her constitucion and determynacioun to þe apostlis, as
touching þe fre preching of þe gospel seiʒing on þis wise 'Comaund- 340
ing to ʒow, we han commaundid þat ʒe schul teche no more in
Cristis name (þat is to seie þe gospel). And, loo, ʒe han fillid
Ierusalem wiþ ʒour lore', þe apostlis answerid 'It is behofful to
obeiʒe more to God þan to man!'

Loo, here þou maist se þat þis argument is unpreued bi | scripture: f. 12ʳ
þis prelacie or holi chirche, taking the chirche after þe witt aboue 346
signyd, haþ þus determenyd; eche þan feiþful man auʒt to accept þat
as feiþ and to obeie þerto. For þou schalt vnderstonde here þat a

332 vndurstondin] vndurstonding

man mai obeie on þre manerys: first into harmyng or lesing of his
350 soule, þe secunde wise into peyne or deeþ of his bodi, þe þrid maner
into lesing of wordli goodis. But þe first of þes þre obediencis ben in
no maner case leefful, for a man schuld not abeiȝe so for to wyn alle
world, as Crist meneþ in þis questioun 'What auailiþ a man to wyn
alle þe world and suffre apeiring of his owne soule?' But into lesing
355 of wordli goodis a feiþful man schal obeie, and also into deeþ raþur
þan to suffre apeiring of his owne soule or parel ⟨of d⟩ampnacioun of
his neiȝboris soule. For þus ⟨pr⟩eiid Crist for preching of þe gospel:
not onli to þe le⟨s⟩ing of his cloþis and of wordli goodis, þat he had
to his owne use, but also to lesing of his owne liif. For, as our beleue
360 techiþ us, he was made obedient to þe deeþ of þe cros. But where þe
prelacie of þe Iewis meuedden amenusing of his owne merite and
harmyng of feiþful mennys soulis, asking þis question of Crist 'Who
f. 12ᵛ ȝaff þe þis power?', as þouȝ þey | wold mene 'þou schuldist not do
þus, but bi leue of our power', he wiþstode hem, and wold not abeie
365 for þat euydence ne for her curs aftur, but prechid the gospel vnto þe
deeþ as deden þe apostlis enformyd bi his ensample. And acording to
þis processe þe apostle Poule techiþ, as he lernyd of Crist wiþout any
mene, houȝ seruantis schuld obeie to her lordis, alþouȝ þei were
heþon, into paiyng and l⟨o⟩sse of her owne goodis and in peynful and
370 bonde seruage of her bodi. But, as touching þe soule and euerlasting
liif, he mesuriþ þe obediens þat þei owen to her curatis, and spekiþ
þus to feiþful peple 'Be ȝe obedient to ȝour curatis'—but seint Poule
restiþ not þer as doþ nouȝ antecrist and his retinew, but addiþ more
to and seiþ þus 'Forsoþ þei ben waker, as þo þat ben to ȝeld a
375 rekenyng for ȝour soulis.' And so seint Poule limitiþ þis obediens þat
þei obeie þus fer—þat is to seie, as ferforth as seche obediens is
saluacioun of mannys soule. And no wonder, alþouȝ seint Poule
limite and determeneþ þus þis obedience, for he knewe bi spirit of
prophecie what deuelich and tyrantlich obedience antecrist schuld bi
380 weie of extorcioun aske of Goddis peple, as cristen men mai
conceyue of seint Poules writing. Of þis processe þan, and of oþur
f. 13ʳ þat myȝt be brouȝt | in here, a man mai wel vndurstond houȝ he
schal obeiȝe to þe determinacioun of þis man aboue specifiid þat
sittiþ in þe chirche of God, or ellis of any oþur man, be he neuer so
385 holi outward.

　　And as the world schapiþ now, it is to done to se houȝ a man
obeiiþ to þe determinacion of þis grete aggregat person þat sittiþ in
þe chirche in þe mater of þe sacrid ooste. For þe deuyl of helle, wiþ

help of his bodi þat sittiþ vppon þe bereschrewe þat I spak of before, haþ knyt a nett so sotilli in þis matir þat [no] man mai ascape clereli 390 þis nett, and he be streitli huntid þerwiþ, but þat he most graunt Cristis wordis and his apostlis, and so reuerse þe determynacioun of þis renegat, and diȝe bodili for Crist and his lawe, or ellis reuerse Crist and his lawe and susteine as beleue þe determinacioun of þis renegat þat sittiþ in þe chirche and beleue of him, to lyue here a 395 while and at þe last to go wiþ him to helle for euer. For Crist and þis antecrist, whom seint Austen (*De civitate li*. 20) calliþ a renegat, ben so contrarious þat it is vnpossible any man to close hem togedre, for þei stonden in contradictorie cornys of þe figure. For Crist seide, sacring þe oost, schewing þe brede þat he hilde in his honde and 400 blessid it, 'þis is my bodi þat schal be bitraid for ȝow.' But antecrist seiþ here euyn þe contradictorie, þat þis is neiþur Cristis bodi, ne brede but accidentis | wiþout soget. And noo wondur alþouȝ he seie f. 13ᵛ so, for antecrist wiþ his comperis and his disciplis ben of þis opinion as þei schewen. For þe grettist enmy þat Crist haþ in Ynglond, þat is 405 þe archebischop of Cauntirberi, Arundel, knowlechid þe same nouȝ wiþin a fewe daiis in presens of þe worþiist audiens in þis reme, þat is to seie þat, if it so were þat Crist were nouȝ here on erþe present in his owne persone, whom he beleued feiþfulli to be uerri God and man, and if þis Crist wold aferme any þing þat holi chirche, þat is to 410 seie after his witt þe pope wiþ his clerge, wolde uarie fro, he wold leue Cristis seiȝing and afferming and beleue þis holi chirche. And wondur not al if þis man seide þus, for þis þei putten in execucioun al dai as we mai seen opinli at iȝe! And ellis, as we knowen wel, her determynacioun were of [no] auctorite and nameli in þis mater of þe 415 sacrid oste, but if her determynacion, þat not onli uariiþ from Crist but also contrarieþ him, sourmounted in auctorite, of þe lest in her owne iugement, þe auctorite of Cristis determinacioun in þis matir.

But, certis, seint Poule had lerned in heuene a better witt bi reuelacioun and teching of Iesu Crist wiþouten any mene. For Poule 420 seiþ þus 'þouȝ we, or an angel of heuene, preche to ȝou ouer þat we haue prechid to ȝou, | be he deuidid for euer from Crist in f. 14ʳ dampnacioun.' þis seint Poule seiþ bi maner of prophecie and not bi maner of malicious wisching, as Crist wischid wo to the scribis and phariseis [and] prophecied to hem euerlasting dampnacioun. Loo 425 þan, houȝ seint Poule demeþ hem worþi euerlasting dampnacioun, þat techen þe peple ouer þat þing þat he haþ tauȝt hem, þat is to seie

396 and²] seiþ *canc*. and   397 20] 20 c.   419 *margin* gal.1

þing þat is not conteined in þe beleue þat he tauȝt. And if seche on is
worþi dampnacioun þat prechiþ ouur þat þe apostle tauȝt, what is he
430 worþi þat techiþ euyn þe contrarie of þe beleue of Crist and of his
apostlis [þat þei] han betake to þe peple? And we mai marke here
acordingli to seint Poule þat fonnyd Eue, teching or supposing ouer
þe beleue whan sche added þis worde 'Anauntir we die' to þe open
and playn beleue, þe wiche almyȝti God haþ tauȝt, sche was made
435 anathena, þat is to mene diuided from God, wiþ alle hir issue into þe
tyme þat our blessid Iesu had made aseeþ for her misbeleue apon þe
cros. And if þer were none euydens in scripture aȝenst þe presumpcioun of þis renegat þat passiþ and contrarieþ Crist, me semeþ
þis folisch presumpsion of Adam and Eue, uariyng from þe beleue
f. 14ᵛ þat God had ȝeuen hem, | were inow to dampne the fonnyd
441 presumpcion of this antecrist. And bi þis feiþful men schuld be
meuyd to stond stifli in Cristis wordis and his apostlis, alþouȝ þe
grete ipocrite and renegat, þe angel of Sathanas transfigurrid into an
angel of liȝt, besiiþ himsilf to dampne Cristis lawe. And here I seie
445 for my partie, I wolle hold me bi þe grace of God wiþ seint Poulis
meuyng, þat seiþ þus þat, if Crist seie any sentens, alþouȝ alle þe
resonable creaturis þat euer God made or schal make wold varie from
Crist or reuerse hym, I wold leue alle hem and hold me to Crist. For
alle þei han be liars in her kinde, alþouȝ not eche seche creature haþ
450 be a lier in his owne persone. But Crist, bicause he is almyȝti, he mai
not liȝe.

Herefor seint Austen in þe first parte of þe Psauter, arguyng
aȝenst eretikis, seiþ houȝ þei leren her doctours for hemself, 'Seiyng
þat "He seiþ so, and he seiþ so weel"', seiþ seint Austen, 'and I seie
455 þat "þat man seiþ so", and "þis man seiþ so." But þan,' seiþ seint
Austen, 'What is þis to purpos þat "He seiþ so, and he seiþ so"?
Take we aweie our scrowis and lete Goddis bokis be brouȝt a place!
For it mai be þat þat man lieþ, but it mai not ben þat truþe lieþ!
Truþe is þe name of Iesu Crist, for he seiþ "I am trouþe and liif."'
f. 15ʳ And of þese wordis of seint Austen | and of ful many othir like to þes
461 (for alle his writing is ful of þis sentens) it sueþ þat he wold leue þat
þat is nouȝ comounli callid holi chirche and cleue onli and holli to
Crist, if he were and had be put in choise as men ben nowe adaiis.
And alþouȝ seint Austen had conflict wiþ diuerse heretikis, ȝit I am
465 not avisid þat he was uexid wiþ any heretike þat durst dampne

434 tauȝt] w canc. tauȝt   435 diuided] anath canc. diuided   445 seint]
seinttis, -tis canc.   458 not] be canc. not

scripture, or ellis seie þat it was fals or eresie, or þat durst determene
euyn þe contrarie of Cristis logic and his wordis, as dar þis renagat
þat sittiþ in þe chirche, and contrariiþ Crist nouȝ, and enhaunsiþ
himsilf aboue Iesu. þerfor, as seint Austen seiþ, it mai be þat þat
man lieþ, but it mai not be þat treuthe lieþ. So seie I: þat it mai be 470
þat, boþ in þis poynt of beleue and also of oþur, þat Ion de Deo lieþ;
it mai be þat pope Innocent lieþ; it mai be þat alle þe foure ordris of
freris lien wiþ munkis and chanouns; also it mai be þat al þe
vniuersite of Oxford lieþ and oþur also; it mai be þat aggregat
persone þat haþ his see in the chirche lieþ. But in no wise mai it be 475
þat truþe þat is God lieþ. And þerfor euery man schuld hard cleue to
Crist and his lawe, for þan as Odo Parisiensis seiþ upon þe gospellus,
'A þe dai of dome, if seche a man were enpugnyd bi Crist, he myȝt |
defend himsilf and seie þus "I beleued þus bicause þat þou tauȝtist f. 15ᵛ
þus. Haddest þou oþurwise itauȝt, I wold haue beleued so. þerfor I, 480
tristenyng in þi truþe, beleued as þou tauȝtist."'

But he þat forsakiþ Crist and his logic haþ no colour to excuse
himself whan Crist schal inpugne him. And herfore seiþ Crist þat
whosoeuer schal schame him and his wordis, þe maidenes Sone schal
aschame seche on whan he schal come in his maiestate of þe Fadur 485
and of holi angellus. He it is þat aschameþ Crist and his wordis þat
takiþ any wordis or lawe in more reuerens and auctorite þan he doþ
Cristis, as þis renegat and his disciplis don.

But seint Poule seiþ þat he schameþ not þe gospel, for it is þe
uertu of God to euery man þat beleueþ. And herefor he seiþ also þat 490
he doþ not auoutriȝe aȝenst ⌜þe word of⌝ God. þat wedded persone
doþ auouȝtrie þat in consenting or word or boþ takiþ a persone þat
he is not weddid to. Siþþen þan þat alle cristen men ben weddid to
Crist and his lawe, he þat leueþ Cristis lawe and takiþ him þat alion
sede, þat the wickid man haþ sowen among Cristis sede, doþ 495
auouȝtrie aȝenst Crist and his lawe. þus þan, as seint Poule soþli
seiþ, he doþ not auouȝtrie aȝenst þe word or sede of God as many
don. But he seiþ | 'Of clerenes as of God before God in Iesu Crist we f. 16ʳ
speken.' And þis is ful soþ, and nameli in þis poynt of beleue of þe
sacrid oste of þe auȝter. For seint Poule writiþ þus 'Forsoþ, I haue 500
take of þe Lord þat þing þat I haue betake to ȝowe', þat is to seie to
feiþful men; so þat he techiþ not þe beleue of þe sacrid oste of his
owun auctorite, or of any of þe apostlis or of alle hem, but of oon þat
neuer myȝt liȝe ne erre. And þan suyngli seint Poule techiþ þe beleue

485 seche] þe maid *canc.* seche   496 *margin* cor.2

505 of þe sacrid ost, as he had lerned of God. þat is to seie, 'þat þe lord
Iesu in þe nyȝt þat he was betraid, toke brede and, doyng þankinggis,
brake it and seide "Take ȝe and ete ȝe; þis is my bodi þat schal be
betraid for ȝowe; do ȝe þis into my mynde." On þe same wise he toke
þe kup aftur he had soupid, seiȝing on þat þat was conteined in þe
510 cup or chalice "This cup is a new testement in my blode; do ȝe þis
into mynde of me as ofte as ȝe schal drinke it."' Loo! so clerli in Iesu
Crist seint Poule techiþ þe beleue of þis oste wiþout any uariacion of
þe gospel, so þat bi þe wordis of seint Poule we most beleue þat þe
pure brede bi þe consecracioun is not after þe consecracioun onli
515 brede but olso verri Cristis bodi, and þe wyne is blode. For, as seint
f. 16ᵛ Cyprian seiþ, 'þe blode | mai not be seien in þe chalice whan þe
wyne lackiþ.' And I merueile þat sum ipocritis, pretending tendurnes
of consciens, mai not here asent wiþ olde seinttis and þe gospel to cal
þis sacrid oste 'Cristis bodi and brede', and han consciens inowe to
520 reuerse alle þat Crist and his apostlis, and seint Austen, and seint
Denyse and oþur olde seinttis han and wreten in þis mater.
    Furþermore in þe same processe seint Poule techiþ þe entent of
Crist in ordeinyng of þis sacrament, wher he seiþ þus 'As ofte forsoþ
as ȝe schal ete þis brede and drink þis cuppe, ȝe schal schewe þe
525 deeþ of þe Lord til he come.' And þis is þe same sentens þat Crist
seiþ, whan he seiþ þus to his disciplis, 'As ofte as ȝe schal do þis, ȝe
schal do it into mynde of me.' For Crist sacrid first þe oste whan he
ȝede to þe deeþ; and aftur whan he was reson from deeþ to liif he
dede þe same, for þe gospel telliþ þat þe disciplis knew him in
530 breking of brede. And seint Austen seiþ þus upon þe same worde of
þe gospel, 'We ben sekir we breken brede, and knowen God. Crist
wold not be knowen þan but þer (þat is to seie in breking of brede);
and þat for us þat were not to se him in flesche, and naþeles we were
to ete his flesche. Who þan euer þou be, if þou be a feiþful man, be
535 þou not nouȝ callid in ueyn a cristen man, ȝif þou here þe word of
f. 17ʳ God wiþ drede and | hope. Lete þe breking of þis brede comfort the,
for þe absens of þe Lord is noon absens. Haue þou feiþ, and wiþ þe
he is whom þou seist not.' þis is Austens sentens in a sermon þat he
makiþ of Estur. So þat breking of þe brede, in wiche þe disciplis
540 knewe Iesu, was þe sacrid oste, as seint Austen vndurstondeþ; and
þus Crist dede þis consecracioun after he was resoun from deeþ. And
þe þrid tyme, as men supposyn, he dede þis consecracion whan he
ascended into heuene. For [þe] text telliþ þat Crist, eting wiþ his

509 in þe] in þe / in þe   543 his] hem *canc.* his

disciplis, ascendid; and, for as meche as he ordeyned þis sacrament to
be do into mynde of hym, as he hymself seiþ and Poule also, clerkis 545
supposen þat he sacrid þis oost among his disciplis whan he ȝede
from hem, as touȝching his bodili presens here for euermore. But for
as meche as I haue ȝit noon euydens of þis last sacring of Crist, þe
wiche I most beleue as feiþ, þerfore I suppose þis as probable bi
credens lasse þan beleue. And þis sacring of þis oost þre tymys bi 550
Crist himsilf, as I suppose, is þe cause whi þat euery prest in his
masse aftur þe consecracioun, in þe persone of himsilf and of alle þe
chirche, seiþ þus: 'We, Lord, and þin holi seruantis, hauyng mynde
of þe most holi passioun and of þe resurreccioun from | hellis and of f. 17ᵛ
þe most glorious ascencioun offren to þi most clere maieste holi 555
brede of euerlasting liif and þe chalice of perpetual helþe.' Loo! houȝ
þe olde vsing, þe logic and þe speche of scripture calliþ, as doþ þe
gospel and seint Poule, þis sacrament 'brede', and so 'holi brede' and
'chalice'.

But God forbede, houȝsoeuer þe gospel, Poule or any oþur seint 560
calle þis sacrament 'brede', þat any cristen man schold wiþdrawe þe
grete reward þat ⌐þei⌐ most haue to þis oost, þat is to seie þat it is
Goddis bodi, for þat men schul reward raþur þan þat it is brede. For
þat we knowen bi obedient beleue þat we honoren to Cristis wordis,
for þe wiche beleue we hope to be rewardid. For whosoeuer rewardiþ 565
þis sacrament chifli as brede and not more extentli as Cristis bodi, he
etiþ vnworþili þis sacrament. For a man mai be vnworþi to receyue
þis sacrament for two skelis: þat is to seie, for his yuel manerus in
breking of þe commaundementis, or ellis for his mysbeleue þat he
haþ no reward to þis brede, but as to oþur comen or usual brede. 570
And herefore seint Poule, teching þat men most araie hem in
manerys and in beleue ȝif | þei wol worþili receiue þis sacrament, f. 18ʳ
also he seiþ þus suyngli in þe same place aboue leide, 'Whosoeuer
schal ete þe brede and drink þe chalis of þe Lord vnworþeli, he schal
be gilti of þe bodi and of þe blode of ⌐the⌐ Lord. þerfor preue a man 575
himsilf (þat is to seie in maneres and in beleue), and so ete he of þat
brede and drink he of þat kupp. Forsoþ, whoso etiþ and drinkiþ
vnworþili, he etiþ and drinkiþ dome to hymsilf, not demyng (or
rewarding) þe bodi of þe Lord.' Lo, houȝ seint Poule techiþ þis oste
to be brede after þe consecracioun! But wiþ þis he techiþ a man not 580
to rest in þat conseite, but chifli to reward þat as Goddis bodi or ellis
for fauȝte of beleue he takiþ þat sacrament vnworþili.

And þis logic of seint Poule, acording wiþ þe logic or þe speche of þe gospel, seiyng þat þe disciplis knewen Crist in breking of brede, 585 ascapid not Poule for fauȝte of avisement; for of pure purpos imeuyd of þe Holi Gost he spekiþ þus of þe same sacrament in þe same sentens, vnder seche a logic þat þis foreseide renegat wiþ alle his glosers schal not mowe peruerte þat logic to her entent, wille and determynacion. For seint Poule seiþ þus 'þe chalice of þe blessing to 590 þe wiche we blessen, it is þe communyng of Cristis blode; and is not þe brede þat we breken | the commounnyng (parting or parte-taking) of Cristis bodi?' And seint Poule meneþ affirmatifli þat it is so. For þis sacrid oste is not onli Cristis bodi bi consecracion personali, but also it is Cristis mystik bodi, þe wiche is þe numbre of alle þo þat 595 schul be saued, þe wiche ben oon togedre among hemself bi loue and oon wiþ Iesu Crist, her heed bi final charite. And herfore seint Poule seiþ 'Oo brede, o bodi, many ben we alle þat taken parte of oo loof or brede, and oo cuppe.' And vpon þis text seiþ seint Austen in oon of his epistlis þat 'Oo brede or oo loff is a sacrament of vnite.' For, as 600 þe same Austen seiþ in a sentence vpon Ion, 'As many cornys rennen togedur and maken oo loff, so many personys, onyd in oo feiþ and beleue, maken oo bodi.' þan seint Poulis wordis now rehersid schulden þus be vndurstonde bi þe witt of seint Austen, þat we many in personys ben oo bodi bi vnite and charite, þe wiche bodi 605 and vnite þerof is figurid bi þis oo loff or brede, in wiche we commounnen. And þat þis b[e] þe witt of seint Poule a feiþful man mai vnderstonde bi þe tretice of þis mater þat seint Denyse wrote, þe wiche he lernyd of Poule his maister, and is cald *De eukaristia uel de collacione.*

610   And seint Austen (*De civitate Dei li.* 16) spekiþ acordingli herto, rehersing þer houȝ þe blessing of Iacob before his elder broþur figuriþ þe blessing and þe benefice of Crist and his | lawe in comparson of þe olde lawe, where seint Austen writiþ þus, 'þe world is ful of þe swte sauour of Crist, as it were a feld. þis blessing of Crist is as þe dewe of 615 heuene, þat is to seie of þe rayn of Goddis wordis, and of þe plente of þe erþe, þat is to seie of þe gadring of þe peple. Of Crist also is þe multitude of whete and wyne, þat is to seie þe multitude of þe wiche whete and wyne is gadrid togedre in þe sacrament of his bodi and his blode.' Lo, houȝ þis word of Austen declariþ þe worde of Poule nouȝ 620 rehersid, seiȝing þus 'O brede, oo loof, many be we alle þat partyn or comenyn of oo brede and oo chalice.'

589 *margin* cor.10   606 be] bi

And lo, furþurmore, houȝ seint Austen, confermyng him to Cristis
wordis and logic and þe apostlis, he agrisiþ not as folis don nouȝ to
calle þis sacrament 'brede and wyne'. And þe same maner of speche
haþ seint Austen in a sermon of Ester, wher he seiþ þus þat þing 625
'þat ȝe haue seien is þe brede and chalice, þe wiche þing also ȝour
iȝen schewen to ȝowe. But forsoþ, þat þat ȝour feiþ to be formyd
askiþ þe brede is þe bodi of Crist, and þe chalice is þe blode of
Crist.' Houȝ þis feiþful ⌐heuenli⌐ logician couȝde not uariȝe from þe
logic of Iesu Crist and his lawe; for he supposid ful auctorite of his 630
lawe and moste | truthe in his logik, and so as he dede schuld al f. 19ᵛ
feiþful men do.

Herefor seiþ seint Gregor (18 *Moralia super isto uerbo* '*Habet
argentum venarum suarum principia, et auro locus est in quo conflatur*')
'In siluur is betokenyd feire speche, in gold is betokened clerenesse 635
of liif or of wisdom. And for as meche as heretikis ben proude of þe
schynyng of her feire speche, þat þei be not sadded in none auctorite
of holi bokis (þe wiche holi bokis ben to us as it were ueinys of syluur
in speking, for of þo holi bokis we drawyn þe begynnyng of our
speche), Iob calliþ aȝen heretikis to þe writinggis of holi auctorite, 640
and þat to þis ende þat, if þei desire for to speke truli, þat þei take of
scripture what þei speke. As þouȝ Iob wold scie opinli: whoso araieþ
him to þe wordis of holi scripturis, [it nediþ] þat he reuoke (or calle
aȝen) al þat he spekiþ to þe grounde of Goddis auctorite, and þat he
sett fast þe bilding of his speche in þat. For, as we haue seide before, 645
ofte tyme heretikis, while þei studien for to afferme her owne
weiword þinggis, þei bringgen forþe seche þinggis þat ben not
holden in holi scriptures. And herfore þe noble prechour Poule
amonestiþ his disciple, seiyng "Tymothie, auoide þou newelteis of
wordis." For þe whilis þat heretikis coueiten to | be preisid of hiȝe f. 20ʳ
witt, þei bringgen forthe as it were sum newe þinggis, þe wiche ben 651
not holden in þe olde bokis of olde fadris.' Lo, of þis processe of
Gregor upon þe heuenli wordis of Iob þou maist se þat holi scripture
is grounde of alle trewe logic, and houȝ perlous it is to uarie from
scripturre in any poynt and specialli of þe sacrid oost. 655

Here seiþ almyȝti God (*Exo*.20) 'Ȝif þou make to þe a stonyn
auȝter, þou schalt make þat of stonys vnhewe or vnkutt; for if þou
rere þin eggetole upon þat it schal be defoilid.' Vpon þis text of
scripture seiþ a grete clerk Parisiensis, and seiþ þus þat 'þe auȝter of
ston is þe feiþ of Iesu Crist, þe wiche Iesu is boþ grounde ston or 660

625 ester] hester   641 if þei] *twice*   652 processe] processes

fundement and corner ston of þe chirche of God, as scripture spekiþ.
ʒif þan þou wilt make þe feiþ as toward God, make it of stonys
vnhewe. Take þi beleue as it comeþ of þe strong rok or quarre, Iesu.
And arere not þe sotilte or scharpnes of þi witt upon or aboue þis
665 ston; þat is to mene, frame not þe feiþ wiþ sotilte and scharpnesse of
þi witt, for if þou do þi feiþ schal be defoulid as to þe, and þi witt
f. 20ᵛ schal be adullid.' And þan after þis sentens | this clerk rehersiþ
Ambrose, seiyng þus 'Wiþouten any disputicioun þo þinggis ben to
be beleued, þe wiche ben spoke of God in scripture.' But here seie
670 folis, þat demen in effect þat Crist and hys apostlis failidden foule in
her logic, and namel[i] in þe mater of þe sacrid oste, þat alle þat
scripture spekiþ of þis oste or olde doctours, calling it brede and
wyne, schal be vndurstonde of þe accidentis wiþout sogett or
substaunce þat þei maken so meche of. But it is open of þe processe
675 of Gregor riʒt nouʒ rehersid þat þes ben ueri folis and in hiʒe weiʒe
of heresiʒe. For þei supposen not scripture as grounde of her logic,
but aʒenward supposyn first her owne lewde logic, and wold drawe bi
her vnredi glosis þe endeles witt of þe Trenyte to her wood rauyng
and folie. And, certis, saue for þe processe of Poule of þat renegat þat
680 we haue so ofte spoke of, I wold meche merueile here whi þat þes
folis glosen so besili þe gospel, and so rechelesli drawen to her wille
and logic and determynacioun þe logik of Crist and his apostlis. For I
kan se no skele whi þat alle þat euer scripture seiþ of þis oste vnder
þe nam⟨e⟩ of brede and wyne schal be vndurstonde of accidentis, but
f. 21ʳ bi þe same skele al þat þei seien of | her accidentis schal be
686 vndurstond of bred and wyne.

And certis, hauyng no reward to þis grete ypocrite and renegat þat
we speken of and of his condicions, houʒ he is wel ny sett al in signys
of perfeccioun and holinesse wiþout þe truþe answering to þise
690 signys, no wonder alþouʒ he determene þat þis sacrament be no
brede, ne substance, ne accidente in soget or substaunce, but an
accident or many accidenttis wiþout substaunce. For riʒt as þis
ypocrite was disposid for to receyue a spirit whan he began þis
werke, so wiþout douʒte he receiuyd it; and for as meche as he was
695 an ypocrite, pretending for to suʒe Crist, and reuersing him openli,
he most be meuyd of þat spirit to speke aʒenst Crist þat is trouthe,
and so to conforme his wordis to his ypocrisie. And so as ypocrisie
haþ outword schewing of substaunce of uertuus lyuyng wiþout þe
þing in himself, so ⌐as þei han⌐ determenyd her sacrament after her

663 strong] and strong   682 þe] to þe   693 began] was *canc.* began

witt haþ al outword signys of substaunce wiþout trew[þ]e answering 700
þerto. But al on þe contrarie wise it is of feiþful and trewe cristen
men and her sacrament, þe wiche haþ not onli þe signys of substance
but also the þing in himsilf. For as it is declarid before bi þe best
wittnesse þat mai be, her sacrament is brede and wyne, and so
conteneþ not onli the tokenys of substaunce but raþur | and meche f. 21ᵛ
better þe uertu and substans of seche signys. But here I wote wel þat 706
þes two wordis *forma* and *species* in Latyn disceyuen our ypocritis þat
ben alle dreint in signys and accidentis. For þei kan not vnderstonde
bi þes wordis but her accidentis and signys, notwiþstonding þat olde
seinttis wiþ Crist and þe apostle Poule þat were not þus iȝeue al to 710
signys and accidentis, vnderstonden comynli bi þes ⌐two¬ wordis 'þe
kinddes' and 'þe substancis' of þinggis, as I wold bi Goddis help
haue declarid here and I myȝt haue had leiser.

And of þis processe nouȝ last seide wondur þou þe lesse, for as
meche as Crist seiþ, þat neuer seiþ but treuthe, 'þer schal ⌐ryse¬ vp 715
pseudo-prophetis, þat meueþ sotil ypocrisie, and þei schal ȝeue
signys so þat þei be brouȝt into errour, ȝe, þe chosyn if it mai be.'
And, lo nouȝ, houȝ þe prophecie of Crist is fulfild and uerrefiid
opinli at iȝe, for unneþe is þer any man þat stondeþ stabulli in Cristis
feiþ and lawe wiþouten any wauuryng or vnstablenes. And so I mai 720
seie to seint Poule þat, if he were as he was sum tyme, he myȝt seie
wiþ Iob 'þe drede þat I dredde is befallen on me!', for seint Poule
seiþ þus 'I drede me lest, as þe serpent disceiued Eue, so be ȝour
wittis corrupt and defilid, and so þat ȝe falle from þe symplenesse þe
wiche is in Crist Iesu.' þis | symplenes þat þe apostle spekiþ of is f. 22ʳ
chastite of feiþ wiþout menging of alien sede, þat þe wickid renegat 726
þat I spake of haþ sowen among Cristis sede. And so þis si[m]pilte is
þe auoiding of þe auouȝtriȝe aȝenst Goddis lawe þat I spak of before;
and so þis semeþ þe witt of seint Austen *De civitate Dei li.* 14, and I
be wel auisid. Naþeles, as euery þing is in his owne kinde whan it is 730
vnmengid, so mai Cristis beleue vnmengid wiþ alien tradicions and
determynacions be callid symple and so pure and chast.

But certis nouȝ seint Poule, where þou know or none, I wote wel
þou maist if þou wilt: þe drede þat þou dreddist is come, for þe olde
serpent þat disceyued Eue haþ transfigurid hymsilf into an angel of 735
liȝt, inhabiting specialli þis renegat antecrist, and haþ disceyued þo
þat schuld be Cristis chirche, and put it fro þe simple, pure, clene

715 ryse] *dh later*   720 wiþouten] wiþout/outen   722 *margin* cor.11
727 simpilte] silpilte

and clere beleue þat our blessid Iesu tauȝt. And so nouȝ, Poule, þi
prophecie is fulfillid þat þou spake of wiþ ful grete sorow and
740 mornyng, houȝ 'þer schal be a tyme whan men schal not susteyne
holsum doctrine, but at her owne desiris þei schal hepe to hemself
maistris, tekeling hem in þe eris; and for soþ þei schal turne her
f. 22ᵛ hering from truthe, and | schul be turnyd to fablis.' Truli, seint
Poule, I wote wel þat þis prophecie is fulfild nouȝ, for neiþer þe
745 peple, neiþer he þat haþ þe see in þe chirche, as I spak of aforehand,
haþ reward to Crist or his wordis, neiþer to þi wordis, Poule, but to
her owne talis, and nameli in þe feiþ of þe sacrid oost. And þis
myschif, Poule, is brouȝt in þe chirche bi þilke viserid fendes and dai
deuyllis, freris, þat þou specifidest of wher þou seidest þus 'þe Spirit
750 seiþ opinlich þat in þe last tyme schal sum parte aweie from þe feiþ,
taking hede to þe spiritis of errour and to þe doctrine of deuyllis,
speking lesing in ypocrisie.' And it is no douȝte þes deuyllus ben also
þis gret renegat and ypocrite, antecrist, for þer myȝt no creature
haue brouȝt in þis, and he had stonde feiþfulli and clereli aftur þe
755 ordenaunce of God and his gospel.

Naþeles, al þis myschif and sorowe myȝ⟨te⟩ be remediid if þe
peple wold do aftur þe consail and doctrine of Poule; for he seiþ
[Heb. *ultimo*] 'Wil ȝe not be led aweie wiþ dyuers doctrinys and
strang. For it is best to stable þe hert in grace.' Certis, al þat is from
760 Crist-ward is aweiward; and so alle þat ȝeueþ effectuelli entent to
doctrine þat is not of Cristis doctrine ben leide aweie from Criste wiþ
f. 23ʳ strang doctrine and wauerring from Cristis, | and seche most nedis
erre. And herefor it is best, as þou Poule techist, to stable þe hert in
grace—ȝe, in þe grace þat þou spekist of, (*Tit.*[2]) wher þou seist
765 þus 'þe grace of God our sauyour haþ aperid to alle men,
enf[o]rmyng us.' And þis grace þat þou menyst þer is our lord
Iesu, in þe wiche grace, if we stable oure hert, we schul neuer
perrische vndur þe woodnus and outrage of antecrist. Furþurmore,
seiþ Poule in his prophecie of antecrist þat he schewiþ hymself as he
770 be God, so þat þis grete apostata from þe religioun of Crist and his
rule is contrarious to God, and enhaunsid aboue al þing þat is seide
God bi office or ellis is God bi kinde, as I haue in parti schewid here
before. And ouer þis he schewiþ himself as if he be God, as I schal
wiþ þe help of God sumwhat declare hereaftur.

775   And wondre ȝe but litil, alþouȝ þis grete ipocrite and renegat, þat
is so fer falle wiþ þe first apostata Lucifer from his owne astate and

degre, holt himself not in oo pliȝte aȝen God, but nouȝ enhaunsiþ
himself and is enhaunsid bi oþur aboue God, and nouȝ schewiþ
hymself as he were God. For he is so woodli proude, and so ful of
Luciferis pride þat inhabiteþ þis grete dampnyd man, þat he | raueþ f. 23ᵛ
and knowiþ not his owne state; and so he sowrmounteþ nouȝ al þat is 781
seide or is God, and nouȝ he comparrisoneþ hymsilf bi euennes to
God in many wises. For himself of himself [is] auctour of his lawe,
for he supposiþ not þe gospel generalli as grounde of his awne lawe,
ne of any oþur lawe þe wiche he supposiþ for to be better or of more 785
auctorite þan is his owne. But, as Crist meneþ, þis antecrist spekiþ of
himself and so secheþ his owne glorie. But so myȝt Crist do, þat is to
seie to seche his owne glorie as to hys manheed; but onli Godd as
God mai riȝtfulli do þat. Herefore he seiþ 'I seche not myn owne
glorie; he is or haþ beyng þat sechiþ and demeþ.' Here schalt [þou] 790
vndurstonde þat þis uerbe *est* in Latyn þat betokeneþ beyng is þe
name of God; and so it is of Ebru, Gru, Englische and al oþur
langage þat answeriþ to þis Latyn word *est*. Herefor God answerid
þus to Moyses, whan he askid of God what was his name, 'I am þat
am; þis is my name wiþout ende.' And þis markyþ seint Ierom, and 795
seint Austen in ful many placis. So þat þis uerbe *sum* in Latyn, þat
betokeneþ a pure beyng or substaunce, betokeneþ | chifli þe purist f. 24ʳ
beyng and substaunce of God, the wiche beyng or substaunce is þe
uerri name of God þat haþ beyng, power, goodnes, riȝtwisenes,
kunnyng and strengþe of himself, wiþ alle seche oþur most uertuous 800
namys wiche alle ben þe foreseid name betokened bi þis uerbe *sum*.
And herefore, siþ he haþ al þis of himself and ȝeueþ graciousli to
euery creature his owne beyng, for he nedeþ none of hem, worþeli
and riȝtfulli he sechiþ his owne glorie in creaturis, not for his owne
nede but for nede of his creaturis, and iust seruice þat þei owen to 805
her maker. þan of þis it sueþ þat, for as meche as þis antecrist sechiþ
his owne glorie and demeþ himsilf, as þe dede schewiþ, so worþi and
glorious þat him nedeþ no þing to founde himself or his lawe vpon
saue his owne grete auctorite, power and wille, he schewiþ himself,
as seint Poule seiþ, as if he were God. And þis transfigurid Sathanas, 810
aftur þe first wille of fende þat inhabiteþ hym, wiþdrawiþ bi fraude
and violens from Iesu the feiþfulnesse and þe truȝe legeaunce, þe
wiche þe peple owiþ to our king and lord, Iesu Crist and his lawe.
For he wol not þat any man ȝeue credence to Crist or to his wordis, 814
but in as meche as it is auctorisid bi hym or acording | wiþ his wil. f. 24ᵛ

812 þe¹] viole *canc.* þe

But he wol þat his owne wil and tradicion be take as ful feiþ, not to be enpugned or douȝtid of any man. For whosoeuer do so obstinatli, be his determynacioun or wil neu⟨er⟩ so contrarious to Cristis lawe, he wil deme him for an heretik and kille him. But þis uissered fende
820 reckiþ nouȝt houȝ douȝteful þe peple be in þe determynacion of Crist and his apostlis, for bi þat he drawiþ þe peple to ȝeue more credence to his lore, and to menteyne hym and his lawe ⌜þe⌝ more stifli.

So þan þat seche feiþfulnes wiþout any douȝting or obstinat
825 reuersing o[r] inpugning is onli dew to God, it is nouȝ opyn þat seint Poule seiþ þat þis renegat sittiþ in þe chirche schewing himsilf to be God. And herefor, wylnyng þat his grete power and auctorite schuld be fulli knowe and magnefiid, he sendeþ out into euery kost of cristendom professours of his lawe in dyuers degreis, þe wiche
830 opyn her mouþe into blasfemie aȝen God of heuene and lacken Cristis lawe to the peple, and seien þat it is not onli insufficiente to gouerne Cristis chirche, but also þat it is fals and heresie, and þat hit killiþ þe peple, for þei seien aftur her owne fals menyng þat þe letter scleeþ, and þat Cristis law is not of none auctorite but in as meche |
f. 25ʳ as it is amittid bi þe chirche, þe wiche ys most famousli told or seide
836 of þis grete ipocrite þat sittiþ in þe chirche, as it is seide before. And ful many of þe professourris of þis lawe seien and holden, opyn and preuei, þat þe popis lawe, þe wiche is nouȝ most famousli callid 'þe lawe of holi chirche', is grete or ellis gretter of auctorite þan Cristis
840 law. And certis þis dede schewiþ þat þis is þe opiniyon of þis grete renegat and of alle his special lemys. And so þei callen þis lawe famousli 'canoun', þat is to [seie] autentik, fulli sufficient to rule þe chirche, so þat diuinite is not nedeful þerto, for nouȝ þei seien þei wote not wherof it serueþ. And þus, what for sufficience þat
845 professourris of þis renegatis tradicions supposen in hem to þe gouernaunce of þe chirche, and what for wynnyng þat þei felen to come bi her decreis and determynacions, and stablisching of her owne wille, and oppressing of Cristis wille and his lore, what also for sclaundur þat is put upon Cristis lawe of falsnesse and insuffi[ci]ence
850 to þe gouernaunce of his chirche, and also for as meche as nouȝ Cristis lawe is raþur matir of persecucion þan of promocion to þo
f. 25ᵛ þat | studien it and labouren it to make it knowen, fewe or welny none of þe clergie þat ben myȝti men and frendid besien hem in þe studie þerof, but abouȝte þat oþur lawe þat is now callid canoun, þe

825 or] on   829 degreis] and degreis

wiche aftur þe power of antecrist nouȝ regnyng is ful of wordli 855
wynnyng and glorie. Naþeles it semeþ bi seint Austen þat in his
tyme was no scripture canoun saue onli Goddis lawe, contenyd
expresse in þe bible, as he writiþ pleinneli in *De civitate Dei li*. 18 *ca*.
38 and *li*. 19 *ca*. 17, as, if God wol, I schal write hereaftur.

   And þus þe compleint and þe mone of Iesu Crist, made bi Iob (19 860
ca.) in þe persone of Iesu, is nouȝ fulfillid of Iesu. For Iob seiþ þus in
þe persone of Crist: 'Mi wiif haþ agrisid my breþe.' And þis word
seint Gregor upon þe same understondeþ of Crist, and of þo þat
schul be Cristis chirche and so his wiif. Cristis breþe is his lawe þat
comeþ out of his mouthe, þe wiche mouþe most specialli and 865
passingli is his manheed, bi þe wiche he spak his lawe. And not
onli þis manheede is Cristis mouþe, but also alle trewe prestis and
prophetis of þe olde lawe and newe lawe, and oþur trewe feiþful men
þat speken Goddis law | to his glorie and edificacioun of his chosoun. f. 26ʳ
Here seiþ God bi his prophete of al his mouþe þat þus spekiþ truthe 870
'Ȝif þou departe þat þing þat is precious from þat þing þat is foule,
þou schalt be as myn owne mouþe.' And, as a mannys spirit or breþe
quekeneþ his bodi, so out of þis mouþe of God, and chifli of Cristis
manheed, comeþ a breþe þat quekeneþ for euer al þe bodi of þe
chosen. And herfore Crist spekiþ þus of þis breþe: 'þe wordis þat I 875
haue spoke to ȝow ben spirit and liif', and 'Whoso kepiþ my wordis
schal not tast deeþ for euer.' And boþ while he was here lyuyng
dedli, and also whan he ascendid into heuene, he putt þis breþe in
his apostlis and truȝe prestis, and chargid hem to blowe þis breþe of
þe gospel vppon þe peple wiche schuld be his spouse, seiyng þus to 880
hem alle wiþ[out] any decepcioun or restreynyng, 'Go ȝe and teche
ȝe', 'Go ȝe and preche ȝe þe gospel to alle creaturis.'

   þis gospel is Cristis breþe, his testament and his last wille, of þe
wiche testament he ordeyned his prestis to be his executourris to dele
þis tresorie to his pore breþurne and sistren and neiȝboris here in 885
erþe. And if alle ben akursid, as bischops seien, þat letten men to
make testementis, þat ful | ofte erren in her last wille and testementis, f. 26ᵛ
or ellis letten þe execucioun of dedli mennys testamentis, houȝ
meche raþur be þei akursid of al holi chirche foure tymys bi þe
ȝere þat letten execucioun of Cristis testement and his last wille, 890
nameli siþ þat Crist myȝt not erre? But, certis, I am sure here þat if
þe truȝe and besiȝe execucioun of Cristis testement sounned no more
aȝen þe wordli wynnyng and glorie of þe prelacie, and proude prestis
þat nouȝ regnyn, þan þe excecucioun of þe testement of an erþeli

895 mannys good, þei wolde not lett þe excecucioun of þe ton no more
þan of þe oþur! But nou3, certis, as we mowe se opinli, þis testement
of Crist þat þis breþe þat came out of his owne mouthe is loþe to þe
peple þat schuld be his spouse.

Naþeles, sum tyme þis breþe was blowe ful besili vpon Cristis
900 spouse, and it was ful swete and ful saueri to hir into þe tyme þat
sche wax so frike and lusti þour grete plente of prouendur þat prekid
hir; and nameli in þat partie of þis spouse þat is callid þe clerge, þat
schuld haue be most sibbe and chast, þis spouse specialli in þis parte
began to loþe þe breþe of hir uerri spouse Crist. And þan, ri3t as
905 vnclene and a schrewid calat þat is weri of hir trewe wedded
f. 27ʳ housbond first turneþ hir from her | housbonde and loþiþ his
breþe, and aftur makiþ open playnt upon his breþe seching a
deuors, and at þe last mariiþ hir ⟨t⟩o housbonde wiþ a newe breþ,
so stondiþ it of þe clergi þat schuld be streitli weddid to Iesu Crist.
910 First þei turnen hem from Crist, but neuer more notabli þan whan
þei turned aweie from Cristis wilful pouerte and became wordli
lordis. And aftur ⌈þat⌉ þei loþid Cristys breþe þat is þe gospel, þe
wiche he blewe upon hem whan he prechid it in worde and dede.
And nameli þei loþen þo blastis of Crist wiche ben euyn a3en her
915 wordli lordschip and glorie and wordli besynesse, as is þis worde of
Crist iseide to alle the clerge and byndeþ hem for euer: 'þe kinggis of
heþen men haue lordschip upon hem, but 3e not so.' And 'Whoeuer
renounsiþ not to alle þo þinggis þe wiche he haþ in possession mai
not be my disciple', þat is to seie of office as ben alle trewe prestis
920 and dekenes. Also [þat þat] Crist answeriþ to þe man þat bade Crist
commaunde his broþur to departe wiþ him þe eritage is ri3t vnsaueri
to our clerge, wher Crist answeriþ þus: 'O man! who haþ ordeyned
me a iuge or a departer upon 3ow?', in þe wiche answere Crist
enformeþ al his clerge to fle secler office and besinesse as he dede.
925 For many seche breþis of almy3ti God ben þer, boþ in olde lawe and
f. 27ᵛ also in þe newe lawe, þe wiche ben as loth as venym | to this
foreseide spouse. And no dou3te, ri3t as weiword clerkis in seint
Austens tyme were encumbrid of þis text of Crist wher he seiþ:
'Vpon Moises chaier schal sitt scribis and phariseis, and alle þat euer
930 þei schal seie to 3owe kepe it and performe it. But wil 3e not do aftur
her werkis, for þei seyn and do not'; and þerfor, as Austen seiþ 'þei
wolden, and þei had my3t, haue do þat worde of þe gospel out of
Cristis lawe.' So oure iolie and frike clerge þat schuld be Cristis

903 þis'] þat þis   928 tyme] bokis *canc.* tyme

special spouse is so sore atenyd wiþ seche blastis of Crist as I haue
rehersid þat þei wold ful fayn be delyuerid from hem for euer. 935

And þis is þe cause whi þei sechen a deuors fro Crist and his
breþe, and playnnen opinli and disclaundrousli vpon his brethe
seiyng þat it is wors þan any stinch. For as þei seien it is heresie
and blasfemye, fals and contrarius to himself and so litteralli þat it
killiþ men; and so it is insufficient to gouerne seche a spouse as þis 940
holi clerge is. And herefore þei forsaken to suȝe Crist and his brethe
þat þei loþen so meche, and so þei turnen hem auouȝtrousli to
anoþur spouse—or raþur auouȝtrer, of anoþur breþe þat haþ a
smacche of wordli lordschip, pompe and pride and wordli wynnyng
and glorie as ben comynli her statutis, determynacions and constitu- 945
cions, þe wiche þe spirit of ⌐lesing⌐ þat euer desirid to | do avouȝtrie f. 28ʳ
wiþ Cristis spouse, haþ blowen upon hem. Naþeles, þis corrupt
spouse delitiþ hir so meche in þis newe breþe of auouȝtrie of Goddis
lawe, and so inwardli hatiþ þe brethe of Iesu Crist þat schuld be hir
ueri housbonde, þat schc lieþ euer in awaite þat no breþe of Crist be 950
blowe upon hir, and nameli no seche blastis as ben aȝen her wordli
lust and wynnyng. And herfore boþ bi her determynacions, constitucions and statutis, and also bi uyolens as cursing, presunnyng
and deeþ, þei oppressen and stoppen trewe prestis þat besien hem to
blowe a blast of þis breþe of Crist upon þis auouȝtresse. And so sum 955
of þise prestis þei exilen bi cruel persecucioun and censuris, and sum
þei peynen to þe deeþ bi hungre, and sum þei murþeren in preson
and sum þei brennen openli. And al þis is for to stop þe brethe of þe
gospel of Crist, þe wiche þis proude calot and auouȝtresse hatiþ
wiþout cause. 960

And þis malice, þat is nouȝ ryue among oure clerge, was
ensamplid in Cristis tyme and his apostlis bi þe fals clerge þat was
þat tyme. For þei had lefte þe lawe of almyȝtti God, her spouse, and
wedded herself to gainful tradicions of mennys bifinddinggis, as
Crist pleyneþ upon hem in þe gospel. And bi alle þe weiis þat þei 965
koude deuyse þey or|deyned for to stop Crist and his trewe prestis, f. 28ᵛ
þat þei schuld not blowe þe breþe of þe spouse upon hem, þe wiche
was so grisful to hem. And herfor we mai rede (*Luc.*12) þat, what
tyme Crist had prechid aȝenst þe synnys of þe clerge, þe scribis and
phariseis began greuously to wiþstonde him, and to oppresse his 970
mouthe and to stop it, awaiting to him of many þinggis, seching to
take sumwhat of his mouþe þat þei myȝt acuse hym. And also we
mai rede (*Act.* 23) þat Ananyas þe prince of prestis commaunded þe

peple to bete or to smyte seint Poulis mouþe, forwhi þe trewe breþe
975 of Crist þat came forth bi þat mouþe tenyd him sore. And wheþur
our princis of prestis do not so nouȝ or none to feiþful prestis, þat
blowen or wold blow þe swete breþe of Cristis gospel vpon hem and
the peple, deme ȝe of þe dede þat is open inouȝ! But I wote wel þat
þe malice of oure prestis þat schewen þis hate aȝenst Crist and his
980 breþe passiþ wiþout comparson þe malice of þe ypocritis of þe olde
lawe. For þei were not weddid to Crist and to his lawe, as our clerge,
iringgid and imytrid, pretenden to be. þus þan, as I haue seide in
parte, þis proude prelacie, auouȝtresse aȝenst Crist and his lawe,
beten Crist and oppressen his mouþe and lien in a stronge waite
f. 29ʳ þerupon to accuse and to pursue Crist. For al | þat seche
986 turmentourris don to seche feiþful prechours or ellis to oþur good
men, Crist takiþ it as idon to himself; and here he seiþ 'Whateuer ȝe
han don to any of my lest, ȝe han don it to me.' And Crist seide to
Saule þat pursued his feiþful peple þus: 'Saul, Saul, whi pursuest
990 þou me?' Crist was þat tyme in his owne persone in heuene, but ȝit
Poule disesid him in his feiþful membris in erþe. And Crist seide
also (*Luc.*10) þus to his trewe prechourris: 'Forsoþ, whoso hereþ ȝow
hereþ me; and whoso dispisiþ ȝow dispisiþ me. And, forsoþ, whoso
dispisiþ me dispisiþ him þat sende me.'

995   þan of þes wordis of Crist wiþ þe persecucioun of antecrist we mai
se opinli at iȝe houȝ þis renegat, þat sittiþ þus in þe chirche, betiþ
Crist aboute þe mouthe for þe breþe þat comeþ out þerof. For certis,
as experience techiþ, þe brethe of Crist is so hateful to þis
auouȝtresse þat schuld be his spouse, þat sche wol not her þankis
1000 suffre no feiþful man to blowe þis breþe vpon hir ne upon any oþur
man, ne sche hirsilf wol blowe þis breþe in þe most nede upon any
man, alþouȝ he be accusid of heresie. For I haue wist many men
examnyd in our londe in dyuers materis þat haue be demed bi
scripture, and sum haue ben conuyct of heresie bi þe chiff lymys of
1005 þis renegat, but I neuer koude wete þat seche antecristis lemys koude
f. 29ᵛ aleie for | hem any hole processe or ellis hole sentens or text of
Goddis lawe, but onli her owne tradicions and determynacions,
notwiþstonding þat þe olde descripcioun of heresie is þis: 'Heresie
is fals lore contrarie to ⌐holi⌐ scripture obstinatli defendid.' And
1010 certis whoso wol rede Austens and Ieromes bokes, þat had ful meche
and grete conflict wiþ heretikis, he schal se wel þat þei demed or
conuictid no man for an heretik, ne any doctrine to be heresie, but bi
hole sentens of ⌐holi⌐ scripture þat is Goddis lawe. But nouȝ is þe

auctorite of Goddis lawe so fer put abak þat it suffisiþ not in our
dyuyne scole to him þat schal rede or answere to make þis   1015
protestacioun: þat it is not his wille or entent for to seie or obstinatli
defende any þing aȝenst Goddis lawe. For, if he make his protestacioun so, anoon he schal be had suspect of heresie or errour. But he
most seie þis sentens in his protestacioun: þat it is not his entent to
seie or obstinatli defende any þing contrarie to þe ful holi determy-   1020
nacioun of þe chirche of Rome—vndurstonde chifli bi þis chirche þe
grete aggregat persone from þe hiȝist unto þe lowist þat sittiþ in þe
temple, þat is to seie in þe chirche, as I seide before. But, certis,
antecrist in þis protestacioun can not se | his owne schame, no more f. 30ʳ
þan kan his heed Lucifer; þat is to seie, houȝ he meueþ in þe wordis 1025
of his protestacioun þat Goddis lawe and his determynacioun
acorden not alweie, and so he schewiþ himself preueli to be an
heretik and an antecrist. And ouur þis, siþ a man mai not, as olde
seinttis seien and supposen, be conuict of heresie bi lasse auctorite
þan holi writt, þis apostata, conui[c]ting men of heresie bi his   1030
tradicions, seiþ in þe same dede þat his owne wille and determynacioun is as meche of auctorite or more þan Goddis lawe; and so he
meneþ and schewiþ himsilf to be of as meche auctorite or more þan
God; for, as lawe is comparrisound to lawe, so in þe same degre is
auctour comparsoned to auctour.   1035

þan of þis processe, and of oþur iwrite before, þou maist se in
partie and vndurstond houȝ pleinli Poulis prophecie of antecrist is
uerefiid of þis renegat, þat sittiþ in þe chirche upon the bereschrewe
þat I spak of before—þat is to seie, houȝ þis antecrist is contrarie to
Crist and enhaunsid aboue al þing þat is God in kynde, or seide God 1040
by weie of office, and houȝ he sittiþ in þe chirche schewyng himself
to be God. And ouer þis þou maist se houȝ þis vnkinde calot and
auouȝtresse, þat schuld be chifli Cristis owne spouse and loue, loþiþ |
and agrisith his brethe, and houȝ sche betith Crist abouȝte þe f. 30ᵛ
mouthe to stop þe breþe of his gospel þat it breke not out upon 1045
hir on any side. Also þou maist see in þis processe houȝ Cristis
wordis of þe wickid seruant þat he spekiþ of (*Mt.* 24) ben fulfillid,
where Crist seiþ þus: 'Forsoþ, if þe wickid seruant schal seie in his
hert "Mi lord makiþ tariyng to come", and if he schal begyn to
smyte his felowis, and if he ete and drynke with drunken men, þe 1050
lord of þat seruant schal come in þe dai þat he hopeþ not and in þe

1029 be] to be   1030 conuicting] conuitting   1033 auctorite] of auctorite
1047 24] 42

oure þat he knowiþ not; and he schal departe him and schal put his parte wiþ ypocritis; þer schal be weping and gnasting of teeþ.' þou schalt vndurstonde here þat, alle þou₃ þe wordis of Crist be seide 1055 condicionalli, ₃it he meneþ in þe same wordis þat seche a ⌜wickid⌝ seruant schal be, and þat he worþeli for his wickidnesse be rewardid wiþ þat greuous euerlasting peyne.

And þou schalt vndurstonde here þat euery man ou₃t to be Goddis seruant, for he haþ lordschip bi kinde upon eche creature. 1060 But specialli cristen men ou₃t to serue God mekeli, for upon hem God haþ lordschip and regalie bi þre maner of title: first bi kinde he haþ lordschip upon cristen men, for he is aboue hem alle in kynde and made hem of nou₃t; and bi title of conqueste, for he gate hem f. 31ʳ from þe fende bi conquest upon | the cros; and also bi eleccioun, for 1065 cristen peple han chosen Crist to her lord and king, and are bicome his lege men bi cristendom and don him omage bi sacrifice. But þe clerge, þat schuld be most meke and seruyable and furþest wiþdrawe from þe world, schuld be most ⌜speciali⌝ Goddis seruantis, for alle clerkis ben sacrid to þis seruice. And so to hem it longiþ not onli 1070 most obedientli to serue God and to conferme her wille to Goddis wille, but also to drawe bi worde and werke alle men to þe same seruyce. Naþeles, alþou₃ it so be þat euery man ou₃t to be Goddis seruant, and whosoeuer wiþdrawe his dewe seruyce from God is a wickid seruant, ₃it, siþ al Cristis wordis ben most notable, his wordis 1075 of þis wickid seruant most be vndurstonde of þe most wickid and harmeful seruant þat is or ellis mai be in Cristis house. And Cristis seruantis ben departid in þre statis, as kny₃thood and presthood and laborers; and þe clerge, feiþfulli besie in his owne office, most profitiþ and mai most profite in Cristis house þat is his chirche. It 1080 wol su₃e þat þe clerge isett a₃enst Crist is þe worst seruant in Goddis house, and moste distroieþ, wastiþ and disturbliþ it. For, ri₃t as a wiif in a wordli mannys house, rebel a₃enst hir lord or housbonde, f. 31ᵛ most teneþ and troubliþ þe lord and his | meyne, so hit is of þe rebel clerge þat schuld [be] the most obedient and seruiable parte in 1085 Cristis spouse, þat is his chirche. And þus imened Crist, whan he vndername Petur þat, as olde seinttis seien and nameli seint Austen (*De uerbis Domini et apostoli sermone* 13) signefiiþ Cristis chirche and so his wiif. For, whan Peter reuersid Cristis wille, Crist seide to him 'Go aftur me, Sathanas!', or ellis 'Folowe me, þou art sclaundrid to 1090 me!', þat is to seie 'þou greuyst me' or 'þou art cause of myn

1057 greuous] wick *canc.* greuous   1065 crist] to *canc.* crist offence'. So it is noo douȝte þe wickid spouse and seruant, þe clerge, þe grete renegat þat I spake of before, is Sathanas transfigurid into an angel of liȝt, for he is Cristis aduersarie under þe name of most holynesse, and most offendeþ Crist and harmeþ his chirche, and is cause whi þe glorious name of God is sclaundrid and blasfemed 1095 among heþen folk, and grettist occasion bi his wickiddest ensample whi þe peple stumbliþ and falliþ into synne and aftur into helle. For þis myddai deuyl wol not suȝe Cristis steppis in wilful pouerte and mekenes, and so ensample þe peple þe weie to Crist; for he wol not go behynde Crist and so suȝe him, but he wol go before hym or ellis 1100 euyn chekmate wiþ him. For, as sei[n]t Poule seiþ, he is enhaunsid aboue alle þing þat is seide God bi office or ellis God in kynde; and so he goþe | before Crist. And also he sittiþ in the chirche, schewing f. 32ʳ himsilf as he be God; and so goþ euyn as ferforth as Crist. And so he wol not suȝe Crist and mekeli serue him, but proudeli rebelliþ and 1105 wiþstondeþ Crist. And so he is most worþi to be callid þe wickid seruant þat Crist spekiþ of. And, as experience techiþ, þis wickid seruant seiþ in his hert þat his lord makiþ tariyng to come; for þys schrewid seruant haþ effectualli no mynde of his deeþ, neiþur of þe dai of dome, but is altogedur ȝeue rechelesli to his owne lust, wille 1110 and liking. For, if he had þis mynde effectualli, he wold not contynue alle his liif obstinatli in heresie of his wordli lordschip, of symonye and of þe sacrid oste, and many oþur heresiis and blasfemye þat ben ryue in þis renegat, þat lyueþ euer in seche a plite þat he most nedes be dampned ȝif he diȝe so—and, if he trist meche of fructeful 1115 penaunce or repentaunce whan he seeþ þat he mai lyue no lengger, him is good to beware, for he mai liȝtli be disceyued so! For seint Austen seiþ (in *Libro de natura et gracia*) þat 'It is þe most iust peyne of synne þat euery man lese þat þing þat he wold not wel use, whan he myȝt wiþouten any | difficulte if he wold; þat is to seie', as seith þe f. 32ᵛ same seint, 'þat he þat wetingli doþ not riȝtfulli, lese he to knowe 1121 what riȝt is; and he þat wold not do riȝt whan he myȝt, lak he power whan he wold.' For, as seint Austen techeþ þer, 'It is no wondur alþouȝ a man for faute of kunnyng haue no fredom of wille [to chese] what he schuld do riȝtfulli, or ellis þat bi carnel custome wiþstonding 1125 þat is growe uyolentli into man and in a maner is kindeliche bi dedli successioun, so þat a man se what ouȝt riȝtfulli to be don and willen to do it [he] mai not fulfil it.' And, certis, þis grete parel of nounpower to gete heuenli help in nede auȝt to be dred of þis

1092 is] þat is   1127 so] and so   1128 he] and

1130 wickid seruant. Naþeles, as Crist meneþ in his wordis, malice haþ so
blyndded þis schrewid seruant þat he haþe effectualli none inward
siȝt of þis perrel.'

þe rote of malice, as seint Poule seiþ, is couetice. And þer, as Crist
meneþ, he schal for defauȝte of drede of God smite his felowis,
1135 nameli þo þat ouȝt to be oon wiþ him in þe same seruyce, as ben
feiþful prestis þat besien hem to serue God wiþ besie performyng of
her office. And not onli þis schrewid seruant betiþ trewe prestis bi
dyuers menys and bi bodili deeþ, as it is seide before, but also oþur
f. 33ʳ peple þat louen and affectualli | labourren boþe wiþ bodi and wiþ
1140 catel þat Goddis law schuld be knowen and performed in his hous in
plesing of alle his houshoold. And ouer þis, þat is wers wiþout
mesure þan any bodili disese or smyting, he smitiþ Cristis peple
gostli in wiþdrawing of her heuenli uytaillus þat schuld be her
euerlasting liiflode, as is good ensample and trewe teching of Goddis
1145 lawe. For of þis liiflode Crist spekiþ þus þat 'Not onli in brede lyueþ
man, but in euery worde þat comeþ out of þe mouthe of God.' And
þus, as þei þat wiþdrawen bodili mete from hem þat þei schuld fede
ben seide in Englische prouerbe to bete hem upon þe wombe, so þis
schrewid and wickid seruant þe clerge, þat schuld be steuward in
1150 Goddis hous to dele þe brede of his lawe to his mene, betiþ hem to
euerlasting deeþ bi wiþdrawing of þis liiflode. And þis is þe sorist
beting þat Cristis mene mai suffre here. And of þis beting spekiþ þe
prophete Ieremye þus 'þe litil children askiden brede, and þer was
noon þat brake it to hem.' For þis stiward is so harde a thinge þat he
1155 wol not dele, ne suffre hem dele þat wolden dele, þis brede. And so
he falliþ vndur þe woo, þat is to seie þe dampnacioun, þat Crist
f. 33ᵛ schewiþ to seche (*Mt.*23) where he seiþ þus: 'Woo to ȝou, | scribis
and phariseis, þat closen the reme of heuene!', þat is to seie, as
Crisostom seiþ, holi scripture. 'Ȝe entren [not], ne ȝe suffre men
1160 entring to entre.' And þus aȝenst Cristis word and ensample þei leue
þe peple fasting in þe weie. And riȝt as a wickid seruant, þat haþe
lost þe loue and drede of his wordli lord and maister, wastiþ his
maistris houshold in gloteny and drunkunschip, so meneþ Crist þat
þis wickid seruant schal do in his house. For he, as Crist seiþ, schal
1165 ete and drinke wiþ drunken folk. And þou schalt vndurstonde here
þat þis worde *ebrius* in Latyn is as meche to seie in Englische aftur þe
composicioun of the worde as 'out of mesure'.

And certis ᵀhouȝᵀ unmesurable þis renegat and wickid seruant is

1144 as] crist spekiþ þus *canc.* and   1168 houȝ] as *canc.* ᵀhouȝᵀ

nouȝ in numbre, and in spoiling and wasting of pore mennes goodis, in wordeli pompe and pride, in wast and proude meyne, in super- 1170 fluite of hors and of wordli arayment, as cloþing, bedding, ymagis of go[l]d and siluur and vessellis also, and in festing of grete men þat neden not seche costis—I suppose þat oo mannys liif wold not suffice to write, in special alle þat þei wasten in vanyte of þe flesche and of þe world! But for as meche as alle seche maner of drunkschip and 1175 vnmesurablenes is open at iȝe to euery man þat wol take hede þerto, it is þe lesse nede to write of þis maner | of drunkeschip. Natheles f. 34ʳ þer is an vnmesurablenes, and so a drunkschip, þat þis renegat and wickid seruant þat sittiþ in þe chirche as God usiþ meche, þe wiche drunkschip stondeþ in þis: þat þis seruant kepiþ not himself vndur 1180 þe mesure of Goddis lawe, neiþur in maneres ne in beleue. But, wher him listiþ, he wiþdrawiþ, addiþ or ellis contrarieþ it aȝenst þe bidding of Goddis lawe in þe boke of Deutronomi and in þe boke of þe Apocalips, þe wiche ben þe last bokis of Goddis lawe, olde and newe, and forbeden adding and wiþdrawing to eiþur of þes lawes. 1185 For it is wreten þus (*Deut.*4) 'Ȝe schal not adde to my worde, ne ȝe schul wiþdrawe þerfro.' And in þe ende of þe Apocalips (*Apoc. ultimo*) seint Ion writiþ þus: 'Who schal adde or putt to þes wordis, God putt upon him þe veniaunsis wreten in þis boke. And if any man schal lesse or wiþdrawe of þe wordis of þe boke of þis 1190 prophesie, God take his parte from þe boke of liif and from þe holi cete.' And also God seiþ (*Deutere.* 12) 'Do þou onli to þe Lord þat þing þat he biddeþ the; adde þou no þing, ne wiþdrawe þou þerfro.'

Hereof þan þou maist se þat God haþ put alle þing in mesure, and 1195 mesurid his lawe on þe best wise, and wolde þat alle his seruantis and nameli þe clerge schuld soburli kepe hemself vndur þe most perfite | mesure of his lawe in þo þinggis þat ben longing to good manerys f. 34ᵛ and trewe beleue. But expereens techiþ us nouȝ houȝ þis drunken seruant passiþ the mesure of þis lawe in maneres and beleue, and þat 1200 in articlis and in poyntis wiþout numbre. Naþeles, nouȝ I purpos to reherse but two: oon is as touching manerys, anoþur as touching feiþe. As anempst God and uertuous maner tauȝt in Goddes lawe, þis wickid seruant is drunken and out of mesure of Goddis lawe in þis poynt specialli and openli: þat he, aȝenst Cristis ensample and 1205 teching and aȝenst his open forbeding, occupieþ wordli lordschippis

1172 gold] god   1179 chirche] schirche, s- *canc.*   1189 veniaunsis] veniauⁿnsis   1206 wordli] and *canc.* wordli

and possessions on wordli wise. And þis renegat is so woodli drunke
in þis poynt þat he wol comyn in þis wiþ noon, saue wiþ seche þat
ben out of þe soburnesse and mesure of Goddis lawe. For he holdeþ
1210 alle þo acursid þat on any wise besien hem to redresse þis drunken
apostata to þe soburnesse of Cristis lyuyng and his teching. And þis
vnsoburnesse of þis vnruli seruant is not onli adding to Goddis lawe,
but also contrariyng and wiþdrawing or amenusing þerfro. First it is
adding to Goddis lawe, for it passiþ þe mesure and the termys þerof.
1215 And it is amenusing of Goddis lawe, for it performeþ not but
f. 35ʳ wiþdrawiþ þat God | biddiþ to be do as anempst the forsaking of al
seche lordschip. And houȝ þis dede contrariiþ Goddis lawe, it is
open in parti of þing þat is seide before.

And so þis drunklewe seruant, þat makiþ oþur vnauisid men
1220 drunken wiþ himsilf, is þe drunken hore or strumpet þat seint Ion
spekiþ of (*Apo.* 17, 19), wher he seiþ þus þat þe grete hore þat sittiþ
upon many watris is drunken of þe blode of seinttis and martris of
Iesu. þis strumpet is þe auouȝtresse, þat I spak of before, þat agrisiþ
þe breþe of hir uerri housbonde þat schuld be Iesu Crist, and falsli
1225 haþ souȝt a deuors and doþ þe worst auouȝtriȝe aȝenst ⌐Crist⌐ and his
sede—þys vnruli woman þat sittiþ upon many watris, þat is to seie
upon meche folk or ellis upon many temperalteis. For þe grete clerk
Gorham upon þe Apocalips, bi þe flode þat is many watris
vndurstondeþ abundaunce of temperal possessions. And þis flode,
1230 as seint Ion seiþ, þe dragon cast out of his mouthe after þe woman
fleyng into desert, þe wiche woman, as Gorham seiþ, bemeneþ holi
chirche, as I wrote onys. And also olde seinttis comynli vndurstonden bi þe see þat ys a gadring of watris þis turbelous world. And
w[e]l we wete þat þis renegat þat sittiþ in þe temple sittiþ effectualli
1235 upon al þe wordli lordschip of þis world, boþ upon men and wordli
lordschippis and poscessions; and so he sittiþ upon many watris, þat |
f. 35ᵛ is to seie vpon meche peple, as þe Apocalips spekiþ. And also he
sittiþ upon many watris, þat is to seie upon many wordli possessions,
as Gorham and Parisiensis wiþ oþur olde seinttis vndurstonden. For
1240 he wol not receyue an heþon man or a Iewe to cristendome, but ȝif
he ȝilde into his hondes alle his possessions and goodis. And liȝttli
þis ypocrite takiþ him a kolour of þe gospel, wher Crist seiþ 'But if a
man renounce to alle his possessions, he mai not be my disciple.'
Naþeles, if þis fende were not iviserid wiþ couetise þat is þe rote of
1245 malice and blyndeþ him, he schold mowe se in þe gospel houȝ Crist

1219 so] also, al- *canc.*   1234 wel] wol

for al his liif here renounsid effectualli to alle wordli possessions and lordschip and wordli title, and made his disciplis of office þat were prestis to do þe same; and ȝit he suffrid many wordli men þat were his disciplis of beleue to weld her owne possessions. And so miȝt þis hore receyue al maner of men to þe feiþ and suffre hem to wilde her owne goodis, nere þe couetise of wordli lordschip þat sche haþ upon alle the world. For þis drunken quene haþ enhaunsid so proudli hir see upon many watris þat meneþ boþ peple and possessions, þat sche and nameli þe heede of hir semeþ þat an emperour or a king, þat is þe vicar of þe godheede of Iesu, is dere inouȝ for to kisse hir stinkking feete. 1250

1255

And þus, as seint Ion seiþ, kingis | han don fornycacioun wiþ this strumpet. For þou schalt vndurstonde here þat euery man in a maner schuld be a king in trew gouernaunce at þe lest of himself aftur Goddis lawe, for euery in a maner hathe a reme to gouurne. For euery man, as philisophris seien, is a world: for þou schalt fynde no notable þing in the grete world, but þou mai fynde sum þing answering þerto in man þat is þe lesse world. þo þan þat ben kinggis of erþe bi weie of office aftur þe comen vndurstonding, and also oþur simple folke þat schold be kinggis bi þis maner of witt, han don and ȝit don fornycacion wiþ þis hore. For þe grete trist and feiþfulnesse and chast beleue þat þei owen to Iesu, þat schuld be her spouse, þei ȝeuen to þis auouȝtresse þat loþiþ Cristis breþe. For ȝif þis hore make any constitucion or ordenaunce,—ȝe, be it neuer so openli aȝenst Crist and his lawe and reson bothe,— þei menteyne þat for plesaunce of þis strumpat, and ben redi at þe request of þis drunken calot to swere to hir drunken wille, and to kille any man þat wol reuerse hir. And wel we se, and alle to ofte, þat, þer as Crist seiþ and doþ o þing, þei wol beleue and do þe contrarie for þe drunken dremys þat þis fonned strumpet blaberiþ. And þis þei schewen wel in þis poynt | of wordli lordschip of the clerge. For, alþouȝ þei se wel, or mai if þei be not dampnable recheles, þat þis lordschip in the clerge is openli dampned in holi writt, boþ in þe olde lawe and in þe newe, as euer was manscleyng, auouȝtrie, tresoun or þeft, and notwiþstonding þat þe clerge [in] immesurable numbre is purueied of liiflode and heling in ful grete habundaunce bi tiþis, offrinccis and oþur deuocions of þe peple, and notwiþstonding into mentenaunce of her owne astate þei ben nedid to pele and spoile þe pore commyns bi dyuerse menys, ȝit þe astate of þe secler lordis, from the king vnto

f. 36ʳ

1260

1265

1270

1275 f. 36ᵛ

1280

1246 renounsid] re/renounsid

1285 þe lowist squyar, as for þe more partie is so bedotid upon þis strong
ladi þat þei ben redi to swere to menteyne hir in þis couetous lust þat
sche haþ to þis lordschip, and also to diȝe in þat cause, and to scle
oþur sobre folk þat kepen hem vnder þe mesure of Goddis law, and
grucchen aȝenst þe vnruli rauyng of þis drunken hore þat þristiþ
1290 aftur innocent bloode, and, as seint Ion seiþ, is drunken þerof. For bi
þe leue of hir lemman þat is drunken wiþ hir and doþ wiþ hir
fornycacion gostli from chast Crist and his lawe, to whom þei schuld
boþe be weddid for euer wiþout any deuors, sum sobir men sche
f. 37ʳ peyneþ in preson wiþout any pete, sum sche murþurreþ | þer, sum
1295 sche brenneþ openli, sum sche cursith and banischiþ and pursueþ on
diuerse wise wiþout any mercy. For, certis, þe strong ladi þat
Heraude held in auouȝtriȝe was neuer more aþrist aftur þe blode
of seint Ion þe Baptist þan þis lecherous fende, þat haþ sett hir see of
hir affeccion vpon alle þe seclere lordschip of alle þe wide world,
1300 þristiþ aftur þe blode of feiþful peple þat grucchiþ, nameli in þis
poynt aȝenst þe fornycacioun þat sche doþe aȝen Crist and his
blessid lawe. þis maner of speche of fornycacioun is not strang in
holi scripture. For þe prophete seiþ þus to God: 'þou schalt lese alle
þo þat don fornycacioun fro þe', þe wiche fornycacion stondeþ in
1305 vnfeiþfulnus aȝenst God and his lawe, and nameli in mauȝmetriȝe,
þat is unfeiþfullist, most euyn aȝenst the maieste of God, and is
callid ryueli in scripture fornycacioun.

　　Furþermore seint Ion in þe Apocalips seiþ in þe text aboue leide
þat þo þat dwellen in erþe ben made drunken of þe horedom of þis
1310 strong ladi. For aftur þe tyme þat sche began to agrise hir
housbondis breþe, þat schuld be Crist Iesu, þe wiche breþe is his
blessid lawe betokened bi þe wyne þat Crist made of watur, þe wiche
wyne gladiþ mannys hert for euer, sche chese hir a newe wyne wiche
f. 37ᵛ sche swolowiþ in stede of Cristis wyne, and is to hir | as wyne; and of
1315 this wyne tho þat dwellen in þe erthe ben made drunke, and rauen
wiþ þe wickid seruant and drunken hore þat seint Ion spekiþ of. But,
certis, þe grounde of refusing of Cristis wyne þat meruellisli
confortiþ and kepeþ men in sobirnesse, and chesing of þis wyne
þat makiþ men hornewoode, is þe grete habundaunce of temperal
1320 possessions, þe wiche þis vnclene woman occupiiþ aȝenst þe lawe of
God, for bi þis sche felle into apostasie aȝenst his lawe. If sche wold
lyue vndur any lawe, siþ sche þouȝt neuer to turne to Cristis sobre
lawe, sche most nedes forsake Cristis breþe and his purid wyne, and

　　1290 bi] bele *canc*. bi　　　　1321 his] and his　　if] þat if

take to anoþur brethe and drasti wyne of her owne tradicions. For þis
liif ys generalli, as seint Ierom seiþ in a pistil, þat whoso wol not lyue 1325
vndur Goddis lawe mai lyue vndur his owne lawe. And, certis, ⌐[þ]is
lawe þat¬ þis apostata is gouerned bi and gouerneþ oþur is like drasti
or vnfyned wyne þat is perlous to drynk. For, and seche wyne were
alle drastis, þer wold no man drinke it; and if it were wel ifyned and
ipurid, it schuld profite and not harme þe mesurable drinker. So, and 1330
þis renegattis lawe were alle fals wiþout colour of truþe, it schuld
begile no man; and if [it] were alle purid and clene wiþout lesing, þer
were no perelle in þe drinkking þerof. But nouȝ, certis, þe fende þat |
inhabitiþ þis man of synne aftur his olde craft medliþ or mengiþ f. 38ʳ
lesing wiþ trouthe in þe pseudo-prophetis mouþe, and medliþ 1335
uenym and wyne, and apoiseneþ þerwiþ Cristis chirche. þis craft
usid þe fende whan he begilid Eue, and also whan he wold haue
begilid our lord Iesu Crist, as whoso wol mai se in scripture. And of
þis poisenned wyne spekiþ þe prophete and seiþ þat 'þe vyne of þis
folk is þe vyne of Sodom, and of þe suburbis of Gomor; þe grape of 1340
hem is þe grape of galle and þe glustris most bitter. þe wyne of hem
is þe galle of dragonnesse and vncurable uenym of addris.' For riȝt as
þe frute of Sodom is feire wiþout and roten wiþynne, as Lyncolne
seiþ in a dicte, so it is of the lore of þis renegat þe grete ipocrite. And
herefor Gregor (31 *Moralia*) lickeneþ seche lore to a feire fonnyd 1345
woman. þis is like, as Salamon seiþ, to a swyne wiþ a golden rynk in
hir nostrel. For, as Gregor seiþ þer 'Heretikis lore is feire bi worde
and fonnysche bi vndurstonding.'

And, certis, þe grete delite in þe florischid enditing of mannys
tradicions drawen many curious and couetous folis to loue it and 1350
studi it, and to be besie þerin, and to sauer litil in homeli speche of
þe wisdom of God, þat conformeþ him in grete partie to þe simplist
mannys witt. But Parisiensis seiþ þat þe loue of Goddis | lawe and f. 38ᵛ
contradiccioun of decreis schuld refreyne men from þe studie of
hem. Naþeles þis newe besynes is in grete parti brouȝt into þe 1355
chirche, as I seide riȝt nouȝ, bi occasioun of þe drunkennesse of þis
yuel seruant and drunken strumpet, taking falsli, and euen aȝenst
Goddis lawe, wordli lordschip wiþ many oþur wordli besynesses
upon hir, þe wiche ben not leefful to hir. And ȝit for alle þis sche
calliþ seche possessions 'þe patrimonie of Crist icroised'; and so þei 1360
mai pertinentli be vndurstonde bi þe blode of seinttis and martris þat
made þis hore drunken as seint Ion seiþ. For þour blynde and vnruli

1326 þis] ⌐[þ]is¬

deuocioun þat folis hadden to Crist, þat is martre of martris, and of
oþur seinttis and martris, þei haue ȝeuen aȝenst þe gospel ful many
1365 lordschippis and possessions to þis grete apostata, þe wiche ben nouȝ
grounde and rote of alle vnrulinesse regnyng in þe chirche. For bi þis
is þe wickid seruant þat schuld lede Cristis peple the riȝt weie to
heuene put [out] of mesure and rule of Goddis lawe, and so, as Crist
seiþ, casting no perel of soule þat is to come, etiþ and drinkkiþ wiþ
1370 fo[l]k drunken þat ben not vndur þe mesure of Goddis lawe, neiþur
in manerys, neiþur in beleue. And so þis poynt, as I seide, among ful
many oþur þat ben longging to good manerys is ful grete, and a
f. 39ʳ notable euydence | in þe wiche þis vnmesurable apostata is fal out of
þe mesure of Goddis lawe.

1375　　　　I seide furþurmore þat among ful many poynttis þat longen to þe
beleue þis wickid and drunken seruant erriþ notabli in oon, and þat
is in þe beleue of þe sacrid ooste, in wiche he is as contrarious to
Cristis lawe and as fer out of þe mesure þerof as he mai be, as I haue
in parti declarid before. For þeras Cristis lawe techiþ þis sacrid ooste
1380 to be brede and wyne and Cristis bodi and his blode, þis drunken
dremer seiþ þat þis oost is neiþur brede ne wyne, ne Cristis bodi ne
his blode, but accidentis wiþout subiect. And so he ȝeueþ it a queynt
name and a strange from trewe philosophie and Goddis lawe, þe
wiche name as I suppose no man may conceyue ne vndurstonde for it
1385 includiþ contradiccioun. And þis renegat wiþ his special lemys, þat,
as I suppose, ben oure phariseis and scribis, besien hem bi many
menys to stablisch þis heresie as for truȝe beleue among cristen
peple, and to oppresse and to dampne þe beleue þat Crist and hys
apostlis wiþ olde seinttis han tauȝt in þis article.

1390　　　　And þus is þe prophecie of Danyel fulfillid nouȝ, wiche he spake
of antecrist vndur colour of the grete tyrant and enmye of Goddis
f. 39ᵛ lawe, Antioch, | as seiþ seint Gregor (3[2] *Moralia*) where he rehersiþ
Danyel prophesiyng þus of anticrist: 'He haþ cast dowun of þe
strengþe of þe mone ⌈and⌉ of þe sterris and he haþ troden hem. And
1395 he is magnefiid anone to þe prince of strengþe, and from him he haþ
taken aweie the besie sacrifice. And he haþ cast downe þe place of þe
halowing of him. Forsoþ, strengþe is ȝeue to him aȝenst þe besie
sacrifice for synnes. And truȝe schal be þrist or cast adowne in þe
weie; and he schal do and be in prosperite.' And as me semeþ
1400 experience openeþ nouȝ alle þis prophesie of Danyel: for þis grete
apostata and renegat haþ cast downe of þe strenthe, for he haþ cast

1392 32] 31

downe and vndo of þe secler lordis whom Poule calliþ potestatis or
strengþis (*Ro*.13),—ȝe, as I suppose of þe more partie of cristendom.
For he haþ cast downe the emperour þat schuld be chiff potestate of
cristendome, and amenusid his power and state, and brouȝt him so 1405
lowe þat he mai not bere up his heede; for he demeþ an emperour
unneþe worþi to kisse his fete, alþouȝ he were sumtyme his lord and
his maister. And if þis viserid fende, so ful of Luciferis pride, sett his
fete upon þe emp[er]ouris heede and crowneþ him wiþ his stinkking
feete, Danielis prophesie in þis poynt is more openli verefiid of | the f. 40ʳ
grete bodi of antecrist that approueþ thys vnmesurable pride in þe 1411
heede þerof. þis renegat haþe also cast downe of þe comente, þat is
betokened bi sterris þat ben many, and þat not onli into synne, bi
wiþdrawing of Goddis lawe in worde and dede, but also he haþ
chastisid hem so þat þei schul not be so hardi onys openli to grucche 1415
aȝenst his most passing abhomynacions, ne auenge hemself, haue þei
neuer so meche wrong, ne detecte the auouȝtrie of oon of his special
lemys, alþouȝ he fynde him upon his wiif, but raþur hele hem and
lete hem liȝe stille. þus þan, as Danyel seiþ, haþ þis antecrist cast
downe þe sterris and troden hem vndur fote! 1420

And þus is þis renegat magnefied anoon to þe prince of strengþe.
For, as Gregor seiþ þer, he is enhaunsid aȝen þe Auctour of uertu or
power. And þis word of Danyel is al oon, as Gregor seiþ vpon Poulis
worde, wher he seiþ of þis apostata þat he sittiþ in temple schewing
himself as he be God. And, as it sueþ furþurmore in Danielus texte, 1425
þis renegat haþ take from Iesu, þat is þe prince of strengþe, þe besie
sacrifice. þis besie sacrifice mai betoken veri repentaunce, of þe
wiche sacrifice þe prophete seiþ þus: 'A soriful spirit is a sacrifice to
God.' And this sacrifice | most nedis be riȝt besie and ryue. For, þouȝ f. 40ᵛ
a man lyue neuer so wel here, he synneþ ful ofte, as seint Austen 1430
seiþ, alegging for him Cypriannys sentence in *De dono perseuerancie*
þe wiche Austen approueþ þer; and Gregor haþ þe same sentence (8
Moralia) and in many oþur placis of olde seinttis þis sentence is ful
ryue and nameli in Austens bokis. þan, for as meche as men ben here
ful of fauȝtis and adden many synnys dai bi dai oon upon anoþur, 1435
and þis sacrifice of uerri forþenking is chiff remedie aȝenst seche
fauȝtis, wherfor þe besie sacrifice þat Danyel spekiþ of mai wel
betoken þis sacrifice of verri repentaunce, þat schuld be contynuel in
worde or dede or in bothe, and þis sacrifice of uerri contriscioun mai
wel be figurid bi the continuel fire þat schuld be upon þe auter 1440

1409 emperouris] emp*ou*ris

norschid bi þe prest iche dai, leiȝing woode þerto (as it is wreten *Leu.*
6). For, as þat fire upon þe auter wastid þe mater þat it brent, so
uerri contriscioun in a feiþ[ful] hert wastiþ synne to nouȝt. And
prestis schuld norische þis feruent fire of contriscioun, bi holi
1445 ensample and bi ful trewe preching, and bi uerri forsaking of þe
lordschip of þis world wiþ alle þe liking þat sueþ þerof. But antecrist
f. 41ʳ haþ nouȝ pissid out þe fire bi his yuyl ensample and stopping | of
Goddis lawe, and wiþ cold muddi water of his owne tradicions and
his large vngrounded absolucions þat bolden men to synne, as
1450 experiens techiþ.

Naþeles, alþouȝ þis be a trewe witt answering to Danyellus wordis
as þe dede schewiþ, ȝit we mai haue anoþur ful trewe witt upon þe
same wordis, vndurstonding bi þis besie sacrifice the blessid sacrament of þe auȝter, þe wiche is nouȝ þe most besie and most ryue
1455 sacrament þat I know usid in þe chirche. þis besie sacrifice was and
schuld be Cristis sacrifice or sacrament þat is þe prince of strengthe,
for he ordeyned þis and was þe first auctour þerof. But nouȝ
antecrist þat euenneþ himself to þis prince, as Danyel seiþ, haþ
take aweie þis besie sacrifice from þis prince. For þis renegat þat
1460 renoieþ openli Goddis lawe wol not þat any man take þe beleue of
þis sacrament bi þe auctorite of Crist and his lawe, but þat euery
man wiþ him reuerse and reneie alle þat Cristis lawe techiþ in þis
poynt, and þat he take þe beleue of þe sacrid oost bi þe auctorite of
his ful holi and most autentik determynacioun, þe wiche is euyn
1465 contrarie to alle þat Cristis lawe techiþ of þe beleue of þis sacrament,
f. 41ᵛ as it is seide before. | And moreouur this renegat, in as meche as in
hym is, besieþ himself þat Crist schuld not be this blessid oost. But
here þou most vndurstonde þat al Crist, as seint Austen seiþ ofte
upon þe Psauȝter, is Crist wiþ his chosyn lemys, þat makiþ wiþ þe
1470 hede oo bodi; and alle his holi bodi, þat takiþ liif and meuyng of þat
holi heede and is onyd bi hote loue to þat heede, schal be an
euerlasting sacrifice or preising, of wiche God seiþ þat 'þe sacrifice
of preising schal wirschip me.' þis ⸢is⸣ [þe] reme þat we praien in
oure Pater noster schuld come to God; and þis reme, as Poule
1475 meneþ, Crist at þe dai of dome schal betake to þe Fader. And þis
sacrefice was groundli sacrificed to þe Fadur in Crist vpon þe cros.
And of þis seint Austen spekiþ þus [10 *De ciuitate* [*Dei*]]: 'Forsoþ, þe
gadring and þe felischip of seinttis is offrid in vniuersal sacrifice to
God bi þe grete prest, þat offrid himself in þe passion for us, þat we
1480 myȝt be þe bodi of so grete an heed.' And so aftur he seiþ in þe same

boke: 'þis is þe sacrifice of cristen men: "Many oo bodi in Crist".
And þis þing', as seint Austen seiþ, 'þe chirche vsiþ in þe sacrament
of þe auter iknow to þe peple.' For not | onli Crist as touching his   f. 42ʳ
personal manhede, but also al Crist, heed and bodi, is offrid to God
in þis blessid oost.   1485

And whi þis bodi is raþur offrid in brede and wyne þan in oþur
þinggis seint Austen techiþ in a sermon (*De pascha*) wher he seiþ
þus: 'Зif þou wilt vndurstonde þe bodi of Crist, here þou þe apostle
seiyng to feiþful men "Зe ben þe bodi of Crist and þe lemys".' And
þan he answeriþ to þis question þus: 'Bring we forþe here no þing of   1490
oure owne witt, but here we eft and eft þe apostle whan he, speking
of þe sacrament, seide "Oo brede oo bodi many be we": vndurstonde
зe and be зe glade, and beþenke зe þat brede is not made of oo corne,
but of many. Whan зe we[re] exorciзed, зe were in a maner igrounde.
Whan зe were cristened, зe were sprengid; and so in a maner made   1495
into paast, and afturword ibake and isaddid bi hote loue.' For þes þre
þinggis, þat is to seie knowleching of synne wiþ grete sorow,
cristenyng in þe water and in þe Holi Goost, and hote loue maken
alle þe chosyn of God to be þus oonyd wiþ Crist her heed, and so to
be oo bodi in Crist, and eche personal parte of þis bodi to be a lyme 1500
of þe same. And herfor bi þe vse of cristendom tauзt bi Crist and his
apostlis, whan any man or woman wol become a lyme of þis bodi,
first bi | himself or mene persone he knowlechiþ his synnys wiþ   f. 42ᵛ
sorowe and forsaking of hem, and aftur þis he is cristened in watur
and in þe Holi Gost, and þan he takiþ upon him þe rule of þe   1505
comaundementis, þe wiche is þe hote and þe charitable loue of his
God and his neiзbore. And aftur þis he vsiþ þe sacrid oost þat is þe
blessid bodi, in tokenyng þat he is incorporat into þe same bodi as a
lyme þerof. And þis mystik bodi of Crist is multepliid of þe whete
corne þat Crist spekiþ of, þe wiche fel into þe erthe and was dede,   1510
and so multipliid into meche frute oonyd in Iesu Crist, rote and heed
þerof. And it is betokened into þe sacrid oost þat is many whete
cornys onyd togedre bi craft of man, and uereli is þe bodi of Crist bi
uertu and wirching of his worde; and so it is boþe figurre and truthe.
For seint Poule seiþ þat 'Alle we þat ben many comoun of oo loff and   1515
of oo bodi.' And her seint Austen conseilid alle cristen men þus in þe
same sermon 'Be зe þat зe seen, and take зe þat þing þat зe ben. þis
haþ þe apostle seide of þe brede'—so þat seint Austen meneþ here
þat cristen men schuld be þat þing þe wiche þei seen, and þat is

1515 comoun] and comoun

1520 brede. 'For þat þe iȝen schewyn wel,' as seint Austen seiþ in þe same
sermon, þe wiche brede Poule calliþ oo loof, þat is sacramenttalli and
uereli þis onyd mystik bodi of Crist; and if men ben þus þat þing þe |
f. 43ʳ wiche þei seen, þan þei taken þat þing þat þei ben; for þei taken þe
sacrid oost, þe wiche is Cristis mystik bodi figurali and uerreli, þe
1525 wiche þe peple is þe same bodi reali and uerreli. And þus as seint
Austen seiþ þer to Cristis chirche 'ȝif ȝe be þe bodi of Crist and þe
membris, ȝour mysterie is putt in þe Lordis borde.' And ȝe han take
ȝour mysterie to þat þing þat ȝe ben,' for seche peple is uerri Cristis
bodi, of wiche þe sacrid oost is mysterie, figure and sacrament and
1530 truthe. Furþermore in þe foreseide sermon of Estur Austen seiþ þus
to þe sacrament of þe chalis: 'Nouȝ houȝ [ȝ]e schul vndurstonde of
þe chalice, þat þing þat is nouȝ[t] seide schewiþ wel inouȝ. Forsoþ,
as many cornys [ben] sprengid or wett togedre þat visible kinde ⌈of
brede⌉ be made, as þouȝ þat þing were don þat scripture seiþ of
1535 feiþful peple "To wiche peple was oo hert and oo soule into God",
so my breþerne beþenke ȝe of þe wyne, wherof is wyne: many cornys
of grapis hanggen at a glustre, but þe likour of þes grapis is hilt into
an vnyte. So oure lord Crist is betokend us, and wold us perteyne to
hymself; and he haþe halowid the mysterie of our pees and vnyte in
f. 43�v his borde. Whoso takiþ þe mysterie of vnyte and | holdeþ not þe
1541 bonde of pees, he takiþ not misterie for himsilf but wittnesse aȝenst
himself.'

Siþ þan Cristys mystik bodi, heed and lymys, schuld be þis sacrid
oost of brede and wyne and aȝenward, as Poule and Austen wiþ oþur
1545 olde seinttis techen, and seche a sacrament is propurli a uisible forme
or kynde of an vnuisible grace, and in antecristis sacrament is no
uisible forme or kinde, wiche forme or kinde uisible myȝt be þis
mystik bodi of Crist, but if antecrist wold seie þat þis bodi schuld be
þe accidentis wiþout soiect þat he spekiþ of (þe wiche a uiserid fende
1550 myȝt not seie for schame). Hit is open inouȝ houȝ þis renegat þat
eueneþ himself to þe Prince of strengþe haþ take from him, as meche
as in him is, þe beleue of þe besie sacrefice—and not onli bereuyng
Crist of þe fundement and auctorite of þis sacrament, as it is seide
before, but also as meche as he mai [he] besieþ himself þat Crist heed
1555 and bodi be not þe sacrament as it is schewid. For antecrist hatiþ þis
sentence þat þis Crist heed and bodi be oo brede and oo bodi. And
þerfor he wol haue it þus in effect, þat is to seie: as alle þis special
antecrist, þat is þe grete ipocrite, þat haþ licknesse or signys bi treuȝe

1531 ȝe] he   1534 þat¹] þat/þat

legeaunce or feiþfulnes to God wiþ|out the truþis answering to tho f. 44ʳ
signys, as Poule spekiþ of þe same antecrist, so þis sacrament schal 1560
haue no subiect or substance in itself, but it schal haue alle þe
outward accidentis and signys of substance or kinde wiþout substaunce or kinde answering þerto. And certis seche a sacrament, and
any seche my3t be, wolde wel answere to þe grete bodi of antecrist
þat is a double ipocrite!—but it wol not acorde wiþ Cristis chosen 1565
bodi, þat is simple and as trewe or trewer þan it semeþ. And herfor
Crist þat is heed of þis bodi wold þat alle seche men schuld deme of
þe dedis of himsilf and his lymes, and be wel war of pseudo þat schul
3eue signes and merueillis to bring alle most þe chosen to errour.

But antecrist bostiþ 3it of þes signes wiþout substance, and seiþ 1570
þat þei haue þe same worching in norsching and in eching of mannys
bodi as haþ brede and wyne, and þat þe accidentis schal haue the
same name as had her substancis or schuld haue 3if þei abode stille
aftur þe consecracion. And, certis, whoso wol mai beleue þis!—and
whoso wol, þat þe grete ipocrite antecrist nou3 and long her afore 1575
regnyng wiþ his ipocrisie, þat is as it were an accident wiþout soiect, |
and is as effectif and spediþ in þe bodi of Cristis chirche, and as wel f. 44ᵛ
echiþ it and norischiþ it as dede Crist and his apostlis, and so worþi
to haue þe same name wiþ Crist and his apostlis, þat ben uerreli þe
brede þat Poule spekiþ of! And herfor þis antecrist, notwiþstonding 1580
þat him fau3tiþ þe substaunce of truthe and so is a ueri ipocrite, 3it
he presumeþ to be callid apostle or apostlich man. But leue þis bost
of antecrist whoso wol! For, certis, I leue no dele þis bost of
antecrist, ne schal wiþ Goddis leeue while he wol lende me my
ri3t witt, alþou3 I were artid to seie þe contrarie bi greuous peyne. 1585

þus þan haþ antecrist power a3enst þe besie sacrifice or signes.
For, as Gregor seiþ upon þe same worde of Danyel, 'þe aduersarie
my3t not haue hem þat ri3tfulli beleued, but if þe synnys of þo þat
perrischen schul aske þat.' Herefor Iob seiþ þat 'God makiþ an
ipocrite man to regne for synnes of þe peple.' For, as Gregor seiþ 1590
upon þe same word, 'Bicause þat þe Iewis wolde not þe ueri king,
þat is God, to regne upon hem, þerfor here meritis asking þei toke an
ipocrite', as Saul and many oþur ipocritis aftur him. So, as Gregor
rehersiþ þer 'þe Truþe seiþ in þe gospel, "I haue come in my Fadris
name, and 3e haue not receiuid me; | 3if anoþur or ellis an alien schal f. 45ʳ
come in his owne name, him 3e schal receyue."' And þis alien, as 1596
Gregor meueþ here and also Austen (*De uerbis Domini*), is antecrist.

1568 be] to be   1575 þat] *twice*   1594 seiþ] and seiþ

And Gregor to þis same purpos rehersiþ Poule seiyng þus: 'For as
meche as þe peple haþ not take þe charite of truthe þat þei myȝt be
1600 made saff, þerfor God schal sende to hem wirching of errour, þat þei
beleue to lesing', þat is to seie to antecrist þat is þis ipocrite. And þan
Gregor spekiþ furþurmore vpon þe same text þus: 'In þat worde þat
scripture seiþ "God makiþ an ipocrite to regne for synnes of þe
peple" mai antecrist, þe heed of al ipocritis, be undurstonde or
1605 betokened. For þat disceyuer þan feyneþ holynesse, þat he drawe
men to wickidnesse. But for þe synnes of þe peple he is suffrid to
regne; for no wondur alle þouȝ þei be þan ordeyned undur þe
gouernaunce of him, the wiche were iknow before þe world worþi his
lordschip.' And as touching þe lemys of þis heed antecrist, Gregor
1610 spekiþ þus: 'Be not þei þe lemys of him þat desiren to be seen þat þei
be not bi a lickenesse or colour of holinesse desired? Forsoþ, he
principali takiþ ipocrisie upon him þat feineþ himself to be Godd
f. 45ᵛ whan | he is a dampnyd man and no spirit. And wiþout douȝt nouȝ
þei comyn forþ out ⌐of⌐ his bodi, þe wiche hiden wickidnesse vndur
1615 a keuur of holi honour; so þat þei desiren to be seien bi professioun
þat þei refusen to be in workis.'

Lo, houȝ þis olde clerk wiþ Austen and wiþ oþur mesuriþ his
wordis and writing of antecrist, so þat þei mai truli be applied to þe
grete ipocrite and renegat þat I haue ofte spoke of, þe wiche is on þe
1620 worst wise most contrarious to Crist, and so þe worst antecrist; to
whom is ȝeue strengþe aȝenst þe besie sacrefice, and so he haþ take
þe beleue of þe besie sacrifice from Crist and þerwiþ, it is to drede,
þe uertuous wirching þerof from þe peple. For houȝ mai he profite
to himself or to þe peple þat beleueþ not as Crist haþ tauȝt? And þus
1625 antecrist, heed of heretikis, haþ don grete uiolens aȝenst Crist and
his lawe in ful many poynttis, in þe wiche he reuersiþ obstinatli
Goddis lawe boþe in maneres and in beleue. For þou schalt
vnderstonde here þat it is þe condicions of heretikis, as Gregor
seiþ (18 *Moralia*), þat 'þei bi uiolens enforcen hemself to bowe to
f. 46ʳ here lewde vndurstonding þe sentence of holi scripture | contenyng
1631 riȝtful loris. And so, alþouȝ thei be not violent to mennys goodis, ȝit,
certis, þei ben uiolent to þe wittis of Goddis lawe or his heestis.'

But Gregor spekiþ of heretikis of his time þat were violent and
dede strengþe aftur her wittis aȝen holi scripture. But nouȝ, as þe
1635 dede expounneþ, þe grete heretik and renegat antecrist doþ wondur
grete uiolence aȝenst feiþful men in her goodis and bodiis bi spoiling,

1633 violent] þa *canc.* violent

presounyng and killing. Ouer þis he doþe uyolens aȝenst her soulis,
in bereuyng hem þe brede of Goddis worde þat schuld be her liif and
her sustenaunce, as þe gospel seiþ. But ȝit grettist uiolens as me
semeþ doþe he aȝenst God and his lawe whan he dampneþ it as he   1640
ofte doþ for heresie, or drawiþ þat to his cursid word and lyuyng, as
contrari to Cristis witt, worde and wille as he mai deuise. I prai þe,
what uiolence is þis aȝenst Crist and his lawe þat þis grete antecrist
wiþ alle his special lemys, vndur colour of Cristis lawe and his name,
þe wiche þei taken falseli upon hemself, wherfor Crist calliþ hem   1645
pseudo-prophetis? For þei enforcen hemself to iustefiȝe in worde
an[d] dede her wordli lordschip, her | wordli lawis, iugementis, office   f. 46ᵛ
and custumable begging, dampned expresseli bi Crist ⌐and⌐ his
apostlis and oþur feiþful prestis and peple in þe begynnyng of
Cristis chirche,—and þat in worde and dede and writing left in holi   1650
scripture into perpetual memorie to alle þe world. And no drede þe
tradicions of phariseis teching þe children to seie *Corbona* to her
eldris was not so violent aȝenst Goddis lawe as ben þe tradicions of
þis grete renegat sitting in þe chirche, reneiyng Goddis lawe in
himsilf and arting oþur to do þe same. For sacrefice deuȝli don is   1655
plesing to God, alþouȝ þe child aȝenst þe lore of þe phariseis houȝt
raþur to releue his fader and his modur þan offre þat releuyng to
God in þe temple; and þus newe cloþe and olde, and newe wyne and
olde botellis, wherbi Crist vndurstondeþ his owne lawe and þe
tradicions of ipocritis þat Crist fonde here, wold wiþ lesse violens   1660
haue be glosid togedre þan þe tradicion of þis grete antecrist and of
many oþur ipocrite sectis incorporat in him.

And þus is þis grete heretik wondur violent aȝenst God and his
lawe in þo poynttis þat I haue spoke of, and in ful many mo þan I
can or euer schal mowe beþenk me on. And nameli he goþe wondur   1665
violentli a|ȝenst the beleue of the sacred oost þat I speke of nouȝ. For   f. 47ʳ
in þis article he goþ euen aȝenst Goddis lawe as it mai be þouȝt. And
so bi þis violence he enforsiþ him to acorde oo contradictorie wiþ
anoþur; and þat mai neuer be do, siþ contradiccion is contrariyng or
a wiþseiyng wiþout any mene. And so none of þo wordis or lawis þat   1670
ben contradictorie mai be brouȝt to acorde ne to a mene. And it is
open inouȝ of þing wreten before þat Cristis law and antecristis
determynacioun ben not onli contradictorie in uoice or worde, but
also in witt and in þe þinggis þat þe wordis betoken. And whoso wol
loke antecristis tradicions in þis mater, he schal se houȝ þis uyolens is   1675
do wiþout auctorite of God⟨di⟩s reson and olde determynacion of

Cristis chirche,—ȝhe, a⟨n⟩d wiþout experience or olde use of þe
chirche or olde doctouris sentence. And þus þis violent witt comeþ
of his owne proude wille þat answeriþ to þe grete boost of his power,
1680 of þe wiche is no mesure as his special lemys bostfulli presumen.
And alþouȝ he had for his parte olde doctourris sentence and newe,
and þe auctorite and determynacioun of þe chirche, and reson as fer
as pure mannys witt mai strecche, or þe use of þe chirche, ȝit alle þis
f. 47ᵛ were not worthe | a piȝe hele in a poynt of beleue wiþout expresse
1685 auctorite of Goddis lawe. For onli of God or of his lawe þis schort
forme of arguyng is good and strong: God or his law affermeþ þis,
þerfor þis is feiþ to be beleu⟨ed⟩; or ellis God or Goddis lawe
defendeþ þis, þerfore þis auȝt not to be do. þis maner of argument
founded upon God and his lawe is strong inouȝ wiþout any faute, for
1690 it halt bi þis necessarie mene þat God mai not erre. And so þis
argument is nouȝt: pure mannes reson, or vse of þe chirche, mannys
determynacioun, or doctour sentence determeneþ or dampneþ þis,
þan þis auȝt to be take as beleue or auoided as heresie. For siþ euery
man ⟨bi⟩ himsilf is synful and a lier, and alle þe men ⟨in⟩ þe world
1695 synnen and liȝen, þis argument wantiþ þe necessarie mene þat I
spake of riȝt nouȝ. And, as I suppos, antecrist schal alle besie for his
parte in þis poynt [to] fynde a colo⟨ur⟩ of scripture! For Goddis lore
in þis beleue and antecristis determynacion, as I seide riȝt nouȝ, ben
so openli repungnyng þat þei mai not be brouȝt to acorde; and so þat
1700 oon in processe of tyme mote nedis were out þe toþur.
f. 48ʳ   And | pure mannys r[e]son without grounde of Crist Iesu, þat is so
nedeful grounde, as Poule seiþ, þat no man mai put anoþur grounde,
is none euidence in an article of beleue. And, as touȝching þe
euidence of þe vse of þe chirche, þat peple þat is nouȝ callid chifli
1705 þe chirche wol not, ne vseþ to calle þe sacrament brede or wyne,
alþouȝ we rede in olde legend⟨e⟩ of seint Dyonise houȝ þe chirche
þat tyme used to calle þis sacrament 'brede þat is ibroke', as Dyonyse
wrote in his daiis aftur þe logic and informacion of Poule his maister,
þe wiche lernyd in heuene of Iesu Crist wiþout any mene. þan, siþ
1710 þe vse of þe chirche not onli uarieþ, but also in dyuerse tymes
con⟨trar⟩iiþ þis poynt, and þe truþe of God, as þe ⟨pro⟩phe[te] seiþ,
abideþ euer, þis is none euydence wiþout faile or euydence of beleue,
and nameli nouȝ after þe losing of ⟨Sa⟩thanas. 'þe chirche vsiþ to
specke of beleue ⟨þ⟩us of þe sacrid oost, þerfor þis is verri beleu⟨e⟩.'
1715   And as touching experience, wel we know þat experience preueþ

1680 his] and his   1701 reson] roson   1712 abideþ] and *canc.* abideþ

no dele þe newe determynacioun of þe chirche but raþur þe
contrarie, as doþe scripture. But as touȝching þe beleue þat Cristis
lawe techiþ in þis article, þat is to seie þat þe sacrid oost | is brede f. 48ᵛ
and Goddis bodi, experience [doþ] þe first, and þe beleue of Cristis
lawe doþ þe first and þe secunde, as seint Austen seiþ in his sermon 1720
De pascha, as I rehersid long before, and holi scri⟨p⟩ture rehersid
before confermeþ Austens wordis. And, as touȝching þe euydence
þat antecrist schuld haue in þis mater bi any determynacioun of þe
chirche aftur þe losyng of þe fende or before, þe determynacioun of
Innocent and his comperis, chifli brouȝt in and menteyned in þe 1725
chirche bi labour of þe newe sectis, þat God hatid to be plantid in þe
chirche, I am ware of noone olde determynacioun þat antecrist kan
leiȝe for his parte in þis poynt. For I suppose þat þer was neuer oþur
determynacioun in þis article þan expresse Goddis lawe into þat
tyme. ⟨And⟩ no wondur, for þis beleue was fulli determenyd ⟨bi him⟩ 1730
þat kouȝde not ne myȝt ⟨erre⟩, Iesu Crist, and full⟨i⟩ accept and
stablischid in his chirche,—ȝe, so ferforþ as I suppose þat antecrist
schal neuer mow wer⟨e⟩ out þe determynacioun bi his newe and
contrar⟨ie⟩ tradicioun, alþouȝ vndur þe name of holi chirche (þe
wiche name ful faseli antecrist takiþ upon hymsilf, as Austen techiþ 1735
De ciuitate Dei li. 20 ca. 19). þis renegat usiþ his owne determyna-
cioun as a stumblyng stole while þe candil is | out, and besiiþ himself f. 49ʳ
to make men fal þer that grucchen aȝenst his wordli lordschip and
vngrounded begging. For no douȝte drede of lesing of wordli
possessions is chiff cause of antecristis persecucioun, alþouȝ 1740
false⟨li⟩ he feyne þe contrarie, not articling aȝenst any man þis
lordschip as cause of his persecucioun.

But, certis, I merueile meche here of þe presumpcion of þis newe
determynacioun in a poynt so fulli determened before bi God and his
lawe, in þe wiche þe chirche was quietid into þe vnbinding of 1745
Sathanas, transfigurid into diuerse sectis þat biiogelen þe peple wiþ
her meruellous signys of kunnyng and holynesse. For þe determynacion was wiþout any nede, alþouȝ it had be as wel acording ⟨wiþ⟩
scripture as it is euen contrarie þerto. For ⟨se⟩int Austen seiþ in De
ieiunio sabbati 'In þo ⟨þ⟩inggis, in þe wi⟨che⟩ scripture haþ no þing 1750
ordeined or determened of certeyn, þe custum of the peple or þe
ordenaunce of þe gretter men ben to be holden for lawe.' Siþþen þan
God in his law had putt in certeyn and fulli wiþout faute determened

1718 brede . . . bodi (1719)] goddis bodi and brede   1740 antecristis] word canc.
antecristis

þe feiþ in þis article, and [þe] feiþful peple was fulli quietid in Cristis
1755 determynacioun, what nede was it to pope Innocent wiþ his new
sectis to attempte or to make a new determynacion in þis | poynt?—
f. 49ᵛ and nameli so contrarious to Cristis lawe, stablischid as beleue, and
euer continued for uerri feiþ among feiþful peple. Certis, I kan not se
no nede of þis newe determynacioun so contrarious to Crist, but if it
1760 were to fulfil þe prophecie of Daniel seiyng þat 'To antecrist is iȝeue
power aȝenst þe besiȝe sacrifice', as it is seide afore. For wel I wote
þat sum antecrist most nedis fulfil þat propheciȝe!

And so þat renegat so reneiyng Goddis lawe is in þe case of
Vincent uictor, of whom seint Austen writiþ þus in his boke *Ad*
1765 *Petrum presbiterum de origine anime*, wher seint Austen rehersiþ þe
opunion of þis Vincent, affermyng þat þo þat were ibore in original
synne schuld entre into þe blisse of heuene alþouȝ þei were not bore
aȝen of water and of þe Holi Goost. And þis foole ⟨seiþ⟩ þat men
schuld holde his parte and opunynoun in þis m⟨ater⟩, alþouȝ þe
1770 principal senten⟨s be⟩ aȝenst him, þe wi⟨che⟩ principal sentens, as
þ⟨e⟩ sa⟨m⟩e Vincent seiþ, is þe go⟨spel⟩ wher Crist seiþ þus 'But if a
man be bore eftesonys of watur and of þe Holi Gost, he mai not entre
into ⟨þe⟩ reme of heuenes.' And, certis, whoso take hede schal se þat
antecrist presumeþ as yuel or wors in his determynacion of þe sacrid
1775 oost þan dede Vincent in his opunioun. For he seiþ in worde and
f. 50ʳ dede þat whateuer Goddis lawe seiþ in þe article of | the sacrid oost,
alþouȝ it be or schuld be þe princepal sentens, ȝit his ful holi
determynacion is to be holde in þis poynt or parte, alþouȝ Cristis
sentence contrarie or wiþstonde it. And þus þe presumpcioun of
1780 antecrist is meche more þan was Vincentis. For Vincent supposid in
his writing þe gospel to be chiff sentence, and I kan not se þat
antecrist wol suppose þat in þis article, ne in þe mater of his wordli
lordschip, or of his symonie, or of oþur poynttis þat his lust is sett
upon wiþout grounde of Goddis lawe. And þis grete apostata wiþ his
1785 newe sectis, þat ben his special lemys to bere him, bi magnefiyng of
his power is þe most schameles heretik þat euer was. For where oþur
heretikis, as we mai ⟨red⟩e in Austens bokis and Ieromys, wolde seke
co⟨lour⟩ of scripture, þis renegat sitting in þe ⟨ch⟩irche reckiþ lit⟨il⟩
⟨of⟩ seche colourris, but wiþout ⟨c⟩har⟨it⟩e affermeþ obstinatli his
1790 owne wille, as we mai se specialli in þe poynt of his wordli
lord⟨s⟩chip, and in þe article of þe sacrid oost, and in ful many
oþur poynttis in þe wiche he reckiþ not houȝ euen and openli he go
aȝenst Crist and his lawe, notwiþstonding þat þe gospelle schuld be

þe rule of þe prelacie from þe hiȝest unto þe lowist. And what ioie
seint Austen | wold haue had of this renegat, that goþ so heedli f. 50ᵛ
aȝenst Goddis lawe, a man ma⟨i⟩ vndurstonde bi his writing aȝenst 1796
þis Vincent, wher Austen seiþ þus: 'Miȝt any man in þis cause of
errour haue a larger fole foli or presumpcion? For Vincent recordeþ
and myndeþ þe Lordis sentence and put it in his writing and feiþ,
alþouȝ þe principal sentence wiþstonde, þat is "But if a man be efte 1800
ibore of water and of þe Holi Gost, he mai not entre into þe kingdom
of heuene", ȝit he is bolde to rere up þe polle of his iugement aȝen þe
principal sentence!' And þan Austen seiþ to Peter þe prest 'Nouȝ
þerfor, I beseche þe my broþur, haue consideracion what sentence
schal he deserue to haue of þe prince, Crist, þat assentiþ to any man 1805
aȝenst þe princepal sentens?' And of þes word⟨is⟩ of Austen þou
maist coniect what Austen wold h⟨aue⟩ felid of þis antecrist, þat
eu⟨ene⟩þ himself to þe princ⟨e⟩ of strengþe, and haþ take from him
þe besiȝe sacrifi⟨ce⟩, and iȝeue a sentence and a determynacioun
aȝenst the same prince and his prinspal sentence, and wol þ⟨at⟩ alle 1810
men beleue it, and artiþ men to leeue þe princepal sentence of
Goddis lawe and to holde his determynacioun in þis article of þe
sacrid oost and in ful many oþur.

þou maist se in þis processe furþurmore houȝ streitli Austen
stondeþ upon þe text of þe gospel, | þat seiþ 'But if a man be bore f. 51ʳ
aȝen of watur and of the Holi Gost, he mai not entre into þe reme of 1816
heuenes.' For Austen kan in ⟨no⟩ wise behote euerlasting blisse to
⟨þ⟩o þat ben not cristened i⟨n⟩ þ⟨e⟩ tyme of þe newe lawe, bicause
þat þei haue ori⟨g⟩inal synne þat is not wasche aweie in water and in
þe Holi Gost, wiþout þe wiche wasching no man mai come to blisse, 1820
as þe gospel seiþ. 'And as streitli toke þe consail of þe bischoppis þis
texte of þe gospel, whan þei dampned þe heresie of þe Pelligianys,
bihoting blisse to uncristened children', as Austen seiþ *Ad Petrum*
presbiterum. And as streitli takiþ þe chirche now þe same wordis of
Crist as touȝching þe nedefulnes of þe sacrament of baptym, so þat 1825
þei meuen wiþ þe gospel and seint Austen and oþur doctouris þat, al
if þe frendis of þe childe do alle here besynesse in keping of þe
⟨chil⟩de, and in hasting of þe childe to þe sacrament, ⟨and⟩ alþouȝ
þei kun asigne no fauȝte in þe childe ⟨wh⟩i it is not cristene⟨d⟩, ȝit
þei holden Cristis wordis ⟨so⟩ streitli here þat þei kun not seie but 1830
þat seche ⟨a⟩ child most nedes be dampned; and ⟨þ⟩ei demen ⟨h⟩em
for heretikis þat piteuousli hopen seche a child bi grace of þe Holi
Gost to come to euerlasting blisse. But ȝit þes ipocritis, þat holden so

streitli þe sentence of þe gospel in þis poynt þat sounneþ no þing
1835 aȝenst her wordli lordschip, lust and liking, as openli as þei mai, þei
f. 51ᵛ gon | [aȝen] þe gospel in the mater of her wordlinesse and in the
article of þe sacrid oost, and ful many oþur poyntis of truȝe beleue.
And þus þis renegat wiþ his retinew is like Makameet and his meyne,
dampnyng and auctorizing, refusing and taking what hem list of þe
1840 gospel.

And þus I am war of noo determynacion of þe chirche þat
antecrist haþ for his parte, deniyng our blessid sacrament of þe
auȝter to be brede and wyne, saue þe woode rauyng of mysproude
Innocent and his comperis and newe vngrounded sectis. Naþeles I
1845 wote wel þat it is croniclid in decreis houȝ þat, in þe tyme of pope
Nichol, a clerk Beringarie bi name, defamed of heresie in þe beleue
of þe sacrid oost, knowlechid aftur þe riȝt logik of scripture þat þe
brede and þe wyne þat ben put in þe auȝter ben aftur þe
consecracion not onli a sacrament, but also þe u⟨erri⟩ bodi and
1850 blode of our lord Iesu Crist. And þi⟨s⟩ knowleche of þis beleue, ⟨a⟩s
Beringarie seiþ ⟨þer⟩, he toke of pope Nichol and þe holi seen of an
hu⟨n⟩drid and fourtene bischopis þan present. þe wick⟨id⟩ seen toke
þe beleue to Beringarie no þing of ⟨her⟩ auctorite but of þe auctorite
of Crist and hys apostlis. And in ful euydence þat þis confession was
1855 at þat tyme þe beleue of alle holi chirche, þis seen of þe pope and
f. 52ʳ bischopis senten þis confession into alle cristendome, as fer as the |
wickid fame of this foreseid Beringarie myȝt come, þat þe feiþful
peple ⟨þ⟩at were sori for þat peruertid man myȝt be glad of his
conuersioun. And wel mai we vndurstonde here þat þis ⟨c⟩o⟨n⟩fes-
1860 sion of Beringarie schuld not a gladen þe seen þan present and aftur
al cristendome, but if cristendome þan had errid in þat poynt and
wold haue drawe Beringarie to the same, or ellis Beringarie had errid
in þis article and þe feiþful chirche gladen his conuersioun; and þat
nouȝ alle men supposen. And no man supposiþ þe raþur, but if it be
1865 þes newe determynouris þat presumen to amende Goddis lawe bi her
contrarious determynacioun. Or ellis her hertis ben so hard endured
þat þei mowe not beleue it to be possible to God to make þe brede
and þe wyne put in þe auȝter to be his flesche and his blode, þe
brede ⟨an⟩d ⟨þ⟩e wyne abiding stille in her substaunce ⟨and⟩ kynde;
1870 for it is alle oon to denie þis as ⟨to⟩ denyȝe þat Crist mai not be God
and man togedur, as many heretikis han don, as Valentyne and
Manicheus wiþ her disciplis. For, and þis sacrament schuld be
accidentis wiþout sogect, þan alle þe peple doþ maumetrie, for þei

wirschippen þat þat þei seen wiþ her bodili iȝe, for bicause it is
Goddis bodi; and siþ þe accidentis ben seien wiþ bodili iȝe, þer mai 1875
noone heretik for schame | seie þat þe accidentis ben Goddis body. f. 52ᵛ
And so þei most nedis graunt þat þe comen peple doþe maumetriȝe
in wirschipping þat sacrament in bodili siȝt, or ellis ⟨þ⟩at þe beleue
of þese newe determenouris is fals heresie. But certis I dar not calle
þis act of þe foreseid seen a determynacioun, for as meche as Goddis 1880
lawe had fulli determened þis ⌜bil⟨e⟩ue⌝ before; wiþ wiche determynacion of God alle Goddis chirche held hemself fulli apaide and
weren quietid þeryn and stablischid fro þe tyme of þe apostlis. In
tokenyng wherof þis seen betoke to Beringarie no þing in þis article
of her owne auctorite, as dede Innocent wiþ his comperis and new 1885
sectis, but onli Goddis lawe. And, as I seide before bi auctorite of
seint Austen, wher Goddis lawe haþe fulli determenyd, mannys
ordenaunce o⟨r⟩ lawe haþ no place.

Naþeles, if men wo⟨l⟩ haue þis act of determynacion in þe beleue
of þe sacrid oste, þan þei mai se houȝ þe chirche in pope Nycholas 1890
tyme and in pope Innocentis han determenyd contradiccioun. And
herefore, seien oure newe glosers, þat glosen Goddis lawe and
Beringaries confessioun aftur her new determynacioun, þat þe feiþ
knowlechid in þat seen bi Baringarie is as perlous as is þe heresie
þe wiche he was sclaundrid | of before,—þat is to seie þat þe brede f. 53ʳ
leide vpon the auȝter is aftur þe consecracioun but onli a sacrament, 1896
and not Goddis bodi. And siþ þe confession of Beringarie aftur his
heresie was aftur þe auctorite of þe gospel and of þe apostlis, þes
schameles glosers seien openli inouȝ þat Crist and his apostlis and
alle olde seinttis suyng her beleue and logic weren heretikis, wiþ alle 1900
þe chirche of cristendom þat beleuen not þis newe determynacioun.

Wherefor, se þou now hereaftur þe consail of seint Gregor in his
Morallis 'Not onli what heretikis seien, but also wheder her wordis
strecchen', and þou schalt se þat þe wordis and determynacioun of
þis grete heretik antecrist strecchen into þe most inconuenient þat 1905
mai be þouȝt. For siþ þan þat þe consail of God abideþ euer and þe
þouȝt of his hert, and þe Sone of þe Fader abideþ from generacioun
to generacioun, and þe truþe of þe Lord, þat is Crist as þe gospel
seiþ, dwelliþ for euer, and whan heuene and erþe schal passe Cristis
wordis schul not passe as he himself seiþ in the gospel, and mannys 1910
wittis and wordis ben riȝt uariant and contrarious in þis poynt of
beleue and in many oþur, man auȝt to be neded to stablische himself

1895 þe wiche] ⌜of⌝ þe wiche

in God and his lawe, seyng what perrel it is to trist in vnstable wittis and wordis of men. And þus a man schuld grounde hymsilf in alle

f. 53ᵛ þynggis þat longgen to good maneres | or trewe beleue onli upon þe

1916 stone Iesu Crist, þe wiche alone mai be grounde of þe feiþful chirche þat schal be saued, figurid bi Petur þat figuriþ Cristis chirche, whos name þat is *Petrus* is formyd of Cristis name þat is *Petra*, in tokenyng þat alle Cristis chirche schuld be enformed and ensamplid in Iesu, as

1920 seint Austen seiþ (*De uerbis Domini sermone* 13) and þe apostle acordeþ herewiþ (*Cor.*1).

And of þis founding of þis stable rock þat is Iesu, Crist spekiþ þus (*Mt.*7): 'Euery man þat hereþ þes my wordis and performeþ hem schal be like to a wise man þat bildeþ his hous upon a stone. And þe

1925 rayn haþ come downe and flodis han come, and wynddis han blowen, and þei han fallen into þat house; and þis hous haþ not fallen, for þat hous was bilded upon a stone.' Þis hous is euery feiþful man, or ellis þe numbre of þe chosen, þat bilden her beleue upon Crist, þat is þe stone as Poule seiþ. Þe reyn, flodis and wynddis betokenen þre

1930 temptaciouns to þre maner of synnys, as of þe flesche, of þe world, and of þe fende, þe wiche schenden and casten downe mennes good manerys; or ellis þre maner of persecucions wherebi trewe beleue is ofte peruertid, as bi þretingis, flatringis and wickid spiritis. Naþeles, whoso groundeþ himself sadli upon þis stone, schal not be cast

1935 downe for euer bi wickid maneres or mysbeleue. But Crist seiþ furþurmore þat 'Whosoeuer here þo his wordis and performeþ hem

f. 54ʳ not, he | schal be like a fonned man þat haþ bilde his hous upon grauel or sonde. Rayn haþ come downe and flodis han comen, and wynddis han blowen and þei han fallen into þat hous; and þe hous

1940 haþ fallen, and þe falle þerof was grete,' for seche an hous falliþ so foule þat it mai neuer be repeired. And here we mai se þat antecrist is more foole þan seche a fonned man, for he waitiþ litil or nouȝt of þis grounde, but he bildeþ hym upon þe grauel þat is mony rounde and scleþur stonys. And so as þis fundement is vnstable, so is alle þat

1945 he bildeþ þerupon and most nedes falle foule at þe last.

For þe clerge, as we mai se nouȝ, makiþ not his auȝter of stones vnhewe, of þe wiche I spake of nyȝ þe begynnyng of þis werke, neiþur of stonys foure square, grete and precious þat Salamon commaunded to be leide in þe fundement of þe temple, for seche

1950 maner stones ben stable and not fluting. And þis auȝter and þis fundement betokenen þe beleue þat, as Poule seiþ, is þe substaunce or þe grounde of þinggis þat men ouȝten to hope. For þis is þe

auȝter or fundement of alle þat euer we sacre to God in good
maneres or feiþful workis, and þis sad fundement of God stondeþ
stable, as Poule seiþ (*Thimoth.* 2); and, as þe same apostle seiþ 1955
(*Col.*2), he was glad seyng þe stedefastnesse | of þat feiþ þat was in f. 54ᵛ
Crist. But, certis, þis auȝter ne the square stones þat betokenen þe
stable wordis of Goddis lawe, wiche ben grete in auctorite and
precious for þei sauen mennes soulis for euer,—but þei liken not our
clerkis, and nameli þo þat ben of þe retinew of þis renegat. And 1960
þerfor þei wol not take þis auȝter or fundement as fundement of her
bilding in maneres or beleue or ellis of her workis. And herefor þei
han crafteli framed, and ful sotilli þweten hem a grounde of ful many
poynttis þat [þei] magnefiȝe as beleue. And þis frame þei han forgid
wiþ þe kene instrument of here sotil wittis and hiȝe resons, and þis 1965
grounde þei callen *canoun,* þat is as meche to seie as a rule or ellis
auctorite. And upon þis grounde þei bilden her maneres and many
poynttis of her beleue. And nameli in þe article of þe beleue of þe
sacred oost, þat I speke of chifli here, þei han framed hem a
fundement not of stones vnhewe, þat is to mene of Cristis playn 1970
wordis as þei comen out of þe precious quarre and grete stone, Iesu,
ne of þe grete ⟨and⟩ precious stones foure square þat meuen al oon,
as I seide riȝt nouȝ, but þei han hewe and iþwete, ipublischid and
istirid þe mater of her fundement of her beleue in þis poynt or
article, þe wiche is her ful holi determynacion, þe wiche þei 1975
supposen as grounde of her beleue and refusen þe oþur stable
fundement þat I spak of riȝt nouȝ.

And bicause | þat þis fundement is scleper and scliding, and seche f. 55ʳ
a[n] ⌜vn⌝stable fundement disceiueþ alle þe bilding (as Crist seiþ
*Mt.*7), þerfor alle þe frame þat þei founden upon þis grounde is riȝt 1980
vnstable and euer drawing to riȝt a foule falle. For þe vnstablenes of
þis grounde discrasiþ þe bilding, for certis it is merueile to here houȝ
antecrist and his lemys ben discrasid and diuided into wondur dyuers
opunyons and merueilous in þis mater. For sum seien þat Crist in his
last soper sacrid preueli brede and wyne, and afterward schewid þe 1985
sacrament to his disciplis; and so þes foolis meuen þat Cristis chirche
haþ alweie lackid þe forme of Cristis consecracion at þat tyme;—and,
certis, in þis masid rauyng liþe meche perrel if it schuld be
comenned. Sum seien þat what tyme Crist seide þus 'Take ȝe and
ete ȝe alle of þis; þis is my bodi', the raþur worde *þis* þat answereþ to 1990
þe raþur *hoc* in Laten schewiþ brede; but, as þei seien, so doþ not þe
secunde worde *þis,* for þat answeriþ to þis aduerbe *hic* in Laten, þat

is as meche to seie as 'here' in Englische. So þat aftur þis witt Cristis
wordis in Laten ben þus meche to seie in Englische 'Take ȝe and ete
1995 ȝe alle of þis; here is my bodi', schewing bi þat worde *here* þe place of
þe accidentis. Sum seien þat bi þe raþur worde *þis* Crist schewid þe
brede þat he hilde in his hondes, and bi the secunde worde *þis* he
f. 55ᵛ schewid his owne dedli | bodi as it was present þer, as þouȝ he wold
haue disceyued his disciplis and alle his chirche aftur. Sum seien þat
2000 þis uerbe *est* in Laten is not as meche to seie as þis worde *is* aftur þe
comen vndurstonding of Englisch men, but þat uerbe *est* þer most
haue anoþur queynt Englische þat answereþ to þis uerbe *transsub-
stanciatur* in Laten; and so þes wordis of Crist in Laten *hoc est corpus
meum* ben not þus meche to seie in Englische 'þis is my bodi'. And
2005 houȝ þis Laten schal be openli englischid aftur þis witt fewe men kan
openli teche! Sum seien þat whan Crist seide þus of þe brede þat he
hilde in his hondes 'þis ys my bodi', this worde *þis* þan answeriþ to
þis Laten worde *hoc* [and] schewiþ not Cristis bodi or any oþur þing,
for þat worde wiþ alle þe clause is itake þere bi maner of rehersing,
2010 betokenyng onli þe same worde; and þis rauyng is like to þe first.
Sum seien þat þis word of Crist in Laten *hoc est corpus meum*
betokeneþ þus þat þis accident wiþout soiect or substaunce signifiiþ
sacramentalli Cristis bodi, so þat þei wol not graunt þat her
sacrament is Cristis bodi in forme of brede, but an accident
2015 wiþout soiect or substaunce þat betokeneþ Cristis bodi. Naþeles,
antecrist and his special lemys ben in a grete perplexite what
f. 56ʳ accident | in kinde is þis sacrament, wheþur it be a quantite as is
lengþe, brede and þiknes of þis oost, or ellis a qualite; and, if it be a
qualite, in what special kinde þis sacrament schuld be—þei ben not
2020 ȝit fulli determened, þat is to seie, wheþur it be whitenesse, rounde-
nesse, heuynes or liȝtnesse, sauour or odourre, or any seche þat ben
to mannys witt wiþout numbre. But up hap þes lemys wiþ þe heed
schal drawe hemself togedur and determene þis douȝte whan þei
seen her tyme, and multepliȝe inconuenientis mony and newe!
2025 And, certis, þe hole cause of alle þe diuersite and diuisioun of
opuniouns in þis mater is þe vnstablenesse of þe fundement, þat þes
opiniouneres supposen as grounde in þis article, þe wiche is her
owne wille and determynacion. Crist þat is uerri fundement and
stone, as Poule seiþ, is left or forsaken. And þis vnfeiþfulnesse and
2030 heresie regnyng in þe chirche, bicause of mystrist to Crist and his
wordis, was ensamplid in Cristis tyme, as we mai rede (*Io.*6) where
Crist enformeþ his chirche in þe feiþ of þe sacrid oost in itself and in

þe þinggis þat it betokeneþ, as wel touȝching his personal bodi as al
his mystik bodi, þe wiche, as Austen seiþ, is al Crist, þat is to seie
Crist and his chosen peple of þe wiche he is heed, as Poule seiþ ooft. 2035
For whan Crist seiþ 'þe brede þat I schal ȝeue to ȝow is my flesche
or my manheed for þe liif of þe world', he enformeþ his chosyn in
two þe first: for he techiþ what þe sacrament is in itself or in kinde,
and what | hit is bi vertu of his worde. And, as touȝching for his f. 56ᵛ
mystik bodi, Crist seiþ þus 'Whoso etiþ my flesche and drinkkiþ my 2040
blood, he dwelliþ in me and I in hym.' And þis is soþ of alle his
chosyn, þe wiche ben his mystik bodi, for alle þo eten effectualli
Cristis bodi and drinken his blood, and dwellen in Crist and Crist in
hem, and so maken oo bodi of þe wiche þe sacrid oost is a sacrament
and truthe, as I seide before. For Austen seiþ upon þe same worde of 2045
Crist 'Hit is al oon to þe feiþful peple to ete þis mete and drink þis
drinke, and to dwelle in Crist, and to haue Crist dwelling in hem.'
And wondur þou not alþouȝ I haue vndurstonde þe raþur text of þe
gospel as feiþ itauȝt of þe sacrid oost, for so doþ seint Austen playnli
in *De ciuitate Dei li.* 17, wher seint Austen rehersiþ þis texte of 2050
scripture 'Cast me into a parte of þi presthood to ete brede.' Vpon þe
wiche texte seint Austen seiþ þus: 'þe scripture haþ nobly schewid
out þe kynde of þe sacrefice, of þe wiche þe prest Crist spekiþ þus
"þe brede þat I schal ȝeue is my flesche for þe liif of þe world."' For
as Austen seiþ sone aftur 'Brede is in þe newe testement þe sacrefice 2055
of cristen men.' Naþeles, as þe gospel seiþ, whan Crist tauȝt þe
beleue of þe sacred oste many of his disciplis ȝeden aweie and walkid
no more wiþ hym; for þei hadden þen questions and euydencis
aȝenst Cristis wordis, to þe wiche þei ȝauen more credence þan to
Cristis wordis, for þei supposid Cristis wordis to be fals and | 2060
vnpossible. And herfore þise feyned disciplis became heretikis f. 57ʳ
diuided from Cristis bodi. And þus and meche wors it stondeþ of
þe grete bodi of antecrist, þat supposiþ Cristis wordis to be fals and
heresiȝe and inpossible. And so þis renegat haþ left Crist and is go
ful fer from him, and wol suȝe him no more in maneres and in 2065
beleue, for he goþ euyn contrarie to Crist in boþe, ⟨a⟩nd is wox into
þe most cruel enmye þat euer Crist had, in quenching of his lawe
and of þe liif of þo feiþful men þat besien hem to make it iknowen.
But I wote wel þat antecrist martriþ Goddis peple þe more boldeli,
bicause þat Godd schewiþ not nouȝ myraclis for his martris as he 2070
dede sum tyme. And þe cause whi þat God wol not is þat God haþ

2068 feiþful men þat] þat feiþful men

so ferforþli repreued antecrist from his grace þat he wol not schewe
him seche euydens to repent himself of his tyrantriȝe, for so God
serued king Antioch, þat figurid and ensamplid þis grete renegat
2075 antecrist, as it is seide before. For antecrist brenneþ þe bokis of
Goddis lawe, and stripeþ awei þe skyn from þe trew prechouris
heede and fingris, and killiþ feiþful peple, as dede þe grete tyrant and
enmye of Goddis lawe Antioch. Naþeles, as God schewid no myracle
to þis repreued Antioch, whan he martrid þe modur and hir seuen
f. 57ᵛ sonys, wher⟨bi⟩ he myȝt | haue be meued to haue sessid of his malice
2081 and repent him of his synnes, as he schewid to his chosyn
Nabugodonosor in þe þre vnharmed men in þe myddis of þe fire,
as seint Austen markiþ in a pistle, so it is of þis dampned man ful of
þe fende sitting in þe chirche euynnyng hymself to God. For in alle
2085 þe martirdom þat antecrist doþ upon Goddis peple, he ne his
mynystris f⟨ro⟩m þe hiȝest, þouȝ it be a king, into þe lowist iailour
or his knaue, þe wiche at þe request of antecrist, alþouȝ þei knowe
not þe cause, ben redi to performe his wille, þei sen not a myracle
schewid to hem of God bi þe martir þat þei so cruelli turmenten.
2090   And it is no wondur alle þouȝ God schewe bi his martris nouȝ no
myracles as he dede sum tyme, for þe cause of ⟨m⟩yraclis among
cristen men, þe wiche is the quekenyng of þe feiþ and confermyng
þerof, r⟨e⟩s⟨o⟩nabli sessiþ nouȝ. For uerri myraclis, as Austen seiþ in
De [uera religione], were not suffrid to dure into his tyme, anaunter
2095 þe feiþ schuld wax dulle þour custome of myraclis bi þe wiche it was
first quekened. For, and myraclis were ȝit ryue and custumable, þan
were þei no myraclis. And, as I seide, riȝt nouȝ antecrist is so fulli
f. 58ʳ and utturli repreued in Goddis iugement þat he is not | worþi to be
movid bi uerri myraclis to amende hymself of his mysbeleue and iuel
2100 manerys. And feiþful peple, þat suffriþ nouȝ turmentriȝe vndur
antecrist, ben saddest in beleue, for þei suffren most bitter deeþ
wiþout any special reuelacion or myracle schewid to hem, or ellis
wrouȝt bi hem, tristenyng fulli to God and his lawe and seching noon
oþur signys; and so þei lacken meche comfort here in her martirdom
2105 þat se⟨i⟩nttis hadden in þe begynnyng of Cristis chirche and cristen
feiþ.
     Naþeles, antecrist in his most cruelte schal do myraclis in þe
presens of martris and of oþur peple. For Gregor seiþ þus (3[2]
Moralia): 'Beþenke what schal þat temptacioun be of mannys mynde,
2110 whan þe martir soiectiþ his bodi to turmentis, and ȝit naþeles þe

2088 þei] siþ þei   2094 uera religione] doctrina christiana   2108 32] 31

turmentour doþ my⟨racl⟩is before þe martris iȝen. Whos uertu þan is
not moued from þe grounde of his þouȝttis, wh⟨a⟩n he þat
tur[me]n[t]eþ wiþ woundis and brennynggis schyneþ wiþ signes?
For antecrist schal þan be hiȝe in wirschip of wondring and hard in
cruelte of turment⟨ing⟩.' þan take hede what myraclis ben magnefied   2115
nouȝ in Ynglonde and ⌜in⌝ oþur placis bi antecrist and his lemys of
þo þat han died in his wordli causis, and what signys of hiȝe kunyng
and holinesse þis transfigurid fende schewiþ wherbi he disceiueþ
almost þe chosen! And take hede furþurmore, houȝ þis renegat
turmentiþ þe | peple þat loueþ Goddis lawe, and þou schalt se houȝ   f. 58ᵛ
Gregories wordis here ben openli uerrefiid in our daiis of þe grete   2121
turmentour antecrist and feiþful peple þat suffren persecucioun
vndur his cruel hondes þan.

þus is þis antecrist gon aweie from Crist wiþ þis first heretikis in
þe beleue of þe sacrid oost þat I spak of before, and is igrowe into   2125
seche a turmentour as I haue tolde, and [it] is likli þat he schal neuer
turne aȝen fructefulli to Crist. For seint Poule seiþ of þis antecrist
þat 'þe Lord schal ⟨k⟩ille him wiþ þe breþe of his mouthe, and he
schal distroie him wiþ þe schynyng of his comyng to þe last dome.'
And in euidence of þe final obstinacie of antecrist and his special   2130
membris, it is ful hard to here and see any of his special lemys repent
hem openli or preuelie of her hidous synnys, as of her wordli
lo⟨r⟩dschip þat þei occupie so euyn aȝenst God and his ⟨l⟩awe, of
her vngrounded custumable begging, ne of þe sclaundre þat þei
putten on Crist of þe same ⟨b⟩egging, or of þe blasfemie and heresie   2135
þat þei putten on God and his lawe, or of þe disceite þat þ⟨ei⟩ don bi
her lettris of fraternite and vngrounded absolucions, or of symonye,
most abhominable lecherie, heresie aȝenst þe sacrid oost and many
seche oþur poyntis of iuel maneres and mysbeleue. In þe wiche it is
not inouȝ for seche a crimous wrecche, þat openli in worde and dede   2140
haþ harmed þe chirche of God, to repent himself preueli, while he
haþe leiser openli to amend hy⟨m⟩ bi open p⟨en⟩aunce | and þe peple   f. 59ʳ
wh[om he] haþ harmed,—or ellis as hit semeth open penaunce for
heresie, auouȝtrie ⌜or⌝ fornycacioun haþ no place in þe chirche. For
alle seche ben gilti of alle þe synne þat þei causen bi wiþdrawing of   2145
Goddis worde, yuel ensample or fals teching, as seint Poule seiþ
(Ro.1). And a man mai neuer fructfulli repent him vnto þe time he
do his deuour to vndo his synne, as meche as he mai while he haþ
time and leiser. As ⟨bi⟩cause þis obstinat renegat doþ ne⟨uer⟩ so at

2113 turmenteþ] turneþ   2143 whom he] whan

2150 any time as touȝching þe grete [synne] specifii⟨d be⟩fore and many
oþur, it is likli þat he is wiþ his maister Lucifer abstinatli sett for
euer aȝenst God, and igo⟨n⟩ so from Crist.

And certis I dar in peyne of my soule seie to þis grete apostata
antecrist, þat is þus in maneres and beleue straied aweie fro Crist, þat
2155 he schal neuer haue rest but if he turne aȝen and suȝe C⟨ris⟩t in
maneres and beleue. And þat meueþ þe gospel (*Io*.6) wher Crist
seide þus to his disciplis, whan þe firste heretikis aboute þe sacrid
oost had forsake him: 'Wheþur ȝe also wolen go ⌐a⌐weie?' To whom
⟨Pet⟩ur, þat signefiiþ and figureþ alle þe chosen chirche of God, in
2160 þe persone of þe same chirche answerid þus: 'Lord, to whom schal
we go? þou hast þe wordis of euerlasting liif, and we beleuen and han
knowen þat þou art Crist, þe sone [of] quyk God.' Lo, houȝ þe
chosen, speking in Petur, meuen þat þei kan not go fro Crist and his
f. 59ᵛ   blessid wordis, | for þei ben wordis of euerlasting liif. But antecrist
2165 seiþ, as I wrote before, þat wher þe chirche varieþ fro Crist or
contrarieþ his wordis, he wol forsake Crist and folow þe chirche, and
so suȝe himself and his owne wille for he is þat chirche. For, as seint
Austen seiþ (*De ciuitate Dei li*. 20 *ca*. 19] 'þe Gru haþ Poulis
prophecie of antecrist vndur þis logic þat "þis grete aduersarie
2170 sittiþ into þe temple", and þat is al oone to seie þat he sittiþ as he
were the temple, þ⟨at⟩ is to seie þe chirche', as Austen seiþ þer.

And, certis, þe wordis of Petur wher he seiþ þus: 'We beleuen and
han knowen þat þou art Crist, þe sone of quyk God' ouȝt to be
knowen notabli to alle cristen men, as þei were notable to seint
2175 Austen in [*Tractatus in Iohannem*] wher he m⟨a⟩rkiþ þe ordre of
Petris wordis, seiyng 'We beleuen and han knowen', for, as he
techiþ, a feiþful man most beleue first and know aftur, for, if he wol
knowe first and beleue aftur, he schal ⌐neuer⌐ beleue and know. And
seint Gregor acordeþ herto (2 *Moralia*) wher he seiþ þat 'Feiþ is our
2180 wisdom, þe prophete bering wittnesse þat seiþ "But ȝif [ȝ]e schal
beleue [ȝ]e schal not vndurstonde." Forsoþ þan we be uerreli wise to
vndurstonde, whan we ȝeue feiþ of oure beleuing to alle þinggis þat
þe Maker seiþ.' So þa[n] we mote begyn at beleue if we wol
vndurstond and be wise. And seint Austen acording herewiþ seiþ
f. 60ʳ   þus in his boke *Contra aduersarium legis et prophetarum* 'Forsoþ, | in
2186 so meche euery man in profiting knowiþ þe liȝtlier a þing, in as
meche as he haþ þe more religiousli or feiþfulli beleued to God or he

2167 as] he *canc*. as   2173 ouȝt] and ouȝt   2175 tractatus in iohannem] de
uerbo domini   2180 ȝe] he   2181 ȝe] he   2183 þan] þat

knowe.' And þis was openli ensamplid in þe Iewis, þat seiden of
Crist hanging on þe crosse 'ʒif he is þe Sone of God, go he nouʒ
downe from þe crosse and we beleuen to him', so þat þei wold first 2190
haue a pref and so knowing, and aftur þat beleue, and þei ⟨f⟩aileden
of boþ—as antecristis lemys, þat enforcen hem bi her hiʒe resons to
grounde hem a beleue, and so wold haue a siʒt of þe beleue first and
þan beleue aftur, and þerfor þei failen nouʒ in both. And so þei erren
foule and maken oþur men to erre, as Poule seiþ (Thi. 3). Naþeles, as 2195
seint Austen seiþ (De ciuitate Dei li.12) 'Alþouʒ reson myʒt not
refuse, feiþ schuld scorne seche argumentis wherbi wickid men
enforcen hem to peruerte our simple or clere feiþfulnesse þat we
make wiþ hem in cumpase from þe riʒt weie. þes ben þo þat Poule
spekiþ of "Forsoþ, þei, comparsounyng hemself to hemself, vndur- 2200
stonden not." Forwhi? Whateuer comeþ to hem into mynde, þei don
wiþ a new consail (forsoþ, þei beren changable mynddis!). Soþeli not
God, whom þei mai not beþenk, but beþenking hemself for him, þei
comparisounen not God but hemself not to God but to hemself.' þus
þan þes presumptuous | folis resten in hemself, considering her owne f. 60ᵛ
power, hiʒe witt and grete auctorite wiþout any wise comparrisoun- 2206
nyng of hemself to God, and sechen not þe glorie of God bi inward
vndurstonding of her owne freelte, synne and vnkunnyngnesse. And
þerfor þei mai not beleue fulli to Crist, no more þan myʒt þe
phariseis to whom Crist seiþ (Io.5) 'Houʒ mai ʒe beleue, þat taken 2210
glorie eche of ʒow to oþur, and ʒe sechen not þe glorie þat is of God
alone?' But, and þes presumptuous folis, þat euenen here wittis to
Goddis or ellis setten her owne wittis aboue, wold inwardli considre
þe witt and þe craft of þe Trenyte, schewid in þe leest creature þat
þei kan not deuyse ne comprehende and meche raþur alle þe grete 2215
world, þei schuld now se her owne lewdenesse and cesse of her
presumpcioun aʒenst þe wisdom of þe Trenyte þat is Iesu Crist.

And so þei schulden vndurstonden wiþ seint Gregor (35 Moralia)
þat 'Al mannys wisdom in reward of Goddis wisdom is b⟨ut⟩ folie.'
For þer seint Gregor writeþ þus upon þis worde of Iob (42 ca.] 'I 2220
haue spoke vnwiseli, and seche þinggis þat passidden my kunnyng
wiþout mesure': 'Blessid Iob schuld haue wende wiseli to haue seide
þo þinggis þat he seide, ʒif he herde not þe wordis of hiʒer wisdom.
In comparison of þe wiche wisdom alle our wisdom is but folie. And,
forsoþ, he þat had wiseli spok to men, hering Goddis sentens, 2225
knowiþ more wiseli himself not to be wise. | Hereᶜfor� Abraham f. 61ʳ

2216 cesse] to cesse

among Goddis wordis sawe himself no þing but dust, seiyng þus "I
schal speke to my Lord, whan I am dust and aske." Herfor Moises,
whan he was enformed in þe wisdom of Egipcianus, vndurstonding
2230 himself to be of tunge more let and more sclow, seiyng "Lord, I am
not eloquent fro ȝisturdai and fro þe þrid dai before þis, and siþ þou
hast ispok to þi seruant, I am of tung more ilett and more tariyng."
Herefore, also aftur þat Isaie had seien þe Lord sitting upon an hiȝe
sete and uprerid, aftur þat he had seien seraphyn to hele her face wiþ
2235 two whinggis and her feet wiþ two wingis, and criyng on to anoþur
"Holi, holi, holi, þe Lord of oostis", he turnyng to himself seide
"Wo to me, for I haue be stille, for I am defoulid in lippis, and I
dwel in myddis of a peple hauyng lippis defoulid." And anoon Isaie
telliþ houȝ he knowiþ þat pollucioun "þe King, þe Lord of oostis I
2240 haue seien wiþ myn iȝen." Herefor Ieremye, hering Goddis wordis,
knewe himself to haue no wordis, seiyng "A, a, a, Lord God I kan
not speke, for I am a child!" And herefore also Ezechiel, speking of
þe same foure beestis, seiþ þat "Whan þer was made a uois aboue þe
firmament þat was aboue her heedis, þei bowedden or leiden down
2245 her whinggis." What is betokened bi fleing of þe beestis, but þe
hiȝenesse of þe gospellers and techers? Or what bi þe wynggis of þe
beestis, but þe contemplacions of holi men rering hem up to heuenli
f. 61ᵛ þinggis? But whan þer was made a | voise aboue the firmament, þat is
aboue her heedis, þei stonding leiden downe her wynggis; for, whan
2250 þei heren an inward voice of þe souereyn wisdom, in a maner þei
leien dowun her wingis of her fleyng, þat is to seie, þei knowen
hemself not of power to behold þe hyȝenes of truthe. þerfor to leie
downe þe wingis at þe voice comyng aboue is þe souereyn power
iknowe, to meke her owne uertues and poweris, and bi consideracion
2255 of þe Maker to fele nouȝt of hemself but abiect þinggis. Also holi
men, while þei here sentencis of þe godhed, þe more þat þei profiten
in contemplacioun, þe more, dispising þat þing þat þei ben, knowen
hemself to be nouȝt or ellis nyȝ nouȝt.'

And þus, of þis processe of Gregor grounded upon holi scripture,
2260 we mai se þat þe inward and depe consideracioun þat þes holi men
hadden of her owne freelte, nounpower and vnkunnyngnes on þat oo
side, and þe grete reward þat þei had to þe excellens and worþinesse
of Goddis maieste on þat oþur, was þe cause whi þei setten so litil bi
hemself and her owne speche. But antecrist haþ not þis reward to þe
2265 excellens of God, but, as Poule seiþ, comparisouneþ himself to

2243 was] mai *canc.* was

himself. And þerfor he hereþ not þe voice þat was made aboue þe firmament, þat is to seie þe voice of þe Fadur, seiyng þus to al þe world of his Sone 'þis is my loued Sone, here 3e him!' For þis Sone, as þe gospel seiþ, came dowun from heuene not to do his owun wil but þe wille of his Fadur; and so he schewid out to al þe world þe | wil and þe lore of þe Fadur, þe wiche ben euerlast⟨i⟩ng truþis wreten in þe boke of liif. And Crist seiþ þat his lore was not his, but it was þe lore of him þat sent him, þat is þe Fadur. For as Crist is not original of himself, but of his Fader, so it is of þe lore þat he tau3t. And acording herto Crist seiþ þus to his disciplis: 'Alle þingis þat I haue hird of my Fadur, I haue made kn⟨ow⟩en to 3owe.' And þus þis Crist dede b⟨i⟩ þe most tru3e and couenable logic þat þe Trinyte my3t deuyse, fort schew out þe truþis hid before in þe boke of liif. And þus þe Trinyte koude not bi his endeles wisdom deuise a truer, a bettur and an esier logic to schew þerbi to þe world þe beleue of þe sacrid oost, þan it is wreten in Goddis lawe þat calliþ it 'brede and Goddis bodi'. And so þis logic of þe Trenyte schewid out bi Crist ou3t to [be] take of cristendom, worþeli and souerenli to be had in auctorite. And þis vndurstode wel seint Ion þe Baptist (*Io.*3) wher he, considring his owne freelnesse, febilnes and vnkunnyngnus and oþur mennys also, remittiþ al þe world to Crist and his logic and his lawe, and seiþ þus: 'He þat haþ comen from heuene is aboue alle', and 'þat þing þat he haþ seien and hirde he wittnessiþ, and no man takiþ his wittnes.' For þo þat taken it vnworþel⟨i⟩ ben as it | wer⟨e⟩ no man in comparisoun of þo that refusen hit. For, certis, þe auctorite þerof is ful litil reuerrensid boþ in sermons and in scolis, and so it is þe lesse wondur alþou3 oþur peple take þe lesse hede þerto.

Naþeles, Ion seiþ þer þat 'Whoso haþ take Cristis wittnesse haþ itokened or ischewid þat God is truþe',—not onli in þe performyng of þe behest of þe incarnacioun, but also þat he is tru3e in his wordis and maner of speche, for þat meueþ a feiþful man to take Goddis wittnesse. For, as seint Ion seiþ to alle men, '3if 3e take mannys wittnesse, þe wittnesse of God is more.' But þis grete renegat refusiþ þis wittnesse in ful many poynttis of good manerys and trewe beleue. And so, as Ion Baptist meueþ in his wordis, þis fende seiþ þat God is fals, and his wittnes þat is his lawe also, and nameli in þe beleue of þe sacrid oost, wher he refusiþ alle þe wittnesse of Goddis lawe and betakiþ him to þe contrarie, as it is in parti3e schewid hertofore. And whoso wol se Innocentis tretice in þis mater mai se hou3 incom-

2294 þat god] þat god þat/god

Marginalia: 2270 f. 62ʳ 2275 2280 2285 f. 62ᵛ 2290 2295 2300

2305 pounnedli and houȝ wilfulli he writiþ, wiþouten grounde of Goddis
lawe or ellis reson, and houȝ vnstabli he writiþ, as þouȝ he wist not
wher to abide, hauyng alweie his recors not to Goddis lawe but to his
owne wille. And no wondur of þis vnstablenesse, for he groundeþ
f. 63ʳ him not upon þe stone Crist | but vpon the grauel, as I seide tofore!
2310   And, certis, I drede me not þe mysvndurstonding of þis word of
þe gospel 'þou art Peter, and upon þis ston I schal bilde my chirche',
and , 'Whateuer þing þou schalt bynde in erþe schal be bounden in
heuene, and whateuer þou schalt vnbynde in erthe schal be
vnbounden in heuene',—þis is a grete cause of errour and striff
2315 þat is in þe chirche. For of þis worde þe pope and al cristendom, and
nameli the clergi, presumen þe pope to be hede of, and grounde of
alle holi chirche, and alle þing þat he affermeþ, and nameli bi
writing, to be ferme and stable and to be inpugned of no man, as it is
specialli schewid in þis point of þe sacrid oost, in þe wiche þe pope
2320 wiþ his comperis haþ ȝeuen a decre and determynacioun euen aȝenst
Crist and his law, and killiþ men þat inpugnen it or ellis beleuen it
not. Naþeles, and men were wel avisid, þei schuld beleue, as Poule
techiþ ofte, þat Crist is heede of þe chirche. For I suppose I haue red
in an hundrid placis wher seint Austen spekiþ of þis heed. But I am
2325 not auisid þat any creature saue Cristis manheede schuld be heed of
holi chirche bi seint Austens writing. For (*83 Questiones* 7[5]) he
techiþ bi auctorite of holi scripture þat al Crist is þe heede and þe
bodi togedre, þat is to seie Cristis manheed wiþ þe chosen. And þe
f. 63ᵛ same | sent⟨en⟩ce he hath *De ciuitate Dei li.*17 et *Super Genesim ad*
2330 *litteram li.*11, where he techiþ Crist and his chosen chirche to be oo
bodi and Crist to be heede þerof, as Lucifer and his retinew ben oon
and he hede. And, siþ Cristis chirche haþ but oon heed, men mote
now dele bitwene Crist and þe pope, wiche of hem two schal be þis
heed. Naþeles, it were good to þe pope not to presume proudli aȝenst
2335 Crist, lest for his pride he be finalli ifounde incorporat into Luciferis
bodi!
    Suppose we þan here þat onli Crist is þe stone þat þe gospel
spekiþ of, whan Crist seiþ 'Upon þis stone I schal bilde my chirche.'
For þis is þe stone and þe fundement þat mai not be meued, as seint
2340 Poule techiþ, alþouȝ folis in ueyn presumen þe contrarie. For boþ
seint Austen and Ierom þus vndurstonden þis text of þe gospel þat,
whan Petur in þe persone of alle þe chirche knowlechid his maistur
Iesu to be Crist, þe sone of quyk God, and in þat he knowlechid his

2315 worde þe] worde/ þe worde þe   2326 75] 70

boþe kinddis, þan Crist seide to him figurring alle his chirche 'I seie
to þe, þou art Petur and upon þis stone I schal bilde my chirche'; so 2345
þat Crist [seide] not 'upon þe', or 'upon þe Petur', or ellus 'upon þis
Petur I schal bilde my chirche.' For Crist meued anoþur grounde of
his chirche, þe wiche differentiþ ful meche from Petur boþ in
persone and in figure, and seid 'Upon þis stone I schal bilde my |
chirche', þat is to seie, as thes seinttis meuen acording wiþ þe f. 64ʳ
apostle, 'Vpon þis sadnes of þe beleue of my two kinddis, þe wiche 2351
þou hast knowlechid, I schal bilde my chirche. And so I schal bilde
þe, þat ys to seie my chirche figurid bi the, upon me, and not me
upon þe.' And in tokenyng hereof seint Austen markiþ (in *De uerbis*
Domini sermone 13) Crist formed to þe figure of his chirche þat is 2355
Petur a name of his owne name, þe wiche is *Petra*. But for a man is
sonyst dede bi beheding, þerfor þe deuyl inhabiting þis man of
synne, antecrist, smytiþ aweie þe heed Crist from þe bodi of þat þat
schuld be his chirche; and so þis bodi heedles wantiþ witt and
mouyng þat cometh groundli from þe heed, þat is to mene heuenli 2360
witt wiþ quyk mouyng to heueneward gouerned bi þat witt. For as
Austen meueþ (in *De uerbis Domini*) antecristis lemys wollen þat þe
chirche be heedles as for Crist, alþouȝ þei sette for him a worme-eten
idol.

Of þe wiche God spekiþ þus bi þe prophete Zacharie (11 *ca.*) 'Ȝit 2365
take to þe vessellis of þe fonned hirde. For, loo, I schal rere an hirde
in erþe þat schal not visite forsaken þinggis; and he schal not seche
þing iscatrid, and þat þing þat is brisid he schal not hele it, and þat
þing þat stondeþ he schal not norische, and he schal ete þe flesche of
þe fatt and he schal dissolue or vndo þe clees of hem. O hirde and 2370
ydol, leuing | þe flok!' Bi þis hirde and idol, þat haþ þe condicions f. 64ᵛ
þat þe prophete spekiþ of here, men vndurstonden resonabli þe grete
antecrist and renega⟨t⟩ þat I haue ofte spoke, of þe wiche bi his owne
presumpcioun and bi þe lewde assenting of þe peple sittiþ in þe
chirche as heed þerof in stede of Crist, pretending to ȝeue, as an heed 2375
schuld, witt and mouyng to alle þe lemys, and for to mynstere gostli
liiflode to alle þe bodi of þe chirche in a maner like as a mannes
heede doþ to alle þe bodi, or ellis þe rote þat is heed of þe tre to alle
þe branchis. But, for as meche as þis is not true but counturfetid in
ipocrisie, þe prophete bi þe witt of God ȝeueþ hym a name aftur his 2380
propurte and calliþ him an hirde or a feder and idol þat haþ
countenaunce of liif and wirching wiþout þe truþe or dede.

And also as þe Apocalips seiþ 'Alle þe kingis of erþe han don

fornycacion' gostli, þat is idolatrie wiþ þis idol. For þe chast beleue
2385 and tru⟨e⟩ þat þei schuld haue ȝeue to Iesu Crist, þe Sone of quyk
God, þei haue ȝeuen to þis herde and idol. þe vesellis of þis ipocrite,
hirde and idol ben þe special lemys of antecrist þat ben his
instrumentis, and so his vessellis aftur þe speche of Ebrew, wherbi
he wircheþ his malice; for eche instrum⟨e⟩nt or tole in Ebrew is callid
2390 a vessel, and so aftur þis speche seint Poule is callid 'þe chosen vessel
f. 65ʳ of Iesu'. And God techiþ þe prophete Zacharie and in | hym al þe
world to take to him þe vessellis of the fonned hirde, þat is to seie to
bring to mynde þes wickid vessellis of antecrist, so þat he be war of
þe wickid lemys of þe fonned hirde and of his vessellis also. For God
2395 seiþ here þat 'he schal arere up in erþe a fonned hirde and an idol',
and in doyng and in suffring [he] schal harme Goddis flok as þe
prophetis wordis sownen. But þat schal be iustli for þe synnes of þe
peple. For, as þe holi man Iob seiþ, 'God schal make an ipocrite to
regn⟨e⟩ for synne of þe peple', þe wiche ipocrite, as Gregor seiþ, is
2400 antecrist whom þe prophete here, bi maner of wondring upon his
grete ipocrisie and malice þat he wirchiþ bi ipocrisie, calliþ him 'an
hirde and idol leuing þe flok'. And on what wise þis idol harmeþ
Goddis flok, as þe prophetis wordis sownen, men mai on diuerse
wise coniecte of þe wickid doing and suffring of þis grete ipocrite þat
2405 is þus hirde and idol, þat falsli bi fauour of þe peple and nameli of
his special lemys presumeþ to be þe stone vpon whom Crist bildeþ
his chirche, and so to be fundement and þe heed of holi chirche.

And as touȝching þe power of byndding and vnbindding ⟨þ⟩at
antecrist presumeþ, and his special membris magnefien in hym, bi
2410 occasion of Cristis wordis seide to Petur, seint Austen seiþ þat þis is
f. 65ᵛ not a power at any tyme singlerli ȝeuen to Petur, but | hit is the
power of al Cristis chirche figurid bi Petur; and so þis power was not
ȝeue to Petur as for himsilf, but to h⟨im a⟩s figurring al Cristis
chirche. And in tokenyng and in ful wittnesses herof þe same power
2415 þat Crist betoke to Petur, nemnyng singlerli to Petur, he ȝaf generalli
to alle þe chirche, seiyng to alle his apostlis 'Whatsoeuer þinggis ȝe
schal bynde vpon þe erþe schul be bounden in heuenes, and
whatsoeuer þingis ȝe schul vnbinde in erþe schal be vnbounden in
heuenes.' And Crist seide also to al his apostlis 'Take ȝe þe Holi
2420 Goost, of whom ȝe schal forȝeue synnes þei ben furȝeue to hem, and
of whom ȝe schal wiþhold þei ben wiþhold', þat is to seie not
forȝeue. And upon þis text of þe gospel Gregor writiþ þus (27

2393 so] and so

Moralia) 'Loo, þe drede of men turned to God is turned to power, for, while þei punschen her owne wickidnesses bi penaunce or forþenking, þei stiȝe up to exercise iugement; þat þei take to 2425 mowe þat þing in God þat þei raþur dredden of God. Forsoþ, þei ben made iugis þat perfiȝtli dredden þe souereyn iugement, and now þei begynnen for to forȝeue oþur mennys synnes, þat raþur dredden lest her owne were wiþholde.' Lo, houȝ þis seint acording wiþ seint Austen vndurstondeþ þis power as power of alle Cristis chirche, and 2430 not as power singlerli ȝeue to Petur. | And þus, alþouȝ þer were no f. 66ʳ pope as oft haþ betid, or alþouȝ al cristendome had forsaken him for a fals renegat, as þe Grekis h⟨an⟩, or alþouȝ þe pope wiþ al his endowid prelacie þat ben temperal lordis were an antecrist and heretik in þe mater of her wordli lordschip and office and symonye, 2435 and in þe feiþ of þe sacrid oost, and in þe sacrament of penaunce, and in many oþur poynttis (þe wiche I suppose few of hem to be clene), ȝit neuer þe latur þis power abideþ in þe chosen chirche of Crist, alþouȝ þei ben here but a litil flok.

And certis houȝ and bi what auctorite þis power of asoiling and 2440 bindding is engrosid into þe popis sceler to be tappid forthe into þe world aftur his mesuris, sum more sum lesse, tel whoso kan for I kan not. Naþeles, I cesse nouȝ to trete furþur of þis maner of asoiling and binding, for it was not myn entent to hang upon þis mater. For I brouȝt not in þe text of Crist as touȝching for þis, but for to schew 2445 houȝ falsli þe pope wiþ folis of his assent presumeþ to be grounde and heed of þe chirche of Crist, and alle to be ferme and stable as beleue þat he determeneþ. For I can not deuise a nerrer weie to schende wiþ cristendome and our beleue þan, as þis renegat wiþ his retinewe enforsiþ him to do, in þis article of þe beleue of þe sacrid 2450 oost, wher his determynacion bynddeþ not, for it a|cordeth [not] but f. 66ᵛ euyn contrariiþ the sentence of þe hiȝe Iuge. For onli þan þe chirche byndeþ whan it acordeþ, as seint Gregor seiþ, wiþ þe sente⟨nc⟩e of þe iuge Crist; and reson mai neuer assent to þe contrarie of þis, alþouȝ þis malice blinde it ofte tyme. 2455

And, certis, grete wondring upon þis newe presumptuous deter-mynacioun, so euen contrarie aȝen alle Goddis lawe, made me astonyed here. For we mote suppose here as feiþ þat Crist, not onli in his last soper, but also before, as I seid bi auctorite of seint Austen, tauȝt brede to be his bodi or his flesche, whan he seide þus 2460 'þe brede þat I schal ȝeue to ȝow is my flesche for þe liif of þe

2456 upon] is *canc.* upon

world.' And Crist di[e]de in þis beleue not an eretike, alþouȝ þis
grete renegat seie þe contrarie, but as most feiþful cristen man and
heed of alle truȝe cristen men. And, alþouȝ þis beleue were dede in
2465 Cristis disciplis as for þe time of her maistris deeþ and sumwhat
aftur, ȝit it was alyue in þe blessid uirgyne Marie, þat neuer fautid in
feiþ but euer kept it sadli in hert and, as men supposid, enformed
oþur vnstable disciplis in þe same, aftur þat þ⟨ei⟩ had fled boþe from
Crist and fro þe beleue þat he had tauȝt; and so among oþur poynttis
2470 sche kept in hert þe beleue of þe sacrid oost aftur þe logic and beleue
tauȝt of hir blessid Sone, to whos wordis sche supposid al men to
owe obedience, as sche meued in hir owne wordis whan he made
f. 67ʳ water wyne. And in þis sacrament Cristis | disciplis boþ of beleue
and office wiþ þe blessid Virgine commenned wondur besili aftur
2475 Cristis deeþ, and nameli aftur his ascencioun and sending of þe Holi
Goost. For, as it is wreten in þe Dedis of þe Apostlis, þe feiþful
peple, hauyng oo hert and oo soule, 'weren enduring in þe lore of þe
apostlis and in commenyng of breking of brede and in praiouris'.
And þis brede þat Luke writiþ of here is þe same þat he writiþ of in
2480 þe gospel, seiyng þat 'þe disciplis knewen Crist in breking of brede',
þe wiche text seint Austen in *Sermone de Pascha* expouneþ of þe
sacrid oost as I wrote before. And sone aftur in þe same chapitur
Luke writiþ houȝ þe feiþful peple were during dai bi dai in þe
temple, and þei breken loues abouȝt housis, token mete wiþ ioiyng
2485 and simplenesse of hert, preising God. And þe Maister of Stories
vndurstondeþ bi þis communyng in breking brede, and bi louys
broken aboute housis or meneis þe sacrid oost or ellis brede of almys.
But, for as meche as the feiþful peple þan was communed eche dai,
and þis brede of þe sacred oost is þe more worþi and notable brede,
2490 and also for as meche as þ[e]r was m⟨a⟩de þan ful purueans aȝenst
euery mannus nede, it is more to purpos to vndurstond þis
communyng in breking of brede, and þis breking of loues of þe
blessid sacrament, as Austen doþ þe gospel acording to þes wordis of
Luke here.
f. 67ᵛ   And of | this processe we most suppose here þat þis holi peple, so
2496 ful of þe Holi Gost, so riueli treting þis blessid sacrament, hadden
sum maner of speche and logic wherbi þeʳiˀ communed in worde and
spak of þis sacrament, þe wiche logic was oon among hem alle,
printid in her hert bi þe plente of þe Holi Gost þat mai not contrarie
2500 Crist seiyng 'þe brede þat I schal ȝeue ȝow is my flesche or manheed

2462 diede] dide   2490 þer] þur   2498 was] sa was

for þe liif of þe world.' For Crist seiþ þus 'þe Holi Gost schal take of
myn and schewe to ʒow.' And it is not lefful to douʒt here but þat þis
logic was oon among hem alle, for ellis þei schuld haue ⌈be⌉ diuided
into diuerse logikis in her communyng, and so haue had mater of
dissencion and striff as men han nouʒ; and so þei schuld not haue 2505
ben in oo hert and soule as þei were, as Luke wittnessiþ. And þis
logic, as we mote nedis suppose, is ful truli reportid bi þe blessid
man and maide Luke, þat bi þe witt of þe Holi Gost perfiʒtli þe
wordis and þe dedis of þe apostlis reportid and oþur perfiʒt men in
his time, as ferforþ as it was spedi and nedeful for Cristis chirche. 2510
And, as I haue seide in partie aboue, Luke in þe Dedes of þe Apostlis
acordeþ in þis point of þe sacrid oost his logic and his writing to þe
gospel þat he wrote before, in þe weche he makiþ special mencioun
of two consecracions of þe blessid oost don bi Crist. þe oon was in
his last soper wher he made brede to be his bodi as he had | behiʒt f. 68ʳ
tofore, seiyng as I haue rehersid 'þe bred þat I schal ʒeue to ʒow is 2516
my flesche for þe liif of þe world.' And þe oþur consecracion Crist
dede aftur his resurreccioun, whan þe disciplis þan conformed in
beleue knoulechiden þat þei knew Crist in breking of brede, þe wiche
beleue aftur þe raþur logic Luke truli reportiþ in his gospel as þe 2520
derling of God, ful of þe Holi Goost. Long aftur þat þe feiþ was
multipliid and confermed [he] reportid þe raþur texte of Crist of þis
blessid oost.

And so Ion þe euangelist þan was of þe same beleue, and vsid þe
same logic in writing and speking of þis blessid sacrament þat vsid 2525
Crist, for time of his lyuing here, and þe þre euangelistis þat wroten
in þis mater long before Ion. For Ion wrote his gospel ful nyʒe þe
ende of his liif, þe wiche was foure score ʒere and nyntene, and Ion
lyued aftur þe passioun of Crist þre score and seuen as þe cronycle
telliþ in *Legenda Sanctorum*. And, aftur time he had founded many 2530
chirchis, he wrote his gospel for to quenche certeyn heresie þat time
regnyng. And so of þis we haue open euidence þat seint Ion and al þe
feiþful peple for his time toke þe beleue of þe sacrid oost aftur Cristis
logic reportid bi þe foure gospellers. And who schuld douʒt here þat,
if Crist had iknowe a better logic to schew to his chirche þe beleue of 2535
þe sacrid oost, he wold as raþe or raþur haue told þat to seint Ion,
þat had so grete plente of Goddis reuelacions, þan to mysproude
Innocent and his comperis aftur þe losing | [of] Sathanas?   f. 68ᵛ
    Also to this purpos we mai rede (*Gal*.2) houʒ seint Poule fourtene

2537 had] he had   2539 fourtene] aftur fourtene

2540 ȝere aftur þe passioun of Crist ȝede to Ierusalem, and toke wiþ him
Barnabe and Tite to se þe apostlis, of þe wiche Luke writiþ (*Act*.15).
And in þat seen, as seint Poule seiþ, he talkid þe gospel wiþ þe
apostlis, and nameli wiþ Iames, Petur and Ion, þe wiche semed pelars
of þe chirche. þis dede Poule, not to lerne ouȝt of þe apostlis, for þe
2545 same Iesu þat tauȝt Iames, Petur and Ion and her felowis tauȝt seint
Poule þe same gospel in heuen wiþout any oþur mene. For, as seint
Poule meneþ, þe best of þe apostlis ȝaf him no þing as touȝching þe
gospel or ellus þe beleue. But Poule dede þus, þat þe apostlis and
oþur feiful peple schuld wel knowe þat Poulis teching and his felowis
2550 among þe heþen men acorded wiþ Cristis teching and þe apostlis
among þe Iewis. And, siþ þe apostlis weren at þat time gadrid to
distroie and dampne heresies and errouris, who schold douȝt but þat
þei wolde haue distroid and dampned þe errour of Poule and his
felowis, if þei had ben infect wiþ any?—as þei were not, and þerfore
2555 al þe apostlis and feiþful peple weren wondur glad, seing þe acord
betwene Poulis teching and þe gospel þat þei had lerned of Crist.
And siþ seint Poule had before þat seen ful oft times tauȝt and
prechid of þe beleue of þe sacrid oost þat was ryue among þe peple,
and also wrete of þe same article, we mote suppose þat al þe apostlis
f. 69ʳ wiþ Barnabe and Tite and oþur feiþful peple acorden wiþ Poule | in
2561 þat article, boþ in logic and beleue. And siþ seint Poule tauȝt and
wrote al oon, for þer was not in him 'ȝe' and 'nai' and so
doublenesse, as he seiþ himself, we mai vndurstond bi Poulus
writing (*Cor*.10 *et* 11) þat þe beleue of al þe apostlis, and of alle
2565 þe feiþful peple and wel enformed at þat time, was þat þe sacrid oost
is brede and Cristis bodi, and wyne and Cristis blode, as Crist tauȝt
his apostlis in his last soper. And afturward seint Poule, as he wrote
(*Gal*.1 *et Cor*.11), lerned þe same beleue of Iesu in heuene; and siþ
þis beleue, tauȝt aftur þe forme of þis logic, was neuer reuokid ne
2570 chaungid in þe time of þe apostlis. In tokenyng wherof Luke, writing
of Poulis last dedes, writeþ of þe same oost vndur þe same logic as I
seide before;—we most suppose þat Crist and his modur, þat
enformed specialli Luke to write his gospel, wiþ þe apostlis and
martris and feiþful peple in þe begynnyng chirche, made an ende of
2575 his liif in þis beleue, þe wiche þis renegat sitting in þe chirche wiþ al
his newe sectis dampneþ for heresie.

And þis consideracioun þus grounded upon scripture makiþ me to
suppos wiþout any douȝte þat þis grete renegat wiþ his special
lemys, þat dampneþ Cristis law in þis article and also his lore aȝenst

his wordli lordschip and custumable begging wiþ ful many oþur 2580
poynttis of trew beleue, is þe kinde of antecrist þat mai be. Alþouȝ he
encrese dai bi dai in numbre and malice, and alþouȝ it be no nede | or f. 69ᵛ
litil to alegge doctour sentencis to conuicte þe heresie of antecrist in
þis mater, þe wiche is so plainli declared bi holi scripture, ȝit I
mynge old sentencis of seinttis wiþ holi scripturre, þat þe vile 2585
presumpcioun of þis antecrist be þe more open in þis mater, and
þat men mai se houȝ olde seinttis confermed hem to þe logic of
scripture, and to schew þat þe conclusion þat I hold in þis point is no
new doctrine but þe first and so þe eldest þat euer was tauȝt of þis
sacrament, and ȝit icontinued in Cristis chirche, alþouȝ antecrist and 2590
his disciplis calle þis a new feiþ and a new doctrine. For seint
Ambrose seiþ þus aȝenst þis antecrist: 'þat þing þat was brede before
þe consecracion is nouȝ Cristis bodi aftur þe consecracioun.' And
seint Ierom writeþ þus aȝenst þis renegat in his epistle *Ad Helbediam*
'Here we beleue þe brede wiche þe Lord brake and ȝaf to his disciplis 2595
to be þe bodi of þe Sauyour himself, seiyng to hem "Take ȝe and ete
ȝe, þis is my bodi."' And Ignacius þat was in þe time of þe apostlis
seiþ, as Lincoln rehersiþ (*Super ecclesiastica ierarchia*), þat þe
sacrament is Cristis bodi. And houȝ seint Denyse writiþ of þis
sacrament aftur þe logic of Goddis law I told in partie before, but for 2600
I haue not nouȝ þe copie of his boke, I write not his wordis here.
And seint Ciprian þe martir, þat was a ful autentike man to seint
Austen, in *Epistola sua de corpore Cristi*, vpon þe wordis of þe
consecracion of chalis, concludeþ þat þat þing was wyne þe wiche
Crist seid to be his blode. | And seint Austen, as I wote wel, and I be f. 70ʳ
wel avisid it is in his boke *De doctrina christiana*, rehersiþ þe same 2606
Ciprian, seiyng þat þe blode mai not be seen in þe chalis whan þe
wyne lackiþ. But antecrist, ⌐aȝenst¬ al þis wittnes of script⟨ur⟩e and
old seintis, seiþ þat he in his consecracion blessiþ aweie boþ þe brede
and þe wyne; but I wote w⟨e⟩l þat antecrist schal finde þis a ful bittur 2610
blessing, whan Crist schal deme wiche partie in þis mater is heresie,
bi his owun blessid lawe and not bi antecristis new determenacioun,
þe wiche is so contrarious to Crist þat it schal not be auoided at þe
dredful dai of dome!

Furþurmore, acording wiþ Crist and þes olde seinttis, Fulgencius 2615
þat is cald *Auctor De diuinis officiis* writiþ þus of Crist, þe hiȝe
bischop and of his sacrifice: 'In þis bisschop and in his sacrefice is
boþe a godli substaunce and also an erþeli. þe erþeli substaunce i[n]

2616 of] of/of   2618 godli] goddli, *altered to* goodli   in] is

boþe is þat þing þat mai be seien bodili and be seen to occupi a place;
2620 þe heuenli substaunce in boþe is þe inuisible Sone of God þat in þe
begynnyng was God at God. For whan þe same grete Bischop seid
holding brede and wyne "þis is my bodi; þis is my blode", þe Sone
of God þat had take mankinde, þe same Sone dwelling in flesche,
toke substaunce of brede and wyne; liif being mene, he ioined brede
2625 wiþ his flesche and wyne wiþ his blode. For riȝt as in bodili felingis
þe tunge as mene goþ betwene þe mynde and þe bodili eire, and
f. 70ᵛ ioinyng boþe togedur makiþ oo | word, þe wiche word leeft into þe
eeris, þat þing þat miȝt be hirde is sone take aweie and passiþ;
forsoþ, þe witt of þe word[is] abideþ hole and vnwastid in him þat
2630 seiþ þat ⟨and⟩ in him þat hereþ þat. So þe Sone of þe Fadur goyng
betwene þe flesche and þe blode, þe wiche ⌐he⌐ had take of þe wombe
of þe maide, and þe brede and þe wyne þat is take in þe auȝter makiþ
oo sacrament; and whan þe prest haþ departid þat into þes mouþus
of feiþful peple, þe brede and þe wyne ben taken aweie and passen.
2635 Forsoþ, þe birþe of þe Uirgen abideþ hool and vnwastid wiþ þe onli
Sone of þe Fadur boþe in heuen and in men. But into him, in whom
feiþ is not, comeþ no þing of þe sacrifice saf þe visible kindis of
brede and wyne; like as an asse reisiþ vp his vnresonable heris to þe
harp and heriþ a soun, but he perceiueþ not þe mesure or þe maner
2640 of þe song.' Her Fulgencius. 'And seche ben likned to þe Iewus, of
þe wiche þe Lord seiþ "Ȝour faduris han eten angellus mete in
desert, and þei ben dede." Forsoþ, þei þat taken it in feiþ be likned
to þo whom þe apostle spekiþ of (*Cor*.10) 'Alle ȝour fadris han ete þe
same spiritual mete, and al han drunken þe same spiritual drink."
2645 For sum ben þe fadris of þe Iewis and heretikis bi mysbeleue; sum
ben fadris of þe apostlis and oþur feiþful men bi beleue. þerfor þer is
inuisible brede þat came fro heuene, and þat is liif; þe[r] is þe visible
brede þat grew on ⌐þe⌐ erþe, for [þis is] al oon brede a[s] he [þat]
f. 71ʳ came | from heuen and was borne of the maidenus wombe is oon.
2650 Wherfor he þat etiþ þe visible brede of þe sacrifice, and bi faute of
beleue puttiþ from his hert þe inuisible brede, scleþ Crist, for he
departiþ liif from thing þat schuld be quekened; and ⟨h⟩e also drawiþ
wiþ his teeþ þe dede bodi of þe sacrifice, and bi þis is gilti of þe bodi
and of þe blod of þe Lord. But þe aduersarie seiþ "þe man Crist is
2655 quyk and sensible in his bodi and moueable, and þe bodi of þe
sacrefice haþ no liif, ne feling, ne it is not moueable." þe wiche þing

---

2619 þing] *twice*   2629 wordis] worde   2647 þer] þe wiche
2648 as he þat] and he   2649 was] he was

grauntid, þis aduersarie concludeþ þat þis sacrefice is neiþur Goddis
bodi ne Crist.' And anoon suyng Fulgencius answeriþ þus to þis
aduersarie: 'I prai þe, what liif sekist þou in þe bodi of þe Lord?
Forsoþ þer is a bestli liif and þer is a spiritual liif. þe bestli liif usiþ   2660
fiue wittis, þat is to seie seing, hering, smelling, tasting and
touȝching. But þe Lord seiþ þat "þe flesche profitiþ not", for al if
the Iewis had wold a kitt þe flesche þat þei crucifiid as þe flesche of
þe lombe, or myȝt haue swolowid it hole and quyk, as þe whale of þe
see swolowid Ionas quyk, it schuld not haue profitid hem, but þei   2665
schuld haue defoulid her conscience wiþ more sacrilege or wrong
aȝenst God. þerfor þe beestli liif, for it is flesche, if it were present in
þe bodi of þe Lord, it schuld not haue profitid to us; and þerfor it is
superfluite to seche þat liif. For wherto schuld þe heuenli man haue
mynystrid here bi his heuenli sacrefice þat þing þat wanteþ vs not?   2670
Forsoþ, it is not a prudence of þe Lord to fede | oure kuriouste wiþ   f. 71ᵛ
myraclis not nedful. þerfor it becometh þe wisdom of þe Lord, and
it was spedi to our nede to mynystre to vs in þe sacrefice onli
spiritual liif, þe wiche is halowing and blessing, merci and truþe,
riȝtwisnesse and pees. Forsoþ, þis spiritual liif of þe Lord is so in þe   2675
bodi of þe sacrefice wiþout þe beestli liif, as þe liȝt of þe sunne
wiþout his hete i[s] present to vs in þe bodi of þe mone. Herefor, our
souereyn Bischop haþe made vs a sacrefice of þinggis togedre, bi þe
wiche al þe man is quekened, þat is to seie þe Sone of þe Lord in
whom a man lyueþ in soule, and of þe frutis of þe erthe wiþ þe wiche   2680
onli þe bodi lyueþ, þe wiche frutis ben þe first of alle—for brede is
þe first þing of þo þat perteinen to mete, and wyne is þe first þing of
þo þat perteinen to drink.' And her Fulgencius.

   Loo, houȝ þis clerk acording wiþ scripture and olde seinttis techiþ
what our sacrament is in kinde, and what it is bi gracious wirching of   2685
Goddis worde, and houȝ Cristis bodi and þis sensible sacrament ben
ooned togedre, and what maner being Crist or his han in þis sacrid
oost, and what maner of being of Cristis bodi feiþful men schullen
seke in oure sacrefice. Alle þis and meche more men mai marke in þe
feiþful wordis of þis clerk. Furþurmore, as touȝching þis poynt seint   2690
Austen, acordingli to his owne wordis þat I | haue wrete before,   f. 72ʳ
writing *Ad Cassulanum presbiterum de ieiunio sabbati*, vndurnemeþ a
man mysteching houȝ þe sacramentis and þe sacramental þinggis of
þ⟨e⟩ olde lawe han ȝeuen place to þe sacramentis of þe new lawe,
wher Austen writiþ þus: 'þis man seiþ þat þe swerde haþ ȝeue power   2695

2677 is] in

to fasting, not hauing mynd of þe swerd scharp on boþe sides, (þat is to seie of boþe testementis, wiþ þe wiche swerd knyʒttis of þe gospel ben armed). He seiþ fire haþ ʒeue place to praiers, as þouʒ þer had at þat time no praiour be brouʒt into þe temple, and nouʒ fire is sent
2700 into þe world of Crist. He seiþ þat þe beest haþe ʒeue place to brede, as þouʒ he knewe not þat þe looues of forþsetting were not wont to be sett in þe Lordis borde, and as þouʒ he knew not himself to take parte of þe bodi of þe lombe wiþout wem. He seiþ þe blode haþ ʒeue place to drink, not beþenking himself nouʒ also to take blode in
2705 drink.' And Austen, amending þe witt of þis man, concludeþ þus: 'þerfor meche better and more congruli he schuld haue seide þus þat þe olde þinggis ben past and made new in Crist, so þat þe auʒter ʒeue place to þe auʒter, swerde to swerde, fire to fire, brede to brede, beste to beste, blode to blode. Forwhi, in alle þes þingis we sen þe
f. 72ᵛ flescheli oldnes to ʒeue place to þe newte of spirit.' So þat | here seint
2711 Austen calliþ þe sacrid oost brede, as he doþe in many oþur placis.

Also seint Austen writiþ þus in þe boke *Contra aduersarium legis et prophetarum*: 'þei þat reden knowen what Melchisedech brouʒt forþe whan he blessid Abraham; for if þei ben parteners þerof þei sen
2715 seche a sacrefice [now] offrid to God in al þe world.' And, as I suppose, þer wol no man seie þat it was Goddis bodi, or an accident wiþout soiect or substaunce þat Melchisedech brouʒt forþ þat time!—but ⌐brede⌐ and wyne, þat is nouʒ þe kinde of our sacrifice, as scripture techiþ wiþ olde seinttis and nameli Austen, as I haue
2720 oofte rehersid, and also Goddis bodi and his blode bi his gracious wirching þour vertu of his worde. For, as seint Ambrose seiþ, 'Not euery brede, but brede þat receiueþ þe blessing, is þe Lordis bodi.' And ful ofte whan seint Austen spekiþ of þis sacrament, he seiþ þat feiþful men knowen it, excepting no feiþful man but speking
2725 generalli as it were of comoun knowleche of feiþful men. But wel I wote þat riʒt fewe can tel clerli what is an accident! For men be not ʒit determened in Oxeford houʒ an accident schal be discriued or diffinid, or houʒ many most general kinddis ben of accidentis. And þerfor it is noo wondur alþouʒ feiþful knowe not an accident wiþout
2730 sogect, no more þan knewe Austen whan he seide þat feiþful men
f. 73ʳ knewen þis sacrament. | And seint Austen spekiþ not onli of þe knowleche feiþful men han bi weie of beleue, for þei mai not so know an accident to be Goddis bodi or brede, but raþur Austen spekiþ of þe knowleche þat þe peple haþe of þis oost bi her outword wittis, as

2722 blessing] lordis *canc.* blessing   2732 feiþful] of feiþful

we conceyue of Austens wordis in *Sermone de pascha* aleide before. 2735
Also seint Austen seiþ *De diffinicionibus recte fidei* þat 'Wyne was in
þe mysterie of our redempcion, whan Crist seide aftur þis "I schal
not drink of þis burioun of þe vine", þe wiche wordis Crist seide
aftur þe consecracion of þe wyne.' And so þat sacrament was wyne,
as seint Austen seiþ; and it was þe burion of þe frute of þe vyne, as 2740
Crist seiþ. And antecrist is to schameles if he seie þat þe burioun of
þe vyne þat Crist spekiþ of was an accident wiþout soiect!

Ful many ⌜seche⌝ sentencis of old seinttis a man þat had leiser
my3t draw togedur. But, for as meche as Goddis lawe in þis poynt
and in al oþur þat perteynen to good maneres and true beleue fulli 2745
quietiþ feiþful men, wherfor it nedeþ not to labour þus, saf for to
schewe þe beleue of olde seinttis acording to Goddis lawe, and hou3
þei hadden scripture in soueren auctorite and reuerence, and also for
to make þe deuyllisch presumpcioun of antecrist þe more open, so
pleynli determenyng a3enst Goddis law and | writing of olde seinttis f. 73ᵛ
þat confermed her belcue, writing and logic to blessid logic of holi 2751
scripture,—and in þat þei schewid þat þei were Cristis disciplis. For
Crist seiþ þus (*Io*.8): '3if 3e schal abide in my word, 3e schal be
uerreli my disciplis; and 3e schal know truþe, and truþe schal deliuur
3ow.' And of alle seche true disciplis þat louen effectuousli Goddis 2755
worde Crist seiþ þus (*Io*.17): 'Fadur, I haue schewid þi name to men
þe wiche þou hast 3eue hem to me, ⌜and⌝ þei haue kept þi worde.
And nou3 þei han knowen þat alle þinggis, þe wiche þou hast 3eue to
me, ben of þe. For þe wordis þe wiche þou hast 3eue to me I haue
3eue to hem; and þei han knowen verreli þat I haue gon out of þe,' 2760
for þei han take first Cristis wordis bi beleue and knowen hem aftur
bi vndurstonding, as I seide before. And, certis, þes fewe wordis of
Crist ileide before þe presumpcioun of þe renegat þat sittiþ in þe
chirche in þis article of þe sacred oost, and in þe mater of his wordli
lordschip and many oþur poynttis, weren sufficient to open þis 2765
antecrist to al þe world, if men wolden do her besines for to
vndurstond hem. For þou schalt vndurstond here þat al Cristis
wordis ben oo word, as Crist meneþ here and *Io*.14, of þe wiche
word Crist spekiþ þus here: 'Fadur, þi word is truthe.' And þis truþe
is Crist, for himself seiþ 'I am truthe', | so þat al wordis and truthis f. 74ʳ
þat Crist spekiþ outward ben substancialli and groundli Iesu Crist 2771
þat is þe worde of þe Fadur, and truþe, and þe scripture þat Crist
spekiþ ⟨o⟩f whan he seiþ þus: 'þe scripture þat þe Fadur haþ
halowid and sent into þe world mai not be vndo.'

2775   Siþþen þen al Cristis wordis ben oo worde þat is truthe and þe
boke of liif, and þis renegat wiþ his retinew demeþ Cristis wordis for
he determeneþ þe contrarie, it is open inouȝ þat þis renegat is of þe
fadur þe fende. For Crist seiþ þer: 'Whoso is of God hereþ Goddis
wordis', and þerfor þis renegat wiþ his special retinew hereþ not
2780   Goddis wordis, for he is not of God. And so, as Crist spekiþ þo
þinggis þat he haþ hirde of his Fadur, so þis grete bodi of antecrist
spekiþ þo þinggis þat he haþ hirde of his fadur þe fende, þat is a lier
and fadur of lesing and stode neuer in truþe, as Crist techiþ (*Io*.8).
And so þis fadur of lesing, inhabiting þe tunge of þis grete pseudo,
2785   diuideþ it into ful diuerse and contrarious opunions bitwene hemself
and to scripture also, and specialli in þe beleue of þe sacred oost, as I
haue wreten before. For it is no wondur alþouȝ þe chirche [be]
diuided from þe trinyte and vnyte of þre statis, answering to þe
trinyte and vnyte of God and expresli grounded in þe olde lawe and
2790   þe newe, and not onli diuided from þis vnyte but also imultepliid
f. 74ᵛ   into diuerse and contrarious vngrounded sectis, wiche ben | diuided
into many contrarious opunions aboute þis sacrament of vnyte. For
as in time of Moises lawe weren opunion⟨s⟩ multeplied aftur þe
[olde] lawe [to a] multitude of new vngrounded sectis of phariseis
2795   and saduceis and esseis, so it is in þe time of þe new law of oure new
vngrounded sectis; and so it was of þe sectis of heþen philesophris,
and sectis of heretikis in Austenus time, of Arrianes, Sabellianis and
Donatistis and ful many oþur þat multipliidden opunions aftur þe
numbre of her sectis, as don nouȝ our newe sectis.

2800   And þe diuisioun of mannes ⟨tu⟩nge into diuerse langagis began in
þe first Babilon, bicause þat þe peple ȝaf not credence to Goddis
wordis seiyng 'Aftur þis schal not euery man be sclayn wiþ watur of
flode.' And so þe tung of Cristis chirche, þe wiche was alle oon in al
poynttis longging to good maneres and truȝe beleue in þe time of þe
2805   apostlis and long aftur, is nouȝ diuided into diuerse and contrarious
opunions aboute þe sacrid oost, þe wordli lordschip of þe clergi and
ful many oþur, þe wiche diuision began in þe secunde Babilon, þat is
Rome, for faute of beleue of Cristis wordis. And þat Rome is Babilon
we mai se in þe first epistle of Petur in þe ende, and Austen (*De*
2810   *ciuitate Dei li.*18) þat 'Babilon is as þe first Rome, and Rome is as
anoþur Babilon.' And, as Austen seiþ þer, 'Babilon is as meche to
f. 75ʳ   seie as confusion or medling togedur.' For in Rome, as | Austen seiþ,
weren ful many diuerse and contrarious opinions among þe

2778 þe fende] of þe fende   2794 olde] newe

philisophris, for, as he writiþ þer, 'It was no charge to þe fende þat
was king of Rome wiþ hou3 contrarious errouris þei striuen bitwene 2815
hemself, while he had al togedur in his possessioun bi þe deser⟨t⟩ of
manyfolde and diuerse vnfeiþfulnes!' And on þe same wise it
stondeþ now of Lucifer, heed and king of þe grete bodi of antecrist
and his lemys, striuing bitwene hemself wiþ diuerse errouris, but al
rennyng into oon vnfeiþfulnesse a3enst God and his law. þan of þis 2820
processe and oþur wreten ny3e þe begynnyng, þou maist se þat þe
prophecie of Daniel rehersid before, whan Daniel seide þat 'Strengþe
haþe be 3eue to antecrist a3enst þe besie sacrefice', is uerrefiid of þis
renegat, þat besieþ himself for to distroie þe beleue of þe sacrid oost
tau3t bi Iesu Crist and his lawe. 2825

Furþurmore as anempst þe wirschip þat cristen peple doþ at þe
schewing of þis blessid sacrament, þou schalt vndurstond þat Crist,
God and man, haþ a special being in þe sacrid oost þour vertu of þe
consecracion bi his owne worde; and þis Iesu feiþful peple seen in þe
sacred oost bi true beleue, and to þis Iesu feiþful peple doþ safli þe 2830
hi3 wirschip of God. For þou schalt vndurstond here þat God haþ a
wirschip onli reserued to himself, þe wiche wirschip is ⟨c⟩ald in Grue
latria and in Laten *pietas*, þat is as meche to seie in Laten as *verus
veri Dei cultus*, as Austen | seiþ *Ad Macedonium et 4 et 5 De ciuitate* f. 75ᵛ
Dei and in many oþur placis. And þis Laten is as meche to seie as a 2835
trew wirschip of verri God; and þis wirschip is betokened bi þes two
uerbis *adorare* and *colere*, þe wiche be put in þe first commaundement þat techiþ þis wirschip to be don onli to þe lord God. And þis
wirschip, as Austen meueþ in *Libello suo de 6 questionibus*, stondeþ in
avou3yng and performyng þerof, in praiouris, in offring and in 2840
sacrefice, þe wiche wirschip and many oþur belongen onli to
Goddis maieste [and] mow be reduced to sacrefice. And of þis it
sueþ þat whosoeuer doþe þis wirschip to any creature þat euer God
made, doþ þe grettist synne, þat is þe grete crime of hirting or of
harmyng of Goddis maieste. For þis wiᴿrᴵschip is þe real protestacion 2845
of Goddis vniuersal lordschip. And so he þat doþ þis wirschip to any
creature seiþ in þat dede þat þe creature þat he doþ þat wirschip to is
vniuersal lord of alle þe world. And so he puttiþ in a practif, as
meche as in him is, þe first purpos of Lucifer, willing to euyn himself
and a creture to þe maieste of God. And so eche seche idolatrer is a 2850
tretour to God, conspiring wiþ Lucifer and his retinew a3enst his
maieste; and so he is worþi to be dede for his treson. And herfor God
haþ 3eue þis iugement vpon alle seche (*Exo*. 22) þat whosoeuer do

sacrifice to goddis schal be sclayn, saf onli to þe Lord. For, as
f. 76ʳ   Austen | techiþ in *De uera religione* bi long processe, [it] is not of
2856   feiþful cristen religion to do þis wirschip to any of þe elementis,
sunne or mone, ne to dede mennes bodies, or holi spirit or soule, ne
to imagis; for he seiþ þer þat 'þei þat make imagis ben better þan þe
imagis, and ȝit men wirschippen hem not so.'

2860   Furþermore, it is not of þis religion, as Austen seiþ þer, to
wirschip angellus þus, for þei wol not be wirschipt so. For Austen
seiþ in *Libro de 6 questionibus* 'It haþ alweie be þe condicions of good
angellus to put fro hem þis wirschip, and to teche it onli to be don to
God.' And herfor Austen in *De vera religione* markiþ þe caase and þe
2865   wordis betwene þe angel and seint Ion in þe ende of þe Apocalips,
and seiþ riȝtfulli: 'It is wrete a man [was] iwarned of an angel þat he
schuld not wirschip him, but oo God vndur whom þei schuld boþe
be seruanttis togedur.' And þerfor Austen seiþ, 'Alþouȝ we honour
angellus bi charite, for we owen hem loue and no þing ellis þat I am
2870   war of, ȝit', as Austen seiþ, 'we honour hem neuer bi seruage, þat is
omage onli duȝe to God.' Of þe wiche Crist spekiþ þus to þe fende,
desiring þis omage and seruage: 'þe lord þi God þou schalt wirschip
and ⟨t⟩o him alone þou schalt serue!' For, as Austen seiþ in þe same
f. 76ᵛ   boke, 'A man schuld wirschip þus þat þing þat þe most | souereyn
2875   angel wirschipiþ, and þat is onli God. And for to teche þis wirschip
onli to be don to God, Crist became man', as seint Austen seiþ. And
seint Poule seiþ þe same (*Tit*.[2]) wher he writiþ þus: 'þe grace of
God our sauyour haþ apperid to alle men, enformyng vs þat we,
forsaking idolatrie and wordli desiris, lyue sobirli, riȝtwiseli and in
2880   trew wirschipping of uerri God.' For siþ *pietas* in Laten is in
Englische 'true wirschip of uerri God', as I seide before bi wittnesse
of Austen, it wol nedes sue þat *impietas* in Laten þat contrariiþ þis
word *pietas* is idolatrie in Englische. And siþþen an aduerbe is
worþe a preposicioun wiþ a casuel, þis aduerbe *pie* [is] as þis worde
2885   *i*[*n*] *pietate*, and so seint Poulus wordis ben taken riȝt as I haue nouȝ
englischid hem.

And so þou maist se of seint Poulis wordis þat distroiyng of
idolatrie was Cristis chef erand hedur, and þe chif cause whi God þe
Fadur sent his Sone Iesu into þis world þe wiche is a grace. For he is
2890   a ȝift ȝeuen to vs freli wiþout any deseruyng. For þou schalt
vndurstond here, as seint Ierom seiþ in a epistle and seint Austen
De questionibus vetere et nove legis, þat, for as meche as þe peple

2866 þat . . . not (2867)] *twice*   2877 2] *gap*   2885 in pietate] impietate

desireful to God souȝt to come to him bi vnlefful menys and dede
idolatrie in many diuerse maneres, Crist ioined God and man in oo
persone to schewe þat man is in kinde nexte to God. For, as seint 2895
Austen techiþ in *De differencia spiritus et anime, et | 83 Questiones 46 et* f. 77ʳ
3 *De libero arbitrio*, mannes soule in kinde is þe best creature, euen in
kinde wiþ angellus, alþouȝ angellus ben aboue hem in office; and so
man haþ no souereyn bi weie of kinde saue God alone. Siþ þan a
man is as good and as worþi as is his soule þat is þe best creature in 2900
kinde, and ouer þis siþ man in kinde is as good and as worþi as it is
good and worþi in Crist, in whom it is bi grace and bi office aboue
alle angellus, þo þat soiecten men bi seruage onli duȝe to God, as
offring and sacrefice to stokkis and stones and worme-eten bonys, to
þe swerdis poynt and water, to olde raggis and many oþur þinggis 2905
þat ben callid imagis, reliquiis, þe wiche in comparson of God or of
man ben but uerri trifelis, don grete wrong aȝenst God, for þei
harmen his maieste and bereuen him of his prerogatif, and aȝenst
man also, for þei maken man þat is þe beest creature boþe bi kinde
and bi grace, to be soiect bi þe hiȝest and worþiest seruage to þingis 2910
of litil price, þe wiche wirschip of seruage ouȝt to be don to no
creature, ȝe, not to Cristis manhede þat is þe best creature, as seint
Ierom seiþ in a epistle. And þe same seint writeþ þus *Ad Uigilancium*
þat put idolatrie vpon Ierom and his felowis wiþ relikis 'I do þe to
wete þat we wirschip neiþur sunne ne mone, heuene ne erþe, 2915
cherubyn ne seraphyn, angel ne archangel, ne any þing þat mai be
nempned in þis world or ellis in þe world to come; | so þat we f. 77ᵛ
wirschip God alone.' But, for as meche as þis mater of idolatrie
[nediþ] a special labour and a leiser þat lackiþ me now, I leue of þis
now, conseiling al feiþful peple þat þei trete þe blessid sacrament of 2920
þe auȝter wiþ reuerens and solennite, and nameli wiþ clene liuing
and truȝe beleue tauȝt expreseli bi Goddis lawe þat onli mai quiete
mannys soule, and þat þei rest her deuocion and her wirschip in Iesu
Crist, uerri God and man whom þei sen in þe sacrid oost wiþ þe iȝe
of þe soule and truȝe beleue.   2925
    Naþeles of þis litil processe touȝching þe abhominacioun of
idolatrie þou maist se houȝ ful of þe deuyl weren þo visered
fendes þat nouȝ late in Ynglond made a constitucioun and artid
men to kepe it, þat no man schuld enpugne þe wirschip þat peple
doþ to imagis and relikis. For þis constitucion is aȝen alle Goddis 2930
law, olde and newe, þat chefli and most riueli forfendeþ þe grete

2913 writeþ] austen writeþ   2914 wiþ] doþ wiþ

synne of idolatrie. And it is aȝen þe chef cause of Cristis incarnacion,
as I wrote riȝt now. And it is dampnyng of alle þe cause of
martirdome of seinttis þat suffredden deþ boþ in þe old law and
2935 in þe newe bi cause þat þei wold [not] offre and so do sacrifice to
creaturis. For seint Austen seiþ þat alle offring is sacrefice. And if
þou þenk here þat þe idolatrers in þe olde law offreden to fendis, as
seint Poule seiþ, sekir, þat is soþe; for þei offreden in effect to fendis,
f. 78ʳ for good angellus alowen | not offring ne seinttis, saf onli þat offring
2940 þat is offrid to God alone. For whan men of blindnesse offridden to
hem, þei refusen þat offring and flen fro it. And þer þe deuel, þat
euer desireþ Goddis wirschip to be don to him, renneþ to and
receiueþ þat offring þat is don to creaturis. For, as seint Austen seiþ
in *Libro de 6 questionibus* God mai not for he wol not alowe any oþur
2945 sacrifice saue þat offring þat is onli to himself wiþout any mene. For,
as I seide, offring is a prerogatif and real knowleching of his vniuersal
lordschip and omage onli duȝe to his kindli regalie and maieste vpon
alle creaturis.

And for no good angel mai not alowe or accept offring don to any
2950 creature, þe deuil receiueþ alle seche offring, as seint Austen seiþ in
Libro de 6 questionibus and in many oþur placis, for he is fedde wiþ
many errouris. For bi þis skele seint Austen preueþ in *De questionibus
veteri et nove legis* þat it was þe fende þat appered in liknesse of þe
holi prophete Samuel to king Saul, whan þe wicche had rerid a spirit
2955 at þe request of þe king Saul, as it is wreten (*Re*.28), þat is to seie for
as meche as he toke upon himself the wirschip þat Saul profrid him.
For, as seint Austen seiþ, ȝif he þat aperid had be uerri Samuel, he
wold not haue take upon him þe wirschip þat Saul dede to þe spirit
þat apperid, for as meche as he tauȝt þe contrarie alle his lyf. For, as
f. 78ᵛ Austen seiþ, seinttis while þei lyued here lettid | men to do idolatrie
2961 wiþ hem, and ȝit wold if þei were present, as ȝe mai rede of Petur
(*Act*.10), and of Poule and of Barnabas (*Act*.14), and of þe blessid
angel þat schewid to Ion þe Apocalips (*Apoc. ultimo*), and of seint Ion
þe Baptist (*Io*.1) þat put from himself þe name and þe wirschip of
2965 Iesu Crist and told þe peple to whom þat wirschip was duȝe, whan
he seide 'Loo, þe lombe of God! loo, him þat takiþ aweie þe synne of
þe world!', for onli God myȝt do þat. Also seint Gregor put fro
himself as meche as he myȝt wordli reuerens and mekid himself, as
Legenda aurea telliþ. For wete þou wel here, alþouȝ þis be an heuy
2970 conclusioun to mennys wittis nouȝ blinded wiþ antecristis tradicions

2949 no] god no   2963 seint] þe blessid angel seint

and olde custome of synne, þat if any seint of heuene wold aproue
seche sacrifice or offring don to creaturis þe wiche is duʒe to God
onli, he schuld no more abide in heuene þan dede Lucifer and his
retinew þat begunnen þis heresie first!

And so it wol suʒe of þis processe þat, as Saul felle so foule for he   2975
wirschipt þe fende whan he had went to haue wirschipt Samuel, as
Austen seiþ in *De questionibus veteri et nove legis*, and þat fal betidde
him bicause he wirschipt anoþir þan God, so it stondeþ of folis þat
don offringgis to angellis, seinttis or to oþur imagis or relikis, for onli
þe fende and his | retinew mowen delite hemself in seche offring.   f. 79ʳ
And so it sueþ furþurmore of þis þat alle þat the blinde peple offriþ   2981
to any creature is offrid to fendis in effect, alþouʒ her effeccioun be
oþur,—as it was of þe heþen idolatrers þat forged hem imagis and
many diuerse liknesses in wirschip of goddis, þat is to seie Goddis
angellis after her entent, and offrid to hem to þis ende þat þei schuld   2985
be mene bitwene hem and þe hiʒe God whom þei callid þe Lord, to
procure for hem good at þis Lordis maieste, as seint Austen techiþ.
And in þis case welny ben nouʒ alle þo þat ben cristened, for hem
semeþ þat þei ben neuer better occupiid þan whan þei offende God
bi apeiring of his maieste, and harmen seinttis, in as meche as in hem   2990
is, for þei ben abouʒte for to bereue hem of her blis. For, if seinttis
wold assent to seche idolatrie, þei myʒt not abide in heuene. But þe
peple vndurstondeþ not þis. For as Lyncolun seiþ in a sermon þat
begynneþ þus *Natis et educatis* 'Long custum of synne for defaute of
preching of truþe makiþ þe grettist synnes to seme noo synnes or   2995
ellus suffreable.' And he puttiþ þer an ensample of þe golden calues
þat þe wickid king Ieroboam made and commaunded to be wirschipt,
þe wiche idolatrie for olde custum and fauʒte of truʒe correccioun
semed suffreable and | also holi, so ferforth þat Hieu, þat zelid for   f. 79ᵛ
God and distride meche maumetrie, left hem vndistroied (4 *Re*.10).   3000
As nouʒ late in Ynglond sum riʒt myʒti men besied hem to haue
distreide þe idolatrie late begun at ʒork, and ʒit þei hemself
continued forþ þe most abhominable idolatrie don at Caunturberi
and in oþur diuerse placis, and wolen not suffre oþur trew men to
inpugne it. And as þis idolatrie semed suffreable for long custome   3005
and fauʒte of true preching, so it was of þe foule synne of Sodom,
comunyng togedre on beestli maner wiþout matrimoin, as Lincoln
seiþ in þe same sermon and scripture wittnessiþ þe same.

And here we mai se houʒ harmeful ipocritis and dampnable ben þe
kinggis and þe lordis of cristendome, þat ben or schold be þe vicaris   3010

of þe godhede and so bi uertu of her office ouȝt to kepe hemself and al her peple from þe abhominacioun of idolatrie and so to kepe þe maieste of God hole upon alle her peple. But þei ben abhominable idolatrers hemself, and so ensamplen þis synne to þe peple and sum 3015 þei compellen þerto. þes schulden raþur be cald þe sones of Ieroboam, þat made Israel to do þis abhominacioun, þan þe sones of Dauid, as were al þe good kingis þat kepten hemself and her peple from þis filthehede. And, certis, ful litil be þei worþi to haue maieste upon þe peple þat recken so litil of Goddis maieste and prerogatif 3020 among his peple. Naþeles, as Iob seiþ, God makiþ an ipocrite to f. 80ᵣ regne for synne. | But I do seche an to vndurstond þat, as he is hiȝest among þe peple, so he schal be deppest in peine, as Austen seiþ *De libro de 12 abusionibus*. For alle þis I wote wel þat foolis wollen answere me here as idolatrers answeredde þe prophete Ier⟨e⟩mye 3025 whan he prechid aȝenst þis synne, as it is wrete (*Ie*.44), for [þei] seiden to him þus: 'We schal not here þi wordis þat þou hast spoke to vs in þe name of þe Lord. But we schal do þe word þat schal come out of our owne mouþe, þat we do sacrefice to þe quene of heuene, as we and our fadris and kinggis and [princis] han do; and we han be 3030 filde wiþ louys, and it was wel to us and we haue seien none iuel. Forsoþ, siþ þe time þat we haue cessid to do sacrifice to þe quene of heuene, we neden alle þinggis, and we ben wastid wiþ swerd and hungre.' And (*Macha*.1) it is wreten þat sum of þes Iewis seiden þus to þe peple: 'Go we and ordeine we a law wiþ þe heþen þat ben 3035 aboute us; for siþ we haue gon fro hem many harmes han founden vs.' So þat folis, as don cristen foolis nouȝ, witen idolatrie her prosperite and cessing þerof her aduersite.

þan of þes few wordis þou maist se houȝ abhominable is þis deuyllisch constitucion, for if it haue his cours it wol stablische þe 3040 chirche of Inglond in idolatrie for euer. And þat it schuld so, þe f. 80ᵛ fende, þat | is chif auctour of þis con⟨st⟩itucioun, and his lemys, þat specialli helpen him, made anoþur constitucion in þe same time þat þe gospel schuld not be prechid. For it is al one to me: no man schal preche þe gospel saue he þat wol not, and so no man schal preche þe 3045 [gospel]. þan for Goddis loue open þin iȝen here, and inwardli behold upon þis renegat þat sittiþ in þe chirche, and stumble no more at antecrist for it nedeþ not, for sekir he is a myddai deuil!

Furþurmore, þe prophete Daniel seiþ þat antecrist haþ cast downe þe place of halowing of þe prince of strengþe. And siþ it is al oon þe 3050 place of halowing and þe holi place, it were to wete here what þe holi place of þis prince is þat antecrist haþ þrow downe. I wote wel þat sum ben redi to vndurstond bi þis place of God þe temple of Ierusalem, sum þe feire bilding of material chirchis in þe newe lawe, and sum and most famousli, as þe world goþ now, wolen vndurstonde bi þis place þe state of þe clerge, and nameli of þe prelacie þat 3055 wolen be cald moost famousli holi chirche. Sum men, and most to purpos as I suppose, wolen vndurstonde bi þis place of halowing Goddis law, teching good maneres and trewe beleue, for þes two halowen a man here þat restiþ in hem. And þis lawe is substancialli Iesu Crist, in whom alle þat | schul be finalli halowid schul be blessid f. 81ʳ and rest in him for euer. And for þis rest of Cristis chosen in þis 3061 place Crist praieþ þus to his Fadur (*Io*.17): 'Fadur, I prai þe þat my chosen be oon as we ben, I in hem and þei in me, þat þei be ended into oon.' And no douȝte here but þat þes blessid peple schul be in Crist, for Crist seiþ þat he haþe spoken þe gospel to his chosen, to 3065 þis ende þat þei haue pees in hym. And also Ion seiþ þat 'God is charite; and whoso dwelliþ in charite dwelliþ in God and God in him.' So almyȝti God is þe place in whom alle þe chosen resten finalli bi ful blis hade in dede. And þis blis and halowing was behote to Abraham, and to his folowers in maneres and beleue, whan God 3070 seide þus to him 'In þi sede alle folk schul be blessid.' And þis sede as Poule seiþ is Crist. Naþeles, þo þat wollen rest in þis place finalli most rest here a while in Goddis lawe, for þat is þe halowing place of mannes soule. And wondur ȝe no more þat mannes soule haþ a place here in Goddis lawe, þan þat a law of man or ellis an argument haþ a 3075 place. And if I knewe a more heuenli place of halowing and any better þing þan mannes soule þat ouȝt to be halowid, I wold vndurstonde Daniellus prophecie of þat place. For I wote wel þat antecrist cast neuer dowun þe holi angellus, þat ben þe holi see | of f. 81ᵛ God as al oþur spiritis ben; and Lucifer and his retinew weren neuer 3080 þis place of halouing, for þei stoden neuer in truþe but failedden in þe begynnyng bi omiscioun; ne antecrist mai not cast downe almyȝtti God, þat is þe most holi place to alle seinttis as I wrote riȝt now. Herefor, [bi] þe casting dowun of þe place of halowing most be vndurstonde Goddis lawe, þat techiþ good maneres and trew beleue, 3085 in þe wiche men ben and mow be halowid, alþouȝ þat God forbede þat þer were no material chirche, ne prest, ne prelate in þis world.

And houȝ antecrist haþ cast down þe place of halowing it is open

3053 ierusalem] gr *canc.* ierusalem   3071 and] in þi sede and   3088 it is]
is it

in partie of þing wreten tofore. For, as fer as he haþ taken power
3090 aȝenst þe sacred oost, he haþ wrouȝt to cast down and distreie þe
trew beleue þerof, as I haue schewid before bi long processe. And on
þe same wise he fariþ wiþ many pointtis touȝching Cristis incarnacioun, for he seiþ þat Crist mai leue þe kinde of man, þe wiche he
haþ take into his owne persone, and become an asse or a toode, or
3095 whateuer abiect þing þat a man wol nempne. And if God mai do so,
houȝ wote antecrist þat it is not so?—seker, no more þan he wote in
case whan he seeþ tw⟨o⟩ postis, wiche is halowid and wiche is
vnhalowid, and so wheþur þei ben boþe substauncis, or accidentis
f. 82ʳ wiþout soiect, | or þat oon a substaunce and þat oþur an accident
3100 aftur his new drunken dremyng, þe wiche he calliþ a determynacioun! And þus þis fole most douȝte of euery creature, if he be
streitli examened, wheþur it be personalli God or no! Naþeles Crist
seiþ (Io.10) þat 'þe scripture, þat þe Fader haþ halowid and sent into
þe world, mai not be vndo', þe wiche scripture is Crist, God and
3105 man, þe boke of liif, as þe cros, in wiche Poule alone wold haue his
glorie, is Iesu Crist, in whom Poule was icrossid to þe world to him,
for þe reuelacion in boþe þes clausis limiten to þis witt. And also
Crist was not so vnavi⟨s⟩id but þat he knew wel þat al mannus
writingis, wordis, and conseitis and þouȝttis of mannus hert schuld
3110 perrische, aftur þat þe inperfeccioun of man were vtturli avoided and
ful perfeccion of man fulli gete. Bi onyng of God and man togedre
for euer bi clere knowing of þe godhed wiþout any mene, man schal
haue clere vndurstonding. And so þe scripture þat Crist spekiþ of
most nedis ⌐be⌐ vndurstonde Iesu Crist, God and man, and þe boke
3115 of liif. And Poule was noon idolatrer, hauing þe glorie þat he spekiþ
of in þe material gebat þat Crist died on, ne in þe passioun of Crist
þat passid wiþ his owne time and schal neuer be aftur þis, but in Iesu
Crist þat is uerri cros þat doþ aweie alle synne and ȝeueþ euerlasting
liif. For Crist seiþ 'Forsoþ, þis is euerlasting liif: þat þi chosen know
f. 82ᵛ þe alone, verri God, and him þat þou | hast sent, Iesu Crist', þe
3121 wiche Iesu Crist is the scripture þat mai not be vndo. And Crist left
neuer his manhede, for bi alle þe time of his deþ þe soule of Crist,
þat is man as Austen seiþ, was knyt wiþ þe godhede; and aftur þe
resurreccioun he myȝt not leue his manhede, for bicause he is almiȝti
3125 he mai not do þe lest inconuenient, but he most nedis do al þing on
þe beest wise þat it mai be do. And herfor seint Austen techiþ (3 De
libero arbitrio) þat 'God made þe a feld-telier'. And seche euidencis

3093 leue] not(?) eras. leue   3122 margin]us ⟨ . . .⟩ 68./]e ci. di. 13

of scripture myȝt þe obstinat heretike fynde in Goddis lawe ȝif he
had grace, bi wiche he myȝt proue many feire poyntis of beleue þe
wiche he falseli denyeþ nouȝ.   3130

Furþurmore seint Austen writiþ þus vpon þe worde of þe
prophete *Si dormiatis inter medios cleros* 'It is sum grete god to
sclepe amyddis þe clergeis, þe wiche sum men seien to be þe two
testementis, þat it be al oon to sclepe amyddis þe clergeis and to rest
in þe auctorite of þo testamentis; þat is to seie, to assent to þe   3135
wittnessinggis of euer eiþur testamentis, þat whan any þing is brouȝt
forþ and proued of þes testementis, al debate or striff ben ended bi a
pesible rest. And siþ it is þus, what oþur þing ben men preching wiþ
meche uertu iseie to be tau⟨ȝ⟩t, saue þat þan þe Lord schal ȝeue to
hem þe word þat þei mow speke or preche, if þei "sclepe amyddis þe   3140
clergies"? For þan þe word of truþe is ȝeue to hem, if þe auctorite of
þe | two testementis be not ileeft or forsaken of hem.' But antecrist   f. 83ʳ
kan fynde him noo rest amiddis þes clergies, for he is so beestli or
flescheli þat he sauureþ not þo þinggis þat ben of þe spirit of God.
And þerfor he haþ araid hym a soft heed of þe most delicat and esie   3145
rulis contened in ciuile, and isprad þerup⟨on⟩ t⟨en⟩dur tradicions þat
he calliþ canoun. And lest þ⟨e⟩ hardnes of þes two bereue him of his
rest, he keuereþ hem boþ wiþ an esie glose, and, aftur his ese askiþ,
addeþ as him likiþ. And if he be awacched bi noise of þ[e] clergies,
he is as wroþe as þe wynde and wol be auengid. Ȝe mai marke also in   3150
þes wordis of Austen þat al þe cause of strif in holi chirche is þat
men quieten not hemself in þes two testementis, and also þat
antecrist for þe same cause and his special lemys worþeli wanten
þe truþe of God. Also seint Austen in *De [d]ono perseuerancie*, writing
aȝenst þe enmyes of þe grace of God, and prouyng bi many feire   3155
euidencis of scripture þat alle þinggis þat we han ben of the purre
ȝift and grace of God, concludeþ þus finalli 'What man of sobur and
waking or quik feiþ receiueþ any voicis of men aȝenst so clere a
trumpe of truþe?' For, as he seiþ, þe hest of God sounnyng or
þundring, it is to obeie and not to dispice. Nouȝ, and it mai be seide 3160
wiþ charite, I prai God þat ⟨al⟩ þe w⟨o⟩rld wondur vpon þis antecrist
þat neuer cessiþ of his kursid liif and beleue of so mony clere
trumppinggis | and þundringgis as ben noisid aȝenst hym in Goddis   f. 83ᵛ
lawe and olde seinttis writing, of þe wiche sum ben rehersid before.

Ȝit, bicause þat antecrist is an armed fende aȝenst þe armurys of   3165

3140 speke] not speke   3154 dono] bono   3157 concludeþ] and concludeþ
margin de ci. d[/ ca.

God, I schal schete to him an arowe of Ionathas þat neuur ȝede backward. Ionathas is as meche to seie as 'þe culuur comyng', or 'þe culuur of þe Lord', þat meneþ þe Holi Gost þat came downe upon Crist and his apostlis in sensible tokenesse. Of þis culuur spekiþ þe
3170 prophete Dauid and seiþ þus 'Mercy schal bilde in heuenes wiþouten ende; whi?—for þou hast seide.' Vpon wiche worde seint Austen writeþ þus: 'þis man whos mouþe serueþ to þe truþe of God haþ behold himself at þe same truþe of God. As whos seiþ "þerfor I schal schew, þerfor I seie—whi?—for þou hast seide. I am sure, (or I
3175 made sure), schal seie whi, for þou God hast seide. For ȝif I schuld wauur or be vnstable in my worde, I schuld be confermed bi þi word. Whi? For þou hast seide."' Loo, schameles heretik, antecrist, fende! I seie þe sureli þat þe sacred oost is brede and wyne, and Cristis bodi and his blode, whi?—for God and his lawe seiþ so. I seie also þat
3180 idolatrie, þat is seruyce onli duȝe to God don to a creature, is a passing grisful abhominacioun, for God speking of þe same seruice seiþ 'þi lord God þou schalt wirschip, and him alone þou schalt serue!' And also, þou fals renegat, þi wordli lordschip is akursid, for
f. 84ʳ God haþe | dampned þat in word and d⟨e⟩de in boþe his lawis. And
3185 þe maner of proue goþ aȝenst þi kursid begrie and oþur abusions þat ben ryue!

ȝit schete we moo arowis of Ionathas, ȝif any grace mai ben to wounde þis fende antecrist or any of his special membris to ueri repentaunce. Seint Austen writiþ þus (super Ps.96): 'Go we not aweie
3190 from þe cornerstone þat is Crist, lest our vndurstonding make a falle; and be þat þing stablischid in him þat wauurred bi an vnstable mouyng, and lete þat þing hang in him þat hing bi vncert[e]in þinggis. Whateuer þing of douȝte a man haþ in his witt, þe scripture of God ihirde, departe he not from Crist.' Also þe same seint (super
3195 Ps. 85 super isto uerbo 'Eruisti animam meam' etc), answering to þis douȝte wheþur þer ben moo hellis þan oon, 'In þis auctorite', as þe same seint seiþ, 'and in þo þinggis þat ben openli put þerin, ben alle þinggis ifounde þat contenen feiþ and maneres or uertuus of lyuyng, as hope and charite; and so þei þat tristen in þis grounde stonden
3200 stable and sadde in þe feiþ, whan oþur þat don not so weten not where to abide.' Of whom seint Austen writiþ þus (De ciuitate li.18 ca.40] 'þe citecines of þe wickid citee isprad aboute bi londis, whan þei reden riȝtwise men whos auctorite semeþ not to be dispisid,
f. 84ᵛ discording bitwene hemself of þo þinggis ido and | furþest from the

3192 vncertein] vncerting

mynde of our age, finden not to whom þei owen raþest ⌐to⌐ beleue. 3205
Forsoþ, we in storie of oure religion, vndursett wiþ Goddis auctorite,
douten not [þat] whateuer þing wiþstondeþ þat to be most falsist.'
And herfor seiþ Austen (19 *De ciuitate ca.* 14] 'Lest a man þour
studie of knowing bi þe infirmyte of mannes mynde falle into þe
pestilence of any errour, he haþ nede of þe maisterschip of God, to 3210
whom he is made certeinli to abowe, and him nedeþ Goddis help þat
he freli obeie.'

For þei þat obeien not, seint Austen (*super Ps.*68) calliþ þem þe
pursuers of Crist, vpon þis worde of þe prophete seiyng 'þei ʒaf me
galle into my mete', wher seint Austen [seiþ] þus: 'Crist receiued 3215
swete mete, whan he ʒete þe pask lombe wiþ his disciplis; þer he
schewid þe sacrament of his bodi. þis mete, so deinte and so swete,
of þe vnite of Crist þe apostle comendeþ seiyng "We many ben oo
brede and oon bodi." And what is galle in þis mete, saue þe
aʒenseiers of þe gospel, þat ben as pursuers of Crist? For þe Iewis, 3220
crucifiyng him walking in þe erþe synned lesse þan þei þat dispisen
(or setten lite) bi him sitting in heuene', as don alle þo þat setten ony
ordenaunce or lawe before þe lawe of God. And of seche peple
plaineþ Crist bi his prophete, and seiþ þat þei han opened her
mouþe vpon hym as a rauenous roring lion. Vpon þe wiche word 3225
seint Austen writiþ þus in þe persone of Crist and his chosen,
complaynyng hem to God þe Fadur 'þei han opened her mouþe
vpon me, not of þi scripturis but of her | covetisis.' þis lioun, as þ⟨e⟩ f. 85ʳ
same seint seith, is antecrist þat, as ⌐þe⌐ prophete seiþ, liþe in awaite
in hidnes as a lion in his kouche. þis hidnesse, as Austen seiþ (*super* 3230
*Ps.*9), is gile or disceite, as is ipocrisie, and þe lion betokeneþ violens
of tirantrie, þe wiche two knyt togedur ben þe werst and þe last
persecucion of antecrist. And þo þat setten so litil bi þe auctorite of
Goddis lawe ben many antecristis þat maken oo grete antecrist, of
whom þe prophete pleineþ and seiþ þat 'Wickid men han tolde to me 3235
fablis or talis, but not as þi lawe.' And þerfor, as þe same prophete
seiþ, 'It is time þat God wirche', for seche antecristis han distreide
his lawe, for antecrist blasfemeþ it and settiþ it at litil or ellis riʒt
nouʒt, as it is oofte rehersid before. But þe chosen chirche of God
doþ not so for, as seint Austen seiþ (*De ciuitate* 19 *ca.* 18) 'þe citee of 3240
God, þat is þis chosen chirche, beleueþ to holi scripturis olde and
newe, þe wiche we callen canoun (or ellis autentik), wherof þe feiþ is
conceiued, of þe wiche a riʒtwise man lyueþ, bi þe wiche we walken
wiþout douʒtting as long as we ben pilgrimes from þe Lord. þe

3245 wiche feiþ or scripture saff and certeyn, we douten wiþout iust
repreff of sum þinggis, þe wiche we perceiuen not bi feling or reson,
neiþur ben made clere to us bi þis autentik scripture, neiþur han
f. 85ᵛ come into our knowing bi wittnessis to whom not | to ʒeve credence
were a dul þing.' Also seint Austen seiþ (*De ciuitate Dei li.* 20 *ca.*
3250 1[0]) 'þer ben sum men þat wenen þat aʒenrising (or resurreccion)
mai not be seide but of bodiis. But what speke þei aʒen þe apostle,
þat seiþ þat þer is a resurreccioun of soule? For þei hadden resen
aʒen aftur þe inner man and not aftur þe vttur man, to whom he seiþ
"Ʒif ʒe han aʒen⌜risen⌝ wiþ Crist, seche ʒe þo þinggis þat ben
3255 aboue."'

So þat Austen meueþ here and in ful many oþur placis þat it is a
grete and a dampnable inconuenient for to reuerse þe wordis of the
apostle, as it was also to Ierom blamyng Helmidie (*Epistola* 55),
enpunnyng þe sentens of the apostle setting mayndeheed before
3260 wedlok, where þat seint seiþ þus: 'What enberkist þou, what
repungnyst þou þe chosen vessel of God þat spekiþ þes wordis or
þinggis?' And of þis it sueþ here þat antecrist and his kursid lemys
schuld not repungne or berke aʒen þe apostle, and meche raþur
aʒenst Crist in þe feiþ of þe sacrid oost or bi mentenaunce of his
3265 wordli lordschip, and ⌜of⌝ mony oþur poynttis þat reuersen holi
scripture for, as Parisiensis rehersing seint Ambrose (*super isto
euangelio 'Ego sum pastor bonus'*) seiþ þat a man ouʒt to beleue
wiþout any disputicion to þo þinggis þat ben expressid in holi
scripture, for in alle seche þinggis a man ouʒte to be riʒt certeyn
3270 wiþout any douʒting. And acording to þis seint Austen writiþ þus
f. 86ʳ (*De ciuitate Dei li.* 20 | *ca.* [3]0): 'No man demeþ or douʒtiþ þe last
dome to be comyng, þe wiche is before seide bi Iesu Crist in holi
scripturis, saue seche oon þat bi an vnlefful boldnes or blindnesse
beleueþ not to þe same lettris, þe wiche han now schewid her truþe
3275 to alle þe world.' And bi þe same skele þer is no man þat demeþ or
dowtiþ not þe sacred oost to be brede and wyne, and Cristis bodi and
his blode, saue seche oon þat beleueþ not to Crist and his lawe þat
techiþ so.

And so no man, saf he þat is out of þe beleue of boþe þes lawis,
3280 beleueþ þat it is leefful to þe clergie to occupie secler lordschip as it
doþ nouʒ. And on þe same wise it is to suppose of ful many oþur
feiþful articlis enpungned nouʒ bi þe grete renegat and his kursid
lemys, þat obstinatli reuersen Crist and his chosen chirche. Of þe

3250 10] 11   3271 30] ⟨2?⟩0   3280 beleueþ] and beleueþ

wiche chosen seint Austen writiþ þus (*De ciuitate Dei li. 20 in fine*):
'þo þat saueren (or vndurstonden) aftur God taken þe uerri 3285
almyʒtinesse of God as f[o]r þe grettist argument of al þinggis þat
ben sen vnbeleueful to men, alþouʒ þei ben contened in holi
scripturis, whos truþe is nouʒ affermed in many maneres. For þis
peple holdeþ þis for certeyn þat God mai not liʒe in þo scripturis,
and þat he myʒt do þinggis þat is vnpossible to an vnfeiþful man.' 3290
And so God mai make brede to be his bodi as his lawe techiþ, alþouʒ
antecrist, þat is þe vn|feiþful renegat þat I haue ⟨s⟩o ofte spoke of, f. 86ᵛ
seiþ þat to be inpossible. Also seint Austen (*De ciuitate Dei li. 21 ca.*
23), arguyng aʒenst þo þat seien þat turmentis of þe iuel angellus and
wickid men ben not euerlasting, writiþ þus: 'þer mai no cause be 3295
more riʒtwise or more openli founde whi it is ferme and stable and
þe most truʒe fidelite (or feiþ) þat þe deuil and his angellus schul
haue no returnyng to riʒtwisenes and liif, saue þat þe scripture þat
deceiueþ no man seiþ þat God haþ betake wickid angellus to be
bronddis of helle. Also Crist seiþ þat þer is euerlasting fire ordeined 3300
to þe deuil and alle his angellis, and to men þat schul be dampned.
And so,' as seint Austen writiþ þus aʒenst þo þat seien þat þis
sentence of dampnacioun schal be trewe upon angellus but not upon
men 'wher þe sentence of God ʒeuen aʒenst yuel angellus schal be
trewe, and fals aʒenst men? Ʒe, pleinli þis schal be if þat God seiþ 3305
schal auaile more þan þat men supposen. And bicause þis mai not be
do, men owen raþur to obeiʒe to Goddis heest while time is, þan to
arguʒe aʒenst God, if þei coueite to wante euerlasting turment.'

But antecrist, þat wantiþ drede of þis turment, ʒeueþ more
credence to a ⌜n⌝[e]we fonned gloce þan to holi scripture, or to 3310
olde seinttis writing and to þe beleue of holi chirche istablischid and
continued | into þe losing of Sathanas. But and he [be] verreli Petris f. 87ʳ
successoure in maneres and beleue, as he falseli presumeþ, he wold
not do so. For Petur spekiþ þus (in *Itinerario Clementis li.* 8) to his
felowis Clement, Niceta and Aquila: 'Be it not tedious to ʒowe in 3315
disputing to enforme and to teche þe vnkunning peple aftur þe
wisdome [þat] is ʒeuen to ʒow bi þe puruyaunce of God, so þat ʒe
ioine þe eloquens of ʒour sermon to þo þinggis þat ʒe han hirde and
ben bitake to ʒow of me. And speke forþ no þing of ʒour owne, and
þat þat is not betake to ʒow, alþouʒ it seme like truþe. But folow ʒe 3320
þo þingis þe wiche, vnfongen of þe uerri prophete, I haue ta⟨k⟩e to
ʒow, alþouʒ þei seme not to be of ful affermyng. For ofte time it

3286 for] fer as   3310 a newe] awe, ⌜n⌝ above -a-   3316 to¹] and *canc.* to

hapneþ sum men to bowe aweie from þe truþe, while þei wenen
hemself to haue ifounde wiþ her owne þou3tis a liknesse of a uerrier
3325 and a strangur truþe. It is wondur to me þat men maken wiþ her
kurious þou3ttis þinggis to be hard, þe wiche my3t li3tli be founde.
And þei don þis most þat semen [to] hemself to be wise, and wiche
also, willing to comprehende þe wil of God, vsen God as a man; for
no man mai knowe þe consail or þe witt of a man, but if he himself
3330 schew out his þou3t. Hou3 meche raþur a man mai not knowe þe
f. 87ᵛ witt or þe worke of þe invisible and incompre|hensible God, but if he
sende a prophete þat schewiþ his conseile as meche as it is lefful to
men to lerne. I hold it but a scorne whan men demen of þe uertu of
God bi weie of kinde, and wenen þat to be possible to h[i]m. And
3335 þus þo þat ben vnri3twise men demen ri3twise God, and vnwise men
demen þe crafti man, and corruptible men demen God þat is
vncorruptible, and þe creature demeþ þe Maker.' And þis is open
at i3e if we take hede: antecrist, þat is vnri3twise, vnwise, corruptible
and a defoulid creature, bi his new tradicions and determinacions
3340 3eueþ dome a3enst Crist and his lawe and feiþful men þat louen it.
    And soone aftur seint Petur spekiþ þus: 'If any man desire for to
lerne, seche he þe uerri prophete. And whan he haþ founden him he
schal wirche wiþ him not wiþ questions and disputicions or
argumentis. But, if þis prophete schal any þing answere or pro-
3345 nounce, þat þing mai not be dou3tid to be vncertein. And þerfor
before al þinggis b[e] þe verri, trew prophete isou3t and bi his wordis
ihold. And considre we ri3t be⟨sil⟩i þe werke of Goddis purueaunce,
for bicause þat philesophris had brou3t in sum sotil wordis and hard,
so þat þe names of þe wordis my3t not be know to alle men and able
3350 to vnderstonde, God haþ schewid to hem demyng hemself to [b]e
f. 88ʳ craft[i] of wordis to be utturli vnwise anempst þe knowing | of truthe.
Forwhi, þe science of þo þinggis þat is betake bi þis uerri prophete is
simple, open and schort, þe wiche science philesophris, walking [bi]
bipaþis and difficulteis of wordis, han not iknow in al þe weie of her
3355 liif.' Of þis processe of Petur we mai vndurstonde what ioie þis seint
wold haue had of þis renegat þat pretendeþ to be his successour, þat
haþ so litil reward nou3 to þis uerri prophete whom he reuersiþ
obstinatli boþe in lyuyn[g] and preching. Furþurmore seint Petur
spekiþ þus (in Itinerario Clementis li. 10): 'þo þinggis þat ben of þe

---

3334 him] hem   3338 antecrist] to antecrist   3344 any] do any
3346 be] bi   trew] of trew   3350 be crafti] þe crafte   3358 lyuyng] lyuyn
margin Itinerarij[/mentis l[

feiþ ben not to be gadrid of mannes coniectinggis and opunions, in 3360
þe wiche men ben huȝgeli disceiued. But þei ben to be gadrid of þe
feiþ of þe truȝe prophete, as oure doctrine is. Forwhi, we speken no
þing of ourself, neiþur we schewen þinggis gadrid of mannes
estimacion; for þat and to disceiue þe herers were al oon. But we
prechen open þinggis betake to us bi þe auctorite of þe uerri 3365
prophete.' Of þis processe of seint Petur we mai se þat seint Petur
wold haue be gretli displesid wiþ þis new frantike determynacion
aboute þe sacrament of þe auȝter, and many oþur vngrounded
tradicions brouȝt into þe chirche bi þe grete renegat and autentike
eretik þat I haue oofte spoken of. 3370

Ȝit, for to schew what feiþ olde seinttis ȝaf to þe wordis of holi
scripture, I purpos to reherse mo of her sentencis | here. Seint f. 88ᵛ
Austen, disputing of þe watris þat ben aboue þe firmament,
concludeþ þus (*Super Genesim ad litteram li. 2 ca.* 1 in þe ende):
'Houȝ and what maner watris ben þere, douȝte we not hem to be þer; 3375
for þe auctorite of scripture is more þan any mannes witt is able to
take or vndurstonde.' And so a feiþful, if antecrist wold suffre, myȝt
boldli seie þat oure sacrid oost is brede and wyne, and Cristis flesche
and his blode, for þe auctorite of scripture rehersid before is more
þan al þe world mai comprehende. And bi þis a man mai se what him 3380
ouȝt to seie of idolatrie, of þe lordschip of þe clerge, of begging of
freris and many seche oþur synnys. For þe auctorite of holi scripture,
dampnyng seche abhominaciouns, is grete wiþout mesure; and þe
wittnesse of antecrist and his lemys, defending seche hidous synnes,
is riȝt nouȝt worþ. For as þe same seint seiþ (*ad Bonefacium epistola* 3385
33): 'þo þat suen not þe wittnessis or þe lawis of God han lost þe
charge (o[r] þe price) of mannes wittnesse', so þat her wittnesse ouȝt
not to be of any charge or auctorite to þe peple. Wherfor siþ antecrist
is falseli and openli forswore, goyng aweie from þe vowe and oþe þat
he made to God and to his lawe in his baptym, he haþ vnablid 3390
himself to be wittnesse in any cause þat is of charge. Also þis seint
writiþ þus (*in prefacione Libri retractacionum*): 'Forsoþ, I trowe mony
maistris to be made | aȝenst Cristis commaundementis, whan þei f. 89ʳ
felen diuerse þinggis and contrarie betwene hemself. But whan þei
se[i]en alle þe same þing and seien soþ, þei gon not from þe 3395
maisturschip of þe uerri Maister. Forsoþ, þei offenden not whan
þei seien many of Cristis wordis, but whan þei adden her owne;
forsoþ, on þat wise þei fallen fro meche speche into fals speche.'

3371 what] þat what   3387 or] of   3395 seien¹] seen

What wondur þan is it þouȝ antecrist be fals and a grete lier þat is so
3400 contrarie in himself, and also not onli addeþ to Cristis wordis but
also contrariiþ hem euen in worde and dede?

Also seint Austen writiþ þus vpon þis word *Omnis enim qui dimittit
vxorem suam et cetera* 'þe ordenauncis of þe Lord ben to be kept
wiþouten any retreting; forwhi, þei han riȝtwisenes, þe wiche is
3405 before himself wheþur þat men approue hem or vnproue hem. And
þerfor it behoueþ not to be seide þat Goddis ordenauncis ben not to
be kept lest men be offended, or lest men be lettid from þe helþe þat
is in Crist Iesu.' Loo, whateuer antecrist and his lemys seien of
Goddis lawe, it is riȝtwise in Goddis siȝt, not onli as ⌜a⌝nempst þat
3410 partie þat techiþ good maneres, but also anempst þat partie þat
techiþ aȝenst trewe beleue! And so, alþouȝ antecrist be offended and
hornewood wiþ many ordenauncis of God aboute trew beleue and
goode maneres, of þe wiche sum ben ooft rehersid before, ȝit þei ben
f. 89ᵛ trewe and riȝtwise, and ouȝt to ben | schewid and kept, and defended
3415 as ful autentik and trewe aȝenst þe foule mouþe of antecrist, þat is
ful of sclaundring, deprauing and blasfemyng of Goddis lawe. And
herfor seint Austen writiþ þus of an aduersarie of þe [lawe] and of þe
prophetis (*libro Contra aduersarium legis et prophetarum*): 'þouȝ it be
not open of what þis blasfemie is, þe scripture of God, þe wiche he
3420 pursueþ wiþ kursid disputicions, is to be defended aȝenst his tunge!'
Furþurmore seint Austen writiþ þus (*libro De mendacio*) how þer
were sum men in his time þat wold raþur suppose þat Poule wrote
fals, þan þat Petur synned whan Poule vndurname him (*Gal.*2). And,
as Austen seiþ þere, 'While þes men wolen defende Petur from
3425 errour, and from þe schrewid weie into wiche he was fallen, þei
enforcen hem to ouurturne þe weie of þe religion of cristendome, þe
auctorite of scripturis ibroke and amenusid in þe wiche helþe is to al
men.' For, as þis seint seiþ in þe same boke, 'Whan þe auctorite of
truþe is broke or liȝtli lackid or amenused, alle þinggis schul leue
3430 douȝteful.'

And acording to þis sentence seint Austen writiþ þus in a epistle
to seint Ierom: 'Forsoþ, I knowleche to þi charite þat I haue lerned
to bring (or ȝeue) þis drede and wirschip onli to þe bokis of
f. 90ʳ scripturis, þe wiche ben nouȝ callid canoun (or autentike), þat | I
3435 beleue most stedfastli noon of the auctouris of hem to han erred in
any þing in writing. Forsoþ, I rede oþur men on þis wise, þat I wene
not any þing þerfor to be soþ bicause þei feledden so, but bicause þat

3399 grete lier] lier grete, *marked for rev.*

þei myȝten make euidence to me bi þe autentike auctoris or probable
reson þat seche a þing abhorreþ not from truþe. And, my broþur, I
trow þat þou fele noon oþur wise. For utturli I deme not þat þou 3440
wilt þat þi bokis be rad so as þe bokis of prophetis and apostlis, of
whos writing it is a kursid þing to douȝte þat þei wanten al errour.
And so', aftur he writiþ, 'þus I schal rede holi writt, isett in þe
souereyn and heuenli heiþe of auctorite, certein and sekir of þe
truthe þerof.' For, as þe same seint seiþ, it mai not be þat þis 3445
auctorite of scripture liȝe in any parte, wher also he writiþ þus (in
Epistola ad Paulinum de uidendo Deo): 'If þou aske wher God mai be
seen, I answere he mai. If þou aske wherof schal I wete þat, I answere
for it is rad in þe most uerri scripture "Iblessid be þo þat ben of
clene hert for þei schul se God."' But seche an euidence is of litil 3450
price at þe grete renegat antecrist and his special membris, þat so
openli reuersen and demen ful many nedeful þinggis expressid in
Goddis lawe.

Ȝit, into þe confusioun of antecrist and his dampnable retinew, þis
seint | writiþ þus (*Super Ps*.66): 'God þat mai do al þinggis is our f. 90ᵛ
filde-telier; we ben sure. In hap sum man seiþ "þou seist God to be 3456
our fild-tilier!" If I seie, no man beleueþ it. If Crist seie, wo to him
þat beleueþ it not! What þerfor seiþ þe lord Iesu? "I am þe vyne, ȝe
ben þe branchis, and my Fader is þe feld-telier."' Lo, þis was a ful
euidence to seint Austen to graunt þat þe Fadur of heuene made his 3460
worde on þe most perfite wise þat it mai be made, for þe
almyȝtinesse of God is þe cause whi he mai make no fauȝte or
synne. For seint Austen seiþ þus (in *De natura et gracia*) 'God
forbede þat we seie þat God mai synne! Forsoþ, he schal not be
vnmyȝti, as folis wenen, bicause he mai ⌐not¬ diȝe in his godheed or 3465
ellis denyȝe himself.' And so God is not vnmyȝtti, alþouȝ he mai not
denyȝe or leue his manhede, as he is not vnmyȝtti, alþouȝ he mai not
punsche an innocent bi þat peyne þat is callid of harme, as he schuld
if he left his manheed. For s[i]þ his manheed oned wiþ God mai not
synne so ioined, þe leuing of þis manhede, þat is þe grettist peine þat 3470
mai be þouȝt to þis manhede, most go before þe synne þerof; and so
God schuld punsche an innocent bi þis peine þat I spak of, and þat
he mai not do wiþ alle the power þat he haþ, alþouȝ he peined his |
owne Sone bi þat peine þat is cald þe peine of feling. And þis proueþ f. 91ʳ
God to be almyȝti and in no þing vnmiȝti. For seint Ancelme seiþ 3475
þus (in *suo Proslogion*) 'Lord God, herfor þou art uerreli almyȝti: þou

3469 for siþ] forsoþ

maist no þing bi nounpower, ne any þing aȝenst þiself', as we mai
and don as ofte as we synnen, or chesen þat þing þat is lesse good,
and leuen þe better.

3480 Sum of antecristis disciplis seien also þat Crist ȝede not to helle,
ne he was beried, ne dede upon þe cros or in þe sepulcre. Also, in as
meche as þei seien Crist mai leue his manheed, þei meuen þat Cristis
manhede was neuer ne schal be blessid, for it lackiþ surete of blisse,
þat is þe chef parte of blisse, as Austen meueþ (Encheridion 18 ca.).
3485 And so [no] man is sekir in þo goodis þe wiche he mai lese aȝenst his
wille, as Austen seiþ (De libero arbitrio 2 [li.]). And Cristis manhede,
as antecristis disciplis seien, mai lese his blisse; þan was it neuer sure
þerof, as Austen seiþ, and so it was neuer ne mai be fulli in glorie or
blisse. But I consail here þat þes folis be riȝt wel war lest þei exclude
3490 hemself from euerlasting blisse bi seche fals opunions aboute þe
articlis of beleue, for þes þat þus deuiden Crist ben antecrist! For, as
seint Ion seiþ, 'Euery spirit þat departiþ Crist is not of God, and he
is antecrist' (Io.4).

f. 91ᵛ   Naþeles, I wondur þe lesse, alþouȝ þei | speke þus hidousli of
3495 Cristis manheed, for þei speken wors of his godheed, for þei s⟨ei⟩en
þat it mai be þat no god or any þing is ⌐or¬ mai be; for, as þei seien
falseli, no negatif includeþ contradiccioun and þerfor eche negatif is
possible. But, certis, and þes foolis weren in her riȝt witt, þei myȝt
vndurstond þat if it were so þat no þing is, þan it were a truþe þat no
3500 þing is; and siþ eche truþe puttiþ þe first truþe, it sueþ þat God is;
and so þis negatif þat no þing is includeþ contradiccion and is
inpossible, alþouȝ þese blinde foolis seien þe contrarie. þes wikkid
sedis and many seche oþur þes newe sectis þat God hatiþ to be
plantid han sowen in þe chirche, þe wiche acumbren þe sede of þe
3505 worde of God þat it grow not freli, as it dede sum tyme. And bicause
þat it wold be a labour wiþout mesure to reherse here in special þe
wickid and blasfemous sedes of doctrine þat antecrist and his lemys
han sowen in Cristys chirche, þerfor I cesse here nouȝ of þis besines.
And I wol schew bi writing of olde seinttis houȝ þei chargeden þe
3510 auctorite of holi scripture, for whi þe liȝt reward þat antecrist haþ to
þis auctorite is grounde of alle errouris and heresies þat infecten þis
world, heþen and cristen.

f. 92ʳ   Seint Austen writiþ þus (super Ps.57): 'Eretikis þat | weren deff
aȝenst þe gospel and suffren us not to rede þe wordis of God, þe
3515 wiche þei bosten to haue kept fro þe fire and wolen do hem aweie
      3485 no] gap

wiþ the tung, speken her owne þingis and speken veyn þingis, seiyng
þus, leiȝing for hem her owne auctouris "He haþ betake to us, and he
haþ betake to vs." Ȝe, and I seie "He haþ betake to us, and he haþ
betake. And I seie soþ. But what is þis to me? For neiþur þou redest
in þe gospel hem þat þou nempnest to me, neiþur I rede of þe gospel   3520
hem þat I nempne. Lete take awei our cartis (or scrowis), and lete þe
boke of God come a place! Here þou Crist seiyng; here þou Crist
speking!" But heretikis seien "Naie, but here ȝe what we seien. For
⌐þat⌐ þe gospel seiþ we wolen not here!"' And þan Austen writiþ
þus: 'Speke we truȝe þinggis þat heren truȝe þinggis; speke we þat   3525
God seiþ and not þat man seiþ. It mai be þat þat man lieþ, but it mai
not be þat truþe lieþ!' Here ȝe mai se what Austen wold haue felid
and haue demed of þe vngronded fantesies of antecrist, for he seiþ
þus [(De natura et gracia)]: 'I am fre in al maner of writinggis of men,
for onli to holi scripturis I owe consentinggis wiþout renying or   3530
recusing.' Wherfor Austen writiþ þus: 'Forsoþ, I a man, and as
meche as it is grauntid of holi scriptures, so meche I dar seie and no
þing of myself. And bicause þat | scripture, to þe wiche it mai not be   f. 92ᵛ
wiþseide, seiþ þus: "Lord, þou hast deliuurred my soule fro inner
helle", we vndurstonde to be as it were two hellis.' Here ȝe mai se   3535
houȝ it wold haue be riȝt hard to haue brouȝt seint Austen to haue
consentid to þe new feiþ abowte þe sacrid oost!

Ȝit þis blessid Ionathas schetiþ at antecrist bi his trew lege man
seint Austen preuing þat God is loue and charite (De Trinitate li. 8
ca. 8) wher he seiþ þus: 'Douȝte we bi noon infidelite of þo þinggis   3540
þat ben to be bileued! Affirme we bi no folie þo þinggis þat ben to be
vndurstond! In þe raþur auctorite it is to holde, in þe secunde
þinggis truþe is to be souȝt. We mai not wiþstonde þe most certeyn
feiþ, þe most strenggist auctorite of scripture seiyng "God is
charite" et cetera.' Nouȝ, lord God, houȝ is þis þat antecrist   3545
wiþstondeþ so many open auctoriteis of þi lawe, affermyng our
sacrid oost to be brede and wyne and þi bodi and þi blode?
Furþurmore seint Austen (De Trinitate li. 15 ca. [2]7), blamyng þo
þat besiedden hem to come to þe knowyng of þe Trenite bi reson
raþur þan bi feiþ of scripture, writiþ þus: 'Whi is it þat þis peple   3550
bileueþ not of þe souereyn Trenite, þat is God, þat þing þat is
founde in holi writt, raþur þan þei aske a clere reson to be ȝeue to
hem, þat is not itake or conceiued of mannes mynde sclow and feble?

3529 de . . . gracia] after þus (3631)   3546 open auctoriteis] auctoriteis open,
marked for rev.   3548 27] 17   3553 mynde] myndee

And whan þei han beleued holli to holi scripturis as to þe most trewe |
f. 93ʳ wittnesse, þan wirche þei in praiyng and seching and asking and in
3556 good lyuyng, þat þei mai vndurstond, and þat þe same þing be iseen
bi mynde as meche as it mai þat is ihold in feiþ. Who is þat þat
warneþ þis? Ʒe, who is þat amonestiþ not to þis?' Loo, what seint
Austen wol here wiþ seint Petre: þat euery man were not onli sad in
3560 þe beleue, but also redi as he mai to proue his beleue bi reson.

But antecristis nouellrie wantiþ boþe beleue and resoun, as wel as
experience or oold seinttis writing. And aʒenst seche rauing þe same
clerk writiþ þus (*li*. 3 *De Trinitate ca*. 10): 'þer is an auctorite of
Goddis scripturis wherfro mannes mynde schal not straiʒe aweie,
3565 neiþur be cast downe bi cleues, rockis or skerris of her owne
suspeccions, þe sadnesse or grounde of Goddis wordis or speche
ilefte, wher neiþur witt of bodi gouerneþ neiþur clere reson of truþe
declariþ.' And þan he rehersiþ þe processe of þe scripture þat seint
Steuen aleggiþ for him (*Act*.6), and concludeþ þus finalli: 'What is
3570 more euidence or open þan þis? What is strengger þan so grete an
auctorite?' And if þe lawe of Moises, þat seint Steuen rehersid þer,
be of so grete auctorite as seint Austen meueþ here, houʒ is it þat the
wordis of Crist ben nouʒ of so litil reward to þo þat pretenden
hemself to be þe chef of þe chirche of Crist?—nameli siþ Austen seiþ
3575 (*De doctrina christiana*) 'Whateuer a man schal lerne out of scripture, |
f. 93ᵛ if it be noious it is dampned þer, and if it is profitable it is ifounde
þer!' And I wold fayn wete of antecrist here wher he fyndeþ in holi
scripture his new determynacioun;—for, certis, I suppose it wol be
harde to him to finde þer a colour of his wilful and woode rauyng!
3580 Wherfor, certis, if his fantesie schuld be a poynt or an article of
beleue þat is so necessarie to mannes saluacioun, he most seie wiþ þe
prophetis of þe olde lawe 'þe Lord seiþ þes þinggis', and wiþ Poule
and oþur apostlis in þe new lawe 'I haue take of þe Lord þat þing þat
I haue betake to ʒow', and in anoþur place he seiþ þat þe gospel þat
3585 he prechiþ is not aftur man, and þat he neiþur receiued or lerned it
of man but bi þe reuelacioun of Iesu Crist. And herefore uppon þis
texte of scripture 'Mi name is glorified in þe heþen or in þe folkis, þe
Lord seiþ' also Austen writeþ þus (*Epistola* 31 *ad Vincencium
donatistam*) 'Ʒe þat presumen upon mannes witt, herkeneþ "þe
3590 Lord seiþ"; he seiþ not "Donat seiþ", or Rogat, or Vincent, or
Ambrose, or Hillari, or Austen seiþ, but "þe Lord seiþ."' Lo what
ioie seint Austen wold haue had of þis nouellrie, or of any oþur not
grounded in scripture!

And I drede me not, and seint Ierom were here nouȝ in oure daiis of þe same condicions as he was in his owne daiis, antecrist and his 3595 mene schuld haue had riȝt a scharp rebuke or chiding for his newe and vngrounded triflis, as had oon þat enforced | himself to susteine f. 94ʳ þe errouris of Origene. To whom seint Ierom spekiþ þus (*Epistola* 40): 'Whoeuer þou be þou affermer of new loris, I beseche þe spare þou Romaines eeris, spare þou þe feiþ þe wiche is ipreisid bi þe voice 3600 of þe apostle. Whi aftur foure hundrid ȝere enforcest þou to teche us þat we knew not before? Whi dost bring a place þat Petre and Poule wold not? Into þis dai þe world haþ be cristen wiþout þis doctrine! I, an olde man, schal hold þat feiþ in wiche I was bore a child.' Acording to þis seint here a feiþful man mai areson antecrist, and 3605 seie þus: 'þou affermer of new lore and feiþ, I prai þe spare þou Romaines eeris, and offende þou hem not wiþ þi nouellries.' For þou ouȝtest to know wel þat it was declared bi pope Nichol and his conseil long before þe new determynacioun, and þat bi auctorite of þe gospel and þe apostlis, þat þo þinggis þat ben put on Cristis borde 3610 ben after þe consecracioun not onli a sacrament, but also uerri Cristis bodi and his blode. And þou glosest þis now bi his contradictorie, and seist þat it is heresie, but if it be vndurstonde so as it is wrete before. And þus þou offendest þe old eris of Rome wiþ þin vnruli noise and clatring of þin new eresie! þou schuldest prinscepalli also 3615 haue spared þe feiþ tauȝt bi Iesu Crist, and ipreisid boþ bi þe voice and þe writing of þe apostle. And whi, fals antecrist and renegat, not onli | aftur foure hundrid ȝere but aftur a þousand ȝere aftur the f. 94ᵛ losing of Sathanas, þou enforcest þe to teche Cristis chirche an article of beleue vnknowen before? Is þer any oþur cause saue into 3620 þyn owne dampnacioun? þou most fulfil þe prophecie of Daniel anempst þe taking aweie of þe besie sacrefice, as it is declared aboue. Whi bringgist þou a place þat Petir and Poule brouȝt not?—ȝe, and þat Crist and Poule han dampned? Wost þou not wel, blinde fende, þat þe world haþ be cristen, and ȝit is wiþout þe newe determyna- 3625 cioun?' For not onli good and feiþful men, but also oþur þat pursuen hem to deeþ, bileuen aȝenst þe newe rauyng þat þe sensible sacred oost is Cristis bodi. And so þe chirche of þe chosen, þat in þe begynnyng of þe new lawe was a child nouȝ bore of þe sede of Crist, and now bi processe of time is now wax olde, schuld now answere to 3630 þis antecrist þat trauelliþ it wiþ new eresies, seiyng þus: 'I, oolde, schal holde þe feiþ of þe sacred ost in wiche I was bore a child!' And

3615 of] of/of

þus a man mai openli se þat þe feiþ of þe sacred oost, as Crist and his
apostlis and oolde seinttis han wreten and tauȝt, and haþ be
3635 continued among feiþful men into þis dai, is riȝt a sure weie
wiþout any perplexite or doute.

And bicause þat þe feling of olde seinttis schold be more open in
þis mater to alle þo þat reden it, I rehers here more acording to her
writing reportid before, in entent þat men mow clerli se þat it is not a
f. 95ʳ new opunioun contrarie to scripture, and olde seinttis | lawis or
3641 seiyngis, and þe beleue of þe chirche to seie þat our sacred oost is
uerri Cristis bodi. Seint Austen, rehersing Ciprian þe marter, writiþ
þus (li. 4 De doctrina christiana): ' "Know þou vs to be tauȝt þat þe
Lordis tradicioun be kept in offring of þe chalis, þat noon oþur þing
3645 be don of us saue þat þat þe Lord raþur dede for us: [þat] þe chalis
þat is offrid in mynde of hym be offrid medlid wiþ wyne. Forwhi
whan Crist seiþ 'I am þe verri vyne', soþeli þe blode of Crist is not
watur but wyne; neiþur his blode, bi þe wiche we ben raunsummed
and iquekened, mai not be seie to be in þe chalis whan þe wyne
3650 lackiþ, in þe wiche þe blode of Crist is schewid, in þe wiche Crist is
prechid bi wittnessis of alle scripturis and bi þe sacrament." ' Nouȝ
marke here houȝ þis sentence likid wel seint Austen, for þis martir
among al oþur doctouris was most autentik to him! Marke we here
also how contrarie ben þe sentencis of þes two olde seinttis and þe
3655 newe iaping of antecrist, for þes seinttis seien þat Cristis blode mai
not be, or be seien in þe chalice whan þe wyne lackiþ, and þat oþur
newe vngrounded tradicion seiþ euen þe contrarie, for it seiþ þat þer
is neiþur brede ne wyne in þe sacred oost! And antecrist most nedis
liȝe, if he seie þat Ciprian and Austen callen þe accident wiþout
3660 soiect wyne, for Cristis blode is as þei seien þat wyne. And antecrist
f. 95ᵛ mai not for schame, | as I suppose, seie þat Cristis blood is an
accident.

And, answering to þis witt of þes two seinttis, seint Austen writiþ
þus (De Trinitate li. 3 ca. 4): 'Poule myȝt signefiyng preche þe lord
3665 Iesu Crist, oþurwise bi tunge, oþurwise bi epistle, oþurwise bi þe
sacrament of his bodi and his blode. And we seien þe bodi of Crist
and þe blode to be neiþur þe tung of Poule, neiþur parchemyn,
neiþur þe betokenyng sounnes made wiþ þe tung of Poule, neiþur
signes of lettris wreten in þe skynnes. But þat þing onli, þe wiche is
3670 itake of þe frutis of þe erþe and ihalowid bi mystik praiour, we take
bi a riȝt goostli help in mynde of þe Lordis passioun for vs. And

3645 þat] in

whan þis þing is brouȝt to þe visible kinde bi þe hondes of men, it is
not halowid þat it be so grete a sacrament saue bi þe spirit of God
wirching vnuisibli.' Loo, þis seint seiþ þat 'We receyue þat þing þat
is itake of þe frute of þe erþe and ihalowid into Cristis bodi', but 3675
antecrist seiþ 'Naie', for no þing, as he seiþ, leueþ aftur þe
consecracion þat was made bi mannes hondes into a uisible kinde
and ihalowid to be a grete sacrament. For þe brede and þe wyne ben
made of þe frutis of þe erþe, and ben Cristis bodi and his blode, as
Austen seiþ here, and þo bi þe werke of þe spirit ben, as antecrist 3680
seiþ, halowid and iblessid into nouȝt! And bi þis fantasie prestis
speken alle in ueyn, | whan þei praien in the begynnyng of þe f. 96ʳ
consecracioun þat þe brede be made þe bodi, and þe wyne þe blode
of our lord Iesu Crist. For it is inpossible, as þat woodnesse seiþ, þat
brede be made Cristis bodi, siþ þe brede is clene anullid and doþ 3685
neuer good aftur þe consecracion.

But þis ⸢vn⸣saueri and newe presumpcioun is euyn aȝenst seint
Ieromes witt and consail (*Epistola* 54 *ad Lucinum*) þat, irequired to
seie his feling of certeyn custummes of þe chirche, answereþ þus: 'I
suppose schortli þis þing to be tauȝt and amonestid: þat þe tradicions 3690
of þe chirche, nameli þo þat greuen not þe feiþ or worche not
þeraȝenst, ben to be kept like as þei ben take of þe gretter men, and
not þe custome of sum men to be ouerturned bi oþur mennes
custome or maner.' Here ȝe mai se þat þis newe determynacioun
abowte þe sacred oost is nouȝt, for it reuersiþ and greueþ þe feiþ and 3695
þe tradicioun of þe grettist and þe best men þat euer were, and also it
is peruerti⟨n⟩g of þe custumable beleue continued generalli in Cristis
chirche into þe vnbindding of Sathanas—and þat continueþ ȝit in
feiþful men and schal into domys dai. Furþurmore seint Austen
writiþ þus to our purpos (*Epistola* 4 *ad Dardanum*): 'Crist is heed 3700
of þe bodi of þe chirche, þe vnite of þis bodi comended in our
sacrefice, þe wiche þing þe apostle haþ schortli signefiid seiyng "We
mony ben oo brede and oo bodi."' And I suppose þat | antecrist wiþ f. 96ᵛ
his accidentis schal fare riȝt foule wiþ himself, or he haue a redi witt
to þis text of seint Poule! Naþeles, houȝ it mai be truli vndurstonde 3705
it is wrete before.

And þis worde of Austen þat sueþ helpeþ also for to declare þe
same. þis seint seiþ þus (*super Ps.*3): 'þe Lord haþ long suffred Iudas
as a good man, whan his þouȝtis weren not vnknowe to hym, whan
he had him to þe fest in þe wiche he comended and betoke to his 3710

3701 of þe bodi] *twice*

disciplis þe figure of his bodi and his blode.' 3it furþurmore seint
Austen (*super Ps.*98) helpeþ vs to vndurstond þis sacrament and derk
wordes of scripture aboute þe same, rehersing Crist þat spekiþ þus
'It is þe spirit þat quekeneþ, forsoþ þe flesche profitiþ not; þe wordis
3715 þat I haue spoke ben spirit and liif.' And þan suen þe wordis of þe
seint: 'Vndurstonde 3e spiritualli þat þing þat I haue spoke: 3e ben
not to ete þat bod⟨i⟩ þat 3e seen, or to drinke þat blode þat þei ben to
schede out þe wiche schul crucifi3e me. And I haue betake to 3ow
sum sacrament þat spiritualli ivndurstond schal queken 3ow. And
3720 alþou3 it nede to be halowid uisibli, 3it neuerþelese it most nedes be
vndurstond inuisibli.' And hou3 þis sacrament schal be vndurstonde,
and what it is, is tau3t before bi wittnesse of þe same seint. Also þis
seint seiþ (*De Trinitate li.* 3 *ca.* [10]) þat 'þe brede imade to þe
misterie is consumed in taking or receiuing of þe sacrament.' But þis
f. 97ʳ stondeþ not | wiþ the witt of þe newe tradicioun of antecrist, þat seiþ
3726 no brede to leue after þe consecracioun. 3it þis seint writiþ þus
(*Epistola* 42 *ad Paulinum et Therasiam*) þat 'þe Lord is iknow of þo
two disciplis in breking of brede. No man ou3t to doute it to be þe
sacrament þat gadriþ vs into þe knowing of God.' Also þis seint seiþ
3730 þus (*Epistola* [42] *ad Paulinum et Therasiam*) how 'þat þing þat is in
þe Lordis borde or it begyn to be blessid, whan it is blessid and
halowed is departid to be delid. In þe wiche sacrament þat þing þat
is our grettist auow is preched, in þe weche we auowen vs to be
mylde in Crist and in þe vnite of his bodi. Of þe wiche þing þis is a
3735 sacrament, þat we many be oo bodi and brede.' For, as þis seint seiþ,
'Oo brede, oo loff' is a sacrament of vnite. 3it þis seint writiþ þus to
our purpos: '3ong children þat knowen what is putt in þe au3ter and
is consumed, þe halowing of fidelite performed, wherof and hou3 it
be made, and whi it is made, and whi it is take into þe vse of fidelite
3740 or religioun, and if þei neuer lerne bi her owne experience or ellis of
oþur mennes and sawe neuer þat kinde of þinggis, þat is to seie brede
and wyne in þe halowing of þe sacramentis, whan it is offrid and
i3eue and is seide to hem bi most sad auctorite, whos bodi and blode
it is, þei schal beleue noon oþur þyng, saue þat þe Lord haþ apered
f. 97ᵛ in þat kinde to | dedli men, and þat on al wise þe same licour had ron
3746 out of his side ismete.' Loo, here 3e mai se hou3 it mai be tau3t bi þe
most auctorite þat þing þat is put upon þe au3ter to be Cristis bodi
and his blode aftur þe consecracioun. 3e mai also here hou3 þe sacred

oost is al oþurwise Cristis bodi þan was þe bodi þat lyued here and died. 3750

Also Thomas Alquin writiþ þus in þis mater (*De ueritate theologie*): 'Foure þinggis ben of þe substaunce of þis sacrament. þe first is þ[at] he þat sacreþ be a prest; þe secunde is brede; þe þridde is þe entent of him þat sacreþ; þe fourþe is þe forme of þe wordis.' Nouȝ, and brede be of þe substaunce of þe sacrament, as þis man seiþ, houȝ is it 3755 þat antecrist, þat auouȝeþ him specialli in þis mater upon þis man, seiþ noo brede leueþ in þe sacrament aftur þe consecracioun? And þes mowen not be vndurstonde as for þe tyme afore þe consecra- cioun, for þan þe brede is no sacrament for it is not þan sacred. For if it schal be seide a sacrament before þe consecracion, and þat a 3760 sacrament of Cristis bodi, þan it sueþ þat brede is of þe substaunce of þe sacrament of Cristis bodi and þat þer leueþ brede in þe sacrament of Cristis bodi. Also seint Barnard spekiþ þus in a tretice þat he makiþ of þe sacrament of þe auȝter: 'þe sacramentis of holi | chirche stonden in foure kinddis: in watur, oile, bred and wyne.' f. 98ʳ

Nouȝ is it not a wondur þing þat antecrist and his lemys stonden 3766 so stifli upon þis ⌈new⌉ determynacioun, siþþen he haþ no colour of holi scripture, of olde seinttis, ne of olde custome of þe feiþ of þe chirche, or ellis of experience? For as Austen seiþ (*Epistola* 87 *ad Optatum*): 'Where a þing is kindlie derk, and ouercomeþ and passiþ 3770 our mesure, and open Goddis lawe helpeþ not, mannes coniecting presumeþ not to diffine or determene any þing þerof.' What a presumpcioun þan was it for to bring in a newe beleue wiþout any help of scripture or reson or experience! Also þe same Thomas writiþ þus in þe boke alegged before 'þe nedeful mater of þe sacred 3775 oost is brede of whete. And þe nedeful mater of þe chalice is wyne, for þe blode of Crist mai not be made in oþur mater þan wyne. Mater imedlid of wyne and watur acordeþ to þis signefiyng, for þe chirche þat is betokened bi watur is ioined to Crist bi feiþ and charite.' And þer a man mai se þat þis frere takiþ þes wordes al for 3780 oon *transubstanciacio* and *consecracio*, and *transubstanciare* and *con- secrare*. Nouȝ we mai see here þat þis frere was to douȝble and hateful to God, if he consentid in worde and dede to þe newe fantesie of antecrist þat euen contrarieþ his sentence here.

And þe seruice of þe chirche i|rad in the dai of Cristis bodi makiþ f. 98ᵛ no þing for antecrist parte in þis poynt. þe wordis of þis seruice to 3786

3752 þat] þe   3754 him þat *twice*   3764 sacramentis] -is *added dh.*
3768 holi scripture] scripture holi, *marked for rev.*

our purpos ben þese: 'þe bodi of Crist is iete of feiþful men but not torente; but raþur, þe sacrament departid, he leueþ hoole vndur euery partie of þe diuision. Accidentis ben wiþout soiect in þe same.'

3790 Nouȝ þis worde in Englische *same*, þat answeriþ to þis word in Laten *eodem*, is a relatif, and referred to Cristis bodi or to Crist or ellis to þe sacrament. þan siþþen þer is noon oþur þing nempned or named here þat it myȝt congruli be referred to saue to þes þre, and if it be referred to Cristis bodi, þan it meneþ þat accidentis ben wiþout

3795 soiect in Cristis bodi, þat is to seie not soiectid in Cristis bodi; and þat is soþ, for ellis Crist schuld be seen þere sensible and iseen wiþ bodilie iȝe, and þat no man graunteþ. And on þe same wise we mote graunt and seie if þe relatif be referred to Crist, for we seen Crist and Cristis bodi in þe sacrament bi feiþ and not wiþ bodili iȝe. And if þat

3800 relatif be referred to þe sacrament, and þe sacrament be take for an accident as antecrist blabereþ, þan it is al on to seie þat accidentis ben wiþout soiect in accident; and þat is soþ, for noon of þes sensible accidentis in þe sacred oost ben soiectid in anoþur, or any of hem in f. 99ʳ itself. And if | antecrist wol seie þat þe whitenes is oure sacrament,

3805 bicause þat it is þe most sensible accident þer as in þe sacrament, þan it is al one to seie accidentis b⟨e⟩n in þe same wiþout soiect, and accidentis ben in þe whitenesse wiþout soiect; and þis is an vnsauerie and a fonned witt, what weie þat euer a man holde. And, certis, as I suppose, if þis relacioun be weel handlid, it wol be riȝt hard to

3810 antecrist to bring þis worde irad in holi chirche to acorde wiþ his drunken dremyng, þat he enforsiþ to bring in now, seiyng þat it is a ful holi determynacioun of holi chirche, and þerfor alle men up peine of bodili deeþ and dampnacioun of soule most nedes stedefastli wiþout any douȝting beleue to þis wondurful holi determynacioun of

3815 þis ful holi chirche of antecrist and his special lemys, wiche falseli calliþ himself holi chirche. And þerfor if þis mater be wel and groundli souȝt out, it schal be founden þe wood rauyng and þe drunken dremyng of þe deuyllus chirche!

Naþeles, I wote wel þat whoso wol arguȝe in þis mater wiþ
3820 antecrist, he schal finde þerin more labour þan frute. And þerfor I kan no better consail but alweie to resort to holi scripture, þat is grounde of alle our feiþ, and to rest sadli in þe wordis and teching of Iesu Crist, þat seiþ to alle þo þat schul be saued 'I ȝeue to ȝow my f. 99ᵛ pees, and in me ȝe schul haue pees', | for mannes soule is bi kinde so

3825 witti þat no þing mai make it to rest or fulfille it saue Crist alone. And herfor sein⟨t⟩ Ierom (*De laude Pauli epistola* 115) seiþ þus to þe aduersarie 'I merueile þat þou hardest þi fronte or thi foreheed whiles þe Lord spekiþ', as whos seiþ þer schuld no disputicion be but euery man ouȝt to obeie. And seint Austen writiþ þus (*Ad Euodium epistola* 47) to conferme us in Crist: 'Hoold we most 3830 stedefastli þat þe feiþ haþ founded bi þe most founded auctorite.' And also þe sam⟨e⟩ seint writiþ þus of Abraham, þat is isett in scripture as an ensample, and as a myrrour or glas of feiþ feiþful men to loke or to beholde inne: 'Abraham is comaunded of God to offre his sone; he haþ not douȝtid, argued, disputid of þe comandement of 3835 God, neiþur he supposid þat þing to be yuil þat he þat was best myȝt comaunde.' And on þe same wise I conseil þe þat desirest to be a childe of Abrahames, whom God came to seche and to make saff, þat no disputicion of þin owne witt or of any oþur mannes moue þe from þe simplenesse, clerenes or chast feiþ þat is in Crist Iesu, vndur- 3840 stonding þat Crist is þe feiþ of alle þo þat schul be saued, and antecrist is þe fals beleue of alle þo þat schul be dampned, and nameli in þe mater of þe sacred oost. Wherfor þou schalt vndur- stonde þat noon schal be saued saue Crist Iesu, þat is to seie al Crist, heed and bodi, | þe wiche bodi is þe numbre of the chosen þat came f. 100ʳ from heuene in þe heed and goþ vp þedur, heed and bodi. 3846

Now I haue no lenger leiser to labour in þis mater, and þerfor I make here an ende, praiyng mekeli almiȝti God þat þis werke turne to his wirschip and stabling of cristen feiþ þat antecrist nouȝ soore enpugneþ. And if any man finde any errour in þis writing, I wold 3850 fayn be warned þerof in purpos to amende it mekeli. And I put it in þe dome of þo þat reden þis, wheþur þis be olde lore or newe, or wheþur I speke of myn owun heed or ellis of þe auctorite of Goddis lawe and þe olde feiþ of holi chirche. For at þe dai of dome Crist schal seie to þat forwaried cumpanye þat on his lift hande schal be, 3855 for þei dede not þe werkis of merci, 'Winde, ȝe forwaried wrecchis, aweie fro me into þe euerlasting fire of helle þat is ordeined to þe deuil and al his angellus! þer schal be weping and gnasting of teeþ', as ȝe þat are hatid of God and alle his halowis. And þe forwariid schul se þat þei are dampned, and knowe þat þer is noon help ne 3860 merci to fynde. þan þei mai seie þe wordis of Iob wiþ siking ful sore: 'þat dai mote perrische þat I was born oon, and þat careful nyȝt þat I was conceiued inne! þat ne I had be ded in my modris wombe! Wherto, my modur, settist þou me on þi | kneis, and wische me, and f. 100ᵛ rockid me, and fed me on thi brest?' Alas, þat while so meche swynk 3865 sche tolt þat norisched me, a bronde to brene in helle fire! For

requiem þat prestis synggen, ne noon oþur þing schal help þes
wrecchis in þat grete woo, þat dien in dedli synne; for in hem God
had no rest while þei lyued in synne, and þerfor þei schul neuer haue
3870 r⟨e⟩st while God is in heuen; and as þei made noon ende of synne
while þei lyuedden he⟨re⟩, þerfor schul þei fynde [noon] ende of her
pe⟨i⟩ne. For, soþeli, to þe riȝtwise domesman it longgiþ þat þei be
neuer wiþout peine whan þei are dede, þat wold not leue her synnes
while þei lyued here. For Ieremye seiþ 'Riȝt as a þef is confounded
3875 whan he is taken, so schal be confounded þe hous of synful men!'.
Alas, what schame and repref schal be whan þe King of kinggis schal
sitt wiþ al þe cumpany of seinttis, and schal blame synful men
bringging in her nek þe fardel of al her wickidnes in þe siȝt of alle þe
world. þerfor, leue we synne and serue we God, þe Fadur of our lord
3880 Iesu Crist and our sauiour, to whom be glorie ⟨and i⟩oie, wirchip and
honour into þe world of wordlis. Amen.

Explicit tractatus de oblacione iugis sacrificii

NOTES

The titles of certain patristic works which are repeatedly quoted in the edited texts have been abbreviated in the notes; their full titles can be found in the Index of non-biblical quotations.

1. EGERTON SERMON AND LAMBETH TRACT

Material is annotated in the order of the Egerton sermon whose line numbers come first; Lambeth line numbers, where relevant, are put in brackets after Egerton's. Those passages found within Lambeth's overlap with Egerton are annotated immediately after the last parallel with Egerton; the material at the end of Lambeth and not appearing in Egerton is annotated at the end of the sequence from Egerton.

Egerton text Matt. 15:13; the text occurs within the gospel for Wednesday of 3 Lent (Matt. 15:1–20) in the Sarum rite, but there is no indication in the sermon that it was intended for this occasion, and its length would seem to preclude use within a liturgical setting.
Lambeth text 1 Cor. 3:11, not used for a Sunday epistle in the Sarum rite.

2 (L2) For this relationship between the Trinity and the three traditional medieval estates in society see G. Constable, *Three Studies in Medieval Religious and Social Thought* (Cambridge, 1995), pp. 251–360; cf. Gower *Vox Clamantis* iii.1 ff. and Arnold iii.184/8, 207/18, 445/8.

7 (L7) Rom. 13:1.

11 (L10) *and also . . . placis* (13): the divergence between the readings of H and ED seems to reflect H's incorporation into his text of information, probably placed marginally in his exemplar, fuller than that of ED. The Latin material may be original. If the reference *in þe Book . . . 91* was originally in the text, rather than in the margin, it seems better placed as in ED.

11 (L11) *vicar of þe godhed*: the idea of the king as *vicarius Dei* (the priest or pope as *vicarius Christi*) goes back to Augustine, as claimed here. See (pseudo-)Augustine *Questiones ex novo testamento*, PL 35.2284.

12 (L11) *groundid*: the Lollard sense of this verb, as of *ground(e* sb., and *(un)groundli* adv., locates the foundation of all authority as scripture; see Hudson (1985), pp. 171–2.

16 (L16) Rom. 12:19.

17 (L17) Jer. 31:16.

19 (L19) *vicaries of þe godhed*: contrasted with *vicar of his manhed* (35); the distinction is sometimes between the two aspects of Christ, divine (kings) and human (clergy). See above notes to 11; cf. Wyclif *De off.reg.* 4/26, 137/18, *Serm.* i.233/33, ii.300/6, iii.211/14, *De blas.* 110/4 and elsewhere, also *EWS* E25/59, BL Add. 24202 f. 5v, T3010.

25 (L25) Mal. 2:7; the text of E and of L has been emended to the reading of HF which is that of the Vulgate.

29 (L29) Matt. 28:19, Mark 16:15.

32 (L32) Augustine PL 39.2287-8.

36 (L36) i.e. as line 11 PL 32.2329.

43 (L44) Eph. 6:5.

45 (L46) Heb. 13:17.

L53 1 Cor. 11:1.

L54 Gal. 1:9.

47 (L60) The implication of the first alternative is that nothing unrecorded in scripture is necessary for salvation. For Wyclif's own position in the *scriptura sola* debate see most reasonably Obermann (1967), pp. 361–411; the position of many Wycliffites was, as suggested here, often more extreme.

L68 1 Cor. 3:11.

58 Matt. 15:13.

61 Matt. 16:12.

62 ff. The condemnation of all forms of 'private religion', that is any rule that separates an individual from the christian community here, and the equation of members of such sects with the biblical sects 'pharisees, essenes and saducees' there is normal in Wyclif's later writings (e.g. *Serm.* i.62/4, 288/10, *Pol. Wks.* ii.477/11, 491/1) and in Lollard texts (*EWS* 6/12, Matthew 2/2, *LL* 39/2). For sects see *PR* pp. 347–51, *EWS* iv.121–34.

67 Corresponding to the *congregatio predestinatorum* and *congregatio prescitum*; see Rom. 8:29–30 and cf. Lombard *Sentences* i.40 (PL 192.631). The opposition is clearest in Wyclif *De eccles.* 415/8 ff., and is taken over into Lollard texts, *EWS* 20/66; *Op.ard.* f. 173va, *LL* 23/3 ff; see *PR* pp. 314–24, *EWS* iv.57–64 and 89–90.

72 The *Maistir of Stories*, Latin *Magister historiarum*, is Peter Comestor; here *Historia scolastica* PL 198.1553, 1607—the work became the standard medieval text on biblical history.

77–87 see *ODCC phylactery*, and more extensively E. Schürer, trans. G. Vermes et al., *The History of the Jewish People in the Age of Jesus Christ (175BC–AD135)* (Edinburgh, 3 vols., revd.edn. 1979), ii.479–81; for the *buysch of þornes* (76) see

Comestor, PL 198.1553 'Isti etiam majores fimbrias aliis ferentes spinas alligabant, quibus puncti in deambulando memores mandatorum Dei fierent.'

78 The preacher doubtless has in mind, though he does not refer to them specially, passages such as Matt. 23:13–33, Luke 18:10–14.

84 Lollard objections to long prayers are found, for example, *VO* 40, Arnold iii.228/25; cf. *EWS* iv.68–9.

86 *ypocritli*: MED records the word only once, as an adverb, but *ipocrit(e* adj. is recorded twice from Wycliffite texts, Matthew 89/15, *ALD* 105/9.

86 Matt. 23:5; cf. *EWS* 32/36–57.

90 Mark 7:6 quoting Isa. 29:13.

93–6 continues the citation of Mark 7:7–9, of which the final clauses *bene . . . seruetis* are not translated till 101–2. The burdensome nature of the rules of monks and friars, which prevents them from helping their fellow Christians, is stressed, for instance, *EWS* 48/30, 81/31.

102 *vngroundid*: see above note to 12.

104 Matt. 23:4; cf. *EWS* 154/25–35.

104 The enrichment of churches which had popular images or relics is well-known; cf. *PPl* B.v.226–7 where Bromholme and Walsingham, two pilgrimage churches in Norfolk, are visited by Avarice.

109 Whether this is a specific charge against a particular preacher, or a vague protest against defenders of the worship of images is unclear. The contrast is commonplace in Lollard writings: that poor men should be the true objects of pilgrimage and are the images of Christ and the saints on earth (Laud 200 ff. 113, 166v-168, *LL* 85/29, *SEWW* 3/99–101, 16/17), *ALD* 88/28, *Plowman's Tale* 909 ff., but also the orthodox *Dives and Pauper* I.lii.1–75, *PPl* B.xi.180. It may derive from pseudo-Chrysostom PG 56.867–8.

117 Mark 7:12.

130 Matt. 15:13.

134 John 3:1; Acts 5:34, 23:6, 26:5, Phil. 3:5.

136 Referring to the destruction of Jerusalem in AD 70 by the Romans. A long account is found in Higden, *Polychronicon* iv.422–56. For similar comment, the first citing Gregory as source, see Wyclif *Op.min.* 62/30, 355/18.

146 *3he al bisi*: the context requires a sense of 'even'; *MED al-bisi* gives the sense 'hardly, scarcely' with only two examples.

150 Matt. 23:9; cf. *EWS* 154/68–73.

154 Matt. 24:24; cf. *MC* 317–50.

155 *ducantur* EDH, *inducantur* F and modern Vulgate; since Wordsworth and White record the EDH reading as a variant, it has not been emended.

159 The contrast between *new sects* and *Christ's sect* is commonplace; see *EWS* E32/56, E39/31, E44/84, Laud.200 f. 191v, Arnold iii.432/35.

162 Matt. 24:23, Mark 13:21.

164–5 The sermon (and its tract version), though the precise date is indeterminable, was certainly written during the period of the Great Schism, 1378–1415. Some of the bitterest vituperation of Wyclif's last years was reserved for the antagonism of the nations supporting the two contenders (e.g. *Op.min.* 25/18 ff., 367/3 ff., *Pol. Wks.* ii.595/11 ff., 674/10 ff.) and this was continued by his followers (e.g. Arnold iii.351/14, Add. 24202 f. 13v, *Op.ard.* f. 132ra).

170 Luke 17:23.

171 The WB translation of Luke 17:23 is entirely inoffensive: both versions read 'Nyle 3e go, nether sue 3e', and *EWS* 143/37 has 'but wole 3ee not go, and sue hem not'. But cf. *friars/fratres* in E2777 note.

180 1 Cor. 1:10.

185 2 Pet. 2:1–3.

196 *marchaundisen* appears frequently in WB as the translation of Lat. *negotiare*; but, despite this similarity, the rendering here is not precisely that of WB.

217 *in scool . . . in sermouns and priuy comynyngis*: the distinction is between academic and more popular discourse.

221–4 for these three 'titles' of Christ, as creator, as innocent and as righteous man, see *De dom.div.* 10–12, *De civ.dom.* i.38–42.

226 apparently a reference to 1 Cor. 3:21 (cf. Wyclif's use of this *De dom.div.* 53/19). For the question of Christ's begging see Scase (1989), pp. 67–8, and below here E3116 ff.

228 Cf. Luke 10:7. The claim was made by Wycliffite preachers (e.g. Arnold iii.312/18, Matthew 252/9), and not unnaturally was seized on as inconsistent by their opponents (e.g. Netter *Doct.* IV.1–20 esp.cap. 10, i.858–9). The question is further examined in E722 ff. below. Cf. also TCD 245 f. 155 'True prestis þat prechen þo gospel, if þei ben boden of þe peple, may leuefully for her traueil, for þe tyme þat þei teche þe puple, take of þem her sustynaunce.' See *PR* pp. 340–6.

230–7 The same two instances are discussed at more length in Taylor 607–58, and reappear again here in lines 2700–2 (see notes); see also Arnold iii.413/14 ff.

231 John 4:7.

232 Luke 19:5.

234 Matt. 21:2.

238 ff. The charge here, repeated later, is an extreme form of that found in Wyclif and other Wycliffite writings: that because opponents gloss the biblical text, they imply that the text itself is inadequate and hence inherently false (cf. *EWS* iv.74–7 and references to *De ver.* i.148/12, ii.133/7, Arnold iii.258/15).

241 Ps. 18:8.

246 For letters of fraternity see W. G. Clark-Maxwell, 'Some letters of confraternity', *Archaeologia* 75 (1926), 19–60, 79 (1929), 179–216; for Wycliffite hostility to them see *EWS* 112/38–78, Arnold iii.377/19, 420/6, *Upland* 187, 335. A benefactor to a religious house was promised, in exchange for his gift, a share in the prayers and spiritual merit acquired by the house or order. The writer here claims that the house or order has no spiritual merit (256–8) because of a lack of charity.

255 1 Cor. 13:1.

260–71 see T403 ff. and notes where this subject is discussed in more detail.

264–7 For the claim that the view propounded by the contemporary church authorities was of only recent origin, and that the Lollard explanation was of greater antiquity cf. Wyclif *De euch.* 47/10, *Op.evan.* ii.143/35 ff.; *SEWW* 1/26 and see *EWS* iv.54.

265 *pure substaunce of þe bileeue*: the sense appears to be 'basic elements for the construction of a system of faith'. The point is that the gospel teaching, to the Wycliffites the only primary authority, remains the same throughout all ages; later writing can only interpret that primary authority, not essentially alter it. The relevant passages are those mentioned in 266.

266 Matt. 26:26, Mark 14:22, Luke 22:19, 1 Cor. 10:16.

277 The implication is that anything not found in scripture is unnecessary or even harmful; cf. *PR* pp. 375–9, *EWS* iv.71–2.

280 *autentik*: a favourite word of the present author (cf. 654, 1112 etc., and T842, 2602, 3369 etc.), but twice found in Thorpe 1010, 1745. The commoner sense in ME (see *MED*) is 'worthy of belief, authoritative', but the more specific 'legally valid or binding' seems often implied here.

283 2 Pet. 2:1, Vulg. *sectas perdicionis*. For the ensuing exegesis of this and the following verse to line 678 compare Wyclif's *De fundatione sectarum* (*Pol. Wks.* i.29/16–33/15).

285 Though Wyclif and his followers often speak of four sects (the pope and his curia, canons, monks and friars), stress is often laid on the schisms within each, and on multiplicity of rules that attempt to add to the gospel teaching, and thus diverge from that and from each other. The hostility of one sect to another is also stressed; cf. *Upland* 101–6, 122–36, Matthew 222/2, 310/4, *EWS* E35/31, and iv.125–6.

297 John 14:24.

301 2 Pet. 2:1 'et eum qui emit eos, Dominum, negant: superducentes sibi celerem perditionem'.

308 The same argument appears elsewhere, more generally, as an objection to private confession; see Arnold iii.255/17, Matthew 327/28, 344/15; cf. *EWS* iv.44–6.

317 2 Pet. 2:2.

318 For the charge of sexual immorality against the sects see *12 Concs.*, *SEWW* 3/25–35, 154–62.

323 2 Cor. 2:17, quoted marginally.

329 Luke 8:11.

332 The reproach is probably primarily against the preaching of tales, even of saints' lives, not found in the bible, a feature regarded as peculiarly characteristic of friars' sermons. Cf. Arnold iii.299/31, Matthew 59/11, 105/29, *Op.ard.* ff. 138vb, 168vb, 182rb; see *EWS* iv.143–4 and refs.

341 The *sectis in þe oold lawe* are the pharisees, saducees and essenes, explicitly compared to the orders of monks and friars in many texts, see also 62 ff., 438 ff.

344 Matt. 13:24–30, expounded vv.36–43.

357 *bastard braunchis*: picking up the metaphor of the text, Matt. 15:13; for this usage cf. *Upland* 248, *FDR* 630–2.

357–68 Isa. 30:9–11; 2 Cor. 2:17 (above 323). The quotation from Isa. 30:9–11, abbreviated by the omission of part of v.10 ('Nolite videre; [Et aspicientibus: Nolite aspicere nobis] ea quae recta sunt'), is explained by the glosses here, marked off by the introductory *id est*, and here enclosed in brackets; these glosses are then partially worked into the translation. So *videntibus* and *videre* 359 are not literally translated. The English in turn adds further glosses, here again (366–8) enclosed in brackets. The glosses are in no way unorthodox, and develop the interpretation of GO; see iv.278 where prophets are held to be the *videntes*, picked up also in Lyra. LV renders *videntibus* and *videre* as *profetis* and *prophesie*. 360 F's addition is correct by the Vulgate but is not translated in the English; hence it is presumably hypercorrection by F.

371 Rom. 10:4, 13:10.

377 2 Tim. 4:3.

382 The difficulty of rendering the Latin, reflected here in the alternative translations, is also found in WB where in EV two renderings are offered (though different from those here).

388 The preference for pleasing tales is mocked outside Wycliffite writings in Langland *PPl.* B.v.400 ff. and *Summoner's Tale*, *CT* D.2017 ff.; cf. Spencer (1993), pp. 78 ff. and above 332.

391 Ps. 33:15, quoted marginally in ED.

393 2 Pet. 2:2.

416–17 The sense requires that *and wolde . . . malice* be parenthetical: 'they have grafted in three other [sects] in their place (and would to God they were of no greater malice than those!), as monks, canons and friars . . .'

417 The writer is thinking of the different orders of monks and friars, with their

various individual customs. For comments on the divergent attitude of different orders of friars, see, for instance, Wyclif *Serm.* i.24/4, 53/17–55/33; *Upland* 144–7 and *FDR* 386–405, *EWS* 29/74.

421 The three estates of medieval tradition: knights, clerks and labourers; see 2.

431–2 *haue her forþ*: F's substitution of *goo* for *haue her* retains the sense but uses a simpler idiom; see *MED ford* n. 2(b)).

450 Gen. 3:4.

452 Gen. 2:17.

463 ff. The idea is that St. Peter (particularly in 2 Pet. 2:3) foresaw the magnitude of the effect of the sects from their small beginnings in his time, just as the Baptist perceived Christ's divinity from the events at the baptism; both made known their insights to the less perceptive.

465 John 1:36.

466 2 Pet. 2:3.

470 cf. 246 ff. and note there.

481 Luke 18:10–14.

493 *lettris of fraternyte*: see 246 and note.

497 An allusion to the reproach, more fully set out elsewhere in the text (672 ff.), of the friars' reluctance to win their sustenance by physical labour.

503 Luke 1:51 alluding to Pss. 32:10–11, 146:6.

505 Luke 14:11, 18:14, Matt. 23:12.

508 Augustine cf. PL 38.1315.

510 Ps. 101:18.

515 James 4:6.

517 Ecclus. 35:21.

521 Lollard objections to the long prayers of the sects are numerous; see *VO* 40, Ps. Bod. 288 ff. 58vb, 98ra, TCC B.15.40 f. 50v.

540–2 Two objections are here combined. The first is to the acquisition by the church of lands or incomes to be held inalienably. According to Edward I's Statute of Mortmain 1279, this became theoretically illegal unless the king issued a licence; but large numbers of licences were granted and alienation continued. See K. L. Wood-Legh, *Studies in Church Life in England under Edward III* (Cambridge, 1934), pp. 60–88, S. Raban, *Mortmain Legislation and the English Church, 1279–1500* (Cambridge, 1982), the crucial passage of the 1279 statute being translated p. 1, Swanson (1989), p. 197; cf. Arnold iii.276/35, 302/26, 307/6, Matthew 278/35. The second objection is to the assumption by a religious house of the revenues of a benefice, with its accompanying duty of providing an incumbent; for Lollard objections see *SEWW* 3/8–9.

545 ff. The argument is that both mortmain and appropriation were claimed by the religious as payments for services rendered, but, in the writer's view, no services were in fact performed.

563 ff. The writer may be thinking of the justificatory treatises written by the monks (cf. W. A. Pantin, 'Some medieval English treatises on the origins of monasticism', *Studies presented to Rose Graham*, ed. V. Ruffer and A. J. Taylor (Oxford, 1950), pp. 189–215). More notorious (cf. 566–9) were the defensive writings of the friars both in response to the division in the Franciscan order (see M. D. Lambert, *Franciscan Poverty* (London, 1961) and to the hostility of FitzRalph (see Walsh (1981), pp. 349–451).

574 *Poul . . . Crist*: referring to 2 Cor. 12:2–4.

578 1 Cor. 1:11–14.

590 The 'Philosopher' is usually Aristotle. Comparable proverbs, though not attributed to Aristotle, are recorded in Walther nos. 7178b and 36579h.

614 That is respectively Benedictine monks, Cistercian monks (from St. Bernard's influence on the order, founded by Robert of Molesme), Franciscan and Dominican friars, Augustinian canons or friars, both of which orders claimed Augustine as their founder, and lastly the Carmelite friars. The last order was actually founded in the twelfth century in Palestine as an eremitical group, but was later reorganized as a fraternal rule. The jibe alludes to Carmelite claims to be descended from Elijah and the 'sons of the prophets' (2 Kgs. 2, see *ODCC*). For Nabal see 1 Kgs. 25:2–39. The association with Mary comes from the Carmelites' particular devotion to the Virgin. For similar ridicule see Add. 24202 f. 55, Wyclif *Trialogus* 362/1, *Op.min.* 17/1, *Pol. Wks.* i.24/20.

618 1 Kgs. 25:36–7.

619 1 Cor. 1:13.

624 ff. The writer seems to be regarding the followers of the classical philosophers as 'sects'. It is unclear how superficial the writer's knowledge of the authors to whom he refers may be. It is tempting to think that he may have known Wyclif's *De logica* iii which refers to all four: Anaxagaras iii.141/17, Democritus 35/7, 132/35, Plato and Aristotle more frequently. The matter is discussed again in *Trial.* 83–5, but though Democritus is there mentioned (84/1), Anaxagaras is not. Cf. Netter *Doct.* I.14 (i.88).

629–32 Plato's view appears in *Laws* x (see *ODCC* sv Plato), and Plato is commended by Augustine (*De civ. Dei* 8.4–10, PL 41.228–33), and this is in turn mentioned in Wyclif *De ver.*i.36/4 and 39/1. Aristotle's opinion *Physics* viii.1–2, 6–8 is of greater complexity than this bald statement. The view attributed to the Aristotelians, that the world had no beginning, was discussed nearer the writer's own time, following Averroes, by Aquinas II Sent.d.1q.1a.2 (ed. R. P. Mandonnet (Paris, 1929–47), ii.47); see *CHLMP* 529.

630 Augustine *De civitate Dei* 8 especially caps 4 and 10, PL 41.227–9 and 234–5.

632–43 See J. Murdoch and E. Synan, 'Two Questions on the Continuum: Walter Chatton(?) OFM and Adam Wodeham OFM', *Franciscan Studies* 26 (1966), 212–88, and *CHMLP* pp. 564–91. Aristotle *Physics* VI.1 and elsewhere stated that no continuum of space, time or motion, could be composed of indivisibles; the atomistic structure of magnitudes was to him not permissible. Wyclif, as outlined there and discussed more fully by N. Kretzmann, 'Continua, Indivisibles, and Change in Wyclif's Logic of Scripture', in Kenny (1986), pp. 31–65, was an indivisiblist, and the present writer evidently followed him in this.

637 *reuersen*: HF's expanded reading 'seiþ þe contrarie and reuersen' may be correct, but in default of D (here lost from 436–657) E's possible reading has been retained.

644 See *OED* whetstone 2b for the allusive use of the word in reference to the custom of hanging a whetstone round the neck of a liar, and the phrase *to lie for the whetstone* 'to be a great liar'. The sense here is 'this seems to be a blatant lie and flagrant enough, even for a master liar'. See Whiting W216.

652–3 The inclusion of the essenes (see *ODCC*), not mentioned in the bible, along with the pharisees and saducees, is commonplace in Wyclif (*De blas.* 12/25, *De apos.* 2/33, *Trial.* 384/18). Though they appear to have imposed strict rules upon members of their sect, the charge that they rejected the Judaic law is unjust and is not mentioned by Comestor (PL 198.1553–4).

654–6 *saduceis*: see *ODCC*; again though the saducees rejected the resurrection of the body (Matt. 22:23) and belief in angels and spirits (Acts 23:8), the alleged refusal to accept the prophets is less clearly established in the bible, but is found in Bede (PL 92.98) and Comestor (PL 198.1553).

656–68 As the writer acknowledges, much of the information about the pharisees derives from Matt. 23 with the addition for the first point of Mark 7:10–13; see also Comestor PL 198.1553.

659 Mark 7:11–13.

665 Matt. 23:13–33.

667 Peter Comestor *Historia scolastica*, PL 198.1607–8. For Wyclif's elaboration on Matt. 23 see *Op.min.* 313–53, and for the English sermon on the same chapter, partly based on Wyclif's tract, *VO*.

672 ff. For the rival claims see above 563 ff. Wyclif had, from the earliest stages of his teaching on ecclesiastical matters, opposed the monastic orders as departing from the teaching of Christ with regard to clerical poverty; his view about the friars changed from cautious approval of their ideals, if not of the contemporary abuses of those ideals, to extreme hostility following their rejection of his eucharistic views. See Gwynn (1940), pp. 211–69.

674 See note to 540–2.

675 *clamarous* : E's form *clamous* is not found in the other copies, nor recognized by *MED*.

678 See, for instance, Matt. 10:9–10, Luke 12:14, Acts 3:6, 18:3.

685 ff. The writer claims that the sects' case is poor: despite *suche colours*, the clear evidence of scripture, of the lives and writings of saints, and even of the sects' own rules (the last of which the sects regard most highly), produces a refutation of their claims. Each sect uses such sources to refute the others' claims.

692–5 As well as the claims mentioned in 563 ff. note, the writer may be alluding to the lengthy disputes within the Franciscan order concerning poverty. See D. Douie, *The Nature and the Effect of the Heresy of the Fraticelli* (Manchester, 1932) and M. D. Lambert, *Franciscan Poverty* (London, 1961). Knowledge of that dispute is evidenced in Wyclif (*Pol. Wks.* i.42/6, *Trial.* 367/16); see also *Op.ard.* f. 174vb. The sophistication of the later Franciscan attitude to possessions produced virulent Lollard polemic (e.g. Matthew 40–51).

696 From the material that follows, it is clear that *trewe clerkis* has its sect meaning of 'disciples of Wyclif'. The important word here is *fundacioun*: many medieval writers had criticized the practices of monastic and fraternal orders alike, but the opposition to their founding ideals is a mark of the later teaching of Wyclif and his followers.

702–19 This long and unwieldy sentence cannot grammatically be split; the main clause starts in 711 *þese sectis ben acordid . . . and . . . maintenen . . . and acorden*.

711 Cf. Matt. 12:25–6, Mark 3:24–6 and the Lollard *Epistola Sathanae ad cleros* (*SEWW* no. 17).

712 Luke 23:12.

713 ff. The author is correct in his assertion that monks and friars dropped their arguments against each other in the face of Wyclif's attack on orthodoxy, as they saw it. At the Blackfriars' Council in 1382 the signatories to the condemnation of Wyclif included friars of all four orders, seculars and monks (*FZ* 286–9). Treatises against Wyclif were compiled similarly by the Franciscan William Woodford, the Cistercian William Rymington, the Dominican Roger Dymmock and the anonymous Dominican author of *Pharetra sacramenti*, the Carmelite John Kennyngham and many others.

718 1 Tim. 6:8, a text cited with great frequency in the writings of Wyclif and his followers; only D has the correct subjunctive *simus*.

722 The affluence of the monastic orders by the fourteenth century is a commonplace, not only in Wyclif(fite texts, but also in the writings of contemporary satirists. For the pursuance of begging beyond the needs for immediate necessities of life by the friars cf. *PPl. Crede* 153 ff., Matthew 222/14,

278/28. Again it is not a criticism limited to Wycliffite writers but is found, for instance, also in Chaucer and Gower.

731 Luke 16:22.

736 Luke 12:18.

740 Luke 19:8; Acts 10:4.

773 Cf. 228 ff. and note. The distinction between the illegitimate claims of the monastic and fraternal orders to possessions and alms respectively, and the legitimate maintenance of *trewe prechours* lies in the words *prestis office duli perfourmed to þe peple*, and in the restriction of payment (777) to that providing immediate necessities for maintenance of life (cf. *SEWW* 2/81–7).

777 Matt. 10:10.

778 1 Cor. 9:11.

781–2 F's transposition of the phrase *to Crist and perfyt folowers of hym* to the end of the sentence avoids the awkwardness of the repetition, in different senses, of *of* in the middle; the sense is 'ordained by the Trinity for Christ and for perfect followers of him'.

787 Prov. 30:8; for the use of this text against religious mendicancy cf. Scase (1989), p. 57.

789 D's reading agrees with both versions of WB in the rendering of Vulg. *dederis*; for the possibility that the original may not have had this reading see introduction p. xxxiii.

800 The topic is further pursued below, lines 1183 ff., 1393 ff.

804 (L71) *clergie* DHFL: E's *chirche* makes sense, but seems incorrect in view of *in alle þo* which suggests an animate subject.

806 (L72) Deut. 18:1. The relevance of this quotation to the issue of clerical wealth is discussed by Netter *Doct.* II.56 (i.539); for the background see Scase (1989), pp. 143–4.

811 (L78) Num. 35:2–3.

813 (L79) Num. 18:20–4

816 (L82) Lev. 27:30–33.

828–9 (L95–6) *as . . . temple*: the corrections in E and in F suggest uncertainty between two constructions 'as to repaire þe temple' and 'as to þe repaire of þe temple'; since the former is found in D and H, it may have been the hyparchetypal reading (though L agrees with E and F).

829 (L96) For the argument that the temporalities of this church should be made available to secular uses in times of national emergency see Gradon (1980), 187 and references there given; cf. Wyclif *De off.reg.* 126/29, 183/14.

830–1 (L97) King Joas (AV Jehoash), 4 Kgs. 12, perceived that the priests were not using the money assigned to them for the repair of the temple for that purpose; he therefore ordered a special chest to collect the money, and that the money should go straight to the workmen charged with the work. Josiah (4 Kgs. 22:1–7) continued the practice.

835 (L101) 3 Kgs. 10:12, 1 Chron. 6:31.

843 (L108) *and Salomon . . . same* (844): as recorded in Neh. 12:44.

852 (L115) The reproach to kings, though they were by no means alone in endowing religious houses, is typical of Wyclif (see *De off.reg.* 97/29, 213/10) and the Lollards. As Wilks has shown (1972), 118–25 and (1977), 63–70, Wyclif looked to the king to initiate the reform of the church. This hope was maintained by his followers (see *EWS* 80/55 and cf. 66/107, Arnold iii.214/8, 240/24, 515/13), and is reflected in their attempts to win parliamentary support for reform.

864 ED read *if alþouȝ*, HF *alþouȝ*. Although HF's reading is the only one that makes possible sense, it seems unlikely to have been original since it will not explain ED's error. It seems probable that the original had *if al* (see *MED al* adv. and cj. 4(a), uncommon according to *LALME* i.193 and iv.56–7) 'even if' (a sense which better accords with the following words), and that the second word was corrected to *alþouȝ* without removal of *if*. See introduction pp. xxiii–xxiv for the textual implications of this.

865 ff. (cf. L122) The question of the relevance of OT teaching to christians was a longstanding issue from Acts onwards. Wyclif and his followers did not depart in general terms from orthodox thinking on this, though on individual issues (as here) they stressed different points.

880 Lollard arguments about images are discussed by Aston (1984), 135–92 and (1988), 96–159; see Thorpe 1055–1227 and notes.

881 The writer is implicitly contrasting the moral precepts of the Old Testament, still binding on the Christian, with the ceremonial ordinances that were superseded in the new dispensation given by Christ and his apostles (cf. Acts 10:9–11:18). Cf. *De mand.* 52/30, 62/1, *Op.ev.* i.116/38, 365/11; *EWS* E43/38 ff., 207/21 ff. and iv.73.

890 (cf. L134) *colege*: cf. Wyclif *Pol. Wks.* i.134/3.

897 (L137) As used by Lollards (e.g. *LL* 60/29), or about them (e.g. *SEWW* 5/114), *conuenticlis* is a strongly pejorative word.

899 (L140) Num. 18:20–24 (omitting vv.22 and part of 23); the beginning of the translation (904–6) is adapted. The English *noon oþir* (910) confirms the HF reading *aliud* (903).

912 (L153) Deut. 18:1–2; again the emendations to E at 914–15 are confirmed by the translation, and conversely that at 918 by the Latin.

920 (L161) Josh. 13:33.

926 (L167) Ezek. 44:28.

L173 Jerome PL 22.531; *God will not be parte*: Jerome 'non vult Dominus esse pars', *MED part* sense 7 is the closest, but still not precisely that here 'God does not wish to be associated (or an associate).'

933 ff. (L179 ff.) Lollard comments on tithes are variable, but always subject to the restrictions mentioned in the note to line 540–2. In general, their criticism of contemporary practice was aimed at the excessive demands made in tithing (e.g. *VO* 170), the use of excommunication to enforce payment (e.g. Matthew 145/2, 437/1), and the illegitimacy of the clergy's regard for tithes as an inalienable right, independent of the merit of the recipient (e.g. Arnold iii.468/28, 517/5, Add. 24202 ff. 34v, 40v); see *PR* 342–5, *EWS* iv.169–70.

L188 1 Cor. 3:11.

942 Eph. 5:8.

946 Matt. 5:3, 10.

950 Gen. 1:28–30: the natural lordship granted to mankind by God in paradise, as explained 950–5.

960–2 Earthly lordship was the result of the fall, a commonplace view (Augustine *De civ. Dei* 19.15, PL 41.643–4, cf. Wyclif *De stat.inn.* 506/28). The sense of the lines is 'And so lordship of this kind (i.e. earthly lordship) could not be, and was not, introduced by God or by man in his perfect state, because of its defects.'

962 1 Kgs. 8:4–22; the passage deals with the introduction of kings as ruler over the children of Israel, against the advice of Samuel who warned them of the consequences. The situation is further explained here in the next paragraph. See also 1381–3 below.

970 Judges 2:16, 18.

982 1 Kgs. 8:11–18.

986 1 Esdras 7:26.

988–9 *shal be . . . liiflood*: Vulg. 'iudicium erit de eo sive in mortem, sive in exilium, sive in condemnationem substantiae eius vel certe in carcerem'.

990 ff. See GP to WB i.11/42–15/6 for the history of the kings of Israel after David in 3 Kgs.

999 Augustine Epistola 102, PL 33.378 'Omnis quippe illa interpretatio ad creaturam refertur, non ad Creatorem, cui uni debetur servitus religionis illa, quae uno nomine *latria* graece appellatur.' *Latria*, the honour and worship which should be paid to God alone; the term figures prominently in contemporary discussions of images and pilgrimages (see Aston (1984), pp. 135–92 and (1988)). Cf. T2833.

1005 ff. The period of Jewish history here in question is not entirely clear. The preceding paragraphs seem to suggest that it refers to the period of Ezra, recorded in Nehemiah and 1 Esdras, after the return from Babylon. See GP to WB i.34/32 ff. Ezra (see *ODCC*) was often regarded as 'the Father of Judaism', hence the reference here to the multiplication of traditions (1013).

1015 The Vulgate uses the word *episcopus* once only in OT at 2 Esdras 11:22 with reference to the chief of the Levites in Jerusalem; it is not clear that his function was particularly important. The *princis of prestis* are the *principes sacerdotum* of biblical usage.

1030–1 A reference to the destruction of Jerusalem in AD 70; see 136 note.

1042 Only H is correct in omitting *þat* after *so*.

1046–55 The period covered by 1046–9 seems to extend beyond the apostolic times to the point when Christianity became an official religion. It is not clear to whom the writer is referring when he speaks of *heþen kyngis and lordis* (1049–50) who converted: the praise for the early secular rulers who favoured Christianity is couched in historically vague terms, and it is not clear which countries or rulers are meant. It seems that his admiration was excited by his belief that such rulers strictly separated secular and ecclesiastical affairs, and confined the clergy to the latter (cf. 1055–7). The secular rule, he considers, is *more acordinge wiþ þe staat of innocence* (1052–3): the king's rule is closer than the priest's to that of Adam in Eden, disposing of the material creation.

1057 Constantine was believed throughout the Middle Ages to have given pope Sylvester I (314–35) by the Donation supremacy over the clergy, primacy over the various patriarchates and dominion over Italy. The document, probably an eighth- or ninth-century forgery, was incorporated into canon law and became the prime instrument in the claims, territorial and spiritual, of the papacy. The legend that on the day of Constantine's act an angel appeared to proclaim 'This opyn 3yfte maad bi Constantyn today is venym sched in þe chirche of God' (*Lollard chron.* Em. 20) is repeatedly mentioned in Wyclif (*Pol. Wks.* ii.669/23, *Op.min.*226/2) and his followers (*EWS* 89/83, Arnold iii.340/34, Matthew 378/5, 475/22), but is not confined to unorthodox writers (cf. *PPl.* B.xv.556–66, Gower *VC* iii.283 ff., *CA* ii.3475 ff.).

1060 The connection between *mawmetrie* 'idolatry', and the loss of royal power lies in the three terms traditionally used to distinguish the different kinds of honour: *latria* (1001), the honour due to God alone, *dulia*, the honour which could be paid to man, angel and lower creatures, and *yperdulia* which might be paid to the Virgin Mary. In the writer's view, the excessive honour which kings and lords had allowed to be paid to images of saints (and to the elements in the eucharist which, as appears T2918 ff., the writer regards as a form of idolatry) upset the proper order of reverence, and hence impugned their own exercise of authority.

1063–6 See further 1088–94 and notes for more particular aspects of this complaint. The writer here is probably thinking of the extension of papal authority in Italy and France with the Avignon capitivity (Rome and Avignon as *citees*). But he may also have in mind the powers of the bishop of Durham who throughout the medieval period exercised civil jurisdiction over county Durham and beyond, and ranked as a Count Palatine (see *ODCC*).

1068 ff. Cf. Wyclif *De eccles.* 291/17 ff., *De off.reg.* 28/16 ff. and 154/23 ff. Lollard objections to the secular jurisdiction and pretensions of the clergy are neatly summed up in the sixth of the *12 Concs.* (*SEWW* 3/62–72) 'þat a kyng and a bisschop al in o persone, a prelat and a iustise in temperal cause, a curat and an officer in wordly seruise, makin euery reme out of god reule'. This view is supported by quotation of Matt. 6:24 *nemo potest duobus dominis servire*, a precept ignored by the 'men of duble astate' who might well be termed *hermofodrita* or *ambidexter*; see further 1183–7 note.

1071 (L191) Luke 22:25.

1078 The manuscripts are agreed that the second name is *Bolayn*; the options seem to be Boulogne or Bologna. The second is found as *Boleyn de Grace* in *The Book of Margery Kempe*, ed. S. B. Meech and H. E. Allen (EETS 212, 1940, p. 65/25) and the notes (p. 287) point out that this name has persisted as *Bologna la grassa*, 'the rich or fertile', until the present day. It seems likely that this name lies behind the comment here: the author heard the name, also knew that Bologna was celebrated as an academic centre of canon law, and has assumed a connection between the two points.

1079 The writer may have been thinking of the Flanders crusade, the enterprise in support of Urban VI against the forces of Clement VII, disastrously led in 1383 by bishop Despenser of Norwich; see *EWS* iv.146–51.

1088–94 Though Wyclif often cited canon law in support of his own positions, he was critical of the claims made for it and especially of its practitioners (*Pol. Wks.* i.169/15, ii.562/2, *Op.min.* 325/3, 440/31, *Serm.* i.377/3). The charge that the laws made by the clergy involve parts of *þe emperours lawe*, i.e. Roman civil law (for Wyclif's hostility to this see *De off.reg.* 188/10 ff.) is only true in the sense that medieval canon law incorporated precepts governing matters beyond the spiritual or moral spheres. The close link between civil and canon law was fostered by the fact that most students took degrees in both.

1094 The cancellation in E of *and noon oper* is in black, not the usual red ink used for the purpose by the main scribe and may be later; the words must be restored.

1096 Eph. 1:22.

1098–9 Lollard hostility to the practice of law is frequent, as in Wyclif; see, for instance, Arnold iii.215/16, 326/26, Matthew 184/5, Add. 24202 f. 37v, *EWS* iv.84–8.

1098, 1101 *mengid lawe*: here refers to canon law, based, as is claimed by its practitioners, on biblical precept, but contaminated in the writer's view with worldly consideration (cf. 1042–3 'a mengid lawe of Goddis lawe, of þe kyngis and of her owne tradiciouns').

1100–20 (L201–20) The notion of a clerical conspiracy to take over the kingdom is found elsewhere in Wyclif (*De civ.dom.* ii.6/20 claims that the possessioners own more than a third of the land, *De eccles.* 338/21 states that more than a quarter of England is now in the dead hand of the church), and in Lollard writings, for instance in Durham f. 10v or in *37 Concs.* 87–8, Add. 24202 f. 13; Matthew (p. 527) compares *Dialogus* 70/11 where Mendacium claims that, rather than secular disendowment of the clergy 'Videtur quod docere debet pocius e converso quod clerici auferant totum seculare dominium a brachio seculari et reservent ex integro ipsum sibi.' The claim that the clergy already has the majority of the lordships in their control (1112, L210) is implausible. But the writer may be thinking of computations such as those embodied in the Lollard Disendowment Bill (*SEWW* 27). Here as there *spiritualtees* (1114, L212) has the technical sense (not recognized by *spiritualte* n.) of income derived from benefices, tithes and similar ecclesiastical sources (as opposed to *temperaltees* (1111, L209), income derived from secular lands or tenements belonging to the church). The claim that the temporal lords are less numerous and able than previously is also unspecific. The writer may be thinking of the effects of the upheavals caused by Richard II's minority, his later deposition and the accession of Henry IV; but as the precise date of the text is obscure, it is hard to determine. From the polltaxes of 1377 the number of beneficed clergy has been estimated at 15,532, of unbeneficed clergy at 16,809 and of regular clergy as 10,623 (J. C. Russell, 'The clerical population of medieval England', *Traditio* 2 (1944), 177–212 at pp. 179 and 212 (cf. Swanson (1989), pp. 30–40); he conjectures that these numbers did not alter much in the fifteenth century).

1101 (L204) For the possible significance of the difference in status between E's first person conversation with 'a greet maistir of þis mengid lawe' and L's questioning of a bishop by a gentleman, see introduction p. xlvii–xlviii.

L222–30 The whole of this passage, which is unique to L and is replaced in E1121–43, derives from the *English Wycliffite Sermons* no. 175/12–13, 18–20, 20–3, 41. The quotation is precise, with only *byleue* 222 departing from the sermon's *trowe*, and *þai* 228 replacing *þe Iewis*. It is extremely rare to find isolated quotations from these sermons.

L222 John 11:48.

1121–54 It is clear that *pore prestis* (1121) has its sect meaning of 'Lollard priests'; the parallel between the treatment of Christ and that of his more recent followers is commonplace in Lollard writings (*EWS* 57/24, 96/41, see *EWS* iv.173–4, Matthew 87/2). Unfortunately, the observations about the recent persecution are couched in ambiguous terms: the references to killing in 1140–3 probably suggest a date after the enactment of *De heretico comburendo* in 1401, after which the death penalty was used against heretics in England as it had long been on the continent; but the ensuing 1144–6 suggest that *killing* may not be physical death actually imposed but spiritual death by deprivation of gospel teaching (cf. *EWS* iv.18–19). The description of episcopal action against the unspecified Lollards in 1130–3 echoes the terms of many proclamations against the heretics from 1382 onwards (e.g. *CPR 1381–1385* p. 153, *CPR 1385–1388* pp. 427, 430, 448 etc.).

1130–3 Cf. Arundel's Constitutions 1–2 of 1407 (Wilkins iii.316), the first concerning condemnation of the unlicensed preacher, the second of the receivers and place where he preaches 'ecclesia, coemeterium, seu locus quiscunque in quo sic praedicatum fuerit, ipso facto ecclesiastico subjaceat interdicto, sixque maneat interdictus'.

1135–43 The comparison echoes closely the analysis in Wyclif's *De blasphemia* p. 62/8–18; in both the hostility of the contemporary clergy is ascribed to their desire to protect their wealth.

1151 ff. (cf. L236 ff.) Lollards echoed and extended Wyclif's desire (e.g. *Serm.* Pref./8, 109/36, 359/4, 377/15) for the wider availability of the gospel by their insistence upon the availability of vernacular scriptures (see *EWS* iv.78–9). The writer's terms here are unspecific: it is not entirely clear from the wording whether Arundel's Constitutions of 1407, which effectively banned new biblical translation and general ownership of existing versions, were in existence when he wrote. In the light of 1160 this seems more probable than that he is thinking of the vaguer terms of earlier provisions for licenses; for which see Pagula's *Summa summarum* v.59, Bodley 293 f. 226ra–va; for licences for preaching see Spencer (1996), pp. 165–7, 179–81. L's wording on the other hand is far less explicit.

L238 2 Cor. 4:3–4.

1153 ff. To the Lollards the primary duty of the priesthood was preaching, not the administration of the sacraments (*EWS* 164/44, 179/80, iv.79–84, Matthew 57/12, 112/17, and see Wyclif *Serm.* i.110/16).

1153 Matt. 28:19–20, Mark 16:15, Acts 1:8.

1160 *þese newe constituciouns and statutis*: probably references respectively to Arundel's Constitutions and the 1401 statute *De heretico comburendo* (see introduction p. xlvi–xlvii). Many of the proclamations that followed the condemnation of Wyclif in 1382 did not mention him by name, but speak more generally of heresy (e.g. *CPR 1381–5* pp. 150, 487, *CPR 1385–9* pp. 145–6, 200). Even Arundel's Constitutions in 1407 specify Wyclif in only two of their thirteen sections (Wilkins iii.314–19).

1162–7 This continues Wyclif's own asserted willingness to accept correction if shown to be at fault from scripture (e.g. *Op.min.* 354/7, 363/6 reproduced in the English *MC* 5, 136, 177, 210, 331, 1014).

1164 For the origin of the term *Lollard* see *SEWW* p. 8 and no. 17/151. The name was first applied to the followers of Wyclif as an insult, and only gradually was it gladly used by the sect itself (cf. *Op.ard.* f. 179ra, Laud misc.200 f. 67v, *LL* 11/11); see *PR* pp. 2–4. The two forms of the name, *Lollardis* (1164) and *Lollers* (1169) are found side by side in E though DHF have *Lollers* at both instances; for suggestions about a distinction between the two forms (not sustainable in relation to E's forms), see Scase (1989), pp. 150–8, and cf. *MED Lollard* and *loller(e* n.

1167 The form of amendment that the preacher would regard as legitimate is revealed at the end of his sermon (2949–62), namely if his use of scripture were illegitimate or inadequate.

1169 The heresy that the preacher would primarily identify is that of departure from scripture (see lines 1177–80), and especially in the matter of the eucharist (see lines 1197–200); in both the offenders are, of course, the accepted clerical authorities. For the orthodox view of the eucharist as 'heresy' see, for instance, *EWS* iv.54 and references there.

1173 ff. The ecclesiastical authorities used hostility to images as prime evidence of the Lollard heresy from a very early period. For instance, William Smith of Leicester was condemned for heresy in 1382 for using an image of St. Catherine as firewood (Knighton 296–8). The questions asked of Lollards regularly included the subject.

1183–7 The evils of clerics in offices which could be held by lay people are often mentioned in Lollard texts (e.g. Matthew 168/16, 247/3, Laud misc.200 f. 184v). For the issue see Hudson (1997), pp. 41–51.

1184 2 Tim. 2:3.

1188 Acts 6:2.

1196 1 Tim. 5:16.

1197–200 For the arguments on the eucharist see Titus 403 ff.

1199 *confederacie*: here, and later, the meaning plainly points to people not to an abstract concept. *MED* does not admit such a sense, though it does give the derogatory abstract 'conspiracy, plot'.

1199 Matt. 26:26–8, Mark 14:22–4, Luke 22:19–20, 1 Cor. 10:16–17.

1200–3 The objections to mendicancy are taken up more fully later in the sermon; see 2654 ff. and notes.

1209 Matt. 2:3, John 18:14.

1212–18 The issue here is that of licenses for preaching. Arundel's Constitutions (Wilkins iii.315–16, 319) reiterated previous legislation on this, and made the penalties for infringement more severe. Though the original legislation had not been designed to impede Lollard preachers (deriving from an earlier period), it was a useful and well-used tool for this purpose; cf. Spencer (1993), pp. 163 ff. From the earlier texts on (e.g. *Op.ard.* f. 157ra), Lollards fulminated against the requirement and objected to the grounds on which licenses were given to others but denied to them (see *EWS* 208/4 and iv.83–4, Arnold iii.333/1, Laud misc. 200 ff. 12, 189v).

1215 *if he wole go begge*: the implication is that the favoured preacher is likely to be a friar. Friars at first saw the 1407 Constitutions as impinging on their rights, but this was swiftly corrected by legislation in 1409 (Wilkins iii.324).

1220 John 5:43; the added material in the translation is placed in parentheses.

1225 The source is not entirely clear, but is reminiscent of PL 38.723–4, a sermon on the verse of John 5:43 just quoted.

1240 Matt. 23:2.

1246 The objection here to *Salisberi vss* (that is the order of services during the ecclesiastical year, in origin a modification of the Roman rite for the cathedral church at Salisbury, but by the fifteenth century in use through most of England south of the Humber) is to the excessive attention paid to the details of its performance, an attention greater than that paid to basic gospel precepts. Cf. *EWS* 161/53, Arnold iii.359/35, 433/1. Elsewhere the *vss* comes under criticism because of its practice of obscuring the words of scripture by singing them.

1251 Mark 7:11; *corbanan*: here apparently 'treasury', but in origin an altar offering, which often (to judge by Christ's words) took precedence over the maintenance of parents in their old age. Cf. *MED corban* n.

1252 ff. The notion of religious houses as guardians of the poor, and of money given to them as being given in trust for distribution to poor folk, is found in the statutes of many religious orders. See, for instance, Knowles *Monastic Orders* pp. 482–6. It is also found in the Statute of Carlisle 1306, *Statutes of the Realm* (London, 1810) i.150. Cf. Add. 24202 f. 8.

1260 The Pater noster, as the basic christian prayer, was one of the elements of religion, knowledge of which was to be ensured by investigation by the parish priest, according to the edicts of the 1215 Lateran Council. Knowledge and understanding of it in English was encouraged by the Lollards (see, for instance, the commentaries on it in Arnold iii.93–7, 98–110, Matthew 198–202, and there are other unprinted commentaries with Wycliffite content). By the mid-fifteenth century, however, knowledge of the prayer in English appears to have been possible evidence of heresy: in 1485 John Smith of Coventry was dilated for heresy because he held 'quod quilibet tenetur scire dominicam orationem, salutacionem angelicam et simbolum in Anglicis' (Lichfield reg. Hales f. 166v, cited *LB* p. 161).

1262 Matt. 23:13.

1263 Pseudo-Chrysostom PG 56.881 'Regnum enim coelorum dicuntur Scripturae, quia in illis insertum est regnum caelorum . . . Clavicularii autem sunt sacerdotes, quibus creditum est verbum docendi et interpretandi scripturas.'

1265 Matt. 23:13 ff.

1266 Comestor PL 198.1607–8; cf. line 667.

1268 Matt. 10:17, Mark 13:9, Luke 21:12.

1277 (L247) See 1231 ff.

1291 Acts 3:17.

1293 For the implication of the secular powers in the machinations of the clergy cf. Wyclif *Serm.* i.268/20, 383/22, *Trial.* 307/9; Arnold iii.152/6, 202/1. 281/29, Matthew 176/18.

1298–9 *to her vndoing*: i.e. to the ruin of the lay powers.

1301 Luke 22:38.

1305 Augustine *Quaestiones veteris et novi testamenti* 104, PL 35.2314 'Ne ergo velut impraescius haec pati videretur, et a quo forte virtus recessisset, haec omnia sic praedixit, ut non dubitaret de his, sed praescius contra haec se pararet.'

1308 Rom. 13:4.

1308 Eph. 6:17.

1311 Matt. 26:52, John 18:11.

1317 The reference is primarily to the activities of the rival claimants to the papal throne at the time of the schism: see above note to 1079.

1323 Augustine PL 38.479, by one numbering sermon *De verbis Domini* 13.

1326 John 1:42, combined with Matt. 16:18 and 1 Cor. 10:4; cf. *PPl* B.xv.212; both writers, following tradition, are bringing together 1 Cor. 10:4 (*petra autem erat Christus*) and Matt. 16:18 (*quia tu es Petrus, et super hanc petram aedificabo ecclesiam meam*).

1333 The three references apparently relate to the power of the sword. That to Numbers may refer to the story of Balaam and his ass, whose way was blocked by the angel with a drawn sword (22:15–35); the second to Kings is less clear, but may allude to the story of Solomon's judgment on the two women, when he decreed to divide the disputed child in two with the sword (3 Kgs. 3:16–28 at vv.24–5); the third is Rom. 13:14.

1334 Rom. 13:14.

1340 (L255) Luke 20:25.

1343 ff. (L258 ff.) The separation of church and state, and the importance of the laity in the *communitas Christianorum*, whilst characteristic of Wyclif and his followers, has a long ancestry behind it; see Wilks (1964).

1364 (L276) John 6:15.

1365 (L277) Luke 12:14.

1371 (L283) 1 Tim. 2:1–2, 6:1, Eph. 6:5–9, Tit. 3:1, all marginally in ED, in the text HF.

1372 (L284) Rom. 13:4; *triuauntis* (1375, L287 *tirawntes*) 'tyrants', Vulg. *vindex in iram*, see *MED tiraunt* for E's form.

1376 (L287) 1 Pet. 2:13–14, Vulg. 'Subiecti igitur estote omni humanae creaturae propter Deum: sive regi quasi praecellenti: sive ducibus tanquam ab eo missis ad vindictam malefactorum, laudem vero bonorum'; despite the reported speech of the introduction, the lines are a close translation.

1379 (L291) 1 Pet. 5:3, Vulg. *neque ut dominantes in cleris.*

1381–3 cf. 960–2 and note; the distinction between *kyndeli lordship*, that which God conferred on man over the creation on the sixth day (Gen. 1:29–30) and lost at the fall, and *lordship bi grace upon creaturis*, that which man *bi grace* exercises over his fellow men and over the lower creation, is found in FitzRalph's *De pauperie Salvatoris* ii.1–9 whence it was taken over by Wyclif in *De dominio divino* 15/13 ff., and further elaborated in *De civili dominio*. See briefly Leff ii.546–9. Wyclif's emphasis on grace, to the exclusion of any authority, material or spiritual, adhering to those not in a state of grace, led to the condemnation by Gregory XI in 1377 (*Hist. Angl.*i.353–4, cf. *FZ* 245–7); for the significance of this view in the later thought of Wyclif, his followers and opponents, see Hudson (1999) 63 ff.

1388 2 Tim. 2:3.

1393 *and so . . . office* (1395): cf. Wyclif's comment on the slaying of archbishop Sudbury by the peasants in 1381 (*De blas.* 194/16) 'Quid, rogo, pertinet ad archiepiscopum occupare cancellariam regis, que est secularissimum regni officium?'

1400–6 The use of clerics as judges in secular courts was widespread in medieval England; see for the earlier period F. Pegues, 'The "Clericus" in the legal administration of thirteenth-century England', *EHR* 71 (1956), 529–59; Swanson (1989), pp. 140–2, 182–90.

1401 1 Cor. 6:1–20, especially vv.1–5.

1403 1 Cor. 6:4 'Saecularia igitur iudicia si habueritis: contemptibiles, qui sunt in Ecclesia, illos constitute ad iudicandum.'

1428 Num. 16:15.

1433 Though all manuscripts include the reference to 1 Kgs. 8:[10–18], none quotes or translates the relevant material; the passage contains the warnings of Samuel to the Jewish people about the powers a king would hold over them if, contrary to his advice, they insist upon the provision of one.

1434 1 Kgs. 12:3–4.

1437 ED include the Latin quotations after *12 capitulo* in line 1434, whereas HF place it immediately before the translation. This latter must be correct, but the error probably derives from a manuscript which had the Latin in the margin. Whether that was its original position is unclear.

1440 *dixerunt* is expanded 1446 'the people bar witnesse wiþ him and seiden'.

1448 1 Kgs. 12:5 accurately translated.

1451 Saul, whose authority had been challenged by the Israelites in the previous chapter (1 Kgs. 11:12), here endorsed Samuel's judgment.

1456 Judges 8:22–3.

1481 See further lines 2654 ff. and notes there.

1487 (L299) Matt. 26:52. John 18:11.

1500 (L310) Rom. 1:32 'Qui cum iustitiam Dei cognovissent, non intellexerunt quoniam qui talia agunt, digni sunt morte; et non solum qui ea faciunt, sed etiam qui consentiunt facientibus.' The passage is quoted in translation in L.

1502–3 *þo two viciouse extremytees . . . of*: see 715.

1503–6 The author has in mind the strictures of 1 Cor. 13:1–3.

1509 For mockery of the extent of condemnation accorded within the sects to those who depart from the rule cf. Matthew 127/19, *Op.ard.* f. 169va, *Upland* 122.

1524 (L321) Matt. 26:52, John 18:11.

1527–8 (L324–6) The allusion to other nations is vague, and it is not clear whether the writer has any specific instance in mind (cf. 1078–81). He may be thinking of the close connection between the Avignon popes and the French throne, though most English observers saw this as dangerous because of the influence of the French upon the supposedly independent papacy rather than the reverse (see G. Mollat, *The Popes at Avignon, 1305–78* (Edinburgh, 1963), pp. 263–8).

1532–3 (L329) *ner . . . us*: 'were it not for the sleep of inertia that has fallen upon us'.

1538 (L335) Cf. Chaucer *Troilus and Criseyde* v.1433 and Knight's Tale A.1838; Whiting I.72.

1540–3 (L336–40) The charge is that gifts to the church, whether to a monastic or fraternal order or to a parish church, were to an institution and not to an individual—institutions, unlike individuals, do not naturally die and hence make no bequests. For the implications of this cf. Raban (1982), pp. 2–4 and *passim*.

1544–6 (L341–3) A blend of the instruction to the young man of Matt. 19:16 ff. with Matt. 10:37, more closely linked in Luke 18:22 and 29. Wyclif discusses the passage in *De civ.dom.* i.87/26 ff. where he cites Augustine Ep. 153 (PL 33.665).

1557–61 *and þus . . . titil*: the author appears to be referring, albeit allusively, to Wyclif's theory of dominion (cf. 1381–3 above and note). For Lollard echoes of this complex view see *EWS* iv.161–2 and especially sermon 78/95–120, *PR* pp. 359–62.

1575–9 Cf. *Benedicti regula*, ed. R. Hanslik (CSEL 75, 1960), cap. lviii.24–6; Smaragdus *Diadema monachorum* PL 102.610–11, 618–19.

1580 H glosses *symylacioun* marginally as *fayneyng*, and **1581** *resume* as *take aʒen*; *MED* suggests that both glossed words would have been uncommon c.1410, though for both the first occurrence is earlier.

1586 2 Pet. 2:22.

1592–4 Cf. *The Customary of the Benedictine Abbey of Eynsham in Oxfordshire*, ed. A. Gransden (Corpus Consuetudinum Monasticarum ii, 1963) p. 55/20 and *Decreta Lanfranci*, ed. D. Knowles (id.iii, 1967), p. 88/4 ff. and note.

1607–10 For legal actions by the clergy in defence of their rights and properties cf. various episodes described in M. Aston, *Thomas Arundel* (Oxford, 1967), esp. pp. 262–84. For a general survey of monastic economy in the later middle ages see Swanson (1989), pp. 193 ff., D. Knowles, *Religious Orders in England* (Cambridge, 1961), ii.309–30, and more particular studies B. Harvey, *Westminster Abbey and its Estates in the Middle Ages* (Oxford, 1977); C. Dyer, *Lords and Peasants in a Changing Society: the Estates of the Bishopric of Worcester 680–1540* (Cambridge, 1980).

1612–13 The medieval tavern was marked outside by a pole with a circle of ivy hanging from it; cf. Whiting W354–5, 361.

1619 (L349) Ps. 24:1.

1621 (L351) *him*: i.e. God.

L360–81 Origen: the passage is given in Latin in lines 1127–44. It derives from Origen on Genesis homily 16 §5, PG 12.250–1. The translation is close but idiomatic, the only strain coming where the Latin question ends with *exponimus* (1141), and the ensuing *qui* is more easily resumptive in Latin than in English (375).

L364 Num. 18:20.

L370 Luke 14:33.

L379 Matt. 19:27.

L382–99 Odo: Odo of Cheriton (c.1185–1246), at one time chancellor of the University of Paris, whence his patronymic T477. See A. C. Friend, ' Master Odo of Cheriton', *Speculum* 23 (1948), 641–58, and the same author's unpublished D. Phil thesis (Oxford, 1936). The *Floretum* quotes three passages (under *columba, prelacia, simonia*) and *ALD* translates two (56/9, 75/12). The reason for Odo's popularity with the Wycliffites is not far to seek: his sermons are full of castigation of contemporary abuses in the church. The quotation, given in Latin in L1189–202) derives from the sermon specified; manuscripts of the text vary considerably, and this is closer to CUL Kk.1.11 f. 131v than to the abbreviated version in Bodley 420 f. 271v.

L383-8 The contrast between Abel the shepherd and Cain the arable farmer is commonplace, based on Gen. 4:2-5 where God seems to value the former's gift over that of the latter.

L389 For the story of Constantine's donation, and the angel's message, see E1057 and note.

L394 Gen. 4:9.

L398 Actually the words are those of Jer. 50:6, though there could be conflation with Ezek. 34:2 which has comparable sentiments and is actually closer in its castigation of the clergy than the Jeremiah quotation.

L401 *Ysydre*: Isidore of Seville, *De summo bono* iii.51, PL 83.723–4, found in canon law C.23 q.5 c.20 (Friedberg i.936–7), a fairly free translation of the final two sentences 'Cognoscant principes seculi Deo se debere esse rationem reddituros propter ecclesiam, quam Christo tuendam suscipiant. Nam siue augeatur pax et desciplina ecclesiae per fideles principes, siue soluatur, ille ab eis rationem exigit, siue soluatur, ille ab eis rationem exigit, qui eorum potestati suam ecclesiam credidit.'

L408 Augustine *Quaestiones ex novo testamenti* 91, PL 35.2284, quoted at the start E11 (L11).

L410 Rom. 13:4.

L412 1 Tim. 2:2.

L416 1 Pet. 2:13–14.

1637 (L430) Luke 22:25–6.

1639, 1643 (L433, 437) Augustine PL 38.758 (after quoting Luke 22:25–6) 'Numquid non, si illis liceret, non delerent illam de evangelio? Quia vero delere illam non possunt, pervertere illam quaerunt.' The passage is quoted again in Titus 927 ff.

1641 (L434) Matt. 23:2.

1644–6 (L438–40) This taunt, that the established church prefers its own glosses to the naked word of the gospel, appears *EWS* 45/16, Arnold iii.258/17, Laud misc.200 ff. 32, 43v, 66. But compare Chaucer's exploitation of the divergence between gloss and obvious literal sense in WBP.

1649 (L443) John 10:38, 14:11 (both mentioned marginally in all manuscripts).

1654 (L447) All manuscripts give John 6 marginally (ED also in the text), and the reference is presumably to v.15; the wording is, however, closer to John 8:58.

L449 1 Cor. 3:11.

1657 Job dwelt 'in the land of Uz', one of the 'men of the east' (Job 1:1, 3): this appears to indicate an area east of Palestine, but its precise location is debated (see S. R. Driver and G. B. Gray, *A Critical and Exegetical Commentary on the Book of Job* (Edinburgh, 1921), pp. xxv–xxxi); he is here regarded as heathen probably because he lived before the christian dispensation.

1658 Acts 10:1–33.

1666 John 6:15.

1668 (L455) Matt. 20:17–19, Mark 10:32–4, Luke 18:31–4.

1674 (L461) Gregory PL 76.1139; the marginal reference to *omelia 17* in ED is correct. The translation 1676–7 (L464–5) is an abbreviated paraphrase.

1681 Gen. 1–3.

1688–90 (L470–2) Simony, so-called from the story of Simon Magus (Acts 8:9–24), was the offering or acceptance of worldly goods or temporal advantage in exchange for spiritual or ecclesiastical benefit or advancement.

1690 (L472) John 6:2–15.

1698 (L479) See E1057 for note on Constantine and Sylvester.

1700 (L481) 4 Kgs. 5:1–19.

1703 ff. (L484 ff.) For the legend of Sylvester see *Legenda aurea* (ed. Graesse), pp. 70–9; see also W. Levison, 'Konstantinische Schenkung und Silvester-Legende' in *Miscellanea Francesco Ehrle* 2 (*Studi e Testi* 38, 1924), 159–247. The story of Naaman, captain of the Syrian host, a leper healed by Elisha, is told in 4 Kgs. 5. Giezi (E1723), AV Gehazi, Elisha's servant, ran after Naaman on his return from the visit to Elisha to ask part of the gifts previous offered to, and refused by, Elisha; because of this, Elisha inflicted leprosy upon him. The term *symonyan* is not, of course, used in the OT; but the story is a fair example of the sin. The writer's point in 1727–30 is that Elisha's discernment as a prophet, greater than that of his servant, would have made him even more guilty had he succumbed to Naaman's offer; Sylvester, living under the new dispensation, in which simony was much more clearly forbidden, was even more culpable.

1721 (L499) 4 Kgs. 5:20–7.

1730 (L508) For the healing of Constantine, following the instruction of Sylvester, see *Legenda aurea* pp. 72–3, and note to E1746–51 (L520–6) below.

1734 (L509) *mouable goodis*: the gifts that Giezi received were transportable, those received by Sylvester consisted of lands (i.e. *vnmoeblis*, cf. E981).

1736 marginal references to 4 Kgs. 5, Num. 22[:1–21], Matt. 26[:14–16], Acts 8[:9–24].

1738 (L513) The story of Balaam is told in Numbers 22; Balaam, at God's instruction, refused to curse the people of Moab and answered Balak's servants (v.18): 'Si dederit mihi Balac plenam domum suam argenti et auri, non potero immutare verum Domini Dei mei, ut vel plus, vel minus loquar.' The writer alludes to the acceptance by Judas of thirty pieces of silver for the betrayal of Christ (Matt. 26:15, Mark 14:11, Luke 22:5). For the story of Simon Magus (Acts 8:9–24) see above E1688–90 (L470–2) note.

1746–51 (L521–6) See *Legenda aurea* p. 71 Constantine, before his conversion, persecuted the church, and Sylvester 'de urbe exiit et in quodam monte cum suis clericis mansit.' Subsequently the emperor, afflicted by leprosy, was told in a vision to send for Sylvester; the bishop (p. 72) 'Videns autem . . . milites statim ad palmam martirii credidit se vocari', commending himself to God, came forward.

1751 (L526) *Legenda aurea* p. 72 tells nothing about Sylvester's reception of what is said to be Constantine's law, issued the fourth day after his baptism 'ut sicut imperator Romae sic Romanus pontifex caput ab universis episcopis habeatur'.

1762–5 (L536–9) Constantine might partially be excused as a layman, and one whose conversion was not, according to the legend, of long standing.

L539 1 Cor. 3:11.

1768–73 The writer is presumably thinking of the implications of the use of money by clerics, directly and indirectly, to gain their own advancement or that of their house.

1777 For the charge that the established clergy impugn scripture as heresy see above 238 ff. and note.

1798 (L550) Gorham: for the relevant passage on Rev. 12:15 see L1203–19. The true author is uncertain: see Hudson (1985), pp. 307–9 and R. E. Lerner, 'Poverty, preaching, and eschatology in the Revelation commentaries of "Hugh of St Cher"', *Studies in Church History*, *Subsidia* 4 (1985), pp. 157–89, where it is argued that the commentary derives from the immediate circle of Hugh of St. Cher. A copy of the text is found in Bodley 716, following Wyclif's own NT postills, ff. 173ra–246vb ascribed to Hugh de Vienna; the passage relevant here is f. 213rb–va. A closely related, but not identical, text was printed in *Sancti Thomae Aquinatis Opera Omnia* (Padua, 1869), pp. 325–511, here pp. 430–1. For the legend of the prophecy see E1057 note above.

L551 Jerome PL 23.53, quoted in L1220–1 immediately after the Gorham quotation above.

1806 (L558–62) See 4 Kgs. 4:8–10, the story of Elisha's sojourn with the Shunemite woman and her husband.

1813 (L565) Luke 8:3.

1819–20 (L572–3) 'and such divergent actions in circumstances that are so similar cannot be linked together'.

1827 (L581) Matt. 26:56, Mark 14:50, Acts 9:1. Cf. Bodley 647 f. 107 'And

Petir and Poule synned also when þei denyed and blasp[h]emed in Crist, bot men schuld not sue hom in þis, for þen þei wente from Iesu Crist.'

1832 (L586) Matt. 26:75.

1833 (L587) 1 Cor. 15:9.

1841 (L593–4) Matt. 11:28–30, Mark 16:15, both chapters cited marginally, though L's marginal reference to the last chapter of Matthew is a clear misreading of abbreviated *Mr*.

1843 (L596) All manuscripts, some marginally, some in the text, give references to 1 Cor. 11 and Eph. 5 (L, which has a simpler version of the sentence, has only the second). The basic allusion, however, seems to be to 1 Cor. 1:12–13 (where Cephas is Peter's other name, see John 1:42). The cited material seems to be 1 Cor. 11:1 'Imitatores mei estote, sicut et ego Christi', and Eph. 5:1 'Estote ergo imitatores Dei, sicut filii charissimi.'

1846 (L599) 1 Pet. 2:21.

1854 (L605) *west empire*: Constantine, after the events which led to his gifts of land and authority to Sylvester, following the battle at Chrysopolis in 324, fixed his capital at Constantinople. This had the effect of enhancing the importance of the papacy in the western areas of the empire.

1859 (L612–13) The saints referred to are Thomas a Beket, archbishop of Canterbury 1162–70, Hugh, bishop of Lincoln 1186–1200, and Swithin, bishop of Winchester who died in 862. Beket was commonly regarded by Lollards as having been killed in defence of the powers and endowment of the church in opposition to the secular ruler (see *EWS* 93/98, iv.163 and J. F. Davis, 'Lollards, Reformers and St. Thomas of Canterbury', *University of Birmingham Historical Journal* 9 (1963), 1–15). Hugh of Lincoln (see *ODCC*) is less frequently mentioned by Lollards, but the author is presumably thinking of Hugh's independence of Henry II and Richard I (see *Magna Vita Sancti Hugonis*, ed. D. L. Douie and H. Farmer (London, 1961) bks.iv–v). It is unclear why Swithin is mentioned, though this is probably a deduction from the wealth of the shrine by the author's date (see the assessment in G. L. Harriss, *Cardinal Beaufort: A Study of Lancastrian Ascendancy and Decline* (Oxford, 1988), pp. 411–12).

1871 (L624) *þouȝ þat þis maner of arguyng of a creature is to short*: compare 1867–8 (L620) 'þis argument is to short'; *short* in both cases has the sense of 'facile' (cf. *MED short* adj. 3(c)). L's substitution of *so* for *þouȝ* here makes easier sense, but the majority reading seems just possible, with *MED*'s sense 'in as much as' for *though* conj.4. Matthew (p. 528) compares *Dialogus* 20/3 'Cum ex fide capimus quod nullus sanctorum, quantacunque sanctitate prepolleat, est in dicto vel consuetudine credendus, nisi de quanto illud consonat cum Christo qui est prima veritas. Et per consequens, habita a Christo vivaciori evidencia ad credendum contrarium, istud est ex illa forciori evidencia dimittendum.'

1879–80 (L632–3) That is 'the day of judgment shall come before they manage to prove the lesser part of the argument.' The *minor* is the minor premise of the syllogism, here that the saints followed Christ's example in their lordship (the *major*, repeated here, is that it is therefore right to follow their example). The scholastic jargon was apparently comprehensible without explanation (see *MED majour* adj. which does not give this technical sense, and *minor* adj. and n. , giving this and Fortescue as the only logical uses). For Gabriel's horn as a sign of the last judgment see Whiting G1–2; cf. also *Op.evan.* ii.152/26, *Op.min.* 213/12, *Religious Lyrics of the Fourteenth Century*, ed. C. Brown, revd. G. V. Smithers (Oxford, 1957) no. 103/67.

1898 ff. (L641 ff.) Cf. note to E1079 above. One of the aspects of the Despenser campaign most offensive to Wyclif and his followers was that the campaign of the bishop was against fellow christians (cf. Wyclif *Serm.* iv.156/3, *Pol. Wks.* ii.466/21, *Op.min.* 25/16; *EWS* 48/19, E11/83, E31/48, 203/26).

1901 (L645) Acts 3:6.

1902 (L646) Matt. 19:27.

1905 ff. (L649 ff.) The papacy claimed primacy by virtue of St. Peter's tenure of the bishopric of Rome.

L650–67 Bernard *De consideratione* ii.6 §10, *Op.* iii.418/1–17, PL 182.748, quoted in Latin L1110–26 and fairly closely translated here.

L651 cf. Acts 3:6, 2 Cor. 11:28.

L654 1 Pet. 5:3.

L657 Luke 22:25.

L663 Hos. 8:4.

L664 Luke 22:26.

L668 1 Cor. 3:11.

1906–8 One Lollard objection to images was that their traditionally elaborate carving and painting, often with gold and jewel adornments, gave a misleading impression to the ignorant of the life of the saints the images purported to recall. See *SEWW* 16/24–33, and the orthodox *Dives and Pauper* I.vii.25–34. For the type of image to which the author is objecting see many of the decorated saints illustrated in E. Duffy, *The Stripping of the Altars: Traditional Religion in England 1400–1580* (New Haven and London, 1992). Cf. *Lollard Chron.* Em. 610–16 for the story of the Emperor's submission at the feet of pope Celestine III.

1908 1 Pet. 2:13–14.

1914 The definition of *anticrist* in Lollard works is variable; compare that here with Titus 61 note. The basic sense is that here, anyone who reverses Christ or his teaching; cf. Arnold iii.457/20, *ALD* 54/16, *LL* 6/15, *Op.ard.* f. 167va.

1920 ff. (L670 ff.) Ownership of property or goods acquired by the church was usually vested in the monastic house, cathedral chapter or similar body. For the background to the writer's claim as it concerns the monastic orders amongst nearly contemporary discussion see Swanson (1989), pp. 191–209, and W. Pantin, 'Two Treatises of Uthred of Boldon on the Monastic Life', in *Studies in Medieval History presented to F. M. Powicke*, ed. R. W. Hunt, W. A. Pantin and R. W. Southern (Oxford, 1948), pp. 363–85. Since the writer deals with the friars later in the text (2654 ff.), it seems unlikely that the arguments over their holding of property are here relevant.

1922 (L673) Acts 4:32.

1929–31 (L680–1) That is, that *lordship* does not descend through inheritance as is the case in normal medieval secular society, but accrues by virtue of the original gift of alms to the house or community. The concept of *perpetuel almesse* concerns the gift of property by a secular person to such a community. Wyclif challenges the same (*elemosinae perpetuae*) in *Pol. Wks.* i.245/25, 277/5 and *Op.min.* 247/1.

1933 (L684) John 5:36, John 10:38, John 14:11.

1935 (L686) Matt. 23:3.

1936 (L688) John 5:36.

1942 (L694) *persoone aggregat*: again a piece of legal terminology; *MED* does not give the adjectival use of *aggregat*. Cf. *De sym.* 90/18.

1943 (L695) cf. Augustine *Enarr.* in Ps. 21:29, PL 36.180–1 (suggested by Parker pp. 204–5).

1944 ff. (L696 ff.) The argument here deals entirely with *temporalities* as opposed to *spiritualities* (see note on E1100–20). The writer is correct in his charge that religious performed the same legal functions on their estates as did secular lords. See Jones (1970), pp. 113–17, Raban (1982), F. R. H. DuBoulay, *The Lordship of Canterbury* (London, 1966), Jones, 'Relations of two jurisdictions', *Studies in Medieval and Renaissance History* 7 (1970), 77–210. The issue here is rather different from that involved in the *Upland* sequence, JU 214–19, FDR 554–76, JUR 266–75, discussed by Somerset (1998), pp. 140–8.

1945 (L698) *knyȝt fee*: L's reading *knyȝtte* is an error, not made in P where the term was still correctly given.

1954 (L706) The technical sense of *fraunchisen togidir* 'are under the jurisdiction of joint possessors' (*MED* sense 3(d) only this text in the Lambeth version) makes it clear that the writer is here speaking of a more complicated position where secular and clerical lords hold jointly estates and properties. For ecclesiastical involvement in control of secular crime see Dyer pp. 76–8. 264–9, 358–60, Swanson (1989), pp. 147–8, also various papers in R. H. Helmholz, *Canon law and the Law of England* (London, 1987), pp. 59–76, 77–99, 119–44; it is clear from the evidence given by Dyer that the bishops of Worcester had the power to hang felons, and exercised it, though the precise charge here is not confirmed. Matthew (p. 529) quotes Pecock's *Repressor* ii.369/2 justifying the use of religious as royal deputies in legal suits.

1958–9 (L709–10) That is, the lordship claimed by the clergy is not just possession of property but involves jurisdiction over ordinary layfolk, even to the extent of involving rights over their continued existence. See previous note and cf. A. H. Thompson, *The English Clergy and their Organization in the Later Middle Ages* (Oxford, 1947), appendix II, extracts from bishop Alnwick's courtbook pp. 206–19; also DuBoulay pp. 297–312.

1971–81 that is, this kind of lordship is no more legitimate for an ecclesiastical corporation than for an individual cleric.

1981–4 For resort by the clergy to civil law for pursuance of their claims see R. L. Storey, 'Clergy and Common Law in the reign of Henry IV', in *Medieval Legal Records edited in memory of C. A. F. Meekings*, ed. R. F. Hunnisett and J. B. Post (London, 1978), pp. 342–408, though most of the cases discussed concern preferment rather than property or cases against the clergy. Jones (1970) deals with the conflict between secular and ecclesiastical law; but clerics by this date were obliged to resort to civil law courts in all questions involving land (see pp. 132–42); also Dyer pp. 51 ff.

1984–90 The writer is reverting to his earlier distinction between rights through innocence, grace or human law (see lines 1381–3 note). The point is that appeal to litigation is not a relevant way to maintain title through innocence or grace; so if the clergy resort, as they do, to legal processes, they must be basing their claim upon purely human, and secular, rights.

1992–6 For struggles of the kind mentioned cf. M. Aston, *Thomas Arundel: a Study of Church Life in the Reign of Richard II* (Oxford, 1967), pp. 262–84.

2004 Acts 4:32–4.

2009–13 The point is that, just as an individual's claims exclude those of another individual, so do the claims of one community, albeit a religious community, exclude those of another community. The writer views this as divergent from the situation in the early church where goods were shared amongst all believers without division of that community into smaller groups. The outright advocacy of communal overship was thought worthy of enquiry of Lollards (see *LB* p. 134 q.37 and p. 135 q.9), but was not a common view (see *PR* pp. 374–5).

2016–32 The writer is exploiting the divisions between different groups of religious: all say they live a more perfect life than the laity, but they squabble amongst themselves about the relative claims of the monastic, fraternal and canons' ways of life. If they were really perfect, each group would help not denigrate the other. In fact the secular clergy were probably most loud in denunciation of the friars' mendicancy, and not the monks as the writer implies (2024–6); for this see below 2704 ff. notes. But arguments against mendicancy are found in recent monastic writers such as Uthred of Boldon (see Pantin art.cit. note on 1920 ff., p. 370 and especially his *Contra fratrum mendicitatem* and *Contra iniustas fratrum querelas* with manuscript details p. 364).

2028 1 Cor. 13:5.

2031 *þat hem nede . . . synne* (2032): 'that it would not be necessary for them, nor would they have had opportunity for them to sin'.

2037 (cf. L711) That is, since the monks will not relieve the friars, it is clear that they assert restrictive claims to their wealth and do not share as did the early christians. Since L does not include the discussion of fraternal ownership, the sentence there relates to the conflict between monks and the laity.

2051 (L723) See Grosseteste Dict 2, MS Bodley 830 f. ivb 'Misericordia est amor siue voluntas releuandi miserum a sua miseria. Et tunc est vera misericordia cum hec voluntas tam intensa fuerit quod compellat voluntatem suum velle in actum producere si possit, hoc est releuare miserum a sua miseria ut compellat eum si possit.'

2053 (L726) Luke 14:14.

2054–67 (L727–37) The implication is, of course, that all of these conditions in which alms should *not* be given are fulfilled in the case of donations to the clergy. The social argument, that money given to the friars removes alms from those genuinely in need, is advanced in a number of Lollard works; see, for instance, Matthew 173/19, 233/12, Arnold iii.415/26, TCD 244 f. 216v; but compare also *PPl.* C.x.98 ff.

2068–75 (L739–45) The implication is that alms should not be given to those better off, or better able to support themselves, than the donor. Cf. Scase (1989), pp. 72–6.

2069 (L739) 2 Cor. 8:10–14; L's marginal reference to '*prima* Cor. ' is erroneous, and is not replicated in P. L's reading is the easier, but E's (supported by DHF) seems justified by the LV translation 'and not that it be remyssioun to othere men, and to ʒou tribulacioun'.

2072 (L742) Cf. Luke 11:41 'Verumtamen quod superest, date eleemosynam: et ecce omnia munda sunt vobis'; LP quote this marginally as 'Quod superest date elemosinam. luc.xiiij'.

2075–6 (L745–7) A reference again to the Donation of Constantine.

2077 (L747) Matt. 22:21, Mark 12:17, Luke 20:25.

L757 1 Cor. 3:11.

2084 *distraccioun* E, *distruccioun* DHF: E's reading involves the superscript letters usually meaning *ra*. E's reading is the more difficult (*MED*'s examples are all later), but also the more appropriate: *MED*'s sense (b) 'subtraction or diversion (of possessions)', recorded only from Bokenham 1447, is exactly that needed here; consequently it has been left. It must, however, be admitted that at

2164 (like the present, not found in L) all manuscripts have *distruccioun or enpeiring*.

2095 (L767–8) The command to win bread by toil came as a result of the fall (Gen. 3:17–19), before which toil was not needed (Gen. 1:27–30).

2096 (L769) Matt. 7:12.

2099 (L771) Num. 18:8–24. Deut. 26:1–4.

2106 (L778) Deut. 15:4.

2110 *partener* because Christ partook of (cf. *MED partener(e* n.), for instance, the fish that Peter and his fellow caught (John 21:10–13) and of the food provided by various friends and disciples (e.g. John 12:2); the clause does not appear in L.

2116 (L788) Luke 14:13; for the three, rather than four, groups of poor, a division traceable to FitzRalph, see Scase (1989), pp. 63–4 and notes.

2121–2 (L792–3) For the distinction between the provision of food and clothing, legitimately provided for the clergy, and the excessive wealth or begging of the contemporary monks and friars see above lines 228 ff. and 773 and notes.

2133 (L803) To Lollard writers the period before the Donation of Constantine represented a kind of 'golden age', corrupted by the endowment of the church (e.g. *Lollard Chron.* Em. 14–26, *Op.ard..* ff. 139vb, 176vb, Arnold iii.418/24). But the most rapid decline was viewed as occurring after the first millennium: it was then, according to many writers, that the fiend was loosed (Rev. 20:7); see *EWS* 231/40.

2136 (L806) *þe opir two statis*: i.e. those of lords and ordinary layfolk.

2144 (L814) Matt. 6:26–9, Luke 12:24–8.

2150–2 (L819–23) Cf. 2068–75 note and reference to Scase.

2157 (L824) *al-amys*: not recognized as a noun by *MED*, but formed obviously from *al + amys*, as a distortion of, and pun on, *almesse*. It seems peculiar to this text.

2175 *a lord . . . kyngis* (2177): the writer is evidently envisaging a situation where the temporal lord of a settlement would act as defender and protector of the church there—a situation similar to that portrayed by Langland in *PPl* B.vi.21–56 (though whether the preacher's knight would accept instruction as meekly as Langland's is unclear!). It is not here stated that the lord would act as patron of the living, but the references to *amortaisyng* (2186) and *apropriaciouns* (2192) would suggest this. Again (as at the start, see note to 11), the temporal ruler is portrayed as *vicarius Dei*, the priest as *vicarius Christi*.

2184–6 (L835–7) See 1100–20 and notes.

2192 For *apropriacioun* see 540–2 note. The writer here outlines some of the abuses that arose from the transference, abuses that were recognized by orthodox members of the church (cf. the petitions sent by the English church to the Council of Pisa in 1408 in *Magni et Universalis Constantiensis Concilii* I.xxvi, ed. H.von der Hardt (Helmstedt, 1697), at 1140–3). Because the religious house usually retained the bulk of the income, the vicar appointed by the house was forced to live on a minimal sum; as a result such vicars often obtained licenses for non-residence, and the curates they were supposed to provide were often incompetent. See Wood-Legh (1934), pp. 127–53, Thompson (1947), pp. 109–23. For Lollard comments see Matthew 419/29, 453/14, *PR* p. 357.

2196–9 Cf. *PPl* B.v.386–423.

2205 *þe curatis of her sustynaunce*, that is, by appropriation; see note above to 2192.

2225–7 The analysis goes back to Augustine's in line 11 note. E's reading *partis* is possible, but DF *propirtees* (H is missing) is more appropriate.

2232–5 i.e. respectively where the ordinary layfolk lack both secular lord and resident cleric (because their church and the lands of the village have been given to a religious house); where the layfolk have a secular lord but no resident cleric; where the layfolk have a priest but no secular lord.

2241–9 For disendowment, and schemes to effect it, cf. *SEWW* no. 27 and Aston (1993) pp. 95–131. Matthew (p. 529) compares *Pol. Wks.* ii.703/5 ff.

2253 *þouȝ þei feelen . . . hemsilf:* 'though they do not perceive it in relation to themselves'.

2256 (L847) Judges 11:30–40.

2257 (L849) Matt. 14:6–12, Mark 6:21–9.

2260 (L852) Augustine PL 35.2239–40; Parker (pp. 209–10) also compares PL 34.811 though this is not the book specified in 2260.

2263–4 (L855–7) The oaths referred to here are those stated or implied in the grants of property made to the church (see note to 1944 ff.).

2278–82 (L868–70) In view of the beginning of the paragraph, which advocates the breaking of foolish oaths, the force of E's sentence would seem to be that lords regard themselves as bound by such oaths. L's sense, omitting 'what þat euere . . . ypocritis' makes easier sense, referring to the obligation to God.

L871 1 Cor. 3:11.

2284–6 Lollard objections to the adornment of the material church by architectural elaboration or painting, or by the addition to its services of bells, and music of any kind are persistent. *LL* 38/15–43/28 gives a good review of many of the arguments advanced; see *PR* pp. 319, 321–7. Objection to bells (found, for instance in the Norwich trials, Tanner pp. 49, 54, 58 etc.) was probably partly because of the charges made on the parish for their provision and ringing (see B. Kümin, *The Shaping of a Community: The Rise and Reformation of the English Parish c.1400–1560*

(Aldershot, 1996), pp. 50, 80, 101, 240), but partly also for the reasons advanced against organs and singing. Here one objection was the use of money for their provision, money that could better have been spent on other charitable or religious purposes (e.g. Matthew 192/12, Ps. Bod. 288 f. 96vb). A more substantial objection was that the use of organs or of chant, especially *knakkyng* to which particular exception was taken, obscured the words of the services and, most importantly, of scripture (e.g. Arnold iii.481/13, Matthew 76/8, 91/29, Ps. Bod.877 f. 82va). Objection to elaborate church building is partly on the theological grounds that it misplaced the importance from the congregation to the material object (cf. *LL* 23/3 'þe chosun noumbre of hem þat schullen be saued' and 35/37 'comyng togiddir of good and yuel in a place þat is halowid' where the definition involves both the mixture of *good and yuel* and the physical church) and that the material object was only of importance insofar as it served man (*EWS* 73/20, Arnold iii.487/14). The other Lollard objection was that of the misapplication of money, diverted from poor men to the adornment of churches (cf. *LL* 38/3). For objections to painting see Thorpe 1119–72.

2299 Isa. 1:13–15.

2301 ff. The objection here is not primarily to the form of monastic prayer, but to the unworthiness and hypocrisy of those praying. Cf. 521 note.

2309 Ecclus. 34:25.

2310–16 For criticism of the worldly prosperity of the monastic orders compare Chaucer's portrayal of the Monk in *CT* A.165–207, and J. Mann, *Chaucer and Medieval Estates Satire* (Cambridge, 1973), pp. 17–37 and notes showing the lineage of such criticisms before the Lollards.

2318 1 Tim. 2:8.

2323 cf. Rom. 12:19.

2326 Gregory *Regula pastoralis* iii.21 (PL 77.88) where the quotations below from Prov. 21:27 and Ecclus. 34:24 follow each other in quick succession.

2328 Ecclus. 34:21; Prov. 21:27.

2333 Ecclus. 34:24.

2335 Matt. 5:23.

2340 Gen. 4:4–5.

2342 Matt. 5:24.

2351 See 2294 ff.

2352–5 These examples are often used by Lollards in refutation of the idea that beautiful or even 'holy' places can induce greater virtue; cf. *LL* 36/21 quoting declaredly Jerome but actually pseudo-Chrysostom on Matthew PG 56.876.

2353 Isa. 14:12; Gen. 2:8–25.

2358 1 Kgs. 2:12–17, 27–36.

2364 See, for instance, Prov. 15:8, Is. 1:11–17, Jer. 6:19–20, 7:21–3, Hos. 6:6.

2370 See above 521 ff.

2380 (L873) *entail* involves the limitation of inheritance by conditions imposed or fixed by the donor, the most important of which conditions is the restriction of inheritance to a particular group of heirs; the donor fixes not only the immediate beneficiary but also the succession to later inheritors. As is implied by 2381 (L875), the restrictions could be for a fixed period or indefinitely. Failure to observe the conditions imposed by the original donor was regarded as incriminating both the unintended beneficiary and the immediate alienator, if any (2384–6, L878–80), regardless of the reasons. The writer ingeniously uses this provision to incriminate the monastic orders, regarded as breaking the *entail* imposed by God in leaving lordship to the laity according to the Levitical law.

2396 ff. (L890 ff.) The writer goes on to deal with a possible objection from the clergy that by the same token of *entail* they are entitled to tithes. But in E he claims that this *entail* was effectively broken by Christ and his apostles: because they did not exercise the right of *entail*, ignoring tithes and living by other means, the right lapsed. The Lambeth text takes a rather different way out of the clergy's logic: the *entail* of tithes were to the kindred of Levy; but Christ was of the kindred of Judah, not Levy, and so was not entitled to the *entail*; in so far as the contemporary clergy were descended from Christ, nor are they. Both texts agree that Christ said nothing to confirm the *entail*. For the discussion cf. White in *FZ* p. 428, saying that tithes ceased at the passion and were only revived under Gregory X. As any of the extant manuscripts stand, the sermon version is expressed in extremely contorted syntax.

L891 Num. 18:21.

L892 Matt. 1:2, Luke 3:33.

L896 Higden *Polycronicon* vii.34 (RS 8.204) where the pope is question is said to be Gregory IX.

2396–407 (L896–902) *and if . . . sacrilege* (2407, L902): as the sermon version stands in all manuscripts, this sentence does not have a main verb since *and so ferforþly cleymen riȝt* (2402) seems to be a completion of *and if . . .* (2396). In the tract version, following wording in place of 2398–402, the wording runs *and ȝitt þai claymen so ferforþli þes tiþis* (L897); this, a new sentence, provides clear syntax. The sense of the sermon is clear, and so the imperfect construction has been left. The sermon version has been emended by the insertion of a pronoun.

2411–15 (L907–10) The point is that, unlike the case of tithes, the *entail* of secular lordship continued unbroken from OT times through to the present.

2416 (L912) For a general survey of tithes see G. Constable, *Monastic Tithes* (Cambridge, 1964), esp. pp. 9–56. Wyclif took the position that tithes were not a legal obligation to be paid to the clergy without question, but alms for the clergy if they were deserving and poor (see *De civ.dom.* i.317/1 ff. and *Serm.*

iii.471/26); the 1382 condemnation included the point 'quod decimae sunt purae eleemosynae, et quod parochiani possunt propter peccata suorum curatorum eas detinere, et ad libitum aliis conferre' *(FZ* 280–1) The removal of tithes from unworthy clerks, and their payment for other charitable causes was often advocated (Matthew 436/5, Add. 24202 ff. 34v, 40v, see *PR* pp. 340–5, *EWS* iv.169–71).

2429 (L921) Gen. 3:14–24.

2433 (L925) 2 Cor. 11:14.

2435–50 (L928–41) *and if . . . expresli groundid* (2450, L941): this unwieldy sentence consists of two complex conditional clauses (2435–40, L928–32; 2440–3, L932–5), here separated by semi–colons, the main question (2443–6, L935–8), followed by an explanatory clause with its subordinates (curtailed in L by the omission of the final clause).

2437–8 (L930–1) The question of the return to a benefactor of property previously given to a religious body but now needed by the benefactor is dealt with in canon law: C.16 q.1 c.61 (Friedberg i.781). The issue was one of considerable interest in the late fourteenth century, and had been debated outside Wycliffite circles in the context of the need for funds to continue war against France. Two Austin friars in the 1371 parliament had urged that, in time of national need, the donors of ecclesiastical wealth could recall it for the defence of the realm (see Aston (1993), pp. 105 ff. and references); the case was continued two years later. Wyclif urged the same (e.g. *De off.reg.*183/14, 185/9); cf. Scase (1989), pp. 103–4.

2439 (L931) *positif lawe*: law laid down by human decree or legislation, as opposed to natural law (see *MED* (a)); here clearly the term is derogatory 'arbitrary legislation'.

2440–3 (L932–4) The recovery of property, originally given to a religious body but in some way subsequently lost to it, is covered by D.3 c.13 (Friedberg ii.512–16).

2443 ff. (L935 ff.) As in 2380 ff. (L873 ff.) the writer ingeniously turns the clergy's arguments against themselves: if the law governing inalienability of clerical property is just, then the same principles apply even more stringently to secular property because, as he has argued in 2396–414 (L890–910), the legal claims of secular inheritance are stronger than those that could be advanced by the clergy. He here goes one step further and urges, 2453–6 (not replicated in L), that the only justification for the clerical position is their own, human traditions and legislation whereas the justification for the secular position is God's own law.

2445 (L937) The agreement of E and L against the evidence of DHF seems likely to be coincidental: both manuscripts have been influenced by *seculer* in the preceding and following wordings. The reading of E has been corrected, but since P confirms L's *seculer* this has been left as, at most, the reading of the archetype of this version.

2459–61 For further ridicule of this position see *SEWW* 26/57.

2461 *tradiciouns* is, as here, regularly a derogatory word in Lollard writings, being of human invention, as opposed to the law of God embodied in scripture; see Arnold iii.295/17, 372/24, Matthew 19/28, 89/1, Add. 24202 f. 52.

2476–83 (L944–52) The argument is that the value of tithes and offerings is sufficient to maintain the clergy, without endowment. Whether the value of tithes was as high as the author claims is difficult to discover. For an analysis of one living's tithes in the fifteenth century see Heath (1969), pp. 166–73, Swanson (1989), pp. 210–15, 229–31, and A. G. Little, 'Personal Tithes', *EHR* 60 (1945), 67–88.

2484–90 (L953–60) The sense of *perquisitis* here is 'gratuities or occasional compensations accruing to an office' (see *MED perquisitives* n. pl., the tract version being the only example). Lollard objections to the fees that had to be paid for the services here mentioned are frequent, and echo earlier objections in many cases. See *Op.ard.* f. 190rb for the case against payments to priests 'pro administracione cuiuslibet sacramentorum'. See above 2284–6 note. Cf. Heath (1969), pp. 156–8.

2487 (L956) L's *chauncellis*, though supported by P, may be an error in the archetype, since, though it follows through from the previous two nouns, the ensuing *opir ournementis* supports the sermon reading *chaliss*.

L962 1 Cor. 3:11.

2496 Matt. 8:19–20, cf. Luke 9:58.

2500 ff. See above 221–4 and notes.

2519–24 For this interpretation of Matt. 8:19–20 cf. Bonaventura *Op.*viii.113, 161, 172. For the background to the tau cross see G. Schiller trans. J. Seligman, *Iconography of Christian Art* (London, 1971–2), ii.125.

2526 2 Kgs. 17:23; Matt. 27:5.

2531 Matt. 8:19.

2545 Luke 19:45, Matt. 21:12, John 2:15.

2560 For the use of *pseudo* as a noun cf. Titus 1568, 2784, Matthew 319/3, 479/23, *Upland's Rejoinder* 99; *MED pseudo* n. shows it to be used only by Lollard authors or by their opponents concerning their usage. In Latin before Wyclif the noun is used by William of St. Amour, for example, *Opera omnia* (Constance, 1632), p. 57).

2560 Matt. 24:24, Mark 13:22.

2562 Matt. 20:16, 22:14.

2570 Perhaps Jerome ep.58, PL 22.583. These lines to 2580 are an imagined riposte to the preacher's views on the monastic orders, and so have been placed in inverted commas.

2573 4 Kgs. 6:1.

2576 Dionysius *De ecclesiastica hierarchia* cap. 6, *Dionysiaca* ii.1392 (PG 3.534) in Grosseteste's translation 'Partibilium non solum vitarum sed quidem et phantisiarum, abrenuntiatio perfectissimam manifestat monachorum philosophiam in scientia unificatorum mandatorum operantem.' Oxford, Lincoln College MS 101 f. 125 with Grosseteste's commentary. The author (see *ODCC*) was probably a late fifth-century Syrian, who passed off his writings under the name of Paul's disciple mentioned in Acts 17:34. Though the attribution was early questioned, the works in various Latin translations became widely known and immensely influential in western Christendom throughout the medieval period and later. For further quotations see T236, 520, 607, 2599. The present writer had probably encountered Dionysius through the translations and commentaries of Grosseteste (see S. H. Thomson, *The Writings of Robert Grosseteste Bishop of Lincoln 1235–1253* (Cambridge, 1940), pp. 55–8, 78–80; there is an unpublished edition of Grosseteste's translation and commentary by C. T. Hogan (PhD thesis, Cornell, 1991)); Wyclif drew on this source (see *De apos.* 62/2, *De ver.* i.41/11, 43/5, 115/7).

2587 John 3:25–36.

2591–621 See cap. 6, *Dionysiaca* ii.1386 (PG 3.531–4).

2599 Acts 17:34.

2613 *and þe peple . . . perfit* (2614): E's haplography (not replicated in DHF) was doubtless caused by the repetition of *perfit*.

2621–3 Jerome, see for instance Ep. 125, PL 22.1077–9; the writer would have been particularly attracted by Jerome's exhortation *ama scientiam scripturarum* (1078) and to live, like the apostles, by the works of their hands.

2628 The author is presumably thinking of the fact that the monks, unlike the friars, did not undertake parochial duties, such as ordinary preaching or the hearing of confessions (cf. 2617 ff.). The charge that this omission is *sumwhat for her owne eese* (2629) may be fair in relation to the abuses of monasticism already described, but it ignores the founding ideals of the monks.

2629–31 For a description of a curate's duties in Lollard eyes see *LL* 34/23–35/ 10 based on 2 Tim. 4:5, amplified by the same text pp. 48/3–69/20 in so far as that section relates to priests.

2633–4 Matt. 5:40, Luke 6:29.

2635 Hildegar: Hildegard of Bingen 1098–1179 (see *ODCC*). The quotation here comes from *Pentachronon*, a collection of extracts made by Gebeno of Eberbach in 1220, the chief way in which her name and ideas were known in the middle ages: see K. Kerby-Fulton, *Reformist Apocalypticism and 'Piers Plowman'*,

(Cambridge, 1990), pp. 28–56, and the same author's 'Prophecy and Suspicion: Closet Radicalism, Reformist Polemics and the Vogue for Hildegardiana in Ricardian England', *Speculum* 63 (2000), 318–41. Here PL 197.1018 'Deus quidem non praecepit ut tunica et pallium alteri filio daretur, et alter nudus remaneret, sed jussit ut isti pallium illi tunica tribueretur. Pallium itaque saeculares propter amplitudinis saecularis curae, et propter filios suos qui semper crescunt et multiplicantur habeant; tunica vero spiritali populo concedatur, ne in victu aut in vestitu deficiant, et ne plus quam necesse sit possideant.' Wyclif cites her *Op.min.* 169/12, *Pol. Wks.* i.67/16, *Trial.* 338/17, and she is mentioned in Lollard works Matthew 11/20, Arnold iii.413/3, 421/27, *PPlCrede* 703.

2641 1 Cor. 1:14.

2642–3 There is no sign of this apparently proverbial saying in Whiting; *MED* gives no parallel. But the sense presumably is ironic: the man who would forsake the world is least likely to find the other as an innkeeper (cf. CT A241).

2643–6 The idea that the gospel precepts could be completely fulfilled by those still involved in secular affairs as a layman was not limited at this date to the Lollards; cf. Hilton's letter to Adam Horsley and his *Epistle of Mixed Life*. For Lollard praise for the christian life of the laity see Laud misc.200 ff. 146v, 198v.

2650–3 With this promise cf. later in the same text 2945–55, and T2599 and 3847 ff.

2654 ff. Though the sermon is not strictly divided into sections, and the preceding material has dealt with questions peculiar to the monastic orders and with those relevant to the monks and secular clergy (such as tithes), the preacher in the previous section has had little directly to say about the friars. The *foure apostasies* (2658) are the four orders, Franciscans, Dominicans, Carmelites and Augustinians. Although one order is not specifically named as the object of the preacher's criticism, it is clear that his points are most relevant to the Franciscan order (cf. the similar position of FitzRalph).

2664 Matt. 7:26.

2667–8 John 4:7 ff., Luke 19:5, Matt. 21:2.

2671 3 Kgs. 17:8 ff.

2678–97 For instance Bonaventura *Apologia pauperum* (*Opera omnia* 8 (Quaracchi, 1898), 324).

2682 John 8:44.

2700–2 The same story is used to a similar end in Taylor 612–46, *Upland* 272–4, *Upland's Rejoinder* 330–41. In Taylor Christ's requests are largely taken spiritually, though their understanding as commands, found here, is briefly mentioned 616 'on comaundinge maner'.

2703 John 4:7 ff.

2704–8 As an example of the friars' interpretation see, for instance, Bonaventura *Expositio super regulam Fratrum Minorum* (*Op.omn.* 8.423–4), a point reiterated by Netter *Doct.* IV.10 (i.860–2). The Lollard denunciation was anticipated by William of St. Amour *Op.omn.* pp. 51–2.

2711 Matt. 21:19.

2718–25 Continual begging is contrary to natural justice as well as to the *moraltees*, the moral teachings of the Old Testament. Natural justice requires that a man should not need to beg indefinitely, but that the rich should make a *puruyaunce*, an arrangement for provisions for his livelihood (cf. *PPl* B.xx.384). Cf. the earlier arguments in the dispute between FitzRalph and the friars, for which see Walsh (1983), pp. 410 ff.

2727 Deut. 15:4–11; EHF have incorrectly *Num.*

2730 Acts 4:32–7.

2732–3 For Clement of Rome see *ODCC*; his legend is *Legenda aurea* (ed. Graesse, 1850), pp. 777–88, this episode being mentioned p. 784 'non sinebat publicae fieri mendicitati subjectos'. The same story is told in *ALD* 110/ 32 and in FitzRalph's *Defensio curatorum*, trans. Trevisa p. 84/21.

2737–9 For these prayers see 246 note, and Owst (1961), p. 561, Netter *Doct.* VI.93–104 (iii.593–662).

2740 *unkunnyngnesse*: E's form *vnkunnesse* here and 2854 is not recorded in *MED*.

2744 Rom. 1:32.

2748 Acts 11:29–30, Rom. 15:26, 1 Cor. 16:1.

2749 *lymytours*: a limiter was a friar assigned to a particular part of the area for begging allowed for the support of the entire convent. See A. Williams, 'The "limitour" of Chaucer's time and his "Limitacioun"', *Studies in Philology* 57 (1960), 463–78 and Scase (1989), pp. 140–1; cf. *Upland* 177–9, *FDR* 477–85.

2749 *quilagis*: this is the form in ED throughout, H has *colletis* or *collectis* (usually with *-lec-* on an erasure, often of *-leg-*) and F *collegis* or *collagi(i)s*. For the *collect* form see *MED collecte* n.; *MED quilet* does not record the *-age* ending. The sense of both is 'collection'. F, and H in its uncorrected form, apparently did not understand the word. For a similar discussion of this passage see Taylor 514, 544, TCD 244 f. 218v, Harley 1203 f. 79; cf. Woodford's *Responsiones contra Wiclevum et Lollardos*, ed. E. Doyle, *Franciscan Studies* 43 (1983), p. 152 reply to question 42.

2763 Gal. 2:9.

2763–9 The qualification concerning these *quilagis* is associated with the provision of necessities to preachers, a question discussed above; see note to 228.

2764 Acts 18:3.

2765 2 Thess. 3:10.

2773 1 Cor. 16:2–3.

2777 ff. 2 Thess. 3:6–15; for use of this passage in antifraternal writings cf. Scase (1989), pp. 94–5. The writer here draws on a pun frequently used in antifraternal polemic: he takes biblical instances of *frater* as 'friar' rather than 'brother'. So in 2 Thess. 3:15 *sed corripite ut fratrem* the last word gives excuse for the interpretation of the entire passage as a reference to the friars. For similar usage see *EWS* i.114 and note 51 regarding 2 Thess. 3:6, Gal. 2:4 and 2 Cor. 11:26; cf. *EWS* iv.135. Although such an interpretation must have been recognized as anachronistic, its influence is evident from its intrusion into straightforward biblical translation, for instance in the non-Wycliffite version of 2 Cor. 11:26 in M. J. Powell, *The Pauline Epistles* (EETS ES 116.1916); cf. further *PPl* B.xiii.68–75.

2784 2 Thess. 3:6.

2786 Francis *Regula Bullata* caps.4–6 (ed. E. Menestò and S. Brufani, *Fontes Franciscani* (Assisi, 1995), pp. 175–7), and *Regula non Bullata* caps.8–9 (pp. 192–5); note esp.cap. 8 (p. 193) 'Et si forte, quod absit, aliquem fratrem contigerit pecuniam vel denarios colligere vel habere, excepta solummodo praedicta informorum necessitate, omnes fratres teneamus eum pro falso fratre et apostata et fure et latrone et loculos habente, nisi vere poenituerit.' Cf. Scase (1989), p. 96 with reference to FitzRalph *Defensio curatorum* trans. Trevisa p. 93/3.

2787 2 Thess. 3:14.

2791 2 John 10–11.

2808 Hildegard *Pentachronon*, (see above 2635 note) here an extract from the *Liber divinorum operum simplicis hominis* III.visio x.cap.28, PL 197.1028 'In eis quoque amaritudo et asperitas orietur, ac tantae haereses fient, ut etiam haeretici errores suos aperte et indubitanter praedicent; tantaque dubietas et incertitudo in catholica fide Christianorum erit, ut homines in dubio habeant quem Deum invocent.' Since Hildegar died in 1179, before the establishment of any of the fraternal orders, it is impossible that she wrote these words with the friars specifically in mind.

2814–15 Preaching friars customarily travelled in pairs (see Moorman (1968), p. 273); cf. *Upland* 310, *FDR* 771–88.

2821 *þe which ordynaunce kept*: note the Latinate syntax, here retained in English.

2825 *incontynence*: neither of *MED*'s senses 'inability to restrain sexual desire', nor 'inability to keep to a religious rule' seems suitable here; a more generalized meaning 'immorality' is more probable.

2829 Matt. 24:24, Mark 13:22.

2830 John 10:38, 14:12.

2834 Matt. 7:15.

2836–46 The whole passage is a fairly accurate translation of pseudo-Chrysostom *Opus imperfectum* PG 56.737; the only slight departure is 2840–2 'vir sapiens, si non confitetur Christum, et manifesta esset gentilitas illius, et si seducebaris per eam, insania erat, qua seducebaris'.

2837 *haþ an auter*: Lat. *altare habentem*, i.e. is fully ordained as a priest.

2857 *up hast*: E's reading (translate 'speedily') is possible, and has been retained as more difficult than H *up haþ* (F *peraventur*, D lost).

2871–3 Arguments were advanced by the friars that biblical condemnations of begging were not relevant to them in, for instance, Bonaventura (above 2678 ff. and 2704–8 notes), and *Apologia pauperum Op.* viii.c.12, pp. 324–30.

2884 Matt. 23:14, Mark 12:40.

2890–1 Cf. Walther no. 32568 for a close Latin parallel, and cf. 32607; Whiting P357. Cf. *Dives and Pauper* I.lvi.4–9, having quoted the same proverb 'It is a comoun prouerbe of truantys þat sone ben wery of preyere . . . Netheles 3if it be wel vndirstondyn þe prouerbe is soth, good and holy, for why eueryþyng is clepyd schort whan þe endys ben ny3h togedre.' The subject of prayer is then discussed in the remainder of the chapter in not dissimilar terms (save the exclusion of references to the friars) as here.

2898 *þat oonli . . . preied*: the question of the address of prayers to saints is here sidestepped, though disapproval is clear. It is considered and its legitimacy denied in, for instance, Arnold iii.467/1; it became a major issue in the final trial of William Taylor (see *TWT* xxi–xxii).

2916–17 Isa. 29:13.

2919 Mark 12:40.

2924 Matt. 15:7–9; Isa. 29:13.

2935–8 Alliance between the possessioners and the friars is contrary to the disputes mentioned often (see note to 285 above), but certainly occurred in opposition to Wyclif and Lollardy (e.g. the signatories to the condemnation of Wyclif's views at the 1382 Blackfriars Council, see FZ 286–91).

2944 Exod. 16:8.

2963–3096 As the writer imagines an opponent observing, this section is something of an appendix to the main text, passing on to eschatological matters. The Apocalypse is frequently quoted by Lollard texts, but is not so often the basis of extended analysis as later radical tendencies might lead one to suppose. The most notable exception is *Op.ard.*; see *LB* pp. 43–65 and Hudson (1996), 99–113.

2973 Rev. 7:1.

2979 ff. 2 Cor. 11:14. *þe foure aungels* who have *sett her feet . . . upon þe foure* *corners of þe erþe* derive from Rev. 7:1; *þe hardist weie of Sathanas* goes back to Rev. 6:5 where the third beast 'habebat stateram in manu sua'; *Sathanas bi ypocrisie transfigurid into aungels of liȝt* derives from 2 Cor. 11:14.

2985 *fatt of þe erþe*: *MED fatte* gives no instance of the phrase 'fat of the land/ earth'; *OED fat* a and sb.[2] B.2c gives *fat of the land* first from AV Gen. 45:18 (WB *the mary* (LV *merow*) *of the loond*), but even there it is more literal than here.

2987 Zech. 2:6, 6:5; cf. T2074.

2991 For this interpretation of Rev. 7:1 see MS Bodley 716 f. 193vb, pseudo-Aquinas p. 381.

2993–8 For Nicholas Gorham see 1798 note; this section, unlike the earlier, does not appear in Lambeth. It seems based on the commentary to Rev. 7:1, MS Bodley 716 ff. 193vb–194ra, pseudo-Aquinas edited text p. 381 as before.

2998–3000 cf. *GO* vi.1523–4.

3000 Phil. 3:20.

3002 Rev. 7:3

3004 Matt. 3:10, Luke 3:9.

3005 Rev. 17:1–6.

3007–8 For the endowed clergy as the scarlet woman of Rev. 17:3 cf. *Op.ard.* f. 192va–b.

3013 The three manuscripts, EHF, available here agree in the reference to John 5, and a distant allusion to John 5:43 may be intended; but closer are Matt. 13:39 and John 10:5.

3014 Augustine on John, PL 35.1631, quoting John 5:43 in commentary on John 7:18.

3020 An allusion to Matt. 3:7–10 'Videns autem multos pharisaeorum, et sadducaeorum, venientes ad baptismum suum, dixit eis: Progenies viperarum, quis demonstravit vobis fugere a ventura ira? . . . Iam enim securis ad radicem arborum posita est. Omnis ergo arbor, quae non facit fructum bonum, excidetur, et in ignem mittetur.'

3022 Matt. 3:7.

3025 Gen. 4:8.

3029 cf. Ps. 149:6 and Prov. 5:4.

3030 Rev. 11:3.

3032 For the two *witnessis* of Rev. 11:3 as Enoch and Elijah see *Op.ard.* f. 167vb; it is traditional, see *GO* vi.1566.

3036 For instance, Jerome *Liber contra Joannem Hierosolymitanum*, PL 23.380–4.

3039 Text as at 1798, here based on Rev. 11:3, MS Bodley 716 f. 206ra, pseudo-Aquinas text pp. 412–13.

3048 Rev. 12:14.

3050 *GO* vi.1586.

3055 Rev. 13:5.

3065 4 Kgs. 9:30–7.

3066 Matt. 14:3–12, Mark 6:17–28, Luke 3:19–20.

3077–83 See above note to 1798; here again based on Rev. 12:15, MS Bodley 716 f. 213rb, pseudo-Aquinas text pp. 430–1.

3080 Rev. 12:16.

3090–9 This section is missing from E (and D became defective long before it); it is restored here from HF in the spelling of E.

L969–81 As the marginal note makes clear, this derives from canon law, C.21 q.3 c.4 (Friedberg i.856); the chapter is indeed from Cyprian (PL 4.410). The translation is close apart from 976–7 *whosoeuer . . . seculere* which renders 'ne quis excedens ad tutelam uel curam clericum nominaret'.

L973 2 Tim. 2:4.

L984 The marginal reference to Luke 16 seems to point to the postscript to the parable of the unjust steward, Luke 16:1–13.

L989 Exod. 20:17.

L995 2 Tim. 2:4.

L1001 Acts 6:2.

L1008–14 It is not clear what the marginal reference here 'iij° decr' in fine' implies. Judging by the other references to canon law in L, this should be to part 1 of the *Decretum*, but dist.3 does not seem relevant (Friedberg i.4–5). The summary that follows resumes arguments of the preceding tract, but does not define the source any further. A possible section which may be the source is C.21 q.3 cc.4–7 (Friedberg i.856–7), drawn from a letter of Cyprian (hence *he* of 1008); parts of this section are previously quoted L969–81 and appear in Latin L1281–5.

L1015–22 D.88 c.4 (Friedberg i.307), quoting Gregory (PL 77.1073) as indicated 1014–15; it is cited in Latin L1295–304.

L1026 Ezek. 33:2–6 paraphrased.

L1046 Mal. 2:7.

L1056 Num. 18:20–1.

L1060 Num. 18:23–4.

L1064 *GO* i.1571 on Deut. 18:1.

L1070 Matt. 10:9–10.

L1072 1 Cor. 9:13.

L1076 Ezek. 44:28–9.

L1079–88 Jerome on Ezechiel bk. 13 c.44, PL 25.443.

L1082 Heb. 5:6.

L1086 Num. 18:20.

L1087 Ps. 72:26.

L1089 Deut. 10:9.

L1091 Josh. 14:4.

L1093 Ecclus. 45:26.

L1095 Matt. 20:25–8.

L1101 Matt. 10:25, Luke 22:24–30.

L1102 1 Pet. 5:2–3.

L1105 1 Tim. 6:8–9.

L1107 Luke 14:33.

L1110–26 Bernard *De consideratione* bk. ii cap. 6.10 (PL 182, 748, or *Opera* iii.418/1–17; this is translated L650–97. The passage is quoted, with some slight variation in wording, in the *Floretum* under *possessio* 4 (Harley 401 f. 236v).

L1114 1 Pet. 5:3.

L1116 Luke 22:25.

L1122 Hos. 8:4.

L1123 Luke 22:26.

L1127–44 Origen PG 12.250–1, translated at L360–81.

L1130 Num. 18:20.

L1137 Luke 14:33.

L1145–62 Peraldus *Liber de viciis* (Paris, 1669), ii.123–4, cap. 10 sub.2.

L1163–88 Odo sermon for 4 Trinity on Luke; cf. Bodley 420 f. 142 though lines 1169–78 and 1183–5 are not present in this later copy; closer is CUL Kk.1.11, f. 64vb–65ra. Neither copy has the verses.

L1174 Phil. 3:8.

L1189–202 Odo, translated at L382–99 and see note there.

L1190 Gen. 4:2–4.

L1197 Gen. 4:9.

L1201 Actually Jer. 50:6, though with allusion to Ezek. 34:2; Odo also has Ezek.

L1203–19 Gorham on Rev. 12:15 (printed Aquinas *Opera omnia* 23 (Padua, 1869), pp. 430–1 with minor differences).

L1203 Rev. 12:15.

L1206 Ps. 61:11.

L1213 Ps. 68:2.

L1220–1 Jerome, *Vita Malchi Monachi Captivi*, PL 23.53 'potentia quidem et divitiis major, sed virtutibus minor facta sit', translated at L551–2. This passage and the next are quoted in *Floretum* under *possessio* 2 (Harley 401, f. 236), though in reverse order and with other intervening Jerome quotations.

L1222–5 Jerome ep.52, PL 22.536.

L1225–42 Jerome ep.52, PL 22.531.

L1230 Ps. 15:5, 72:26.

L1237 1 Tim. 6:8.

L1245 2 Tim. 2:4.

L1251 D.88 c.3 (Friedberg i.307) derived, as the text here repeats 'ex Septimo canone Apostolorum'.

L1253 D.88 c.8 (Friedberg i.308); as correctly indicated this is from Gregory ep.12 no. 27 (PL 77.1237).

L1256–65 The reference in 1256 to 'ibidem . . . capitulo *neque*' must refer to D.88 c.14 (Friedberg i.310) which is indeed a quotation from Cyprian. However, lines 1263–5 form the opening sentence of this section (with substitution of *non* for *neque* of canon law). Cyprian ep.66 (PL 4.410–11) has the sense, though not the precise wording of the material, and the passage here is extended beyond what is in canon law. A version of the entire quotation is given L969–81.

L1266–9 D.88 c.10 (Friedberg i.308), rightly attributed to Augustine (PL 35.2385).

L1269–72 D.88 cc.5–6 (Friedberg i.307–8), derived from legislation of the fourth Council of Carthage.

L1273–7 C.11 q.1 c.30 (Friedberg i.634–5).

L1277–80 The marginal reference is incorrect, since this is C.21 q.3 c.2 (Friedberg i.856), derived from the first Council of Carthage; presumably *xxi* was simplified to *xi*.

L1281–5 C.21 q.3 c.6 (Friedberg i.857), from Cyprian ep.66 (PL 4.411); cf. above L1008–14.

L1285–94 C.11 q.1 c.29 (Friedberg i.634).

L1295–304 Despite the absence of any marginal reference, this passage derives from canon law D.88 c.4 (Friedberg i.307), and was taken from Gregory ep. bk. 10 no. 10 (PL 77.1073). The passage appears in English L1015–22.

2. TRACT *DE OBLACIONE IUGIS SACRIFICII*

The title derives from the colophon at the end; there is no heading at the start. For the words of the title see Dan. 8:11 'Et usque ad principem fortitudinis magnificatum est, et ab eo tulit iuge sacrificium, et deiecit locum sanctificationis eius', and 12:11 'Et a tempore cum ablatum fuerit iuge sacrificium, et posita fuerit abominatio in desolationem, dies mille ducenti nonaginta'; both make clear the eschatological emphasis found repeatedly in the tract. Tissyngton in his rebuttal of Wyclif's views on the eucharist quotes the verse in connection with his allegation that, as a result of Wyclif's teaching, many abstain from receiving the eucharist at Easter since it is only *panis sanctificatus*; he adds 'hoc doctores exponunt de sacra eucharistia, quae est iuge sacrificium in domo Domini' (*FZ* p. 178).

1 ff. Apocalyptic vocabulary is pervasive in Wycliffite writings, but is rarely translated into chronological terms; see A. Patschovsky, '"Antichrist" bei Wyclif', and A. Hudson, 'Lollardy and Eschatology', in *Eschatologie und Hussitismus*, ed. A. Patschovsky and F. Šmahel (Prague, 1996), pp. 83–98 and 99–113 respectively, and C. V. Bostick, *The Antichrist and the Lollards: Apocalypticism in Late Medieval and Reformation England* (Leiden, 1998). Where the word is spelt out, as here, the normal form in Titus in *antecrist*, whereas in Egerton it is *anticrist*. The two forms, however, though distinct in etymological sense, were used interchangeably in medieval Latin and English texts (*MED* does not separate the two), especially in eschatological contexts: the enemy of Christ (*antichristus*) foreshadows the coming of Christ to judgement (*antechristus*). For the sense in Wycliffite texts see note to Taylor 263 (*TWT*), and the usage in the two texts here.

3 The point is that taken up further below, and repeatedly elsewhere, that everything necessary for salvation is within the gospels and epistles.

4 The expectation of persecution, to the extent of death, is here a reference to the 1401 introduction of the penalty of burning for heresy in the statute *De heretico comburendo*. For the parallelism between Christ's persecution by the Jews and the experience of contemporary *true men* see the references in *EWS* iv.173–82.

16 2 Thess. 2:3–4.

23 Rev. 12:12 'diabolus . . . habens iram magnam', combined with 12:17 'iratus est draco . . . et abiit facere praelium cum reliquis de semine eius, qui custodiunt mandata Dei, et habent testimonium Iesu Christi'.

29 It is not clear that this is a quotation rather than an allusion; comparable sentiments are expressed in the work mentioned PL 35.2217–18.

32 ff. For attempts by the authorities to prevent Lollard preaching see Thorpe 707 ff., *EWS* iv.83–4.

39 Rev. 20:7.

42 Gregory *Moralia* 33.56 ff., PL 76.709 ff.

43 See above 16.

45 The idea that the clergy was the source of spiritual health or corruption goes back to Matt. 5:13–16, and was repeated constantly in the christian tradition. For the stomach as the most vital part of the body for physical health compare Trevisa's translation of Bartholomeus Anglicus v.38 (i.245/14) 'þe stomak is puruyour and housbonde of al þe body, and fongiþ fedinge for alle þe membres, and serueþ alle þe membres þerof as it nediþ.'

56 Tit. 1:16.

61 ff. The author's definition of antichrist as multiple, consisting of all those with the will and the power to pervert Christ's church from its pristine state (85–6) is a useful one, but one that is difficult at any particular point to sustain. The writer here immediately particularizes (87) the prelates; cf. Taylor 263 and note, Matthew 63/30, *LL* 15/21. More frequently the pope is regarded as antichrist, with the prelates and other priests as his limbs or disciples: cf. *EWS* E50/77, 87/54, 100/92, Arnold iii. 457/20, *PR* pp. 332–4.

66 2 John 7 'multi seductores . . . hic est seductor et antichristus'; cf. 1 John 2:18 'sicut audistis quia antichristus venit: et nunc antichristi multi facti sunt.'

67 Matt. 24:5.

71 Matt. 24:24, Mark 13:6.

74 John 5:43.

78 Those of Matt. 24:5, 24, Mark 13:6 which speak of *antichristi* in the plural, as against John 5:43 which uses a singular.

80–1 Augustine *De verbis domini* sermon 129, PL 38.723–4; Gregory as above line 43.

90 2 Thess. 2:3–4, see line 16.

92 A marginal note by the original scribe, now partially cropped, gives a reference to Augustine *De civ. Dei* 20 cap.19 (PL 41.685–7) which discusses this passage from 2 Thess. 2:1–11 and equates *in templo* with *in ecclesia* (685–6).

96–8 For the logical point cf. TCD 244, f. 215 'þis man is in synne and þis man synneþ, as it is alle one þis man is in his rennynge, and þis man renneþ'.

100 Matt. 23:2–3.

105 Augustine *De verbis domini* sermon 137, PL 38.757–9; Jerome PL 26.167 '*super cathedram Moysi* . . . per cathedram doctrinam legis ostendit'.

110–14 The author's point is that the episcopal office is not inevitably corrupt:

provided that the bishop 'spekiþ not of his owne auctorite' but with the 'auctorite of þe lawe of God', his teaching should be accepted. The second part of the sentence is apparently corrupt as it stands in the manuscript; *as many* (110) . . . *spekiþ* (113) is parenthetical, and the 'whoso þus prechiþ' (110) is provided with a completion by the deletion of *for* before *neiþur* (113). For *at þe hardest* (111) see *MED hard* adj.4(f) 'in the worst case, at worst, at least'.

113 2 Thess. 2:4.

117 *bereschrewe* (cf. 389, 1038): the reference is presumably to the beast on which the scarlet woman of the Apocalypse (Rev. 17:3, usually interpreted as the devil, see *GO* vi.1635) sat. The etymology is unclear (the word is not in *MED*): the second element is presumably *shreue* (*MED* sense 2(a) 'devil, evil creature'; the first is perhaps *ber(e* n(1) for which the basic sense is 'bear' but which is used as a type of the sins of sloth and gluttony (sense 3).

120 *þe bodi of antecrist*: here identified as the prelates, regularly a condemnatory term in Wyclif(fite) writing; cf. *EWS* iv.102–11.

127–31 cf. Luke 12:14 and discussion of this in E1365 ff., and the wider discussion throughout that text of the legitimacy of clerical temporalities.

134–5 cf. E1160 and note.

134 *furbarre the fredom*: for the shutting away of Christ's law cf. L222–30 and note.

135 f. For hostility to traditions, opposed as here to the *gospel*, and to the promulgation of these traditions whereas access to the bible was restricted, cf. Arnold iii.295/14, Matthew 38/10, 89/1, 93/18, 157/12, Laud misc. 200 ff. 43v, 66v. One of the pieces of legislation that provoked particular anger was Innocent III's at the Lateran Council of 1215, imposing the duty of annual confession on the laity; cf. Matthew 337/12, Arnold iii.255/17.

143–4 2 Thess. 2:4.

147 Gregory *Moralia* 28.18, PL 76.486–7; the sentence is a paraphrase rather than a translation, but its core derives from Gregory: having quoted Exod. 7:1, Gregory comments 'Deus vero coli purus homo non potest'.

149 Exod. 7:1.

155–6 *but in as meche . . . wille*: 'except in so far as they agree (as if it were himself) with his proud will'.

162–9 For the corruption of the authority of scripture by the clergy cf. Laud misc. 200, ff. 141v, 143, *EWS* iv.76–8.

172 See 90 ff.

174–6 Henry IV died on 20 March 1413. This reference, taken together with that in 406 to the continued tenure of the see of Canterbury by Arundel who died 19 February 1414, fixes the composition of the text within eleven months.

There is little obvious support for the idea that Henry IV acted in defence of Lollardy: it was during his reign that the 1401 and 1407 determinations came into force. For the possibility that the Lollard knights, if no others, hoped for support from Richard II, see Wilks (1978), pp. 63–70. Henry IV, however, did not always act against the Lollards with the energy that Arundel might have wished: see *PR* pp. 112–16, Taylor *TWT* xiii–xiv, and McNiven (1987). For the Lollard claim that secular rulers were forced by the clergy to take action against Lollards that they themselves found distasteful cf. Arnold iii.165/24, 324/12, TCC B.14.50, f. 43.

179–83 *and þus . . . office*: the preacher's point is that men might be deemed heretics for their refusal to accept, for instance, contemporary teaching on the eucharist but not for constant infringement of the ten commandments.

186–7 Again a reference to *De heretico comburendo* 1401.

198 *in schauyng of crownys*: i.e. in marking clerical status by a tonsure.

205 cf. E1100 ff. and note.

221 Matt. 15:13. Unfortunately, although this allusion gives the relative dates of the two tracts, it does not give any clear indication of the length of time that had elapsed between their composition; *onys* may suggest an interval of several years. Actually the subject of the earlier sermon may perhaps more accurately be attached to the preacher's first point here (189–215).

225 ff. As the writer says, 229, the matter is more fully treated below lines 499 ff., 1451 ff., with more precise references to his various authorities.

236 Jerome and Augustine are quoted both in the sermon and the present tract; *Dyonyse*, i.e. Dionysius the (pseudo-)Areopagite (see note to E2576–621) is used under his anglicized name of *Denys(e* in the sermon (as here 521, 607, 2599); Cyprian appears only in L (969, 1256) and here (516, 2607).

257–8 *brou3t our bileue into an insolible*: for the logical vocabulary of this text see p. lii–liii and cf. 281 ff., 3497 ff. See *MED insolible* n. sense (b) 'an unanswerable question or problem for which there is no solution'.

260–2 'he shall be divided from Christ through censures and condemnation for heresy, to the lengths that antichrist's power may extend'. For this use of *til to* 'extend to' see *MED tillen* v.(2).

283–6 For the authorities' claim to determine true belief cf. Thorpe 1020 ff., and many abjurations in trials for heresy (e.g. *LB* p. 136, *Norwich Trials* pp. 63, 65 etc.).

290 Augustine *De verbis Domini* sermon 129, PL 38. 725, from an anti-Donatist commentary on Luke 9:22 'Tollere vis ecclesiae caput, et capiti credere, corpus relinquere, quasi exanime corpus'.

291 For the Lollard understanding of the church, opposed to this, cf. *LL* 22/ 11–23/7, *Op. ard.* f. 173va, *ALD* 35/23, Add. 24202, f. 8 etc.

296–301 Matt. 18:15–17 provides for one rebuke by the offended brother alone, and a second by the brother accompanied by witnesses; only if these fail should open rebuke in the church follow. The current ecclesiastical hierarchy interprets *to þe chirche* (298) as 'to the bishop', hence equating the two.

296 Matt. 18:15–17, v.17 repeated 312.

319 *not worþ a piȝe hele*: cf. 1684; cf. Whiting P177 'Not worth a pie', so here literally 'not worth a magpie's heel'—i.e. absolutely nothing.

322–31 The terms specified make it clear that the writer is thinking of the 1407 Constitutions, devised by Arundel. For the terms see Constitutions 1–2, Wilkins iii.315–16; the most remarkable is that mentioned 330–1 which reproduces no. 2 'alioquin ecclesia coemeterium, seu locus quiscunque, in quo sic praedicatum fuerit (by an unlicensed preacher), ipso facto ecclesiastico subjaceat interdicto . . .'. Cf. E1130 ff.

336 Acts 4:5–20, 5:28–32, the quotation 336–8 being 4:19–20. For the syntax of 340–1 cf. 5:28 'Praecipiendo praecepimus vobis ne doceretis in nomine isto'.

353 Matt. 16:26.

354–7 *but . . . soule*: for the conditions under which compliance with contemporary authorities is allowable cf. *EWS* iv.180–2.

360 Phil.2:8.

362 Matt. 21:23, Mark 11:28, Luke 20:2.

367, 371, 374 Heb. 13:17.

387 *aggregat person*: cf. 474, 1022. The sense here must be the pope and his followers in contrast to the sense of E1942 ff. where it is 'community'; only the latter is recognized by *MED* 'a number of persons . . . regarded as a unit'. The implication here is presumably that the pope represents the sum of the institutional church.

390 The emendation seems necessary. The author is describing the devil's devising of a dilemma: either man follows Christ's teaching and loses his life, or he follows the determination of antichrist and loses his soul.

399 *contradictorie cornys*: underlying this seems to be Dan.7:20–24, especially vv.21–2 'ecce cornu illud faciebat bellum adversus sanctos, et praevalebat eis, donec venit antiquus dierum, et iudicium dedit sanctis Excelsi'. Augustine *De civ. Dei* 20.23 (PL 41.694–6) quotes this passage, and understands the fourth king as antichrist who will be overcome by Christ.

401 Matt. 26:23–6, Mark 14:21–2, Luke 22:19–21.

403 ff. Cf. Thorpe 1026 ff., *EWS* iv.53–6, *PR* 281–90. The accidents are those of the physical appearance, taste, texture and dimensions of the bread, the substance the 'reality' or 'essence' of bread. See *SEWW* 1 and notes, and further below.

405–12 Not surprisingly, there is no record of this alleged admission by Arundel, but compare E1135 and intro. pp. xlix–l.

406 Cf. the view of Ralph Fryday of Leicester reported after the Oldcastle rising that 'Thomas Arundell achiepiscopus Cantuar' est vnus discipulorum antechristi et murdrator hominum' (PRO KB 9/204/1 no. 141).

414–18 The emendation, though it reverses the sense given by the manuscript, seems the only way to make sense of the passage. The point is that the only way in which authority can be attributed to the contemporary hierarchy is by assuming they have credentials superior to Christ's pronouncements.

419 2 Cor. 12:2–3.

421 Gal. 1:8.

424 The comparison between Christ's prophecy of punishment to come for the contemporary misdeeds of the scribes and pharisees, and Paul's prophecy warning against hypothetical misleaders to come, depends upon the fact that neither were *malicious* (424).

424 Matt. 23:13 etc.

433 Gen. 3:3 *ne forte moriamur*: for this interpretation of Eve's alteration of Gen. 2:17 *morte morieris* cf. Lyra's comment *GO* i.92.

443 2 Cor. 11:14.

446 Cf. Gal. 1:8–9.

453 *þei leren her doctours for hemself*: 'they teach the doctors they recognize as their own'.

453–9 Augustine *En. in Ps.*57, PL 36.678–9, quoted at more length at 3513–27. The quotation here is paraphrased rather than translated; it is slightly obscure, since Augustine's introductory words of sarcasm concerning the activities of those who suppress Christ's law is omitted.

459 John 14:6.

471 *Ion de Deo*: a canonist c.1190–1267; see A. D. de Sousa Costa, 'Animadversiones criticae in vitam et opera canonistae Ioannis de Deo', *Antonianum* 33 (1958), 76–124; his works, genuine and attributed, circulated widely in medieval Europe. See further 1996–9 where John's view seems to be specifically refuted.

472 *Pope Innocent*: the author certainly refers to Innocent III (for whom see *ODCC* and J. Sayers, *Innocent III: Leader of Europe 1198–1216* (London, 1994)), who, as the man who called the Lateran Council of 1215 at which the doctrine of regular oral confession was instituted and as one determined to assert the feudal as well as the spiritual powers of the church over the secular rulers, was particularly disliked by the Lollards. Cf. here 1745 and *EWS* 231/40, MC 896, Arnold iii.255/21, Matthew 328/21.

474 Cf. 2727 for the reference to Oxford, and the dismissive tone concerning an academic question.

477 *Odo Parisiensis*: see L382 note. The passage here is similar to one in MS Bodley 420 f. 225v.

483 Mark 8:38, Luke 9:26.

489 Rom. 1:16.

490 2 Cor. 4:2, 6. The discussion depends on the precise wording of the Vulgate, concealed in AV, 2 Cor. 4:2 reads 'neque adulterantes verbum Dei', LV 'nether doynge auoutrye bi the word of God'. 498 using words from 4:6 'ad illuminationem scientiae claritatis Dei, in facie Christi Iesu'.

500 1 Cor. 11:23.

504 1 Cor. 11:23–5.

515 Cyprian Ep. 63, PL 4.386 quoted roughly in D.2 de cons. c.2 (Friedberg i.1314), but here abbreviated from its original form: 'Nec potest videri sanguis ejus, quo redempti et vivificati sumus, esse in calice quando vinum desit calici, quo Christi sanguis ostenditur, qui scripturarum omnium sancramento ac testimonio praedicetur.'

520–1 See the quotations from both authors that follow in the text. For Dionysius see note to E2576–621.

523 1 Cor. 11:26.

526 Luke 22:19.

527 Luke 24:30, 35.

530–8 Augustine sermon 235 for Easter, PL 38.1118, translated fairly closely (parenthetical gloss added). The preceding biblical quotation, upon which the sixteenth-century reformers' memorial doctrine of the eucharist was largely based, is used here for a different purpose. The aim here is to show the continued existence of bread after the words of consecration.

543 Mark 16:14–19.

545 1 Cor. 11:25.

547–50 The author's point is that the account of the ascension that he is here following, Mark 16:14–19, does not mention the breaking of bread. The similarity between Mark 16:14 and the story in Luke 24:13–35 makes it likely that this occurred but only 'as probable bi credens lasse þan bileue'. For the author's supposition cf. *EWS* 197/15 where Mark 16:14–19 is taken as starting point for a discussion of the eucharist.

553–6 See Legg p. 223.

560 Wyclif constantly affirmed that his eucharistic doctrine did not imply disrespect, let alone a devaluing, of the sacrament, but on the contrary restored its primary importance: see, for instance, the discussion in *Serm.* ii.457/37 ff. and note 463/14 ff. and cf. J. I. Catto, 'John Wyclif and the Cult of the Eucharist', *SCH Subsidia* 4 (1985), 269–86.

561–3 Cf. *De blas.* 24/24 replicated in *SEWW* 1/7 'but as a man leeues for to þenk þe kynde of an ymage, wheþer it be of oke or of asshe, and settys his þou3t in him of whom is þe ymage, so myche more schuld a man leue to þenk on þe kynde of brede.'

566 1 Cor. 11:27–9, quoted more accurately at 573–9 where the translation is close to EV.

576–7 The point is that *so ete he of þat brede* must refer to the host after consecration, still described as *brede*.

578 *not demyng or rewarding*: Vulg. *non diiudicans*, WB *not wiseli demyng*.

583 Luke 24:30, 35.

589 1 Cor. 10:16.

594 1 Cor. 12:27.

594 Eph. 2:20.

597 1 Cor. 10:17.

599 Augustine *epistola* 185, PL 33.815, quoted again at 3735.

600 cf. 1492 and the source PL 38.1247 'Recolite quia panis non fit de uno grano, sed de multis' . . . 1248 'Sicut enim ut sit species visibilis panis, multa grana in unum consperguntur, tanquam illud fiat, quod de fidelibus ait scriptura sancta "Erat illis anima una, et cor unum in Deum" (Acts 4:32).'

606 Acts 17:34.

607 See above note to 520; the reference is probably the same.

610–19 Augustine *De civ. Dei* 16.37, PL 41.515–16; as far as 613 *þus* the passage is an abbreviated paraphrase but the following section is a fairly accurate translation. The sentence structure is plainer in Latin where *benedictio* governs a sequence of phrases introduced by *de*; in the Engish *of þe rayn* . . . *of þe plente* . . . *of þe gadring* should be understood as dependent on *blessing of Crist* (614)— this is reinforced by the new sentence *Of Crist* . . . (616).

611 Gen. 27:18–29.

615 Gen. 27:27–8.

620 1 Cor. 10:17.

622 *confermyng*: here and elsewhere (see glossary) the meaning is plainly 'conforming'; *MED* under *conformen* queries whether the example in *ALD* (sense 1) that they cite is a mistaken spelling, but in view of the usage in Titus this seems unlikely.

625 Augustine sermon 272 (PL 38.1246) for Pentecost (but cf. 1530 where the same sermon is described as *of Estur'*. 'Hoc quod videtis in altari Dei, etiam transacta nocte vidistis: sed quid esset, quid sibi vellet, quam magnae rei sacramentum contineret, nondum audistis. Quod ergo videtis, panis est et calix; quod vobis etiam oculi vestri renuntiant: quod autem fides vestra postulat instruenda, panis est corpus Christi, calix sanguis Christi.' Cited in canon law, D.2 de cons. c.58, Friedberg i.1336; quoted also *SEWW* no. 21A/23. *þat þat . . . askiþ* translates 'quod autem fides vestra postulat instruenda'.

633 Job 28:1.

635–52 Gregory *Moralia* 18.39, PL 76.58. The quotation is closely translated, apart from the omission of the repeated opening words of the biblical text before as *þouȝ Iob* (642). At 643 the English text is evidently defective and a verb has here been supplied. The omission may be even longer: the Latin reads 'necesse est ut causarum origines a sacris paginis sumat, ut . . . revocet'. Haplography due to the repetition of *þat* is possible, but the Latin text the author used may here have been defective; only the minimum alteration necessary has been made. *reuoke* in 643 renders Lat. *revocet*, of which the alternative *calle aȝen* is the better translation.

649 1 Tim. 6:20.

656 Exod. 20:25.

658–69 Parisiensis: here the Dominican, more usually known as Peraldus; see Taylor 83 and note. Here *Summa virtutum* (Paris, 1668–9), i.120 elaborated and expanded; Ambrose 'Auferantur argumenta vbi fides quaeritur: non enim recipienda sunt argumenta fidei contraria', is here referred to before not after the quotation of Exod. 20:25.

660 Matt. 21:42, Mark 12:10, Luke 20:17, Acts 4:11, 26:26, 1 Pet. 2:7, cf. Ps. 117:22.

672 ff. For the view of the eucharist underlying this discussion of accidents and subject see more fully 1543 ff. The accidents are those aspects apprehensible by the senses (taste, smell, weight, texture, susceptibility to corruption etc.) which remain unchanged by the words of consecration. Debate, some of it resumed in this text, centred on the effect of the words of consecration on the substances, the 'breadness' and 'wineness' of the elements: did they, as the words of institution implied, become the body and blood of Christ? and if so how did the accidents inhere in the changed substances? For a general view see G. Macy, *The Banquet's Wisdom: A Short History of the Theologies of the Lord's Supper* (New York, 1992), and the same author's more detailed surveys of doctrine in the medieval period, *The Theologies of the Eucharist in the Early Scholastic Period* (Oxford, 1984), and 'The Dogma of Transubstantiation in the Middle Ages', *JEH* 45 (1994), 11–41.

675 referring to 2 Thess. 2:3–4 quoted at 16, and subsequently.

692 *riȝt as . . . werke* (694): alluding to 2 Thess. 2:10 'mittet illis Deus operationem erroris ut credant mendacio'.

707 *forma . . . species*: Wyclif discusses the differing senses of these words in *De apostasia* 84/19–85/16 in the context of the eucharist, and it may be this discussion the English writer is recalling. Wyclif there quotes Phil. 2:6–7 for the sense of *forma*, where Christ in his two natures is said to be *in forma Dei* and *formam servi*, commenting that this must imply that 'Christus est duplex substancia, scilicet deus et homo'; this he calls the *forma substancialis*. Accidental form is where *forma* is used in scripture (no examples are given) 'pro qualitate secunda ex substancia quantitate et qualitate prioribus resultante'. From this he concludes 'Et sic corpus Christi videtur per fidem sub forma panis, quando forma substancialis panis videtur oculo mentali et forma accidentalis panis videtur oculo corporali, sed corde creditur quod corpus Christi veraciter est in pane.' *Species*, Wyclif says, is used similarly, *substancialis* in Gen. 1:12, 21, 24, *accidentalis* as at Ps. 44:5.

715 Matt. 24:24.

722 Job 3:25.

723 2 Cor. 11:3.

728 see above 490 ff.

729 Augustine *De civ. Dei* 14.7, PL 41.414.

735 2 Cor. 11:14.

738 2 Tim. 4:3–4.

745 cf. 96 ff.

748–9 For the translation of Lat. *fratres* as *freris* in ME texts see *EWS* E14/48, i.114 and n. 51. The reference is here introduced partly because of the identification of the doctrine of the eucharist just rejected with that propounded by the friars; see *SEWW* 1/35.

749 1 Tim. 4:1–2.

758 Heb. 13:9.

761 *leide*: 'led'; *MED leden* v(1) gives parallels to this spelling of the pa.p.

764 Tit. 2:11–12; the emendation of *enfermyng* to *enformyng* follows Vulg.*erudiens*, WB EV *techinge*, LV *and tauȝte vs*.

769 2 Thess. 2:4.

772 see above 16 ff.

783–6 For the necessity of grounding in the gospel cf. *EWS* E6/83, 231/47, Arnold iii.460/21, Matthew 145/20, *37 Concs.* f. 26v (p. 44).

786 John 7:18.

789 John 8:50.

793 Exod. 3:14 'Dixit Deus ad Moysen: Ego sum qui sum. Ait: Sic dices filiis Israel: Qui est, misit me ad vos.'.

795–6 For example Jerome commentary on Isaiah, PL 24.630, and Augustine *De trinitate* I.i–ii, PL 42.819–22.

810 2 Cor. 11:14.

819–23 For ignorance of scripture and Lollard explanations of this along similar lines see Aston (1984) pp. 193–217 and *LB* pp. 141–63. Cf. *Opus arduum* ff. 143va, 156vb, 187rb, Laud misc. 200 f. 198v, Arnold iii.186/13.

826 2 Thess. 2:4.

827–36 For the neglect of scripture in favour of canon law cf. *Rosarium* sub *lex*, Matthew 156/18, 437/31, *Opus arduum* f. 156va; and for the avarice of ecclesiastical lawyers cf. Arnold iii.153/21, Matthew 182/16, 184/5.

833 2 Cor. 3:6.

850 Cf. Wyclif *De off.reg.* 72/9 'Et ex istis colligitur quod sciencia theologie est pernecessaria ad stabilimentum cuiuscumque regni . . . 26 Quomodo ergo sine theologis staret regnum?' and 125/13. Even opponents of Lollardy admitted that the study of theology was neglected in fifteenth-century England: Gascoigne *Loci e libro veritatum* pp. 35, 61, 181–5 condemned Arundel's Constitutions for silencing orthodox theology and orthodox preaching by the majority in order to silence a handful of heretics.

854–6 The claim that study of canon law was more popular than study of theology in the early fifteenth-century university seems justified: see *HUO* ii.281 and references.

858–9 Augustine *De civ. Dei* 18.38 and 19.18, PL 41.598 and 646–7.

860 Job 19:17.

863 Gregory *Moralia* 14.44, PL 75.1066; a summary, not precisely accurate in all its details, rather than a translation.

871 Jer. 15:19.

875 John 6:64, John 8:51.

878 John 20:22.

881 Matt. 28:19, Mark 16:15.

886 ff. For provisions concerning wills see canon law Decretals X 3.26 esp. cc.19–20 (Friedberg ii.538–46); cf. John of Freiburg *Summa confessorum* (Rome, 1518) ii tit.xv. q.100 ff.; Durandus *Speculum iuris* (Frankfurt, 1592) bk. iv part 3, pp. 366–90.

889–90 *akursid of al holi chirche foure tymys bi þe ȝere*: this was the so-called Great Curse, repeated as described here and covering those offences which incurred automatic excommunication; see E. Vodola, *Excommunication in the Middle Ages* (Berkeley and London, 1986). For English versions see *IMEPP* no. 122 and

O. S. Pickering, 'Notes on the Sentence of Cursing in Middle English; or A Case for the Index of Middle English Prose', *Leeds Studies in English* new series 12 (1981), 229–44; a Wycliffite commentary on this general form is Arnold iii.271–337, where wills are covered in cap.14 and where again the contemporary venality of the clergy is seen as a breach of 'þe trewe testament of Jesus Crist' (304/7).

897 Job 19:17 (as 860).

899–902 For the origin of all ills of the church in the Donation of Constantine see E1057 note.

916 Mark 10:42–3, Luke 22:25–6.

917 Luke 14:26.

922 Luke 12:13–14.

927–33 Augustine sermon 137, PL 38.758 'Nam audivi quosdam pervertere velle istam sententiam. Numquid non, si illis liceret, non delerent illam de evangelio?'

929 Matt. 23:2–3.

938–40 For the allegation of the clergy concerning the literal sense see *EWS* iv.76 ff. and references; and for Lollard stress on the literal sense Ps Bod. 288 f. 73ra, Laud misc.200 f. 66.

945 *statutis . . . constitucions*: see E1160 note.

952–5 The idea that persecution of Lollards by the established church is the result of their exposure of clerical vices is repeatedly voiced; see, for instance, EWS 63/44, 119/29, 157/84, E48/14, Arnold iii.309/4, 495/25, Matthew 124/25, Ps. Bod. 288 ff. 22va–b, 85ra.

955–8 The penalties for heresy were excommunication (*cursing* 953, *censuris*), various penances for recanted minor offences, imprisonment and, in the case of obdurate heresy by a relapse, burning. The allegation 'sum þei peynen to þe deeþ bi hungre' is difficult to substantiate; the accusation presumably relates to death in prison, and would have been explained by the authorities as accidental death. Exile ('sum of þise prestis þei exilen') was not a formal penalty, but was probably a not infrequent self-imposed consequence of heresy. The best documented case was that of Peter Payne, who was in Prague by the autumn of 1414 and possibly left England a year earlier (see A. B. Emden, *An Oxford Hall in Medieval Times* (Oxford, 1968), pp. 150–7). An earlier instance of temporary exile was that of Nicholas Hereford between 1382 and 1385, for which see *LB* pp. 58–9.

963–4 Matt. 15:6.

968 Luke 12:1. 13:31.

973 Acts 23:2.

976 *princis of prestis*: derived from the gospel *principes sacerdotum* (e.g. Matt.

26:3, 14, 47 etc.). It is in the light of this usage that the Lollard description of Henry V as *princeps sacerdotum* should be understood.

987 Matt. 25:40.

989 Acts 9:4.

992 Luke 10:16.

1002–7 Whatever the justice of this allegation with regard to judicial proceedings for heresy (and the abbreviated accounts of trials in many registers do not allow for reconstruction of the establishment's case, or whether one was made), it is very unfair with regard to the numerous defences against Lollardy. The crux came in the interpretation of scripture.

1008 Cf. Grosseteste in the sermon 'Natis et educatis et assuefactis', BL MS Royal 6 E.v f. 123rb 'Heresis est sentencia in terris fidei vel vite agende humano sensu electa sentencie sacre scripture contraria palam edocta pertinaciter defensata.'

1013–21 Cf. the argument between Thorpe and Arundel with his clerks, briefly summarized by the exchange in lines 2005–75. The preacher's implication here and in the next two lines may be malicious, but his charge is in essence true.

1034 *for as lawe . . . auctour* (1035): i.e. since the law of the established church is set above that of the gospel, so its author (the pope and hierarchy) is implicitly set above God, author of scripture.

1037 2 Thess. 2:4.

1043 Job 19:17.

1048 Matt. 24:48–51.

1055 *condicionalli*: the story of Matt. 24:48–51 is told not as history but as a hypothetical case. Nonetheless, according to the present author, it may be understood as a prophecy of contemporary affairs. *MED* does not give this sense for the adverb, but it is a natural extension from sense 4 of the noun.

1059 Gen. 1:28–30.

1061–6 For the three titles of Christ to lordship cf. *De dom.div.* 15/13. Fiona Somerset (1998). p. 147 n. 20 points out that the three titles of *kynde*, *conqueste* and *eleccioun* are those used in the coronation oath of Henry IV.

1077 *pre statis*: cf. E2 and note.

1087 Augustine sermon 76, PL 38.480.

1089 Matt. 16:23 Vulg. *scandalum es mihi*, WB *thou art (a) sclaundre to me*, Mark 8:33.

1091 2 Cor. 11:14.

1098 Ps. 90:6.

1101 2 Thess. 2:4.

1108 Matt. 24:48–51.

1118–28 Augustine *De natura et gratia* cap.67, PL 44.287 quoting his own *De libero arbitrio* iii.52, PL 32.1296. Lines 1118–23 in the original follow the material in 1123–8; the author has rearranged them to give the result first, and its justification second. The first part is a close translation; the second part here seems to be textually corrupt. In 1124 *to chese* is added to translate Latin *ad eligendum*. 1125 *or ellis . . . fulfil it* (1128): the passage (as emended by the omission of *and* 1127) is a close rendering of 'vel resistente carnali consuetudine, quae violentia mortalis successionis quodam modo naturaliter inolevit, videat quid recte faciendum sit, et velit, nec possit implere'. The point is that evil habit may become so strong that, though a man may perceive what should rightfully be done, and even may in a sense desire to do that, habit prevents him from enacting his perception and desire. In 1128 *he* replaces *and* to clarify this sense.

1133 1 Tim. 6:10.

1139 see 955–8 and note.

1139 *labourren bope wip bodi and wip catel*: the author is presumably referring to the financial help given not only to Lollard preachers but also to the funding of the copying of books. As has been noted (see Hudson, 'Lollard Book Production' in *Book Production and Publishing in Britain 1375–1475* (Cambridge, 1989), pp. 131–4 and *PR* pp. 197–206), quite apart from copies of the Wycliffite Bible which (despite Arundel's prohibition) could have been made in orthodox circles, the majority of Lollard books are professionally produced; even if they lack illumination, their materials and writing cannot have been of negligible cost. In view of 1139–41 *labourren . . . wip bodi* may refer to the (possibly free) labour of sympathetic scribes (cf. *PR* pp. 76n.101, 206–7).

1145 Matt. 4:4, Luke 4:4.

1148 Whiting does not appear to record the alleged proverb, though *OED womb* bears out the sense of the passage.

1153 Lam. 4:4.

1155 *ne suffre hem dele pat wolden dele*: i.e. Lollard preachers.

1157 Matt. 23:13.

1159 Pseudo-Chrysostom *Opus imperfectum* 44, PG 56.881.

1166 *ebrius*: presumably by 'aftur þe composicioun of the worde' the author means 'by etymology'. In fact the etymology of the word is dubious; see A. Walde, revd. J. B. Hofmann, *Lateinisches Etymologisches Wörterbuch* (Heidelberg, 1938–54), i.387–8. The author seems to have in mind the opposite *sobrius* and to have interpreted *e-* as a negative prefix; this etymology is rejected p. 388 though it had some currency until much later.

1183 Deuteronomy is the last book of the Pentateuch, the law of Moses.

1186 Deut. 4:2.

1187 Rev. 22:18–19.

1192 Deut. 12:32.

1202–3 *oon . . . feiþe*: the first concerns the wealth of the church, discussed here to 1632, the second concerns the eucharist, discussed 1663 ff., the transition being the persecution of those who hold the correct view on either.

1210 *alle þo . . . þat . . . besien hem*: for the antecedents to Lollard attempts towards disendowment see Aston (1984); subsequent moves by the ecclesiastical hierarchy (not acknowledged here) included the 1409 petition to the Council of Pisa (text in H.von der Hardt, *Magnum Oecumenicum Constantianse Concilium* i. pars xxvi (Helmstedt, 1697), cols.1126–71).

1221 Rev. 17:1, 19:2.

1223 Job. 19:17.

1226 Rev. 12:16.

1227–37 For Gorham see E1798 note. The quotations here are very brief and are identifiable roughly with passages in the commentary used in Egerton. The reference in 1232 to the preacher's previous writing seems to be to the final section of Egerton, where Gorham is again cited, lines 2993, 3077. 1230 *after þe woman . . . chirche* (1232) cf. Bodley 716 f. 213rb, pseudo-Aquinas p. 431 'post mulierem, idest Ecclesiam'; 1233 *bi þe see . . . world* cf. Lyra GO vi.1634 '*quae sedet super aquas multas* id est dominatur populis multis'. 1236 *upon many watris . . . possessions* (1238) cf. Bodley 716 f. 231ra, pseudo-Aquinas p. 472 'Super has aquas sedet mundana vanitas, quia fere mones subjecti sunt vanitati mundanae . . . Laborem, et studium, et amorem suum totaliter circa temporalia expendendo.'

1230 Rev. 12:16.

1232 *as I wrote onys*: see E3077 note.

1239 *Parisiensis*: here Peraldus (1668–9), ii.123.

1239–41 For the conditions under which a heathen or Jew might be received on conversion into the church see *Summa summarum* MS Bodley 293 f. 177ra–178ra (bk. V.ix), Penafort *Summa* (Rome, 1603), pp. 32–8, John of Freiburg *Summa confessorum* (1518), bk. I tit.iv q.iiii, f.x^v. See D.45 c.5 (Friedberg i.161–2).

1242 Luke 14:26.

1249 For this view of secular rulers cf. Wyclif *De off.reg.* 4/26, 12/1 quoting Augustine; Add. 24202 f. 5v, *Tractatus de regibus* 8/9, Arnold iii.214/4. See further E19 note.

1257 Rev. 17:2.

1263–5 *þo þan . . . witt*: those who are kings according to the usual understanding of that word, and those who are in worldly terms lesser men but are in the microcosmic sense rulers (of themselves).

1280 *in immesurable numbre*: for the excessive number of the clergy see *De off.reg.* 107/15, 159/9.

1282 *deuocions*: the parallel with *tipis* and *offringgis* makes it plain that the word has a concrete sense; *MED* does not admit such a meaning. The sense is 'gifts paid out of a misplaced sense of piety'.

1284 *þe astate . . . lordschip* (1287): for the responsibility of the secular powers in encouraging clerical worldliness cf. *De off.reg.* 92/15, 215/1.

1289 Rev. 17:6.

1294–6 cf. 955–8.

1296 Matt. 14:3–11, Mark 6:17–28.

1307 Ps. 72:27.

1309 Rev. 17:2.

1311 John 2:9.

1313 Ps. 103:15.

1321 It is possible that the passage is more corrupt, probably by loss of a clause or clauses, than the two emendations correct. But as emended the passage makes sense.

1325 Compare Jerome Ep. 121, PL 22.1024–5.

1336 Gen. 3:1–5; Matt. 4:3–10, Luke 4:2–13.

1339 Deut. 32:32–3.

1342 *uenym of addris*: Vulg. Deut. 32:33 has *venenum aspidum* but WB agrees in translating *venym of eddris*.

1343 Grosseteste Dict 6, MS Bodley 830 f. 9va; cf. Augustine *De civ. Dei* 21.8, PL 41.722.

1345 Gregory *Moralia* 31.2, PL 76.572 quoting Prov. 11:22 'Nam quia in nare fatuitas solet intelligi, Salomone attestante didicimus, qui ait "Circulus aureus in naribus suis, mulier pulcra et fatua" (Prov.11:22). Haereticam namque doctrinam nitore vidit eloquii resplendere, nec tamen sapientiae apto intellectu congruere . . .'.

1353 Peraldus *Summa viciorum* (1668–9), ii *De avaritia* p. 106 'deberet homines cohibere ab officio amor legis divinae et conditiones scientiae decretorum', quoted in Wyclif's *Opus evangelicum* ii.37/12.

1360 *þe patrimonie of Crist icroised*: *patrimonium Christi crucifixi* cf. Wyclif *Pol. Wks.* ii.683/15, where the habit of antichrist is described 'facit suos episcopos in castris dominorum temporalium residere, vocans totum hoc furtive conquestum patrimonium crucifixi'; cf. *De blas.* 58/3, *De eccles.* 311/27 and *EWS* iv.165. See also *MED patrimonie* n.

1362 Rev. 17:2.

1384–5 *it includiþ contradiccioun*: because, according to Wyclif's philosophy, it is impossible for accidents to exist without a subject. See Leff ii.500–10 and Kenny (1985), pp. 82–90.

1390 Dan. 8:10–12 (also 12:11); 1396 *besie sacrifice*: Vulg. *iuge sacrificium*, WB *contynuel sacrifice*.

1392–9 The quotation is entirely derived from Dan. 8:10–12 without Gregory's commentary (actually *Moralia* 32.26, PL 76.651). 1398 *truȝe*: Vulg.(v.12) *veritas*; 1399 *and he schal do . . . prosperite*: *et faciet, et prosperabitur*. The passage with Gregory's interpretation reappears at 1426.

1393 *haþ cast dowun of þe strengþe*: see Dan. 8:10 Vulg. 'et deiecit de fortitudine', WB EV 'castide doun of strengthe', LV 'castide doun of the strengthe'.

1403 Rom. 13:1.

1404 The relations between pope and emperour had long been uncertain and fluctuating. The author probably has in mind the theory of pope Innocent III (see *ODCC*) which held the view that 'no king can reign rightly unless he devoutly serve Christ's vicar' (i.e. the pope).

1422 Gregory *Moralia* 32.26–7, PL 76.651–2, where 2 Thess. 2:4 is quoted.

1423 2 Thess. 2:4.

1428 Ps. 50:19.

1430 Augustine *De dono perseverantiae* cap.2, PL 45.996, referring to Cyprian *De oratione Dominica* (PL 4.543–4).

1432 Gregory *Moralia* 8.56, PL 75.836.

1437 Dan. 8:11–12.

1441 Lev. 6:8–13.

1449 *large vngrounded absolucions*: the writer is probably thinking of plenary absolutions and absolutions *a pena et a culpa*; cf. *EWS* iv.47–9, Arnold iii.257/6, 356/5.

1464 The *determynacioun* is doubtless that of the 1215 Lateran Council which was generally taken to affirm transubstantiation, though the explanation of this was developed in the following century. For a discussion of the justice of the attribution to the Lateran Council, and of the varied interpretation of its wording see Macy (1994). Macy quotes the crucial section of the Council's creed p. 11 n. 3; as he points out the wording allows for (and foreshadowed) widespread variation. The most important words are 'Iesus Christus, cuius corpus et sanguis in sacramento altaris sub speciebus panis et vini veraciter continentur, transsubstantiatis pane in corpus et uino in sanguinem potestate divina.' The writer here objects to this (1465) because it implies that bread and wine cease to exist in their substances, a change that he believes Christ's words of institution do not allow (cf. Berengar below 1844–64 note and Chadwick (1989), p. 423).

1466 *and moreouur . . . oost* (1467): the point seems to be that this definition is contrary to that favoured by the later stages of the argument (see 2615 ff.) that both bread with wine and Christ are simultaneously in the consecrated elements. This is implied by the analogy in the following sentence: that Christ is united with his chosen in a single body.

1468 See for instance Augustine on Ps. 57:1, PL 36.692–3, on Ps. 62:2, 750–2 and on Ps. 65:1, 785–7.

1469 Col. 1:18.

1472 Heb. 13:15, Ps. 49:14.

1475 1 Cor. 15:24.

1477–83 Augustine *De civ. Dei* 10.6, PL 41.284; the two sections are separated by some fifteen lines. 1483 *iknow to þe puple* translates rather unidiomatically Latin *fidelibus noto*.

1487–542 The whole section is based on quotations from Augustine's sermon 272, PL 38.1246–8, a sermon there for Pentecost. The quotations are not in Augustine's order: in the original sermon the material appears in the order 1520–1 (a quotation curtailed here, see note to line 1717–20 where the passage recurs), 1488–9, 1526–8, 1490–6, 1517–18, 1531–42; lines 1496–516 and 1521–5 expand on Augustine.

1489 1 Cor. 12:27.

1492 1 Cor. 10:17.

1495 *and so . . . loue* (1496): this expands on and paraphrases Augustine (cols. 1247–8) 'Quando Spiritus sancti ignem accepistis, quasi cocti estis.'

1509 John 12:24–5.

1515 1 Cor. 10:17.

1517 Augustine (cols. 1247–8) 'Estote quod videtis, et accipite quod estis. Hoc Apostolus de pane dixit.'

1526 *3if . . . ben* (1528) Augustine (col. 1247) 'Si ergo vos estis corpus Christi et membra, mysterium vestrum in mensa Dominica positum est: mysterium vestrum accipitis. Ad id quod estis, Amen respondetis, et respondendo subscribitis.' The English writer has altered the syntax in the last sentence and ignored the second half (or had a defective exemplar). The punctuation here makes sense of the English text.

1532 *nouзt*: the emendation is made in the light of Augustine (col. 1248) 'Jam (*nouз* 1531) de calice quid intelligeremus, etiam non dictum, satis ostendit.' The translation of the last section is very literal in some sections: 1534 *as þouз* . . .

don, tanquam illud fiat; 1535 *to wiche peple, illis*; 1535 *into God, in Deum*; 1538 *and*
. . . *hymself* (1539), *nos ad se pertinere voluit.*

1535 Acts 4:32.

1546 *antecristis sacrament*: the eucharist as 'antichrist' explains it. According to this explanation there remains no *uisible forme* since the substance of bread has been annihilated at the words of consecration. The only possible *uisible forme* are 'þe accidentis wiþout soiect', to a Wycliffite a philosophical impossibility.

1560 2 Thess. 2:9.

1568 *pseudo*: see E2560 note.

1569 Matt. 24:24, Mark 13:22.

1572–4 Any explanation of transubstantiation had to account for the fact that the bread and wine after consecration have the same nutritional effect as beforehand; cf. *EWS* 197/27 where it is pointed out that the accidents of the wine after consecration can still make men drunk. 1575 the infinitive *beleue* is understood again after the second *whoso wol* (cf. 1584).

1587–9 Gregory *Moralia* 32.26, PL 76.651 'nisi pereuntium merita exigerent, eos qui recti credebantur, obtinere adversarius nequaquam posset'; the English is not very clear since *haue* 1588 has the sense of 'gain possession of', *aske þat* 1589 that of 'demand that punishment'. The same passage is referred to, though not quoted, at 1392 and quoted 1422.

1589 Job 34:30.

1590–6 Gregory *Moralia* 25.34, PL 76.343; Gregory quotes John 5:43 as the author says.

1592 *here meritis asking*: Gregory's absolute construction *exigentibus meritis* is replicated.

1593 *as Gregor . . . gospel* (1594): the scribe has mistaken the construction, not realising that *Truþe* is here substituted for *Crist* : Gregory 'sicut ipsa quoque Veritas in evangelio dicit'.

1594 John 5:43.

1597 Augustine sermon *De verbis Domini* 45, PL 38.723.

1598 2 Thess. 2:10–11; *þe charite of truthe*: Vulg. *charitatem veritatis*; *wirching of errour*: *operationem erroris.*

1601–16 Gregory *Moralia* 25.34, PL 76.343, following straight on from the passage in 1590–6 and the quotation there from John and 2 Thess. 1608–9 *the wiche . . . lordschip*: Gregory 'qui ejus dominio digni ante saecula praesciuntur'. The second part from 1610 is obscure in the English. Gregory's original for 1610–11 has 'An non ejus membra sunt, qui per affectatae sanctitatis speciem appetunt videri quod non sunt?' In the ME *desiren* 1610 translates *appetunt*, but confusingly *desired* 1611 is used for *affectatae*, this latter the result of mistranslation, since *affectatae* has the sense of 'assumed, feigned'; translate 'Are they not limbs of him [sc.antichrist] who wish to appear to be what they are not, through an appearance, or pretence of coveted holiness?' The forms *seen* 1610 and *seien* 1615 are both past participial forms of the verb 'to see' (1615 Gregory *videri*; see glossary). 1613 *no spirit* appears again a mistranslation, this time of *nequam spiritus*—perhaps misread as *nequaquam spiritus*. 1615 *bi professioun*, Gregory *professione* 'in public appearance'.

1629–32 Gregory *Moralia* 18.20, PL 76.48; the translation is again very literal: *þei . . . loris*, Gregory 'haeretici . . . qui scripturae sacrae sententias recta dogmata continentes ad intellectum pravum conantur violenter inflectere'.

1633 *but . . . scripture* (1634) paraphrases Gregory's sense.

1639 John 6:48–51 etc.

1646 Matt. 7:15, 24:11, 24, Mark 13:22.

1648 Matt. 10:10, Mark 6:8, Luke 9:3, 10:4.

1652 Mark 7:11; cf. E659, E1251 note.

1655 Matt. 15:5–6.

1658 Matt. 9:17, Mark 2:22, Luke 5:37.

1661 *glosid*: there seems to be a pun here on *closid togedre* 'linked together' and *glosid togedre* 'erroneously interpreted' (see E1820).

1669 *siþ contradiccion . . . mene* (1671): *mene* 1670 seems to have the sense of 'qualification' implied in *MED* n(3) sense 3(d); *mene* 1671 'compromise' (see *MED* n(3) sense 3(c)). Here, and at 3496–502, the author is plainly drawing on academic terminology of logic, terminology which would become familiar to any arts student in the first two years of the university course. Aristotle discussed the nature of contradiction in *De interpretatione* vi–vii.

1673 *contradictorie . . . betoken* (1674): i.e. not only in the signifier but also in the signified.

1681–96 The basis of Wyclif's belief in *scriptura sola* is here set out in clear and uncompromising terms. It should be noted that the human authorities listed in 1691–2 are not rejected out of hand; they are only removed from a position where unquestioning credence must be given to them to one where they are open to discussion—and, most vitally to the Lollards, to testing against scripture.

1686 ff. cf. E1871 ff.

1702 1 Cor. 3:11.

1704–5 *þat . . . chirche*: i.e. the pope and prelates.

1706–9 Pseudo-Dionysius *De ecclesiastica hierarchia* (*Dionysiaca* 2) III.3, for instance pp. 1177, 1219, 1245, and see his legend *Legenda aurea*, ed. Graesse p. 685.

1707 Acts 17:34.

1709 2 Cor. 12:2.

1709–14 *þis* in 1712 anticipates the claim in 1713–14; since the claim is that of the establishment and is rejected by the author, it is here put in single inverted commas.

1711 Ps. 118:142.

1713 *after . . . Sathanas*: for the origins of eucharistic error in the second millennium cf. *De apos.* 46/8.

1715 For the importance of pragmatism in Lollard thought about the eucharist, commoner later than this preacher but not unknown from the end of the fourteenth century, see Hudson 'The Mouse in the Pyx: Popular Heresy and the Eucharist', *Trivium* 26 (1991), 40–53.

1717–20 The emendation is made in the light of the quotation from Augustine referred to, sermon 272, PL 38.1246 (see 1487–542 for other quotations from this sermon). The passage runs 'Quod ergo videtis, panis est et calix; quod vobis etiam oculi vestri renuntiant; quod autem fides vestra postulat instruenda, panis est corpus Christi, calix sanguis Christi.'

1724 *þe determynacioun of Innocent*: see above 1464 note.

1725–6 The association of the eucharistic doctrine particularly with the friars arose from the predominant teaching of the Dominican Aquinas and the Franciscans Duns Scotus and Ockham. The views that Wyclif and his followers set out to refute were those of the Franciscans Scotus and Ockham. Wyclif, like his disciples, often identified the opponents of his eucharistic views as the friars, and it was his teaching on this subject that alienated all support for him from the friars. For a brief summary of Franciscan views see Macy (1992) pp. 109–14; see here further 2011–15 note. For this identification cf. *EWS* 8/28, 67/111, 162/49, *MC* 970 etc. and iv.53–5, Arnold iii.403/8, *Upland* 394.

1726 Matt. 15:13.

1727 *I am ware . . . tyme* (1730): the author is right to suppose that the early church made little attempt to provide a precise formulation concerning the eucharistic doctrine though, as his own quotations show, individual fathers express views. Paschasius Radbertus in the ninth century and Berengar in the eleventh century provoked further thought, and the latter's retraction led towards the definition of the 1215 Lateran Council. This was the first point at which the doctrine was embodied in canon law. See *ODCC*.

1736 Augustine *De civ. Dei* 20.19, PL 41.685 speaking of 2 Thess. 2:1–11.

1739 *for no douȝte . . . persecucioun* (1742): the author may well be right in his analysis that the Lollards' chief threat was perceived to be their attack on the worldly wealth and power of the church rather than their views on the eucharist. These latter, and Wyclif's initiation of them, played into the hands of enemies already looking for a simple test of heterodoxy. For evidence that the starting point of opposition was Wyclif's views of dominion see Hudson '*Peculiaris regis clericus*: Wyclif and the Issue of Authority', in *Authority in the Medieval West*, ed. M. Gosman, A. Vanderjagt and J. Veenstra (Groningen, 1999), pp. 63–81. The prime position of the eucharist in fifteenth-century enquiries into Lollardy is clear from the 1428 listing (*LB* pp. 133 nos. 1–4, 135 nos. 1–4), anticipated in the 1382 Blackfriars Council (*FZ* 277–8).

1745 *into þe vnbinding of Sathanas*: Wyclif saw this as occurring near the start of the second millennium (*Pol. Wks.* ii.391/1 ff.), though occasionally dated it more precisely 'tempore . . . Innocencii tercii circa quod tempus sathanas est solutus et fratres intraverant' (*Pol. Wks.* ii.622/22).

1749 Augustine Epistola 36, PL 33.136 'In his enim rebus de quibus nihil certi statuit scriptura divina, mos populi Dei, vel instituta majorum pro lege tenenda sunt'.

1760 Dan. 8:12.

1764–73 Augustine *De anima et eius origine* (addressed to Peter presbyter) c.10, PL 44.503. This section is a reported paraphrase not a quotation; use of the text continues at 1797 and again 1821. The citation of John 3:5 is within Vincent's speech as reported by Augustine.

1771 John 3:5.

1785 *newe sectis*: here especially the friars. The fraternal orders were outside the traditional episcopal jurisdiction, owing allegiance direct to the papacy.

1797–803 The same text col. 505 'Numquid in hac causa erroris audaciam, temeritatem, praesumptionem habere quispiam posset ampliorem? Ipse sententiam dominicam recordatur . . . et audet tamen suae censurae levare cervicem contra sententiam principalem'; the author here supplies the name Vincent for Augustine's *ipse*.

1800 John 3:5.

1802 *þe polle of his iugement*: though *MED polle* n. gives no abstract sense, the meaning here is clear 'the chief part', Lat. *cervicem*.

1803–6 Again the material derives from the same passage; *þe princepal sentens*: Augustine *sententiam . . . principis*; for the sense 'royal, princely' see *MED principal* adj.3. One sentence is omitted from the Latin after this.

1815 John 3:5.

1821–3 This is reported from Augustine, where it follows immediately on from the sentence quoted 1803–6.

1821–3 *þe consail of þe bischoppis*: interestingly abbreviated from Augustine 'consiliorum catholicorum et sedis apostolicae . . . auctoritas'. *Pelligianys* (1822): see *ODCC* Pelagianism. The basic tenet of the heresy was that man was able to take the initiative towards salvation without divine grace. One implication of this was a denial of the transmission of original sin, and hence the possibility that an unbaptised child might achieve heaven. The *consail of þe bishoppis* refers to the Council of Carthage in May 418 which reaffirmed earlier condemnation of Pelagius's teaching. The ideas, despite their rejection by the church, resurfaced in modified form in the thirteenth to fourteenth centuries and provoked Bradwardine's reaffirmation in more extreme form of Augustine's predestinarian theories. Wyclif in turn pushed further Bradwardine's ideas.

1824–33 The author does not unequivocally question the need for infant baptism, but only contrasts the strict adherence of the church to the letter of John 3:5 with its departure on the eucharist from literal interpretation of NT statements. Lollard questioning of the need for a child born of, and brought up by, christian parents for baptism was persistent; see *PR* pp. 291–2.

1838 For medieval knowledge of Mahomet and the beliefs of Moslems see R. W. Southern, *Western Views of Islam in the Middle Ages* (Cambridge, Mass., 1962).

1844–64 Berengar, c.1010–88, was for much of his life associated with Tours. His teaching on the eucharist was first condemned at a court under Nicholas II in 1059. His recantation was embodied in canon law as *De cons.* II.42 (Friedberg i.1328–9). His opponents regarded Wyclif as reviving Berengar's heresy (see Woodford *De sacramento altaris questiones lxxii*, MS Bodley 703, ff. 129vb–131rb, Netter *Doctrinale* V doc. 12 (ii.35), and the Dominican author of *Pharetra sacramenti*, MS CUL Ff.6.44, f. 60); for Wyclif's knowledge of Berengar see *LB* pp. 214–15. Wyclif, as the author here, stated himself to be in agreement with the condemnation of Berengar embodied in the recantation (*De apos.* 68/4, *Trial.* 249/26; cf. *Op.ard.* f. 136vb), though his understanding of it as stated *De euch.* 26/7 that the confession should *not* be understood 'quod panis et vinum sit formaliter vel essencialiter corpus Christi et sanguis, sed figurative et tropice' led opponents to argue that he departed from the intention of that recantation. The knowledge of the first part of Berengar's story probably came both to Wyclif and his followers from Higden's *Polychronicon* VI.27 (RS vii.206–11). Knowledge of Berengar's later troubles, and of the 1079 confession under Gregory VII, seems to have been less widely disseminated. The author here (1851, 1860, 1880) seems aware of only one *seen* 'synod, council', that of pope Nicholas. For Berengar see most recently H. Chadwick, '*Ego Berengarius*', *JTS* ns 40 (1989), 414–45, for his theology especially pp. 421–6.

1859 *and wel mai . . . supposen* (1864): that is the publication of Berengar's confession must imply *either* that Berengar had been induced to follow the error of the whole church, *or* that Berengar had erred and been brought to the right faith, that of the church. Noone takes the first option—unless it be these new-fangled hairsplitters who try to alter God's law to their folly.

1865 *determynouris* (cf. 1879): *MED* does not record the word. The meaning here seems based on Med. Lat. *determinator* 'a bachelor qualifying for a master's degree' (see *DML* sense 2), here in the sense, derived from the method of so doing, 'arguer, debater', with the added association of the hated *determynacioun* (1880)—ie 'the confectors of such a false law'.

1866 *or ellis . . . togedur* (1871): the view propounded here anticipates that explained more fully later (see 2615 ff.), where it is associated with an author named as *Fulgencius*.

1871 *Valentyne*: see *ODCC* Valentinus, a second-century Gnostic theologian. One of the most characteristic elements in Gnostic thought was a denial of the human nature of Christ.

1872 *Manicheus*: see *ODCC* Mani and Manichaeism. His teaching was a highly radical version of Gnostic thought.

1873 *maumetrie*: for connection between Lollard dislike of images and their condemnation of the contemporary cult of the eucharist compare Wyclif *De euch.* 316/10 ff. and J. I. Catto, 'Wyclif and the Cult of the Eucharist', *SCH Subsidia* 4 (1985), 269–86 at pp. 273–82.

1877 *and so . . . heresie* (1879): the author argues that those who assert that after the consecration only the accidents of bread and wine remain imply thereby that the common people idolatrously honour such accidents—or that their own dogma is heresy.

1886 see above 453 ff.

1890–3 Berengar's confession in canon law mentions only 'auctoritate evangelica et apostolica'; for Innocent III's provisions see the edition by A. García y García, *Constitutiones concilii quarti Laterensis* (Vatican City, 1981), pp. 41–118. Innocent commented on the 1059 confession in his own *De sacro altaris mysterio* IX.x, PL 217.862–3. For the glosses cf. Wyclif *De apos.* p. 169/30 ff.

1892 For Wyclif's criticism of one such gloss see *De eucharistia* 225/11 ff. See the glosses in the edition of canon law put out in Louvain (1624), ii.1932–3; that of Johannes Teutonicus is in García y García (above 1890) pp. 187–270.

1903 Similar sentiments are found in Gregory *Moralia* xvi.68, PL 75.1153, but the parallel is not exact.

1906 Ps. 32:11.

1908 John 14:6.

1909 Matt. 5:18, 24:35, Mark 13:30, Luke 21:33.

1915 John 1:42.

1918 Matt. 16:18; cf. E1326 and note.

1918–21 Augustine sermon 76, PL 38.480; a summary only.

1921 1 Cor. 10:4.

1923 Matt. 7:24–5.

1929 1 Cor. 10:4.

1930 1 John 2:16.

1936 Matt. 7:26–7.

1946 Exod. 20:25 (see line 656)

1948 3 Kgs. 7:31.

1951 Heb. 11:1.

1955 2 Tim. 2:19.

1956 Col. 2:5.

1979 Matt. 7:26–7.

1981–2029 The author is correct in claiming that there was not uniformity amongst those who supported the orthodox view of transubstantiation. See for the early period Macy (1984), and for the later period Macy (1994); cf. Wyclif *De apos.* 151/1. In this section the author appears to be alluding to discussions, many founded on Lombard's *Sentences* iv.dist.9–12 (PL 192.856–67), of the actual words of institution. These discussions focussed especially on two problems in the second part 'Hoc est corpus meum': the sense of the verb *est* and the referent of the demonstrative *hoc*. The latter was of particular interest to logicians, and came to the fore in the work of Duns Scotus and those who responded to him. This is the dominant concern of the present text here, and is an area of interest recently analysed (mainly in regard to authors some half century or more before the present text) by Rosier, de Libera and Bakker (see bibliography and especially de Libera and Rosier-Catach (1997[1]), pp. 171–9). Whilst it is impossible to identify precisely the proponents of the views here ridiculed, the ensuing notes endeavour to indicate parallels.

1984–9 For the view mentioned cf. Alexander of Hales *Glossa in Quatuor Libros Sententiarum* (Bibliotheca Franciscana Scholastica Medii Aevi 15, Florence, 1957) d.11 §21–2 (pp. 183–5); Woodford *De sacramento altaris* MS Bodley 703 f. 141ra alleging Innocent. Rosier (1990), p. 416 mentions also Prepositinus of Cremona *De sacramentis et de novissimis* (ed. D. E. Pilarczyk, Collectio Urbaniana ser. 3 Textus ac documenta 7, Rome, 1964), p. 77/19 'Sed melius dicimus quod Dominus non ad hec verba transubstantiavit, sed sua secreta et spirituali benedictione hoc fecit. Dedit tamen vim illis verbis ut per ea in posterum fieret.'

1989–96 The words of consecration used in the mass (Legg p. 222) 'Accipite et manducate ex hoc omnes. Hoc est corpus meum' are a combination and expansion of the three gospel records (Matt. 26:26 'accipite et comedite: hoc est corpus meum', Mark 14:22 'sumite, hoc est corpus meum', Luke 22:19 'hoc est corpus meum, quod pro vobis datur'). It would seem that the proponents of the view set out here thought the second *hoc* either a corruption of *hic* or its synonym. For this view cf. Woodford, Bodley 703, f. 143va; cf. Wyclif *Trial.* 252/23 though the argument there takes *hic* as a pronoun. Dr Fiona Somerset has suggested orally that this same disagreement underlies *Jack Upland* 390–3, *Daw's Reply* 838–52, and *Upland's Rejoinder* additional marginal material printed Heyworth notes p. 172/1–10. For earlier stages of the idea see Rosier (1990), pp. 413–33, Bakker's analysis (1997), pp. 427–8 of Bonaventura, and for Scotus's discussion de Libera and Rosier-Catach (1997¹) p. 188 and quotation n. 48.

1989 Matt. 26:26, Mark 14:22, Luke 22:19.

1990 ff. For Wyclif's consolidated discussion of current interpretations of *hoc* and *est* see *Trial.* 250/25 ff., though the interpretations reviewed are not in every particular those of the English text and cannot be its sole source.

1996–9 For this view, attributed by Wyclif to John de Deo (see 471) in *Trial.* 251/10 and *Op.min.* 213/35, see Arnold iii.406/12 ff. As the author implies (1998–9), the words of 1 Cor. 10:16–17 are hardly compatible with such an explanation. There is probably here a reflection of the logical debate on the force of *hoc* which, in the eucharistic formula, appears to have one referent at the start of the utterance, another at the end (see de Libera and Rosier-Catach (1997²), especially pp. 33–58); the issue is the precise point of consecration in the utterance. Here the force of *hoc* and that of *est* (the verb being present indicative rather than future *erit*, the subjunctive *sit* or the verb *fiat*) interrelate.

1999–2006 The view put forward here could have been subscribed to by either Aquinas or Scotus since it makes no attempt to explain how the change occurred. Wyclif discussed the force of *est* in the words of consecration many times, arguing that, as often in scripture, its force was that of *signat* or *figurat*: see *EWS* iv.52–3, *De apos.* 51/13, 115/28. For the difficulties of understanding *transsubstanciacio* compare *De euch.* 52/18. The author here may have in view the issue of *demonstratio ad sensum* discussed by Alexander of Hales and Bonaventura, analysed by de Libera and Rosier-Catach (1997¹), pp. 172–3 and quotation from the second n. 8.

2002 *queynt*: see *MED queint(e* adj.2(c).

2006–10 The explanation again turns on the problem of the meaning of *hoc*, assuming that it, and the English equivalent *þis*, are merely grammatical prop-words, necessary for the completeness of the sentence but having in themselves no meaning; this view is alluded to by Wyclif *De apos.* 196/19. See the quotation from Fishacre in de Libera and Rosier-Catach (1997¹), p. 194 n. 22, and Bakker (1997), p. 431.

2011–15 The view of Aquinas was that at the words of consecration the substance of bread was annihilated, leaving only the accidents of quantity in which the other accidents inhered (cf. *De euch.* 29/27); no substance took the place of that which had been annihilated (see Macy (1992), pp. 104–9 and references). This view Wyclif regarded as philosophically impossible and abhorrent: see *De apos.* 65/18. He was prepared to use the verb *transsubstanciat* (*De apos.* 218/31, *De euch.* 219/27), but not to accept accidents without a subject.

2015–22 In medieval philosophy following Aristotle nine accidents were distinguished. An accident (cf. *ODCC*), *ens in alio*, something which (with the disputed exception of the consecrated elements) could only exist in another entity; it is contrasted with substance or subject (*ens per se*). Three accidents were of quantity, six of quality. For Aquinas's view in relation to discussions alluded to in the previous lines here, see Rosier (1990). The English author pushes the Thomist view to its logical conclusion: that somehow, since the substance of bread has been annihilated and no new substance has taken its place, one of the accidents of bread must have assumed the nature of a substance to which the other accidents can then adhere. He mocks the Thomists that they have not yet decided which of the original accidents has assumed dominance. For the objections to the subsistence of accidents without a substance in Aristotelian philosophy see Chadwick (1989), p. 427.

2029 Eph. 2:20.

2034 For instance Augustine *Tract.in Ioh.* 26.13–15, PL 35.1612–14.

2035 1 Cor. 11:3, Eph. 4:15, 5:23, Col. 1:18, 2:10,19.

2036 John 6:51–2.

2040 John 6:57.

2046 Augustine as 2034 PL 35.1614 'Hoc est manducare illam escam, et illum bibere potum, in Christo manere, et illum manentem in se habere'.

2049–54 Augustine *De civ. Dei* 17.5, PL 41.535–6; the last part is in Augustine 'ideo hic dixit *manducare panem*; quod est in novo Testamento sacrificium Christianorum'.

2051 1 Kgs. 2:36.

2054 John 6:52.

2056 John 6:67.

2069–81 The reason for the decline in frequency of miracles was a question often discussed in the late medieval period. Cf. Wyclif *Serm.* ii.420/4, *Pol. Wks.* i.250/9; *ALD* 92/3.

2074 cf. E2987: for Antiochus Epiphanes, probably implied here, see *ODCC*, and for the allusion here cf. Dan.11:35–40, 1 Mach.1:57–60 especially vv.59–60 'et libros legis Dei combusserunt igni, scindentes eos: et apud quemcumque inveniebantur libri testamenti Domini, et quicumque observabat legem Domini, secundum edictum regis trucidabant eum'.

2075 *antecrist brenneþ þe bokis of Goddis lawe*. The charge, based on the wording of 1 Mac., is inexplicit; it could refer to the undoubted confiscation and destruction of manuscripts of the WB after Arundel's Constitutions of 1407 (Cf. Hudson (1989), pp. 125 ff. and Aston (1984), pp. 196 ff.) or more generally to destruction of Lollard works (cf. *Op.ard.* f. 174va–vb).

2080 2 Mach. 7:20.

2082 Dan. 3:19–30.

2083 Augustine Ep. 102, PL 33.383.

2084–9 The corruption here may well be greater than the emendation of only one word may suggest. The deleted word *siþ* (2088) has a capital in the manuscript, although that may well not indicate a new sentence but only a new clause. The sentence construction has become more than usually complicated (with the concessionary clause 2087–8 embedded in a relative clause 2087–8, itself between subject and verb), and it may well be that the main verb has been lost either before *siþ* or after *turmenten*. But since the single emendation gives sense to the sentence and leads on to the next, it has been accepted. *þei* 2088 resumes *he ne his mynystris* of 2085–6.

2094 Augustine, but not *De doctrina christiana* as the manuscript states, rather *De vera religione* cap.25, PL 34.142 'nec miracula illa in nostra tempora durare permissa sunt, ne animus semper visibilia quaereret, et eorum consuetudine frigesceret genus humanum, quorum novitate flagravit.'

2108–15 Gregory *Moralia* 32.24, PL 76.650; the emendation of *turneþ* to *turmenteþ* (2113) is necessary for sense and as a translation of Gregory's *cruciat*. **2111** *whos vertu . . . signes* (2113): 'Cujus tunc virtus non ab ipso cogitationum fundo quatiatur, quando is qui flagris cruciat signis coruscat?' The English author supplies the subject for the last sentence: Gregory after *signes* (2113) reads '*Stringit caudam suam quasi cedrum*, quia nimirum et altus tund erit veneratione prodigii (*wirschip of wondring* (2114), et durus crudelitate tormenti'. The emendation of the book number derives from the Latin.

2115–19 The reference is unspecific but may be to claims made for miracles at the tomb of Beket; cf. J. F. Davis, 'Lollards, Reformers and St. Thomas of Canterbury', *University of Birmingham Historical Journal* 9 (1963), 1–15 and *SEWW* 3/110–13 note. Cf. E1859 and note.

2119 Matt. 24:24, Mark 13:22.

2128 2 Thess. 2:8.

2137 *lettris of fraternite*: see E246 note. *vngrounded absolucions*: cf. *EWS* iv.41–9.

2138 *most abhominable lecherie*: for Lollard accusations of sexual offences amongst the religious see *SEWW* 3/25 ff., 154 ff., and Carolyn Dinshaw, *Getting Medieval: Sexualities and Communities, Pre- and Postmodern* (Durham NC, 1999), pp. 55–99.

2140 *crimous*: *MED* only gives the form *criminous*, and this from the late fifteenth century, but this seems a possible derivative adjective from *crime* sb.

2143 *open penaunce . . . fornycacioun* (2144): for public penance for abjured heretics see N. Tanner, 'Penances imposed on Kentish Lollards by Archbishop Warham 1511–12', in *Lollardy and the Gentry in the Later Middle Ages*, ed. M. Aston and C. Richmond (Stroud, 1997), pp. 229–49; Tanner gives the canon law justification for these penances.

2146 Rom. 1:32.

2156 John 6:67–9.

2165 See lines 405–12 and note.

2168–71 Augustine *De civ. Dei* 20.19, PL 41.685–6; the Latin shows the difference by variation between dative and accusative cases 'rectiusque putant etiam Latine dici, sicut in Graeco est, non *in templo Dei*, sed *in templum Dei sedeat*, tanquam ipse sit templum Dei, quod est Ecclesia.' Augustine explain this usage of *in . . . sedeat* in his next sentence 'sicut diximus, *Sedet in amicum*, id est, velut amicus', a sentence unhelpfully omitted in the English. *vndur þis logic*: MED offers no suitable sense for *logic* here, nor is the word a straight rendering of the Latin; it appears here to mean 'mode of speech'.

2169 2 Thess. 2:4.

2172 Matt. 16:16.

2175–8 Augustine, not *De uerbo Domini* but *Tract.in Ioh.* 27.9, PL 35.1619. The passage here is a rather inaccurate summary, and the last clause misses the point of Augustine's statement 'si prius cognoscere, et deinde credere vellemus, nec cognoscere nec credere valeremus'.

2178–83 Gregory *Moralia* 2.71, PL 75.588; *be wise to vndurstonde* (2181) renders *ad intelligendum sapimus*.

2180 Isa. 7:9; the emendations correct to both biblical original and Gregory's citation.

2185–8 Augustine *Contra adv.* 1.7, PL 42.609.

2193 Matt. 27:40, 42, Mark 15:32.

2193 *a siȝt of þe beleue*: 'a revelation of faith'.

2195 2 Tim. 3:13.

2196–204 Augustine *De civ. Dei* 12.17, PL 41.366–7. Lines 2202–4 in the Latin run 'profecto non Deum, quem cogitare non possunt, sed semetipsos pro illo cogitantes, non illum, sed se ipsos, nec illi, sed sibi comparant.'

2200 2 Cor. 10:12.

2210 John 5:44.

2215 *alle þe grete world*: modern English would repeat *in* (2214) here.

2218–58 The whole section is an accurate translation of Gregory *Moralia* 35.3, PL 76.751–2. 2222 *wiseli* belongs with *to haue seide* (Gregory *dixerat sapienter*). 2226 *knowiþ . . . wise*: 'sapientius se cognoscit non esse sapientem'. 2232 *more tariyng*: *tardioris*. The rather awkward final sentence, where *holi men* 2255 governs the verb *þe more . . . knowen hemself* 2257, reflects precisely the Latin but, lacking the variety of Latin inflections, is less comprehensible: 'Sancti itaque viri dum divinitatis sententias audiunt, quanto magis contemplando proficiunt, tanto amplius despiciendo quod sunt, aut nihil, aut prope nihil se esse cognoscunt.'

2220 Job 42:3.

2224 1 Cor. 1:19–21.

2226 Gen. 18:27.

2228 Exod. 4:10.

2233 Isa. 6:1–5.

2240 Jer. 1:6.

2242 Ezek. 1:25.

2265 2 Cor. 10:12.

2268 Mark 9:6, Luke 9:35.

2269 John 6:38, cf. 4:34, 5:30.

2272 John 7:16.

2275 John 15:15.

2281 1 Cor. 10:16.

2284 John 3:31–2.

2289 1 Cor. 11:27, 29.

2291 Cf. above 405 ff., and *EWS* 45/28, Arnold iii.186/3, *Pol. Poems* ii.244. The distinction is between popular modes of instruction (*sermons*), and academic debate (*scolis*).

2293 John 3:33.

2297 1 John 5:9.

2304 The reference is presumably to Innocent III's treatise *De sacro altaris mysterio*, PL 217.763–916. The charge that he wrote *wiþouten grounde of Goddis lawe* is unfair, since scriptural references abound in the work. It seems likely that the author had not actually read Innocent's treatise, which is far from an extreme statement (see, for example, PL 217.859–62).

2308 Matt. 7:24–7, Luke 6:48–9.

2311 Matt. 16:18–19.

2315 ff. The basis of papal claims was, as the author correctly states, the commission to Peter of Matt. 16:18–19. Wyclif understood this commission as a representative assignment to Peter for the priesthood as a whole; he also considered that, if it were right to recognize any as 'vicar of Christ on earth' this should be the most righteous man alive, an individual recognizable only by God himself. See *De pot.pap.* 271/22, 365/21, *De eccl.* 563/7, *Serm.* ii.353/11. For his followers' views, which adhered to these principles but often concerned themselves more with the abuses of the contemporary papacy, see *SEWW* 2/88, *37 Concs.* ff. 26v-31v (pp. 44–54), *Op.ard.* f. 183va–vb, BL Add. 24202 ff. 2–4; cf. *EWS* iv.93–101. For the development of the doctrine of papal infallibility see B. Tierney, *Origins of Papal Infallibility 1150–1350* (Leiden, 1972).

2318 *as it is . . . not* (2322): for the incorrectness of this claim, but for evidence that the author was not alone in holding it, see Macy (1994), pp. 11–32.

2322 Eph. 1:22, 4:15, 5:23, Col. 1:18.

2325 1 Cor. 12:12.

2326 Augustine *De diversis questionibus 83*, no. 75 (rather than 70 as the manuscript has), PL 40.86–7.

2329 Augustine *De civ. Dei* 17.16, PL 41.548–50 and *De Genesi ad litteram* 11.24, PL 34.442.

2338 Matt. 16:18.

2340 Eph. 2:20.

2341 Implied by Augustine, *De doctrina chris.* 1.18, PL 34.25 and Jerome commentary on Matt., PL 26.118.

2342 Matt. 16:16.

2350 *acording . . . apostle*: as in Eph. 2:20.

2354 Augustine sermon 76, PL 38.479 paraphrased rather than translated; note especially 'Ideo Petrus a petra, non petra a Petro: quomodo non a christiano Christus, sed a Christo christianus vocatur.'

2362 Augustine sermon 129, PL 38.725; the material drawn from here is paraphrased in lines 2356–64, before the reference as well as after; note 'Quid tibi fecit Ecclesia, ut eam velis quodam modo decollare? Tollere vis Ecclesiae caput . . . Erubescunt negare Christum, et non erubescunt negare verba Christi.'

2365 Zech. 11:15–17; *take to þe vessellis*: Vulg. *sume tibi vasa*: *þe* is the pronoun, but it is possible that the text should be emended to *to þe [þe]*, though compare WB 'ʒit take to thee vessels (one MS the vessels) of a fonned scheepherde'.

2372 2 Thess. 2:4.

2381 *feder*: *hirde* and *idol* come from Zech. 11:17 but *feder* appears to be an addition inferred from *he schal ete þe flesche* (2369); the hostile sense implied by the biblical verse is not acknowledged by *MED feder(e* n. 'one who feeds, sustains or supports'.

2383 Rev. 17:2, 18:3.

2389–91 *eche . . . Iesu*: Hebrew *keli* (see concordance for examples); Greek *skeuos* (according to the concordance). Paul's name is given in Acts 9:15 where it is explained as *vas electionis*; see *Unger's Bible Dictionary*, ed. M. F. Unger (Chicago, 1957), p. 831.

2390 Acts 9:15.

2398 Job 34:30.

2399 Gregory *Moralia* 25.34, PL 76.343.

2410 Matt. 16:18–19; the Latin pronouns and verbs are distinctively second person singular.

2410 Cf. Augustine sermon 295, PL 39.1349 and *Enar.in Ps.* 108, PL 37.1431–2 quoted in Wyclif *De pot.pap.* 98/7, where the same interpretation of the Petrine commission is given. For the powers of absolution cf. Thorpe 1827 ff. and notes.

2419 John 20:22–3; here the Latin verbs are distinctively second person plural.

2422–9 Gregory *Moralia* 27.34, PL 76.419. Again the translation is over-literal, and the obscurities are clarified by the Latin 'Ecce conversorum terror vertitur in potestatem, quia dum mala sua poenitendo puniunt, usque ad exercendum judicium ascendunt; ut hoc in Deo posse accipiant, quod prius de Deo ipsi metuebant. Judices quippe fiunt qui supernum judicium perfecte timuerunt, et aliena jam peccata incipiunt dimittere qui prius formidaverant ne retinerentur sua.' In 2425 *to mowe* renders Lat. *posse* 'so that they assume they are able to do in God's power what they the more dread from God [i.e.judgment]'. The final clause *þat raþur . . . wiþholde* (2428–9) is a relative clause dependent on *þei* 2426.

2431–3 After the death of a pope and until the election of a successor there is, of course, no pope; longer gaps occurred between Clement IV (1265–8) and Gregory X (1271–6) and effectively in the disputes following the death of Nicholas IV (1292). The Greek (see *ODCC* Orthodox Church) and the Latin churches began to move apart at a fairly early date and by the ninth century the estrangement was considerable; the complete schism is usually dated as beginning in 1054. One of the causes of the schism, and of its continuaunce, was the claim of the Roman papacy to primacy. Cf. Wyclif *De pot.pap.* 234/11. *Supp. Trial.* 446/3.

2439 Luke 12:32.

2441 *sceler*: *MED seler* n. does not give the sense of the office, only senses relating to persons 'an official affixing a seal'; here the sense must be 'chancery' with a pun on *celer* (see *MED* n(1) sense 2(a) 'cellar for wine' and (b) 'department of household in charge of receiving and dispensing wine and ale'), and hence *tappid forthe*.

2453 Gregory *Hom.in evang.* 26, PL 76.1200 quoted in the *Floretum/Rosarium* under *absolucio* (see English text p. 56/10); the paraphrase here is not entirely accurate. The view attributed here to Gregory is central to Wycliffite doctrine on absolution, see *PR* 294–9 and *EWS* iv.41–6.

2456 *þis newe presumptuous determynacioun*: i.e. the 1215 Lateran Council imposition of annual oral confession and (though cf. 2318 note) the introduction of doctrine concerning the eucharist.

2460 Augustine *Tract.in Ioh.* 26.13, PL 35.1612.

2461 John 6:51–2.

2465–9 For the idea that faith remained only in the Virgin during the triduum, see Y. Congar, 'Incidence ecclésiologique d'un thème de dévotion mariale', *Mélanges de science réligieuse* 7 (1950), 277–92; in Lollard writings see *SEWW* no. 24/132.

2468 Matt. 26:56, Mark 14:50.

2472 John 2:5.

2476 Acts 1:14, 2:42.

2480 Luke 24:30, 35.

2481 Augustine sermon 235, PL 38.1118–19; a summary. See above 1487–542. It may be that the author had a manuscript where these two sermons had been run together, as their subject matter would encourage.

2483 Acts 2:46.

2485 Peter Comestor on Acts 2:46, PL 198.1655.

2490 Acts 2:45; for the *ful purueans* and its implications, see E2116 ff.

2500 John 6:51–2.

2501 John 16:14.

2506 Acts 2:46.

2514 Luke 22:19.

2516 John 6:52.

2517 Luke 24:35.

2530 See Jacobus de Voragine *Legenda aurea*, ed. Graesse (1850), p. 61 sect.11 quoting Isidore.

2538 Rev. 20:7.

2539 Gal. 2:1.

2541 Acts 15:2 ff.

2543 2 Cor. 12:2–3.

2547 Gal. 1:12.

2564 1 Cor. 10:16–17, 11:23–9.

2568 Gal. 1:12; 1 Cor. 11:23.

2575 2 Thess. 2:4.

2581 *is þe kinde of antecrist þat mai be*: *kinde* here seems to have the sense of 'essence' (*MED* 1(b)), quintessence; *þat mai be* 'in so far as that may exist'. It is tempting to conjecture that a superlative adjective such as *verriest* has been lost before *kinde*, but, since the text makes possible sense as it stands, it has not been emended.

2592 Ambrose *De sacramentis* 4.4, PL 16.439–43; quoted in canon law D.2 de cons. c.55 (Fried. i.1334–5) and found in *SEWW* no. 21A/27.

2594–7 Jerome Ep. 120, PL 22.986; quoted *SEWW* nos. 2/59, 15/238 and 21A/ 26.

2596 Matt. 26:26, Mark 14:22, Luke 22:19.

2597–9 Grosseteste commentary on pseudo-Dionysius *De eccles.hier.* cap.3a in MS Lincoln College Oxford 101 f. 106v 'Est enim eukaristia secundum beatum Ignacium caro salvatoris nostri Iesu Christi', referred to by Wyclif *De apos.* 227/ 2. For Ignatius (c.35–c.107) see *ODCC*.

2599–601 See above 520, 607, 1706. For the implications of this observation concerning the composition of the present tract see introduction pp. lii.

2602 Cyprian Ep. 63, PL 4.386; *þat was a ful autentike man to seint Austen*: compare Augustine Ep. 151, PL 33.648.

2606 Augustine *De doctrina chris.* 4.21, PL 34.111; *þe blode . . . lackiþ* 'nec potest videri sanguis eius . . . esse in calice, quando uinum desit calici'.

2615–83 The whole section derives from Rupert of Deutz's *De divinis officiis*, PL 170.40–41; it is unclear why this should be attributed to Fulgentius, an attribution also found in Thorpe 1010, and marginally in two manuscripts of Wyclif's *De apos.* 95/37. In TCD 242, a manuscript containing Wyclif's *Opus evangelicum* and other works, a flyleaf at the start has a note from 'Autor Fulgencius de diuinis officiis', further identified by its incipit as identical to Rupert's text; the same note appears in Herrenhut AB II. R.1.16a f. 82, a notebook which also contains some of Wyclif's sermons. It was under the title of *auctor De diuinis officiis*, as here, that Wyclif cites the work *De apos.* 73/18–75/25, 95/36–9, 106/36–107/16, 248/4– 249/37 adding a tentative identification with Ambrose. For Wyclif's unease about the author's name, but his conviction of his antiquity, and for early fifteenth-century research about the identity of the text, see Hudson (1985), pp. 309–12. A substantial part of this section of Rupert's work is cited in Wyclif's *De apos.* 73/ 18–75/25 but the passage here cannot come from this source since 2640–4 is not in Wyclif's work (between 74/20–1). The text of Titus is close to the version printed in CCCM 7, here 41/361–44/436; the variants given by P. Classen, 'Zur kritischen Edition der Schriften Ruperts von Deutz', *Deutsches Archiv für Erforschung des Mittelalters* ns 26 (1970), 513–40 at pp. 519–27, are not reflected here. The translation is very literal, and the ensuing notes are designed to elucidate the English text. **2618** *godli*: MS *goodli* but Rupert *diuina*, which is picked up **2620** *heuenli*, Rupert again *diuina*; **2621** cf. John 1:1–2; **2622–3** *þe Sone of God*: the English omits Rupert 'uox erat Verbi incarnati, uox aeterni principii, verbum antiqui consilii' before resuming; **2624** *liif being mene: uita media*; **2627–8**

þe wiche . . . eeris: 'quo in aures dimisso, id quod audibile est, cito absumitur et transit'; 2625 in grammatical construction *for riȝt as* is completed by *so* 2630, but to simplify the meaning in modern English the two sections have been divided; 2635 *þe birþe of þe Virgen*: *partus autem Uirginis*. The quotation continues straight on after *her Fulgentius* 2640, there is no gap in the Latin; 2640 *þe Iewus*: *Iudaeis uel patribus eorum*, wording that is taken up in what follows. The emendations in 2647–8 are to bring the English closer to the Latin: 'Panis ergo inuisibilis, qui de caelo descendit, uita est, et panis uisibilis, qui de terra creuit, unus tamen panis est, quomodo qui de caelo descendit, et qui conceptus et natus est de utero virginis, Christus unus est.' Again there is no interruption of the quotation at 2658. 2660 *bestli liif*: *uita animalis*; 2662 *touȝching*: after this Rupert adds 'Haec vita animalis est, carnalis est, caro est'; 2672 *nedful*: after this four sentences are omitted (43/421–44/430).

2641 John 6:49.

2643 1 Cor. 10:3–4.

2653 1 Cor. 11:27.

2660 1 Cor. 15:40.

2662 John 6:64.

2665 Jonah 2:1.

2674 cf. Ps. 84:11.

2680 Deut. 8:3.

2684 Wyclif similarly expresses his approval for the views of *auctor De divinis officiis*, but they had caused controversy and accusations of heresy in Rupert's own time (for which see van Enghen (1983) pp. 135–80). Those accusations described Rupert's view as impanation—but Wyclif strongly rejected what he understood by that theory (see *De apos.* 209/18, *De euch.* 228/4, *Trial.* 269/17).

2690–710 Augustine Ep. 36, PL 33.147.

2696 Heb. 4:12, Rev. 1:16, 2:12, 19:15; the parenthetical gloss is added by the English writer.

2699 Luke 12:49.

2701 Exod. 25:30; *looues of forþsetting* is a calque on the Vulgate *panes propositionis* (WB *looues of proposicioun*).

2702 cf. Luke 22:7–20. There is no gap in the quotation of Augustine at 2705.

2712–15 Augustine *Contra adv.* 1.39, PL 42.627; *now* is added to reflect Latin *nunc*, making the conventional parallel between Melchisedech's action and the christian mass clearer.

2713 Gen. 14:18–19.

2721–2 Cf. Ambrose *De sacr.* iv.4, PL 16.439–43 cited in slightly varied form in canon law D.2 de cons. c.58 (Friedberg i.1334–5) but closer to the version here is the sentence in D.2 de cons. c.61 (Friedberg i.1337) attributed there to Augustine.

2723 For instance Augustine *Tract.in Ioh.* 26 caps.6, 8–20, PL 35.1610–15.

2725–8 Consideration of the nature of accidents, and their involvement in the eucharist, was inevitable in all lectures on the *Sentences* following the Lombard's use of the term in *Sent.* iv.xi ff. (PL 192.862).

2730 see above 2723.

2735 See above lines 1487–542.

2736–9 Cf. Augustine *De questionibus evangeliorum* i.43, PL 35.1331–2.

2737 Matt. 26:29, Mark 14:25, Luke 22:18.

2753 John 8:31–2.

2756 John 17:6–8.

2768 John 14:12.

2769 John 17:17.

2770 John 14:6.

2773 John 10:35.

2778 *þe fadur þe fende*: the emendation is based on 2782.

2778 John 8:47.

2780 John 8:26.

2782 John 8:44.

2785–6 *ful . . . scripture*: 'into opinions very diverse, and contrary both amongst themselves and against scripture'.

2794–6 For the author's views on these OT sects see E62 ff., 497 ff., and those of the *heþen philesophris* see E624 ff. and notes.

2797–8 For these groups see *ODCC*. In simple terms the Arian heresy, flourishing in the fourth century, denied the divine nature of Christ; the Sabellians of the second and third centuries did not fully distinguish the Father from the Son; the Donatists of the fourth century and later maintained that sacraments given by sinners were of no validity. Some of his opponents (e.g. Netter *Doctrinale* II.8 (i.277), V.146 (ii.846)) maintained that there was a dangerous contiguity between the view of Wyclif that authority depended upon merit and the heresy of the Donatists.

2800 Gen. 11:1–9; Babel is a variant of the more usual Babylon.

2802 Gen. 9:11.

2808 1 Pet. 5:13.

2809–11 Augustine *De civ. Dei* 18.2, PL 41.561, and 18.41, PL 41.601 'Babylon quippe interpretatur Confusio'.

2814–17 this continues from the second passage in 2811 'Nec interest diaboli regis ejus, quam contrariis inter se rixentur erroribus, quos merito multae variaeque impietatis pariter possidet.'

2822 Dan. 11:31.

2826 Cf. Thorpe 934 ff. Wyclif (contrary to the assertions of his opponents) did not condone irreverence towards the eucharist (see for instance *Serm*.iv.350/9 and cf. *EWS* 162/54–76), but did condemn the cult of the eucharist (*Serm*.i.165/14, ii.165/18, 460/39, cf. *EWS* 67/134, 46/75).

2831 Cf. E999 and discussion in Thorpe 1059 ff. and notes; see *Rosarium* under *ydolatrie* and *ymage* (English text pp. 96–101).

2834–5 Augustine Ep. 155, PL 33.673 and *De civ. Dei* 4.15, PL 41.160 and further in 7.32 (col. 221), 19.17 (col. 646).

2837 Cf. Exod. 20:5 'non adorabis ea neque coles'.

2839 Augustine Ep. 102, PL 33.376–7 summary.

2853 Exod. 22:20.

2855–9 Augustine *De vera religione* 55, PL 34.169–70, a summary apart from lines 2858–9 'Meliores enim sunt ipsi artifices qui talia fabricantur, quos tamen colere non debemus'.

2861–4 Augustine Ep. 102, PL 33.378, slightly abbreviated.

2863 Rev. 22:8–9.

2864–76 Augustine *De vera religione* 55.110, PL 34.170; the English author has rearranged the material which in the Latin is in the order 2874–6, 2868–71, 2866–8.

2872 Matt. 4:10, Luke 4:8, not quoted by Augustine.

2877–86 The discussion depends upon the wording of the Vulgate, Titus 2.11–12 'Apparuit enim gratia Dei Salvatoris nostri omnibus hominibus, erudiens nos ut abnegantes *impietatem*, et saecularia desideria: sobrie, et iuste, et *pie* vivamus in hoc saeculo' (AV translates the italicized words 'ungodliness' and 'godly', EV 'vnpite' and 'piteuously', LV 'wickidnesse' and 'piteuousli'). *MED* gives the noun *casuel* only twice and not in a possible sense. It seems that *casuel* (2884) has here the sense of 'a word having grammatical case'. The emendation in 2885 was suggested to me by Dr David Thomson, who further noted that the error could have been suggested by the *impietas* of four lines earlier. The nasal in MS *impietate* is written out, not indicated by an abbreviation mark.

2891–2 Cf. Jerome Ep. 100, PL 22.821, and Augustine PL 35.2304–5, a summary rather than an exact quotation.

2896 Augustine *Liber de spiritu et anima* PL 40.782, and *De diversis questionibus 83* c.46, PL 40.29–31.

2897 Augustine, *De libero arbitrio* 3.11, PL 32.1287, paraphrased.

2899–913 Cf. Thorpe 1030 ff.; the author has moved on from the honour due to the eucharistic elements to images in general; he returns briefly 2918 ff.

2913 Jerome Ep. 109, PL 22.907; the manuscript attributes the letter marginally to Augustine but the prefixed *þe same seint* makes it plain that this is an error.

2928 The author seems to be referring to section ix of Arundel's Constitutions, Wilkins iii.317–18 which, though it has a general heading 'Ut nullus disputet de articulis per ecclesiam determinatis, nisi ad verum intellectum habendum', is largely concerned with images, the honour due to them, and pilgrimages.

2936 Cf. Augustine Ep. 102, PL 33.377.

2937 1 Cor. 10:18–20.

2943–52 Augustine Ep. 102, PL 33.376–9, general sentiments but not an exact quotation.

2952 Augustine *De questionibus veteris et nove legis*, PL 35.2231.

2955 1 Kgs. 28:7–20.

2962 Acts 10:25–6.

2962 Acts 14:11–15.

2963 Rev. 22:8–9.

2964 John 1:29.

2967–9 Gregory in *Legenda aurea*, ed. Graesse p. 192 sect.5.

2977 Augustine as at 2943–52.

2994 Grosseteste sermon 34, BL Royal 7. E.ii, f. 372va–vb.

2997 3 Kgs. 12:28–33.

3000 4 Kgs. 10:18–31; *Hieu* is AV Jehu.

3001–5 The cult to which the author objected at Canterbury was, of course, that of Beket; see Thorpe 1255. For the *idolatrie late begun at Ȝork*: for indulgences to those making gifts for the fabric at York see Wilkins iii.226–7 dated 1396. It is probable, however, that the writer is referring to the cult of Archbishop Scrope at York, beheaded in 1405 for alleged treachery to Henry IV; see *ODCC* under Scrope, Richard le, and J. W. McKenna, 'Popular Canonization as Political Propaganda: the Cult of Archbishop Scrope', *Speculum* 45 (1970), 608–23, and for the case P. McNiven, 'The Betrayal of Archbishop Scrope', *BJRL* 54 (1971), 173–213, and R. G. Davies, 'After the Execution of Archbishop Scrope: Henry IV, the Papacy and the English Episcopate, 1405–8', *BJRL* 59 (1976), 40–74 esp.p.41. Despite Henry IV's prohibitions, the cult flourished and at the Reformation the treasure in St. Stephen's Chapel, where the Scrope tombs and chantry were located, were amongst the richest in the minster (see *Victoria County History Yorkshire: The City of York*, ed. P. M. Tillott (London, 1961), p. 346).

3006–8 Grosseteste sermon 34, BL Royal 7 E.ii, f. 372vb.

3011–12 For the secular lords as *vicaris of þe godhede* cf. *EWS* E25/59, Matthew 362/22, Add. 24202 f. 5v and E19 note.

3015–18 see 2 Chron. 13:4–12.

3020 Job 34:30.

3022 Augustine *De 12 abusionum gradibus*, PL 40.1086, 'Attamen sciat rex, quod sicut in throno hominum primus constitutus est, sic et in poenis, si justitiam non fecerit, primatum habiturus est'.

3025 Jer. 44:16–18; the emendation in 3029 derives from the Vulgate *principes*; *it was wel to us* (3030): 'bene nobis erat'; *we haue seien* (3030): *seien* is pa.p. of 'see', Vulg. *vidimus*.

3033 1 Mac. 1:12.

3039 see above 2928.

3040–3 The author refers to sections i–iii of Arundel's Constitutions, Wilkins iii.315–16 that concern the need for preachers to obtain licences. His point is that those who by their orthodoxy could obtain such licences have no inclination to preach, whereas those who want to preach are considered Lollards and hence cannot gain licences. Cf. Matthew 57/25, 79/5, *LL* 17/26, *EWS* iv.83–4.

3047 Ps. 90:6.

3048 Dan. 11:31.

3049–56 For such glosses on Dan. 11:31 see GO (iv.1656) where Jerome is quoted, referring to the destruction of Jerusalem but also to the *lex Dei* as the symbol of true religion.

3057 ff. For this understanding of *þis place of halowing* cf. the Lollard definition of the church for which see Thorpe 898–917 and note.

3062 John 17:20–1; *ended into oon*: Vulg. *unum sint*.

3064 John 16:33.

3066 1 John 4:16.

3069 Gen. 22:17–18.

3071 Gal. 3:16.

3078 see 3049.

3082 *omiscioun*: i.e. by lack of obedience.

3086–7 The force of the final clause is 'even if God should forbid there to be material church, priest or prelate in this world'. The value of church building was questioned by the Lollards: the more extreme saw no virtue in material churches (see *PR* pp. 321–3), the more moderate saw buildings as merely convenient (e.g. *EWS* 73/19—they keep off the rain). All agreed that over-elaborate adornment should be avoided (*LL* 37/7, Matthew 321/22, Arnold iii.273/13) and that the church is hallowed by man not man by the church (Arnold iii.487/14, *LL* 36/13, *ALD* 48/8). Although there is rarely argument about the existence of priests and bishops in the church, because of the mention of such offices in the NT, there is constant comment on the duties and purposes of such men.

3091–119 Cf. Wyclif *De veritate sacre scripture* i.5/1 ff. where allegorical language is discussed. See *EWS* 30/37–94 and notes for a parallel to this discussion and some of the issues involved. The basic issue involves the meaning of the verb of predication *esse*, as this is used in scripture. Wyclif points out, following Augustine (PL 34.703) that *est*, *sunt* etc. are often used in scripture with the meaning more precisely rendered by Latin *signare* or *figurare*. He concludes (*Trial.* 267/14) 'sacramentum est corpus Christi, hoc est, ipsum corpus sacramentaliter signat vel figurat'. The author's point here is the same: Paul (3115–16) was not glorying in the physical object on which Christ actually died, but in Christ himself; the cross *figurat* Christ. In a sense the whole argument on the eucharist between the Lollards and their opponents was an argument on the philosophy of signs.

3096–8 *in case . . . vnhalowid*: cf. Arnold iii.405/28–35 where it is pointed out that if consecrated hosts were mixed with unconsecrated, none could distinguish them or 'knowe accident fro bred'—the end of the sentence here makes the eucharistic implications clear.

3103 John 10:35–6.

3105 Gal. 6:14.

3119 John 17:3.

3123 Cf. Augustine *De civ. Dei* 13.23, PL 41.395–8.

3126–7 1 Cor. 3:9. Cf. Augustine *Enar.in Ps.*66:2, PL 36.802–6, and *De libero arbitrio* iii.5, PL 32.1276–8, but the latter not quoting Ps. 66:2. Cf. 3455.

3131–42 Augustine *Enar. in Ps.*67:14, PL 36.823. The translation in lines 3138–41 is somewhat obscure: the Latin runs 'Quod si ita est, *quid aliud admoneri videntur evangelizantes* virtute multa, nisi quia tunc eis Dominus dabit verbum ut evangelizare possint, si dormiant inter medios cleros?' The writer has translated *videntur* 'seem' by *ben iseie*, 'been seen'. Translate 'And, since it is so, of what else are men preaching with much virtue seen to be instructed, but that the Lord will then give them the word that they may speak or preach if they "rest between the learned men"? (i.e. rest between the testaments)'. At 3140 *not* has been removed since the force of *saue* is sufficient translation for *nisi*.

3132 Ps. 67:14.

3145–50 The two parts of medieval law, customarily linked in legal training at the universities. The *gloss* is here a vague term, but covers all the various commentaries and explanations of both legal codes. The *noise of þe clergies* (3149) is, according to the account of Augustine above, the teaching of the bible.

3154–9 Augustine *De dono perseverantiae* 15, PL 45.1002; *waking or quik*: *vigilantisque*. A marginal note in the original scribe's hand gives the reference *De civitate D[../capitulo*.

3166 1 Kgs. 20:20–40.

3168 Matt. 3:16, Mark 1:10, Luke 3:22, John 1:32–3; Acts 2:1–4.

3170–1 The Vulgate in Ps. 88:2–3 has nothing corresponding to *whi* (WB likewise nothing). The author has supplied it as an understood antecedent for *quoniam* (WB *for*).

3171–7 Augustine *Enar. in Ps*.88:1, 3, PL 37.1121; *þis man . . . God* (3172–3) Augustine 'tenuit se ipse, cujus os servit veritati Dei, ad ipsam veritatem Dei'. The gloss in 3174–5 is on Latin *securus*.

3182 Matt. 4:10, Luke 4:8.

3189–94 Augustine *Enar. in Ps.* 96:1, PL 37.1237. There seems to be an awkwardness in 3192 *hang . . . hing*, translating Augustine *in illo incumbat, quod per incerta pendebat*, where the English has used parts of the same English verb to translate two different Latin verbs.

3190 Ps. 117:22; cf. Eph. 2:20.

3195–201 Augustine *Enar. in Ps.* 85:13, PL 37.1093–4; for clarity the material has been put in quotation marks, but strictly the English is a summary rather than a direct quotation.

3201–7 Augustine *De civ. Dei* 18.40, PL 41.600; *discording . . . age* (3204–5): 'inter se de rebus gestis ab aetatis nostrae memoria remotissimis discrepantes'; *douten . . . falsist* (3207): 'quidquid ei resistit, non dubitamus esse falsissimum'.

3208–12 Augustine *De civ. Dei* 19.14, PL 41.642; 3210–12 *to whom . . . obeie*: 'cui certus obtemperet, et adjutorio, ut liber obtemperet'.

3213–22 Augustine *Enar. in Ps.* 68:22, PL 36.859, a close translation apart from the parenthetical gloss; 3217–18 *þis mete . . . vnite*: 'In hanc escam tam suavem, tam dulcem unitatis Christi'.

3214 Ps. 68:22.

3216 Luke 22:19.

3218 1 Cor. 10:17.

3225 Ps. 21:14.

3225–8 cf. Augustine Ep. 140, PL 33.553, and *Enar. in Ps.* 21:14, PL 36.175.

3228–33 Augustine *Enar. in Ps.* 9B:9, PL 36.128, a paraphrase ending 3233 *antecrist*.

3235 Ps. 118:85.

3237 Ps. 118:126.

3240–9 Augustine *De civ. Dei* 19.18, PL 41.646–7. The translation is, considering the inversion of Augustine's Latin in the second sentence, a clear one; *þe whiche* 3244 . . . *þing* (3249) is an absolute construction, Latin 'qua salva atque certa, de quibusdam rebus, quas neque sensu, neque ratione percepimus, neque nobis per scripturam canonicam claruerunt, nec per testes quibus non credere absurdum est, in nostram noticiam pervenerunt, sine justa reprehensione dubitamus.' It is worth noting that Augustine's *canonic-* is glossed the first time (3242), and replaced by *autentik* the second (3247).

3249–55 Augustine *De civ. Dei* 20.10, PL 41.675; the English author has clarified by adding *of soule* (3252).

3254 Col. 3:1.

3258–62 Jerome Ep. 55, *De perpetua virginitatis B. Mariae adversus Helvidium*, PL 23.203, quoting 1 Cor. 7:29, 32–3.

3259 1 Cor. 7:1–11.

3266 Peraldus: cf. sermons for 2 Easter in Magdalen 204, ff. 97r-v, but without reference to Ambrose; closer seems to be the passage cited before 658–69 *Summa virtutum* (Paris, 1668–9), i.120 'Ambrosius: Auferantur argumenta vbi fides quaeritur: non enim recipienda sunt argumenta fidei contraria. In hic quae fidei sunt peccatoribus creditur, non dialecticis, iuxta verbum eiusdem. Ambros.'

3267 John 10:11.

3270–5 Augustine *De civ. Dei* 20.30, PL 41.708.

3284–90 Augustine *De civ. Dei* 20.30, PL 41.708 The sense of the Latin is somewhat obscure, but seems better reflected by the emendation; 'Qui vero secundum Deum sapiunt, omnium quae incredibilia videntur hominibus, et tamen scripturis sanctis, quarum jam veritas multis modis asserta est, continentur, maximum argumentum tenent veracem Dei omnipotentiam, quem certum habent nullo modo in eis potuisse mentiri, et posse facere quod impossibile est infideli.' The Loeb edition translates 'But those who are wise according to God hold that the strongest argument in favour of all things that seem incredible to men, yet are found in the holy scriptures whose truth has already been upheld in many ways, is the reliable omnipotence of God; they are sure that he could in no way have lied in the scriptures, and that he can do what to the unbeliever is impossible.'

3293–308 Augustine *De civ. Dei* 21.23, PL 41.736; the first part is compressed and then paraphrased. At 3305–6 Augustine reads 'si non quod Deus dixit, sed quod suspicantur homines plus valebit'; the English *3e . . . supposen* 'Yes, certainly this must be so if what God says shall prevail over what men conjecture.'

3300 2 Pet. 2:4; Matt. 25:41.

3312 Rev. 20:7.

3314–66 The whole section derives from Clement *Recognitiones*: 3315–25, bk. 8.37, PG 1.1389; 3325–37, bk. 8.58, PG 1.1398; 3341–7, bk. 8.60, PG 1.1399; 3347–55, bk. 8.64, PG 1.1400; 3359–66, bk. 10.51, PG 1.1444–5. For the *Recognitiones* see *ODCC Clementine literature* (2); they survive in a Latin translation by Rufinus. 3321 *vnfongen of þe uerri prophete*: 'a vero propheto suscepta'. There is a long gap between the two sentences in 3325. The emendation in 3334 is necessary in view of the Latin *ei*, referring to God. There is another long omission after this. The emendation in 3344 is to bring the sense into line with the Latin *si quid responderit*. 3345 *þat þing . . . vncertein*: 'hoc certum esse non potest dubitari'. 3345–7 translates Lat. 'Et ideo quaeratur verus propheta ante omnia, et ejus verba teneantur'. The translator has changed the Latin 'qui sibi artifices verborum videbantur' to 'demyng hemself to [b]e craft[i] of wordis' (3350–1); the emendation is to bring this into line with the sense of the Latin. 3346 *þe verri trew prophete*, Lat. *verus propheta*, with double translation of the adjective.

3372–7 Augustine *De Genesi ad litteram* 2.1, PL 34.263.

3385–7 Augustine Ep. 185, PL 33.794; *þe charge . . . wittnesse*: 'pondus humani testimonii perdiderunt'.

3391–8 Augustine preface to *Liber retractationum*, PL 32.585. The Latin 3895 has 'dicunt . . . dicunt', and hence the emndation.

3399 John 8:44.

3402–8 Augustine, *De adulterinis coniugiis*, PL 40.467.

3417–20 Augustine *Contra adversarium legis et prophetarum*, PL 42.603.

3421–8 Augustine *De mendacio*, PL 40.517–18; lines 3421–3 summarize a section of Augustine; the rest is translated, 3426–7 'þe auctorite . . . amenusid' translating the ablative absolute 'confracta et comminuta scripturarum auctoritate'.

3423 Gal. 2:11–14.

3428–30 Augustine *De mendacio*, PL 40.500 'Fracta enim vel leviter diminuta auctoritate veritatis, omnia dubia remanebunt.'

3431–45 Augustine Ep. to Jerome 82, PL 33.277; there is, as the author observes (3443), a gap at that point in the material translated; there is also a gap unnoted in 3436. Again (cf. 3240–9 note) the author is reluctant to apply *canoun* to scripture, glossing *canonici* 3434 and substituting *autentike* for *canonicos* in 3438.

3445–50 Augustine Ep. 147, PL 33.612.

3449 Matt. 5:8.

3454–9 Augustine *Enar. in Ps.* 66:2, PL 36.802–3; cf. *Dialogus* 20/17, *De ver.s.s.* i.46/18.

3458 John 15:1, 5.

3463–6 Augustine *De natura et gratia* c.48, PL 44.274; *in his godheed* (3465) is a gloss by the English author.

3463–4 Rom. 3:5–6.

3465 2 Tim. 2:13.

3466–74 The distinction between *peyne of harme* (3468) and *peine of feling* (3474) reflects the Latin *pena dampni* and *pena sensus* discussed by Wyclif in *De stat.inn.* 478/8 ff., *Trial.* 289/5 ff. and elsewhere. The first 'consistit in habitu tanquam privacio, cum sit defectus boni utilis, quod creatura racionalis habere debuit sine maioris commodi recompensa' (*De stat.inn.* 478/9). Christ could suffer only the second since he had no such *defectus*; only had he been separated from the divine could he have suffered in such a way. 3471 *so* has the force of 'in such a way'.

3475–7 Anselm *Proslogion* cap.7, ed. Schmitt i.105–6. 3477 *maist* translates *potes*; English would supply an infinitive.

3480–93 The precise, apparently contemporary, speculations that the writer is opposing are not clear, but they seem to turn on debates about the dual nature of Christ and, in particular, the status of his humanity after the ascension. 3480–1 presumably turns on the use of *Crist*, the divine name, and asserts that the divinity never died or went to hell but only the humanity. The debates to which the writer alludes probably occurred in the course of the obligatory lectures in the university theology course on Lombard's *Sentences*, here on 3 *Sent.* dist.21–22 (PL 192.800–8); for examples of such discussions from a somewhat earlier period see Aquinas *Scriptum super Sententiis* 3, 658–78, Albertus Magnus *Opera omnia* 28, 383–9, Alexander of Hales *Summa theologica* 4, 226–32 and 279, Bonaventura *Opera omnia* 3, 436–54. The writer's objection, as is clearer in 3494 ff., is not only to the heterodoxy of the views advanced (which are clearly put down in the examples just noted) but to the relentless application of logic to issues of the faith (cf. his objections to such analyses of the words of eucharistic consecration above 1981–2029). Wyclif's *De apos.* 183/25 ff. may refer to similar questions. The speculations condemned may be those current in the Oxford schools in the mid-fourteenth century, for which see W. J. Courtenay in *HUO* ii.30–34 and references.

3484 Augustine discusses these issues in the *Enchiridion*, PL 40.231–90, but the precise reference seems to be incorrect; a closer analogy is cap.105 (col. 281).

3486 Augustine *De libero arbitrio* 2.14, PL 32.1261, actually book, not chapter, 2.

3492 1 John 4:3; *departiþ*: Vulg. *solvit* (WB EV *dissolueth or fordoith*, LV *fordoith*).

3497 *no negatif includeþ contradiccioun*: cf. Wyclif's *De logica* ii.107 and

J. A. Robson, *Wyclif and the Oxford Schools* (Cambridge, 1961), p. 108 for Nicholas Aston and the 'logic of contradictories'. Cf. 1669 note. That the issue was under contemporary debate is suggested by the notebook of Stephen Patrington O. Carm. where one entry concerns 'An pura negativa includat contradiccionem' (St. John's College Cambridge D.28 f. 33rb); see L. A. Kennedy, 'A Carmelite Fourteenth-century Theological Notebook', *Carmelus* 33/1 (1986), pp. 70–102 at p. 78. Patrington took part in the early opposition to Wyclif in 1381–2: see Emden *Oxford* iii.1435–6 for this and his later career.

3503 Matt. 13:7, 22.

3507 Matt. 13:25, 39.

3513–27 Augustine *Enar. in Ps.* 57:4, PL 36.678–9; there is a gap in the quotation at 3522 where Augustine quotes Luke 24:47. 3516–17 *seiyng þus . . . auctouris*: an added gloss; in 3517 *haþ betake* renders Lat. *tradidit*. There is another gap at 3524 where Augustine quotes Ps. 57:4. The passage has been paraphrased before at 453–9.

3525 Heb. 6:18.

3529–31 This passage is from *De natura et gratia*, PL 44.282 '[Maxime quoniam me,] in hujusmodi quorumlibet hominum scriptis liberum (quia solis canonicis debeo sine ulla recusatione consensum), [nihil movet quod de illius scriptis, cujus nomen non ibi inveni.]' The English author has used those words not enclosed in square brackets. The source reference was probably originally supplied in the margin, and was subsequently transferred to the text at the wrong point.

3531–5 Augustine *Enar. in Ps.* 85:13 (PL 37.1093), previously quoted at 3195–201. A short passage is omitted after the first sentence.

3534 Ps. 85:13.

3539–45 Augustine *De trinitate* 9.1 (PL 42.961); the detailed reference is not correct, though the discussion goes back to 8.8. The beginning of the quotation, whilst keeping the rhetorical construction, elaborates Augustine 'De credendis nulla infidelitate dubitemus, de intelligendis nulla temeritate affirmemus: in illis auctoritas tenenda est, in his veritas exquirenda . . . quoniam resistere non possumus certissimae fidei, et validissimae auctoritati scripturae dicentis, *Deus charitas est*.'

3544 1 John 4:16.

3548–58 Augustine *De trinitate* 15.27 (PL 42.1096). 3553–4 'raþur þan . . . feble' translates 'quam poscunt liquidissimam reddi sibi rationem quae ab humana mente tarda scilicet infirmaque non capitur'; *þat* 3553 is a relative referring back to *reson*; 3556–7 *þat þe same þing . . . feiþ*: 'ut quantum videri potest, videatur mente quod tenetur fide'; 3558 *warneþ*: *prohibeat*.

3559 1 Pet. 5:9.

3563–71 Augustine *De trinitate* 3.10, PL 42.882 and 885; *cleues rockis or skerris* (3565) is the author's own elaboration on Augustine's single word *abrupta*. The absolute phrase 3566–7 *þe sadnesse . . . ilefte*, 'nec relicto solidamento diuini eloquii', is particularly awkward since the translator has ill-advisedly moved it far from the clause introduced by *wherfro*. There is a substantial gap before the concluding material of 3569–71 (col. 885).

3569 Acts 6:5–8, 7:2–53.

3574–7 Augustine *De doctrina christiana* 2.42, PL 34.65 'Nam quidquid homo extra didicerit, si noxium est, ibi damnatur; so utile est, ibi inuenitur.'

3582 e.g. Jer. 28:2, 29:25 etc., Hag. 1:2.

3583 1 Cor. 11:23.

3584 Gal. 1:12.

3587 Mal. 1:11.

3588–91 Augustine Ep. 93, PL 33.331; the English author has supplied the subject. The epistle is indeed to Vincent, though modern numbering differs.

3598 *þe errouris of Origene*: see *ODCC*. Origen's doctrinal errors (not all of which can be found in his surviving works) related to the eternal nature of the world but the finite nature of God, and to the ultimate salvation of all creatures, even the devil.

3598–604 Jerome Ep. 84, PL 22.750, closely translated.

3605–32 In the expanded imitation of Jerome the writer seems to switch out of direct speech at 3626–31, though using some of Jerome's words. The author's claim in 3631 that not only the Lollards held dubious views on the eucharist fits with other assertions that obscurity on the subject was general (*EWS* E35/9, E47/68, *VO* 257, Arnold iii.503/17, Matthew 465/7).

3608 *Pope Nichol*: Nicholas II, pope at the time of Berengar's confession; see 1844–64 and note above.

3618 Rev. 20:7.

3621 Dan. 8:11, 11:31; see note to 1390.

3629 *a child nouʒ bore*: for the use of *nouʒ* see *MED nou* adv.3(a) example from *Legend of Cross* a.1500 (despite the spellings of the next line, Titus's use of *nouʒ* is paralleled frequently elsewhere).

3642–51 Augustine *De doctrina chris.* 4.21, PL 34.111, quoting Cyprian *Ad Donatum.* 3643 *know . . . tauʒt*: 'admonitos autem nos scias'. The emendation in 3645 is made to bring the translation into line with the Latin where *calix* is the subject of *offertur*. 3649–50 *mai not be seie . . . lackiþ*: 'nec potest videri sanguis eius . . . esse in calice, quando vinum desit'.

3647 John 15:1.

3655–6 In the orthography of Titus *seien* may be pl.pres.ind. of 'say', as in the first example here, or past participle of 'see' as in the second (3656).

3663–74 Augustine *De trinitate* 3.4, PL 42.873–4. 3668 *þe betokenyng sounnes* . . . *Poule*: 'significantes sonos lingua editos'. 3672 'is brouȝt to þe visible kinde' (is brought to that visible form) renders 'ad illam visibilem speciem perducatur'.

3680 *þo*: 'those things', that is 'þe brede and þe wyne' (3678).

3682–4 Legg p. 223—see note to 3785 and add here cf. Arnold iii.522/2 and its source 'in canone misse post consecracionem "Offerimus preclare magestati tue panem sanctum vite eterne et calicem salutis perpetue"', quoted in Arnold iii.521/25 and its Latin source, ed. I. H. Stein, 'The Latin Text of Wyclif's *Complaint*', *Speculum* 7 (1932), 87–94 at 94/7; cf. Legg p. 218 n. 8.

3688–94 Jerome Ep. 71, PL 22.672. 3690 'suppose . . . to be tauȝt and amonestid', translating Latin 'admonendum puto'; 3693–4 *not . . . maner*: 'nec aliorum consuetudinem, aliorum contrario more subverti'.

3699–703 Augustine Ep. 187, PL 33.839.

3702 1 Cor. 10:17.

3708–11 Augustine *Enar. in Ps.*3:1, PL 36.73; 'þe figure of his bodi and his blode' (3711) rendering Lat. 'corporis et sanguinis sui figuram'.

3711–21 Augustine *Enar. in Ps.* 98:5, PL 37.1265; in the original the elucidation given follows directly upon the quotation of John 6:63, as a continuation of Christ's speech.

3714 John 6:63.

3723–4 Augustine *De trinitate* 3.10, PL 42.880; the part used in the English comes from a longer sentence of which this is the conclusion 'ministerio transitura, sicut panis ad hoc factus in accipiendo sacramento consumitur'.

3726–9 Augustine Ep. 149, PL 33.644; *no man . . . God* (3728–9) 'sacramentum esse quod nos in agnitionem suam congregat, nullus debet ambigere'.

3730–5 Augustine Ep. 149, PL 33.636–7; in the Latin the sense is less obscure since the material is part of a longer argument. 3731–2 *whan . . . delid* 'cum . . . et ad distribuendum comminuitur', a section involving discussion of the Greek text is then omitted; *in þe wiche . . . brede* (3732–5) 'voventur autem omnia quae offeruntur Deo, maxime sancti altaris oblatio; quo sacramento praedicatur nostrum illud votum maximum, quo nos vovimus in Christo esse mansuros, utique in campage corporis Christi.' 3733–4 *to be mylde in Crist*: Lat. 'in Christo esse mansuros'. The future participle *mansuros* must be part of the verb *maneo* 'to remain'. Either the English translator has confused this with part of the verb *mansuesco* 'to make tame', or his medieval text of Augustine read not *mansuros* but *mansueturos*. In the passage as a whole, indeed, it seems that either the

English writer's text of Augustine differed from that in PL, or the English text is greatly corrupted.

3735 Augustine Ep. 185, PL 33.815.

3737–46 cf. PL 33.368.

3745 The marginal reference at the top of f. 97v *Epistola 33 ad Bonifacium* may relate to the quotation that begins 3736 or to that beginning 3737 since both were addressed to Boniface, though neither is recorded in any numeration as '33'.

3745 John 19:34.

3751–4 The text is *Compendium theologicae veritatis* vi.12 in the edition published under the name of Albertus Magnus, *Opera omnia* 34 (1895), p. 210 col. a. This work was usually attributed in the medieval period to Aquinas, occasionally to Albertus or to Bonaventura. It seems in fact to be the compilation of Hugh of Strasburg (see L. E. Boyle, *Pastoral Care, Clerical Education and Canon Law, 1200–1400* (London, 1981), no. 3 p. 246 and note 5). The work is brief and uncontroversial; almost the whole of it is quoted in the *Floretum* and it is frequently cited in other Lollard works.

3755 Aquinas, the supposed author of the *Compendium*, was the first to provide a philosophical explanation of transubstantiation, and was often credited with the composition of the office for Corpus Christi day though this has been questioned (see *ODCC Thomas Aquinas*). For Aquinas's part in the evolution of the office see P.-M. Gy, 'L'office du Corpus Christi et la théologie des accidents eucharistiques', *Revue scientifique de philosophie et théologie* 66 (1982), 81–6, and the same author's earlier article 'L'office du Corpus Christi et S. Thomas d'Aquin: État d'une recherche', ib.64 (1980), 491–507. The claim here is that, since the word *sacrament* (Lat. *sacramenti*) is used, the text must refer to the consecrated elements.

3763–5 It is not clear to which work of Bernard the author is referring: his sermon 'In cena Domini de baptismo, sacramento altaris et ablutione pedum', PL 183.271–4 seems nearest to the description here, but does not contain the statement attributed. The microfiche concordance to Bernard (Turnhout, 1987) further suggests that the attribution is not correct. Since the statement is such a commonplace, it seems fruitless to search for it elsewhere.

3769–72 Augustine Ep. 190, PL 33.862 'Sed ubi res naturaliter obscura nostrum modulum vincit, et aperta divina scriptura non subvenit, temere hinc aliquid definire humana conjectura praesumit.'

3774–80 *Compendium* (see above 3751) vi.12 (p. 210 col. b). The passage is abbreviated but its sense is not distorted. In fact *transubstanciacio* and its derivative verb are not used in the *Compendium*.

3785–818 See Aquinas, *Opuscula theologica*, ed. R. A. Verardo and R. M. Spiazzi (Turin and Rome, 2 vols., 1954), ii.273–81 'Officium de festo Corporis Christi', here Lectio 3 (p. 277). The wording of 3787–9 is 'Manducatur itaque a fidelibus, sed minime laceratur: quinimmo diviso sacramento integer sub qualibet divisionis particula perseverat. Accidentia autem sine subiecto in eodem subsistunt.' The lections are not included in either Legg or Dickinson, but appear in modern breviary editions.

3791 *relatif* (cf. 3798, 3800): *MED*'s definition '(a) *Gram*. A relative pronoun' will not fit here, though the sense is an extension of it. The point is that *same*, Lat. *eodem* refers back to a noun previously given; 'pronoun/adjective of reference' is nearer to the sense required (cf. *MED relatif* adj. (a) '*Gram*. referring to an antecedent').

3823 John 14:27.

3826–8 Jerome Ep. 108, PL 22.901; the person praised is not St. Paul but Paula, the mother of Eustochius to whom the letter is addressed.

3829–31 Augustine Ep. 164, PL 33.715 'Quamobrem teneamus firmissime, quod fides habet fundatissima auctoritate firmata.'

3832–7 Augustine *Enar. in Ps.* 30:13, PL 36.244; 3836–7 *neiþur . . . comaunde*: 'nec malum putavit quod jubere optimus potuit'.

3834 Gen. 22:1–19.

3845 Eph. 5:23, Col. 1:18.

3856 Matt. 25:41.

3862 Job 3:3, 10–12.

3866–8 The uselessness of prayers for the dead is stressed in many Lollard writings; see, for instance, *EWS* 237/8, iv.68–9, Matthew 8/12.

3874 Jer. 2:26.

GLOSSARY

The Glossary is a selective one, intended to provide a guide for readers accustomed to Chaucerian English. Line references prefixed with E refer to the sermon *Omnis plantacio*, with L to the Lambeth tract version of this, and with T to the *Tractatus de oblacione iugis sacrificii*. To avoid unnecessary repetition of line numbers, the text in Lambeth is only glossed when it is not replicated in E or when its spellings might give the reader difficulty. The actual forms found in E and T (and in L where given) are entered, not hypothetical uninflected forms. The commonest spelling in E is generally treated as the head word; variant spellings or forms that are not easily referable to a head word are entered in their alphabetical place with a cross reference. Tolerance of varying spellings in the usage of each scribe, together with the coverage here of three different scribes, makes simple presentation hard to achieve; brackets are used in head words to indicate letters not found in all instances, but the alphabetization includes or excludes these bracketted letters according to the common usage of the texts. Where the infinitive of a verb is found, other parts of the verb are only given in the case of strong verbs, or in weak verbs where any difficulty may arise; where the attested verbal forms do not include an infinitive, a full list of forms is included. Normal abbreviations for grammatical terms are used; (*see note*) after a line reference refers to comment in the notes.

Words are only glossed if their meaning departs from that of modern English, or if their form within the texts is likely to cause difficulties of recognition; thus, when one Middle English sense of a word here coincides with modern English, but another does not, only the second is regularly included here. Hence the material under each head word is not necessarily a full inventory of either paradigms or senses in the texts (e.g. a full repertory of the verb *be* is not given). Phrases likely to cause difficulty are entered under the word within them that departs from its normal sense.

Throughout *i/y* variation is included under *i*; ʒ follows *g*, þ follows *t* initially but is interpreted as *th* medially. The scribes normally use *v* initially, *u* medially for both the consonant and the vowel; in the glossary these are sorted into modern usage.

a *see* **haue**

a, *prep.* ~ *place* about E1617, T3602, T3623, forward T83, T457, T3522

abak, *adv. put* ~ put back T1014

abeggid, *adv. þei comen* ~ they come begging E2798

abei(ʒ)e, *v.inf.* submit T364, render obedience T352

abhorreþ, *3sg.pres.ind.* ~ *not from* is not alien to T3439

abiect, *adj.* wretched T2255, T3095

abite, *sb.* religious habit, garb E62, E71, E73 etc., habit, customary use E1510

ablynde(n, *v.* (**ablinded** *pa.p.*) blind, mislead E1056, E1207, E1884 etc.

abode, *v. pl.pa.sj.* remained T1573

abouʒt, *prep.* ~ *housis* from house to house (Vulg. Acts 2:46 *circa domos*) T2484

abouʒte, *adj. þei ben* ~ they are eager T2991

abowe, *v.inf.* be subject to T3211

abregynge, *ger.* curtailment L67

abstinatli, *adv.* obstinately T2151

abusio(u)n, *sb.* abuse E2741, T272, T3185

accept, *v.3sg.pa.ind.* accepted T1731

acomptiþ, *v.* accounts E2624

acord(e, *sb.* agreement T1671, T1699, T2555

acorde, *vb.* agree E647, E704, T156 etc., make agree T1668, agree with T2451, reconcile T2512, is suitable T3778; **acordid**, *pa.p.* in agreement E712; *acording(e wiþ* in agreement with E396, E2791, T583 etc., *according in* allied in T64

according(e, *adj.* ~ *to* in accordance with E681, T2275, T2493 etc., suitable for

E1809; ~ wiþ in accordance with E2260, ~ to in agreement with E3

acordingli, *adv.* ~ *to* in agreement with T237, T253, T432 etc.

acountis, *sb.pl.* explanations L1030

acumbren, *v.pl.pres.ind.* impede T3504

admitte, *v.* admit, approve E655

ado *sb. he haþ* ~ *wiþ* he has any dealings with E1934, *þei han not* ~ *wiþ* they have nothing to do with E2638

adullid, *v.pa.p.* made dull T667

afeerd, *adj.* afraid E307

afer, *adv.* far E2659

affeccioun, *sb.* ~ (*to*) sympathy (for) E1605, E2517, E2519 etc.

affect, *sb. in* ~ in effect, in actuality E1605

affectualli, *adv.* earnestly, zealously T1139

affermyng, *sb.* certainty T3322

afore, *adv.* previously T43, T1575, T1761

afore, *prep.* before T3758

aforehand, *adv.* previously T745

aftur, *adv.* afterwards T1999

aftur, *prep.* according to T3585, in accordance with E845, T1898, T2000 etc., behind T1089

aggregat, *pa.p.adj. perso(o)ne* ~ community E1942, E1978, T63 etc., ~ *person* collective person (ie pope?) T387 (*see note*), T474, T1022

aggreggide, *v.3sg.pa.ind.* make heavier, increase E1742

agrise, *v.* abhor T862, T1044, T1223 etc., hesitate T623

a3en, *adv.* again E182, E591, E1105 etc.

a3en, *prep.* in respect to T777, against E159

a3enrisen, *v.pa.p.* risen again T3254

a3enrising, *sb.* resurrection T3250

a3ens, *prep.* against E177, E324, E325 etc.

a3enseiers, *sb.pl.* deniers, opponents T3220

a3enward, *adv.* on the contrary T677, in the reverse order T1544

akursid, acursid, *pa.p.adj.* excommunicate, acursed T313, T314, T328 etc.

al, *adj.* ~ *Crist* the whole Christ T1468

al, alle, *adv.* entirely T688, T3749, T3780, ~ *most see* **almo(o)st**

al-amys, *sb.* disaster E2157 (*see note*), E2183, E2379

al-bisi, *adv.* even E146 (*see note*)

alegge, aleie, *v.* (**aleggid, aleide** *pa.p.*)

plead T288, adduce as proof E36, E317, E1960 etc.

alien, alion, *adj.* alien, aberrant, abhorrent E327, E332, E695 etc.

alien, *sb.* stranger, foreigner E1223, E1225, E3013 etc.

aliene, *v.* (**aliened** *pa.p.*) alienate, remove (property) E2418, E2436, E2444 etc., estrange E1226, E2999

al if, all 3if, *cj.* even if E1888, T413, T1826 etc.

alyue, *adj. suffren hem* ~ allow them to live E2251

almesse, *sb.* alms, charity E740, E1257, E1931 etc.

almesse-3yuyng, *sb.* almsgiving E2154, E2166

almy3tinesse, *sb.* omnipotence T3286, T3462

almo(o)st, alle most, *adv.* almost, nearly E1296, E2225, very nearly T2119

alowd, *adv. a lesyng* ~ blatantly a lie E644

alowe(n, *v.* permit, allow E2109, T2939, T2944 etc., **alowid** *pa.p.* authorized E1108, E1167

al so, *cj.* just as E1501, E1579

altogedur, *adv.* entirely T1110

amenusing, *sb.* reduction, impairment E843, T361, T1213 etc.

amenusiþ, *v.3sg.pres.ind.* (**amenusid,** *pa.p.*) decrease, impair E996, T1405, T3427 etc.

amyddis, *prep.* between T3133, T3134, T3140 etc.

amittiþ, *v.3sg.pres.ind.* (**amittid,** *pa.p.*) admit, authorise T329, T835

amonestiþ, *v.3sg.pres.ind.* (**amonestid,** *pa.p.*) urge, admonish T649, T3558, T3690

amortaisyng, amorteisyng, *sb.* alienation of property (in mortain) E1946, E2186, E2229 etc.

amorteise, *v.* alienate property and title in mortmain E541, E674, E2480

an, *num. seche* ~ such a one T3021

anathena, *sb.* ~ *þat is to mene diuided from God* anathema, cast out from God T435 (*not MED*)

anaunter, *cj.* lest perchance T2094

anauntir, *adv.* peradventure, perhaps T433

and, *cj.* if E196, E277, E350 etc.

and so, *adv.* in the same way E207

anempst, anentis, *prep.* concerning
T3351, T3410, T3622, *as* ~ as concerning T1203, T1216, T2826 etc., in regard
to L1022

anett, *sb.* dill E1243

an(n)exid, *v.pa.p.* ~ *to* attached to E799,
E1362, T100 etc.

a(w)nswere, *v.* correspond to E22, E2172,
E2175 etc., correspond E3, E42

antecrist, anticrist, *sb.* opponent, or
antithesis, of Christ E1226, E1656,
E1917 etc.

anullid, *v.pa.p.* annihilated T3685

apaid(e, apai(e)d, *pa.p.adj.* satisfied E773,
E795, E911 etc.

apairing, apeiring, *sb.* impairment, harm
E842, T354, T356, diminution T2990,
~ *of* impairment to E2085

apoiseneþ, *v.3sg.pres.ind.* poisons, cor-
rupts T1336

apon, *prep.* upon, on T436

apostasie, *sb.* abandonment of faith E684,
E1172, E1497 etc., abandonment of holy
orders without dispensation E2659,
E2868

apostata, *sb.* (apostatas *pl.*) apostate
E689, E1510, T770 etc.

apostilhede, *sb.* the office of an apostle
L659

apostlich, *adj,* evangelical, following the
example of the apostles T1582

applie, *v.* ~ . . . *to* compare . . . with
E196, relate to T1618

ap(p)reued, *v.pa.p.* approved E2064,
E2068, E2155 etc.

ap(p)ropre, *v.* set aside, assign E4, E21,
E41 etc., appropriate E542, seize E674

ap(p)ropriacioun, *sb.* annexation of
endowment E2192, E2222, E2231 etc.

arai, *sb.* estate, rank E1720, display E2314

araye, *v. with refl.* prepare self, furnish self
T571, T642, T3145

arayment, *sb.* equipment, gear T1171

arere, *v.* raise up, exalt E2287, T664,
T2395

areson, *v.* rebuke E2835, T3605

argument, *sb.* piece of evidence T3286

armurys, *sb.pl.* war equipment T3165

arten, *v.* induce E1180, T1811, force,
compell T1585, T1655, T2928

articling, *v.pres.pa.* specifying T1741

artyng, *sb.* force E981

as, *adv.* ~ *for* during E2521, E2728,
E2729 etc., ~ *for* as representing E2640

as, *cj.* as if T115, T1104, T1425 etc.

as, *prep.* in accordance with T3236

asaied, *v.pa.p.* investigated E1288

ascape, *v.* escape, evade responsibility
E305, escape T390, escape notice T585

aschame, *v.* feel shame about T484, do
shame to T486

aseeþ, *sb.* satisfaction, atonement T436

asent, *v.inf.* ~ *wiþ* agree with T518

as(s)igne, *v.* specify E2160, E3042, T54
etc.

aske, *sb.* ask T2228

aske, *v.* require E231, E2630, T628 etc.,
demand, call for T1589 (*see note*)

as(s)oile, *v.* refute E2143, settle T333

asoiling, *ger.* absolution T2440, T2443

aspi(3)e, *v.* discern E2563, T53

assent, *sb. of his* ~ in collusion with him
T2446

assenten, *v.pl.pres.ind.* agree to E288

astaat, *sb.* position E702, E2077, office L413

astonyed, *pa.p.adj.* astonished T2458

at, *prep.* in, with E167, E2112, E2825, to
E522, by E2320, from T2987, in comparison with T3173, with T3451

atenyd, *pa.p.adj.* annoyed, vexed T934

atteyne, *v.pl.pres.sj.* attain, reach E2538

atwynne, *adv.* apart E2892, E2894, E2906

aþrist, *pa.p.adj.* ~ *aftur* thirsty for T1297

au3t see owen

auncetr(er)is, *sb.pl.* ancestors E2188,
E3075, L839

autentik(e, *adj.* authoritative E1112,
E2814, T2602 etc., legally binding
E280, E654, T842 etc., ~ *eretik* certain
heretic T3369

au(3)ter, *sb.* altar E261, E1198, T500 etc.,
haþ an ~ has a cure E2837 (*see note*)

au(c)torisen, *v.* give authority to E1180,
E2448 etc.

autorite, *sb.* justification E145

auaile, *v.* be effective T3306

avarous, *adj.* avaricious E736, E746, E747

avenge, *v.inf.* champion L411

avisid, *v.pa.p.* advised E1636, *I am/be
(not)* ~ I (do not) know T465, T2325,
and I be wel ~ if I am well informed
T730, T2322, T2606

avisement, *sb.* due consideration E988,
T585

avoide, *v.* avoid E1685, T649, reject E785,

E1362, E1369 etc. deny T2613, cast out T3110

avoiding, *ger.* rejection E939, E994, avoidance T728

auouȝeþ *see* **avowe**

avouȝyng, *sb.* avowal T2840

avouȝtrer, *sb.* adulterer T943

auouȝtresse, *sb.* adulteress T955, T959, T983 etc.

auouȝtrousli, *adv.* adulterously, immorally T942

auou(ȝ)tri(ȝ)e, *sb.* adultery, hence moral adultery E324, E3074, T492 etc.

avourie, *sb.* protector E610

avow, *sb.* vow E2254, E2256, E2259 etc.

avowe, *v.* pledge with a vow E109, E659, ~ *hem* make a vow for themselves E605, ~ *vs* dedicate ourselves T3733; *auouȝeþ v.3sg.pres.ind.* ~ *him . . . upon* bases his declaration . . . upon T3756

avowing, *sb.* vow of E997

awacched, *v.pa.p.* awoken, aroused T3149

awaite, *sb. lieþ . . . in* ~ takes care that T950, *liþe in* ~ lies in ambush T3229

awaiting, *v.pres.p.* watching, waiting T971

aweiward, *adv.* in the opposite direction T760

ax, *sb.* axe E3005, E3028

ax(e, *v.* demand L380, L386 etc.

bade, *v.3sg. and pl.pa.ind.,* **boden, bodyn** *pa.p.* ordered, commanded E110, E808, E892 etc.

baily, *sb.* king's officer in town, county or hundred E206, L984, L985

barony, baronrye, *sb.* domain as a *baroun* E1945, L697

bastard, *adj.* illegitimate E354, worthless E357, E372, E374 etc.

be- *see also* **bi-**

be, bi, *prep.* according to E1943, in T1348, through L662, L1033

be, *v.inf. to* ~ *tauȝt* ought to be taught (*Lat. admonendum*) T3690, *what schal* ~ what shall happen L380; *imper.pl.* ~ *ȝe no sectis* do not form sects E172; *pa.p.* been E833, E958, E1436; **art** *2sg.pres.ind.* ~ *wo* are grieved E1636; **ben** *pl.pres.ind.* ~ *of* belong to E226, *þei it* ~ those are the ones E473; **is** *3sg.pres.ind. it* ~ *not of* it does not befit T2855; **bi** *3sg.pres.sj.* be ~ *. . . ihold* let . . . be held T3346; **nar, ner(e.** *3sg. and pl.pa.sj.*

were (it) not (that) E1532, E2466, E2808 etc.; **was, were** *as auxiliary of past tense (and pa.p of motion)* had E1278, **be(n,** *pa.p.* E84, E85, E191 etc.

becometh, *3sg.pres.ind. it* ~ it is fitting to T2672

bedel, *sb.* town crier E566

bedotid, bidotid *pa.p.adj.* besotted E1056, T1285

beest, *adj.superl.* best T2909, T3126

be(e)stli, *adj.* brutish, sensual E2291, E2565, T2667 etc.

beestli, *v.inf.* ~ *hemself* wallow, make themselves brutish E2284(*not MED*)

beggerie, begrie, *sb.* mendicancy (esp.that of friars) E707, E716, E770 etc.

begynnyng, *adj.* ~ *chirche* early church T2574

behest(e *see* **biheest(e**

behofful, *adj.* necessary T343

behold(e, *v.* behold T2252, T3046, T3834 etc.; **behold** *pa.p.* ~ *himself* consider himself T3173

behote, *v.* (**bihotinge** *pres.p.,* **behiȝte** *pa.ind.,* **behiȝt, behote** *pa.p.*) promise E944, E945, E2658 etc.

beleuing, *sb.* belief T2182

bemeneþ, *v.3sg.pres.ind.* symbolises T1231

benefice, *sb.* beneficence T612

bere, *v.inf.* maintain T1785; **beren** *pl.pres.ind.* ~ *. . . on hand* accuse E2748; **berynge** *pres.p.* maintaining L973; **(i)bore** *pa.p.* born E106, T1766, T1767 etc.

bereschrewe, *sb.* devilish beast T117 (*see note*), T389, T1038 (*not MED*)

bereue, bireue, *v.* deprive E2227, E2228, T1552 etc.

beried *see* **biried**

berke, *v.* bark, i.e. speak T3263

besi(ȝ)e, *adj.* busy, engaged T1078, T1351, careful T892, earnest T1136, ~ *sacrifice, as translation of* Dan. 8:11–12 *iuge sacrificium* continual sacrifice T1396, T1397, T1426 etc.

besie, *v.inf.* (**besieþ, besiiþ** *3sg.pres.ind.,* **besien** *pl.pres.ind.,* **besiid** *3sg.pa.ind.,* **besied(den** *pl.pa.ind.*) *often with refl.* concern self, be anxious about T134, T444, T1467 etc., be active T131, exert (themselves) E1950

besili, *adv.* eagerly T2474, carefully T282

besines, *sb. do her* ~ exert themselves
T2766; besynesses *pl.* concerns T1358
betake, *v.inf.* (betoke *pa.ind.*, bytaken
pa.p.) entrust E848, T431, T501 etc.,
commit T1884, T3299, ~ *hemsilf*
devote themselves E2880
beþenk(e, biþenke, *v.* (biþouȝte
3sg.pa.ind. and *pa.p.*) recollect, consider
(*often with refl.*) E1271, T1493, T1536
etc., comprehend T2203
betidde, bitidde, *v.pa.ind.* (betid *pa.p.*)
occurred E1703, T2432, befell T2977
betoken, bitokene, *v.* signify T1427,
T1438, T1674, symbolise, represent
E1592, E1593, E2634 etc., ~ . . . *to*
equate . . . to T1929
betokenyng, *adj.* symbolic T3668
bi- *see also* be-
bie(n, *v.* (bouȝte *3sg.pa.ind.*) buy, redeem
E193, E292, E296 etc.
biers, *sb.pl.* buyers E2546
bifinddinggis, *sb.pl.* inventions, devices
T964
bigile, *v.* ~ *hem* trick them E258, ~ *of
him* trick by him E2844
bihalf, *sb. on Goddis* ~ in God's name
E2782
biheest(e, *sb.* pledge, promise E470,
E2434, T2295
biiogelen, *v.pl.pres.ind.* bind with spells
T1746 (*not MED*)
bilde, *v.* (bilde(d) *pa.p.*) construct, found
T1924, T1927, T1937 etc.
bilding, *sb.* building E2286, T1979, T1982
etc., edifice, foundation T645, moral
edification T1962
bile(e)ue, *sb.* faith E263, E264, E266 etc.,
article of the faith T550
bilie, *v.* slander 190, E2698, E2713
bilongiþ, *v.3sg.pres.ind.*, bilongen *pl.pres.
ind.*, bilongide *pl.pa.ind.* pertain, belong
properly E14, E16, E18 etc.
bynde(n, *v.* (boond *3sg.pa.ind*, bounden
pl.pa.ind., boundun, ybonden *pa.p.*)
bind, oblige E294, E1247, E2254 etc.,
put under obligation E935
bynd(d)ing, *sb.* condemnation (i.e.refusal
to give absolution) T2408, T2441,
T2444
bipaþis, *sb.pl.* side tracks T3354
birewid, *v.pa.p.* regretted E1286
biried, beried, *v.pa.p.* buried E731,
T3481

biside, bysidis, *prep.* over and above
E586, L55
bisili, *adv.* eagerly E169, E1192
bissynes, *sb.* exertion, activity L653, attention L369; *pl.* affairs L366
bitwix, *prep.* between L361
biwope, *v.pa.p.* lamented E1286
blaberiþ, *v.3sg.pres.ind.*, blabren *pl.pres.
ind.*, blaberide *pl.pa.ind.* babble, talk
foolishly E609, E1515, E2917 etc.
blame, *v.* condemn, blame E614, E1312,
E1401 etc., *is to* ~ is to be condemned
T263
blasphemes, *sb.pl.* blasphemers E1904
blasten, *v.pl.pa.ind.* ~ *out* exhale violently
(like a dragon) E446, E568
bleren, *v.pl.pres.ind.* delude E258
boden, bodyn *see* bade
bolden, *v.pl.pres.ind.* encourage T1449
boond, *sb.* obligation, legal constraint
E894, E897, E937 etc.
boone, *sb.* prayer E2320
bord(e, *sb.* table E1191, E1196, E1808 etc.
bost, *sb.* boast T1582, T1583
bostiþ, *v.3sg.pres.ind.* (bosten *pl.pres.ind.*)
boasts T1570, T3515
boþe, *adj. of þer* ~ *astaat* of the position of
both of them E702, *of her* ~ *sectis* of
both their sects E704, *his* ~ *kinddis* both
his natures T2344
boþe, *adv.* also E695
botiler, *sb.* butler E2691
bouȝte *see* bie(n
boundun *see* bynde(n
bowe, *v.* (bowedden *pl.pa.ind.*) turn, bend
E366, T2244, T3323, twist T1629
brede, *sb.* breadth T2018
brake(n, *v.3sg.and pl.pa.ind. and sj.*
(breken *pl.pa.ind*, i)broke *pa.p.*) broke
E451, T1154, T1707 etc.
bren(n)e, *v.* burn T212, T327, T1295 etc.
brennynggis, *ger.pl.* burnings T2113
bribours, *sb.pl.* bribers E2547
briddis, *sb.pl.* birds E2145, E2498
bringging, *v.pres.p.* carrying T3878
brisid, *v.pa.p.* broken, bruised T2368
brond(d)e, *sb.* piece of firewood T3300,
T3866
brouȝt, *v.pa.p.* ~ introduced E962, *is* ~
to (Lat. *perducatur*) brought to T3672
buysh, *sb.* bunch, wisp (of brambles) E76
buysshels, *sb.pl.* bushels E204

burio(u)n, *sb.* fruit T2738, T2741, product T2740

but, *adv.* only E2237, ~ *onli* only T1896

but, *prep.* except T532, L971

but if, *cj.* unless E306, T248, T255 etc.

ca(a)s, case, *sb.* situation E1104, E1233, E1703 etc., *in* ~ *þat* in a situation such that E1106, E1753, E1782

calot, calat, *sb.* harlot T905, T959, T1042 etc.

canoun, *adj.* canonical T3242

canoun, *sb.* canon law T3147

careful, *adj.* unfortunate T3862

careyns, *sb.pl.* corpses E1578

cartis, *sb.pl.* (Lat. *chartae*) papers T3521

cast, *v.imper.sg.* put T2051; **casting** *pres.p.* caring about T1369

casuel, *sb.* word with grammatical case T2884 (*see note*)

catel, *sb.* goods, wealth T1140

ce(e)sse, *v.* turn away E368, E2356, T141 etc., stop E1026, E2368, T2443 etc., come to an end E1560, E2727, E3078 etc.

ce(e)ssyng, *ger.* ceasing E1286, cessation T3037

censuris, *sb.pl.* condemnations by the church T138, T262, T956

certein, *adj.as sb. for/in/of* ~ as a matter of certainty E2484, T1751, T1753 etc.

certified, *v.pa.p.* reported officially E594

certein, *adv.* indeed E535, E1751, E2026

certis, *adv.* indeed E196

cete, citee, *sb.* city T1192, T3202

chalenge, *v.* claim E603, claim as a right E1347, E1350, accuse E1447

chaliss, *sb.pl.* chalices E2487

chanoun, *sb.* canon (i.e. Augustinian or Premonstratensian canon) E167, E417, E540 etc.

charge, *sb.* care, solicitude E1246, E2074, burden E106, importance T2814, T3388, T3391, weight (Lat.*pondus*) T3387; pl. responsibilities L1036

charge, *v.* (**charchid** *pa.p.*) command E793, E810, E818 etc., impose as a duty E2762, burden E103, value T3509, ~ *moche* consider of great importance E1243, E2761, *more to* ~ to be valued more highly E1245, ~ *wiþ* entrust with L970

chargeouse, chargiouse, *adj.* burdensome E100, E148

charging *sb.* valuing T181

charite, *sb.* grace T3432

chaunserie, *sb.* chancery E1185

cheer, *sb.* welcome E2804

chef *see* **chif(f**

chef, *sb.* head T3574

chefli *see* **chif(f)li**

chekmate, *adv. euyn* ~ *wiþ him* exactly equal with him T1101

chese, *v.* (**chees, chese(n** *pa.ind. and sj.*) choose E840, E1803, T263 etc., adopt E690, E792, E2656 etc.

chesing, *ger.* choice T1318

cheuysshaunce, chefesaunce, *sb.* profit E1889, L638

chif(f, che(e)f, *adj.* main, most important T70, T1004, T1404 etc.

chif(f)li, che(e)fli, *adv.* especially, particularly T48, T118, T1725 etc., primarily T566, T581, T797 etc.

chynche, *sb.* niggard E732, E736, E745

choise, *sb. put in* ~ confront with an alternative T463

citecines, *sb.pl.* inhabitants T3202

ciuile, *adj.as sb.* civil law T3146

ciuilite, *sb.* civil power, E1952, E1992, E1997, civil position E1958

clarge, *sb.* clergy T272

clatring, *sb.* idle noise T3615

clees, *sb.pl.* claws T2370

cleyme, *v.inf.* ~ *hem* claim for themselves E1843

clene, *adj.* free from T2438

clepe, *v.inf.* call E2613, L980

clerenes, *sb. of* ~ in openness of moral purity (*Vulg. in manifestatione veritatis,* cf WB 1 Cor.5:8 *of clernesse: sinceritatis*) T498

clergeis, clergies, *sb.pl.* learned men T3133, T3134, T3141 etc.

clerke, *sb.* priest L176

cleue, *v.* remain faithful T462, T476

cleues, *sb.pl.* cliffs T3565

clippen, *v.pl.pres.ind.* ~ *to hem* embrace E762

close *sb.* see **glose**

close, *v.* shut up E1262, T1158, obstruct by fortification E1610, ~ *hem togedre* bring them together T398

cloþid, *v.pa.p.* ~ *wiþ* supported by E1883

cloutid, *v.pa.p.* patched (with derogatory sense) E407

cockil, *sb.* cockle (trans. Vulg. *zizania*, prob. darnel) E346

coyn, *sb.* design on coin E2712

colege, colage, *sb.* fellowship E890, E893; *pl.* resident body of ecclesiastics, esp.-chapter of a cathedral E1947, E1996, E2003 etc.

coligiens, *sb.pl.* members of endowed religious body E895

colour, kolour, *sb.* reason, justification (often derogatory, implying specious) E146, E147, E685 etc., pretence E431, E1255, E2432, T1611 etc.

colourable, *adj.* plausible E213

coloure, *v.* disguise, misrepresent E433, E683, E1089 etc.

comaundingis, *sb.pl.* commandments E1677

comen, *v.pl.pa.ind.* came E895

comente *see* comounte

comyn, *sb.* cumin E1244

comyn, com(m)oun(n)e, comen, *v.* communicate, converse T1208, T2474, T2497, partake T1515, share T606, T621, disseminate T1989, give communion T2488, have sexual intercourse T3007

commynyng, com(m)(o)un(n)yng, *ger.* conversation E218, E694, participation T590, T591, T2486 etc., sharing E2010, E2031, 2039, ~ (. . .) *to* sharing with E2013

comoun, *adj.* common, shared E64, E218, E230 etc.; ~ *peple* ordinary folk E499, E2233

comoun, *adj.as sb. in* ~ in shared ownership E1922, E1924, E1999 etc., together E1976, E1979

comunes, *sb.pl.* common people E2207

comounli, *adv.* often, usually E336, E1522, T462

com(o)unte(e, comente, comynte, *sb.* community E42, E2012, E2013 etc., *in* ~ as a community, group E1942, E1980

compar(i)so(u)n, *sb.* comparison T980, *in* ~ *of* in comparison with T612, T2906

compar(r)(i)so(u)ne, *v.* compare T782, T1034, T1035 etc.

compe(e)r(i)s, *sb.pl.* companions E1141, mates (derogatory) T203, T293, T404 etc.

complaynyng, *v.pres.pa.* ~ *hem* making their complaint T3227

comprehende, *v.* grasp (Lat. *comprehendere*) T3328

comuners, *sb.pl.* commoners, ordinary lay folk E440

conceyue, conseyue, *v.* perceive E1182, E1813, imagine T1384; conceiued *pa.p.* derived T3243

concurraunt, *adj.* ~ *wiþ* existing alongside E3059

condempnyng, *ger.* forfeiture (Vulg. *condempnationem*) E989

condicionalli, *adv.* as part of a conditional clause T1055 (*see note*)

condicions, *sb.pl.* attributes T688, characteristics T3595

confederacie, *sb.* conspiratory band, gang E1199, E1261, E1265 etc.

conferme, *v.* conform (to) T622 (*see note*), T1070, T2587 etc., make fast T3830

confermyng, *ger.* confirmation T2092

confortiþ, *v.3sg.pres.ind.* strengthens T1318

confoundid *v.pa.p.* ruined E1280

congruli, *adv.* appropriately T2706, T3793

coniect(e, *v.* deduce T1807, T2404

coniecting, *ger.* surmise T3360, T3771

conquere, *v.inf.* win E1386, ~ *to him* win for himself E1318

consail, *sb.* plan T2202, opinion T3688

conseil, *sb.* council T3609

conseit(e, *sb.* opinion T581, T3109

consentyng, *ger.* acquiescence E247, agreement T3530

consideracio(u)n, *sb.* consideration T2254, T2260, T2577, *haue* ~ take thought T1804

constitucio(u)n, *sb.* decree (of church) E1160, E1179, E1182 etc.

conteneþ, *v.3sg.pres.ind.* contains T705

contradictorie, *sb.* opposite T402, *bi his* ~ by its opposite i.e.to a sense opposite to that intended T209, T3612 (*not MED*)

contradictorie, *adj.* opposite T399, T1668, T1671 etc. (*not MED*)

contrarie, *adj.* discordant E149, E184, E623 etc., opposite E512, E1563, E3034 etc., opposed E1077, E1566, E2039 etc., contradictory E937 contrarie, *sb.* opposite E257, E452, E631 etc.

contrarie, *v.* oppose T122, T226, T267 etc., acts contrary to T224, conflict with T1217, T2452

contrariyng, *ger.* contradiction T239, T1669, opposition T1213

contrari(o)us(e, *adj.* hostile E79, E767, T21 etc., contradictory E700, E1819, T79 etc.; ∼ *to* contrary to E1320, E1916, E1918 etc., rebellious against E1912, T119, T144, T771, at variance with E240, E445, T939

contrariousing, *ger.* ∼ *of* opposition to T8 (*not MED*)

contrariousli, *adv.* differently, in opposing fashions E706, L197

contrari(o)uste, *sb.* hostility, contradiction T140, T184

contrarite, *sb.* opposite T187

conuenticlis, *sb.pl.* secret gatherings E897, E1256

conuicte, *v.* prove T2583

conuyct(id, *pa.p.adj.* convicted, found guilty of T1004, T1012, T1029

corbanan, *sb.* treasury E1251 (*see note*)

corbona, *sb.* a gift (*see* Mark 7:11) T1652

corne, *sb.* grain of wheat T600, T1493, T1533, *whete* ∼ wheat grain T1510, ∼ *of grapis* fruit in bunch of grapes T1536

cornys, *sb.pl.* horns T399

corrupt, *pa.p.adj.* corrupted E796, E1564, T724 etc.

corruptible, *adj.* corrupt, fallible T3336, T3338

costis, *sb.pl.* expenses E1889, T1173

costlew, *adj.* expensive E2286

coueite(n, *v.pl.pres.ind.* wish T650, T3308

cou(3)de see kan

countenaunce, *sb.* appearance T2382

counteruailen, *v.pl.pres.ind.* are as profitable as E2477

coupable, *adj.* blameworthy L1022

cours, *sb. after þe* ∼ *of þe world* through the succession of history T99

couenable, *adj.* reasonable T2277

couent, *sb.* convent (of monks, nuns etc.), group of monks, nuns etc. E1947, E1974, E1976 etc.

couetice, couetise, *sb.* avarice E107, E195, T1133, *pl.* covetous desires T3228

craft *sb.* skill T2214

crafti, *adj.* skilful T3336, ∼ *of* clever with T3351

credens, *sb. bi* ∼ through belief T550

crimous, *adj.* sinful T2140 (*see note*)

crist-ward, *adv. from* ∼ away from Christ T760

cropun, *v.pa.p.* crept E1210, E2548

crownys, *sb.pl. schauyng of* ∼ shaving of heads in clerical tonsure T199

culuur, *sb.* dove T3167, T3168, T3169

cumpase, *sb. in* ∼ (Lat. *in circuitu*) in a circle T2199

curat, *sb.* priest E2205, E2231, E2630 etc., parish priest T372

curious, *adj.* ingenious (derogatory) E2285, E2286, sophisticated (derogatory) T1350

curs, *sb.* cursing T365

cursid, cursed, *pa.p.adj.* cursed E375, E697, E1134 etc., dampnable E2030, E2540, T1641, dampned E2790, E3076

cursyng, *sb.* cursing E1026, excommunication T953

custumable, *adj.* habitual E723, E2659, E2661 etc.

custumabli, *adv.* habitually E470, E675

dampne, *v.* condemn E61, E63, E1777 etc.

dampned, *pa.p.adj.* condemned, damned E737, E1772, E1772 etc.

damp(n)yng, *ger.* condemnation E714, E1801

dar, *v.1 and 3sg. and pl.pres.ind.*, darst *2sg.pres.ind.*, durst(e, dirst *sg. and pl.pa.ind.* dare E269, E846, E849 etc.

daren, *v.pl.pres.ind.* lurk E2553

debate, *sb.* disagreement T3137

declare. *v.* clarify T3707

declaring, *ger.* exposition E696, clarification, explanation T22

decre, *sb.* law T312, T847, T2320, decision E1190, E1623, *pl.* papal legal code T1354, T1845

dede, *sb.* fact E2250, *in* ∼ in action E1250

deed, *adj.* dead E542

de(e)dli, *adj.* mortal E1034, E1589, T888 etc., mortal, human T1126, T1998

de(e)dli, *adv.* grievously E1485, heinously E2270, mortally E3037, T878

defamed, *pa.p.adj.* accused E442, T1846

defau(3)te, defawt, *sb.* lack T1134, T2994, mistake E2948, L127

defendeþ, *v.3.sg.pres.ind.*, **defending**
pres.p. forbid T1688, T3384

defensoure, *sb.* defender L1015 (*see note*)

defilid, *pa.p.adj.* defiled T724

defoilid, *v.pa.p.* broken to pieces T658

defoulid, *pa.p.adj.* polluted E243, T666,
T2237 etc.

deinte, *adj.* fine T3217

dele, *sb.* *no* ~ not at all E2642, T1583,
T1716

dele, *v.* divide, share E538, E2101, E2480
etc., give E2073, decide T2333, ~ *wiþ*
have to do with E2037

delitable, *adj.* pleasing E435

delyuere, deliuur, *v.* hand over E1104,
E2459, E2467 etc., release E1462, T2754

de(e)me, *v.* (**dempten** *3pl.pa.ind.*) consider, judge E1352, E1355, E1406 etc.,
decide E525, T1003, argue T3271,
T3275; *not demyng* not perceiving T578
(*see note*)

departe, *v.* divide E922, T871, T921 etc.,
separate E126, T1052, T2652 etc., ~
into set aside for E911

departer, *sb.* divider E1369, T923

departing, *ger.* break up T18

depraued *v.pa.p.* disparaged E2959, T167

deprauing, *ger.* condemnation T3416

dere, *adj.* good T1255

derk, *adj.* obscure T3770

derkli, *adv.* secretly, obscurely E276,
E3091, E3093 etc.

derling, *sb.* favourite T2521

desert, *sb.* *bi þe* ~ *of* as a deserved result
of (Lat. *merito*) T2816

desired, *pa.p.adj.* coveted T1611 (*see note*)

desireful, *adj.* ~ *to* desiring of, anxious
for T2893

determene, *v.* declare, decree T300,
T305, T466 etc.

determenouris, -ynouris, *sb.pl.* arguers
T1865 (*see note*), T1879

deuelich, deuyllisch, *adj.* fiendish T379,
T2749, T3039

deuȝli, *adv.* properly T1655

deuyse, *v.* ~ *me* conceive E1319

deuocions, *sb.pl.* gifts T1282 (*see note*)

deuors, *sb.* divorce T908, T936, T1293
etc.

deuour, *sb.* *do his* ~ exert himself T2148

dicte, *sb.* saying (title given to writings of
Grosseteste, in subject similar to ser-

mons but with shorter exposition)
E2051, T1344

differentiþ, *v.3sg.pres.ind.* differ T2348
(*not MED*)

diffine, *v.* define T2728, T3772

dynyed, *v.pa.p.* denied E611

dirst *see* dar

disceyueable, *adj.* deceptive T244

disceiueþ, *v.3sg.pres.ind.* undermines
T1979

disclaundrousli, *adv.* shamefully T937
(*not MED*)

discording, *v.pres.p.* disagreeing T3204

discrasiþ, *v.3sg.pres.ind.*, **discrasid**, *pa.p.*
undermine, corrupt T1982, T1983

discryue, *v.* describe E322, T2727

disese, *sb.* affliction T1142

disesid, *v.3sg.pa.ind.* harmed T991

dispence, dispense, *v.* ~ *wiþ* release
from E885, E894, E2281

dispice, *v.* *it is . . . not to* ~ it is not to be
despised T3160

disposid, *v.pa.p.* inclined T693

disposinge, *ger.* distribution E1354

dispreue, *v.* disprove E244, E709, disallow
E2777

disputicio(u)n, *sb.* debate T668, T3268,
T3343 etc.

disputing, *v.pres.p.* debating T3373

dissolue, *v.* annul E2723, E2724, destroy
T2370

distinccioun, *sb.* discrimination E1000

distraccioun, *sb.* diversion (of possessions)
E2084 (*see note*)

distr(e)ie, *v.* destroy, eradicate E884,
E1168, E1173 etc.

disturbliþ, *v.3sg.pres.ind.* troubles T1081

dyuers, *adj.* various E64, L409

dyuerse, *v.* deviate E63, change E126

diuinite, *sb.* theology T843

do, done, *v.inf.* act E19, put E1639, E1640,
cause E181, E1303, perform E1175, ~
aweie abolish T3118, T3515, *it is to* ~ *to*
one should make an effort to T386; do
1sg.pres.ind. ~ *þe to wite* I make known to
you T2914; do *imp.sg.* perform T1192;
doiþ *imp.pl.* ~ *þe weie* get yourselves
away E366; doyng *pres.p.* ~ *þankinggis*
giving thanks T506; dide *3sg.pa.ind.* ~
us to vndirstonde made us understand
E1337; y)do(n *pa.p* put T313, T932,
done T545, T3204, finished E2939

doctour, *sb.* teacher E268, E699, E2623

etc., ~ *sentencis* statements of (post-scriptural) teachers T2583

doctrine, *sb.* instruction L53

doing, *ger.* action E398

dome, doom, *sb.* judgment E1405, T20, T34 etc., last judgment E1158; *þe last* ~ last judgment T2129, T3272; *dai of* ~, *domys dai* day of judgment T17, T28, T478 etc.

domesman, *sb.* judge T3872

doublenesse, *sb.* duplicity E1579, E2037, T2563

douȝble, *adj,* deceitful T3782

douȝte, *v.pl.pres.sj.* ~ . . . *of* have doubts about T3540; douȝtid *pa.p mai not be* ~ *to be vncertein* cannot be thought to be uncertain T3345

douȝteful, *adj.* ~ . . . *in* uncertain about T820

dowyng, *sb.* endowment E1790

dragonnesse, *sb.pl.* dragons (Vulg. *draconum*) T1342

drasti, *adj.* ignorant, worthless E2537, T256; ~ *wyne* unpurified wine T1324, T1327

drastis, *sb.pl.* dregs T1329

drawe, *v.* (drowe(n *sg. and pl.pa.ind.*, drawe, y)drawun *pa.p.*) approach E946, T1981, tear E55, E59, E413 etc., draw E1311, T1862, taken away from E3054; ~ *into* came into (a state of) E1012

drede, dreed, *sb.* hesitation E563, *no* ~ (there is) no doubt (that) T1651

drede, *v.* (*often with refl.*) fear E321, T2310, T2426, *it is to* ~ it is to be feared T1622, *I* ~ *me not* I do not doubt E1345, T3594

dreedles, dredeles, *adv.* without doubt E1212, E1495

dreint, *v.pa.p.* drowned, overwhelmed T708

dritti, *adj.* filthy, worthless E759, E2439

drunklewe, *adj.* drunken T1219

drunk(e)schip, drunkunschip, *sb.* intoxication T1163, T1175, T1177 etc.

dul, *adj.* stupid T3249

duli, *adv.* properly E1187

dure, *v.* continue E1485, T2094, T2483

durste *see* dar

dute, *sb.* duty E237

echiþ, *v.3sg.pres.ind.* enlarges T1578

eching, *ger.* enlarging T1571

eende, *sb.* culmination E371, E391

eerlis, *sb.pl.* earls E2081

effeccioun, *sb.* intention T2982

effect, *sb. in* ~ in fact, in reality E2594, E2913, E2962 etc.

effectual(l)i, *adv.* effectively, properly E277, E1267, E1651 etc., satisfactorily E1025, E1494, E2051 etc., actually, in reality E2646, E2648, T1246 etc.

effectif, *adj.* effective T1577

effectual, effectuel, *adj.* efficacious E2345, T241

effectueli, *adv.* completely, sincerely E277, E1025, E1651 etc.

effectuousli, *adv.* sincerely T316, T2755

eft(e, *adv,* again T1491, T1800

eftesonys, *adv.* again T1772

egge, *sb.* blade E3029

eggetole, *sb.* tool with cutting edge T658

eire, *sb.* air T2626, sky L391

eiþur, *adj. euer* ~ both T3136

eke, *adv.* also E801

eldest, *superl.adj.* oldest T2589

eleccioun, *sb.* choice T1064

ellis, *adv.* otherwise E1066, E1855

enberkist, *v.2sg.pres.ind.* rail at (Lat. *oblatres*) T3260 (*not MED*)

ende, *sb.* , *for þis, to þis* ~ for this purpose T641, T2985, L998

endeþ, *v.3sg.pres.ind.* dies T317; ended *pa.p.* ~ *into oon* brought into unity (Vulg. *ut . . . unum sint*) T3063

enditing, *ger.* composition T1349

endured, *pa.p.adj. hard* ~ strongly hardened T1866

enduring, *v.pres.p.* continuing T2477

enforcest, *v.2sg.pres.ind.*, enforsiþ *3sg.pres. ind.*, enforcen *pl.pres.ind.*, enforced *pa.ind.*, enforcid, *pa.p.* constrain E1717, E1754, T1668 etc., attempt T3601, T3811

enfo(u)rme, *v.* instruct E111, T366, T2878 etc., guide T766, T1919

englischid, *pa.p.adj.* translated into English T2005, T2886

engrosid, *v.pa.p.* gathered together T2441

enhaunciþ, enhaunsiþ, *v.3sg.pres.ind,* enhaunsen *pl.pres.ind.*, enhaunsing *pres.p.* enhaunsid *pa.p.* raise up, exalt E507, T153, T182 etc.

enhaunsing, *ger.* elevation T158, T180, T185

enpeiring, *sb.* injury E2164

enpu(n)gne, v. dispute E1120, E1181, E1213 etc., challenge the authority or validity of E1171, E2290, E2738 etc., condemn E2964, E3006, resist E450

enpungyng, ger. disputing E454

ensaumple, sb. example E629, E753, E854 etc., parable E480, bi ∼ from the example E313

ensa(u)mple(n, v. set an example (for) E1686, T1099, T1919 etc., prefigure E2174, T2074

ensuraunce, sb. pledge E2140

ensuren, v.pl.pres.ind. assure E522

entail, sb. limitation of inheritance by conditions imposed by donor E2399, E2412, E2413 etc. (see MED entaille n.(3))

entailid, v.pa.p. assigned (property) to particular class of heirs E2380 (see note), E2380, E2386, E2393 etc.

entent, sb. purpose T522, T588, T1016 etc., in ∼ þat for the purpose that T3639

enterditen, v.pl.pres.ind., enturditid pa.p. bar from its ecclesiastical function E1132, T331

entirmete, v.3sg.pres.sj. ∼ hym wiþ concern himself about L997

entrikiþ, v.3sg.pres.ind., entriken pl.pres. ind., entrike 3sg.pres.sj., entrikid pa.p. entangle E1184, E1392, E1395

entriþ, v.3sg.pres.ind. engages T219

enuenymed, v.pa.p poisoned E1794

er, cj. before E1550, E1880, E2538 etc.

eritage, sb. inheritance E1366

erþetyller, sb. tiller of the soil L385, L388

ese, sb. salve E1779, leisure L378, L381

estimacion, sb. opinion T3364

euen(e, adj. equal E955, E1970, T2897, just E969, L1001

euene, euyn, adv. equally E871, E956, E1070 etc., plainly E1177, E1647, E2895

euen, euyn, v. make equal T1458, T2084; ∼ himself makes himself equal T1551, T1808

euenli, adv. properly E961, justly E1151

euennes, sb. bi ∼ as an equal T782

euydence, sb. proof E1207, T1373, T1703 etc., testimony E2581, T2058, in ∼ of as proof of T2130, make ∼ to produce evidence for T3438, more ∼ or open greater or plain evidence (Lat. evidentius)

T3570; pl. authorities, proofs E683, E686, E692

euery, adj.as sb. everyone T1260

ex(c)ecucio(u)n, sb. putting into effect T888, T890, T892 etc., enforcement L1020, do ∼ cause enforcement E972, put(ten) in ∼ put into effect T323, T413

excepting, v.pres.p. excluding T2724

excusacion, sb. excuse L1021

experience, sb. confirmation T1677

expown(n)eþ, v.3sg.pres.ind., expowne pl.pres.ind. expound E199, E346, E3091 etc., reveal T1635

expownyng, ger. expounding E198

expresse, adj. plain T1729

expresse, adv. expressly E1789, T858

expresli, adv. blatantly E855, E858

extentli, adv. widely T566 (not MED)

extremyte, sb.. excess E715, extreme E721, E769, E771 etc.

fablis, sb.pl. falsehoods E384, T743, fictions, stories E388, T3236

faile, sb. defect T1712

faile, v. fail, disappoint E1932, E2142, E2146 etc., neglect E2144, be lacking T207

fayn, adv. wold(e ∼ would be glad E2291, T935, T3577 etc.

fayned, adj. misleading, dissembling E474

faintiþ, v.3sg.pres.ind. exhausts E205

fair, adv. properly E84, E167, E2289 etc.

fal(len, v.pa.p. fallen T1373, ∼ into changed into E1066

famousli, adv. commonly T835, T842, T3054 etc., notoriously T838

fardel, sb. burden T3878

fare, v. act T3092, ∼ riȝt foule go badly astray T3704

faseli, adv. falsely T1735

fat, adj. rich, well endowed E542

fau(3)te, sb. sin E227, E276, E871 etc., lack E256, E2148, E2192 etc., deficiency E722, E2660, E2822 etc.

fau(3)ti, adj. defective, at fault E48, E51, E399 etc., deprived E2120, sinning T297

fauȝtiþ, v.3sg.pres.ind., him ∼ is lacking to him T1581; fautid pa.p. was lacking T2466

fautours, sb.pl. abettors, supporters E1161, E1269

fauoren, v.pl.pres.ind. assist, look with favour E1132, E3060

feder, *sb.* devourer T2381 *(see note)*

feelen, *v.pl.pres.ind* perceive E2253 *(see note)*, **feelide**, *3sg.pa.ind.* thought E550, ~ . . . *of himsilf/hemsilf* considered himself/themselves E486, E492, **feledden**, *pl.pa.ind.* felt, thought T3437

feerd, *adj.* afraid E285

feyneþ, *v.3sg.pres.ind.*, **feyne** *3sg.pres.sj.* pretend T1605, T1612, T1741

feyned, *pa.p.adj.* misleading E195, E468, E470 etc.

feiþ, *sb. bring in . . . a* ~ make into an article of belief T165

feiþful, *adj. as sb.* faithful man T2729, T3377

feld-telier, fild(e)-tilier, *sb.* ploughman, husbandman T3127, T3456, T3457 etc. *(compound not MED)*

fe(e)ld, *sb.* field E345, T614

feledden *see* **feelen**

feling, *ger.* opinion T3637, T3689

fer, *adv.* far E93, E1120

ferforþ, *adv. so* ~ *(þat)* to such an extent (that) E825, E1298, E1838 etc., *as* ~ *as* as far as T52, T376, T1104 etc.

ferforþli, *adv. so* ~ *þat* to such an extent that, so extensively . . . that E351, E2402, T2072, *as* ~ *as* to the extent that E2230

ferme, *adj.* firm, certain T2318, T2447, T3296

ferþe, *num.ord.* fourth E1711

ferþer, *adv.* further E1838, E1844, E1892

ferþermor(e, *adv.* furthermore E101, E291, E317 etc.

feruent, *adj.* ardent T1444

fest, *sb.* feast T3710

festing, *ger.* feasting T1172

fidelite, *sb.* faithfulness T3297, faith T3738, T3739

figurali, *adv.* symbolically, as a symbol T1524

figur(r)e, *sb.* symbol E942, T1514, T1529 etc., likeness T2349, T2355, representation, diagram T399

figure, *v.* symbolise E369, E1289, E1306 etc.

filow, *v.pl.pres.sj.* should follow L599

fylowers, *sb.pl.* followers, disciples L53

filthehede, *sb.* depravity T3018

final, *adj.* complete T596

fynde, *v.inf. to* ~ to be found T3861; **fonde** *3sg.pa.ind.* found; **i)founde(n**

pa.p. found E1449, E1467, E1848 etc., come upon T3035, devised T3296, discovered T3324, discovered to be T3817; **foundun** *pa.p.* ~ *in* based upon E143

fynding, *sb.* sustenance E1807

fleing, *ger.* flight T2245, T2251

fleschly, *adj.* earthly E326

florischid, *pa.p.adj.* ornamented T1349

fluting, *adj.* moveable T1950

foly, *adj.* foolish E2267

fonned, fonnyd, *adj.* foolish T432, T440, T1275 etc.

fonnysche, *adj.* erroneous T1348

foole, *adj.* foolish T1942

for, *cj.* ~ *bicause* since T1874

for, *prep.* in exchange for E471, as T2432, during T71, T2526; ~ *al his liif* throughout his life T1246; ~ *him* in his place T2363

forbede, *v.3sg.pa.sj.*, **forbodun**, *pa.p.* forbid E1661, E2735, T560 etc.

forbeding, *ger.* prohibition T1206

fordo, *v.inf. and pl.pres.sj.* destroy L225, L227

forfendiþ, *3sg.pres.ind.*, **forfenden** *pl.pres. ind.*, **forfendide** *3sg.pa.ind*, **forfendid** *pa.p.* forbid, prohibit E767, E898, E934 etc.

forgoer, *sb.* leader L666

forȝete, *v.inf. and pa.p.*, **forȝite** *imp.sg.* forget E77, E113, E2783 etc.

forme, *sb.* form, outline T284, T307, T310 etc., manner T1987, T2569, T3754; ~ *of* model for L655; *uisible* ~ outward manifestation; *in* ~ *of brede* having assumed the form of bread *(see note)* T2014

formede, fo(u)rmed, *v.3sg.pa.ind.*, **fo(u)rmed** *pa.p.* created T627, T2355; ~ . . . *to* created for E1326; ~ *of* formed from E1325, E1327

forsoþ(e, *adv.* truly E153, E190, E362 etc.

fort, *cj.* in order to T184, T2278

forþ, *sb. haue her* ~ have free course E431 *(see note)*

forþenking, *ger.* repentance E311, T1436, T2425

forþsetting, *sb. looues of* ~ shewbread (Vulg. *panis propositionis*) T2701 *(see note, not MED)*

forwaried, *pa.p.adj.* accursed T3855, T3856; *as sb.* accursed T3859 forwhi, *adv.* for (may translate Lat. *quippe* or *enim*) T2709, T3352, T3362 etc.

forwhi, *cj.* because T974

forwhi, *inter.* why T2201

foul(e, *adv.* grievously E620, E1172, E1280 etc.

founded, *pa.p.adj.* firm T3831

founded, *v.pa.p.* established T3831

foundun, *pa.p.adj.* devised E402

frame, *sb.* framework T1964, edifice T1980

frame, *v.imper.sg.*, framed *pa.p.* fashion T665, T1963, T1969

fraternyte, *sb. lettris of* ~ letters of brotherhood E493 (*see note*), T2137

frantike, *adj.* crazy T3367

fraunchisen, *v.pl.pres.ind.* ~ *togidir* are under the jurisdiction of joint possessors E1954 (*see note*)

fre, *adj.* at liberty E983, T3529, uninhibited T335, T340

fredom, *sb.* liberty T134, T1123, body of rights claimed T13

freelnesse, *sb.* frailty T2285

fre-hertid, *adj.* generous, liberal E738

frendid, *pa.p.adj.* having (powerful) friends T853

frike, *adj.* eager (i.e. lascivious) T901, T933

fro, *prep.* from E93, E176, E182 etc.

fronte, *sb.* face T3827

fructeful, *adj.* profitable T1115

fruct(e)fulli, *adv.* fruitfully, profitably T2127, T2147

fructuous, *adj.* profitable E309, E765, E2357

fructuousli, *adv.* profitably E307

ful, *adj.* complete E2741, T3459

ful, *adv.* completely E280, very E306, E2639

fundement, *sb.* foundation T661, T1553, T1944 etc.

furbarre, *v.inf.* obstruct T134

gadrid *v.pa.p.* collected together T618, T2551, T3361 etc.

gadrid, *pa.p.adj. a grete* ~ *persone of* a great person composed of T84

gadring, gedering, *ger.* collection E1087, T616, T1233 etc.

gaynful, *adj.* profitable E1017, T964

game, *sb.* sport E389

gate see get

gebat, gibat, *sb.* gallows (i.e. cross) E2530, T3116

gedering see gadring

gete, *v.* (gate *3sg.pa.ind.*, gotun *pa.p.*) obtain E23, E538, E543 etc., beget E330, E331, E355 etc., ~ *into* obtain for E1541

getyng, *ger.* acquisition E1110, E1983

gibat see gebat

gladiþ, *v.3sg.pres.ind.*, gladen *pa.p.* gladden, rejoice T1313, T1860, T1863

glo(o)s(e, gloce, close *sb.* gloss, sophistical interpretation E937, E1632, E1646 etc.

glose, *v.* gloss E1647, E1648, E1662 etc., gloss over E2492, E2817, T681 etc.; ~ *togidir* linked E1820, T1661 (*see note*)

glosers, *sb.pl.* glossers, falsifiers E2540, T588, T1892 etc.

glosing, *ger.* glossing T196

glustre, *sb.* bunch T1341, T1537

gnasting, *ger.* gnashing T1053, T3858

go, igon, *v.pa.p.* gone E2674, T2064, T2152

godward, *sb. to* ~ towards God E928, E2318, for God E1390, E1392

good(e, *sb.* property E259, E537, E1141 etc., money E523, benefit T2987; *it is sum grete* ~ it is a great good T3132; *doþ neuer* ~ is no use T3686

good, *adv. him is* ~ it is well for him T1117

go(o)stli, *adj.* spiritual E322, E331, E337 etc.

gostli, *adv.* in spirit T1143, T2384

gotun see gete

gouernail, *sb.* authority E2182

gouernaunce, *sb.* administrative control E848, E1005, E1007 etc., authority E1015, E2770, government E1032

graffid, *v.pa.p.* grafted E416

gratter, *adj.comp.* the greater L665

graunt(e, *v.* agree T1877, T2013, T3460 etc., agree to T256, T391, concede T3797

grauel, *sb.* sand E2665, T2309, gravel T1938, T1943

grauen, *v.pl.pres.ind.* carve E1907

greet, *adj.as sb.* a great thing E780, *in* ~ in general E1032

greueþ, *v.3sg.pres.ind.*, greue(n *pl.pres.ind.* harm T3691, T3695; ~ *3ou* disturb yourselves E1518 greuous, *adj.* burdensome E2189

grisful, *adj,* horrible T968, T3181

ground(e, *sb.* basis E165, E273, E3018 etc., justification E213, E477, E1559 etc., *pl.* justifications E184

grounde, *v.* base E149, T1914, T1934 etc., justify E12 (*see note*), E55, E185 etc.

groundli, *adv.* as is shown in scripture E455, E1068, T1476, basically T2360, T2771, thoroughly T3817

i)growe *v.pa.p.* ~ *forþ* increased E3024; ~ *into* grown into T2125

grucche, *v.* complain E1259, E2288, E2296, E2857 etc.

grucching, *sb.* complaint E2944

gru(e, *adj.* Greek E1001, T792, T2168 etc.

ȝaf(f, ȝauen see ȝeue

ȝate, *sb.* gate E2675

ȝeld, *v.* (ȝilde *3sg.pres.sj.*, ȝildiþ, ȝeldiþ *imper.pl.*) give E1341, T374, T1241

ȝeer, ȝere, *sb.pl.* years E2132, T3601, T3618

ȝete, *v.3sg.pa.ind.* ate T3216

ȝeue, ȝyue, *v.* (ȝaf(f *3sg.pa.ind*, ȝaf, ȝauen, ȝeuen *pl.pa.ind.*, ȝoue(n, ȝeue(n, iȝeue *pa.p.*) give E108, E115, E120 etc.; yȝouen *to* addicted to E2283

ȝ(h)e, *adv.* yes, indeed E146, E535, E631 etc.

ȝide(n, ȝede(n, *v.3sg. and pl.pa.ind.* went E482, E489, E1301 etc.

ȝif, *cj.* if T47, T206, T287 etc.

ȝisturdai, *sb.* yesterday T2231

ȝit, ȝut, *adv.* yet, still E78, E287, E632 etc

ȝyue see ȝeue

ȝyuer, *sb.* giver E2384, E2387, E2390

ȝyuyng, *ger.* giving E2059, E2160, E2417

ȝongar, *adj.comp.* more humble L665

ȝou, *pron.2pl.obj. and refl.* you, yourselves E91, E152, E191 etc.

ȝoue(n see ȝeue

ȝut see ȝit

habundaunce, *sb.* plenty E1604, E3053, T1281 etc., riches E2657, quantity E2996

halidaies, *sb.pl.* holy days E2300

halowen, *v.pl.pres.ind.*, i)halowid *pa.p.* sanctify T1539, T2774, T3059 etc., consecrate T3670, T3673, T3675

halowing, *ger.* sanctification T1397, T2674, T3081 etc., consecration E2487, T3738, T3742

halowis, *sb.pl.* saints T3859

halt see hold(e(n

hammes, *sb.pl.* back of legs E75

han, a, haue, *v.inf.*, hast *2sg.pres.ind.*, haþ *3sg.pres.ind.*, han *pl.pres.ind.*, haue *pl.pres.sj.*, have E113, E120, E191 etc., possess T2161, take possession of T1588; ~ *himsilf/hemsilf* behave E512, E928; ~ *leuer* would rather E763, ~ *in hond* own, have in their power E1076; hade *pa.p.* experienced T3069

hand, *sb.* *beren him on* ~ accuse him E2748

handlid, *v.pa.p.* treated T3809

hang, honge, *v.*, hyng *3sg.pa.ind.* hang E75, E1613, E1956 etc., dwell, linger T2444; ~ *bi, in* depend on T3192; ~ *on* is the responsibility of E2313; ~ *at* pertain to, belong to T1537

hap, *sb.* *in, up* ~ perhaps, perchance E1634, E2567, E2833 etc.

hapneþ, *v.3sg.pres.ind.* happens T3323

hard, *adj.* unusual T2131

hard, *adv.* firmly E819, T476

hardest, *adj.superl. at þe* ~ at the least T111

hardest, *v.2sg.pres.ind* ~ *þi fronte* frown T3827

hardli, *adv.* vigorously E1234

harme, *sb. peyne of* ~ (Lat. *pena dampni*) damnation T3468 (*see note*)

harned, *pa.p.adj.* hardened, confirmed E563

hast, *sb. up* ~ speedily E2857

hastiþ, *v.3sg.pres.ind.* hastens T33

hasting, *ger.* hastening T1828

hatouse, *adj.* hateful E2301

haue see han

hawnte, *v.3pl.pres.sj.* take trouble over L368

he(e)d(e, *sb.*(1) head, chief E68, E1094, E1095 etc.

he(e)de, *sb.*(2) heed, notice E342, E350, E1112 etc.

hede, *v.3sg.pres.sj.* heed, take notice T298

hedur, *adv.* hither T2888

heedles, *adj.* without a head T291, T2359, T2363

heedli, *adv.* headlong T1795

heering, *sb.* hearing E383

heiþe, *sb.* summit T3444

hele, v. cover T2234
helid, v.pa.p. healed E1706, E1707, E1708 etc.
heling see hilyng
hellis, sb.pl. hell (Lat. ab infernis) T554
helt, hilt, v.pa.p. poured E1798, T1537
helþe, sb. salvation T556, T3407, T3427
helþful, adj. wholesome E2611
hem, pron.pl.obj. and refl. them, themselves E23, E30, E31 etc.
hemsilf, hemself, pron.3pl.refl, and emphatic themselves E193, E708, T1882 etc.
hengen, v.pl.pa.ind. hanged E2526
hepe, v. gather E381, T741
her, pron.pl.poss. their E3, E73, E75 etc., hers theirs E495, E1218
he(e)re(n, v. (i)hird(e, herd(e pa.p.) hear E1494, E1546, E2320 etc.; þe scripture of God ihirde (Lat. auditis scripturis Deo) having heard the word of God T3194
herbifore, adv. before this E2371
herd, adj. strict L403
heris, sb.pl. ears T2638
herself, pl.pron.refl. themselves T964
herupon, adv. on top E348
hertly, hertili, adv. eagerly E1717, L317
he(e)st(e, sb. commandment E101, E178, T1632 etc.
heþenesse, sb. paganism E2841
heuenward, prep.phrase to ~ (to lead) towards heaven E331
hewe, v. (hewe 3sg.pres.sj, and pa.ind. and pa.p.) hew E3020, E3021, E3022 etc.
hidnes(se, sb. hiding place, secrecy T3230
hiest, adv.superl. most highly E268
hiȝ(e, adj. (hiȝer comp., hi(ȝ)est, hiȝist superl.) high, exalted E425, E2587, E2694 etc., important E5, loud E568
hiȝenes(se, sb. high position T2246, height T2252
hilde see hold(e(n
hilt see helt
hilyng, heling, sb. covering, i.e.clothing E718, E773, T1281 etc.
him, pron.3sg.obj. and refl. him, himself E14, E173 etc.
himself, himsilf, pron.refl. itself E205, T939
hing see hang
hir, pron.f.sg.obj., poss. and refl. her E235, E325, E327 etc., herself E3072, T908
hir, pron.pl.poss. see her

hird see he(e)re(n
hirde, he(e)rde, sb. shepherd T2366, T2370, T2371 etc.
his, pron.poss. its E1312, T3039
hogeli, adv. greatly E867
hold(e(n, v. (halt, holt 3sg.pres.ind., hilde 3sg.pa.ind., heelde(n pl.pa.ind., i)hold(e(n pa.p.) keep E1608, E1621, E1899 etc., maintain E98, E1890, E2048 etc.; ~ him maintains himself E749; ~ him/hem consider himself/ themselves E795, E2121, E2955 etc.; ~ of possess (power) from E1621; ~ his parte uphold his side T1769; ~ wel is very effective E1863; ~ not does not follow T301; bi . . . ihold (Lat. teneatur) be . . . held T3347; ben holden are obliged L1023
holding, ger. possessing E2043
hole, hool, adj. complete E422, E842, T1006 etc., healthy T48
ho(o)l(l)i, adv. wholly, completely E1278, E1671, E1862, etc.
ho(o)lsum, adj. wholesome E381, T741
holpen, v.pa.p. helped L1013
homeli, adj. familiar T1351
hond(e, sb. more and more ~ more and more control E1533, sett ~ attempted, put his hand to the task T175
honge see hang
hool, adv. completely E2728
hoolsumly, adv. properly L976
hope, sb. hope T3199, trust T536
hope, v. believe E1100, E2958, T1832 etc., expect E1119, T1051, trust T565
hordam, hor(e)dom, sb. prostitution E375, E3073, T1309
ho(o)re, sb. whore, strumpet E337, E3011, E3064 etc.
hornewood(e, adj. mad with rage T1319, T3412
hors, sb.pl. horses E2315, T1171
houȝ, interj. lo T629
houȝ, rel.adj. what T2815
houndish, adj. doglike E1590
huȝeli, adv. greatly T3361
husbondrie, sb. farming E2110

i-/y- for these as pa.p.prefix see infinitive forms; included here are only those whose infinitives do not occur; cross references are only given for difficult cases
iailour, sb. jailer T2086

iaping, *ger.* foolery T3655
ibake, *v.pa.p.* baked T1496
ybooldid, *pa.p.adj.* confident E560
icche, *v.* itch E382
iche, *adj.* each T1441
icontinued, *v.pa.p.* continued T2590
icroised, *pa.p.adj.* marked with a cross, i.e.
   sanctified T1360 (*see note*)
icrossid, *v.pa.p.* crucified T3106
ierarchies, *sb.pl.* rulers in sacred order
   E2609, E2615, E2617 etc. (*see note*)
iete, *v.pa.p.* eaten T3787
if al, *cj.* even if E864
ifyned, *v.pa.p.* fined (of wine) T1329
igrounde, *v.pa.p.* ground (as flour) T1494
iȝe, *sb.* (iȝen *pl.*) eye E258, T271, T1874
   etc.; *at* ~ openly, plainly E465, E797,
   E1940 etc.
iȝeue, yȝouen see ȝeue
imytrid, *pa.p.adj.* mitred T982
impertynent, *adj.* irrelevant E878, E880
imultepliid, *pa.p.adj.* multiplied T2790
in, *prep.* on E836, T3221, T3737, by E84,
   amongst E191, T3587, as (worthy of)
   T487, for E701
incompounnedli, *adv.* unsubtly T2304
   (*not MED*)
incontynence, *sb.* immorality E2825
inconuenient, *sb.* offence T1905, T2024,
   T3125 etc., misfortune T98
incorporat, *adj.* ~ *in(to* absorbed into
   T2335, contained in T1508, T1662
indett, *v.pa.p.* obliged E2755
indifferent, *adj.* impartial E1165, E1352
indifferentli, *adv.* carelessly E1665
infectiþ, *v.3sg.pres.ind.*, infecten *pl.pres.*
   ind. corrupt, infect E1976, T3511
infect, *pa.p.adj.* corrupted E758, E1683,
   E1792 etc.
infidelite, *sb.* weakness of faith T3540
informacion, *sb.* instruction T1708
inhabite, *v.* take possession of T34, T41,
   T48 etc.
ynow, *adj.* enough E148, E404, T10 etc.
ynow, *adv.* enough E244
inpugne, *v.* dispute T2318, T2321, question T3005, repudiate T2, T483
inpugning, *ger.* disputing T825
insolible, *sb.* unanswerable question T282,
   T333, situation from which there is no
   escape T258
insufficience, *sb.* inadequacy T849

insufficient(e, *adj.* inadequate E2134,
   T831, T940
interrupt, *v.pa.p.* suspended, abrogated
   E2399, E2412
into, *prep.* in E66, E179, E577 etc., onto
   E193, T1926, T1939, until E632, E977,
   E1158 etc., up to the point of E1887,
   E2412, E2490 etc., to E511, for E1378,
   T1282, T3215 etc., until E643, E3026,
   T3603, as regard to E1576, against E9,
   L411; ~ *þe tyme* until the time E81,
   E172, E991 etc.
inwardli, *adv.* intensely T949, earnestly
   T2213
ioie, *sb.* pleasure T1794, T3355, T3592,
   delight E550, T3880
ioiyng, *ger.* gladness T2484
ypikid, *v.pa.p.* plucked E1296
ypocrit, *adj.* hypocritical T119
ypocritli, *adj.* hypocritical E86
ipurid, *v.pa.p.* purified T1330
irad, *v.pa.p.* read T3785, T3810
iringgid, *pa.p.adj.* ringed, adorned with
   rings T982
iscatrid, *pa.p.adj.* dispersed T2368
iseen *see* seen
ysete, *v.pa.p.* sat E1641
ismete, ysmytun, *pa.p.adj.* smitten E1739,
   pierced T3746
isouȝt *see* seche
istablischid, *pa.p.adj.* established T3311
istirid, *v.pa.p.* considered T1974
itake see take
itauȝt, *v.pa.p.* taught T137, T480, T2049
itokened, *v.pa.p.* indicated T2294
ivnderstond, *v.pa.p.* understood (Lat.
   intellectum) T3719
iuel, yuele, *adj.* evil E557, T2099, T2139
   etc.
yuel, *adv.* badly E1636, T1774
iviserid, *v.pa.p.* covered over T1244
ywounde, -un, *v.pa.p.* embroiled in
   E1397; *pa.p.adj.* wound E1604

kan, *v.1sg.pres.ind.*, can, kan, kun *pl.pres.*
   ind., koud(e, cou(ȝ)de, cowde pa.ind.
   be able to E80, E1545, E1770 etc., know
   (how to) E1888, T3821
kepe, *sb. take* ~ pay attention to L656
kepen, *v.* guard E27, care E565, want
   E2351; ~ *hemsiilfe* protect themselves
   L1028, L1041
keuereþ, *v.3sg.pres.ind.* covers T3148

keuur, *sb.* covering T1615

kynde, *sb.* nature E949, E952, E955 etc., form T1546, T1547 etc., substance E1274, T2637, T3765, essence T2581 (*see note*)

kynd(e)li(che, *adj.* proper E1331, E1336, E1520 etc., natural E726, E1383, E1682 etc.

kindli(e, *adv.* by nature E2720, T3770

kynred, *sb.* kindred, tribe E822, E827, E832 etc.

kitten *v.pl.pres.ind.*, kitt *pa.p.* cut E120, T2663

knaue *sb.* boy, servant T2087

kny3t fe(e, *sb.* landed property of a knight E1945

knyt(t, *v.pa.p.* joined, united E435, E1124, E2899 etc, woven T390

knowen, *pl.pres.ind.* acknowledge T2257; i)know(e(n *pa.p.* known T2068, T2535, T3349, recognized E2294, T2254, T3354, made manifest T1483, foreknown (Lat.*praesciuntur*) T1608

knowing, *ger.* knowledge (Lat.*cognitionis*) T3209, T3729

knowleche, knouleche, *sb.* knowledge E754, E1145, E2295 etc., understanding E1702, E2778, E3097 etc., recognition E573, information E2946, E2497

know(e)leche, knouleche, *v.* acknowledge E1833, T56, T250 etc., profess E2837, E2840, T316 etc.

knowleching(e, *ger.* confession T1497, recognition T2946

kolour *see* colour

kost, *sb.* country T828

kouche, *sb.* lair T3230

kunnen see kan

kunnyng(e, *sb.* knowledge E22, E23, E27 etc.

kunnynge, *adj.* knowledgeable, skilful E1016, E1019, E1127 etc.

kurious, *adj.* ingenious T3326

kuriousite, *sb.* curiosity, desire for novelty T2671

labouren, *v.pl.pres.ind.* toil at T852

lackiþ, *v.3sg.pres.ind.* is lacking T517, T2608, T3650 etc., hem ~ they lack E2188, ~ me is lacking for me T2919; lacken *pl.pres.ind.* ~ . . . *to* deprive . . . from T830; lackid *pa.p.* deprived T3429

lad *see* led

large, *adj.* (larger *comp.*) ample E72, T1798, comprehensive E2653, extensive T1449

large, *adv.* widely E1215, E1217, at length E121

largenesse, *sb.* abundance E2635

lasse, *adj.comp.* lesser T1029

lasse, *adv.comp.* less T223, T550

late, *adv.* recently E114, E1102, T174 etc.

late *see* lete

latur, *adv.comp. neuer þe* ~ nevertheless T2438

led, *v.pl.pres.ind.*, lad, *v.pa.p.*, lead T57, L396

leef, *sb.* leaf E1538

le(e)f(f)ul, *adj.* lawful E1887, T352, T1359 etc.

leefully, *adv.* lawfully E1879

leene, *v.inf.* rest, put E2499

le(e)syng, *ger.* losing E1141, E1209, E1228 etc.

leet *see* lete

lege, *adj.* loyal T1066, T3538

legeaunce, *sb.* allegiance T812, T1559

leide, *v.pa.p.* led T761

lei3e, *v.* (leiþ *3sg.pres.ind.*, ileide *pa.p*) allege, cite T573, T1308, T1728 etc., place T1441; ~ (. . .) *up* accumulate E733, E737

leiser, *sb.* leisure E1206

lemys, *sb.pl.* limbs, members (i.e. followers) T841, T1005, T1385 etc.

lemman, *sb.* paramour T1291

lende, *v.* grant T1584

lenger, *adj.comp.* further T3847

lenger, *adv.comp.* longer (in space or time) E2894, E2939, E3096; ~ *þan* longer than, beyond E304

leren, *v.pl.pres.ind.* teach T453

lerned, *v.pa.p.* instructed E559

lesse, *v.* abridge T1190

le(e)se, *v.* lose E1028, E1061, E1289 etc., ruin T1303, lose ability T1121

lesing, *ger.*(1) losing E1209, E1228, T349 etc., destruction L237

lesyng, *ger.*(2) lie E212, E213, E242 etc., *make(n a* ~ tell a lie E208, E212, E260 etc.

le(e)st, *adj.superl. at þe* ~ *weie* finally E1570; *as sb. of þe* ~ at least T417, *my* ~ the least of mine T988

lete, *v.sg./pl. pres.sj.* late, *imper.sg. and*

pa.p., **letiþ** *imp.pl.*, **leet**, *3sg.pa.ind.* let, allow E439, E2118, T457 etc., cause E367, E841

lett, *sb.* impediment E1597

lett(e, *v.* (**let, lettid, ylett** *pa.p.*) prevent E1120, T886, T888 etc., impede T27, T33, hinder E1126, E1216, T2230 etc., keep away T3407

letting, *ger.* hindrance T220

lettre, *sb.pl.* letters E74, E258

le(e)ue, *sb.* permission E1214, E1621, E1964 etc., authority E2270, E2272, E2383 etc., *wiþ Goddis* ~ by God's grace T1584

le(e)ue, *v.*(1) (**ileft(e** *pa.p.*) leave, abandon E97, E312, E390 etc., remain T3429, T3676, T3726 etc., leave behind E2187, let alone L222

le(e)ue, *v.*(2) believe E1025, E1649, E1650 etc.

leuer, *adj.comp. han* ~ *to be deed* would rather be dead E763

leuing, *ger.* loss, leaving of T3470

lewdenesse, *sb.* ignorance, worthlessness T2216

lewid, lewde, *adj.* stupid, misguided E99, T677, T2374, ignorant T1630, lay, secular T169

liberal, *adj.* generous E743, E746

liberalte, *sb.* generosity E750

lickeneþ, *v.3sg.pres.ind.* compares T1345

licli, likli, *adj.* probable E2478, T2151

ligge, *v.* (**liþe** *3sg.pres.ind.*) remain, lie E1398, E2030, T1988 etc.

liȝe, *v.* (**lieþ** *3sg.pres.ind.*, **lien** *pl.pres.ind.*) lie, tell lies E245, E562, T451 etc.

liȝt, *adj.* easy E69, slight E146

liȝt(t)li, *adv.* (**liȝtlier** *comp.*) readily E185, E1115, E1214 etc., quickly E1519, E2283, E2861 etc. gladly E1638

liiflood, -lode, *sb.* food E718, E773, E790 etc., means of providing the necessities of life E817, E824, E832 etc.

liik *adj.* alike E1704, E1820, similar E1800, probable E1529

like as, *cj.* just as if T3692

liking, *sb.* pleasure T31, T1111, T1446 etc.

lykynge, *adj.* pleasing L237

likiþ, *v.3sg.pres.ind.*, **liken** *pl.pres.ind.*, **likid** *3sg.pa.ind.* please E2941, T1959, T3652, like T295; *with refl.* it pleases him etc. T157, T3149

likned, *pa.p.adj.* similar T2640

limitiþ, *v.3sg.pres.ind*, **limiten** *pl.pres.ind*, **limite** *3sg.pres.sj.*, **lymytid** *pa.p.* specify E849, E1355, E2445 etc., ~ *to* are restricted to T3107

lymytours, *sb.pl.* mendicant friars whose begging was limited to one of the subdivisions of the territory of a religious house E2749 (*see note*)

lyne, *sb.* lineage L892, L893

list, listiþ *v.3sg.pres.ind. with refl.* it pleases him/them etc. T1182, T1839

litarge, *sb.* lethargy, inertia E1532

lite, *adv. setten* ~ account of little worth T3222

liþe *see* **ligge**

litil, *adj.as sb. a* ~ *and a* ~ little by little E1294

lyuyng, *ger.* means of livelihood E815; *pl.* manner of life E797

loff, loof, *sb.* (**looues** *pl.*) loaf E2708, T597, T599 etc.

logic, *sb. vndur þis* ~ in this mode of speech T2169 (*see note*)

lond, *sb. a* ~ into existence E895

long(g)iþ, *v.3sg.pres.ind*, **long(g)en** *pl.pres.ind.*, **longide** *pl.pa.ind.* pertain, belong E63, E882, E1345 etc., is the responsibility of T3872; **long(g)ing(e** *pres.p.*, ~ *to* belonging to E1351, ~ *to* associated with T1198, T1372, T2804

lo(o)re, *sb.* teaching, doctrine E97, E113, E406 etc.

lordshiping, *ger.* power (including that afforded by ownership) E761, E804, E873 etc.

losel, *adj.* roguish E2197

losid, *v.pa.p.* loosed T40

losing, *ger.* loosing, release T1713, T1724, T2538 etc.

loten, *v.pl.pres.ind.* lurk E2553, E2554

loþe, loth, *adj.* reluctant E1465, E1467, hateful T897, T926; *me were* ~ I would be sorry E2495

loþe, *v.* hate E1509, E1512, E1547 etc.

loþeli, *adj.* hateful E337, E1588

loþing, *ger.* hatred E1421

lust, *sb.* delight E3064, T208, T952 etc., desire T1783

lusti, *adj.* spirited T901

magnefien, *v.pl.pres.ind.* enlarge T2409

mayndeheed, *sb.* virginity T3259

maieste, maiestate, *sb.* royal power E992, E993, T485

maintenaunce, *sb.* conduct E2934; *in* ~ *of* for the preservation of E702

maintene, *v.* ~ *wiþ* defend E1857, E1859, support E2817

mair, *sb.* mayor E206

maist, *v.2sg.pres.ind.* are able to do (Lat. *potes, see note*) T3477

maisters(c)hip, *sb.* lordship E1012, E1022, T3210 etc.

maistirdom, *sb.* superiority E1684

maistirfulli, *adv.* vigorously E570

maistrie, *sb.* special skill E201, E203, E204 etc., mastery E571, exercise E1058

make, *v.* produce T3438, bring about E479; cause T3825; made *3sg.pa.ind.* ~ *an ende of* ended T2574; made *pa.p. to be* ~ are set up T3393

makyng, *ger.* creation E1557

maner(e, *sb.* kind of E951, E1992, E1997, fashion E1749, manner of speaking T1494, T1495; *bi* ~ *of* in fashion of T2009; *pl.* habits of behaviour E1084; *þese* ~ *wises* these kinds of fashions E459

manglid, *pa.p.adj.* perverted E1232, E1275

manhed, *sb.* humanity E35, E36, E39 etc.

mankinde, *sb.* human form T2623

manly, *adv.* resolutely E1750

manscleyng, *ger.* murder T1279

marchaundise, *sb.* trade E475, E534, E2110 etc.

marchaundise, *v.* engage in commerce, traffic E196, E467, E531 etc.

mark(e, merke, *v.* observe, point out E1234, E2054, E2115 etc.

masid, *pa.p.adj.* crazed T1988

mater, matir, *sb.* material T3775, T3776, cause T851

material, *adj.* physical E2534, T3116, ~ *swerd* physical sword, as symbol of secular authority E1297, E1307, E1316 etc.; ~ *chirche* church buildings T3053, T3087

matrimoin, *sb.* marriage T3007

mau(3)matri(3)e, mawmetrie, idolatry E880, E995 etc., idols T3000

maundement, *sb.* commandment E97, E98, E108 etc.

me, *pron.indef.* one T83

meche, *adj., adv. see* moche

medling, *ger.* mingling T2812

medliþ, *v.3sg.pres.ind.* mixes T1334, T1335, medlid *pa.p. be 3e not* ~ have nothing to do E2788; imedlid, *pa.p.adj.* blended T3778

meede, *sb.* wage E777, reward E1504

meedful, *adj.* meritorious E249, E251, E254 etc.

meedfulli, *adv.* meritoriously, justifiably in the light of precedent E1862

meke, *v.* humble E506, E518, T2254

memorie, *sb.* reminder T1651

mene, *sb.* condition T116, T289, T302 etc., method E539, E1685, E2032 etc., intermediary E175, E183, E634 etc.; *vertuous* ~ golden mean, virtuous way E690, E717, E720 etc.; qualification T1670 (*see note*), T1695, compromise T1671; *pl.* arguments E2986

mene, *adj.* intermediary E607, T1503

me(e)ne, *v.* imply E405, E2148, E2715 etc.

menes, *sb.pl. make* ~ complain, make petition E2327

me(e)nyng, *ger.* sense E2964, T62, interpretation T833

meynee, mene, meyn3e *sb.* (meneis *pl.*), household E818, E1310, E1911 etc., crew E1155, E2706, T1150 etc.

mengiþ, *v.3sg.pres.ind.*, mengen *pl.pres. ind.*, mynge *inf.* mix E432, E1084, T1334 etc.

mengid, *pa.p.adj.* mixed E1042, E1089, E1092 etc.; ~ *lawe* canon law E1092, E1101 etc.

menging, *ger.* mingling, admixture T726

menteyne, *v.* defend T822, T1286, sustain T1725

mentenaunce, *sb.* support T5, T1282, T3264

mescheuous, *adj.* evil, pernicious E2024, E2104, E2268, wretched E2168, E2191

mes(c)heuousli, *adv.* miserably E2019, E2099, E2120

meschif, *sb.* (mescheues *pl.*) vice E179, E181, evil E2734, E2737, E2971 etc., poverty, destitution E2734

mesels, *sb.pl.* lepers E1705

mesurable, *adj.* moderate T1330

mesure, *sb.* proper proportion T1195, T1198, T1200 etc., intellect, understanding T3771; *wiþout(e* ~ immeasurably E1142, E1193, E1472 etc., *out of* ~ without limit T1167 mesuriþ, *v.3sg.pres.ind.*, **mesurid** *pa.p.* proportion T1196, T1617, limit T371

mete, *sb.* food E777, E2692

meue, *v.* (imeued *3sg.pa.ind.*) exhort, persuade E1911, T164, T211 etc., argue E2579, T1986, T2163 etc., practice T716; **imeuyd** *pa.p.* ~ *of* inspired by T585

meuyng, *ger.* persuasion, argument T446

mylde, *adj. to be* ~ to be at one (Lat. *mansurus, see note*) T3734

mynde, *sb.* remembrance, reminder T189, T251, T553 etc., imagination E504; *haue* ~ remember E2336, *into my* ~ in remembrance of me T508, T511, T527 etc.

mynde, *v.* recall T15, T1799

mynge *see* **menge**

mynystracioun, *sb.* management E2021, E2421

minor, *adj.as sb.* minor premise of a syllogism E1880

myntis, *sb.pl.* mint (*Vulg. mentham*) E1243

misbele(e)ue, *sb.* lack of belief E457, T569, T1935 etc., error in faith T2645, disobedience T436

myschif, *sb.* trouble T748, T756

mysdoiþ, *v.3sg.pres.ind.* does wrong E9

mysese, *sb.* distress E2050, E2052, E2054 etc., hardship E1816

mysgouerned, *v.pa.p.* ~ *þee* gone astray E2578

myspaid, *v.pa.p.* displeased, dissatisfied E2136

mysproude, *adj.* unduly arrogant T1843, T2537

myssvss, *sb.* abuse E1633

mysteching, *v.pres.p.* teaching falsely T2693

mysterie, *sb.* sacrament (Lat. *mysterium*) T1527, T1528, T1540 etc., mystery T1529

mystik, *adj.* mystical, sacramental T594, T1509, T1522 etc.

mystrist, *sb.* ~ *to* lack of faith in T2030

mo(o, *adj.comp.* more (in number) E53, E251, E253 etc.

moche, meche, myche, *adj.* many E114, E566, E1884 etc., much E116, E297, E429 etc., a great deal of E2902; a great number of T1227, T1237, T1511; *as sb.* much T674

moche, meche, myche, *adv.* much,

greatly E66, E293, E296 etc.; *for/in as* ~ *as* in so far as T1, T212 etc., because T138, T275 etc.; *also as* ~ *as* just as much as T1554; *as* ~ . . . *as* as much as T1966

moeblis, *sb.pl.* movable goods E981

mone, *sb.* lament T860

mon(e)þis, *sb.pl.* months E3055, E3057, E3058

mony, *adj.* many T321, T1943, T2024 etc.

moote hallis, *sb.pl.* courts of law L1017

moral, *adj.* concerned with morality E882, ethical E2719

moraltees, *sb.pl.* moral precepts E2725

more, *adj.comp.* greater E1107, E1113

mossel, *sb.* morsel, small piece E2678, E2699

most, *adj.superl.* greatest T2107

moue, *v.1sg.pres.ind.* urge E1703

mou(e)able, *adj.* movable E1114, capable of movement T2655, T2656; *goodis* ~ movable property (as opposed to *vnmouable* lands and buildings) E1714, E1715, E1734 etc.

mouyng, *ger.* movement T97, T2361, T2376 etc., persuasion E3052, ability to move T2360

mow(e, *v.* (**moun, mow(e(n** *pl.pres.ind.*) be able to E2563, T142, T588 etc., may E106, E1477, T2842 etc., be able to [do] T2426 (*see note*)

muse, *v.* ponder E1474, T10, T14 etc.

mut, *v.3sg.* and *pl.pres.ind.*, **most(e(n** *pa.ind.* must E48, E59, E677 etc.; **mote** *3sg.pres.sj.* (*in imprecation*) may T3862; **moste** *pl.pa.ind.* were able to E1009

nakid, *adj.* bare, worthless E1882, poor, inadequate E1885

nameli, *adv.* especially, in particular E89, E386, E486 etc.

nar, ner(e *see* **be**

naþeles, neþeles, *adv.* nevertheless E685, T77, T331 etc.

ne, *adv.* not, *it is no doute þat* ~ there is no doubt but that E1672

ne, *cj.* nor E171, E256, E275 etc., *ne . . . ne* neither . . . nor T691

nede, *adv.* necessarily L986, T301

nede, *sb. at* ~ in time of necessity E829; *it were* ~ it is needful E1524; **nedis** *pl.* affairs L974 nedeful, *adj.* essential T3775

nedes, nedis, *adv.* of necessity E221, E459, E677 etc.

nedeþ, -iþ, *v.3sg.pres.ind.*, nede(n *pl.pres. ind.*, nede *3sg.pres.sj.*, neded, nedid *pa.p.* be necessary (*often with refl.pron.*) E244, E384, E739 etc., be forced E2722, E2867, T1283 etc.; hem nede *not* it would not be necessary for them E2031

needles, *adj.* unnecessary, superfluous E2073

ne(i)þur . . . (ne(i)þur), *cj.* neither . . . (nor) E1463, T3567, L177

nem(p)ne, *v.* name T2917, T3095, mention T233, T3521, specify T2415

ner *see* be

nerrer, *adj.comp.* ~ *weie* quicker way T2448

neþeles see naþeles

neuer, *adv.* ~ *þe latur* nevertheless T2438

newelteis, *sb.pl.* novelties T649

newte, *sb.* newness T2710 (*not MED*)

ny3, ny, *adv.* near E635, E639, E641, nearly E3047, T2258, *ful/wel* ~ almost E1253, E2037, E2167 etc.

ny3(e, *prep.* near to E2578, T1947, T2527 etc.

nile, *v.imper.pl.* (cf. *wol(l)e*) ~ *3e* do not E152, E171, E364

no, *adv.* ~ *more* any more T895, T1024

noious, *adj.* harmful T3576

noisid, *v.pa.p.* reported T3163

none, *adv.* not T976

notabli, *adv.* especially T2174

nou3, *adv.* now T59, T99, T174 etc.; ~ *bore* recently born T3629

nou3t, *pron.* nothing T3681, of no effect T3695

nounpower, *sb.* impotence T1129, T2261, T3477

nouellrie, novelty, innovation T3561, T3592, T3607

o, one, oo, oon, *num.* one E284, E954, E1137 etc; *al* ~ all one, the same thing E298, E299, E1943 etc.; *for* ~ as the same thing T3781; *ton*, *þe* ~ the one T895

obeie, *v. it is to* ~ it is to be obeyed T3160

occasioun, *sb.* occurrence E1724, opportunity E311, E313, E1726 etc.

oc(c)upie, *v.* have possession of E889, E1356, E1582 etc., take up E2902

of(f, *prep.* from E28, E232, E233 etc., out of T2940, T3228, concerning E60, E108, T679 etc., by E162, T2, T3645

offence, *sb. myn* ~ my being offended T1091

office, *sb. of* ~ by virtue of their office T1247

offrid, *v.pl.pa.ind.* made offering T2985

olso, *adv.* also T515

omage, *sb.* homage T1066, T2871, T2872 etc.

omiscioun, *sb.* sin of omission T3082

on, *prep.* over T509; oon on T3862, about E239, in E811

o(o)ned, o(o)nyd, *pa.p.adj.* united T65, T601, T1471 etc.

ony, *adj.* any E142, E144, E174 etc.

onyng, *ger.* unifying T3111

o(o)nys, *adv.* once E1537, T220, T1232 etc., *at* ~ at one time E204

oonly, *adv. he is not* ~ *worþi deþ* not only is he worthy of death L311

o(o)st(e, *sb.* the bread consecrated in the eucharist E261, E1200, T243 etc.

oostis, *sb.pl.* hosts of men T2236, T2239

o(o)þ(e, *sb.* oath E2253, E2257, E2258 etc.

open, opun, *adj.* evident, plain E282, E2206, E2218 etc., clearly visible T14

open, *v.* reveal E461, T20, T2765, make clear T1400

openyng, *ger.* revelation E372

opynyoun, *sb.* reputation E1018, thought E1774

opiniouneres, *sb.pl.* theorists, speculators T2027 (*not MED*)

or, *cj.* before T2187, T3704, T3731

ordeyne, orden, *v.* establish E53, E1480, E2089 etc., order, decree E836, E2719, E2818 etc., arrange E1191, E2089, E2120, provide (for) E810, E851, E2446 etc., make ready T966

ordeinyng, *ger.* establishing T523

ordynaunce, ordenaunce, *sb.* ordering, arrangement E49, E399, E801 etc., command E50, E90, E2067 etc., determination, direction E294, E969, E973 etc., *pl.* decrees E88, E1010, E1208 etc., commandments T133, T3406, T3412 etc.

original, *adj. not* ~ *of himself but of his fader* not derived from himself but from his father T2274

orysons, *sb.pl.* devotions L973

orrible, *adj.*, horrible E321, fearful E1204

ostiler, *sb.* innkeeper E2643

oþur, oþer, oþir, *adj.* different T2983; ~ *wise þan* in a fashion different from E1941; *pl.as sb.* others E1639, E2765

oþurwise, *adv.* in another fashion T480, T3749; ~ ... ~ ... ~ at one time ... at another time . . . at another time T3665 (Lat. *aliter*)

ouȝt, *pron.* anything E493, E497, T2544

oure, *pron.* ours E1240, E1245, E2594 etc.

ournementis, *sb.pl.* ornaments E2487

outrarously, *adv.* violently E2544

ouer(e, *adv.* excessively E1172, beyond E408

ouer(e, *prep.* beyond E226, E554, E648 etc.

ouerlede, *v.* gain superiority over E206, oppress E2189

ouerse, *v.* look over E2941

ouertrauaile, *v.* overburden E2495

owiþ, *v.3sg.pres.ind.*, owe(n *pl.pres.ind.*, (h)ouȝt(e, auȝt *3sg.pa.ind.* ought T347, T1129, T1656 etc.; *hem/him* ~ they/he should E119, T3381, own E2209

paast, *sb.* dough T1496

payde, *v.pa.p.* satisfied L151

panter, *sb.* officer in charge of pantry E2691

parel, *sb.* peril, danger T356, T1128

part(e, *sb.* lot T1053, assignment L366; *on her owne* ~ on what had been assigned to them E841; *haue* ~ *of* be a partner in E2794; *take(n* ~ partake T597, T2703; *into a* ~ *of þi presthood* into a priestly office (Vulg. *ad unam partem sacerdotalem*) T2051; *for antecrist* ~ to antichrist's purpose T3786; *God will not be* ~ God will not be an associate (Lat. *pars*) L178 (*see note*)

parte, *v.* ~ *aweie* depart T750

partener, *sb.* sharer E248, E257, E471 etc.

parte-taking, *ger.* sharing T591

particuler, *adj.* individual E2174

parti(ȝ)(e, *sb.* part E297, E391, E436 etc., side T2611, T3410, company, order of society E1115, E1339, E1343 etc.; *at* ~ alone E2858; *for my* ~ for my part T445; *in grete* ~ to a large extent T1355

partyn, *v.pl.pres.ind.* share T620

parting, *ger.* sharing T591

pask, *sb.as adj.* ~ *lombe* paschal lamb T3216

passe, *v.* pass E2494, E2663, T1910 etc.,

go beyond, surpass E270, E409, E410 etc., exceed T2221, depart T2634

passing, *adj.* preeminent T1416

passing, *adv.* preeminently T3181

passingli, *adv.* preeminently T86, T120, T866

patroun, *sb.* founder E592, E603, E605 etc.

peyne, *sb.* *vnder grete* ~ with [threat of] great penalty T137

peyneþ, *v.3sg.pres.ind.*, peynen *pl.pres. ind.*, peined *pa.p.* hurt E205, T3473, torment T957, T1294

peyrynge, *ger.* harm L108

pelars, *sb.pl.* pillars T2543

pele, *v.* plunder T1283

perfeccioun, *sb.* salvation E603, E605

perfit, *adj.* perfect E673, E781, E784 etc.

perfourmen, *v.pl.pres.ind.*, performed *pa.p.* put into practice E1477, T3738

perlous, *adj.* dangerous T654, T1328, T1894

perlousli, *adv.* dangerously T86

perquisitis, perquisitiuys, *sb.pl.* payments accruing from an office E2485 (*see note*)

perschen, *v.pl.pres.ind.* are lost L241

personal, *adj.* individual T1484, T1500, T2033

personali, *adv.* individually T593, in person T3102

persones, *sb.pl.* parsons L1039

perteyne, *v.* belong E1297, T1538, T2682 etc.

pertinentli, *adv.* appropriately T1361

pesible, *adj.* peaceful T3138

pete, *sb.* pity T1294

piȝe, *sb.* (literally) magpie, *not worþ a* ~ *hele* not worth a thing T319 (*see note*), T1684

pilagis, *sb.pl.* robberies E2190

pipe, *v. mai* ~ *wiþ an iuy leef* may as well whistle in the wind E1538 (*see note*)

pissid, *v.pa.p.* ~ *out* extinguished T1447

pistil, pistle, *sb.* letter T1325, T2083

piteuousli, *adv.* mercifully T1832

playne, pleyne, *v.* (pleniþ *3sg.pres.ind.*) complain E2135, E2249, T965 etc., ~ *upon* complain against E104, E116, E356

playnt, *sb.* complaint T907

pleniþ *see* playne

plente, *sb.* fullness E2645

plesaunce, *sb.* pleasure E413, E663, E966 etc.

plesaunt, *adj*, pleasing E436, E957, E1866 etc.

plesible, *adj.* pleasing E2330

plete, *v.* go to law E1607, E1986, E1988

pleting(e, *ger.* carrying on a law suit, litigation E1615, E1983

pli(3)te, pliyt, *sb.* condition E2317, T1114, state T777

poerte *see* pouert

poynt, *sb. in ~ to* on the point of E1295

poisies, *sb.pl.* poems E388

polecie, *sb.* government E2199

polle, *sb.* head T1802 (*see note*)

positif, *adj.* arbitrarily instituted E2439

possession, *sb. hap in ~* owns L371, L373

possessioners, *sb.pl.* members of a religious order having endowments (i.e.monks and canons but not friars) E220, E540, E672 etc.

potestate, *sb.* power (Rom.13:1) T1402, ruler T1404

pouert, poerte, *sb.* poverty E680, E1122, E1127 etc.

power, *sb. of ~* of sufficient power T2252, *3eue ~* given way (Lat. *cessisse*) T2695; *done not her ~* do not exert themselves L313

powerous, *adj.* powerful T85 (*not MED*)

practif, *sb. puttip in a ~* puts into effect T2848

prauylegies, *sb.pl.* evil privileges E895

preesside, *v.3sg.pa.ind.* went forward E483

pref, *sb.* proof E1932, T2191

prekid, *v.3sg.pa.ind.* incited T901

prelacie, *sb.* body of major ecclesiastical figures (usually derogatory) T52, T95, T293 etc.

prelat(e, *sb.* ecclesiastical dignitaries (usually derogatory) E1142, E1159, E1211 etc.

prerogatif, *sb.* prior and exclusive right T2908, T2946, T3019

preson, *sb.* prison T957, T1294

preson *v.*, presounyng *ger. see* prisone, priso(u)nyng

presume, *v.* undertake, venture E2955, E3085, proceed on the assumption of right E856, E2415, E2417 etc., arrogantly pretend E425, E525, T1680 etc., take as a right T2409

preue, *v.* prove E299, E1880, E2025 etc.,

~ a man himsilf let a man judge himself T575 (Vulg. *probet*)

preue(li *see* priue(li

preuyng, *ger.* proving (legally) E2486

price, priis, *sb.* value T2911, T3387, T3451; *to ~* for money E2490

prinspal, *adj.* princely (Lat. *principis*) T1810

prynt, *sb.* impress on coin E2712

printis, *sb.* apprentice E559

prisone, *v.* imprison E1956

priso(u)nyng, pres(o)un(n)yng, *ger.* imprisoning E985, E1948, T953 etc.

priue, priuy, *adj.* secret E218, E694, E3069 etc.

priue, preuei, *adv.* secretly E1166, T838

priueli, preueli(e, *adv.* secretly E444, E561, E1120 etc.

priuyte, *sb.* secrecy E565

processe, *sb.* argument E121, E123, E665 etc., discourse E509, E705, E1231 etc., course E590, E2186, T1700 etc., narrative E1333

procuratour, *sb.* agent E2112, E2760

procure, *v.* obtain E2435, E2755, T2987, win E3071

professioun, *sb.* public appearance T1615 (*see note*)

profite, *v.* be of benefit T1079, T1330, T2662 etc., advance E2992, increase T2256; *~ in/to* do good to T1079, T1623

profiting, *sb.* advancing T2186

profride, *v.3sg.pa.ind. ~ himsilf* gave himself up E1668

propre, *adj.* private E1981, E1985, E2038 etc.; *as sb.* individuality L717; *in ~* as private property E1944

proprete, propirte, propurte, *sb.* private ownership E1997, E2009, E2012 etc., attribute E3, T2381

proue, *sb.* proof T3185

pseudo, *sb.* false person, pretender E2560 (*see note*), E2564, E2829 etc.

pseudo-prophetis, *sb.gen.sg. and pl.* false prophet T716, T1335, T1646

punsche, *v.* punish T2424, T3468, T3472

pured, purid, *pa.p.adj.* purified, uncontaminated E129, E134, E182 etc.

purpos, *sb.* aim, desire T33, T585, T2849; *to ~* relevant to the point at issue E1632, E2525, E2651 etc., effectively E2533; *to oure ~* effectively for our intention E2898

purpos(e, *v.* intend E835, E2847, E2963 etc.

pursue(n, *v.* persecute E703, E1121, E1128 etc.

pursuers, *sb.pl.* persecutors T3214, T3220

purtenance, purtynauncis, *sb.* trappings, things which pertain to possession E1338, E1343, E1348 etc.

puru(e)(y)aunce, *sb.* provision E1303, E2147, E2721 etc., foresight T3317, T3347, provision of victuals E2114, E2119, T2490

purveynge *v.pres.p.,* carrying out L975, **purvei(e)d,** *pa.p* provided E2087, T1280

putten *v.* establish L68, L188 etc., presuppose T3500; ~ *to* add to T1188, ~ *on/upon* allege against E276, E1202, E1427 etc., ~ *awei* expel E2221, ~ *in choise* made to choose T463, ~ *in* place on T1527, ~ *out* expel E1268, ~ *hemsilf . . . to* to commit themselves to E679

quarre, *sb.* large mass of stone T663, T1971

queynt, *adj.* ingenious T1382, elaborate T2002 (*see note*)

queken, *v.* (**iquekened** *pa.p.*) quicken, bring alive T873, T874, T2096 etc.

quekenyng, *ger.* bringing alive T2092

quenche, *v.* put down E2587, T2531

quenching, *ger.* stifling T2067

quene, *sb.* harlot T1252

quiete, *v.* make quiet T2922, satisfy T1745, T1754, T1883 etc.

quyk, *adj.* living, lively E1145, E1599, T2162 etc., alive T25, T2664, T2665

quilagis, *sb.pl.* collections E2749 (*see note*), E2758, E2768 etc.

quytte, *v.3pl.pa.ind.* exonerated E1422

rad *v.pa.p.* read T3441, T3449

rasyng, *ger.* ~ *awei* taking away E1593

raþe, *adv.* quickly T2536

raþer, raþur, *adj.comp.* former T1864, T1990, T1991 etc., earlier T2520, T2522

raþer, raþur, *adv.comp.* more readily E315, E389, E866 etc., more E2152, E2157, E2248 etc., previously T3645

raþest, *adv.superl.* most particularly, soonest T3205

rauyng, *ger.* madness T2010

raunsome, -summe, *v.* ransom E829, T3648

real, *adj.* fit for a king T2845, T2946

reali, *adv.* actually, substantially T1525

recheles, *adj.* careless E2845, E2846, negligent T1277

rechelsli, *adv.* carelessly T1110, rashly T681

rechelisnesse, *sb.* carelessness E2441, E2741, E2855

reckiþ, *v.3sg.pres.ind.,* **recken** *pl.pres.ind.* care T820, T1788, T1792, ~ *. . . of* care about T3019

recors, *sb.* recourse T2307

recusing, *ger.* refusal T3531

redi, *adj.* appropriate E1495, T3704

redili, *adv.* quickly E2950, properly E616, E619

redresse, *v.* recall E182, E591, E601 etc.

reduced, *v.pa.p.* mow be ~ *to* may be summarized as T2842

refreyne, *v.* ~ *. . . of* restrain *. . .* from E1178, restrain T1354

regalie, *sb.* royal prerogative E841, E1055, T1061, kingship E1058, T2947

regnen, *v.pl.pres.ind* prevail E1169

regnynge, *adj.* dominant, prevalent E457

reherse, *v.* repeat E1775, E2328, T3506 etc., call to mind E16

rehersing, *ger.* repetition T2009

reioisiþ, *v.3sg.pres.ind.,* **reioisen** *pl.pres. ind.* rejoice E601, ~ *hemsilf* have delight E1951

rekenyng, reknynge, *sb.* account L406, L1031, T375

relacioun, *sb.* account T3809

relatif, *sb.* relative word, word relating to an antecedent term T3791 (*see note*), T3798, T3800

releue, *v.* help T1657

releuyng, *ger.* (means of) help T1657

religioun, *sb.* religious order E1927

religious(e, *adj.* bound by formal vows to a religious order E220, E682, E1017 etc.

religi(o)use, *sb.* people bound by formal vows to an order of religious life E125, E1127, E1134 etc.

religiousli, *adv.* devoutly T2187

reliquiis, *sb.pl.* relics T2906

reme, *sb.* realm, kingdom T407, T1158, T1260 etc.

remitte, *v.* resign E1412, T2286, refer E1845

renegat, *sb.* renegade, apostate E2681, E2925, T393 etc.

reney, *v.* (renoieþ *3sg.pres.ind.*) deny T1460, T1654, T1763, ~ *to* renounce E1552

renying, *sb.* denial T3530

renne, *v.* run E1598, E1653, ~ *togedur* unite T600, ~ *into* coalesce into T2820, ~ *to* run up T2942

renounsiþ, *v.3sg.pres.ind.*, renounce, *3sg.pres.sj.*, renounsid *3sg.pa.ind.*, ~ *to* renounce T918, T1243, T1246

repref, *sb.* reproof E86, E88

repreue, *v.* reprove E71, E124 etc., cast out T2072

repreued, *adj.* accursed T2079

repungne, *v.* oppose T3261, T3263

repungnyng, *adj.* contrary T1699

requiem, *sb.* service for dead T3867

requirid, irequired, *v.pa.p.* asked E1365, T3688

rere, *v.* raise T658, T1802, T2247 etc.

resen, reso(u)n, *v.pa.p.* risen T528, T541, T3252

ressaueris, *sb.pl.* recipient L884

resume, *v.pl.pres.sj.* take again, repossess E1581

retreting, *ger.* diminution T3404

reuersc, *v.* overturn E885, E1819, T393 etc., oppose, contradict E637, E657, E676 etc.

reuersing, *ger.* contradiction T825

reuoke, *v.inf.* call back T643 (Lat *revocet*, *see note*)

reward, *sb.* regard E511, E514, E567 etc., care E1003, reverence T562, T570, T2262 etc., value T3573; *in* ~ *of* in comparison with T2219

reward(e, *v.* regard, pay attention to T563, T565, T579 etc.

rewme, *sb.* realm, kingdom E695, E711, E829 etc.

rialte, *sb.* royal estate E1760

richelisnesse, *sb.* carelessness E2843

richesse, *sb.* wealth E1023, E1806, E2593; richessis *pl.* riches E789

riȝt, *adj.* straight E633, E638

riȝt, *adv.* very T3536, T3704, T3809, directly T3596, certainly T3635, absolutely E545, E546

riȝt as *cj.* just as E324

riȝtful *adj.* righteous E224

rynk, *sb.* ring T1346

ryue, *adj.* common E320, E1178, T292 etc., frequent T1429, T1434, T1454 etc.

ryueli, *adv.* frequently T1307, T2496, T2931

rulid, *v.pa.p.* ordered E2069

ruþe, *sb.* matter for grief E1285

ruþeful, *adj.* sorrowful E1517

sacreþ, *v.3sg.pres.ind.*, sacre *pl.pres.ind.*, sacring *pres.p.*, sacrid *3sg.pa.ind.* and *pa.p.* consecrate T400, T527, T546 etc.

sacrifieþ, *v.3sg.pres.ind.* sacrifices E2334

sacring, sakering, *ger.* consecration E2488, T548, T550

sad(de, *adj.* steadfast T2101, T3200, T3559, trustworthy E2878, T1954, T3743

sadded, isaddid, *v.pa.p.* confirmed T637 (Lat. *solidentur*), made firm T1496

sadli, *adv.* steadfastly T1934, T2467, T3822

sadnes(se, *sb.* constancy T2351, T3566

sale, *sb.* sett to ~ put up for sale E2490

salued, *v.pa.p.* saluted E2803

saruandis *see* seruande

saumple, *sb.* example E750

sauacioun, *sb.* salvation E1149, saving E1313, E1314

sauer, *v.* value T3144; ~ *aftur/in* have pleasure from T1351, T3285

saueri, *adj.* pleasing T900

sauour(e *sb.* pleasure E1012, savour (Lat. *odore*) T614, taste T3285

scarste, *sb.* limitation E51

sceler, *sb.* chancery T2441 (*see note*)

schame, *v.* be ashamed of T484, T489

schapiþ, *v.3sg.pres.ind.* fares T386

schende, *v.* destroy T1931, T2449

schete, *v.* shoot T3166, T3187, T3538

schewe, *v.* (ischewid *pa.p.*) indicate, reveal T1995, T2008, T2052 etc., recognize T1520, acknowledge T2294, make manifest T524 (Vulg. *annuntiabo*); ~ *out* reveal T3330

schortli, *adv.* in brief T3690

schrewid, *adj.* evil-disposed, wicked T905, T1109, T1131 etc.

schrewis, *sb.pl.* vicious people E1378

science, *sb.* knowledge T3352, T3353

sclayn *see* scle

sclaundre. sclaundur, *sb.* defamation T173, T175, T849 etc.; ~ *to* defamation of E2796 sclaundrid *v.pa.p.* defamed L1014, T170, T1095; *þou art~ to me* you are an offence to me T1089 (*see note*)

sclaundring, *ger.* defamation T3416

scle, *v.* destroy T1287, kill T834, T2651, sclayn *pa.p.* killed T2854, ~ *wiþ* killed by T2802

s(c)lei3t, slei3tþe, *sb.* trick E543, E2548, T133

sclepe, *v.* sleep T3133, T3134, T3140

scleper, *adj.* unstable T1978

scleþur, *adj.* smooth T1944

scliding, *adj.* slippery T1978

sclow, *adj.* slow T2230, T3553

scool, *sb.* university E694, E709

scorne, *sb.* something contemptible T3333

scrapan, *v.pl.pres.ind.* gather greedily together E1251

scrowis, *sb.pl.* small rolls of paper E73, E87, T457 etc.

se(e, *sb.* seat (with extension to bishop's see) T95, T96, T112 etc., throne T3079

seche, *adj. and dem.sg. and pl.pron.* such T56, T71, T97 etc.

seche, *v.* (sike *imper.sg.*, i)sou3t *pa.p.*) seek E28, E1897, T907 etc.; *be . . . ~ be . . .* sought (Lat. *quaeratur*) T3346; *sou3t out* examined T3817

seching, *ger.* seeking T3555

seculerli, *adv.* in secular fashion E889, E1394, E1944

seculerte, *sb.* secular position E1952

se(e)meþ, *v.3sg.pres.ind.*, semen *pl.pres. ind. with refl.* it seems to me etc. E499, E570, E1660 etc., thinks T1254; *hou ~ þee* what do you think E1913

seen, *v.* synod etc. T1851, T1855, T1860 etc.

seen, *v.* (seist, *2sg.pres.ind.*, seeþ *3sg.pres. ind.*, se(e)n *pl.pres.ind.*, seinge, *pres.p.*, saie(n *pa.ind. and sj.*, seie(n, seyn, i)seen *pa.p.*) see E551, E553, E1025 etc.; *ben sen* appear T3287, *be not seyn* do not appear to be L367

seew, *v.3sg.pa.ind.* sowed E345, E346, E347 etc.

seie, *v.* (seist, *2sg.pres.ind.*, seiþ *3sg.pres. ind.*, seie(n *pl.pres.ind.*, sei(3)ing(e, *pres.p.*, seide *pa.p.*) say T3532, T3581, T3606 etc., ~ *hemsilf* claim themselves E1994

seing, *ger.* sight T2661

sei(3)ing(e, *ger.* speech E398, *pl.* words T412, T3641

sekir, sikir, *adj.* certain, assured E2296, T531, T3444 etc.

sekir, seker, sikir, *adv.* certainly, indeed E2035, T271, T272 etc.

sende, *v.3sg.pa.ind.* sent T994

sensible, *adj.* having perception E2283, E2284, T2655, perceptible by the senses T2686, T3169, T3627 etc.

sentence, sentens, *sb.* statement E10, E1778, T600 etc., interpretation E3039, meaning T323, judgment T1804, T3303, T3304, opinion, affirmation T461

sepulture, *sb.* grave L978

sermon, *sb.* speech T3318

seruage, *sb.* servitude T370, obedience due only to God T2870, T2872, T2903 etc.

seruande, *sb.*, saruandis *pl.* servant L15, L990

seruyable, *adj.* ready to do service T1067, T1084

sessiþ, *v.3sg.pres.ind.*, sessid *pa.p.* come to an end T2080, T2093

sete, *sb.* seat T100, T2234

settiþ, *v.3sg.pres.ind.*, sette(n *pl.pres.ind.*, sett *sg.pres.sj.*, setten *pl.pa.ind.*, sett, isett *pa.p.* base T645, place T1080, T3443, T3832; ~ *lite/at litil/litil bi* consider of little account T155, T3222, T3233 etc.; ~ *. . . to* raise E1206; ~ *upon* attach to E1118, establish T165, ; ~ *. . . in* furnish with T688

shenship, *sb.* disgrace E1284

shewen, *v.pl.pres.ind.*, shewid *pa.p.* reveal E509, E764

s(c)hort, *adj.* facile E1868, E1872, simple T1685

shorun, *pa.p.adj. newe* ~ newly shorn E1594

s(c)hul(en, *v.pl.pres.ind.* shall T864, T3071, T3823 etc.

shuldris, *sb.pl.* shoulders E107

sibbe, *adj.* peaceful T903

siche see seche

signefiyng, *ger.* signification T3778

signefiiþ, *v.3sg.pres.ind.*, signefiyng *pres.p.*, signefiid *pa.p.* represent E2997, T2012, T2159 etc., declare T3664

signyd, *pa.p.adj.* indicated T347

significacioun, *sb.* meaning T151

siik, *adj.* sick E1711
sike *see* seche
siking, *sb.* sighing T3861
sikirnesse, *sb.* security E2139
sille, *v.* sell E467, E473, E531 etc., *is to* ~
  is for sale E1613
sillers, *sb.pl.* sellers E2546
symylacioun, *sb.* deception E1580, E1598,
  pretence E2427
symonyan, *sb.* simoniac E1723, E1725,
  E1728 etc.
sympilness, *sb.* innocence L665
simpilte, *sb.* innocence T727
singlerli, *adv.* singly, particularly T2411,
  T2415, T2431
singuler, singular, *adj.* single, unique
  E1980, T63, T85
synguler, *adv.* individually E1219
siþ, *adv.* afterwards T2568
siþ, siþþen, *cj.* since E67, E242, E300 etc.
skill, skele, *sb.* reason, cause E60, E543,
  E1304 etc.
skerris, *sb.pl.* precipices T3565
slei3t, slei3tþe, *see* s(c)lei3t
sleuþe, *sb.* sloth E1508
smacche, *sb.* ~ *of* taste for T944
smacchiþ, *v.3sg.pres.ind.*, smacchen
  pl.pres.ind. ~ *of* smack of E1570, E2485
so, *adv.* such T1701, in this fashion E1659,
  T2859, in such a way T3470, ~ *þat* so
  E821; ~ *as* just as E36, E1579, E2173
  etc.; ~ *as . . .* ~ *as* in the same way
  T699; *al* ~ *long as* as long as E1501
so þat, *cj.* in so far as E2143, that T724,
  provided that L395
soiect, soget(t, subiect, *sb.* subject
  (usually in phrase *accident wiþout* ~)
  T403 (*see note*), T673, T1382 etc.
soiectiþ, *v.3sg.pres.ind.*, soiecten *pl.pres.*
  ind., soiect(id *pa.p.* subject T2110,
  humiliate T2903, subjected T2910, provided with a subject T3795, T3803
sokourid, *v.pa.p.* nurtured E2923
soler, *sb.* upper room E1808
sonde, *sb.* sand T1938
soore, *adv.* seriously E818
soriful, *adj.* sorrowful T1428
soþ(e, *sb.* truth E394, T499, T3395 etc.
soþ(e, *adj.* true E201, E1162, E1283 etc.
soþ(e)li, *adv.* truly T496, T2202, T3647
  etc.
soudiours, *sb.pl.* soldiers E1110
souereyn, *sb.* lord L49, T2899

souerenli, *adv.* to a supreme degree T2283
souere(y)nte, *sb.* highest point E677,
  E1992, T190
soun, *sb.* sound T2639, T3668
sowe. *v.pa.p.* sown E779
sowneþ, *v.3sg.pres.ind.*, sownen *pl.pres.*
  ind., sounnyng *pres.p.*, sowned(e,
  pa.ind. argue E159, T892, T1834,
  imply T2397, sound T3159; ~ *into*
  lead toward E202, E1014; ~ *to* have a
  tendency to advance E90
special, *adj.as sb. in* ~ especially E2778,
  T1174, in detail T140, T3506; *in more*
  ~ more particularly E166
spedy, *adj.* profitable E1866, E2368, T281
  etc., beneficial T2510
spediþ, *v.3sg.pres.ind.* flourishes T1577
speke, *v.* (spikiþ *3sg.pres.ind.*, spak(e
  sg.pa.ind., spak, speken *pl.pa.ind.*,
  i)spok(e *pa.p.*) speak E556, E925, T7
  etc.
spicis, *sb.pl.* kinds E417
spiritualtees, *sb.pl.* income from benefices, tithes etc. E1114 (*see note*)
spitten, *v.pl.pa.ind.* spat E448
spoile, *v.* (spolid *pa.p.*) rob L215, T1283
spoiling, *ger.* robbery T1169, T1636
spotil, *sb.* spittle E448
spous(e)brekers, *sb.pl.* adulterers E335,
  E338
sprengid, *v.pa.p.* sprinkled T1495, T1533
stable, *v.* make firm T759, T763, T767
stabling, *ger.* making firm T3849
stablisch, *v.* establish T1387, make secure
  T163, T1732, T1757 etc.
stablisching, *ger.* strengthening T847
stappis, *sb.pl.* steps E1847, E2534
startlen, *v.pl.pres.ind.* rush about E1603
sta(a)t(e, *sb.* estate E2, E5, E11 etc.,
  proper function E19
statutis, *sb.pl.* laws (usually of the ecclesiastical authorities) E1160, E2460,
  E2989 etc.
stede, stide, *sb.* place E416, T1314,
  T2375
stifli, *adv.* resolutely E576, T46, T442
  etc., obstinately E655, T3767
sti3e, *v.pl.pres.ind.* mount T2425
stille, *adj.* silent T2237
stinch, *sb.* stench T938
stonde, *v.* (stonde *pa.p.*) stand E319,
  E464, E685 etc., remain E244, E623;
  ~ *wiþ* be consonant with E253, E1972,

E2045 etc.; ~ *forþ* remain E428, E439; ~ *in* consist of T3765; ~ . . . *upon* insist upon T3766; ~ *þerwiþ* in agreement with it E2876; *stondinge þis apostasie* during this apostasy E1507; *stondinge her astaat* in view of their position E2281; ~ *wiþ* be compatible with E1506

stonyn, *adj.* made of stone T656

storie, *sb.* legend E1709, E1712, account E1747, history T3206

strang, *adj.* (**strangur** *comp.*) strange T759, T762, T3325, unfamiliar T1302

strecche, *v.* extend T1683, T1904, T1905

streyt, *adj.* strict E680

strei(3)tli, *adv.* (**streitloker** *comp.*) strictly E89, E825, E934 etc., rigorously E1258, E2736, E2988 etc., firmly T138, unsparingly T391

strengþe, strenthe, *sb.* violence T1634; *of þe* ~ some of the host (Vulg. *de fortitudine*) T1401 (*see note*); **strengþis** *pl.* hosts T1403

strengþing, *ger.* strengthening E704

strenkiþ, *v.3sg.pres.ind.* strengthens E2936

stripeþ, *v.3sg.pres.ind.* strips, tears T2076

striuen, *v.pl.pa.ind.* strove T2815

stryues, *sb.pl.* quarrels E594

striuyng, *ger.* contending E1615

stronge, *adv.* strongly E2413

studie, *sb.* *wiþ* ~ after consideration E1109, E1272, E1891

studied, *pa.p.adj.* considered E1293

stumble, *v.imper.sg.* ~ . . . *at* trip over T3046

stumblyng stole, *sb.* stumbling block T1737

subarbis, suburbis, *sb.pl.* country estates just outside town E812, T1340

subiect *see* soiect

substaunce, *sb.* *of þe* ~ *of* be essential to T3752, T3761

substancial(l)i, *adv.* in substance E298, T2771, T3059

sue, su3e, swe, *v.* follow E194, E318, E691 etc., follow as a consequence E243, E680, E2054 etc., imitate E334, E351, E1128 etc.

suers, *sb.pl.* followers E782

suffragiis, *sb.pl.* prayers, intercessions E471, E474, E524 etc.

suffre, *v.* allow E119, E589, E797 etc., endure E1119, treat T3708

suffreable, *adj.* permissible T2996, T2999, T3005

suffring, *ger.* tolerating T2396

suyng, *adv. anoon* ~ immediately afterwards T2658

suyngli, *adv.* consequently T504, subsequently T573

sum, *adj.* a certain (Lat. *aliquod*) T3719, *in* ~ *place . . . in* ~ *place* in one place . . . in another E1941

sumdel, *adv.* to some extent E1763

sumwhat, *adv.* ~ *aftur* for a while afterwards T2465

sunner, *adv. comp. þe* ~ the more quickly E1531

superflue, *adj.* excessive L743

superfluite, *sb.* excess T3

suppose, *v.* think, consider, conclude E29, E113, E272 etc., *it is to* ~ *of* it is to be concluded from T3281

sure, *adj.* certain T3174

sureli, *adv.* certainly T3178

surete, *sb.* certainty T3483

susteyne, *v.* endure E380, maintain T394, T740

sutes, *sb.pl.* companies of disciples E177

swen *see* sue

swerd, *sb. beriþ þe* ~ holds civil authority E7, E8

swynk, *sb.* toil, labour T3865

swiþe, *adv.* rapidly E2495

swte, *adj.* sweet T613

take, *v.* (**i)take(n** *pa.p.*) take E228, E350, E1112 etc., receive T3377, understand T2009, T2885, T3553, consider T169; ~ *of* receive from E1430, T501, T3583 etc., derive from T3670, T3675; ~ *to* receive T2366, give to T3321, adopt T1324, taken in (i.e. killed) L1029

tappid, *v.pa.p.* discharged T2441

tari(e, *v.* delay E2939, E3095, T27, put off L1021, linger L1022

tariyng, *adj.* slow T2232 (*see note*)

tariyng, *ger.* delay T1049, T1108

teelde, *v.3sg.pa.ind.* told E1112

te(e)me, *sb.* text E56, E65, E130 etc.

teenful, *adj.* troublesome E2095, E2630

tekeling, *v.pres.p.* tickling (i.e. flattering) T742

temperal, *adj.* secular E839, E850, E1065 etc., worldly E1103, E1106, E1545 etc.

temperali, *adv.* ∼ *endowid prestis* priests endowed with temporal goods E896

temperalte(e, *sb.* temporal possessions E849, E857, E1111 (*see note*) etc., secular power E842

tendirli, *adv.* carefully E1496

teneþ, *v.3sg.pres.ind.*, **tenyd** *3sg.pa.ind.* vex T975, T1083

tent(e, *sb.* heed E1525, L366

termes, *sb.pl.* terms, words E1927, limits T1214

til, *v.inf.* (1) ∼ *to* extend to T261 (*see note*)

tylynge, *ger.* cultivation L368

tiliþ, *v.3sg.pres.ind.* tills, cultivates E2994

tymes, *sb.pl.* *bi* ∼ in time, quickly E1525

tyrantlich, *adj.* tyrannical T379

tira(u)ntri(3)e, *sb.* tyranny E2236, T2073, T3232

titil, title, *sb.* legal right E222, E223, E225 etc.

to, *adv.*(1) too E1867, T2741

to, *adv.*(2) thereto T374

to, *prep.* for E659, E734, E931 etc., as L381, T1065, towards E308, concerning E2253, T1531, amongst T1535, up to the point of L1044

tofore, *adv.* previously T90, T2309, T2516 etc.

togider, togidir, *adv.* together E106, E633, E701, immediately beside each other E635

tokenesse, *sb.pl.* signs T3169

tokenyng, *sb.* signal E50, *in* ∼ *þat* as a sign that E2769

tolt, *v.3sg.pa.ind.* brought forth T3866

ton *see* o, oo, oon

too *see* two

toode, *sb.* toad T3094

torente, *v.pa.p.* torn to pieces T3788

tou(3)ching(e, *prep.* concerning E71, E824, E939 etc., *as* ∼ as far as T547

toward, *prep.* towards obtaining E252, *as* ∼ as regarding E1516

trace, *sb.* path E85

trauel(l)e, *v.* labour E1389, E2766, E2767 etc., trouble E205, distress E1431, T3631

tre, *sb.* wood E115

trenyte, *sb.* trinity T678, T2214, T2217 etc.

treting, *v.pres.p.* partaking of T2496

tretour, *sb.* traitor T2851

tr(e)u3e, *adj.* true, faithful T1558, T1837

trist, *sb.* trust T1266

trist(en, *v.* trust T1115, T1913, T3199, believe T14, T481

triuauntis, *sb.pl.* tyrants E1375 (*see note*)

trowe, *v.* believe T3440, think E2829, T3392

tru3e, *adj.as sb.* truth (Vulg. *veritas*) truth T1398 (*see note*)

trumpe, *sb.* trumpet T3159

trumppinggis, *ger.pl.* trumpetings T3163

turbelous, *adj.* troubled T1233

turmentri3e, *sb.* torment, vexation T2100

turne, *v.inf.* put back E1312, E1520, E1524, ∼ *a3en* reform L1020; ∼ *to* be converted to E110, T2423

tweyn *see* two

twelþe, *num.ord.* twelfth E1798, E3083

two, too, tweyn, *num.* two E391, T297, ∼ *þe firste* the two first E752, T2038

þan, *cj.* than E112, E115, E145 etc.

þanking(g)is, *ger.pl.* thanks E598, E2641, T506

þankis, *sb.* *her* ∼ by their will E373, T128, by her will T999

þan(ne, *adv.* then E86, E175, E211 etc.

þat, *cj.* in that E101, E411, so that E754

þedur, *adv.* thither T3846

þeefli, þeuely, *adv.* stealthily E2248

þef, *sb.* thief T3874

þenke, *v.* (þou3t 3sg.pa.ind., þou3ten *pl.pa.ind*, þou3t *pa.p.*) think E819, E2567, E2825 etc.; *me þenkiþ* it seems to me E2644, E2957; ∼ *to sle* considered how to kill L228

þera3enst, *adv.* against it T3692

þer(e)as, *cj.* where E982, E983, T1379 etc.

þere (þat), *cj.* where E701, E728, E1133 etc.

þes(e, *dem.adj.sg. and pl. and pron.* this E281, E839, E1800 etc.

þidir, *adv.* thither E2908

þilke, *dem.pl.* those same T748

þing, *sb.* ∼ *of dou3te* matter of doubt T3193

þo, tho, *dem.adj.and pron.pl.* those E31, E160, E229 etc.

þou3t *see* þenke

þour, *prep.* through T901, T1362, T2095 etc.

þretingis, *ger.pl.* threats T1933

þrid(de, *num.ord.* third E40, E752, T225 etc.

þrist, *v.pa.p.* thrust T1398

þristiþ, *v.3sg.pres.ind.* thirsts T1289, T1300

þrow, *v.pa.p.* thrown T3051

þweten, iþwete, *v.pa.p.* shaped T1963, T1973

vnablid, *v.pa.p.* disqualified T3390

vnauysi, *adj.* ill-advised E2263

vnauysid, *pa.p.adj.* imprudent E3051, E3074, T1219 etc.

vnauysili, *adv.* imprudently E1890, E2264

vnbeleueful, *adj.* incredible T3287

vnbynde, *v.* (vnbounden *pa.p.*) unbind, absolve T2313, T2314, T2418 etc.

vnbind(d)ing, *ger.* release T1745, T3698, absolution T2408

vncorruptible, *adj.* incorruptible T3337

uncristened, *pa.p.adj.* unbaptised T1823

vncurable, *adj.* incurable T1342

vndefoulid, *pa.p.adj.* undefiled E241

vnder, *prep.* ∼ *grete peyne* with (threat of) severe penalty T136

vndirnymmeþ, -nemeþ, *v.3sg.pres.ind.*, vndernam(e *3sg.pa.ind.*), rebuke E593, E1023, E3065 etc.

vndo, *v.* (vndo *pa.p.*) destroy E1296, E1644, E2075 etc., ruin E2082, E2184, E2186 etc., abolish E426, E1793, E2134 etc.

vndoing, *sb.* ruin, destruction E1299, E2071, E2230 etc.

vndurnemyngis, *ger.pl.* rebukes T297

vndursett, *v.pa.p.* ∼ *wiþ* supported by T3206

vndurstondeþ, *v.3sg.pres.ind.*, vndurstond(e *pa.p.*), understand T673, T684, T686 etc., mean T1659, interpret T1361, T2048

vndurstonding(e, *ger.* meaning L1032, T1348

vnequite, *sb.* wickedness E1189, E1194, L1005 etc.

vnfyned, *pa.p.adj.* unrefined T1328 (*not MED*)

vnfongen, *v.pa.p.* received T3321

vngroundid, *pa.p.adj.* unfounded in scripture E102, E295, E332 etc., unjustifiable E2910

vnhalowid, *pa.p.adj.* unconsecrated T3098

vnhewe, *pa.p.adj.* not fashioned by cutting T657, T663, T1947 etc.

vnkinde, *adj.* unnatural T1042

vnkindli, *adj.* unnatural E1969, E1971

vnkyndli, *adv.* unnaturally E1920, E2909

vnknowe, *v.pa.p.* unknown T3709

vnkunning, *adj.* ignorant T3316

vnkun(n)yngnes(se, *sb.* ignorance E1292, E1763, E2740 etc.

vnlefful, *adj.* unlawful T2893, T3273

vnmengid, *pa.p.adj.* uncontaminated T731 (*not MED*)

unmesurable, *adj.* immeasurable T1373, T1411, beyond reason T1168

vnmesurablenes, *sb.* lack of moderation T1176, T1178

vnmesurabli, *adv.* unrestrainedly E1128

vnmy3t(t)i, *adj.* lacking in power T3465, T3466, T3467 etc.

vnmoeblis, *sb.pl.* immovable possessions E981

vnneþe, *adv.* scarcely E2197, E2555, E2563 etc.

vnpacientli, *adv.* impatiently E2539

vnperfeccioun, *sb.* imperfection E961, E1963

vnperfit, *adj.* imperfect E406, E953, E956 etc.

vnperfitnesse, *sb.* imperfection E1585, E2512, an imperfect arrangement E2014

vnpossible, *adj.* impossible T44, T47, T398 etc.

vnpreued, *pa.p.adj.* not proved E1870, T345

vnproue, *v.pl.pres.sj.* reject T3405

unreuerentli, *adv.* disrespectfully T179

vnredi, *adj.* ill-prepared T678

vnresonable, *adj.* incapable of reason T2638

vnruli, *asj.* uncontrolled E1688

vnrulynesse, *sb.* insubordination E1499

vnsaueri(e, *adj.* offensive T3687, T3807, unattractive T921

vnsoburnesse, *sb.* lack of moderation T1212

vnstabli, *adv.* uncertainly T2306

vnþrifti, *adj.* harmful E2524

vnuisible, *adj.* invisible T1546

vnuisibli, *adv.* invisibly T3674

vnwastid, *pa.p.adj.* undiminished T2629, T2635

vp, *prep.* on L695, T285, T3812, ∼ *hap* perchance E2836, ∼ *hast* speedily E2857

uphepid, *pa.p.adj.* piled up E1274

vpon, *prep.* over E974, E1369, E1533, for

E1405, at T907, concerning E689, E2700, T147

uprerid, *pa.p.adj.* raised up T2234

vse, vss, *sb.* usage T1683, T1704, T1710, practice T1501, profit E110, E112, E827 etc., liturgical form E1246

vsiþ, *v.3sg.pres.ind.* receives T1507, **vside** *pl.pa.ind.* practised E666

vsing, *ger.* usage T557

vttirli, *adv.* completely E1411, E1582, E1656 etc.

vttur, *adj.comp.* outer T3253

vtward, *adj.* external E2285

uariant, *adj.* different T1911

vari(3)e, *v.* diverge E264, E645, T411 etc., change T1710

velony, *sb.* defamation E297

veniaunce, *sb.* vengeance E16, E2325, punishment E1378, E1739, T1189

venym, *sb.* poison E1797, T279, T926 etc.

ver(r)eli, *adv.* truly E1391, T1513, T1522 etc.

ver(r)i, *adj.* truthful, true E1579, E2376, E2778 etc., T3346 (*see note*), complete T675, T2907; **verrier**, *adj.comp.* more complete T3324

ver(r)ified, *v.pa.p.* proved true E353, E374, E376 etc.

uertu, *sb.* moral strength (Lat. *virtus*) T2111

vessels, *sb.pl.* utensils for the table E2315

vicar, *sb.* vicar, deputy E11, E35, E38 etc.

vicaries, *sb.pl.* vicars, deputies E19

vis(s)er(i)d, *pa.p.adj.* concealed E2547, T748, T819 etc.

vitail(lu)s, *sb.pl.* food E2693, T1143

waast, *adj.* unnecessary E1515, E2059, E2314

waite, *sb.*(1) trap T984

wayte, *sb.*(2) guard L1027, L1030, L1032

waitiþ, *v.3sg.pres.ind.* observes T1942

wake, *v.inf.* watch L48, L50

waker, *adj.* watchful T374

waking, *adj.* watchful T3158

wakinge, *ger.* watching E472

wante, *v.* lack T1695, T2359, T3308 etc., *wanteþ vs* is lacking to us T2670

wanting, *adj.* lacking T3

war(e, *adj.* aware E561, E2519, E2828 etc.

ware, *sb.* production E1089

warli, *adv.* carefully E2845

warneþ, *v.3sg.pres.ind.* forbids (Lat. *prohibeat*) T3558

wastiþ, *v.3sg.pres.ind.*, **wastid** *pa.p.*, consume, destroy T1442, T1443, devastated T3032

wastour, *sb.* spendthrift E745, E747

wauerring, wauuryng, *ger.* faltering T720, T762

waueringe, *adj.* faltering E458

wauur, *v.* falter T3176, T3191

wax, *v.* (**wax** *3sg.pa.ind.*, **woxen** *pl.pa.ind.*, **wax, wox** *pa.p.*) grow E1022, T901, T2066 etc.

weche, wiche, *rel.pron.* which T9, T2513, T3733, *to þe* ~ which (Lat. *cui*) T590 (*see note*)

weer, *sb.* hesitation E464

wei(3)e, *sb.*(1) way E24, E194 etc., *bi* ~ *of* by right of E6, *euery weies* in all directions E1610

weie, *sb.*(2) balance E2979 (*see note*)

wel, *adv.* very E1767

weld(e, *v.* control E1118, have power over T1249

welny, *adv.* almost T37, T168, T852 etc.

wem, *sb.* blemish E242, T2703

wene, *v.* (**wende(n** *pa.ind.*, **went** *pa.p.*) think E82, E1772, E3032 etc.

wenten, *v.pl.pa.ind.* ~ *forþe* were published abroad L224

were, *v.* ~ *out* exhaust T1700, T1733

werris, *sb.pl.* wars E1889

wers, *adj.comp.* worse T1141

werst, *adj.superl.* worst T3232

werste, *adv.superl.* worst L247

wete(n see **wite(n**

wetingli, *adv.* knowingly T1121

wett, *v.pa.p.* moistened T1533

whan(ne, *cj.* when E131, E162, E179 etc.

what, *cj.* as far as E2878, E2936; ~ *bi/in/for* (. . . ~ *bi/in*) what with (. . . what with) E2933, E2983, T11

wheder, *cj.* in what direction T1903

wher(e, wheþer, *cj.* whether E1443, T174, T733 etc., *interrogative cj. introducing a question* E597, E2787 etc.

wherfor, *adv.* therefore T2746

wheston, *sb.* whetstone E644 (*see note*)

wheþersoeuer, *cj.* whether L405

whilis, *cj.* as long as E250

whinggis, *sb.pl.* wings T2235, T2245

who, *pron.* whoever T1188

whos, *pron.* whoso T3173, T3828

wicche, *sb.* witch T2954
wiche *see* weche
wilde, *v.inf.* control T1250
wilful, *adj.* voluntary E1127, E2816 etc., arbitrary T276, T3579
wilfulli, *adv.* voluntarily E680, E2181, E2592 etc.
will, *sb.* ~ *of* desire to E2049
wylnyng, *v.pres.p.* desiring T827
winde, *v.imper.pl.* go T3856
wynnyng, *sb.* profit E90
wirche, worche, *v.* (wrouȝt *pa.p.*) act T2401, T3237, T3555 etc., carry out E343, E1237, T2389
wirching, worching, *ger.* action E833, E860, T1600 (*see note*), T2685, T2721, activity T1514, T2382, effect T1623
wirschip, *sb.* reverence T2826, T2832, T2836 etc., honour T3849
wische, *v.3sg.pa.ind.* washed T3864
wise, *sb.* manner, fashion E264, E278, E459 etc.; *any* ~ in any way T2206; *no* ~ no way E51
wite, wete, *v.*(1) (wo(o)t(e *1 and 3sg. and pl.pres.ind.*, wo(o)st *2sg.pres.ind.*, wist *3sg.pa.ind.*, wist *pa.p.*) know E215, E616, E1157 etc.
wite, *v.*(2) blame E2867, account T3036
wiþ (. . .) þat, *prep.phrase* besides, as well as that E883, E1113
wiþdrawe, *v.pa.p.* ~ *fro* remove from E943
wiþhold(e, *v.* retain, withhold E2248, E2403, E2416 etc., hold back L983
wiþynforþ, *adv.* inside E2516
wiþout, *prep.* except for T3625, ~ *any nede* beyond anything needed T1748
wiþseide, *v.pa.p.* contradicted T3534
wiþseiyng, *ger.* denial T1670
wiþstonde, *v.* (wiþstonde *pa.p.*) oppose T3207, T3543, T3546
witt, *sb.* understanding E832, E1564, E2864 etc., intelligence E1116, T651, T664 etc., way of thinking E149, E2461, interpretation T1451, T1452, T1993 etc.; *pl.* mental faculties E1474, T724, T1634 etc., senses E2285, T2661, T2734 etc., meanings T1632

witti, *adj.* ingenious T204, intelligent T3825
wol(l)e, *v.1sg.pres.ind.*, wolt, wilt *2sg.pres. ind.*, wol(l)(e(n *3sg.and pl.pres.ind.*, wold(e(n *pa.ind.*, wold *pa.p.* wish, will E132, E289, E322 etc.; *wolde God* God grant E416
wondir, wundir, *sb.* marvel E2457, T3325
wondir, wundir, *adv.* very E323, E1934, E2275 etc., wonderfully E1714, E1720, E1908, strangely E1704
wondirfull, *adv.* badly L544
wondring, *ger. wirschip of* ~ wondering honour T2114
wondur, *adj.* strange T3766
wondur, *v.3sg.pres.sj.* ~ *vpon* should marvel at T3161
wood(e, *adj.* mad E2846, T678, T1843 etc.
woodli, *adv.* ferociously T1, insanely T779, T1207
woodnesse, woodnus, *sb.* frenzy E2061, E2236, madness E2842, T768, T3684
worche(n *see* wirche
worching *see* wirching
word(e)li, *adj.* worldly T77, T126, T1082 etc.
worldli, *adv.* in worldly fashion E1552, E2216
wor(l)dlynesse, *sb.* worldliness E2316, T1836
wo(o)st, wo(o)t(e *see* wite
worre, *sb.* war T26
worre, *v.* fight T166
worshipful, *adj.* honoured E57
worshiping, *ger.* honouring E109
worþ(e, *sb.* value E501, E1664, E1883 etc.; *a* ~ as useful E2651
worþeli, *adv.* justly T1056
worþi, *adj.* worthy of E2298, T429, T430 etc.
writen, *v.pl.pa.ind.*, (i)wrete(n, iwrite *pa.p.*) write T137, T189, T237 etc.
wrooþ, wroþe, *adj.* angry E2327, fierce T3150
wrouȝt *see* wirche

zelid, *v.3sg.pa.ind.* was zealous for T2999

INDEX OF PROPER NAMES

Coverage, notably the omission of L save where that adds to E, and abbreviations are the same as those used in the Glossary. Latin forms in L1055–310 are only spelt out where the name does not occur in the texts in English; references otherwise are subordinated to the English headwords. The index does not include names for the persons of the Trinity, nor author or, in the case of New Testament epistles, recipient names of biblical books where these can be found through the scriptural index. Full references are given for most names, but because of their frequency (well over a hundred instances in each case) not for Peter, Paul or Augustine; again use of the scriptural index will assist with locating the first two, of the index of non-biblical quotations with the last. The names are indexed under the form(s) found in the texts (though normal inflexional instances, usually of the possessive, are not set out separately), and modern equivalents are only given in cases of obscurity in medieval spelling or ambiguity of identity. The notes to the texts provide further information about some of the people and places named, and these are indicated by *n*. following the relevant line number.

INDEX OF BIBLICAL QUOTATIONS

The coverage and abbreviations are those found in the Glossary. Again E and T are fully indexed, L only when its text differs from that in E. Longer quotations are listed before shorter within the same span of verses.

INDEX OF NON-BIBLICAL
QUOTATIONS

The coverage and abbreviations are those found in the Glossary. Again E and T are fully indexed, L only when its texts differ from, or are additional to, those in E; the authorities of L's three appended sets are fully indexed. As the notes make clear, many of the quotations are very accurate, normally closely translated; some, however, are summaries or appear to be paraphrased. No differentiation between these types is made here, and uncertainty of identification is not marked; this information is to be found in the notes. The majority of patristic texts are referenced from PL or PG, in each case by volume and column number; others are referenced from editions listed in the Bibliography section 2, or in the case of Grosseteste section 1. The index is arranged by the sequence of the source text (and therefore have the PL or PG numeration first, with the edited text line number(s) following); where several texts by the same author have been used, they are arranged in alphabetical order of title. Canon law quotations are indexed under *c*, and use the modern conventions listed by Brundage (1995), pp. 193 ff.